MW00629493

Advance Praise for *Heaven Is Not the Last Stop*

A major impact on religious understanding

In a user-friendly form, Sheila Keene-Lund has made *The Urantia Book* accessible to countless people who may have been daunted by the sheer size and dense language of the original. The insights it conveys should have a major impact on religious understanding in the 21st century.

—Peter Laurence EdD,
Author and consultant on religious diversity and spirituality

A new wave of advanced thought

Sheila Keene-Lund bravely steps out of the box and integrates science, philosophy, evolved religions, metaphysical sources, and common knowledge with the gift of revelation. Her intelligent and sensitive approach offers genuine truth seekers a deeper understanding of the universe and our role in it.

—Pato Banton, International recording artist and minister

A practical, must-have reference

This must-have reference introduces the most important and most helpful concepts in *The Urantia Book*. Sheila's book also reconciles these new concepts with existing religious beliefs in a meaningful and practical way.

—Dr. B. Dale Sams, DMin (McCormick Theological Seminary)

Heaven Is Not the Last Stop

Exploring a New Revelation

A Vision for Personal Transformation,
Spiritual Unity, and Cultural Progress

SHEILA KEENE-LUND

Document It! Publishing
Lady Lake, Florida

DISCLAIMER: This work uses quotations from *The Urantia Book*, ©1955, by Urantia Foundation. http://www.urantia.org. The views expressed in this book are those of the author and do not necessarily represent the views of Urantia Foundation or its affiliates.

Keene-Lund, Sheila.

Heaven is not the last stop : exploring a new revelation : a vision for personal transformation, spiritual unity, and cultural progress / Sheila Keene-Lund. -- Lady Lake, Flor. : Document It! Pub., c2010.

p. ; cm.

ISBN: 978-0-9815038-0-6
Includes bibliographical references and index.

1. Spiritual life. 2. Religion. 3. Philosophy of religion. 4. Future life. 5. Urantia book. 6. Teleology. I. Title.

BL624 .K44 2009   2008933685
299.93—dc22   0811

Printed in the United States of America

10 9 8 7 6 5 4 3 2 1

Interior layout by www.tothepointsolutions.com

In memory of
John K. Primm,
friend, mentor, and inspiration

Contents

SECTION THREE
OUR INDIVIDUAL AND COLLECTIVE DESTINY

SECTION FOUR
LIVING THE RELIGION OF THE SPIRIT

List of Illustrations

Preface

I was born in Vigo, Spain, to an English father and a Puerto Rican mother. I was two years old when my father was transferred to Cuba and he relocated us with him. Six months after our arrival, the Castro revolution began; fighting broke out in the streets, with strikes and shootings becoming common occurrences, often within hearing distance of our house. Two years later, fearing for our safety, my father moved his family out of danger to Puerto Rico, remaining behind in Cuba to fulfill his duties for another three months before joining us.

The seed for this book was planted on the island of Puerto Rico. As my early life unfolded there, meaningful events subconsciously anchored the realization that there was more to me than a physical self, the prelude to a long journey of inquiry into questions of life after death.

The first event was a near-drowning experience at the age of eight on a beautiful beach. One moment I was happily walking into seemingly gentle waters and the next I was underwater, being tossed helplessly by turbulent waves. I could "see" my body rolling in the waves, as if in slow motion. There was a distinct absence of fear as I watched myself with great calm and no sense of urgency. I seemed to have no attachment to my body and was not afraid, anxious, or worried.

The next experience happened at the age of eleven. Given an overdose of nitrous oxide anesthesia during a dental procedure, I felt as if I were leaving my body through the head. My attention suddenly shifted to a tunnel that I was approaching at great speed but which seemed too small for me to fit through. As I struggled to enter the tunnel, I "heard" my deceased grandfather's voice call out to me. Turning to look for him, I saw a bright light and "heard" his voice telling me to go back—that it was not my time to pass on. I immediately regained consciousness, still in the dentist's chair.

These poignant experiences remained in the back of my curious mind for many years.

My father was transferred to the island of St. Lucia, where he managed improvements to the island's communication services. It was there that I married, had three sons, and began reading metaphysical books, seeking to find significance in my childhood experiences. I started practicing Transcendental Meditation, a mental technique that promotes deep relaxation through the silent repetition of a simple sound, known as a mantra. Through this practice, I found the inner calmness that helped me overcome many challenges in my marriage. Eventually I found the strength and courage to follow an inner leading and, with my sons, left my husband and St. Lucia. We moved to Fairfield, Iowa, where another experience changed my life forever and laid the foundation for this book.

One day, friends invited me to join them in seeing a woman from India who was considered a wise guru; some thought her to be a saint. Her name was Ammachi. There was a long line of people waiting to receive her advice, and I wondered what was foremost on my mind. Should I ask her about my children, my relationships, my career, my health, or my future? These were things that others were asking. Looking around the room, I reflected about my marriage and became painfully aware that I had never experienced devotion. When my turn came, during the customary hug, I found myself asking, "Will I feel devotion in this lifetime?" Ammachi pulled me back and stared deeply into my eyes. As she hugged me her translator gave me her response: "Love God because only God loves you." I would reflect on her words for years.

Soon afterward, I started attending St. Gabriel and All Angels Liberal Catholic Church, a church of open communion. Its ceremony stirred in me a deep longing for God I had never felt growing up as a Roman Catholic. I realized that my attendance at the services was not as important as the attitude I brought with me, and my quest for devotion took on a life of its own. I became an altar server at the church and eventually a deaconess.

During this time, I became aware of my fear of dying and the general reluctance of others to talk about death. I knew that to overcome this fear I had to know more about the dying process and develop an expanded perspective that included life after death. So I began various activities, including joining an organization of caregivers and volunteers who serve terminally ill patients and their families. Working as a hospice volunteer provided the perfect opportunity to come to terms with my fear and to study other people's attitudes about death; it disclosed that many people at the end of life are in denial of their impending transition.

I also delved deeply into the theologies of different religions, including Christianity, Buddhism, and Hinduism. I studied the Rosicrucian and Theosophy philosophies and the popular concepts described in *The Complete Ascension Manual*. I developed workshops on spiritual care for living and dying. As a deaconess, I conducted these workshops to assist those who sought deeper meaning in their grief and more fortitude when serving loved ones who were facing death.

This extensive research and analysis, along with my teaching efforts, revealed that essential pieces of the Big Bicture of Existence were missing. There had to be greater significance to the similarities and differences in the many distinctive philosophies. I concluded that to have a better perspective of individual destiny after death, and to discover the highest meaning and purpose of our existence, I had to find these missing pieces and objectively connect the fragmented information into a whole so that a full picture could emerge. I knew that to increase my understanding of humanity's destiny, a deeper exploration of humanity's origin was essential.

Soon the many unanswered questions I had about the Christian teaching of Adam and Eve began to recur. One day, a notice on the bulletin board of a health food store caught my attention: "WHO ARE ADAM AND EVE?" I wondered if the person who posted the note was looking for an answer as I was . . . or had found the answer. I called and was invited to attend a study group of *The Urantia Book*. This was the first time I had heard the word "Urantia."

Returning home, I did some research and discovered that Urantia is the celestial name of planet Earth, and that the mysterious book was filled with teachings about God and the universe. Adding another "coincidence" to the chain of events, I discovered that my companion at the time had owned a copy of *The Urantia Book* for over twenty years! He "loaned" me the book—which I have to this day.

I cautiously opened the tome, intimidated by its size. I found the chapters on Adam and Eve and eagerly absorbed what they revealed. Excited, I then turned to the chapter about the heavenly rebellion, a biblical teaching that I instinctively knew had great significance but also missing elements.

I was not prepared for what came next. I was ecstatic to finally explore these unknown events in the history of our planet that had affected humanity so deeply. I knew in my heart that this big blue book contained answers to the questions that had confounded me for so long. But then I came upon a teaching about Sons of God that conflicted with a Christian doctrine that had been the foundation of my childhood beliefs. Confusion clouded my objectivity, and the process of reconciliation was delayed. I closed the book and did not open it again for six years.

The spiritual agitation that some of the teachings in *The Urantia Book* had stirred in me came to a head six months later when I approached my regional bishop. As I expressed my doubts and fears, he gave me a long, hard look and, with a loud chuckle, clapped his hands in congratulations! He said that beliefs should leave room for expansion; that if I released my fears about letting go of the familiar, my faith would lead me to greater truth and the discovery that my existing beliefs have a place within an expanded perspective. His wise response was a pivotal moment in my life.

As I embraced this possibility, I had casual thoughts of writing a book. People who attended my workshops encouraged the idea, but at the time I was managing a successful consulting business; writing a book was not on my list of priorities. Turning to God, I prayed for help. If I was to write a book, I needed a positive indication; the perfect sign would be if one of my sons brought up the subject of death. Like most young men, they felt immortal so it was unlikely that they would bring up the subject on their own. I also asked God for help with the title of the book.

Not long after my request for a sign, my youngest son unexpectedly dropped by for a visit. After dinner, we settled down to watch a movie and I asked him to select one. He looked at the choices and picked *Marvin's Room*. He said it was about a woman who was dying . . . and then he asked me what I thought happened, if anything, after death. I was surprised, but I should have known God would not waste time! Then panic set in; I felt that God had responded with the sign—but where would I find the time to write a book? I rationalized that God still needed to give me a title . . . and wondered how he would manage that.

A while later, without forethought, I picked up a book I had left by my desk, considered the title, and wondered what my book would be called. Before I had time for another thought, I heard the words *"Heaven Is Not the Last Stop"* in my right ear. I jumped, dropped the book, and found my mind blank. "What was that?" I asked myself. Immediately the words *"Heaven Is Not the Last Stop"* were repeated clearly in my ear! I fumbled with my pen and excitedly wrote down the title: *Heaven Is Not the Last Stop*. That was it! The end of excuses! I had received the sign I had asked for, plus the title. My mission was set: I was to create a book. But . . . if heaven was not the last stop, what is?

Such a provocative title demanded a more logical and comprehensive account of the soul and its journey after death. A common factor that surfaced in my research was the concept of planes, representing realms of existence from the most spiritual to the most material. I was particularly drawn to the theory of spiritual evolution through seven cosmic planes. In general, however, the descriptions were either too abstract or didn't stand up to critical analysis. I kept praying for inner guidance to help me discover the relationships that exist between the cosmic planes and the soul's journey after death.

After six months of further study, research, reflection, and constant requests for clarification, I was vacationing abroad when I happened upon *The Urantia Book*—the very tome I had rejected because it challenged one of my cherished beliefs. I picked it up and randomly opened it. The title staring back at me was "The Seven Superuniverses." The connection between my request and what I was reading became obvious. Once again, I felt the synchronicity of spiritual guidance and instinctively knew that my mind was ready to work with my heart to explore concepts outside my comfort zone.

Upon returning home, I retrieved my copy of *The Urantia Book* and eagerly began to read and reconcile. I knew that opening my mind to an expanded perspective of God and creation would be no easy task, but I also knew my faith would lead me to greater understanding.

I dove into the profound text with a renewed dedication, breaking through boundaries in long-held concepts and beliefs. My life seemed to change in every aspect, and for some time it felt as if I were undergoing a deep relearning process. This spiritual agitation was mirrored in a letter to a friend:

> "I am feeling overwhelmed not only because my life seems to be moving so fast, but also because of how I am relating to people and how I am perceiving others relating to me feels different and even confusing. Words and expressions do not provide the same meanings or convey what I once took for granted. My past seems foggy. The concepts that once gave me comfort and provided me with my identity are not holding up and I find it difficult to remember them. Everything is a question. In my reality, I feel as if I am in no-man's land, in a vacuum, or suspended animation. It feels as if a fog is covering what I once considered my world, and all that exists is the certainty of the unknown and the strong sound of silence . . ."

My spiritual conflict was eventually resolved through the process of reconciliation. A new perspective of existence was unfolding along with a deeper, more vibrant relationship with God and those around me. I was ready to begin writing.

After reading *The Urantia Book*, I knew why I had been guided to it. It opened my eyes to the marvels of God's creation in a way that transformed my life forever. The revelatory concepts in this epic text shed light on the under-pinnings of my faith, helping me discover the essential truths about God that had been missing in my religious framework.

The Urantia Book provided the most consistent presentation of philosophy, theology, cosmology, and history I had ever read. Openness to this wisdom, along with resolution of the personal conflicts it raised, clarified and expanded my worldview—my understanding of humanity's spirit origin, history, and destiny—enabling me to stitch together my research and derive greater meaning from that information.

I did not know that in trying to quench my fears about death, I would be deepening my knowledge about my relationship to God *and* the universe. I did not know that my pursuit of devotion would deepen my personal connection with God *and* with others. Yet the two go hand in hand, for one activates the other. Thus, from the fragments of knowledge and life, the Big Picture of Existence emerged, more clear and compelling than ever before. And that is how this book came to be.

Writing a book that abridges a revelation is a daunting task, one that I undertook with a great deal of respect and humility. It is my hope that *Heaven Is Not the Last Stop* will instill into the heart of every reader the significance to the world of the epic text called *The Urantia Book*. I know from personal experience that a clearer and more expanded perspective of our place in the universe can inspire a renewed and consecrated commitment to become one's best for the sake of future generations. And it is this passionate dedication on the part of each individual that will advance collective peace and social progress on our beautiful world.

Connecting

It is my goal to help readers deepen their relationship with God and expand their capacity to love selflessly. If reading this book inspires you in some way, or if you find something particularly meaningful, I would love to hear from you. Your critiques and suggestions are also welcomed. Please send your emails to: skl@sheilakeenelund.com.

Acknowledgments

A book of this nature is possible first and foremost only with the help and inspiration from God. I feel tremendous love and gratitude for the Universal Father and his many helpers who guided me throughout this long and transforming journey.

Many people supported my efforts directly and indirectly and I acknowledge my indebtedness and appreciation to all. There are some people, however, whom I wish to especially acknowledge:

My father, Richard Keene, and late mother, Maria Antonia Bonilla Keene, for never cringing at my eternal curiosity. My stepmother, Grata, for her encouragement and loving care of my father, which allowed me to focus on my writing.

Michael Cuddehe, for lending me a copy of *The Urantia Book* and never asking for its return.

The late Lawrence J. Smith, regional bishop emeritus of the Liberal Catholic Church, who congratulated me when many of my cherished religious beliefs seemed to crumble.

My ex-husband, Jeru Hall, for encouraging me to make writing this book a priority.

My friend and mentor the late John Kenton Primm, for his wisdom, unwavering support, and meticulous editing, and his loving wife Carol for her patience and kindness throughout our work together.

My sisters Mary and Helen, for their continued enthusiasm; my sister Jane, for encouraging me to continue writing when I felt so drained and on the verge of giving up.

My three sons—Guy, Leon, and Erik—for giving me the opportunity to love and care for them; and my grandchildren—Emilio, Laylani, and Amelie—who are my inspiration to make a difference in the world.

Stuart Kerr III, author of *God, Man, and Supreme*, whose emotional support and encouragement helped me through many uncertain moments.

Ken Ronshausen, for his web consulting services, and Joe DiMaggio, for developing and maintaining our website; *the*BookDesigners, for designing the creative cover of the book; my cousin Juan of Lopez-Bonilla Resources, LLC, and Pete Masterson, author of *Book Design and Production: A Guide for Authors and Publishers*, for their creative suggestions and unwavering encouragement; Mary Jo Zazueta for her excellent design services. Mary Jo's patience and professional guidance helped my sanity during the production process.

My many thanks and deep appreciation to everyone who reviewed the manuscript or parts of it and to those who generously provided endorsements, including Dr. and Mrs. Gerry and Milly Fisher; Chris Halvorson, PhD; Gard Jameson, PhD; Dr. B. Dale Sams; Peter Laurence, EdD; Dr. Clay Tucker-Ladd, and Loretta Thomas. A special thanks to Chirag Patel, PhD, director of research of The Vedic Foundation, for answering so many questions and helping me gain a more expanded perspective of Vedism so that I could better understand the relationships between Christian and Eastern doctrines.

A special thanks to James A. Woodward, friend and former Reader Services Manager of Urantia Foundation, who for years supported, encouraged, and inspired me to study *The Urantia Book* and who patiently answered my countless questions. Sharing my vision for this book, James added harmony and wisdom to this work through his meticulous and devoted editing.

To the final midwife of this book—she knows who she is—my sincere thanks and appreciation for her sharp mind and meticulous attention to detail. She had that rare ability to perceive the meaning behind the meaning and bring even more clarity and precision to the expression of my ideas.

AND to my husband Bart, the love of my life, without whom this book would not have been written. I thank him for his love, support, patience, caring, belief in what I was doing, and the many sleepless nights he spent reviewing, editing, and helping put my work in layman's terms.

Introduction

Have you ever asked yourself why our world is burdened with intolerance, prejudice, and hate when the foundations of all major religions are love, peace, and service? Do you wonder why we can't seem to align our human actions with our divine ideals?

In the search for meaning our world has reached a plateau of spiritual beliefs, a blending of philosophies and theologies from east to west, from mainstream to the esoteric, from the ancient to the latest. Despite a growing interest in personal spiritual development, much of the world suffers from moral and religious confusion. Peace, the measure of social evolution, continues to elude us. Our challenge is not so much to do things differently but to perceive them differently, in a new light that is graced with the wisdom of an epochal revelation. Embracing new insights into our understanding of God and God's relation to humanity will stimulate devotion, spiritual humility, and a selfless attitude of service. The faith grasp of the fatherhood of God makes obvious its corollary: the brotherhood of all humans. This simple yet profound spiritual understanding holds the potential to reshape our world.

Today's stubborn adherence to rigid thinking divides a weary humanity, locked in conflict and afflicted with violence. We see our own beliefs as truth, but too often our actions are not aligned with the essence of those beliefs. The brotherhood of man gets lip service but is largely ignored in the march of personal and political interactions. The never-ending quest for dominance breeds power struggle and religious upheaval, distracting us from our human commonality. Living as true members of the family of God is more than an intellectual concept or optimistic hope, and the doing of righteousness is not enough. It is *being* righteous, the result of deliberate and steadfast efforts to cultivate true spiritual character, that nourishes unity and fosters the spirit of cooperation.

It took me twelve years to write this book and reconcile my beliefs with an epochal revelation, *The Urantia Book*. During that time, my connection to God deepened and my worldview expanded out to cosmic levels I had never imagined. With this new conceptual experience of my relation to God and the universe, spiritual development took on new meaning. The last section of this book offers you the insights I gained in that process. I see it as a roadmap that integrates spiritual practice with a universal framework for the progressive and balanced development of human consciousness. Section four could have been a book in itself—short, compelling, and easy to read like so many other self-help spiritual books. However, it would have lacked the powerful new concepts and teachings that are presented in sections one through three. This revealed knowledge challenges the outdated models of our spiritual origin, history, and destiny. It produces an upgraded and comprehensive frame of reference for every reader that can be passed through you to others and into the wider community. Elevating the consciousness of our world is an urgent imperative, and this calling hinges on the discovery of new and higher spiritual meanings and values and in the progressive reconciliation of science with religion, nature with God.

Heaven Is Not the Last Stop is intended to be a soul shaker. Its message is designed to inspire the reader to develop deeper levels of spiritual understanding and growth; to promote humility and greater expressions of loving service. Some may find the content too challenging, while others may embrace only that which requires small effort. Spiritual progressives will be inspired to examine some widely held beliefs and emerge with personal faith insights and fresh reconciliations of their own. It will take resolve—and the dedication of individuals with foresight and courage—to objectively explore the revelations in this book and attain a cosmic perspective that transcends our instinctive preoccupation with personal enlightenment and salvation.

In sections one and two, "Humanity's Spiritual Origin" and "Humanity's Spiritual History," bold new insights into faith and religion will lead you beyond existing concepts to undiscovered ideals and unexplored realities. Historical and theological gaps are filled, upgrading human speculation with reasonable revelation. You will explore the vast celestial hierarchy involved in the evolution and ascension of humanity and gain valuable new insights into the relationships between soul, spirit, and personality, including the profound importance of family.

Section three, "Humanity's Spiritual Destiny," offers expanded detail and clarity about the individual and collective fortunes awaiting us. Myths and distorted concepts of heaven are dispelled; the "fires of hell" are extinguished. You will examine a widespread belief that could be thwarting social progress. And the great adventure that awaits you after death is fully revealed as is the destiny of future generations.

Collectively, the four sections expand your worldview, empowering you to develop and embody a contagious philosophy of living that enlivens your experience and expression of compassion and love. You will discover higher values that will influence you in making superior choices, attracting all that is good in the mind and challenging you to express that which is best in your soul.

The challenge is there for the taking: Are you willing to take the ultimate journey of mind and spirit? Are you open to the realization of deeper understanding? Are you prepared to make faith a priority, to question prevailing attitudes and beliefs? Are you ready to envision a new and appealing universe perspective that lifts human hope for an enlightened era of spiritual vitality—the next age of humanity? If you answer "yes" to any of these questions, you are ready to embark on a journey that is certain to both agitate and satisfy your mind, heart, and soul. Prepare to be amazed and uplifted!

Note to the Reader

Readers who are familiar with *The Urantia Book* will recognize its content throughout *Heaven Is Not the Last Stop*. I have relied heavily on the information that is unique to that tome, through both direct quotes and a substantial amount of paraphrasing. Both my language use and paraphrasing style were chosen to present the material in a way that maintains its meaning and message according to my best understanding.

Greater insight into the expansive nature of God is gained when we overcome human gender bias in discussion of spirit. In *Heaven Is Not the Last Stop*, the term "God the Father" is used. In choosing to do this, it is not my intention to exclude women or the feminine aspect of the Godhead. I believe that God transcends all gender, but gender-neutral language is awkward, impersonal, and uninspiring. When we challenge our prejudices and allow ourselves to consider the highest concept of God as "Father," we stimulate feelings of tender affection and selfless devotion and promote our acceptance of one another as brother and sister.

Similarly, the term "brotherhood of man" is used to represent the unity and cooperation among all people that is founded on this loving recognition of our familial relationship. Terms such as "man" and "mankind," which reflect the writing style of the first half of the twentieth century, are preserved only in direct quotes from *The Urantia Book*. Otherwise, the more gender-inclusive style of the present time is used. Please also note that the word "Urantia" represents our planet, Earth, and the term "Thought Adjuster" is equivalent to "the Indwelling Spirit."

Biblical references noted in brackets within a direct quotation were added by the author. Unless otherwise noted, all Bible quotes are from the King James Version.

SECTION ONE

Humanity's Spiritual Origin

I can see how it might be possible for someone to look around on Earth and not believe in God, but I cannot conceive how anyone could look up into the heavens and say there is no God.

ABRAHAM LINCOLN

Introduction

Hamlet: *"There are more things in heaven and Earth, Horatio,*
than are dreamt of in your philosophy."

William Shakespeare's *Hamlet*, Act I, Scene V

Throughout *Heaven Is Not the Last Stop* you will find a recurrent theme that is crucial to the evolution of both the individual and our civilization: knowing God better in order to establish a more meaningful relationship with him as parent and with one another as his beloved children. This concept, the fatherhood of God and the brotherhood of man, centers on an emergent cosmic perspective and imbues us with spiritual reverence for the rewarding challenges that beckon to us from beyond our comfort zone.

To some, the concept of God is abstract and confusingly rendered by theologians through the ages. This section offers clarification of the entire concept of religion and presents a logical chronology of "the Beginning." An enlarged perspective of the origin and creation of the universe and the superhuman alliance working on behalf of humanity is presented. This information sets the stage for a deeper understanding of our dramatic history and unfolding destiny. The cosmic philosophy portrayed in section one requires patience of the reader—but is ultimately satisfying. It will greatly expand your concept of God and his creation and will lay the foundation for the rest of the book.

1.

Reason and Faith

I don't think that by studying science you will be forced to conclude that there must be a God. But if you have already found God, then you can say, from understanding science, "Ah, I see what God has done in the world."

Carl Feit, cancer researcher from Yeshiva University in New York

Reason and faith are two essential factors in the development of both individual consciousness and world peace—two sides of the same coin that can be harmoniously linked to arrive at a Bigger Picture of Existence.

Reason is the understanding technique of the sciences, introducing us to the material world of nature and facts. *Faith* is the insight technique of religion, initiating us to a world of values, divinity, and personal religious experience.[1]

In science, well-defined evidence is collected to support a theory. Once demonstrated, the theory is considered to be proven and attains universal acceptance. In religion, the existence of God is verifiable only in the reality of *personal experience*. True religion emerges when faith awakens the personal consciousness of God and assures the survival of the believer after physical death.

Without faith, reason is cold . . . but without reason, faith is blind.
David Pyle

Despite the apparent disparities, faith and reason complement one another. Faith challenges us, through personal transformation, to achieve what scientific knowledge and reason alone cannot sustain. Though reason can always question faith, faith can always illuminate both reason and logic. Reason reveals those probabilities that the alchemy of faith can transmute into moral certainties, even spiritual experience. Without symmetry of faith and reason, development of consciousness follows a path of partial wisdom and spiritual confusion.

Facts may quarrel with theories but never with faith. Conflict emerges when faith devolves into dogmatic belief and when reason becomes self-serving.

When beliefs are supported by an integral worldview that incorporates science, religion, and progressive spiritual attainment, faith and reason achieve an elegant balance.

The Development of Consciousness: Faith and Reason

Faith, ". . . the substance of things hoped for, the evidence of things not seen,"[2] lures the seeker into a personal search for deeper meanings and infinite values. A faith suffused with reverence inspires the artist through creative expression to unify her notions of Creator with creation. Faith motivates the philosopher to reconcile reason with the unknown, science with religion, the universe with God. Theology emerges only when the human mind attempts to define God and clarify, explain, and validate personal religious experience.

In the Neolithic era, the religion of the primitive people was not based on faith or belief, but rather on membership in the tribe or group. The individual, the tribe, and the world were intertwined. The spirit of self-reflection was minimally active and there was a negligible concept of space and time. The social meaning of the unexplainable was generally taught through a set of stories or myths, and myth governed the collective mind. The mythologies of the early settlements were mainly matriarchal, partly based on the appreciation of the earth and her fertility (the Great Mother). With the development of larger settlements and cities, the center of divinity shifted to the sky and the spirits who dwelt there, giving way to patriarchal mythologies. In ancient Mesopotamia the Sumerians believed that anthropomorphic gods and goddesses created and governed the universe. In ancient Egypt, science, law, ethics, and philosophy operated together within the framework of the Egyptian religious worldview.

During the Greek classical era, starting around 800 BC, individual thought and philosophy began to emerge from the collective thinking of the time. The sixth century BC was a unique century of spiritual progress as great planetary religious and philosophic traditions were developed from the insights of individuals such as Gautama Siddhartha, Confucius, Lao Tzu, the pundits of the Upanishads, the prophets of Israel, and the philosophers and poets of Greece. Carl Jung lectured about this era: "We find the first signs of a 'Weltanschauung' [worldview] in the Greek philosophers."[3] Toward the end of the classical period, anthropomorphic myths were increasingly discarded, and greater self-reflection and the exercise of individual will were increasingly manifested. The Greek mind strove to discover a natural explanation for the cosmos through observation and reasoning. Nature took on an impersonal dimension that forged a separation from divine forces. It was during this period that the geometer and philosopher Pythagoras of Samos produced a synthesis of religious belief and science that influenced European thought for more than a thousand years—right through the medieval period to the seventeenth century AD. Toward the end of the classical era, a Hellenized Jew, Philo of Alexandria, merged Greek philosophy and Hebrew theology into a compact and fairly consistent system of religious belief and practice that laid the foundation for the development of Christianity.

The classical period was also the era of Roman conquest and rule, and it was not until AD 313 that Emperor Constantine legitimized Christianity. The Edict of Milan officially granted tolerance and restitution. The fourth century saw the center of power move to the church, with the first ecumenical council in AD 325 heralding a millennium of Roman Catholic ascendancy.

By the Middle Ages, ". . . the pluralism of classical culture with its multiplicity of philosophies, its diversity of polytheistic mythologies, and plethora of mystery religions, gave way to an emphatically monolithic system—one God, one Church, one Truth."[4] The hierarchical rule by one supremely powerful, all-knowing and beneficent God had been firmly established. Reflective awareness found itself at home in the cathedral; theology and dogmatism flourished in Western culture. During the medieval period, the tendency was ". . . to diminish the value of observing, analyzing, or understanding the natural world, and thus to emphasize or negate the rational and empirical faculties in favor of the emotional, moral, and spiritual."[5] The divine becomes more and more distant. No longer immanent in the world as in the classical period, God is separated from nature and the divine attributes of goodness are split away from all evil. A distinction between spirit and matter is firmly established. Evil is considered endemic to the human condition, and the doctrines of devils, original sin, and heresy reflect the human capacity to project evil and inflict pain upon others.

Religious persecution reached its apex with the Roman Catholic Inquisition in the thirteenth and fourteenth centuries, when the church blamed so-called heretics for the many famines, plagues, and "sins" against church doctrine. When the heliocentric cosmology of Nicolaus Copernicus's epochal text, *On the Revolution of the Heavenly Spheres*, disclosed that Earth was not the center of the universe, it displaced the human being to a relative and minor position in a vast impersonal universe. This radical shift of the human being from the cosmic center was reinforced and intensified a few centuries later by Darwin's publication of his revolutionary book, *On the Evolution of Species by Means of Natural Selection*. The human being was ". . . no longer divinely ordained, no longer absolute and secure, no longer the crown of creation, the favored child of the universe, but rather just one more ephemeral species."[6] It was Copernicus's discovery that initiated the cosmological estrangement of modern consciousness.

The modern era began with the Scientific Revolution, inaugurated by thinkers such as Francis Bacon and Galileo Galilei. During this stage, the existence of the "spirit" was increasingly denied and evil was greatly deemphasized. The distant God of medieval times is cast even further to the outer reaches of the universe by Enlightenment thinkers such as René Descartes, the empiricist John Locke, and the Deists, such as Voltaire, Thomas Jefferson, and Benjamin Franklin. Deity was removed from reality altogether by the French philosophers Denis Diderot, Julien La Mettrie, and Auguste Comte. Personal estrangement from God and the cosmos was completed by Immanuel Kant's theory that there are no possible means by which the individual can know the universe in its essence. The religious explanations of "who" and "why" were replaced with the scientific explanations of "what" and "how." In *The Passion of the Western Mind*, Richard Tarnas lists several attributes that characterize recent stages of Western consciousness, three of which follow:

1. In contrast to the medieval Christian cosmos, created and governed by a personal and actively omnipotent God, the modern universe was an impersonal phenomenon governed by regular natural laws, and understandable in exclusively physical and mathematical terms. God was now distantly removed as creator and architect of the physical universe, and was now less a God of love, miracle, and redemption, and more of a supreme intelligence and first cause, who established the material universe and its immutable laws and then withdrew from further direct activity.

2. The Christian stress on the supremacy of the spiritual over the material was now largely inverted, with the physical world becoming the predominant focus for human activity.

3. Science replaced religion as the preeminent intellectual authority. Human reason and empirical observation replaced theological doctrine and scriptural revelation as the principal means for comprehending the universe. [7]

In our modern world, science has produced a crisis: its unprecedented progress is one of civilization's greatest dangers. Religion is also in crisis: the living brotherhood of man cannot be established when the fatherhood of God is ignored or denied, or when individuals harbor an attitude of indifference toward God and alienation toward their fellows. Nor can it be established when humanity exhibits so little of the spirit of the life and teachings of Jesus, that devotion which transforms selfishness into selflessness, anger into peace, fear into love and greed into joy through the inward illumination of worship and the outward dedication to the service of humanity. For a considerable time, modern humans have been experiencing an obstinate rift between the mind and the soul.

We pay little heed to the possibility of real and progressive spiritual experience in and with a multilevel universe that extends to God's sphere of infinity. We have lost sight of the fact that "The vast gulf between the experience of the truth of God and ignorance as to the fact of God can be bridged only by living faith. Reason alone cannot achieve harmony between infinite truth and universal fact."[8]

Social Effect

In the nineteenth century, a perilous internal conflict within Christianity loomed. In the West, the general feeling prevailed that institutional religious doctrine did not reflect personal religious experience. Christian sectarianism and fragmentation increased and the more flexible metaphysical approach of Eastern religious worldviews was readily embraced by the creative class. Greatly influenced by Eastern ideas were philosophers and writers such as Goethe, Shelley, Emerson, and de Balzac. Ralph Waldo Emerson is credited with fashioning the modern idea of spirituality as distinct from religion and emphasizing the import of personal religious experience.

Liberal Christianity emerged in the twentieth century, advocating individual freedom of religious thought and expression. It was willing to mix theology with modern scientific theories, adopt broader views of salvation, and embrace Eastern philosophies and esoteric traditions. But these ancient thought systems did not promote the progressive recognition of God as a loving father, the evolution of personal worship, or the increasing discovery of supreme values and divine ideals.

In response to liberal Christianity and to new interpretations of the Bible, Christian fundamentalism took a literal stand, seeking to preserve traditions and a "fundamental" set of Christian beliefs. This reactionary stance fueled massive evangelical, Pentecostal, and charismatic revivals after World War II. It also produced the Christian Right, with its powerful effect upon individual belief and politics. Fundamentalism, however, brings with it a paradox: its rigidity is incompatible with the dynamic spiritual growth needed to herald a brotherhood of man, and its restrictive culture inhibits its members from experiencing a new and fuller revelation of the very gospel it seeks to promote.

Despite good intentions and a growing concern for the environment, the living brotherhood of man cannot be established when the fatherhood of God is ignored or denied, or when individuals harbor an attitude of indifference toward God.

Groups describing themselves as Islamic anarchists reappeared in the latter half of the twentieth century, rekindling Muslim militancy. Contrary to the message of love and peace in the Qur'an, these extremists promote a violent and external interpretation of jihad, not the original meaning: the inward path of self-mastery. This misguided approach to Islam encourages holy war in Allah's name.

Secularism, the modern movement that champions the separation of church and state, was the offspring of the sixteenth-century revolt against the medieval Christian church and the agnostic drift of science in the nineteenth and twentieth centuries. Early secularism promoted increased tolerance, social service, democratic government, and civil liberties. But it also tended to elevate politics and power over ethics and religious thought, leading to secularization and a passive attitude toward God.

With the rise of secularism and the postmodern advent of the New Age movement, it became more common to distinguish between the spiritual and the religious. Many began to link religion with inflexibility and with obsolete practices and values. Spirituality was associated with "spiritual liberty, mystical experience, meditative interiority, universal brotherhood, and sympathetic appreciation of all religions."[9] By the 1970s, Eastern gurus were considered to have high spiritual status. In the 1980s, this reverence shifted to channeled guides—human mediums through which entities from other dimensions are perceived to communicate wisdom. By the end of the twentieth century, the attitude of reverence had shifted to ordinary people—the elevation of the individual to God-like status: "I am a spirit being having a human experience."

Amidst the indifference of many liberal Christians, the rigid stance of Christian fundamentalism, and the free-flowing New Age spirituality, there has been considerable confusion about religion, with many abandoning it altogether. A parallel of social decline has become increasingly evident. The twenty-first century is witnessing an unprecedented lack of personal mutual respect and an increased tendency toward religious divisiveness, exploitation, and violence. Growing social unrest, wide polarization, war, and genocide continue to plague our world.

The Merging of Faith and Reason: the Blossoming of a Cosmic and God-conscious Humanity

The great science scholars, past and present, have shown that amidst religious and secular chaos, faith and reason can prevail to bring higher understanding and ever-perfecting ideals. William Sloane Coffin in his book *Credo* expresses the integration of science and religion: "There is nothing anti-intellectual in the leap of faith, for faith is not believing without proof but trusting without reservation. Faith is no substitute for thinking. On the contrary, it is what makes good thinking possible. It has what we might call a limbering effect on the mind, by taking us beyond familiar ground, faith ends up giving us that much more to think about."[10]

We have arrived at a profound point in history where poignant disparities exist between intelligent design and scientific evolution. Faith and reason play a direct role in responding to this debate but lack the deeper insight required to resolve it. Revelation, specifically epochal revelation as unveiled in chapter 2, reconciles the faith of religion and the reason of science while it unifies them with philosophical wisdom.

Science has sometimes been said to be opposed to faith, and inconsistent with it. But all science in fact rests on a basis of faith, for it assumes the permanence and uniformity of natural laws—a thing that can never be demonstrated.

Tyron Edwards (1809–1894)

In his book *Integral Consciousness and the Future of Evolution*, Steve McIntosh reports that ". . . as we are increasingly confronted with the growing problems of the world, we begin to realize that the solutions to these problems require large-scale cultural evolution. And when we examine the past historical instances of such large-scale cultural evolution, we can see that this most often comes in the form of new, values-based worldviews—new reality frames enacted through enlarged understandings of reality explained through new forms of metaphysics. Thus, as we try to bring about cultural evolution, we can see that the time has come to advance a new philosophical synthesis in the form of a new reality frame . . . a synthesis that moves far enough beyond post-modernism so as to achieve a usable, inspiring and worldview-enacting philosophy that transcends and includes the premodern, the modern, and the postmodern."[11] Likewise, in *The Passion of the Western Mind*, Tarnas suggests that the central factor of the modern predicament is knowledge, and it is here that we should look for an opening.[12]

An enlarged and inspiring worldview can only be attained if individuals are willing to expand their concept of God and their understanding of humanity's relationship to God and the universe. This willingness to consider new philosophical perspectives is enlivened by the exercise of faith. Faith and the discovery of new and higher spiritual meanings work in harmony with the development of a progressive philosophy of living, inspiring us to seek higher values to live by. In the context of expanding our cosmic understanding, epochal revelation invites serious consideration.

When we complement faith and reason with the insight afforded by epochal revelation, we can critically adjust the spiritual meanings and values of today's philosophies and theologies. Epochal revelation offers newfound clarity and significance; the result is a natural uplift of beliefs and the actions they drive. Revelation, *together* with faith and reason, can lift humanity beyond today's parochial mindset to correlate science, religion, and personal experience—thus creating the expanded worldview, the new God-consciousness, that elevates ideals and builds the spiritual family of God.

2.

Religion and Revelation

There is one thing even more vital to science than intelligent methods; and that is, the sincere desire to find out the truth, whatever it may be.

Charles Sanders Pierce, American polymath

True religion may be defined as the progressive experience of finding and knowing God, with the goal to become Godlike. This experience starts on Earth and continues through the multilevel universe to eternity.

When the true meaning of religion is forgotten, religion becomes stagnant and associated with beliefs, institutions, and systems; it becomes fertile soil for corruption and manipulation, and that is what leads to conflict.

Religious conflict is the eight-hundred-pound gorilla sitting squarely in the middle of so many of history's most horrific transgressions against humanity. Kenneth C. Davis, author of *America's Hidden History*, explains that the underlying lesson that history has taught us is that people fear what they do not understand, or what is different. This fearful ignorance moves in tandem with the arrogance of claiming to possess the exclusive truth. Davis explains that these volatile dynamics lead one group to demonize or dehumanize the other. Once they are firmly established in society, it becomes easy to hang people as heretics, burn them at the stake or in ovens, fly jetliners into their buildings, and bomb their railway stations.[1]

> *Always keep in mind: True religion is to know God as your Father and man as your brother. Religion is not a slavish belief in threats of punishment or magical promises of future mystical rewards.*
>
> The Urantia Book

The detrimental effects of forgetting the true meaning of religion are not only evident in the religious conflicts that still plague our world today but are also evident in the growing indifference between individuals; in the violence in our schools and society; and in the quality of the decision-making of our leaders. Joshua Cooper Ramo, author of *The Age of the Unthinkable*, observes that rather than becoming more stable or easier to comprehend, our world is in crisis and requires higher and more progressive thinking to successfully address the complex problems we face. In the following statement, Ramo reveals the setback to social progress as he points to the solution: ". . . whether they are running corporations or foreign ministries or central banks, some of the best minds of our era are still in thrall to an older way of seeing and thinking. They are making repeated misjudgments about the world."[2]

The intellectual earmark of religion is certainty; the philosophical characteristic is consistency; the social fruits are love and service.

The Urantia Book

This observation is relevant not only in business, finance, and politics, but also in religion. Religious and spiritual leaders today are hanging on to ancient ways of perceiving and thinking that hinder the development of the cosmic perspective that can support a growing spiritual nature. Leaders shape our history. The soundness of their decisions and the effectiveness of their leadership in advancing peace and social progress are very much influenced by the accuracy of their worldview—factually and philosophically.

When the true meaning of religion is forgotten, religious institutions become inflexible and excluding, beliefs become rigid and dividing and religious practices become stultified. Decisions influenced by myopic or erroneous beliefs (an inaccurate worldview) are unable to garner the power to transform or advance spiritual unity and social progress.

True religion is about harmoniously developing the three endowments of the human mind: cosmic insight, moral awareness, and spiritual perception. When we are actively engaged in this process, we grow in God-consciousness, the highest attainment of the human mind. As we expand our capacity for God-consciousness we fine tune the accuracy of our worldview; our reasoning becomes increasingly more objective, inclusive, moral, loving, and selfless. As a result, decisions become more effective, socially progressive, and peace-enhancing.

Refining the accuracy of our worldview progressively leads to a more logical, consistent, philosophic framework that illuminates our place in the universe and our responsibility as cosmic citizens. This refinement involves expanding our concept of God, recognizing our relation with the universe in progressive spiritual experience, and discovering greater meanings in our understanding of soul, spirit, and personality. Such wisdom is always attainable through faith-insight and revelation, specifically epochal revelation, as explained further in this chapter.

When we open our hearts and minds to *progress in meanings*, true religion becomes a way of life, a religion of the spirit devoted to harmoniously developing God-consciousness. Living the golden rule becomes the instinctive response of a spiritually progressive cosmic citizen.

True religion deepens our personal connection with God as it blossoms by faith and spiritual insight into the mighty realization of the father-child relationship between God and all humans. "Religion, as a human experience, ranges from the primitive fear slavery of the evolving savage up to the sublime and magnificent faith liberty of those civilized mortals who are superbly conscious of sonship with the eternal God."[3] The religious drive is innate, but religious growth is optional. It is our choice to embrace faith, to take steps to know God and emulate his nature, and to expand our understanding of universe relationships so that worship and altruistic service become a way of life. True religion seeks to evolve and transform mortals into the image and likeness of God—that is, to instill in our decisions the unselfish attitude of a wise and loving parent.

> *Civilization, science, and advanced religions must deliver mankind from those fears born of the dread of natural phenomenon.*
> The Urantia Book

When the religion of the spirit guides our soul, we allow for critical adjustments to our beliefs. We are open to the progressive development of spiritual insight and the appreciation of cosmic values. This living faith transcends any social, religious, economic, or political alliance. We avoid fanaticism by staying attuned to scientific discoveries and reconciling them with our beliefs. And we develop personal associations that are creative, comforting, and love-expanding.[4]

The Evolution of Organized Religion

Primitive religion was born of ignorance and uncertainty about nature, the instinct to fear mysterious energies and worship higher forces. The impulse of religion drove primitive people to seek understanding of the unseen, first by personalizing the forces of nature as fate, then as ghosts and spirits, and later as gods. The inability of the primitive human to understand death fostered the growth of superstitions. Superstitions became the moral and social police force, with the ancients claiming that their olden laws, the taboos or prohibitions, had been given to their ancestors by the gods. Religious rituals evolved as archaic humans sought to appease the unseen forces. Sacrifices were introduced first to ward off the calamities brought on by evil spirits, and later to appease the gods.

The evolved concept of the invisible world became more complex as the medicine people, the shamans, and the priests emerged as the mediators between humans and the unseen world. Belief in good and bad spirits was sanctioned and set the stage for the concept of sin. Sin was the transgression of taboo, bringing a death penalty. The concept of sin led the way to the practices of confession and forgiveness, renunciation and humiliation, and the sacraments and prayers of organized religions. As primitive religion evolves, it creates its gods in the image and likeness of mortals: after death, tribal chiefs are deified and great souls are sainted.

The human attempt to explain the nature and content of personal religious experience resulted in the development of diverse systems of human thought and conduct. These belief systems eventually evolved into the theologies of organized religion, with diverse rituals and practices immersed in superstition forming an integral part of religious conduct. As religion became institutionalized, the high ideals of the ecclesiastics were lowered before the challenge of human greed and lust for power. This resulted in behavior, still evident today, that encourages animosity and dissension among the congregations:

- Fixation of beliefs and stagnation of doctrine
- Accumulation of vested interests
- Tendency to standardize and fossilize truth
- Diversion from the service of God to the service of the church
- Inclination of leaders to become administrators instead of ministers
- Tendency to form sects and competitive divisions within the church
- Establishment of inflexible ecclesiastical authority
- Creation of the "chosen-people" attitude
- Fostering of false and exaggerated ideas of sacredness
- Creation of religious processes that petrify thinking and formalize our worship
- Tendency to venerate the past while ignoring present demands
- Entanglement with functions of lay institutions
- Creation of religious castes for the purpose of discrimination
- Becoming an intolerant judge of orthodoxy
- Failing to hold the interest of adventurous youth and gradually losing the saving message of the gospel of eternal salvation

To rise above these legacies is no easy task. A main function of organized religions is to provide a degree of social stability and spiritual guidance to civilization. But traditional stability can inhibit the expansion of human wisdom by becoming fundamentalist and excluding progressive thinking. Leaders of organized religions have long feared that independent thought might reduce their group's authority by undermining the doctrines they hold to be sacred. This fear has dimmed the passion for the discovery of higher meanings and values; it has inhibited a greater grasp of universal truth and the joyous living of a religion of service. The uncommitted may find easy reason to have contempt for the word "religion," associating belief in God with the manipulation of followers.

Revelation

A rigid orthodoxy within any organized religion reflects irreverence to the soil from which it sprang: the gift of revelation. "Revelation is a technique whereby ages upon ages of time are saved in the necessary work of sorting and sifting the errors of evolution from the truths of spirit acquirement."[5] When there is resistance to progress in human wisdom, religious groups become inflexible, impacting the spiritual growth of the institution, its members, and society.

Revelation is in essence a download of divine knowledge, a gift from God that expands our understanding of his divine nature and creation. Revelation may be personal or epochal.

Personal revelation is generated by the spirit influences resident in the mind. Such insights may be discovered through study, visions, or reflection on personal beliefs and convictions; they may even arise as a result of divine wisdom imparted by celestial beings to selected God-knowing individuals. These personal insights often transform individual lives or advance humankind's morality, philosophy, and theology. But the emotional nature of human beings makes the connection between mind and spirit difficult, sometimes resulting in faulty interpretations and the rise of conflicting religions and strange "isms." Some personal insights can be meaningful to scores of individuals and people of like mind, but not contain enough creative and spiritual impetus or universal religious values to uplift a society or nation.

Many outstanding personalities have inaugurated great religious epochs. Their personal insights have contributed to their particular national or racial illumination and served as the foundation for organized religions. The interpretation of their spiritual experiences was embedded in the teachings that have guided and inspired the lives of their followers. The natural human craving for help from above contributes to the tendency of enshrouding these religious leaders with legends pertaining to supernatural origins and miraculous careers. The idolization of such leaders often comes at the expense of their teachings, with followers sometimes losing sight of the truth that these inspiring leaders proclaim.

> *Revelation unifies history, co-ordinates geology, astronomy, physics, chemistry, biology, sociology, and psychology.*
> The Urantia Book

As an epochal phenomenon, revelation is periodic, imparted by celestial personalities as the inspiration for a new era of planetary evolution. The illumination of epochal revelation and the pressure of the slowly advancing mores are the only two influences that can modify and advance the dogmas of religion.[6]

An epochal revelation is a most blessed gift to humankind, expanding awareness of our origin, history, and destiny; ". . . such revelations are of immense value in that they at least transiently clarify knowledge by:

1. The reduction of confusion by the authoritative elimination of error.

2. The coordination of known or about-to-be-known facts and observations.

3. The restoration of important bits of lost knowledge concerning epochal transactions in the distant past.

4. The supplying of information which will fill in vital missing gaps in otherwise earned knowledge.

5. Presenting cosmic data in such a manner as to illuminate the spiritual teachings contained in the accompanying revelation."[7]

Illustration 1
THE FIVE EPOCHAL REVELATIONS TO DATE

Approx. Time Period	Concepts Revealed or Expanded (brief)	Impetus of Revelation	Birth of Organized Religion	Teachings Disseminated or Founded by	Influence
First epochal revelation 500,000 years ago Revealed by Caligastia, Earth's Planetary Prince (cf. chapters 6 and 8)	Paradise Trinity, the First Source and Center and the one God of all.	Primitive humans developed the capacity to choose path of eternal survival.	Teachings were forgotten soon after the planetary rebellion approximately 200,000 years ago.	Revealed truth disseminated by Caligastia's visible volunteer staff and their modified Andonites. (cf. chapters 8 and 12)	Teachings spread out from the Mesopotamian headquarters.
Second epochal revelation 37,000 years ago Revealed by Adam and Eve (cf. chapters 6 and 9)	Paradise Trinity. Expanded concept of the one Father of all.	The confused affairs of a planet impeded by rebellion needed to be untangled.	The disruption of the first Eden halted the course of the Adamic revelation. By 2500 BC humanity had mostly lost sight of this revelation.	The aborted teachings of Adam were carried on by the Sethite missionaries—founded by Adam and Eve's son.	Greece, Mesopotamia (now Iraq) and India.
Third epochal revelation 1980–1886 BC Revealed by Machiventa Melchizedek (cf. chapters 6 and 10)	Paradise Trinity. Trust in the omnipotent benef-icence of the Universal Father. Salvation through faith, not sacrifices and burnt offerings. The coming of another Son of God. Machiventa Melchizedek initiated the age of righteous servants of the Lord God.	Revealed truth was threatened with extinction during the millenniums that followed the miscarriage of the Adamic mission on Earth.	Teachings did not result in the immediate appearance of religions, but formed the foundations on which later teachers of truth would build religions on Earth.	Revealed truth disseminated by Abraham and the Salem missionaries, who were taught by Machiventa Melchizedek.	Mesopotamia, Egypt, Asia Minor, all of Europe, even to the British Isles, Iceland, China and Japan.
1500–800 BC	An all-pervading Absolute Reality—Brahman. A supreme trinity. Personal form of God—Brahma. Atman as a spark of Brahman.		Hinduism	Originated from Aryan-Andite Vedic settlers. Then the Brahmans of India compiled what has come down through the times as the Vedas and the Upanishads.	Hinduism is now the third largest world religion.
1000 BC	Concept of Deity evolves from the primitive god of Mount Horeb, to God of Israel, to a loving and merciful Creator Father.		Hebrew religion	Moses, followed by the prophets.	
600 BC		Many men arose to proclaim truth, including:			
	The Four Noble Truths; the Eightfold Path; salvation by human effort, apart from divine help.	Siddhartha Gautama	Buddhism		Buddhism is the fourth largest world religion.
	Exalted the idea of one eternal Deity and ultimate victory of light over darkness. Final judg-ment. Resurrection of the dead.	Zarathustra (Zoroaster)	Zoroastrianism		
	Placed morality in the place of magic.	Confucius	Confucianism		
	Tao as the One First Cause of all creation. Man's eternal destiny is the everlasting union with Tao.	Lao Tzu	Taoism		

Illustration 1 *(continued)*

Approx. Time Period	Concepts Revealed or Expanded (brief)	Impetus of Revelation	Birth of Organized Religion	Teachings Disseminated or Founded by	Influence
Fourth epochal revelation 2,000+ years ago Revealed by Jesus of Nazareth (cf. chapters 6 and 11)	Personality of the Universal Father revealed in the life of Jesus. Ever-ascending citizenship in the eternal universe was revealed. Salvation through love and service was proclaimed. The meaning of the golden rule was elevated. Jesus inaugurated the age of the faith-sons and daughters of the Universal Father.	The need to end the planetary rebellion and for the universe to have its established sovereign.		Revealed truth disseminated by the followers and disciples of Jesus; the ministry and writing of the apostles.	
AD 30	Presented a majestic concept of Deity—God as a loving, forgiving Father. Individual salvation. Selfless service.		Prior to the spring of AD 30 Christianity did not exist.	Christianity had been in a state of intense preparation for more than three years spanning the ministries of John the Baptist and Jesus of Nazareth. In time, the teachings of Jesus were acculturated and the new evolving religion became known as Christianity.	Christianity is the largest world religion.
AD 600	Earthly life is a preparation for eternal life. Final judgment.		Islam	Mohammed, founder, born in Mecca, Arabia.	Islam is the second largest world religion.
Middle 19th century	Oneness of God. Oneness of the human family. Oneness of religion. "The earth is but one country and mankind its citizens."Spiritual development begins with life on Earth and continues in the spiritual world. The purpose of God in creating man is to enable him to know his Creator and to attain His Presence.		Baha'i	Founded by Mirza Hoseyn 'Ali Nuri, who is known as Bahá'u'lláh (Arabic: "Glory of God").	
Fifth epochal revelation Revealed by numerous celestial beings and published in *The Urantia Book* AD 1955	*The Urantia Book* presents the Universal Father's profound policy of self-distribution. Provides a clear depiction of the celestial hierarchy. Expands information about the history, structure, and dynamics of the universe. Expands the geologic and biological history of Earth. Clarifies the life and teachings of Jesus. Reveals the nature and mission of the Indwelling Spirit and its relation to the soul and the human personality. Reveals the mortal ascension plan.	Concepts of spirituality and cosmology were in need of clarification and expansion.	N/A	*The Urantia Book* published by Urantia Foundation, Chicago, Illinois. Teachings may be disseminated by all who choose to embrace them.	A grand expansion of religious realities that affirms the truth, beauty, and goodness of all the world's religions, setting the stage for a new vision of cosmic spirituality.

The content of epochal revelation is determined by how much the collective human mind has progressed and can assimilate. *The Urantia Book* states that although there have been many events of religious revelation, only five have been of epochal significance, the first imparted over five hundred thousand years ago and the fifth being disseminated today. Each epochal revelation contributes to major advances in human wisdom when reconciled with the knowledge of the time, and each visitation builds upon the previous one. These kernels of revealed truth can be recognized in the belief systems of organized religions today. Illustration 1 presents the relationship between the events associated with each epochal revelation and organized religions as depicted in *The Urantia Book.*

Epochal revelation expands the ethical horizon of evolved religion while also expanding the moral obligations of all prior revelations. For example, the religion of the Hebrews was one of moral inspiration; the Greeks evolved a religion of beauty; the organizer of Christianity, Paul of Tarsus, and his supporters founded a religion of faith, hope, and charity. The religion of Jesus of Nazareth offers security in the Father's love with the joy and satisfaction that result from sharing this love in the service of humanity.

Materialistic science and organized religion cannot successfully create a perspective of existence that simultaneously generates harmony in the mind and satisfies the spirit. But an evolving philosophy strengthened and guided by the superhuman insights of epochal revelation can reconcile both science and religion to synchronize fact and truth. Such an enlightened philosophy provides an intelligent explanation of the nature and content of religious experience that can serve as a springboard for the further transformation of humanity and our religious institutions. The exploration of current religious beliefs in the light of epochal revelation helps develop the cosmic perspective that motivates individuals to do the following:

- Establish a dynamic and meaningful mode of living
- Create lasting peace in the human experience
- Establish a superior civilization based on enduring spiritual unity and mutual cooperation
- Respond to the needs and sufferings of others
- Join in teamwork for service on the basis of ideals and purpose rather than on the basis of ideas, opinions, and theological beliefs
- Foster a life experience in which the sovereignty of truth, beauty, and goodness prevails

Religion and Revelation

Revelation has been operative in our world since deep prehistoric times, with epochal revelation imparted as humanity developed the capacity to assimilate spiritual information. With the passage of time these revelations commingled with the beliefs and practices of the era, helping religion evolve. Belief systems change as they appropriate the content of other belief systems, for example, the functional levels of Deity are well depicted in Hinduism but underwent further changes in response to Buddhism, Jainism, and later Islam and Christianity. The revealed teachings about the Seven Master Spirits are best represented in the Zoroastrian concept of the seven supreme gods. This theology had a major impact on the later Levantine religions including Judaism, Christianity, and Islam. New branches of religious thought are therefore seen to be fresh expressions of old beliefs with new adaptations and adjustments, all laced with elements of revealed truth. All religious teachings include complementary perspectives that can be integrated into other faiths.

The human flaw of fundamentalism infects followers of all religions. It's a challenge to admit that belief systems may be based on inaccurate or incomplete information, but honestly questioning any belief is how a reflective child comes to understand the world. In the face of unprecedented scientific achievement, social progress is now being threatened by spiritual confusion and philosophic chaos. As science improves our physical world through research and experimentation, epochal revelation can revitalize and broaden our philosophies and theologies to shift humanity's awareness toward greater values and unity of ideals, to uplift the decision-making process essential to social progress.

> *God answers man's prayer by giving him an increased revelation of truth, an enhanced appreciation of beauty, and an augmented concept of goodness.*
> The Urantia Book

The embrace of epochal revelation is vital to the development of the cosmic perspective that supports a growing spiritual nature. How can we assess the credibility of epochal revelation?

1. It provides a coordinated and unbroken explanation of both science and religion as well as a *consistent* and *logical* universe philosophy that harmonizes the mind and satisfies the spirit, giving rise to an internal conviction of the truth of its teachings.

2. It answers questions in the human mind about how the will and plans of Deity are implemented.

3. It naturally leads the individual to translate ideals into actions.

4. It is never ambiguous or inconsistent.

5. It does not threaten religious beliefs, but rather uplifts them, exalting and upgrading *all* world religions.

Examining new knowledge about the relation of God to the universe is not without inner tension; it provides the opportunity to either expand understanding or at least face up to fear and bias. With the aid of revelation, humanity has progressed from the fear of the unknown to the all-powerful love of God that sweeps through the human soul. We must now take the next step to ensure that humanity's relationship to the Universal Father is clearly established and the truth of the Father's limitless love for all is not only intellectually recognized but also awakened in the experience of all individuals.

Authoritative Source

In 2005, the British hierarchy of the Roman Catholic Church published a teaching document, *The Gift of Scripture*, instructing the faithful that some parts of the Bible are not literally true. It is quoted as saying: "We should not expect to find in Scripture full scientific accuracy or complete historical precision."[8] The official recognition of scriptural inaccuracies in the first chapters of Genesis and the apocalyptic prophecies of Revelation is a timely recognition that opens the way for further clarification by epochal revelation. Scriptural inaccuracies do not minimize the intrinsic message of the Bible.

The Urantia Book, the fifth epochal revelation to our world, reconciles many existing philosophies and theologies, which I further reconcile throughout this book. The epic text is not a "new gospel" but an expansion upon virtually all gospels. It reveals their spiritual genesis while widening our perspectives of the eternal and infinite. The conceptual teachings presented in *The Urantia Book* are designed to enhance the rudimentary comprehension of humanity's spirit origin and destiny, filling in missing links in ancient history while also providing detailed knowledge about life's beginnings and the future of the human race. This epochal revelation is unique in that it had the benefit of being presented in writing at a time when printing was widespread, to ensure the preservation of content over time. It now serves as a credible source that individual truth seekers may employ in conjunction with existing scriptures across religions, to uplift religious beliefs and enhance existing spiritual wisdom.

The strategic delay between the compilation of the text and its publication may be of particular significance. The Papers that comprise *The Urantia Book* were received and audited in the 1920s and 30s, after the discovery and initial translations of ancient Sumerian tablets, but before the Nag Hammadi codices and Dead Sea Scrolls were discovered in 1945 and 1947 respectively. However, *The Urantia Book* was not released for publication until 1955. This delay enabled humankind to expand its knowledge and independently confirm and question the accuracy of many existing sources of information regarding religion, history, and anthropology. This self-inquisition and exploratory phase was helpful to humanity as a part of the new and enhanced coordination of planetary knowledge. *The Urantia Book* verifies, clarifies, and expands upon these significant human discoveries. The celestial beings imparting the revelation were directed to use concepts and information already available in the world and to only resort to revelation when a suitable statement of the truth that was being conveyed did not otherwise exist.

They recognized that certain limitations were therefore inevitable: ". . . We full well know that, while the historic facts and religious truths of this series of revelatory presentations will stand on the records of the ages to come, within a few short years many of our statements regarding the physical sciences will stand in need of revision in consequence of additional scientific developments and new discoveries. These new developments we even now foresee, but we are forbidden to include such humanly undiscovered facts in the revelatory records. Let it be made clear that revelations are not necessarily inspired. The cosmology of these revelations is *not inspired*. It is limited by our permission for the coordination and sorting of present-day knowledge. While divine or spiritual insight is a gift, *human wisdom must evolve.*"9

The concepts in *The Urantia Book* gain greater significance when reconciled with existing knowledge. *Heaven Is Not the Last Stop* is an attempt at such reconciliation. With the postulation that organized religions are the cocoon in which the concept of divine brotherhood is evolving, they will be used as a base to reconcile and expand current understanding with the revelatory content of *The Urantia Book*. Such an expanded perspective challenges many belief systems, including present-day Christianity. Scholastic disciplines such as history, astronomy, archeology, geology, and anthropology will also be reviewed. Like any challenge, the ideas presented in this book can be perceived as an obstacle, a heresy, or an opportunity. Approached as an opportunity, they can serve to clarify our worldview. This achievement, accomplished one person at a time and manifested in our society as growing peace and progress, will testify to the value of this epochal revelation in the generations to come.

The Challenge

Spiritual stagnation and philosophic divisiveness have impaired social progress. "Institutional religion is now caught in the stalemate of a vicious circle. It cannot reconstruct society without first reconstructing itself; and being so much an integral part of the established order, it cannot reconstruct itself until society has been radically reconstructed."10

The teaching of the fatherhood of God and the brotherhood of man is the highest concept of religion the world has ever known, able to transform the civilizations of all humankind by lifting them from their quarrelsome depths of interreligious divisiveness. Jesus of Nazareth portrayed God the Father as the ideal of infinite reality and declared that this divine source of values and Paradise—the eternal center of the universe—can be attained by every mortal creature who chooses to acknowledge and accept sonship with God and brotherhood with man. The assimilation of this teaching can shift our world toward the social readjustment, moral acceleration, and spiritual enlightenment necessary to live in peace.

Spiritual revitalization and philosophic harmony are dependent on the willingness of individuals to develop the cosmic perspective that nourishes religious unity and fosters cooperation among all people. The personal realization of the dependability and friendliness of the cosmos will empower humankind to construct a society with new supernal ideals in which everyone loves her neighbor as she loves herself, eventually leading

Progress is impossible without change; and those who cannot change their minds cannot change anything.
George Bernard Shaw

to progressive and trustworthy economic and political leadership. "Religion must not become organically involved in the secular work of social reconstruction and economic reorganization. But it must actively keep pace with all these advances in civilization by making clear-cut and vigorous restatements of its moral mandates and spiritual precepts, its progressive philosophy of human living and transcendent survival. The spirit of religion is eternal, but the form of its expression must be restated every time the dictionary of human language is revised."[11]

The time has come to enliven and uplift our spiritual development efforts with a vision that creates new levels of love and devotion, of service and fellowship. Jesus of Nazareth lived a life of spiritual inspiration for every person, of every age, on every world of the universe. Thus, it is time for Christianity to reconcile or correct any doctrine or dogma that obscures his saving message for all of humanity. Then every religion will be able to recognize and experience "the vitalizing spark of the dynamic love portrayed in the original gospel of the Son of Man."[12] What the world needs now is to see Jesus living again on Earth through the words and actions of those individuals, of every nationality, culture, and creed, who have discovered a new revelation of the life of Jesus and have been illuminated with a new understanding of his teachings.

The reconciliations throughout *Heaven Is Not the Last Stop* should stimulate the exploration of existing wisdom. It is with such an expansion of faith-bolstered cosmic insight that we are enabled to better discern "facts," to more clearly recognize "truth," and to more accurately conceive of final "destinies."

3.

Cultural Progress and the Brotherhood of Man

The ultimate goal of human progress is the reverent recognition of the fatherhood of God and the loving materialization of the brotherhood of man.
The Urantia Book

The golden rule that admonishes us to treat others as we would like to be treated has been known to humanity for thousands of years. How well have we learned to live in accordance with the golden rule? Is Earth's cultural progress proportional to material comforts and scientific advancement? The giant leap of the civilized world in the last hundred years has given us modern communications, transportation, medicine, and science, spawning a worldwide corporate business culture. How easy it is to now communicate with anyone across the globe via telephone and the Internet! We drive in automobiles on highway networks to local airports where aircraft transport us anywhere on the planet. Multinational corporations market products worldwide. Humans have landed on our planetary satellite, live in space stations, and are becoming bionic with the replacement of blood, organs, bones, and teeth. All this and so much more—impossible to humankind just a hundred years ago! In a relative split-second of time, we have come such a long way . . . but have we really?

Peace is not the absence of affliction, but the presence of God.
Author Unknown

What about peace, the social yardstick that measures the advancement of civilization? International quarrels have escalated and terrorism is a constant threat. Genocide is still a dark cloud hovering over the brotherhood of man. What is it that eludes humankind on its path to social progress? What is it that makes our collective lives so full of fear and stress?

There are many causes for the world's problems, but one stands out above the many: humankind's innate self-serving characteristic. Today so much decision-making is self-serving, individually and collectively, in business and in politics. *Unselfish intention*, where the solution or outcome of a decision is of benefit to all parties, is still elusive in our world culture. Self-will is heavily marketed, and though an underlying morality of altruism resides within every individual, in most cases the motivator remains self-reward.

What would it take to have unselfish intent guide all of our interactions? Harmonious living encompasses the genuine desire to be of help and to enhance the well-being of others. If we became conscious of what effect our choices and actions have on the lives of others, and apply a selfless attitude of finding solutions that benefit all, cultural progress would take a giant step forward.

Selfless intention is inherent in the golden rule that summons us to treat others as we are willing to be treated. Unselfishness, however, is not altogether natural; we do not naturally love or serve others. When material and scientific achievements are not enhanced with moral and spiritual insight, selfless growth is inhibited and the result is cultural decline. "Unless the moral insight and the spiritual attainment of mankind are proportionately augmented, the unlimited advancement of a purely materialistic culture may eventually become a menace to civilization. A purely materialistic science harbors within itself the potential seed of the destruction of all scientific striving, for this very attitude presages the ultimate collapse of a civilization which has abandoned its sense of moral values and has repudiated its spiritual goal of attainment."[1] The *ideals* that advance civilization which are born in the spiritual dimension of human experience, have been superseded by a continuous promotion of material progress by way of intellectual *ideas*. Our world of sensory and material values is deeply lacking higher ideals. True cultural progress can only emerge if humanity chooses the spiritual ideals of the human experience.

Conflicts and confrontations can be avoided only when our hearts are not feeling troubled or fearful. "Personal peace integrates personality. Social peace prevents fear, greed, and anger. Political peace prevents race antagonisms, national suspicions, and war."[2] To achieve peace, we must strive to develop the cosmic perspective necessary to realize the highest personal and social goals of human endeavor:

- The clear understanding of the nature and will of God and his relation to humanity and the universe, which contributes to the personal realization of God-consciousness and the increased capacity to love.

- The social achievement of living the brotherhood of man, which leads to peace.

The Brotherhood of Man

Peace is based on brotherhood, the goodwill of love and mutual trust and respect. We begin to live this ideal when we treat others as we would like to be treated, maintaining a balance of interests. At its highest level of expression, the brotherhood of man is lived when we treat each other with the unselfish attitude of a wise and loving parent.

Humanity is far from living a true brotherhood. Weapon makers supply aggressive regimes and religious fervor aggravates historic rivalries. Politics seems to have abandoned diplomatic win-win discussion. These realities are a far cry from any brotherhood, yet brotherhood is the remedy for the major ills that have befallen our society.

The following worldwide adjustments promote the establishment of a world family:

- **Social Fraternity:** Social fraternity arises from associations and open communications made through travel, commerce, and competitive exchanges as well as the international exchange of students, teachers, industrialists, and religious philosophers. All activities promote the use of a common language.

- **Intellectual Cross-fertilization:** With the impetus of social fraternity comes the development of an active international exchange of knowledge and literature. This fosters an intellectual advancement in the character, customs, needs, and development of individual nations worldwide.

- **Economic Interdependence:** Commercial trade lessens the likelihood of armed conflict by increasing the value of mutually supporting commerce over the alternative of competitive aggression. According to Richard Rosecrance, author of *The Rise of the Trading State*, when states are highly interdependent, "the incentive to wage war is absent," since "trading states recognize that they can do better through internal economic development sustained by a worldwide market for their goods and services rather than by trying to conquer and assimilate large tracts of land."[3]

While the above adjustments are in place to promote the establishment of a world family, we still have yet to achieve a brotherhood, as evident in the two world wars of the twentieth century and the continued strife of regional conflicts and international terrorism.

The brotherhood of man cannot be successfully achieved without the spiritual growth of its worldwide family members. When intellectual advancement, supported by emotional maturity, is influenced by enhanced moral and spiritual insight, the results are far-reaching:

> *The true and solid peace of nations consists not in equality of arms, but in mutual trust alone.*
>
> Pope John XXIII (1881-1963)

- The evils of national envy and jealousy surrender to the emerging national and international ethical conscience.

- International suspicion and ignorance surrenders to the attitude of empathy and love.

- War is precluded as the instrument to solve the world's problems. The welfare of humanity and the enduring values that ensure world peace are promoted by wise leaders internationally.

To achieve a social brotherhood first demands a collective growth in God-consciousness to finally recognize a common denominator that links all people from all corners of the earth. The recognition of God as every individual's source and destiny *and* the loving universal Father whose spirit is bestowed upon all is the common denominator that will enable humanity to achieve a unity of ideals. The twentieth-century Indian philosopher Sri Aurobindo referred to this religious harmony as ". . . a dominant sense of unity and commonality."[4]

The recognition of the father–child relationship between God and mortal brings to life the consciousness of being a member of the family of faith children, an insight that inevitably leads to the selfless service of one's brothers and sisters in the effort to enhance and enlarge the spirit of brotherhood.

The challenge of living the brotherhood of man must be complemented by the willingness of organized religions to divest all ecclesiastical authority and involvement in commerce and politics, and fully devote themselves to the monumental task of helping establish religious unity. As humankind locks arms in brotherhood, sovereign nations will participate in international decisions in a world government representative of all humanity, franchised to legislate win-win processes between all nation-states. Under conditions such as these, peace on Earth will blossom and brotherhood, the goodwill of love and mutual trust will prevail. The responsibility to move civilization toward this goal lies with each generation.

Cultural Progress

Growth in moral thinking gives rise to moral behavior. Empathy, kindness, trust, respect, and a sense of justice are central components of moral behavior. Growth in spirituality fills these components with the love and unselfish attitude that promotes unconditional social service, which is essential to the establishment of the brotherhood of humanity and world peace. The concepts of justice and ideals of brotherhood are the most powerful and most fragile of all the factors of human civilization. The sincere effort of each individual toward developing these values contributes to the growth of the whole.

> *A lasting social system without a morality predicated on spiritual realities can no more be maintained than could the solar system without gravity.*
>
> The Urantia Book

In a progressive society, education elevates itself to new levels of value and expands from the classroom to the challenges of daily living. Present-day education, however, is localized, struggling with basic standards and achieving less in the process. To ensure progress, education should become more world-based and idealistic, reaching for cosmic meanings and the attainment of higher moral and spiritual values. The goal of education should be the development of a well-balanced personality; its curriculum must embrace not only the acquirement of skills but the pursuit of wisdom. Education must be continued throughout a lifetime so that individuals can gradually experience the ascending levels of wisdom, which include the following:

- Basic knowledge

- Meanings and associations

- Appreciation of values, such as respect for one another, individually and internationally
- The nobility of work and responsibility—duty
- Goal motivation—morality
- The love of service to humankind—character building
- Cosmic insight—the grasp of universe meanings

By achieving these steps of human wisdom, humanity can ascend to the ultimate of mind attainment—God-consciousness—". . . an experience mightily confirmative of the preexistent truth of the religious experience of knowing God."[5] With increase in the faculty of spiritual insight comes greater understanding of the relation between God and his creation; the intellectual recognition of God as Father and people as brothers and sisters grows to its experiential acknowledgement and expression. "The new loyalties of enlarged spiritual vision create new levels of love and devotion, of service and fellowship; and all this enhanced social outlook produces an enlarged consciousness of the Fatherhood of God and the brotherhood of man."[6]

Growth in God-consciousness will make peace possible. But social evolution will continue to falter if the confusion and superstition regarding the nature and will of God are not sifted from the current cultural base. The most expedient way to achieve this is to reconcile our understanding of origin, history, and destiny with epochal revelation.

It is wise to separate religious institutions from education and government, but to constrain living faith in all civil interaction is like removing the sails from a ship. True religion is an addition of empowerment, the impulse that organizes the soul in an ascent to higher levels of service. The recognition of the fatherhood of God and the brotherhood of man will drive humanity forward and upward from its natural state of fear, superstition, and intellectual inertia to the higher levels of reason, cosmic wisdom, and personal spiritual experience.

"Man's greatest spiritual jeopardy consists in partial progress, the predicament of unfinished growth: forsaking the evolutionary religions of fear without immediately grasping the revelatory religion of love. Modern science, particularly psychology, has weakened only those religions which are so largely dependent upon fear, superstition, and emotion."[7]

4.

The Origin and Nature of Universe Reality

Reality is that which, when you stop believing in it, doesn't go away.

Philip K. Dick, science fiction author

As we move into a study of uncharted reality, this chapter presents deep, even paradoxical concepts. You may stumble in these profound explorations, but take heart! A better understanding of Deity, its functions and relations, is central in our quest ". . . to expand cosmic consciousness and enhance spiritual perception."[1]

In his 1996 book *The Nature of Space and Time*, theoretical physicist Stephen Hawking stated: "Today almost everyone believes that the universe, and time itself, had a beginning at the big bang."[2] Current astrophysical evidence places the origination of the material universe at some point in the finite past before which it did not exist. We are thus confronted with the question: What caused the big bang? Physicist P. C. W. Davies points to a stark choice: ". . . One might consider some supernatural force . . . or one might prefer to regard the big bang as an event without a cause. It seems to me that we don't have too much choice. Either . . . something outside of the physical world . . . or an event without a cause."[3]

> *The mind's highest good is the knowledge of God, and the mind's highest virtue is to know God.*
>
> Benedictus de Spinoza,
> Dutch philosopher (1632–1677)

The recognition that something *must* have caused the beginning raises the consideration of a supernatural cause. As the early twentieth-century astrophysist Sir Arthur Eddington opined, "The beginning seems to present insuperable difficulties unless we agree to look on it as frankly supernatural."[4]

When we consider the supernatural, we are confronted with the concept of God—the God that embraces consciousness, will, and character, the very core of revealed religions. Both intuition and reason suggest that a God exists: the universe exhibits purpose, design, and intent; it appears to function according to universal laws of cause and effect; and moral conviction suffuses all human cultures. Yet none of these statements prove that God exists, for neither scientific experiment nor logical deduction can prove the existence of God. On the other hand, consider that billions of people of every ethnicity throughout history have believed there is a God, and it is impossible to prove that this faith is misplaced.

Mortals who know God hold in their personal experience the only positive proof of the existence of God. But there is ambiguity: to those who have had a religious experience, no argument about the reality of God is necessary, and to the doubtful, there are few arguments that would convince them.

To find proof of God in the material universe has always been a human quest. Prior to the big bang theory, philosophers and theologians hypothesized first-cause arguments revolving around a deity of supreme wisdom and intelligence who was the creator of the cosmos. Since the advent of the big bang theory, astronomers and astrophysicists agree that the universe originated from a singular point in the past. But what is that singular point? Did a personal God create the world out of nothing? Was the big bang a result of undirected natural forces? Or was the universe the result of a unitary Divine Consciousness-Force losing itself in matter?

> *If God does not exist, one will lose nothing by believing in him, while if he does exist, one will lose everything by not believing.*
>
> Blaise Pascal, French mathematician and philosopher (1623–1662)

Disagreements concerning the origin and nature of reality are much more than polite intellectual arguments about diverse interpretations of reality. They can, and often do, lead to bitter conflict; and the resulting strife and suffering caused by religious conflicts worldwide are reason enough to seek a logical and satisfying reconciliation between religious, mystic, and scientific theories. We can now best achieve this reconciliation by admitting the facts of universe reality *and* reconciling our beliefs in the light of epochal revelation. With faith and open minds, we can explore the insights of epochal revelation to refine our worldview. There must be faith because "[t]he vast gulf between the experience of the truth of God and ignorance as to the fact of God can be bridged only by living faith. Reason alone cannot achieve harmony between infinite truth and universal fact"[5] Trying to find the cause of the universe by examining its elements is like searching for a cow in the milk.

When our concept of God and our understanding of God's relation to us and the universe are illuminated by epochal revelation, we discover concepts that may be challenging:

- A physical body is not indispensable to personality.
- God does not personally administer the universes of time and space.
- Mind is not inherent in energy, but energy is responsive to mind.
- Mind can be superimposed upon energy, but consciousness is not inherent in the purely material level.

- Spirit is always intelligent.
- Material and spirit energies are not two ends of the same spectrum.

As we engage in this adventure we may find our faith validated by the insights of revelation and even discover that the First Cause of science and religion's God of salvation are one and the same. "The infinite and eternal Ruler of the universe of universes is power, form, energy, process, pattern, principle, presence, and idealized reality. But he is more; he is personal; he exercises a sovereign will, experiences self-consciousness of divinity, executes the mandates of a creative mind, pursues the satisfaction of the realization of an eternal purpose, and manifests a Father's love and affection for his universe children."[6]

These profound matters should be the subject of all the effort of our human intelligence, so that it may raise itself to that simplicity where contradictories coincide.

Nicholas of Cusa, German cardinal and philosopher (1401-1464)

The I AM: the Primeval Cause of Causes

In the mortal mind, the reality of Deity is best captured in the concept of a Supreme Being, God, characterized by the quality of unity and the comprehensible elements of divinity—truth, beauty, and goodness.

Deity, always minded, is able to communicate with all similar entities, beings, or personalities whether it functions on a prepersonal level (as in the Indwelling Spirit), or personal and impersonal levels (for example, Creator Sons and adjutant mind-spirits respectively.) These examples will be discussed later.

Universe reality consists of *deified* and *nondeified* reality. Deified reality is all that which is minded and can be personalized, and nondeified reality ranges from force to physical matter.

To better understand Deity relationships that have no beginning, it is helpful to explore the eternal past in terms of sequential events, best presented by using the philosophical concept of the I AM as the primeval cause of all causes. While the complexity and abstract nature of the subject is recognized, a basic and brief consideration of these realities in the light of epochal revelation is offered for a better understanding of the origin and nature of universal reality.

Deity is said to be "liberated" from static, changeless infinity in the following sequence:

1. **Static Deity** is absolute. In this primal reality state, Deity is self-existent, containing all potentials of energy, spirit, and mind. Static Deity is motionless and subject to the limitations of perfection, changelessness, eternity, and infinity. Static Deity is known as *Nirakar Brahm* in Hinduism, *the Tao* in Taoism, and *Dhammakaya* in Buddhism. Also expressed as the Infinite One, the Unmanifested God, the Absolute, the Unmanifested Reality, the One Absolute Cause, the Source of Light, the Center of Pure Being, the Unknowable God, the God Beyond All Names,

the *Eyn Sof*, and other names. As a visualization, the I AM can be pictured as the whitest, brightest of all light.

2. **Potential Deity** is self-willed and self-purposed. In the potential reality state, Deity enlivens the basic potentials of force, spirit, and mind energy, thereby preparing them for transmutation into actuals.

3. **Associative Deity** is self-personalized and divinely fraternal. In the associative reality state, the I AM achieves perfect and complete liberation from the static bonds of infinity. As personal Deity the I AM is the Eternal Father of the Original Son (spirit) coexistent with the Infinite Spirit (mind). As impersonal Deity, the I AM is the Eternal Source of the Isle of Paradise (living energy). This eternal Deity union of the Father, Son, and Spirit in the presence of Paradise is the Paradise Trinity, and their collective dynamic represents the personalization of the I AM. Deity expansion, personality expression, and universe evolution result from the free-will act that forever separated the spirit-mind-personal potentials and actuals from the nonpersonal. The Paradise Trinity therefore relates to the universe as follows:

   • The **Isle of Paradise** as *undeified* reality is the pattern and primary origin of all creation—the source of all energies, of all material reality. It acts as the gravity center that draws the actualized gravity forces of the physical universes toward itself. The Isle of Paradise is the hub of the central universe of Havona, which made its appearance simultaneously with the appearance of the Infinite Spirit.[7]

   • The **Universal Father** is the First Source and Center, deified reality and unified spirit personality—the origin and destiny of all personalities. He is also the Controller of energy, the Upholder of the universe, and the donor of personality, a unique value characterized by self-consciousness and free will. Through the personality circuit centered in his person, the Universal Father is conscious of all self-conscious existence throughout Creation. The Universal Father as personal Deity has the divine attributes most often associated with the term "God." While "Deity" may or may not refer to divine personalities, "God" always denotes divine personality.

   • The **Eternal Son** is the Second Source and Center and the spirit gravity center that draws all actualized universe spirit values, energies, and realities toward Paradise. The Eternal Son, through his Divine Sons, is devoted to the revelation of the God of love to the universes of time and space.

   • The **Infinite Spirit** is the Third Source and Center, the universal manipulator of the forces and energies of Paradise, and the source of mind. It is also the mind-gravity center that draws all actualized mind forces toward Paradise. From the Infinite Spirit springs: (a) groups of beings that deal with the intelligent control and regulation of force and energy, and (b) mind-ministering spirits dedicated to ". . . revealing the combined love of the Father and the Son to the individual minds of all the children of each universe."[8]

While the Paradise Trinity is existential—perfect and complete—all potentials existing in the Trinity are experiential—they have an origin, share relationships, and are subject to progressive achievement. This explains the universe phenomenon of the self-actualization of God the Supreme, God the Ultimate, and God the Absolute. While these concepts are outside of the scope of this book, brief descriptions are given below for God the Supreme and God the Ultimate.

4. **Creative Deity** is self-distributive and divinely revealed. In the creative level of reality, Personal Deity as the Universal Father manifests his purpose and plan by drawing upon and activating the great reservoirs of energy potentials. Through the function of a myriad of created spirit and divine but finite beings, the Universal Father creates, organizes, and administers the physical universes of time and space. As the new universes expand, worlds of unsettled physical development and imperfect nature emerge, some of them spheres on which life is initiated and free-will creatures of imperfection eventually appear.

5. **Evolutional Deity** is self-expansive and creature-identified. In the evolutional level of reality, Deity as God the Supreme evolves concurrently with the evolving free-will personalities and universes of time and space. This stage encompasses the supreme activity of "Man finding God and God finding man,"[9] the search for personal recognition of and contact with the Father and the striving to become as perfect as the Father. The notion that the evolving universe is a *living organism* reflects the perceivable reality of the Supreme. Every individual actually lives, moves, and exists within the immanence of the Supreme. "He is the oversoul of the grand universe, the consciousness of the finite cosmos, the completion of finite reality, and the personification of Creator-creature experience."[10] Epochal revelation tells us, "In certain phases the concept of the One Universal Oversoul as the totality of the summation of all creature existence led the Indian philosophers very close to the truth of the Supreme Being, but this truth availed them naught because they failed to evolve any reasonable or rational personal approach to the attainment of their theoretic monotheistic goal of Brahman-Narayana."[11]

6. **Supreme Deity** is self-actualized. The Supreme Being experiences Creator-creature partnership, unifying all evolutionary experience. In this level of unity reality, the completed evolution of God the Supreme results in the eternal fusion of the finite and the infinite—the eternal union of energy and spirit personality.

7. **Ultimate Deity** is self-projected and time-space transcending. In this transcendental level of reality, all of the activities of transcendent reality are consolidated and unified.

According to epochal revelation, the philosophy of the ancient Brahmins included many facts of the universe and approached cosmic truth, but failed to differentiate between the several levels of reality: absolute, transcendental, and finite.

The Personal God: Personal Deity

The German philosopher Joseph von Schelling argued ". . . that deity, to have personality, must hold within itself the limiting factors that define personality."[12] When we pray, most of us address God as a personality, a personalized Deity. But what does this approach really mean? Our quest is to expand the concept of personality in the light of epochal revelation so that humanity may unify its ideals . . . as a world family beloved by a Universal Father.

The higher concepts of personality imply identity, self-consciousness, self-will, self-revelation and the possibility of fellowship with other personalities.[13] Associating God with such characteristics makes God personal in our minds. In the supreme sense, divine personality is the revelation of God as a personal mind presence in the universe, with the loving character traits of the Father best understood as they were revealed in the life of Jesus of Nazareth.

Misunderstandings about the concept of personalized Deity arise because of our association of personality with the physical body. Epochal revelation explains:

If man's personality can experience the universe, there is a divine mind and an actual personality somewhere concealed in that universe.

The Urantia Book

"In the contemplation of Deity, the concept of personality must be divested of the idea of corporeality. A material body is not indispensable to personality in either man or God. The corporeality error is shown in both extremes of human philosophy. In materialism, since man loses his body at death, he ceases to exist as a personality; in pantheism, since God has no body, he is not, therefore, a person. The superhuman type of progressing personality functions in a union of mind and spirit."[14]

The Urantia Book divulges great clarity in the relation between divine personality and human personality, never before expressed.

In the personalization of the I AM, the presence of self-consciousness and will was liberated from static infinity as God the Father in union with living spirit (God the Son) and absolute mind (God the Spirit), in the presence of Paradise (living, nonspirit energy). Personality unifies the associations of spirit, mind, and energy so perfectly that divinity becomes known by both its indivisibility and oneness, and is referred to in the universes of time and space as God, the Universal Father. Thus, the I AM is the identity of the Universal Father who reveals to Moses that his name is I AM (cf. Exodus 3:14).

The farther away from Paradise, the greater is the divergence of spirit and nonspirit energy and the greater the intervening function of mind. Cosmic mind correlated with spirit does not compare with the human mind that coordinates spirit and matter, or with the animal mind that functions on lower levels related to matter. Mind is inherent in pure spirit. "Spirit is ever conscious, minded, and possessed of varied phases of identity."[15] On the other hand, mind consciousness is not inherent in material energy. In the physical realm, consciousness is the result of mind superimposed upon living energy. An animal is a living physical energy system with mind superimposed on it, enabling the creature to be conscious of his surroundings. The human personality is also a living physical mind-energy system, but it has a *spirit nucleus*. This physical-spirit-mind energy system is endowed with self-consciousness and free will, enabling a personal being to experience *reflective* consciousness—to be conscious of consciousness, even the superconsciousness of God.

Personality, therefore, whether human or divine, exhibits self-consciousness and free will, functioning in a union of mind and spirit in the presence of living energy. The difference between human and divine personality is revealed in the level of harmony that exists within them. Divine personality functioning from Paradise is unity. Human personality functioning in a physical world experiences great deviation between material and spiritual existence. Only through the increased spiritualization of the intervening mind and constant spiritual decision-making can the human personality align itself with spirit and triumph over the material levels of time-space personality expression.

Someone who denies the personality of God is left with two choices—two extreme philosophic dilemmas: materialism, which reduces the individual to a soulless automaton in a mechanistic universe, or pantheism, which attaches God to nonminded matter and mostly overlooks the existence of the myriads of free-will beings scattered through a vast universe. "Only a philosophy which recognizes the reality of personality—permanence in the presence of change—can be of moral value to man, can serve as a liaison between the theories of material science and spiritual religion."[16]

The personal concept of God has evolved from the primitive fear of ghosts to a belief in many gods (polytheism), then to a system of several gods with one dominant (henotheism), and finally reaching the belief of one universal God (monotheism). One-God religion then continues through its own process of evolution: from a stern and all-powerful monarch who delights in punishing wrongdoers, to a God of mercy, and finally to the recognition of God as the loving Universal Father.

Although the word-symbol "God" and the concept of divinity exceeds that which the human mind can fathom, a personal God cannot possibly be anything less than an eternal, true, good, and beautiful personality that can be known, loved, worshiped, and emulated. "The concept of the personality of Deity facilitates fellowship; it favors intelligent worship; it promotes refreshing trustfulness. Interactions can be had between nonpersonal things, but not fellowship. The fellowship relation of father and son, as between God and man, cannot be enjoyed unless both are persons."[17]

According to epochal revelation, "Jesus employed the word God to designate the *idea* of Deity and the word Father to designate the *experience* of knowing God. When the word Father is employed to denote God, it should be understood in its largest possible meaning. The word God cannot be defined and therefore stands for the infinite concept of the Father, while the term Father, being capable of partial definition, may be employed to represent the human concept of the divine Father as he is associated with man during the course of mortal existence."[18] Deity as Universal Father is the supreme *ideal* and highest concept that the human mind can assimilate, and exhibits the highest personal attributes we know: unity, perfection, justice, righteousness, love, mercy, truth, beauty, and goodness.

The concept of the personality of God is elevated through revelation but can be validated only through personal experience. The personal experience of a God-knowing mortal is the only proof of the existence of the living God that one human being can offer to another. Epochal revelation provides a reasonable and expansive narrative on the personality of God that complements the faith-insight of the spirit of God. But the loving nature of God is best reflected by the revelation of the Father that Jesus of Nazareth unfolded in his life as a mortal. The divine nature can also be better understood if we regard ourselves as children of God and look to the Paradise Creator as a true spiritual Father. Personal experience of God is always expanded through increased understanding of the personality of God.

The Paradise Trinity: Existential Deity

The doctrine of the Trinity is a revealed truth: the eternal Deity existing in the union of the three Paradise personalities—the Universal Father, the Eternal Son, and the Infinite Spirit—in the presence of Paradise. This association provides the mechanism whereby personal Deity becomes self-revelatory to the creatures of the evolving universes. If the nature of the never-ending association between the three beings of infinite perfection can be understood and embraced, the relation between God, mortals, and the universe comes into sharper focus.

According to revelation, four epochal presentations of the Trinity concept have been made to humanity:

1. The first presentation was made five hundred thousand years ago. This first revelation of truth to our world was largely lost due to a series of rebellion-related events.

2. A second presentation of the Trinity concept was made by Adam and Eve over thirty-seven thousand years ago and passed down through the ages. Despite the default of their mission, this teaching persisted due to the Sethite missionaries in both Mesopotamia and Egypt and perpetuated in India via Agni, the Vedic three-headed fire god mentioned in the Rig-Veda: "I laud the seven-rayed, the triple-headed Agni all perfect in his Parents' bosom." (Rig-Veda Book 1, Hymn CXLVI: 1)

3. The third presentation was made by Machiventa Melchizedek almost four thousand years ago and disseminated by the Salem missionaries. ". . . this doctrine was symbolized by the three concentric circles which the sage of Salem wore on his breast plate."[19]

   a. "In Kish and Ur there long persisted Sumerian-Chaldean groups who taught a three-in-one God concept founded on the traditions of the days of Adam and Melchizedek. This doctrine was carried to Egypt, where this Trinity was worshiped under the name of Elohim, or in the singular as Eloah. The philosophic circles of Egypt and later Alexandrian teachers of Hebraic extraction taught this unity of pluralistic Gods, and many of Moses' advisers at the time of the exodus believed in this Trinity. But the concept of the trinitarian Elohim never became a real part of Hebrew theology until after they had come under the political influence of the Babylonians."[20]

   b. "The Hebrews knew about the Trinity from the Kenite traditions of the days of Melchizedek, but their monotheistic zeal for the one God, Yahweh, so eclipsed all such teachings that by the time of Jesus' appearance the *Elohim* doctrine had been practically eradicated from Jewish theology. The Hebrew mind could not reconcile the trinitarian concept with the monotheistic belief in the One Lord, the God of Israel."[21]

   c. Despite this challenge, the Trinity concept of three Gods did find its way into the religion of the Hebrews. In Genesis 1, the scriptures begin by asserting that "In the beginning the Gods [*Elohim*] created the heavens and the earth." The plural noun *Elohim* is used in the Old Testament over two thousand times. Its original usage to denote the three-in-one-God concept was lost with the passage of time and is now generally used to denote the single God of Israel.

   d. The Old Testament, however, does reveal an evolving Deity: "The most unique and amazing feature of the religious history of the Hebrews concerns this continuous evolution of the concept of Deity from the primitive god of Mount Horeb up through the teachings of their successive spiritual leaders to the high level of development depicted in the Deity doctrines of the Isaiahs, who proclaimed that magnificent concept of the loving and merciful Creator Father."[22]

4. Jesus of Nazareth made the fourth presentation of the Trinity concept to his disciples: "Jesus taught his apostles the truth regarding the persons of the Paradise Trinity, but they thought he spoke figuratively and symbolically. Having been nurtured in Hebraic monotheism, they found it difficult to entertain any belief that seemed to conflict with their dominating concept of Yahweh. And the early Christians inherited the Hebraic prejudice against the Trinity concept."[23] The first five books of the New Testament, taken together, provide the narrative and history of the first sixty years of Christianity and the context from which the books that followed were written.

   a. "Paul knew of the Paradise Trinity of Father, Son, and Spirit, but he seldom preached about it and made mention thereof in only a few of his letters to the newly forming churches."[24]

   b. The Gospel of Matthew offers a clear depiction of the trinity concept.

In Matthew 28:19, Jesus tells the apostles: "Go ye therefore, and teach all nations, baptizing them in the name of the Father, and of the Son, and of the Holy Ghost."

In the sixth century before Christ, a Chinese philosopher named Lao Tzu who had a most discerning understanding of the idea of ultimate causation wrote: "'Unity arises out of the Absolute Tao, and from Unity there appears cosmic Duality, and from such Duality, Trinity springs forth into existence, and Trinity is the primal source of all reality.' 'All reality is ever in balance between the potentials and the actuals of the cosmos, and these are eternally harmonized by the spirit of divinity.'"[25] With the passage of time, much of his teaching was lost or corrupted by his followers, but his concept of the Trinity has survived in the Tao Teh Ching: "The Tao produced One; One produced Two; Two produced Three; Three produced All things."[26]

In the West, the term "trinity" was first used in AD 181 by Theophilus of Antioch, and consisted of God, his Word, and his Wisdom. In the second century, the church leader and author Tertullian (AD 155–230) and Christian scholar and theologian Origen of Alexandria (approximately AD 185–254) used it freely. At first, this concept implied only the threefold nature of the Godhead; later it came to include the unity of the Three Persons of the Trinity as well. But it was the Athanasian Creed, probably completed in the fifth century, that stated it most clearly: "We worship one God in trinity, and trinity in unity, neither confounding the persons, nor separating the substance."[27]

Only by virtue of the Trinity could the I AM conceived as Father enjoy the personality association of the Son and the Spirit. As the Universal Father, the I AM becomes the origin of personality and the personal God and Father of all future personalities. The Paradise Trinity thus enables Deity to be personally free from the limitations of the static infinite, while retaining and maintaining the absolute unity of Deity. This relationship between the three personalities of the Paradise Trinity and Paradise Deity may be clarified as follows:

- The Paradise Trinity can be defined as an organization or entity—the entity of *undivided* Deity. In contrast, the working association of the Father, the Son, and the Spirit can be termed as the First Triunity. The first association of three beings who are *separately* cooperating with a shared purpose, much like the board members of an organization.

- The functions of the Paradise Trinity reflect the *impersonal* and collective attitude of undivided Deity. For example, justice is the Trinity attitude of all three personalities while "goodness, mercy, and truth" are the universal ministry and *personal* expressions of the divine personalities collectively administering justice.

To broaden our cosmic horizon is to recognize the reality of the Paradise Trinity as universal law, its sovereignty extending outward from Paradise to all of creation. This faith-understanding paves the way for an expanded perspective of God and his relation to the universe.

Expansion of the Trinity Concept

The teachings in *The Urantia Book* offer an elevated vision of the Trinity, providing insights into the transcendence of the Father and his self-distribution policy: "The Universal Father all along has divested himself of every part of himself that was bestowable on any other Creator or creature. He has delegated to his divine Sons and their associated intelligences every power and all authority that could be delegated."[28] The above concept is a significant disclosure that clarifies and expands our Trinity concepts; there is only one God who exercises his unlimited power through ". . . the interlocking activities of the celestial beings and the divine spirits who, in accordance with cosmic law, unceasingly labor for the honor of God and for the spiritual advancement of his universe children."[29]

The self-distribution technique of the Father in no way negates the indivisibility of the Father. "Indivisibility of a human father's personality does not prevent the reproduction of mortal sons and daughters."[30] Thus, the self-distribution policy of the Father brings clarification to the paradoxes of "unity in diversity" and the "transcendence and immanence" of God further explained below.

The personality expression of Deity is facilitated by the technique of trinitization and the associated self-distributing technique of the Universal Father. White light can serve as a functional illustration to explain this technique and the creation of the numerous spirit beings involved in the administration of the universe.

Although a beam of light may appear to be white, it is composed of the full spectrum of colors with different wavelengths.

1. White light is the equal wavelength combination of *three* primary colors: red, green and blue.

2. From these three primary colors there are only *seven* potential combinations (i) red, (ii) green, (iii) blue, (iv) red and green, (v) green and blue, (vi) red and blue, and (vii) red, green, and blue.

3. By varying the amount of the individual light sources, a full rainbow of colors can be obtained, evidenced by holding a glass prism against a beam of white light.

Following this analogy, the Paradise potentials of personality, spirit, and mind may be represented dynamically as a three-frequency personification—God the Father, God the Son and God the Spirit, collectively referred to as the Paradise Trinity. As in white light, the *three* divine personalities possess only *seven* possible associations.

a. Three primary associations (unassociated): (i) the Father, (ii) the Son, and (iii) the Spirit

b. Three secondary associations (in shared duality): (iv) the Father and the Son, (v) the Father and the Spirit and (vi) the Son and the Spirit

c. One tertiary association in shared triunity (vii) the Father, Son, and Spirit

Just as a full range of colors may be obtained by adjusting the light source, the personalities of the Trinity, functioning together or in their individual capacities, create associate spirit beings to assist in manifesting the Divine Purpose and Plan.

- Any one of the Paradise Deities, or any one being of direct or indirect descent from them, creates the single-origin beings of the grand universe, such as the Local Universe Mother Spirit or the seraphim.

- Any two of these Paradise personalities, or any two beings of direct or indirect descent, create the dual-origin beings of the grand universe, such as Creator Sons and archangels.

- All three Paradise Deities, individually or as the Trinity, create the triune-origin beings of the grand universe, including the Ancients of Days and Master Spirits.

All Deity personalization in time and space reflects the sevenfold association of the Paradise Deities. "It would also be consistent to refer to the liaison of all spiritual ministry as the spirit of God, for such a liaison is truly the union of the spirits of God the Father, God the Son, God the Spirit, and God the Sevenfold[31]—even the spirit of God the Supreme."[32]

To explore the paradox of the immanence and transcendence of God, we may use the analogy of an idea. An idea must be enlivened by a person. For example, a person may have an idea to build a state-of-the-art retirement community and that idea becomes her goal. A chief executive officer (CEO) forms a board of directors and sets up the headquarters from which they will function. The board is intimately involved in developing and implementing the action plan, but the actual work is delegated to many associates—the managers and contractors—who in turn procure and manage the services of many subcontractors and workers.

A CEO chooses to create a project from her headquarters and to leave the implementation of the master plan to her board members and trusted representatives. So does the I AM, as a personal God, through his profound policy of self-distribution, choose to oversee the implementation of his Divine Plan from Paradise, relying on the perfection inherent in the function of the associate representatives. Thus the I AM as the Universal Father and Original Creator is a transcendent, personal God having the *characteristics* of the I AM— omnipotence, omniscience, and omnipresence—but functioning on Paradise and outside of infinity in the universes of time and space as follows:

- As physical controller, through the patterns and energy gravity center of Paradise.

- As spirit, through the spirit gravity center of the Eternal Son.

- As creator, through the divine children of the Eternal Son, who ". . . provide the mechanism whereby the mortal becomes immortal and the finite attains the embrace of the infinite."[33]

- As mind, through the mind gravity center of the Infinite Spirit and its far-flung family, including the Holy Spirit.

Our CEO functions from a faraway location, maintaining personal contact with her managers via the use of cell phones. The Universal Father, as an immanent, personal God

- Maintains parental contact with all personal creatures through his personality circuit, and

- Acts *directly* within human culture via the prepersonal fragments of Deity in the minds of mortals, discussed later in this chapter.

The advanced perspective of the Trinity that includes the self-distributing technique of the Universal Father may prove an intellectual challenge. To some, this will involve acknowledging one Deity existing in a triune manifestation of divinity and personality; others may balk at the concept of Creator Sons, failing to grasp that their existence does not diminish notions of God as the Eternal Maker and Infinite Upholder of all creation; and to others, the challenge might lie in the concept of a myriad of free-will celestial personalities doing much of what has been attributed to God himself.

History shows that what was considered impossible at one time becomes accepted later. For example, prior to the twentieth century, travel by air was considered impossible, yet aviation and rocket technologies are now converging to produce a vehicle that will make traveling in space as commonplace as airline travel is today. Similarly, by resolving the mysteries of *diversity in unity* and the *transcendence and immanence of God*, this expanded revelation of the Trinity will slowly gain acceptance. It will be embraced as the panorama of our spirit ancestry begins to shine in the hearts and minds of all people, just as a diamond shines brighter as it is polished. Increased understanding of spiritual realities brings the promise of further revelation. We stand at a turning point for humankind, when the scientific understanding of material creation can be coupled with a deeply comprehensive vision of spirit realities. Adopting this holistic outlook will lead to evolution in cosmic consciousness and the consecrated dedication to cultivating and expressing the qualities of divinity.

The Indwelling Spirit: Prepersonal Deity and Immanent God

The presence of an indwelling, immortal divinity has been sensed by individuals since ancient times. Three thousand years ago, Hindu teachers referred to it as the *atman*; the Greeks called it *soul*; New Age proponents refer to it as the Higher Self; the book *A Course in Miracles* calls it the Internal Teacher; while others have called it the Mystery Monitor, the Dweller on the Threshold, the Eternal Spark of God, and the Still Voice Within.

This indwelling divine presence makes it difficult for the human mind to detect the copresence of an *evolving* entity that is *potentially* immortal, the soul. According to epochal revelation, spirit and soul are not interchangeable terms; they refer to discrete entities. The implications of understanding the nuances of their distinct natures and intimate

Indivisibility of personality does not interfere with God's bestowing his spirit to live in the hearts of mortal men.

The Urantia Book

relationship are far-reaching. This clarity gives greater meaning to concepts that range from spiritual growth and personality survival to the establishment of the brotherhood of man. In this section we explore the subject of Indwelling Spirits as presented and clarified in *The Urantia Book*.

> *If there was a controlling power outside the universe, it could not show itself to us as one of the facts inside the universe—no more than the architect of a house could actually be a wall or a staircase or a fireplace in that house. The only way in which we could expect it to show itself would be inside ourselves as an influence or a command trying to get us to behave in a certain way. And that is just what we do find inside ourselves. Surely this ought to arouse our suspicions?*
>
> C. S. Lewis, *Mere Christianity*

The Indwelling Spirit, or Thought Adjuster, is a prepersonal fragment of the Universal Father. The bestowal of his spirit on every individual is the greatest demonstration of the Father's love for mortal beings. It is through this fragment that the Universal Father, as an immanent God, directly experiences material creation, living within the mind of evolving creatures and guiding their progress. Spiritual insight is "... that faculty of human personality which accrues as a consequence of the presence of the God-revealing Thought Adjuster in the God-hungry mortal mind."[34]

The recognition of the factual presence of the Indwelling Spirit is a progressive step in forming an integral perspective of Deity. "The essential doctrine of the human realization of God creates a paradox in finite comprehension. It is well-nigh impossible for human logic and finite reason to harmonize the concept of divine immanence, God within and a part of every individual, with the idea of God's transcendence, the divine domination of the universe of universes. These two essential concepts of Deity must be unified in the faith-grasp of the concept of the transcendence of a personal God and in the realization of the indwelling presence of a fragment of that God in order to justify intelligent worship and validate the hope of personality survival."[35]

The indwelling presence of the spirit of the Father cannot be proven by science but only confirmed through direct spiritual experience as a result of increased understanding and faith. God the Father may be domiciled in far-away Paradise, but he is in each and every one of his universe children as the Indwelling Spirit entity. "Thus does the Father, who is the farthest from you in personality and in spirit, draw the nearest to you in the personality circuit and in the spirit touch of inner communion with the very souls of his mortal sons and daughters."[36]

Indwelling Spirits possess individuality but are not like personalities or the created beings of our limited comprehension. Like the atman in Hinduism, they "... are fragmentations of God on an absolute level of reality which is not only prepersonal but also prior to all energy and spirit divergence."[37] The mindedness of Indwelling Spirits, therefore, is like the mindedness of the Universal Father and the Eternal Son, which is ancestral to the Infinite Mind Spirit which mediates between energy and spirit.

Indwelling Spirits are pure spirit and pure energy. They can plan, work, and love because they have powers of selfhood that are commensurate with mind.[38] Indwelling Spirits are able to traverse time and space instantaneously, unaffected by any constraints. They apparently never lose awareness, being fully conscious when indwelling the human mind.

Indwelling Spirits—perfect and immortal—do not grow and develop, though they gain ministerial experience through living association. Humans—mortal and imperfect—attain perfection through decision-making and gain immortality only through soul development and growth in self-identification with the Universal Father. *Both evolve.* "Thus, while you are in nature evolving inward and upward from man to God, the Adjusters are in nature evolving outward and downward from God to man; and so will the final product of this union of divinity and humanity eternally be the son of man and the son of God."[39]

According to epochal revelation, "Adjusters pass through a definite developmental career in the mortal mind; they achieve a reality of attainment which is eternally theirs. They progressively acquire Adjuster skill and ability as a result of any and all contacts with the material races, regardless of the survival or nonsurvival of their particular mortal subjects. They are also equal partners of the human mind in fostering the evolution of the immortal soul of survival capacity."[40]

The Will of God

The Will of God is reflected in his Divine Purpose: to elevate all free-will beings toward the highest level of spirit attainment—the experience of sharing his righteousness and selfless love. The Universal Father's supreme mandate to all his children of faith is: "Be you perfect, even as I am perfect."[41] In eternity, perfection is absolute, however, in the universes of time and space, perfection is a relative term. For humankind, doing the will of God is reflected in our genuine efforts to develop a well-balanced God-knowing personality, progressively growing in love, trustworthiness, wisdom, and righteousness. According to epochal revelation, the universal command to become Godlike should be the first duty and highest ambition of all of God's free-will creatures. "This possibility of the attainment of divine perfection is the final and certain destiny of all man's eternal spiritual progress."[42]

To do the will of God, therefore, is the progressive experience of becoming more and more like God, and God is the source and destiny of all that is good and beautiful and true.

The Urantia Book

When we choose to do the will of the Father, we experience "[p]eace in this life, survival in death, perfection in the next life, service in eternity . . ."[43] Socially we contribute to cultural progress and collectively each generation gets closer to an age of world peace. This is the supreme purpose of living, the reason for our existence—ideally, superimposed on all other objectives that we pursue throughout our lives.

To do the will of God is not a surrender of will. It is a gradual expansion and perfecting of will that harmonizes human will with God's will. "God *adjusts* with the mind of imperfection—with Urantia mortals through the Thought Adjusters."[44] Epochal revelation informs us that Indwelling Spirits begin their work with a definite and predetermined plan for the intellectual and spiritual development of their human subjects. Efforts to expand God-knowingness and cultivate the qualities of divinity increases attunement with the Indwelling Spirit, and enables the predetermined plan to be revealed in the developing mind with growing vividness and conviction. "When man consecrates his will to the doing of the Father's will, when man gives God all that he *has*, then does God make that man more than he is."[45]

We can validate the accuracy of our interpretation of God's will by the depth of love and gratitude we feel toward God, the corresponding degree of love we feel for our fellow humans, and the urge for unselfish social service that grows out of this love. "So does the true believer exist only for the purpose of bearing the fruits of the spirit: to love man as he himself has been loved by God—that we should love one another, even as Jesus has loved us."[46]

The Divine Plan

The Divine Plan, or Divine Plan of Progress, is "... the universal plan for the creation, evolution, ascension, and perfection of will creatures."[47] It was formulated by God the Father and God the Son, in cooperation with God the Spirit to elevate creatures with free will "... to the high destiny of the experience of sharing the Father's Paradise perfection."[48]

The Divine Plan embraces these three unique but correlated ventures that spiritually advance ascending mortal personalities to the perfection of eternity:

1. **The Plan of Progressive Attainment**. This plan of the Universal Father embraces the progressive spiritual development of individuals with free will through the universes of time and space and on to Paradise. The assurance of personality survival and progress is found in the Universal Father's bestowal of personality, the gift of his spirit, and the birth of the soul. This technique of salvation finds representation in the various *spiritual evolution* theories that have been proposed throughout the ages by many philosophers, scientists, and educators, including: Aristotle (384–322 BC), F. W. Joseph von Schelling (1775–1854), George Hegel (1770–1831), Max Theon (1848–1927), Henri Bergson (1859–1941), Alfred North Whitehead, (1861–1947), Sri Aurobindo (1872–1950), Pierre Teilhard de Chardin (1881–1955), Jean Gebser, (1905–1973), Arthur M. Young (1905–1995), Edward Haskell (1906–1986), E. F. Schumacher (1911–1977), Clare W. Graves (1914–1986), Erich Jantsch (1929-1980), P. R. Sarkar (1921–1990), and Ken Wilber (1949–).

2. **The Bestowal Plan:** This is the Father-revelation venture of the Eternal Son. This plan consists of the bestowal of the Sons of God upon the worlds of time, to incarnate and reveal the love of the Father, the mercy of the Son, and the way of salvation to the free-will creatures of all universes.

3. **The Plan of Mercy Ministry:** This is the plan formulated by the Infinite Spirit, essential to the practical and effective operation of both the attainment and the bestowal ventures, involving the mercy ministry by the spiritual personalities of the Infinite Spirit throughout the grand universe.

Nothing in existence is accidental—all of creation is activated and motivated to fulfill the Universal Father's divine purpose. The implementation of the Divine Plan embraces the following activities:

1. **The grand universe creation and organization.** This activity is a personal and impersonal universe reality that encompasses Deity expansion, personality expression, and universe evolution. It embraces:

   a. The creation of spirit beings through the self-distribution technique of the Father, organized to assist in the creation and administration of the universe and in the spirit ministry to the creatures of all universes.

   b. The creation of the physical universe and the architectural worlds of universe administration through the intelligent manipulation of energy.

   c. Life establishment, as well as the biological and spiritual evolution of the living species.

2. **The ascension and perfection of mortals** involves the survival and advancement of free-will individuals to the heights of spirit perfection. Through steadfast efforts to know God and become increasingly Godlike, ascendant beings grow in their recognition of the intimate and personal relationship of the Creators with their creatures. This conscious and joyous act of sincere worship fully and completely satisfies the divine heart of the Gods, thereby giving full satisfaction to the infinite love of the Creator Father and bringing to fruition the eternal plan and purpose of the Gods.

> *The realization that God is personal to all who are receptive to the Divine influx, enables one to communicate with the Spirit, receiving a direct answer from it. This Jesus was able to do.*
>
> The Urantia Book

5.

The Creation and Organization of the Universe

Matter—energy . . . are but diverse
manifestations of the same cosmic reality . . .
The Urantia Book

The creation of the universe is one of the great mysteries that continues to fascinate the best minds in our world. When the universe is studied using physical science and logical analysis, results reveal the physics of space energies; when viewed exclusively from the perspective of religion, ". . . all creation appears to be spiritual in nature."[1] Theories and beliefs about creation have always left unanswered questions. "A logical and consistent philosophic concept of the universe cannot be built up on the postulations of either materialism or spiritism, for both of these systems of thinking, when universally applied, are compelled to view the cosmos in distortion, the former contacting with a universe turned inside out, the latter realizing the nature of a universe turned outside in. Never, then, can either science or religion, in and of themselves, standing alone, hope to gain an adequate understanding of universal truths and relationships without the guidance of human philosophy and the illumination of divine revelation."[2]

Advances are made by answering questions. Discoveries are made by questioning answers.
Bernard Haisch,
German-born American astrophysicist

Human philosophy attempts to organize and correlate the findings of science and religion into a reasonable and unified attitude toward the cosmos. "But logic can never succeed in harmonizing the findings of science and the insights of religion unless both the scientific and the religious aspects of a personality are truth dominated, sincerely desirous of following the truth wherever it may lead regardless of the conclusions which it may reach."[3] Revelation compensates for the imperfections of evolving philosophy while it validates both reason and faith, inspiring the genuine truth-seeker to discover new and higher levels of spiritual meanings and values in the study of the universe.

Christians recognize the universe as a creation of God. Some believe that the first two chapters of Genesis must be interpreted literally; others consider Genesis to be an allegory suggesting that God controlled the evolutionary process to originate the "heavens and the earth." The true story of the creation of the universe will remain a point of contention for the Christian faithful until they are willing to reconcile the Bible with the facts of science and further profit from the illumination of progressive revelation to logically unify and expand the divergent perspectives.

The metaphysical viewpoint that God is immanent in the universe has been expressed in various forms by philosophers in past centuries. Georg Wilhelm Friedrich Hegel, one of the most influential thinkers of the nineteenth century, proposed that the universe is Geist (Spirit/Mind) and has an innate purpose— to become *Weltgeist*—the World Spirit, the Absolute Spirit, God fully conscious and actualized. This view had much in common with the idealist and theocentric metaphysics found in Gottfried Leibniz (1646–1716).[4]

In the increasingly secular twentieth century, the Indian scholar Sri Aurobindo (1872–1950) fused the scientific concept of evolution with a divine consciousness supporting all existence. According to Aurobindo, in the process of *involution* the One Consciousness concealed in force emerges as matter; in the process of *evolution*, increasing perfection is achieved through a heightening of the descending force of consciousness ". . . from matter into life, from life into mind, from the mind into the spirit."[5]

The British evolutionary biologist Sir Julian Huxley (1887–1975) deemed ". . . that the universe in its entirety must be regarded as one gigantic process, a process of becoming, of attaining new levels of existence and organization, which can properly be called a genesis or an evolution."[6] The Swiss thinker Jean Gebser (1905–1973) saw the process of creation as the "unfolding of consciousness."

Mystic perspectives were reinforced in the middle 1990s by a most compelling analysis using quantum theory and Einsteinian relativistic physics, which showed that ". . . the solid, stable world of matter appears to be sustained at every instant by an underlying sea of quantum light."[7]

Metaphysical worldviews recognize the intimate connection between energy, mind, and spirit. However, the human mind can never succeed in unifying all the levels of reality (absolute, transcendental, and finite) unless it can harmonize its relationship to spirit *and* matter. Epochal revelation explains: "In cosmic evolution matter becomes a philosophic shadow cast by mind in the presence of spirit luminosity of divine enlightenment, but this does not invalidate the reality of matter-energy. Mind, matter, and spirit are equally real, but they are not of equal value to personality in the attainment of divinity. Consciousness of divinity is a progressive spiritual experience."[8]

Matter, mind, and spirit are three functioning levels of finite reality and manifest as separate measurable circuits:

"Matter. Organized energy which is subject to linear gravity except as it is modified by motion and conditioned by mind.

"Mind. Organized consciousness which is not wholly subject to material gravity, and which becomes truly liberated when modified by spirit.

"Spirit. The highest personal reality. True spirit is not subject to physical gravity but eventually becomes the motivating influence of all evolving energy systems of personality dignity."[9]

Energy is responsive to mind *and* subject to physical laws operating in the universes of time and space. Mind is not inherent in energy but can be superimposed upon energy to mediate between the physical and the spiritual. Consciousness is not inherent in the material level, although some delight in ascribing it thereto. The cosmos *can* be thought of as conscious when considering the well-nigh infinite number of personal intelligent beings who inhabit it. Spirit is innately conscious and always intelligent, unaffected by the physics of time and space; attainment of spirit status is the goal of every spiritual seeker.

To know the expanse of the universe has been a human quest throughout the ages. "For the Sumerians the universe was a tripartite structure—heaven (the place of the high gods), earth (the realm of humans), and the netherworld (the realm of deceased humans and the mortuary gods) . . . According to the Akkadian text [German translation] *Keilschrifttexte aus Assur religiösen Inhalts* 307, the cosmos is composed of six levels: three celestial and three terrestrial."[10]

"The first attempt to construct a systematic cosmology that was grounded in physical theory was the model of Aristotle [384–322 BC]. Aristotle developed a theory of motion, and defined the concepts of "natural motion" and "force." In Aristotle's view, the Earth was the center of the universe and the center of all natural motions."[11]

The Ptolemaic model (second century AD) of the cosmos, a modified version of Aristotle's universe with Earth at its center was widely accepted until the Middle Ages. The Catholic Church reconciled the Ptolemaic theory with scriptural understanding: "The universe had the Earth at its center with all heavenly bodies circling it. Beyond the last sphere (that of the fixed stars) lay paradise; hell was in the bowels of the Earth (a sort of "under-Earth"), and purgatory was in the regions between Earth and the Moon. One of the main architects of this vision was Thomas Aquinas whose view was adopted by Dante in his Divine Comedy."[12]

During the Renaissance period, Nicolaus Copernicus (1473–1543) founded modern astronomy. Without the use of a telescope, he developed a model of our solar system with ". . . the sun at the center, the Earth rotating about a polar axis and the Earth and planets circling the sun, essentially as we know it today."[13]

In 1576, the theory of an infinite universe with stars scattered throughout space was first proposed by the English astronomer Thomas Digges (1546–1595) in an augmented edition of his father's *Prognostication Everlastinge*. It is, however, the Italian philosopher Giordano Bruno (1548–1600) who is often credited for this idea and for paving the way for Newtonian cosmology.

With increased precision of science and technology, physics and astrophysics began to play a central role in shaping modern cosmology. Galileo's (1564–1642) passion was physics rather than astronomy; and with his improved telescope, he determined that the celestial bodies did not revolve exclusively around the earth.

Through the late seventeenth century and for the next two hundred years, Isaac Newton's laws of motion and theory of gravity explained most phenomena related to the universe. "In Newton's universe, space existed independent of the matter in it. Both space and time were absolute, regardless of the motion of the observer and the matter contained within space. No substance controlled the motions of the moon, Earth and planets; only the force of gravity."[14] Newton removed the terrestrial-celestial relationship that had driven Aristotle's theory for two thousand years.

In 1905, Albert Einstein propelled the world beyond the unchanging "clockwork universe" of Newton into a *relativistic* universe in which space and time are woven into a single fabric—space-time. Using Bell's Theorem (1964), experiments have proven Einstein's proposition of 1935 to be correct, that ". . . a change in the spin of one particle in a two-particle system would affect its twin simultaneously, even if the two had been widely separated in the meantime."[15]

More recently, string theory ". . . predicts seven undiscovered dimensions of space that give rise to much of the apparent complexity of particle physics. The discovery of extra dimensions would be an epochal event in human history; it would change our understanding of the birth and evolution of the universe."[16]

Reconciling the domains of science and religion has long been the challenge of philosophers, but revelation is the divine unifier. "Metaphysics, but more certainly revelation, affords a common meeting ground for the discoveries of both science and religion and makes possible the human attempt logically to correlate these separate but interdependent domains of thought into a well-balanced philosophy of scientific stability and religious certainty."[17] For a long time, we have known that science stabilizes philosophy by eliminating error, and purifies religion by destroying superstition, but we have yet to deepen our recognition and appreciation for revelation as the technique that helps us to sort and sift ". . . the errors of evolution from the truths of spirit acquirement" which would otherwise take us ages upon ages of time.[18]

With the aid of epochal revelation, our knowledge and understanding of universal reality now includes its origin, scope, organization, and administration. Additionally, we've been introduced to the many spirit beings of diverse levels of identity and origin involved in the creation and administration of the physical universe. This broadened perspective interrelates with all existing beliefs and theories and will be addressed under the following topics:

- Paradise, the source and center of all creation.
- Celestial manipulators of force and energy.
- Physical emergence and organization of the universe.
- Relation of heaven to the grand universe.

Paradise, the Source and Center of All Creation

In Judeo-Christian scripture, the term "Paradise" is generally identified with heaven. In the Bible, it is found in Luke 23:43, 2 Corinthians 12:4, and Revelation 2:7. It is also found in Ecclesiasticus 44.16, an apocryphal book written c. 190 BC that identifies Paradise as the place to which Enoch was translated.

Is Paradise a universe location, the spiritual abode of God, or both? Is Paradise synonymous with heaven? Epochal revelation tells us that from the abstract perspective of eternity, Paradise is the material (living, nonspiritual energy) aspect of the personalization of the I AM, existing outside of space and without time. From a religious perspective, revelation confirms that Paradise is the central abode of God the Father and the destiny of the human soul and personality. To understand the function of Paradise as it relates to the universe, it is important to first expand the meaning and scope of the term "universe" in light of epochal revelation.

Merriam-Webster's Collegiate Dictionary defines the word "universe" (cosmos) as:

1. The whole body of things and phenomena observed or postulated:
    Cosmos: as

    a. A systematic whole held to arise by and persist through the direct intervention of divine power

    b. The world of human experience

    c. i. The entire celestial cosmos

        ii. Milky Way Galaxy [1920 pre-Hubble]

        iii. An aggregate of stars comparable to the Milky Way galaxy [1920 pre-Hubble]

Expanding upon our understanding of the universe, epochal revelation informs us that the master universe embraces the *inhabited* "seen and unseen" grand universe and the currently uninhabited outer space levels (Illustration 2, on page 54). The grand universe, with the "seen" worlds being a minute portion of the universe, may be broadly illustrated as a wheel divided into seven multilevel superuniverses, each approximately the size of the Milky Way, with the central universe as the hub. "*The Seven Superuniverses* are not primary physical organizations; nowhere do their boundaries divide a nebular family, neither do they cross a local universe, a prime creative unit. Each superuniverse is simply a geographic space clustering of approximately one seventh of the organized and partially inhabited post-Havona creation."[19] The reconciliation of the cosmology presented in *The Urantia Book* with modern astronomy is still in its infancy and will not be attempted in this book.

Science is in the continuous process of trying to realize the full expanse of the cosmos, ever redefining its existing terms and definitions. The cosmologic classifications in *The Urantia Book* depict a grand physical creation on a scale that is now being discovered by science. Illustration 2 offers this enlarged perspective, including the names of the parallel and "unseen" functional worlds that are built for specific purposes, such as universe administration and education in the ascending scheme of spiritual evolution. For example, Jerusem and Salvington serve as the headquarters for our local system and universe respectively, and Uversa serves as the seat of government for our superuniverse. The Urantia revelation offers a significant update to traditional religious models by revealing that spirit activities are always oriented around specially created material worlds.

The grand universe embracing the "heavens and the earth" (Genesis 1:1), has been referred to in some traditions as "cosmic planes or dimensions," or

Illustration 2
THE COSMIC LOCATION OF EARTH

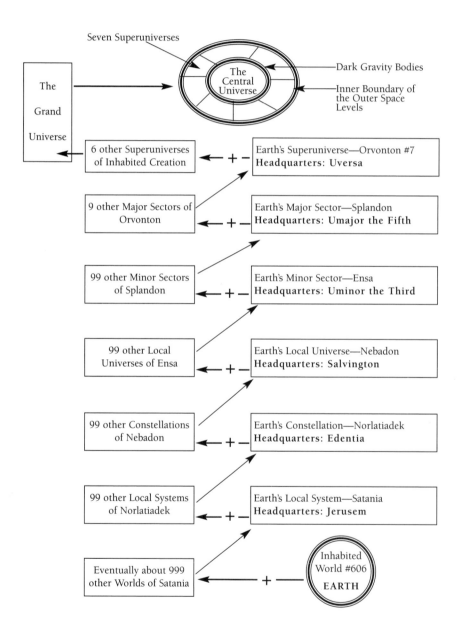

more localized as the "visible and invisible worlds around us," or "the seven levels associated with the soul's evolution." Epochal revelation now expands upon these vague terms. Illustration 3 offers clarity by equating each cosmic dimension with the various ascending levels of universe organization. It is important to note that "the world of God," Paradise, is outside time and space. The illustration shows delineation for clarity.

Epochal revelation continues to expand our knowledge of the relationship between Paradise and the universe:

1. **Paradise is the source and center of gravity.** "The perfect and divine universe occupies the center of all creation; it is the eternal core around which the vast creations of time and space revolve. Paradise is the

Illustration 3
THE DIVINE PLAN OF UNIVERSE ORGANIZATION

Geographic Center of Infinity
Paradise/Havona
The divine and central universes

Cosmic Levels of Time-space Creations

1st Level		Superuniverse
2nd Level		Major Sector
3rd Level	Spirit Realm	Minor Sector
4th Level		Local Universe
5th Level		Constellation
6th Level	Morontia Realm	Local System
7th Level	Physical Realm	

Individual Worlds (Planets)

gigantic nuclear Isle of absolute stability which rests motionless at the very heart of the magnificent eternal universe."[20]

Since the 1980's, astronomers have concluded that many galaxies, including the Milky Way, are being drawn by gravity toward the center of a gigantic concentration of mass known as the Great Attractor. The original Great Attractor was thought to be about 150 million light-years away, but more recent studies involving five times as many galaxies have shown that the Great Attractor still remains to be discovered. "Only now, to keep all these extra galaxies in motion, it would have to be even more massive than the 10,000-trillion-sun figure"[21] the original researchers suggested.

While Paradise will never be identified by scientists, its gravity pull on the cosmos (as downstepped through the dark gravity bodies), will undoubtedly one day be recognized. Healthy scientific inquiry abounds, and researchers trying to prove the existence of a Great Attractor will continue the search.

2. **Paradise is the source and center of all physical force-energy**, ". . . the actual source of the physical universes—past, present, and future."[22] The force that originates from Paradise eventually transmutes to matter. Various theories exist as to the origin and composition of matter. In 1913, Albert Einstein and Otto Stern first proposed the concept of the zero-point field, a universal sea of zero-point energy that pervades space. In the Standard Model of particle physics, this field is needed to impart the property of mass on the fundamental particles.

In 1964, Peter Higgs of the University of Edinburgh, Scotland, and Thomas Kibble of Imperial College, London, England, proposed the existence of a new and specific fundamental particle that binds to other particles and gives them their mass. This particle is referred to by physicists as the Higgs Boson and by journalists as the God Particle. In Europe, scientists are currently using a "giant atom smasher" called the Large Hadron Collider (LHC) to search for the Higgs particle, "to crack the code of the physical world; to figure out what the universe is made of."[23]

Epochal revelation confirms that space is not empty; it is not able to attain a temperature of absolute zero because of the universal presence of gravity and the consequent action of gravity-responding energy currents, power circuits, and organizing electronic energies.[24] There are also the energy activities of the smallest units of material energy in the universe, the ultimatons, ". . . the energy particles which go to make up electrons."[25] As the LHC slams particles into one another in an effort to detect the Higgs Boson, researchers will not discover the ultimaton. The ultimaton is a subelectronic form of energy that is not recognized by current scientists and is not detected by current instruments. When these particles are eventually discovered, they will provide true insight into the nature and dynamics of the physical universe.

As scientists and philosophers hypothesize about the source of force-energy activation, epochal revelation explains that it originates from Paradise, the universe location of the activators of pure energy. In accordance with the self-distribution policy of the Father, the transmutation of space-force into physical matter is carried out by the celestial manipulators of energy, as further described in this chapter. Physical reality is therefore the result of the intelligent manipulation of ultimatons inherent in space-force and their transmutation into the circuits and revolutions of the electron.[26] Einstein's postulate that mass and energy are interchangeable through the equation $E = mc^2$ is expanded to: matter is ". . . organized energy which is subject to linear gravity except as it is modified by motion and conditioned by mind."[27] And "[t]he increase of mass in matter is equal to the increase of energy divided by the square of the velocity of light."[28]

Paradise is thus the focal point ". . . of all phases of universe reality. Paradise, properly qualified, may connote any and all forms of reality, Deity, divinity, personality, and energy—spiritual, mindal, or material. All share Paradise as the place of origin, function, and destiny as regards values, meanings, and factual existence."[29] But scientific inquiry faces an enigma as long as it searches within our physical universe for its origin. The origin of creation exists at the nexus of the multilevel universe: "To assign *causes* as an explanation of physical phenomena is to confess ignorance of ultimates and in the end only leads the scientist straight back to the first great cause—the Universal Father of Paradise."[30]

Celestial Manipulators of Force and Energy

While the universe functions in conformity with the gravitational laws of force, energy, and matter, the organization and administration of universe creation remain forever under the control of the infinite creators and their associates. Two groups of beings previously unknown to us are dedicated to the intelligent control and direction of space-force and the regulation of energy. They are the Master Force Organizers resident on Paradise and the Universe Power Directors. "Of all the universe personalities concerned in the regulation of interplanetary and interuniverse affairs, the power directors and their associates have been the least understood on Urantia. While your races have long known of the existence of angels and similar orders of celestial beings, little information concerning the controllers and regulators of the physical domain has ever been imparted."[31]

Epochal revelation provides us with insights into their function.

"Paradise force organizers are nebulae originators; they are able to initiate about their space presence the tremendous cyclones of force which, when once started, can never be stopped or limited until the all-pervading forces are mobilized for the eventual appearance of the ultimatonic units of universe matter. Thus are brought into being the spiral and other nebulae, the mother wheels of the direct-origin suns and their varied systems."[32]

Once puissant energy (pre-Paradise gravity energy) has been evolved to the ultimatonic level, ". . . the power directors and their associates . . . begin their

Illustration 4
THE UNIVERSE POWER DIRECTORS

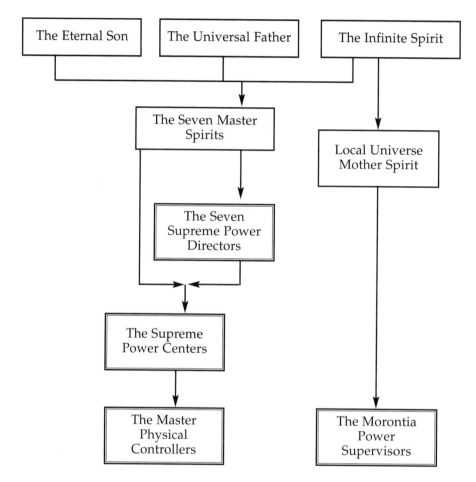

never-ending manipulations designed to establish the manifold power circuits and energy channels of the universes of time and space."[33] The Universe Power Directors are responsible for maintaining the equilibrium between energy and matter and their lineage and divisions are shown in illustration 4.

"The living power directors and force organizers are the secret of the special control and intelligent direction of the endless metamorphoses of universe making, unmaking, and remaking. Nebulae may disperse, suns burn out, systems vanish, and planets perish, but the universes do not run down."[34]

Physical Emergence and Organization of the Universe

The formation of energy into complex structured physical systems, from the headquarters worlds of the superuniverse government to the galaxies and solar systems of human habitation, begins in Paradise, ". . . the center of force-energy activation in the cosmos."[35] "'God is spirit,' but Paradise is not. The material universe is always the arena wherein take place all spiritual activities; spirit beings and spirit ascenders live and work on physical spheres of material reality."[36] *The Urantia Book* describes the transmutation of space-force (nonspirit energy) into physical matter as it responds to the personal will of the Universal Father in Paradise, through the skillful manipulation of energy by the Master Force Organizers and the Universe Power Directors:

- Force-energy exists in the Infinite and its space potency is responsive only to the personal grasp of the Universal Father. Space potency is passive, and its activation as space-force is in itself ever existent. Force-energy is imperishable, indestructible; it may be subject to unlimited transmutation, endless transformation, and eternal metamorphosis, but it can never suffer extinction.

- The passive presence of the Primary Master Force Organizers transmutes space potency into cosmic or primordial force, which is not yet responsive to direct Paradise gravity, and is sometimes spoken of as pure energy. By their active operation, these beings originate and manipulate the "energy cyclones of space" (puissant energy); and they continue to evolve the "premAterial potential" of primordial force until it begins to respond to the Paradise-gravity pull, at which time they give way to the functioning of their secondary associates. Through the presence and actions of the Associate Master Force Organizers, puissant energy transmutes to Paradise-gravity-responding energy, the active ancestor of all universe matter, ultimatons, ". . . the basic units of materialized energy." Further energy manipulation is in the hands of the Universe Power Directors.

> *There can be no living science unless there is a widespread instinctive conviction in the existence of an* Order of Things . . . *The inexpugnable belief that every detailed occurrence can be correlated with its antecedents in a perfectly definite manner . . . must come from the medieval insistence on the rationality of God.*
>
> A. N. Whitehead,
> *Science and the Modern World*

- The directors, centers, and controllers work with ultimatonic energy and its elaboration up through electronic level systems, and to a limited extent, up through the level of atomic systems, when the materialization is fully responsive to local gravity. Universe power is energy that has been ripened to the point where it can be directed into channels of power and made to serve the manifold purposes of the universe creators. The number seven is basic to the spiritual self-distributing technique of the Father—material creation reflecting its spiritual creator. It is therefore inevitable that the atomic world displays a certain periodic characterization which recurs in groups of seven, indicative of its far-distant spiritual origin.[37] Other examples of sevenfold character: in the realm of minerals and crystallography there are seven crystal systems; in the natural light spectrum, there are seven colors; and in traditional Western music, the scales have seven notes. *The Urantia Book* explains: "Such a fact of the physical world unmistakably points to the sevenfold constitution of ancestral energy and is indicative of the fundamental reality of the sevenfold diversity of the creations of time and space."[38]

- "Local or linear gravity becomes fully operative with the appearance of the atomic organization of matter."[39] Free, unattached, and uncharged electronic-energy particles and unassociated ultimatons are only held in the universal space drift of circular Paradise gravity.

- The Universe Power Directors continue the mobilization of the space-energies to provide and maintain the material foundation of the universe, its suns, and its planets. Planets then begin their long journeys of evolutionary stabilization, some of which will support life.

- With regard to the currently evolving superuniverses, when energy-matter has attained a certain stage in mass materialization, Creator Sons take up the task of establishing an orderly administration of their local universes. These plans proceed in conformity to the gravity laws of force, energy, and matter. Upon the arrival of these divine sons, work is begun on the architectural spheres, planets without evolutionary origins that will become the headquarters of the projected local universe. Headquarters worlds also function as power-energy regulators and serve as focal points for directing energy into the local universes.

- Once the physical plan of a local universe has been completed, the Creator Son and the Local Universe Mother Spirit begin the creation of a vast population of celestial personalities to perform myriad duties.

- When a local universe has been organized and a management team is in place, the Creator Son acts upon the Father's proposal to create mortal beings in their divine image—endowed with an indwelling fragment of God and the prerogative of personality—able to know God and become Godlike. Thus, "The foundation of the universe is material, but the essence of life is spirit."[40]

Relation of Heaven to the Grand Universe

The word "heaven" has been synonymous with one or more of the following, as defined in *Merriam-Webster's Collegiate Dictionary*:

1. The expanse of space that seems to be over the earth like a dome (firmament)
2. The dwelling place of God and the joyful abode of the blessed dead
3. A spiritual state of everlasting communion with God
4. A place or condition of utmost happiness
5. In New Thought religion: an inner state in which sin is absent and the harmony of Divine Mind is manifest

Illustration 5
HEAVEN IN RELATION TO THE GRAND UNIVERSE

The Divine Universe	**PARADISE**	7th Heaven
The Central Universe	**Havona**	6th Heaven
	Eternal Creation	

OUTWARD DESCENT OF SPIRIT PERSONALITIES

INWARD ASCENT OF HUMAN PERSONALITIES

Cosmic Levels of Time-space Creations

1st Level	Superuniverse	
2nd Level	Major Sector	5th Heaven
3rd Level	Minor Sector	
4th Level	Local Universe	4th Heaven
5th Level	Constellation	3rd Heaven
6th Level	Local System	2nd Heaven
	Mansion Worlds (John 14:1) 7th 6th 5th 4th 3rd (Third Heaven: 2 Corinthians 12:1-4) 2nd 1st	1st Heaven
7th Level	**PHYSICAL PLANETS INCLUDING EARTH**	

None of these definitions portray heaven as it is in the context of this writing, in which we define "heaven" as the vast expanse of the multilevel universe that is traversed by an ascending personality on the inward journey to God in Paradise. It includes both the morontia and spirit realms of existence, "morontia" being a new term that designates an intermediate level of reality between the material and the spiritual. The existence of this transition state, taught in previous times, can be found in distorted forms in present-day religions. The unawareness and misunderstanding of such an elemental afterlife experience increases the difficulty of a harmonious coordination between science and religion. "The local universe consists of three degrees, or stages, of reality manifestation: matter, morontia, and spirit. The morontia angle of approach erases all divergence between the findings of the physical sciences and the functioning of the spirit of religion."[41]

Illustration 5 clearly shows the relationship between the celestial and human perspectives and further clarifies the definition of heaven.

The writers of the Old and New Testaments vaguely captured the relation between heaven and the administrative structure of the universe, with the term "heaven" sometimes used to mean the seven mansion worlds: "The heaven conceived by most of your prophets was the first of the mansion worlds of the local system. When the apostle spoke of being 'caught up to the third heaven' [2 Corinthians 12:1–4], he referred to that experience in which his Adjuster was detached during sleep and in this unusual state made a projection to the third of the seven mansion worlds. Some of your wise men saw the vision of the greater heaven, 'the heaven of heavens' [Deuteronomy 10:14, 1 Kings 8:27 and Psalms 148:4], of which the sevenfold mansion world experience was but the first; the second being Jerusem; the third, Edentia and its satellites; the fourth, Salvington and the surrounding educational spheres; the fifth, Uversa; the sixth, Havona; and the seventh, Paradise."[42] The mansion worlds in the morontia realm are humankind's first postmortal residence.

To celestial personalities "looking out" from the hub of Paradise, the grand universe is the sphere of their time-space descent. To humanity "looking in," the grand universe is perceived as heaven and is the sphere of their time-space ascent. Divinely created beings travel *outward* in their ministry to mortals while surviving personalities of creature origin journey *inward* in their quest for God. Heaven includes Paradise, but Paradise is not the immediate destination of the soul upon death of the physical body. From the perspective of human spiritual progress ascending from our world through the universes of time and space toward God, it may be better said that Paradise is in the "heaven of heavens"; and that throughout the long adventure in this greater heaven, the soul ascends through various heavens, mastering the technique of choosing the Father's will.

Indeed, HEAVEN IS NOT THE LAST STOP!

6.

The Celestial Organization

There is but one uncaused Cause in the whole universe. All other causes are derivatives of this one First Great Source and Center. And none of this philosophy does any violence to the free-willness of the myriads of the children of Deity scattered through a vast universe.

The Urantia Book

While Paradise is the pattern for all material creation, the three personalities of Paradise Deity, the Universal Father, Eternal Son, and Infinite Spirit serve as a springboard for the vast and complex celestial organization that administers and guards the Divine Plan of Progress. The Universal Father is thereby enabled to function outside of Paradise through his representatives who carry out his purpose. "And the whole scheme of living existences on the worlds of space is centered in the divine purpose of elevating all will creatures to the high destiny of the experience of sharing the Father's Paradise perfection."[1]

The foundation of the universe is material, but the essence of life is spirit.

The Urantia Book

The diverse array of associate representatives is attuned with divinity in varying levels of function throughout each superuniverse. These spirit beings move freely throughout time and space. They are not subject to the physical laws that affect material and morontia energy because the gravity control of spiritual realities, controlled by the Eternal Son, operates independently of time and space. Spirit energy supersedes our physical laws, operating without any reduction in power across enormous distances.

Subordinate spirit beings may be equated to the cocreators and demigods of Vedic traditions who assist in creating and maintaining the physical dimension. They generally serve unseen by mortal eyes, but celestial beings do materialize as part of the Divine Plan. Local universe spirit personalities sometimes incarnate into visible bodies; their lives and teachings have been woven into our history as they serve humanity. Stories of events involving both seen and unseen helpers were verbally passed from generation to generation, and eventually people developed the ability to record history on clay tablets, pottery, papyrus, and parchment. Those records served as the foundation for the sacred texts of today, and many legends and myths have become intertwined with the facts of time.

Epochal revelation clarifies our grasp of scripture and expands our knowledge of God and his universe. It opens us to a better understanding of the interrelation between canonical texts, ancient Sumerian/Babylonian tablets, and the "apocryphal lost manuscripts." *The Urantia Book* identifies spirit beings and illuminates their role in the defining events of planetary history, revealing a comprehensive vision of reality. This reconciliation, however, brings a great challenge to religions of the world. Religious tolerance and interfaith inquiry are desperately needed. To achieve peace among all religions, increased perspective and greater doctrinal elasticity are necessary, including the recognition of the ancestry and history shared by all. Humanity can adopt an empowering perspective from which to launch a lasting brotherhood, gradually evolving beyond parochial traditions.

Humankind now has the chance to correct the misconceptions that divide our planet into so many warring factions. Reconciling and expanding our knowledge of the celestial organization deemphasizes the differences between religions while still continuing to honor noble traditions. In doing so, we can forge a common bond with each other and discover a more meaningful personal connection with God.

This chapter presents a shortened depiction of God's diverse helpers, some who may be familiar. It is important to clarify their lineage and roles to better recognize their interrelatedness within religions. The organizational charts offer a visual representation of my findings. They are intended to give an expanded perspective of the function of these beings in relation to us and the universe and provide fertile ground for the inquiring mind.

We have a choice in how to process the pageant of spirit ancestry and history that has now been revealed. Embracing it with reason and humility will expand our perspective of the Big Picture of Existence. With this expansion of wisdom, unity and love can flourish.

The Celestial Organization

Archaeologists have shed scientific light on the distant past, greatly expanding our understanding of written knowledge. They have unveiled the culture of many ancient civilizations, revealing the many gods in their deity hierarchy: creator gods who produced the world and sustained its position in the cosmos; the gods and beasts that created humanity; fertility gods and mother goddesses who sustained the earth; and the dark gods of war and death who were appeased only by sacrifices and offerings. Enigmatic records tell of strange beings that came from the heavens to live on our planet: extra-terrestrials, angels, and demons. This cornucopia of historical discovery has also unearthed mysteries that can now be reconciled through revelation.

Concepts of God and celestial beings have evolved from depictions in ancient Babylonian tablets, Egyptian papyri, Vedic texts, Old Testament writings and documents (such as the Dead Sea Scrolls and the Apocrypha), and the New Testament. There is also a treatise named the "Celestial Hierarchy," which is considered a classic of Western spirituality, supposedly originating in the first century AD but later penned under the pseudonym Dionysius the Areopagite in the late fifth or early sixth century. The treatise is based on two assumptions:

1. God directly created our world and all celestial beings in heaven.

2. All celestial beings are angels.

Contemporary revelation imparts knowledge of a much broader and organized superhuman realm consisting of a multitude of spirit beings, including angels, but also beings whose lineage, function, and range of influence are different from that of angels. These created beings ". . . live and worship and serve in the swarming universes of time and in the central universe of eternity."[2] Many are involved in mortal ascension, administering and implementing the Father's Divine Plan of Progress. Of these, only the following are within the scope of this book and will be addressed in this chapter:

1. The Seven Master Spirits

2. The Ancients of Days

3. Sons of God

4. Angels: ministering spirits

5. Gabriel and the archangels

6. The seven adjutant mind-spirits

1. The Seven Master Spirits: Central Supervisors of the Seven Segments of the Grand Universe

The Seven Master Spirits have been woven into cultural beliefs and substantiated in religious doctrine throughout recorded history. In Egypt, they were termed the "Seven Mystery Gods." Hindus call them the "Seven Prajapatis" (Lords of Creation). Jews refer to them as the "Seven Sephiroth" and in the Theosophical teachings, the term "Seven Planetary Chain Logoi" is generally used. The founder of Zoroastrianism, a monotheistic faith of ancient Iran, "created a galaxy of seven supreme gods with Ahura-Mazda at its head."[3] In the Bible, the Book of Revelation mentions the Seven Spirits of God four times. These references are found in 1:4, 3:1, 4:5, and in 5:6. Now epochal revelation sheds light on the grand universe's organizational structure, recovering these majestic realities from legends and doctrines.

Who, then, are the Seven Master Spirits? What are their origin and their function in the Divine Plan of Progress?

According to *The Urantia Book*, the Seven Master Spirits are the sevenfold creative act of the Infinite Spirit in collaboration with the Father and the Son. They are one of the Seven Supreme Spirit Groups that coordinate the administration of the grand universe as represented in illustration 6.

The Seven Master Spirits derive their individual characteristics from the seven associations within the Trinity, which are (i) the Father; (ii) the Son; (iii) the Spirit; (iv) the Father and Son; (v) the Father and Spirit; (vi) the Son and Spirit; and (vii) the Father, Son, and Spirit. Our own seventh superuniverse is presided over by the seventh Master Spirit, who equally portrays the individual characteristics of the Father, Son, and Spirit. The *nature* of each superuniverse is therefore determined by the Master Spirit that presides over it. Like the spokes

Illustration 6
THE SEVEN SUPREME SPIRIT GROUPS

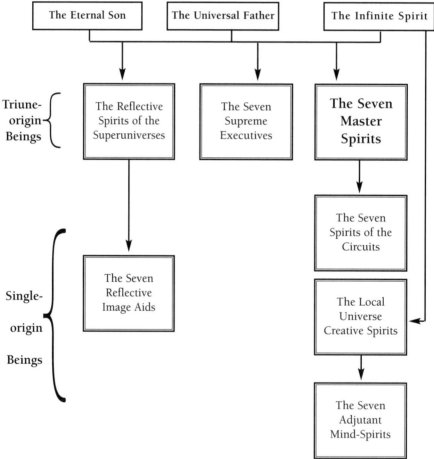

in a wheel, the powerful influence of the Master Spirits radiates out from the central isle serving as ". . . the mind-spirit balance wheel . . ."[4] of the grand universe.

Broadly, the Seven Master Spirits

- supervise the seven segments of the grand universe, functioning on all levels of superuniverse activities. This validates the Zoroastrian and Hindu points of view.

- represent the Infinite Spirit to the evolutionary universes in the relationships of energy, mind, and spirit. While the Infinite Spirit is the source of mind, the Seven Master Spirits further distribute mind to the grand universe as the cosmic mind. They are responsible for equalizing and stabilizing the cosmic-mind circuits of the grand universe that influence the intellectual levels of all known existence. In Trinitarian Christian theology, the Holy Spirit is associated with the Third Person of the Trinity.

- assist Creator Sons in the work of shaping and organizing the local universes.

2. The Ancients of Days: Rulers of the Seven Segments of the Grand Universe

The meaning of the title "Ancients of Days" differs in different traditions. For example:

- In the Western Christian Churches, the title is generally identified with God the Father (Book of Daniel 7:9, 13, 22) while the Russian Orthodox Church identifies the Ancient of Days with God the Son (*The Tome of the Great Council of Moscow* [1666–1667 A.D.], Ch. 2, 43–45; tr. Hierodeacon Lev Puhalo, *Canadian Orthodox Missionary Journal*).

- In the Church of Jesus Christ of Latter-day Saints, the title is identified with Adam (*Doctrine & Covenants* 27:11. lds.org. Retrieved on 2009–06–19).

- In Buddhism, in the Kevattha Sutta (Digha Nikaya #11), the term "ancient of days" is referred to the creator God Brahma: "I am the Great Brahma, the Supreme, the Mighty, the All-seeing, the Ruler, the Lord of all, the Controller, the Creator, the Chief of all, appointing to each his place, the Ancient of days, the Father of all that are and are to be." (http://www.statemaster.com/encyclopedia/Ancient-of-Days)

According to epochal revelation, the term "Ancients of Days" designates one of seven orders of Supreme Trinity Personalities created by the Paradise Trinity and depicted in illustration 7.

Whereas the Seven Master Spirits determine the *nature* of their respective segments of the grand universe, the Ancients of Days, governing in groups of three, manage the *administration* of these same segments.

The Ancients of Days are the most powerful of the direct rulers of the time-space creations. They are the only arbiters in the vast universe that can render

Illustration 7
THE SUPREME TRINITY PERSONALITIES

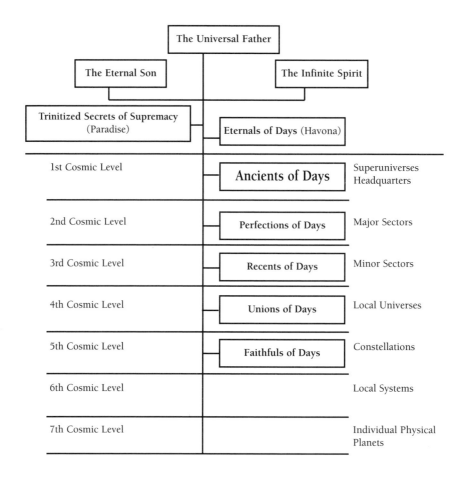

judgment as to whether a free-will creature attains eternal life. "Throughout the grand universe, these Supreme Trinity Personalities represent the administrative policies of the Paradise Trinity; they represent the justice and are the executive judgment of the Paradise Trinity. They form an interrelated line of administrative perfection extending from the Paradise spheres of the Father to the headquarters worlds of the local universes and to the capitals of their component constellations."[5]

The seven orders of Supreme Trinity Personalities are part of a group called the Stationary Sons of the Trinity, who are responsible for administering just and fair judgment to the seven superuniverses. Together the groups comprise the grand corps of Trinity administrators, rulers, executives, advisers, counselors, and judges. The titles, function, and jurisdiction of these Trinity Sons are presented in illustration 8.

Illustration 8
THE STATIONARY SONS OF THE TRINITY

Title	Function	Jurisdiction
Perfectors of Wisdom	Personify the *wisdom* of Deity May and do engage in the work of revealing truth to the individual planets and systems	Superuniverse, under the service of the Ancients of Days
Divine Counselors	Personify the *counsel* of Deity	Superuniverse, under the service of the Ancients of Days
Universal Censors	Personify the *judgment* of Deity	Superuniverse, under the service of the Ancients of Days
Supreme Trinity Personalities		
Trinitized Secrets of Supremacy	Administrators	Supervise Paradise Spheres
Eternals of Days	Administrators	Supervise Havona Spheres
Ancients of Days	**Supreme Rulers**	**Superuniverse**
Perfections of Days	Rulers	Major Sectors
Recents of Days	Rulers	Minor Sectors
Unions of Days	Counselors/advisers (report applicable information to the Recent of Days, Perfection of Days, and Ancients of Days)	Local Universes (Rulers are the Creator Sons)
Faithfuls of Days	Counselors/advisers (Report directly to the Union of Days)	Constellations (Rulers are the appointed Local Universe Vorondadek Sons, commissioned by Gabriel as "the Most High")

3. Sons of Gods

Human beings are possessed of an instinctive longing for superhuman help that is designed to anticipate the appearance on earth of the sons of God. "Many races have conceived of their leaders as being born of virgins; their careers are liberally sprinkled with miraculous episodes, and their return is always expected by their respective groups. In central Asia, the tribesmen still look for the return of Genghis Khan; in Tibet, China, and India it is Buddha; in Islam it is Mohammed; among the Amerinds it was Hesunanin Onamonalonton; with the Hebrews it was, in general, Adam's return as a material ruler. In Babylon, the god Marduk was a perpetuation of the Adam legend, the son-of-God idea, the connecting link between man and God. Following the appearance of Adam on earth, so-called sons of God were common among the world races."[6]

In the New Testament, the phrase "Son of God" refers to the relationship between Jesus and God. Christian theology elevated Jesus' status to the "only begotten" Son of God, synonymous with the second person of the Trinity. This may have been a shrewd bid for theological hegemony, but it has been a source of bitter contention between Christianity and both Islam and Judaism.

When we attempt to understand the present by studying historical events and their causes, we run the risk of distorting facts and misrepresenting truth. It has been said that the present can be truly interpreted only in the light of the correlated past and future. To separate interpretive error from truth in the many theologies related to the "Sons of God," it is instructive to view humanity and its planetary problems from the infinite perspective—from the center of all reality and all cosmic existence. Proceeding from that vantage point with the guidance of epochal revelation, we gain new insight into the pantheon of divinity and Jesus'

> *The lack of a knowledge of the multiple Sons of God is a source of great confusion on Urantia.*
>
> The Urantia Book

place therein. Christian theology presents a paradox: Jesus is more than some understand and less than others believe.

The second deity of the Trinity, referred to throughout this book as the Eternal Son, has the following characteristics that align with the generally accepted tenets of Christianity with regard to God the Son:

1. "The Eternal Son is the original and only-begotten Son of God. He is God the Son, the Second Person of Deity and the associate creator of all things."[7]

2. "The Eternal Son is just as changeless and infinitely dependable as the Universal Father."[8]

3. "God the Son is just as divinely real and eternal in nature as God the Father."[9]

4. "The Son not only possesses all of the Father's infinite and transcendent righteousness, but the Son is also reflective of all the Father's holiness of character. The Son shares the Father's perfection and jointly shares the responsibility of aiding all creatures of imperfection in their spiritual efforts to attain divine perfection."[10]

5. "The Son shares the justice and righteousness of the Trinity but overshadows these divinity traits by the infinite personalization of the Father's love and mercy; the Son is the revelation of divine love to the universes. As God is love, so the Son is mercy."[11]

6. "The Eternal Son is the great mercy minister to all creation."[12]

The Bible refers to Jesus with the words "only begotten" or "one and only" five times (John 1:14 &18; 3:16 &18, and 4:9). This interpretation, the understanding of the people of that day, places human restrictions on God's immense plan of creation. Expanding the meaning of this doctrinal belief does not to diminish one's exalted notions of Christ—but it does open the possibility for great wonder. The literal interpretation of "only begotten" is actually true as regards our local universe, but it is destined to be outgrown like the ancient version of an Earth-centered cosmos. Epochal revelation offers new visions of God the Son, challenging but yet again expanding traditional Christian theology:

- "The Universal Father never personally functions as a creator except in conjunction with the Son or with the coordinate action of the Son."[13]

- "The Eternal Son does not personally function in the physical domains, nor does he function, except through the [Infinite Spirit], in the levels of mind ministry to creature beings. But these qualifications do not in any manner otherwise limit the Eternal Son in the full and free exercise of all the divine attributes of spiritual omniscience, omnipresence, and omnipotence."[14]

- "The Father, in eternalizing the Original Son, bestowed upon him the power and privilege of subsequently joining with the Father in the divine act of producing additional Sons possessing creative attributes . . ."[15]

The above are significant updates that amplify the old meaning of the "only begotten Son" concept. The revelation that God the Son does not personally function in the physical realm except through his Sons who possess mighty creative attributes, clarifies a burdensome tenet of Christianity. We discover that Jesus is a Son of God but not a member of the Trinity. At the same time, it introduces us to the extended family of God the Son—the *multiple* Sons of God of composite origin. This opens our vision to incredible new insights into the personality and divinity of Jesus.

Christian theology presents a paradox: Jesus is more than some understand and less than others believe.

As they function in our superuniverse, Sons of God are classified under three general headings: the Trinitized Sons of God, the Ascending Sons of God, and the Descending Sons of God.

- The Trinitized Sons of God are a group of beings of multiple origins and they are outside the scope of this book.

- The Ascending Sons of God include mortal creatures, such as human beings who have achieved immortal status. Prior to that time, humans are known as *faith sons*. Our status as sons and daughters of God is clearly depicted in the New Testament.

- Descending Sons of God are celestial beings of high and divine origin, depicted in illustration 9. They are dedicated to assisting all free-will creatures of evolutionary origin, such as humankind, in their ascent to Paradise. There are many orders of Descending Sons, but of particular interest are two groups:

    1. Paradise Sons of the Order of Michael.

    2. Local Universe Sons.

Illustration 9
THE DESCENDING SONS OF GOD

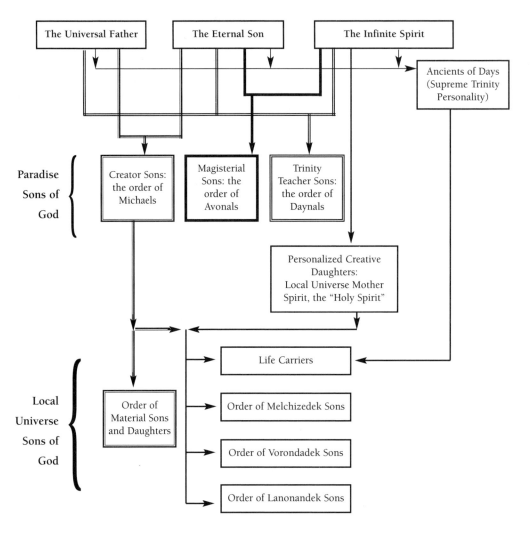

Creator Sons: Paradise Sons of the Order of Michael

Paradise Sons of the order of Michael are known as *Creator Sons*. Throughout their local universe realm, Creator Sons are known as Michael Sons, and in studying them we greatly expand our understanding of human spirit lineage.

Just as many roses spring from the same bush, each unique and complete in itself, every Creator Son is the "only-begotten son," a unique creation of God the Father and God the Son, destined ". . . to incarnate and make real, the love of the Father and the mercy of the Son to the creatures of all universes."[16] Just as each rose from the same bush is perfect in itself, so is each Creator Son, fully embodying and expressing the divinity of his creators.

The Universal Father functions outside of Paradise through these associate beings. Therefore, while the Universal Father is the personal creator of Paradise and the central universe of perfection, the universes of time and space are designed, created, organized, and administrated by Creator Sons as part of the Father-revelation plan. Creator Sons are also responsible for the overall life plans of their respective realms. When a Michael Son embarks upon his universe-building career, his creator prerogatives are subject only to certain limitations:

- *"Energy-matter* is dominated by the Infinite Spirit. Before any new forms of things, great or small, may be created, before any new transformations of energy-matter may be attempted, a Creator Son must secure the consent and working cooperation of the Infinite Spirit.

- *Creature designs and types* are controlled by the Eternal Son. Before a Creator Son may engage in the creation of any new type of being, any new design of creature, he must secure the consent of the Eternal and Original . . . Son.

- *Personality* is designed and bestowed by the Universal Father."[17]

According to epochal revelation, Creator Sons represent in their local universes the Universal Father and the Eternal Son, and for all practical intents and purposes may be considered God by the creatures of the realm. "These Universe Sons receive, in the name of the Father, the adoration of worship and give ear to the pleas of their petitioning subjects throughout their respective creations."[18]

In their universe adventure, Creator Sons are accompanied by the Creative Daughters of the Infinite Spirit. These Creative Daughters are destined to become the Mother Spirits of the new local universes, and often become known in the individual worlds as the *Holy Spirit*. In Christian theology, the Holy Spirit is considered to be synonymous with the Third Person of the Trinity. Epochal revelation clarifies this misconception: "The Holy Spirit is the spiritual circuit of this Creative Daughter of the Paradise Infinite Spirit. The Holy Spirit is a circuit indigenous to each local universe and is confined to the spiritual realm of that creation; but the Infinite Spirit is omnipresent."[19] The Infinite Spirit, like the Universal Father, functions outside of Paradise only through his spirit family.

The Holy Spirit expands our perspective of moral values, religion, and spirituality. The influence of the Holy Spirit is pervasive in all mind activity, even without our conscious cooperation, but it becomes much more effective when the mortal individual invokes a willingness to be influenced by this ministry.

The Creator Son and the Local Universe Mother Spirit create a range of beings that serve to manage and minister to their creation (refer to illustration 10).

To achieve the recognized sovereignty of his local universe, a Creator Son willingly incarnates seven times. On each occasion he lives as a different type of being of his own creation (for example, as a Melchizedek Son, a Lanonandek Son, as seraphim, or a local universe pilgrim). Only once does he experience birth and death as a planetary mortal. How a Son of God incarnates is a divine mystery, the secret of such a mission is only revealed to those who have gone through the experience.

Illustration 10
FAMILY TREE OF
CREATOR SONS AND CREATIVE DAUGHTERS

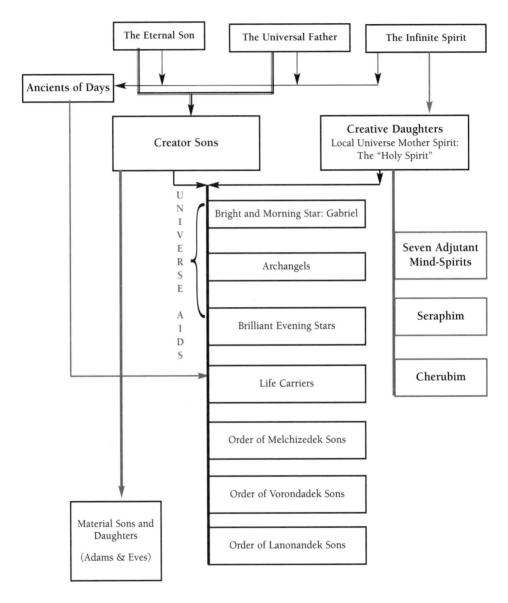

"The purpose of these creature incarnations is to enable such Creators to become wise, sympathetic, just, and understanding sovereigns. These divine Sons are innately just, but they become understandingly merciful as a result of these successive bestowal experiences; they are naturally merciful, but these experiences make them merciful in new and additional ways. These bestowals are the last steps in their education and training for the sublime tasks of ruling the local universes in divine righteousness and by just judgment."[20] "These bestowals are not essential to the wise, just, and efficient management of a local universe, but they are absolutely necessary to a fair, merciful, and understanding administration of such a creation, teeming with its varied forms of life and its myriads of intelligent but imperfect creatures."[21]

After each bestowal, the Creator Son ascends to the "right hand of the Father" to receive the Father's acceptance of the completed mission and instruction for the next universe service assignment. "Following the seventh and final bestowal a Creator Son receives from the Universal Father supreme authority and jurisdiction over his universe."[22]

The Creator Son of our local universe is known as Michael of Nebadon. According to epochal revelation, Michael selected the disintegrating Andronover nebula as the site to build his local universe of Nebadon over three hundred billion years ago. [Note that *The Urantia Book* reveals a cosmic timetable of staggering measure, as yet unconceivable to our scientists.] As soon as the decision was made, the creation of the architectural worlds that would serve as his universe headquarters began. Local creation of galaxies continued to evolve, with suns becoming stabilized and planets forming and swinging into their orbits. With the passage of unimaginable eons of time, Earth would enjoy the singular honor of becoming the mortal bestowal planet of the Creator Son and Sovereign of our universe. Section two explores the relation between Michael of Nebadon and Jesus of Nazareth and reconciles his life in the light of epochal revelation.

Local Universe Sons of God

Local Universe Sons are of special interest because they are part of the family of the Creator Sons who assist in the administration of the local universes and physical planets. Our shared spirit ancestry comes into focus as we study them.

Creator Sons, together with the Mother Spirits, are responsible for the creation of the Local Universe Sons of God, depicted in illustration 10. Other "local" Sons are involved in various functions, including the administration of planets, the fostering of life, and the uplift of the human races. Our ancient history gains new and greater meaning when we understand how divine activities influenced the social and spiritual evolution on our planet, addressed in section two. Here we address the nature and general functions of these local universe Sons.

LIFE CARRIERS

The Life Carriers are the offspring of the Creator Son, the Local Universe Mother Spirit, and one of the three Ancients of Days. They are entrusted with establishing physical life on the evolving worlds and fostering its development.

THE MELCHIZEDEK SONS

The Melchizedeks are the offspring of the Creator Son and Local Universe Mother Spirit. They are the first to respond to all types of emergencies on inhabited worlds. It was a Melchizedek named Machiventa who bestowed himself on Earth when higher truth was threatened with extinction. His mission sparked the beginning of the Hebrew religion. See the beginning of chapter 10 for more on Machiventa Melchizedek.

THE LANONANDEK SONS

The Lanonandek Sons of God are the third order originating in the Creator Son and the Mother Spirit of the local universe. "The Lanonandeks are the continuous rulers of the planets and the rotating sovereigns of the systems."[23]

Prior to assuming service in their local system, the Lanonandek Sons must pass certification by their older brothers, the Melchizedeks. Once this is completed, they are divided into three classes:

1. Primary Lanonandeks function as System Sovereigns—chief executives and rulers of local systems each made up of approximately one thousand inhabited planets. They are always supported by at least two or three other Lanonandek Sons.

2. Secondary Lanonandeks preside over a planet as Planetary Princes.

3. Tertiary Lanonandeks function as subordinate assistants, messengers, custodians, commissioners, observers, etc.

When life on a planet has evolved to the point where evolving mortals can choose to worship and make moral choices, the System Sovereign assigns a Secondary Lanonandek Son to preside as *Planetary Prince*. It is the responsibility of the Planetary Prince to foster human civilization—to elevate primitive people to an advanced level of tribal functioning and usher in the emergence of family life. Although the Planetary Prince is invisible to the physical beings of the planet, he functions effectively through a group of materialized volunteers who accompany him as advisers and helpers in the work of early cultural improvement. In section two, we will discover the identity of Earth's first Planetary Prince and his role in the history of our planet.

Satan and Lucifer

Satan and Lucifer are two Primary Lanonandek Sons who adversely affected the moral and spiritual development of many planets, including Earth. Lucifer was the local System Sovereign and Satan was his lieutenant. With the passage of time, their participation in the planetary rebellion became distorted and embedded in myths and legends.

The name "Satan" surfaced in Zoroastrianism in the sixth century before Christ as part of its concept of the struggle between cosmic good and evil. Zoroaster had come directly in contact with the descendants of the earlier Melchizedek missionaries. His interpretations of their teachings became central in the religion that he founded in Persia, one which later influenced the Hebrew and Christian religions.

The Old Testament correctly presents Satan as a celestial personality that personally opposed God (Job 1:6–12; 2:1–8). The transition of Satan from "adversary" into devil and then synonymy with Lucifer emerged with time as Christianity became a preeminent religion.

The merging of Satan with Lucifer likely arose from the reference to the devil Satan being cast out of heaven in Revelation 12:9–12 and in Luke 10:12. In Isaiah 14:12, the arch rebel is referred to as the "morning star," translated into Latin as "Lucifer" both in the Septuagint and the Latin Vulgate. The King James Version of the Bible is based on these two texts. The passage from Revelation, along with passages from Job 11:17 and 2 Peter 1:19, appear to link the devil Satan with light and the sky/stars, perhaps fueling the assumption that Lucifer and Satan are one and the same. The popular religious fictions *The Divine Comedy* by Dante Alighieri [1265–1321] and *Paradise Lost* by John Milton [1608–1675] finally established Lucifer as another face of Satan. Dante's vision of hell and Milton's view of Satan came together to reflect the position of the church.

The apocryphal Book of Enoch, thought to have been written in the first century, and banned at the First Council of Nicaea in AD 325, describes the rebellion of the angel Satanail and his fall from heaven (2 Enoch, chapter 29, long manuscripts [MSS] only). In the apocryphal *First Book of Adam and Eve*, Satan takes the form of an angel and falsely promises Eve the "bright light."[24] The Qur'an (S. 2:34) relates that Satan told Adam and Eve that his fall from heaven was the result of his refusal to worship Adam, the image of God. These legends reflect the accurate theme of "personal pride" that led to the so-called fall of Satan.

In section two, we will discuss the relationship between Satan and Lucifer, their role in the history of our planet, and their connection to the combat myths—one of the most long-lived genres in ancient literature.

THE MATERIAL SONS AND DAUGHTERS

The Material Sons and Daughters are brought into being by the Creator Son. They are usually known on a planet as Adam and Eve, and are materialized to function as biologic uplifters. Legends about Adam and Eve are to be found in Jewish, Christian, and Islamic sources, as well as apocryphal books and very ancient myths. The miscarriage of their mission on Earth had moral, spiritual, and biological repercussions and will be addressed further in section two.

THE VORONDADEK SONS

The Vorondadeks are the creation of the Creator Son and the Local Universe Mother Spirit. They are the rulers of the constellations and are generally known as the Most Highs. The responsibilities of these Sons are outside the scope of this book.

4. Angels: Ministering Spirits

The belief in angels as "messengers of the gods" has been traced to the ancient Sumerian civilization that existed between the Euphrates and Tigris Rivers in present-day Iraq. The mythology of the Sumerians embraced a wide variety of gods and spirits—including the angelic forces that ran errands between gods and humans—eventually finding its way into Egyptian theology. When the polytheistic Semitic tribes conquered Sumer around two thousand years before Christ, the Sumerian angelic order was adopted and later expanded into the Babylonian and Persian theologies that included corps of angels ranked in a "vertical" hierarchy.

With the passage of time, the messenger concept of angels survived the transition from polytheistic religion to the monotheistic Judaism; angels were incorporated into Jewish writings and, later, into Christian cosmology. According to the *Encyclopedia Britannica*, "The medieval philosophers Aristotelized or Platonized them, the early mystics Neoplatonized them, and the Kabbalists continually invented new ones and fitted them into their complicated network of cosmic existence."[25]

Much of our understanding of angels has been gathered from early artistic depictions of spirits, usually taking form as winged creatures. The Sumerian culture left abundant evidence of such images in stone carvings. The Egyptian Goddess Isis, protector, eternal virgin, and mother, is sometimes pictured with wings. In Greek mythology, Thanatos, the brother of Sleep and the son of Night, is the personification of death, sometimes presented as a winged human. In Plato's writings, gods and the souls of men have wings.

Celestial beings in Western religions have been traditionally called angels. From the Book of Genesis to the Book of Revelation, celestial beings perceived to be closest to God have received names such as "seraphim," while the general designation "angels" is relegated to those of lower rank. In the "Celestial Hierarchy" treatise attributed to Dionysius the Areopagite, the seraphim are of the first and highest order of celestial beings, ". . . the most fully Godlike, and the most closely and immediately united to the First Light of the Godhead."[26] Accordingly, the order of angels is the last and lowest, ". . . since they are the last of the Celestial Beings possessing the angelic nature . . . and because their choir is more directly in contact with manifested and mundane things."[27]

Angels are widely considered to be a familial link between God and mortals. In times of great trial or danger, angels are a source of comfort to many.

The vast celestial organization first revealed in *The Urantia Book* provides us with comprehensive information and the opportunity to expand our understanding of angels—their lineage, function, and relation to other celestial beings as well as their relation to humanity and the ascending scheme of progress.

The Lineages of Angels

Although God is the ultimate creator of all, the Infinite Spirit is the ministering personality, the Paradise Deity who reveals the love of the Father and the personality of the Son to the creatures of time and space.

Angels comprise one of three groups of the Infinite Spirit's functional family. The Old Testament provides validation of their ministering function. Hebrews 1:14 states: "Are they (angels) not all ministering spirits, sent forth to minister for them who shall be heirs of salvation?" The three main groups that comprise the functional family of the Infinite Spirit are depicted in illustration 11.

The lineage of groups one and two, the Seven Supreme Spirit groups and the Universe Power Directors, has been shown in illustrations 6 and 2 respectively.

The third group, the Personalities of the Infinite Spirit, is the most relevant to humanity and is divided into three grand divisions: Powers, Authorities, and Angels. These divisions broadly found in the "Celestial Hierarchy" are clearly identified by the apostle Peter when he wrote about Jesus' ascension, "Who is gone into heaven, and is on the right hand of God; angels and authorities and powers being made subject unto him." (1 Peter 3:22) According to epochal revelation:

- *Angels* are the Ministering Spirits of time
- *Authorities* are the Messenger Hosts of space
- *Powers* are the Higher Personalities of the Infinite Spirit

Illustration 11
FUNCTIONAL FAMILY OF THE INFINITE SPIRIT

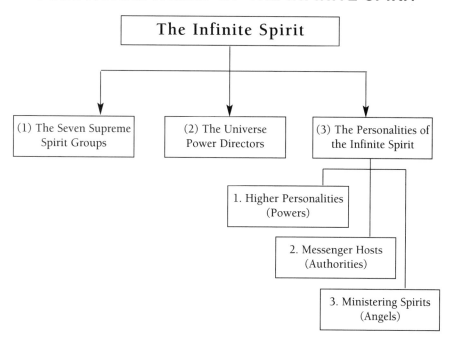

The three divisions are concerned with teaching and ministering to the free-will creatures of ascending mortals, but only the division of angels is within the scope of this book.

When we consider that we live in a multilevel universe extending from Earth to Paradise, the ancient angelic teachings can now be reconciled with epochal revelation and expanded to include the universe territories in which they function (See illustration 12).

The seraphim are part of the third choir of angels that work close to evolving humanity, serving the farthest from Paradise. True to Jacob's dream of a stairway from Earth to heaven with angels ascending and descending on it (Genesis 28:12), these ministering spirits of various orders are encountered throughout our multilevel universe, from the Isle of Paradise to the worlds of time and space. In the revealed scheme, the *seraphim* in the local universe, the *seconaphim* in the superuniverse, and the *supernaphim* in the central universe, play key roles in the ascending adventure of humans. These three orders, whose lineage is depicted in illustration 13, appear in the shaded boxes.

The expanded portrayal of the angelic hierarchy as depicted in illustrations 12 and 13 provides us with a strong foundation to continue familiarizing ourselves with the ministering spirits that directly serve humanity.

Illustration 12
ANGELIC HIERARCHY

BY DIONYSIUS THE AREOPAGITE

1st Choir	2nd Choir	3rd Choir
Seraphim Cherubim Thrones	Dominions Virtues Powers	Principalities Archangels Angels

RECONCILED ANGELIC HIERARCHY
By Territories Within the Multilevel Universe

Division of the Personalities of the Infinite Spirit	The local universe including physical planets	The superuniverses	The central and divine universes
3rd Choir Angels Ministering Spirits	SERAPHIM Cherubim Midwayers	SECONAPHIM Tertiaphim Omniaphim	SUPERNAPHIM Primary, Secondary, and Tertiary orders
2nd Choir Authorities Messenger Hosts	Morontia Companions	Universal Conciliators Technical Advisers Celestial Recorders	Havona Servitals Custodians of Records on Paradise Paradise Companions
1st Choir Powers Higher Personalities	Assigned Sentinels Associate Inspectors	Universe Circuit Supervisors Census Directors	Personal Aids of the Infinite Spirit Solitary Messengers Graduate Guides

The seraphim and their cherubim assistants are primarily assigned to the plans of mortal survival. The *midway creatures*, who operate mostly unseen, are considered to be permanent citizens of the inhabited worlds. They do not accurately belong to the angelic orders but are included because they are indispensable to the work of the seraphim. The gap between the material and spiritual worlds is therefore perfectly bridged by the serial association of mortals, midwayers, cherubim, and seraphim.

Illustration 13

LINEAGES OF ANGELS

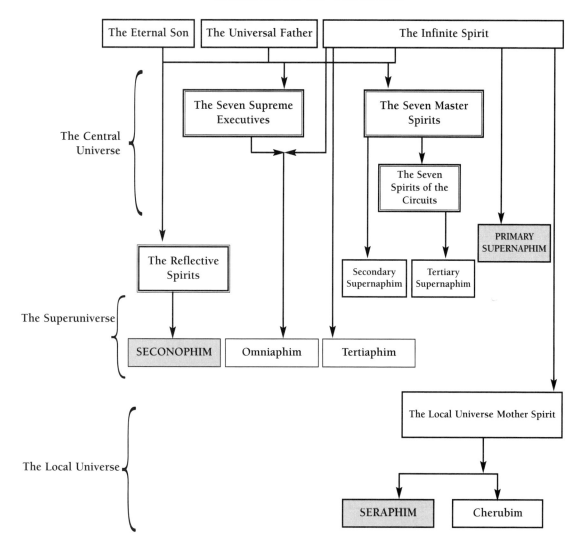

Some of the general characteristics of the angelic corps presented in *The Urantia Book* that resonate with or expand our current knowledge of angels include:

- Angels and human beings share many emotional and personality traits, these similarities becoming even more pronounced after mortal death when the human soul assumes a semispirit form.

- Although angels do not possess physical bodies, they are nevertheless distinct spirit personalities, generally invisible to mortal eyes but able to "see" and provide spiritual guidance.

- Angels grow to love their human associates and appreciate their efforts in music, art, and humor. Angels share all of man's nonsensuous emotions and feelings. The one emotion that angels find hard to understand is fear, so abundant in the mental life of the average person.[28]

- Angels, like humans, are evolving personalities. They are continuously engaged in efforts at self-improvement as they work their way toward the perfection of Paradise.

- The word "host" is occasionally used in the Bible to mean an "organized army" of angels.[29] In Luke 2:13, there is reference to a "multitude of heavenly hosts." In Matthew 26:53, Jesus alluded to a legion of angels that night in the garden of Gethsemane when he asked: "Thinkest thou that I cannot now pray to my Father, and he shall presently give me more than twelve legions of angels?" Illustration 14 depicts the "armies of heaven" as clarified and expanded by *The Urantia Book*.

Illustration 14
THE "ARMIES OF HEAVEN" COMMANDED BY GABRIEL

Title	Contains	Comprising	Directed by
One group		12 pairs, 24 individual angels	
One company	12 groups	144 pairs, 288 individual angels	A leader
One battalion	12 companies	1,728 pairs, 3,456 individual angels	A commander
One seraphic unit	12 battalions	20,736 pairs, 41,472 individual angels	A director
One legion	12 units	248,832 pairs, 497,664 individual angels	A supervisor
A host	12 legions	2,985,984 pairs or 5,971,968 individual angels.	An archangel
An angelic army	12 hosts	35,831,808 pairs or 71,663,616 individual angels	A Brilliant Evening Star

THE SERAPHIM

The seraphim and their cherubim assistants are the direct offspring of the Local Universe Mother Spirit. Seraphim continually seek to promote spiritual decisions of morality in the human mind. "They do this, not as does the Adjuster, operating from within and through the soul, but rather from the outside inward, working through the social, ethical, and moral environment of human beings."[30]

The seraphic hosts are classified into seven groups, with each further subdivided according to the varied functions they perform throughout the local universe. The ministry of angels becomes increasingly relevant to us as they enter the realities of the inhabited worlds, serving those men and women who are preparing themselves for the goal of eternity. Of particular interest are the seraphim designated as Planetary Helpers,[31] subdivided into seven groups; five are described below:

- **The Voices of the Garden:** the seraphim assigned to the Gardens of Eden, the planetary centers of moral, cultural, and spiritual training. They assist in the physical and intellectual evolution of the human race. It was a seraph of this order, not the voice of God, who reprimanded Adam and Eve for disobedience and informed them that they had defaulted in the execution of their planetary mission.

- **The Spirits of Brotherhood:** the seraphim who work to foster racial harmony and social cooperation among the diverse races.[32]

- **The Souls of Peace:** the seraphim whose ministry fosters peace on the willful worlds. As a planet evolves, ". . . these seraphim are instrumental in supplanting the atonement idea by the concept of divine attunement as a philosophy of mortal survival."[33]

- **The Spirits of Trust:** These seraphim instill trust into the minds of evolving humankind. "In the more advanced planetary ages these seraphim enhance man's appreciation of the truth that uncertainty is the secret of contented continuity."[34]

- **The Transporters:** "All groups of ministering spirits have their transport corps, angelic orders dedicated to the ministry of transporting those personalities who are unable, of themselves, to journey from one sphere to another."[35] The planetary helpers who serve as transporters operate from the local planets. They use "energy insulators" for interplanetary travel that give the appearance of wings. The tradition that angels have wings probably originated with those individuals who, according to revelation, were allowed to observe transport seraphim preparing to receive passengers. This belief that angels have wings dates back to ancient times, as recorded by Sumerians and Egyptians claiming contact with "winged beings"—a belief first evidenced on archaic stone tablets and murals that have survived to this day.

THE GUARDIAN ANGELS

Throughout history, guardian angels have been the most recognized group of angels and considered to be the closest spiritual protectors of human beings.

The ancient Sumerians believed that each person had a "ghost" of some sort that remained as a constant companion throughout his or her life. The Egyptian *Hunmanit* may be an early version of the guardian angel, having the responsibility to look after the sun, indirectly fulfilling a responsibility to look after humanity. "This belief in guardian angels can be traced throughout all antiquity; pagans, like Menander and Plutarch (cf. Euseb., "Praep. Evang." xii), and Neo-Platonists, such as Plotinus, held it. It was also the belief of the Babylonians and Assyrians, as their monuments testify, for a figure of a guardian angel now in the British Museum once decorated an Assyrian palace, and might well serve for a modern representation . . ."[36]

Epochal revelation expands our understanding. "The teaching about guardian angels is not a myth; certain groups of human beings do actually have personal angels." Jesus recognized this when speaking for our children: "'Take heed that you despise not one of these little ones, for I say to you, their angels do always behold the presence of the spirit of my Father.'" [37]

Guardian angels are volunteer seraphim assigned to humanity according to each person's ability to develop intellectually, classed as follows:

1. Those individuals with below-average intelligence, who lack the capacity to know and intelligently worship God, are ministered by one company of seraphim assisted by one battalion of cherubim.[38]

2. Those individuals with average intelligence who are assigned guardians according to the level of human progress achieved:

    a. Every group of one thousand human beings in the initial or seventh circle of human progress (see section four) is assigned one guardian angel with one company of assisting cherubim.

    b. Every group of five hundred human beings who have attained the sixth circle of human progress is assigned a seraphic pair with one company of cherubim.

    c. Every group of approximately one hundred mortals who have attained the fifth circle is assigned a pair of guardian seraphim with a group of cherubim.

    d. Every group of ten humans who have attained the fourth circle is assigned a pair of seraphim assisted by one company of cherubim.

    e. A human who attains the third circle of mental, moral, and spiritual development receives the undivided assistance of a pair of personal guardians to help her complete the third circle, pass through the second, and achieve the first.[39]

3. Those rare individuals who are assigned personal angels, including ". . . those of great decision and undoubted potential for spiritual achievement; men and women who enjoy more or less contact with their indwelling Adjusters; members of the various reserve corps of destiny."[40] The reserve corps is made up of individuals of every

generation who have been chosen to assist the superhuman administration of the planet as human liaisons and assistants because of their high level of intellectual, moral, and spiritual achievement.

"Seraphim are not known as guardians of destiny until such time as they are assigned to the association of a human soul who has realized one or more of three achievements: has made a supreme decision to become Godlike, has entered the third circle [of human progress], or has been mustered into one of the reserve corps of destiny."[41]

Personal guardians generally work in pairs, and once they have been assigned, they serve the individual for the remainder of his or her life. "On the spiritual level, seraphim make personal many otherwise impersonal and prepersonal ministries of the universe; they are coordinators. On the intellectual level they are the correlators of mind and morontia; they are interpreters. And on the physical level they manipulate terrestrial environment through their liaison with the Master Physical Controllers and through the cooperative ministry of the midway creatures."[42] Many physical phenomena that humans attribute to ghosts and spirits may well be the actions of midwayers.

Guardian angels protect—it is not their function to be of direct influence. "They do not (ordinarily) arbitrarily intervene in the routine affairs of human life. But when they receive instructions from their superiors to perform some unusual exploit, you may rest assured that these guardians will find some means of carrying out these mandates . . . They are the beings who are going to follow you for many an age . . ."[43]

5. Gabriel and the Archangels: Local Universe Aids

No other order of celestial beings is the subject of more elaborate and conflicting information than the archangels. Discrepancies in their numbers, in their names, and in their individual functions abound in spiritual literature. But there is no confusion regarding their supreme purpose: archangels are linked with service to mortal ascenders. They are intimately involved in humanity's well-being and spiritual advancement, not only during physical life but after death.

Several religions rank two spirit beings as archangels: Gabriel and Michael. There is debate as to the name and number of the other purported archangels. For example, in addition to Michael and Gabriel, Christianity recognizes five other archangels, two of whom are Raphael and Uriel; for centuries theologians have disagreed about whether the other three actually exist. There is consensus that the remaining three may be found among the following angels, their names subject to a variety of spellings: Chamael, Jophiel, Zadkiel, Raziel, Remiel, Sariel, Metatron, Anael, Rahuil, Barakiel, Jeduhiel, Simael, Zaphiel, and Aniel. In Islam, four archangels are recognized: Djibril, Mikhail, Azrael, and Israfil—although the Qur'an actually names two: Djibril (Gabriel) and Mikhail (Michael). The recurring appearance of the names "Michael" and "Gabriel" in both canonical and apocryphal texts suggests previous revelation.

How accurate is the historical depiction of archangels? Michael is the most powerful and well-known angel in history, art, literature, and scripture. In the famous war in heaven (Revelation 12:7), Michael is the legendary angel who casts the rebellious Satan out of heaven after defeating him. The Dead Sea Scrolls reference Michael prominently. In the Old Testament he is called the Prince of princes (Daniel 8:25), and prince of the host (Daniel 8:11). In Hebrew, the name "Michael" means "who is as God." Michael's leadership status is undisputed, yet confusion as to his position in the spirit hierarchy is evident in this case of mistaken title.

Epochal revelation confirms that indeed Michael is a Prince, a ruler of the heavenly kingdom; he defeated Satan and is the champion of all people, but he is *not* an archangel. The magnificence portrayed by Michael as an archangel exemplifies and mirrors the splendor of Michael of Nebadon, the Creator Son of our universe. This is not to say that in all instances the archangel Michael referenced in scriptures is Michael of Nebadon. *The Urantia Book* provides an example: "The roll call of a dispensation termination is promulgated by an attendant archangel. This is the archangel of the resurrection, sometimes referred to as the "archangel of Michael."[44]

The confusion over the status of Michael as an archangel also extends to Gabriel. The Bible does not define Gabriel's status as an angel but he is mentioned ". . . four times in scripture, each time bringing a momentous message: twice to Daniel (Daniel 8:16–17; 9:21–22); to Zechariah, father of John the Baptist (Luke 1:11–20); and to Mary, the mother of Jesus (1:26–38)."[45] And Gabriel appears in the Book of Enoch (Enoch 9, 20, 40) as an archangel. The many legends surrounding Gabriel and his close association with Jesus of Nazareth have led to his being considered, among other things:

1. The archangel of annunciation, resurrection, heavenly mercy, vengeance, death, revelation, truth, and hope.

2. The angel who dictated the Qur'an to Mohammed.

3. The angel who will blow the horn announcing the Second Coming of Christ.

Gabriel, however, is not an archangel; Gabriel is the name associated with the Bright and Morning Star—the first order of Universe Aids, created by the Creator Son and the Local Universe Mother Spirit, as depicted in illustration 10.[46]

The Universe Aids consist of at least seven orders of revealed spirit beings whose function is to help in the administration of their local universe. Only the three orders below are addressed in this book, being the direct creations of the Creator Son and the Creative Daughter and involved in the evolution and history of humanity:

1. The Bright and Morning Star: Gabriel

2. The Brilliant Evening Stars

3. The archangels

There is only one Bright and Morning Star in every local universe, a title given to the first being created in that universe. Gabriel, as the Bright and Morning Star of our local universe, functions as the chief executive and administrator of Nebadon. He is the personal associate and right-hand helper of the Creator Son and also the commander in chief of the celestial hosts, "the armies of heaven" depicted in illustration 14.[47]

Gabriel supervises the entire judicial mechanism of the local universe of Nebadon and does not usually depart from his administrative duties. However, when Michael incarnated on Earth as Jesus of Nazareth, Gabriel was always in attendance. Because of this close association, Gabriel has been cast into the religious culture since those times and has been mistakenly identified as an archangel.

When the local universe was in its early stages of development, Gabriel was the sole assistant of the Creator Son and Mother Spirit. As the universe grew, Gabriel was given a personal staff to assist him that expanded when the corps of Brilliant Evening Stars was created. The Brilliant Evening Stars are the second order of Universe Aids who assist Gabriel in maintaining contact with all other universe affairs while he personally attends to administrative duties.

Archangels are the third of the three orders of Local Universe Aids. "They are the highest type of high spirit being produced in large numbers in a local universe, and at the time of the last registry there were almost eight hundred thousand in Nebadon."[48] Gabriel's command does not generally extend to archangels, who are directed chiefly by the first one of their order.

The main focus of archangels is the survival scheme of free-will creatures and their ascending journey to Paradise subsequent to physical death. Some archangels are responsible for keeping a record of all human personalities: "This enormous corps of recorders busy themselves with keeping straight the record of each mortal of time from the moment of birth up through the universe career until such an individual either leaves Salvington for the superuniverse regime or is 'blotted out of recorded existence' [Psalm 69:28] by the mandate of the Ancients of Days."[49] Other functions of archangels include:

- Assisting bestowal Sons on their missions to the inhabited planets
- Promulgating the roll call of a dispensation termination
- Commanding seraphic hosts.

An interesting note in *The Urantia Book* reveals that archangels maintain a divisional headquarters on our planet Earth—a privilege that ". . . lends a tremendous and solemn import to the Master's personal promise, 'I will come again.'"[50]

6. The Seven Adjutant Mind-Spirits

The seven adjutant mind-spirits are the offspring of the Local Universe Mother Spirit and constitute her personal ministry to the creature minds of her realm. They are not personal entities, but more appropriately described as circuits of the mind, a sevenfold level of directed consciousness from the Mother Spirit. The seven adjutant mind-spirits are called by names that are the equivalent to the influence they send forth to all inhabited worlds (refer to illustration 15).

Biblical reference to the adjutant mind-spirits can be found in:

1. **Isaiah 11:2:** "And the spirit of the LORD shall rest upon him, the spirit of wisdom and understanding, the spirit of counsel and might [courage], the spirit of knowledge and of the fear [worship] of the LORD." The Greek interpretation of Isaiah 11:2 also includes these seven human

virtues as found in the Septuagint, the most ancient translation of the Old Testament, invaluable for understanding the Hebrew text.

2. **Revelation 4:5:** "And out of the throne proceeded lightnings and thunderings and voices: and [there were] seven lamps of fire burning before the throne, which are the seven Spirits of God."

3. **Revelation 5:6:** "And I beheld, and, lo, in the midst of the throne and of the four beasts, and in the midst of the elders, stood a Lamb as it had been slain, having seven horns and seven eyes, which are the seven Spirits of God sent forth into all the earth." If these horns are interpreted to represent specific spiritual influences encircuited to the local universe, the "seven spirits" of Revelation may refer to the sevenfold ministry of human virtues gifted by the Holy Spirit.

The Local Universe Mother Spirit, through the seven adjutant mind-spirits, influences the course of organic evolution on primitive worlds. All life forms are connected to and directed by these circuits, offering a new and spiritual perspective on the term "instinct" in regard to both behavior and environmental adaptation.

The evolving influence of the mind-spirits has been associated in modern spirituality with the concepts of "involution" and "evolution"—the evolutionary conscious force driving the cosmos forward since the dawn of creation. Epochal revelation clarifies: "On the inhabited worlds the Spirit begins the work of evolutionary progression, starting with the lifeless material of the realm, first endowing vegetable life, then the animal organisms, then the first orders of human existence; and each succeeding impartation contributes to the further unfolding of the evolutionary potential of planetary life from the initial and primitive stages to the appearance of will creatures. This labor of the Spirit is largely effected through the seven adjutants, the spirits of promise, the unifying and coordinating spirit-mind of the evolving planets, ever and unitedly leading the races of men toward higher ideas and spiritual ideals."[51]

The mind-spirits exert their influence on the inhabited worlds as a differential urge; the Life Carriers, who are responsible for establishing and directing the course of evolution (see section two), collaborate to ensure that all evolving forms are encircuited by the mind-spirits. This suggests that spirit interaction occurs via organic agency, and that the Life Carriers' task is to produce differentially tuned organic centers that can respond to and accommodate the differential urges of these seven adjutant circuits. What manner of organic interface, what kind of neural psychobiochemical configuration, might this require? It may be that the centers for adjutant interaction through which they are able to influence our inner world are related to the seven energy centers identified by Eastern traditions as chakras, which spiritual healers claim to be able to identify, repair, and even enhance.

This previously unknown influence of the adjutant mind-spirits on the evolving creature mind is indispensable to the evolution of human intellect:

• Animal mind is only receptive to the first five adjutants: intuition, understanding, courage, knowledge, and counsel.

Illustration 15
THE SEVEN ADJUTANT MIND-SPIRITS

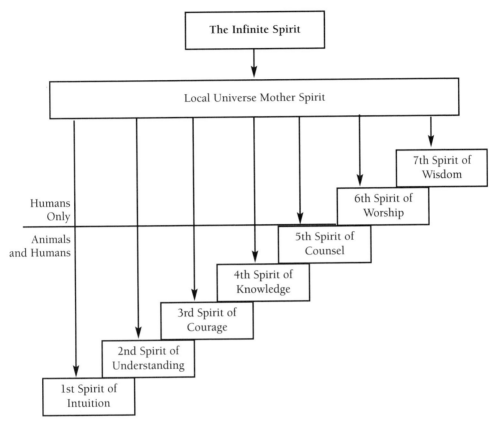

- When the evolving animal mind attains receptivity of the adjutants of worship and wisdom, mind crosses a critical threshold of spirit ministry.
- When the mind is linked with all seven spiritual circuits of the Local Universe Mother Spirit, it signals the planetary arrival of self-conscious will creatures, endowed with the attributes of spiritual responsibility and the potential for eternal survival. This occurred on Earth about one million years ago and marked the official dawn of the human race.

Animal intellect does not have the capacity for worship or wisdom. Animals are not self-observing (reflective) and they do not experience spiritual realities. They cannot discriminate moral meanings or choose spiritual values; their minds are directed outward into the objective physical world.

In contrast, human beings are equipped with a complex brain and endowed with remarkable mind capacity, necessary for the functioning of all seven adjutant mind-spirits. The lower five adjutants function from birth, preparing the mind for the activation of the spirits of worship and wisdom and the reception of the Indwelling Spirit. Our unique personality and genetic endowments, together with our responses to adjutant influence, define the quality of our interface with the adjutant circuits. These interacting dynamics also condition the capacity of the adjutants to create a more or less ideal emotional climate for decision-making. As we cultivate the soul, our choices are increasingly influenced by the guidance of the Indwelling Spirit.

Illustration 16 shows the influence of the seven adjutant mind-spirits. *Note:* In this regard, the order of Virtues under the second choir in the "Celestial Hierarchy" treatise may be said to correspond with the influence of these seven adjutant mind-spirits.

Illustration 16
INFLUENCE OF THE SEVEN ADJUTANT MIND-SPIRITS

Mind Adjutant	Influence
The Spirit of Intuition	• Quick perception • Primitive physical and inherent reflex instincts, such as maternal love and self-preservation
The Spirit of Understanding	• Intellectual coordination • The spontaneous and apparently automatic association of ideas, quick reasoning, rapid judgment and prompt decision • In humans, enables allegiance to grand concepts
The Spirit of Courage	• The intellectual root of moral stamina and spiritual bravery, e.g., parental protective urge • Loyalty, devotion, commitment • In personal beings, the basis of character acquirement
The Spirit of Knowledge	• The scientific spirit: ignites curiosity, the desire for adventure and discovery • The urge to direct the endowments of courage into useful and progressive paths of growth
The Spirit of Counsel	• The social urge • The endowment of species cooperation • Encourages altruism and friendship
The Spirit of Worship	• The impulse to worship is the first differential urge separating the human mind from the animal mind • Fosters the development of spiritual emotions such as awe, reverence, humility, and gratitude
The Spirit of Wisdom	• The inherent tendency of all moral creatures toward orderly and progressive evolutionary advancement • Together with the Spirit of Worship, ability to make a moral choice • Ignites the craving for spiritual survival • Fosters the unification of facts, meanings, and values, through the love of truth, beauty, and goodness

Section One Summary

In the study of our shared spirit origin, we expand our concept of God by bringing clarity to the paradoxes of unity in diversity and divine transcendence and immanence, subjects of misunderstandings throughout the ages. We discover an expanded perspective of our place in the universe and meet the vast hierarchy of spirit beings involved in our personal and collective evolution. We also begin to see the historical connections that highlight the truths in our myths, reconciling the wisdom of the ancient past with ongoing scientific discovery.

The following concepts are useful in organizing a new frame of reference that opens us to higher universal meanings and values:

- Epochal revelation *together* with faith and reason can create the expanded worldview that elevates ideals and builds the brotherhood of man.

- Material and spirit energies are not two ends of the same spectrum. Spirit is always minded—intelligent.

- Paradise is the spiritual and central abode of God the Father and the destiny of the human soul. Paradise is the center of all creation, the source of all energies (matter in all its metamorphic states), and the source and substance of physical gravity.

- The Paradise Trinity is undivided Deity—the eternal Deity union of the Universal Father, the Eternal Son, and the Infinite Spirit. Our highest possible concept of God is embraced within the human idea and ideal of *Father*.

- The working association of the Universal Father, the Eternal Son, and the Infinite Spirit may be termed the First Triunity, or the first association of three beings separately cooperating in a shared purpose.

- The Universal Father is spirit personality, the Original Personality, and origin of all personality. Personality abroad, throughout creation, is the exclusive gift of the Universal Father.

- Personality, whether human or divine, exhibits self-consciousness and free will, functioning in a union of mind and spirit in the presence of living energy.

- The Universal Father is both transcendent and immanent. God is transcendent because he can be found and recognized in Paradise by ascending mortals. God is immanent because his spirit indwells the human mind. Every normal-minded human receives the gift of the Indwelling Spirit, a prepersonal fragment of the Universal Father that is eternal and spiritualizes the mind. The greatest manifestation of the Father's love for mortal beings is this bestowal.

- Mind is not inherent in energy, but energy is receptive and responsive to mind. Mind can be superimposed upon energy, but consciousness is not inherent in the purely material level. As the human mind becomes increasingly spiritual—Godlike—it becomes less responsive to material gravity.

- The Universal Father does not personally administer the universes of time and space. In accordance with the Universal Father's profound policy of self-distribution, the personalities of the Trinity, functioning in their personal capacities, create associate beings of any combination of origin who ". . . unceasingly labor for the honor of God and for the spiritual advancement of his universe children."[1]

- A Divine Plan of Universe Creation and Organization guides the materialization of the grand universe, its physical organization, and its administration.

- A Divine Plan of Progress guides the creation, evolution, ascension, and perfection of creatures with will.

- Humanity shares a common spiritual and physical origin and history, notwithstanding the diverse origins and histories of its many cultural and religious groups.

- Creator Sons are responsible for designing, creating, building, and administering the local universes, which includes the overall life plans of their respective realms.

- Local Universe Lanondadek Sons are involved in the administration of systems and planets as System Sovereigns and Planetary Rulers. Lucifer and Satan were two Lanondadek Sons who impacted the spiritual and social development of our planet.

- Life Carriers are an order of local universe Sons who foster life on the evolving worlds.

- The seven adjutant mind-spirits are the circuitry for response to the cosmic mind and influence the development of the arena for conscious thought.

- Adam and Eve are the names by which the Material Sons and Daughters of a local universe are known. They are responsible for the planetary biological and spiritual uplift of creatures with will.

- Melchizedek Sons are mainly concerned with the vast educational and training organization within the local universe, akin to our professors and philosophers. They are also the first to respond when there is a crisis on an inhabited world.

Some of these teachings conflict with long-held beliefs. But if we are sincere in our commitment to spiritual growth, then honest reflection and new insights will lift us into higher spiritual meanings and values, discovered and integrated into our thinking to create an expanded worldview. In this process, we develop a deeper conviction that what we have in common far exceeds our human differences.

A new spirituality is spreading by means of books, seminars, courses, and lectures—with as many approaches to enlightenment as there are authors and teachers. Progressive and unifying ideals are emerging, but a full blossoming of religious brotherhood awaits the teaching of broader concepts of God and the universe. Our world needs courageous leaders who will help us discover new meanings in ancient wisdom while stretching the boundaries of modern knowledge. There is currently a gap between human thinking—which evolves—and cosmic truth, which is revealed. Because so little is known of our shared origin, history, and destiny, closing the gap will take time and the courage to compare the content and consistency of newly revealed teachings with our personal beliefs. A clearer and more expansive understanding of cosmic relationships, universe facts, and spiritual values is attainable through exploration, debate, and reflective thinking. Every time the truth in our beliefs is expanded, we gain a deeper understanding of our common origin, history, and destiny. This broader perspective allows for spiritual development to be anchored in progressive revelation, a powerful source of personal transformation; it also activates a humble appreciation for our collective responsibility—to live as a true member of the family of God. A new vision of the journey inspires us to modify our framework for conscious living and develop ourselves to express a higher standard of good.

We *can* effect meaningful and permanent change in our world, one person at a time. As we unite in faith and reason, our strength of character and personal quality of spiritual unity is impressed upon the world at large and experienced as increased:

- Intellectual peace
- Social progress
- Moral satisfaction
- Spiritual joy
- Cosmic wisdom[2]

As this coordinated enhancement of the innate recognition of supreme meanings and values emerges, the enhanced comprehension benefits both the individual child of faith (microcosm) and the totality of all cosmic reality (macrocosm).

Each organized religion has followed a unique path of evolution, but a common thread of Universal Truth is woven through them. And with a nod to the symmetry of our shared spirit ancestry, the soul of every human will traverse the same course of shared spirit destination, Paradise. The only difference of consequence between one human being and another is how brightly love is expressed in each heart—the flowing of unconditional love that brings forth salvation of the soul and promises immortality, regardless of religious or ethnic background.

SECTION TWO

Humanity's Spiritual History

We can chart our future clearly and wisely only when we know the path which has led to the present.

ADLAI E. STEVENSON I

Introduction

Science discovers the material world, religion evaluates it, and philosophy endeavors to interpret its meanings while coordinating the scientific material viewpoint with the religious spiritual concept. But history is a realm in which science and religion may never fully agree.

The Urantia Book

History has recorded wars, greed, poverty, immorality, and the injustices that have destroyed earlier civilizations. These social ills continue to plague us despite our knowledge of the past and the universal recognition of the ideals of selflessness, love, tolerance, and compassion. To discover the unknown origins of our selfish and warlike tendencies is to inform our progress as cosmic citizens capable of creating a better world. It is therefore imperative to expand the limited boundaries of recorded history to include and assimilate an expanded perspective of our spiritual history.

Section two, "Humanity's Spiritual History," reconciles science and religion in the light of epochal revelation. What we may gain from such an admittedly unconventional source is profound, even startling, and limited only by the individual's receptiveness. "Revelation is evolutionary but always progressive. Down through the ages of a world's history, the revelations of religion are ever-expanding and successively more enlightening. It is the mission of revelation to sort and censor these successive religions of evolution. But if revelation is to exalt and upstep the religions of evolution, then such divine visitations must portray teachings which are not too far removed from the thought and reactions of the age in which they are presented. Thus must and

Revelation unifies history, co-ordinates geology, astronomy, physics, chemistry, biology, sociology, and psychology.

The Urantia Book

does revelation always keep in touch with evolution. Always must the religion of revelation be limited by man's capacity of receptivity."[1]

The unprejudiced study and reconciliation of origin, history, and destiny is the most effective strategy to understand our current state and approach our present problems. In the previous section, revelation-based information enlightened us about God and our origin. Now epochal revelation illuminates the theory of human evolution to disentangle this polarizing issue. The scientific source of information about our ancient past is preserved in stone, much still awaiting discovery. *The Urantia Book* fills many of the gaps, although skepticism about its remarkable assertions can be expected. But science is progressively confirming a growing number of these. For example, the stupendous size of the physical cosmos as revealed in the text has only recently been affirmed by scientific discovery

There is still no evidence as to why some races advanced more rapidly than others; whole civilizations have been lost to time or buried by natural cataclysms with only myths to hint of their existence. Modern excavations of sunken cities and ancient ruins offer tantalizing clues to illuminate our hazy human prehistory, but many enigmas continue to tease scientists, such as the lineage of the human species and the origin and migration of the various races. Intriguing legends of advanced beings improving civilization are largely ignored. Reclaiming this lost history affirms that we live in a friendly and orderly universe, greatly enhancing our worldview. Can the natural sciences and the religious theologies be synthesized into a consistent and coherent universe philosophy? "Through long ages the human race has struggled to reach its present position. Throughout all these millenniums Providence has been working out the plan of progressive evolution. The two thoughts are not opposed in practice, only in man's mistaken concepts."[2]

The blueprint of this plan for humanity has only been partially discovered by science. Similarly, the mysterious role of a celestial order of existence is only partially revealed by the scriptures. In the process of demystifying and expanding both history and science, epochal revelation fills the gaps in our knowledge while validating what has correctly been ascertained by science; and it also satiates human wonder about spirit beings, explaining how those assigned to our planet uplift human biology, spirituality, and culture.

Scientific minds are not expected to casually accept the facticity of some of the extraordinary events presented in section two. But when *The Urantia Book* is studied for its wealth of scientific, religious, philosophical and historical content, we should be intrigued by it sufficiently to probe deeper into what has been revealed and to search for clues in our pursuit of what can be proven.

7.

Life Establishment and the Evolution of Humanity

The beginning of the evolutionary process raises a question which is
as yet unanswerable. What was the origin of life on this planet?
John W.N. Sullivan, *Limitations of Science*

In a Gallup poll conducted in the United States in May 2006, forty-six percent of the respondents selected the following statement when asked for their belief about the origin of humanity: "God created human beings pretty much in their present form at one time within the last 10,000 years or so." A slightly larger percentage, forty-nine, chose one of the two following evolution-oriented statements: thirty-six percent agreed that human beings have developed over millions of years from less advanced forms of life, but God guided this process; thirteen percent believed that humans evolved, but with no guidance from God."[1] Worthy of note was the fact that this statistical breakdown had not changed much in over two decades.

There are various reasons why so many people believe in creationism versus evolution; adherence to the literal interpretation of the Book of Genesis is one. Another is summed up by David Quammen: "Creationist proselytizers and political activists [are] working hard to interfere with the teaching of evolutionary biology in public schools . . ."[2] This stunts the reasoning capacity of young minds. Never having learned to reason objectively, many people draw their opinions solely from random sources, such as cultural osmosis, documentaries, and references in magazines and newspapers.

Most scientists subscribe to Darwin's theory of evolution: that all life is related and has descended from a common ancestor. But how did that common ancestor originate? It is known that the mineral composition of humankind and all existing creatures on Earth is similar to that of ancient organisms that originated in the sea. We can, therefore, conclude that on the self-contained microcosm called Earth, life in general evolved from the sea.

Nevertheless, evolutionary scientists have many hypotheses of how the first life form emerged. Most of these theories start by addressing the formation of organic molecules, the building blocks of modern life. There are two major theories for the creation of life-producing organic molecules on Earth:

1. They spontaneously formed through chemical evolution in an environment with no preexisting life molecules.

2. The same complex molecules are of stellar or interstellar origin in a nebula.

Several theories exist about the evolution of these complex organic molecules into self-replicating life forms. The popular RNA world hypothesis first proposed in 1986 promoted the idea that RNA may be the ancestral molecule of life because it can function as both a gene and an enzyme. However, not until recently were scientists able to demonstrate that RNA replication is self-propagating. Scientists have now shown through a process called in vitro evolution that RNA enzymes have the amazing ability to replicate themselves without the help of any proteins or other cellular components, thereby furthering the postulate that RNA is the ancestral molecule of life.[3]

Other theories abound, including

1. A primitive metabolism based on chemical esters emerged.

2. *Archaea*, a microbial life form, originated below the earth's surface as in an incubator.

3. Comets encrusted with dark layers of complex organic compounds rained on Earth.

4. Primitive life formed in outer space and transported to Earth.

But science alone cannot explain how life began on Earth or how human beings evolved out of the primeval protoplasm of the early seas. Solutions to these mysteries will remain unsatisfactory as long as scientists persist in discounting the existence and activities of a Creator.

The development of higher organisms from lower groupings of life is not accidental. According to epochal revelation, the human intellectual and philosophic endowments did not originate in primitive life, which was devoid of thinking and feeling; rather it originated as a response to spirit ministry influencing the evolving mind of primitive life. Adult logic can tolerate the concept of truth alongside the observation of fact. Thus, "Organic evolution is a fact; purposive or progressive evolution is a truth which makes consistent the otherwise contradictory phenomena of the ever-ascending achievements of evolution. The higher any scientist progresses in his chosen science, the more will he abandon the theories of materialistic fact in favor of the cosmic truth of the dominance of the Supreme Mind."[4]

The above point of view allows room for both God and Darwin and reflects a more dynamic and progressive thinking, for it accepts the possibility that there is divine initiative in the life process and that evolution is the adaptive function. This view, according to various papal pronouncements, is compatible with Roman Catholic dogma, although still considered controversial in many Christian circles. With this leap in understanding and acceptance, however, the teachings in *The Urantia Book* help us clarify the spiritual and physical relationships existent in the evolution theory.

How then, is life established on a planet?

Section one detailed the creation of the grand universe and the superhuman hierarchy of its spiritual corps. Only when a local universe has been physically organized and "spiritually staffed" is life esablished with the potential to achieve perfection. This inclusive perspective unites the spiritual and the scientific concepts of evolution—the emergence of life is orchestrated and its evolution is encoded.

"The creation of energy and the bestowal of life are the prerogatives of the Universal Father and his associate Creator personalities. The river of energy and life is a continuous outpouring from the Deities, the universal and united stream of Paradise force going forth to all space. This divine energy pervades all creation. The force organizers initiate those changes and institute those modifications of space-force which eventuate in energy; the power directors transmute energy into matter; thus the material worlds are born. The Life Carriers initiate those processes in dead matter which we call life, material life."[5]

Life Carriers

According to epochal revelation, "Life does not spontaneously appear in the universes; the Life Carriers must initiate it on the barren planets. They are the carriers, disseminators, and guardians of life as it appears on the evolutionary worlds of space."[6] Life Carriers are an order of Local Universe Sons; the progeny of the Creator Son and Mother Spirit of a local universe in collaboration with one of the three Ancients of Days of the respective super-universe (refer to illustration 10).

"The majority of inhabited worlds are peopled in accordance with established techniques; on such spheres the Life Carriers are afforded little leeway in their plans for life implantation. But about one world in ten is designated as a *decimal planet* and assigned to the special registry of the Life Carriers; and on such planets we are permitted to undertake certain life experiments in an effort to modify or possibly improve the standard universe types of living beings."[7]

A decimal planet is designated as an experimental planet, but this does not mean that the establishment of life is left to chance. "The evolution of life is a technique ever progressive, differential, and variable, but never haphazard, uncontrolled, nor wholly experimental, in the accidental sense."[8] When adjustments to life forms on a decimal planet are authorized and attempted, they usually result in unexpected variations to the life patterns of that planet. On Earth, which is an experimental planet, one such variation was the early appearance of human will. Likewise Earth has many forms of life that are not found elsewhere and lacks common species generally found on other planets.

The Creator Son provides the Life Carriers with the original life designs for a planet. It is then the responsibility of Life Carriers to fulfill the plans by formulating these patterns, organizing the energy systems, and nurturing their progress. Life Carriers impart the "vital spark" or "breath of life" that turns inert physical patterns into living matter. While Life Carriers impart the life energy, only the Mother Spirit can provide it.

When, through evolution and spirit mind ministry, animal fear arouses the expression of worshipfulness and creatures capable of making moral will decisions emerge, the work of the Life Carriers terminates. From that point forward the biological evolution of all living things proceeds according to the inherent nature and tendencies in the planetary life formulas and patterns. "During the ages intervening between life establishment and the emergence of human creatures of moral status, the Life Carriers are permitted to manipulate the life environment and otherwise favorably directionize the course of biologic evolution."[9]

Life Establishment and Evolution of the Species

The Urantia Book provides a comprehensive account of life establishment and species evolution, which is briefly summarized below:

1. Life cannot be initiated on a planet until it can support and accommodate physical progress. Approximately six hundred million years ago, the commission of Life Carriers arrived here from the system capital, Jerusem, and began the study of physical conditions preparatory to launching life. A sodium chloride pattern of life had been chosen; therefore no steps could be taken toward implantation until the ocean waters had become suitably salty. All ancestral life—vegetable and animal—evolved in a salt-solution habitat, later to include the highly organized land animals that have this same essential salt solution circulating in their bloodstreams.[10]

2. Approximately five hundred and fifty million years ago, the Life Carrier corps returned to Earth to organize, initiate, and plant the original life patterns of this world in hospitable waters. All indigenous planetary life originated in the three original, identical, and simultaneous marine-life implantations identified as the central or Eurasian-African, the eastern or Australasian, and the western, embracing Greenland and the Americas.[11] Life Carriers manipulate evolving life to eliminate inferior strains until they succeed in producing a being with will, the power of moral decision, and spiritual choice.

3. "In the development of planetary life the vegetable form always precedes the animal and is quite fully developed before the animal patterns differentiate. All animal types are developed from the basic patterns of the preceding vegetable kingdom of living things; they are not separately organized."[12] Transition from vegetable to animal life is gradual.

4. Biological evolution progresses on Earth, as documented through scientific discoveries and depicted in the chart at the end of this section. As planetary life evolves, the influence of the first five adjutant mind-spirits triggers the emergence of protomoral behavior, such as courage, industriousness, prudence, and the beginnings of mental acuity and

reason. The ever-present circuit of the Holy Spirit also contributes to enlivened moral expression. As a result of this guidance, coupled with instinct and experience, certain species display extensive cooperative behavior as well as sophisticated social intelligence and moral emotions such as empathy and remorse.

5. Scientists have long searched for those gaps in the human evolutionary record between modern humans and the primates, but *The Urantia Book* states: "Although the evolution of vegetable life can be traced into animal life, and though there have been found graduated series of plants and animals which progressively lead up from the most simple to the most complex and advanced organisms, you will not be able to find such connecting links between the great divisions of the animal kingdom nor between the highest of the prehuman animal types and the dawn men of the human races. These so-called 'missing links' will forever remain missing, for the simple reason that they never existed.

   From era to era radically new species of animal life arise. They do not evolve as the result of the gradual accumulation of small variations; they appear as full-fledged and new orders of life, and they appear *suddenly*. The *sudden* appearance of new species and diversified orders of living organisms is wholly biologic, strictly natural. There is nothing supernatural connected with these genetic mutations."[13]

   These sudden jumps may be said to be "spring-loaded," released by design from within the genetic information stored in the original life plasm implanted by the Life Carriers. Scientific studies into the genetic basis of human brain evolution at the University of Chicago have revealed that rapid mutation in hundreds, even thousands of genes developed a sophisticated and exceptionally large brain in select lineage leading to humans. The trend in current genetic research is to posit the continuing mutation of some of our genes. Thus evolution continues, propelling homo sapiens to a rapid increase of brain size and complexity.[14]

6. Slightly more than a million years ago, a series of mutations began to occur from a lemurlike animal. There arose a mid-mammal, showing the beginnings of superior mental traits. This improved creature, after thriving for about fifteen thousand years, suddenly produced a pair of highly intelligent offspring, the first of the new species of primates. This pair did not fit in well with the tribe and fled to raise their family and establish a new advanced species of primates.

7. At the time the primate twins were born, the same mid-mammal tribe produced a regressed mutant pair that would become the founders of the modern simian tribes.[15] "And so it may be readily seen that man and the ape are related only in that they sprang from the mid-mammals, a tribe in which there occurred the contemporaneous birth and subsequent segregation of two pairs of twins: the inferior pair destined to produce the modern types of monkey, baboon, chimpanzee, and gorilla; and the superior pair destined to continue the line of ascent that evolved into

man himself. Modern man and the simians did spring from the same tribe and species but not from the same parents."[16] The independent evolution of the ape and human lineages was appreciated by Charles Darwin, but recent studies of the skeleton of the hominid "Ardi" discovered in 1994, confirm it. "Rather than humans evolving from an ancient chimp-like creature, the new find provides evidence that chimps and humans evolved from some long-ago common ancestor—but each evolved and changed separately along the way."[17]

8. The superior primate line flourished for about twenty-one thousand years, when suddenly a mutation produced twins, male and female, the first true human beings, born in the highlands of what is now Afghanistan.[18] From a cosmic perspective what determines an evolving animal to be human is its response to the sixth and seventh adjutant mind-spirits of worship and wisdom. These responses indicate the emergence of a self-conscious being with free will who has the potential to exercise moral choice and recognize his Creator. The arrival of free-will dignity is a milestone in the nurtured evolution of a planet. It signals a major junction in the Divine Plan, attended by various administrative and spiritual adjustments relative to a planet's celestial management. With a full complement of adjutant spirit ministry to the human mind, true morality is henceforth an innate impulse.

9. As occurred with their progenitors, friction within their tribe caused the superior pair to flee northward away from their inferior relatives, unaware that they were the dawn creatures of a new species, setting out to establish humankind.

Appearance of Moral Choice: Earth Recognized as an Inhabited Planet

The Urantia Book reveals these protohumans as Andon and Fonta, the founders of the human race. "Andon is the Nebadon name which signifies 'the first Fatherlike creature to exhibit human perfection hunger.' Fonta signifies 'the first Sonlike creature to exhibit human perfection hunger.' Andon and Fonta never knew these names until they were bestowed upon them at the time of fusion with their Thought Adjusters. Throughout their mortal sojourn on Urantia they called each other Sonta-an and Sonta-en, Sonta-an meaning 'loved by mother,' Sonta-en signifying 'loved by father.' They gave themselves these names, and the meanings are significant of their mutual regard and affection."[19]

Andon and Fonta experienced new feelings of vanity and admiration early in their lives. "But the most remarkable advance in emotional development was the sudden appearance of a new group of really human feelings, the worshipful group, embracing awe, reverence, humility, and even a primitive form of gratitude."[20] This new set of feelings, unique to humans, signaled response to the adjutant mind-spirit of *worship*. Fear and ignorance of the true causes of physical events was about to birth primitive religion.

When Andon and Fonta, as a result of meditative thought and purposeful decision, resolved to migrate northward, this signaled a response to the adjutant mind-spirit of *wisdom*. This quality of mind far exceeded the lower intelligence that characterized their ancestors and later descendants who retrogressed due to mating with their inferior cousins.[21]

When these evolving creatures' minds became responsive to the adjutant mind-spirits of worship and wisdom, the new consciousness attained human levels of spirit receptivity. This planetary achievement fully opened the spiritual circuits of the Local Universe Mother Spirit—the Holy Spirit of the inhabited worlds. It announced the appearance of "human mind" and the existence of self-conscious creatures with free will, endowed with the attributes of spiritual responsibility and the potential of eternal survival.

With Andon and Fonta, biologic evolution achieved the human levels of moral free will capable of responding to the leadings of the Indwelling Spirit (also called the Thought Adjuster). With this achievement approximately one million years ago, Earth became formally recognized in the local universe of Nebadon as a populated world. The descendants of Andon and Fonta are called Andonites and will be discussed further in this section.

8.

Arrival of "the Gods"

*Over the centuries we have transformed the ancient myths and
folk tales and made them into the fabric of our lives. Consciously
and unconsciously we weave the narratives of myth and
folk tale into our daily existence*

Jack Zipes

According to myth, legend, and ancient records, the early rulers of our planet were the Anunnaki, anthropomorphic yet superhuman and immortal beings that helped create human civilization and culture. The ancient Sumerians did not call the Anunnaki "gods"; rather, they called them by their nickname, *din-gir*, meaning "righteous ones of the bright pointed objects." *Din-gir* was later translated into the word "god."

Sumerian mythology tells about the arrival of the gods on Earth, the subsequent mutiny between the gods, a deluge, and the creation of a hybrid race. Many other ancient sacred writings describe the gods and their adversaries that physically dwelled on the planet. Indians, Egyptians, Akkadians, Assyrians, Babylonians, Hittites, and Hebrews all drew from Sumerian culture for some of their inspiration.

Laws, legends, allegories, myths, poems, and chronicles . . . reflect the winnowed moral wisdom of many centuries, at least up to the time and event of their being assembled as a "sacred book."

The Urantia Book

Is there a connection between the Anunnaki in ancient legends and the sons of God in chapter 6 of Genesis? Much speculation has arisen as to these "sons of God" (*benáy ha-elohím*). Bryan T. Huie, in his article entitled "Genesis 6: Who Were the Sons of God?" offers three common perspectives:

"1. The first and oldest belief is that 'the Sons of God' were fallen angels who consorted with human women, producing giant offspring called *Nephilim* (Heb. נפלים). This view was widely held in the world of the first century, and was supported by Flavius Josephus, Philo, Eusebius and many of the 'Ante-Nicene Fathers,' including Justin Martyr, Clement of Alexandria, Origen, Tertullian, Irenaeus, Athenagoras and Commodianus.

2. The second view is one which was first suggested by Julius Africanus and later advocated by Saint Augustine, the Catholic Bishop of Hippo. Augustine rejected the concept of the fallen host having committed fornication with women. In his early fifth century book *The City of God*, he promoted the theory that "'the sons of God' simply referred to the genealogical line of Seth, who were committed to preserving the true worship of God. He interpreted Genesis 6 to mean that the male offspring of Adam through Seth were 'the sons of God,' and the female offspring of Adam through Cain were 'the daughters of men. 'He wrote that the problem was that the family of Seth had interbred with the family of Cain, intermingling the bloodlines and corrupting the pure religion. This view has become the dominant one among most modern biblical scholars.

> *The farther backward you can look, the farther forward you are likely to see.*
> Winston Churchill

3. The third view is that 'the Sons of God' were the sons of pre-Flood rulers or magistrates. This belief became the standard explanation of rabbinical Judaism in the second century C.E. after Rabbi Simeon ben Yochai pronounced a curse upon those Jews who believed the common teaching that the angels were responsible for the Nephilim. This interpretation was advocated by two of the most respected Jewish rabbis of the Middle Ages, Rashi and Nachmanides, and became the standard explanation of rabbinical Judaism. However, it is not widely accepted by modern scholars."[1]

In the field of "alternative archaeology" the term "sons of god" is applied to the Anunnaki, who are described as a super race of aliens. The first shamans are thought to be the creation gods themselves, or at least their offspring, who brought the knowledge of shamanism from the heaven worlds to an emerging humanity.

Who were these sons of god and what was their relation to humanity? Is there truth within the myths and legends? Epochal revelation clarifies and expands existing information and fills in the gaps.

The Planetary Prince and Volunteer Staff

Five hundred thousand years after the appearance of the Andonite race, a primal religion of fear and ignorance prevailed. Lucifer, the sovereign of the Satania System to which Earth belongs, appointed Caligastia as Planetary Prince of Earth. Caligastia and a staff of one hundred volunteers from other worlds were charged with inaugurating human civilization—to teach and minister to the nearly half billion primitive inhabitants scattered over Europe, Asia, and Africa. This mission was the first epochal revelation to our planet.

The Prince's headquarters and world center of culture was named Dalamatia and was established in the Persian Gulf region of Mesopotamia (current-day Iraq). The Prince's staff were considered to be gods by the local inhabitants. Their arrival on the planet, as it was eventually recorded in ancient texts, gave rise to many origin myths, including legends of sons of gods coming down to mate with mortals.

The one hundred staff members were ascendant beings who had experienced mortal life on other worlds. As materialized planetary missionaries on Earth, they had flesh-and-blood bodies, unlike the invisible Planetary Prince. DNA from selected local tribe members was transplanted into the life forms created for this mission. "These transactions, together with the literal creation of special bodies for the Caligastia one hundred, gave origin to numerous legends, many of which subsequently became confused with the later traditions concerning the planetary installation of Adam and Eve."[2]

In their work to develop world culture, these one hundred staff members served in ten autonomous councils of ten members each, collectively geared toward the social advancement of the inhabitants on the planet. This organized enterprise of social evolution was brought to a halt almost two hundred thousand years ago when Caligastia and most of his staff (materialized and otherwise) joined with Lucifer and his assistant Satan in mutiny against the Creator Son, Michael of Nebadon. System Sovereigns are self-governing, and such administrators are prone to disloyalty. "These rulers are not supervised by Trinity observers from the central universe. They are the executive division of the local universe, and as custodians of the enforcement of legislative mandates and as executives for the application of judicial verdicts, they present the one place in all universe administration where personal disloyalty to the will of the Michael Son could most easily and readily intrench itself and seek to assert itself."[3]

The Planetary Rebellion: Origin of the "War in Heaven"

Many of the tribulations experienced by the human race cannot be understood without knowledge of certain prehistoric events. One that looms large is the planetary rebellion of two hundred thousand years ago. The events surrounding this epic drama, passed from generation to generation, were the origin of the most venerable genre in ancient literature—the combat myth that depicts a battle between good and evil, order and chaos.

The oldest recorded combat myths can be traced to Mesopotamia. They include the myths of *Lugale*, *Anzu*, and the epic of *Enuma Elish*. The latter epic is centered on the elevation of the chief Babylonian god Marduk above other Mesopotamian gods. Each of these combat myths influenced its successor; but in the *Enuma Elish*, the victorious god not only reestablishes the normal political and social order amongst the gods, he also creates the human race to work and provide for them. Hence the *Enuma Elish* is known as the *Epic of Creation*.

One of the combat myths of India is depicted in the Sanskrit tale of the final battle between Indra and the "demon" Vritra. In Greek mythology, the Olympian war with the Titans describes how Zeus, the supreme ruler of the Olympian gods, along with siblings, fought a series of wars with the Titans to gain total control of the universe. In Scandinavian mythology, the war between the two races of gods broke out when the Aesir refused to give the Vanir the same status and privilege that the Aesir enjoyed. The Hittite version of the Sumerian conflict between the gods, which modern scholars have titled the *Kingship in Heaven*, tells of the lingering and bitter struggles between the House of Anu and the House of Alalu, a generational enmity that erupted into a war that set the gods in heaven against the gods who descended upon dark-hued Earth. The planetary rebellion in religious circles became known as the "war in heaven," described in the Book of Revelation, when Michael and his angels fought against the dragon and his angels (Revelation 12:7). The combat myths are likely the root of the successive apocalyptic perspectives.

> *Much, very much, of the difficulty which Urantia mortals have in understanding God is due to the far-reaching consequences of the Lucifer rebellion and the Caligastia betrayal. On worlds not segregated by sin, the evolutionary races are able to formulate far better ideas of the Universal Father; they suffer less from confusion, distortion, and perversion of concept.*
>
> The Urantia Book

According to the *Encyclopedia of Apocalypticism*, there are at least four recurrent elements in the combat myths, which suggests that there is truth in the narratives:[4]

1. The gods in heaven are faced with cosmic threat.

2. There is combat between the gods and dark forces that are often depicted as monsters or demons.

3. The gods triumph.

4. One god is exalted above all others.

As we identify the above elements as presented in *The Urantia Book*, we recognize the origin of our combat myths and discover deeper meanings:

1. **The gods are thrown into confusion when faced with cosmic threats and rebellion.** Lucifer had reigned as System Sovereign for more than five hundred thousand years before he aligned himself against the Universal Father and the Creator Son. Advocating "self-assertion and liberty," Lucifer and his first lieutenant, Satan, launched a rebellion against the local universe government of Michael, three hundred thousand years into Caligastia's rule on Earth.

   Lucifer condemned the plan of mortal ascension and advocated that mortals should enjoy the liberty of individual self-determination. He promised any Planetary Princes who allied with him that they would rule the worlds as supreme executives. "Satan proclaimed that worship could be accorded the universal forces—physical, intellectual, and spiritual—but that allegiance could be acknowledged only to the actual and present ruler, Lucifer, the 'friend of men and angels' and the 'God of liberty.'"[5]

In attempting to point out the exact cause or causes that finally culminated in the Lucifer rebellion, epochal revelation explains that "There must have been a pride of self that nourished itself to the point of self-deception, so that Lucifer for a time really persuaded himself that his contemplation of rebellion was actually for the good of the system, if not of the universe."[6] This insight supports the Christian interpretation of Isaiah 14:12–14 that depicts the fall of a spirit being through pride. In fact, epochal revelation confirms the actual claims Lucifer made as he sought to displace his superiors, as they are recorded in Isaiah 14:13–14: ". . . I will exalt my throne above the stars [sons] of God: I will sit also upon the mount of the congregation, in the sides of the north: I will ascend above the heights of the clouds; I will be like the most High."

2. **There is a battle between the gods and dark forces that are often depicted as monsters or demons.** The outbreak of rebellion in the system of Satania challenged the authority of the Creator Son and ruler of the local universe, Michael of Nebadon. It also threatened the divine privilege of all personalities in the system to participate in the creation of their own destinies.[7] In response, the government of the local universe immediately severed the circuits of communication to the rebelling planets (thirty-seven in all) and quarantine the system to prevent Lucifer from spreading his scheme through that medium. There was "war in heaven" and it spread to every planet in the local system.[8]

Celestial beings that chanced to be on Earth at the time of its isolation found themselves cut off, suddenly and without warning, from all outside support. They were detained on the planet and compelled to choose between sin and righteousness—between the ways of Lucifer and the will of the unseen Father. Only after every personality had made a final decision did the Melchizedeks seize authority and begin planetary rehabilitation. The chief rebels were divested of all administrative control in the local system. Yet because there was no sovereign local universe authority to refrain them at the time, they were able to wander the isolated planets, promoting their doctrines of discontent and self-assertion for almost two hundred thousand years.[9] In their defiant mission they were accompanied by rebel leaders such as Abaddon (cf. Revelation 9:11), who was the former chief of Caligastia's staff, and Beelzebub (cf. Matthew 12:24, 27, Mark 3:22, and Luke 11:15), the leader of the rebellious secondary midwayers. Unable to occupy human minds without their consent, the arch-rebels were nonetheless able to influence weak-minded individuals and dominate their minds as it is recorded in the New Testament.

Lucifer, Satan, Caligastia, and Daligastia (Caligastia's assistant) are the original evil personages often depicted as monsters, dragons, and demons in the various ancient combat myths. The dragon eventually became their symbolic totem. These arch-rebels did not work alone. They were joined by many celestial personalities and ascendant beings, including:

a. **The rebellious or fallen angels:** A vast number of angelic hosts—seraphim, cherubim and midwayers—joined forces with the disloyal Sons. Of the seraphic rebels it is written in Jude 1:6: "And the angels which kept not their first estate, but left their own habitation, he hath reserved in everlasting chains under darkness unto the judgment of the great day."

b. **Caligastia's volunteer staff:** Sixty of the one hundred materialized staff members of the Planetary Prince joined the rebellion. They became known as "the sons of God" captivated by the "daughters of men" (Genesis 6:1–4). Their offspring became known as the Nephilim, "the hybrid race" who dwelled in the "land of Nod" (Genesis 4:16).

Illustration 17 depicts the functional hierarchy on Earth at the time of the rebellion.

3. **The gods procure victory over the demons.** To the volunteer ascendant staff who supported the rebellion, the irresponsibility of their alliance to Lucifer was soon evident. They lost their "immortality status" and were reduced to living their lives as mortals—because of their disloyalty to God they were destined eventually to suffer extinction by death.[10] In contrast, thirty-nine of the forty loyal staff members, along with those humans that had achieved immortal status, were allowed to resume their Paradise journey. Van, the leader of the loyal staff, remained on the planet and along with some loyal humans, continued to provide leadership to the world.

The seventh bestowal of Michael of Nebadon as Jesus of Nazareth terminated the Lucifer rebellion on the thirty-seven planets in Satania whose Planetary Princes had rebelled.[11] Since the bestowal of Michael, all of the unrepentant supporters of the rebellion and their leaders, except for Caligastia and Daligastia, have been detained and are awaiting their final adjudication.

Jesus expressed the termination of the Lucifer rebellion to his disciples. In Luke 10:18 it is written: "And he said unto them, I beheld Satan as lightning fall from heaven."

The triumph of Michael over the arch-rebels is expressed in Revelation 20:1–2: "And I saw an angel come down from heaven, having the key of the bottomless pit and a great chain in his hand. And he laid hold on the dragon, that old serpent, which is the Devil, and Satan, and bound him a thousand years." Gabriel was the angel who came down from Salvington and bound the dragon (he imprisoned the rebel leaders) for an "age."

Illustration 17
FUNCTIONAL HIERARCHY ON EARTH AT THE TIME OF THE PLANETARY REBELLION

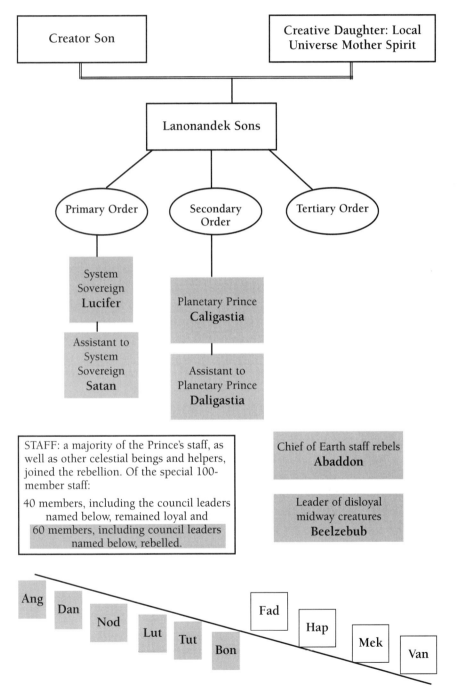

4. **One god is exalted above all others.** Michael, Creator Son of the Universal Father, prevailed over the rebellion, claiming sovereignty over his local universe in accordance with his Father's will. Even those who had rejected Michael ultimately recognized his sovereignty although some among them refused to submit to it.

Physical Aftermath of the Rebellion

The betrayal of Caligastia severed the local spiritual circuits to the planet and immediately isolated Earth. This deprived its people from the superhuman assistance necessary to assuage the natural tendency of humanity to be argumentative, distrustful, and extremely self-absorbed. "Hunger and love drove men together; vanity and ghost fear held them together. But these emotions alone, without the influence of peace-promoting revelations, are unable to endure the strain of the suspicions and irritations of human interassociations. Without help from superhuman sources the strain of society breaks down upon reaching certain limits, and these very influences of social mobilization—hunger, love, vanity, and fear—conspire to plunge mankind into war and bloodshed."[12] Peace, therefore, is derived from assimilating the teachings of revealed religion, from the accumulated experience of the progressive races, and more recently from rediscovering the true teachings of Jesus, the bestowal Son who terminated the rebellion and one day will reestablish the interplanetary lines of communication.

The planetary rebellion of two hundred thousand years ago was not a physical battle, but it did have social, intellectual, and spiritual consequences: "Although this upheaval did not seriously interfere with the progress of organic evolution, it did markedly modify the course of social evolution and of spiritual development. The entire superphysical history of the planet was profoundly influenced by this devastating calamity."[13]

Without the active rulership and guidance of a legitimate Planetary Prince and staff, rebellious self-will flourished. "Great confusion reigned in Dalamatia and thereabout for almost fifty years after the instigation of rebellion. The complete and radical reorganization of the whole world was attempted; revolution displaced evolution as the policy of cultural advancement and racial improvement . . . Liberty was quickly translated into license by the half-evolved primitive men of those days."[14]

In an effort to increase their numbers, the materialized rebel staff members resorted to immediate sexual reproduction with the local inhabitants. "The presence of these extraordinary supermen and superwomen, stranded by rebellion and presently mating with the sons and daughters of earth, easily gave origin to those traditional stories of the gods coming down to mate with mortals."[15] The children of this union were more advanced than the people of the time. "This unexpected excellence characterized not only physical and intellectual qualities but also spiritual capacities."[16] These mutant traits appeared in the first Nodite generation (addressed in a later chapter).

The rebel staff members were hardly sons of the gods, but they were considered so by those who knew them, and their stature came to be magnified by tradition. "And thus originated the thousand and one legends of a mythical nature, but founded on the facts of the postrebellion days, which later found a place in the folk tales and traditions of the various peoples whose ancestors had participated in these contacts with the Nodites and their descendants."[17]

The staff rebels eventually died a natural death, having been deprived of the sustenance of the system life circuits. "And much of the subsequent idolatry of the human races grew out of the desire to perpetuate the memory of these highly honored beings of the days of Caligastia."[18] The rebellion experience of "the sons of gods" who became men was immortalized through the combat myths.

Our status as an isolation planet does have its rewards: "On first thought it might appear that Urantia and its associated isolated worlds are most unfortunate in being deprived of the beneficent presence and influence of such superhuman personalities as a Planetary Prince and a Material Son and Daughter. But isolation of these spheres affords their races a unique opportunity for the exercise of faith and for the development of a peculiar quality of confidence in cosmic reliability which is not dependent on sight or any other material consideration. It may turn out, eventually, that mortal creatures hailing from the worlds quarantined in consequence of rebellion are extremely fortunate. We have discovered that such ascenders are very early intrusted with numerous special assignments to cosmic undertakings where unquestioned faith and sublime confidence are essential to achievement."[19]

Evil Spirits, Demons, and "the Devil"

According to epochal revelation, "When the doctrine of good and bad spirits finally matured, it became the most widespread and persistent of all religious beliefs. This dualism represented a great religio-philosophic advance because it enabled man to account for both good luck and bad luck while at the same time believing in supermortal beings who were to some extent consistent in their behavior."[20]

"Evolutionary religion has, however, paid a terrible price for the concept of dual spiritism. Man's early philosophy was able to reconcile spirit constancy with the vicissitudes of temporal fortune only by postulating two kinds of spirits, one good and the other bad. And while this belief did enable man to reconcile the variables of chance with a concept of unchanging supermortal forces, this doctrine has ever since made it difficult for religionists to conceive of cosmic unity. The gods of evolutionary religion have generally been opposed by the forces of darkness."[21]

Ancient humans developed ways to coerce spirit action and compel spirit assistance, including the practice of exorcism. "Exorcism was the employment of one spirit to control or banish another and these tactics were also utilized for frightening ghosts and spirits."[22]

"The tragedy of all this lies in the fact that, when these ideas were taking root in the primitive mind of man, there really were no bad or disharmonious spirits in the world. Such an unfortunate situation did not develop until after the Caligastia rebellion and only persisted until Pentecost. The concept of good and evil as cosmic coordinates is, even in the twentieth century, very much alive in human philosophy; most of the world's religions still carry this cultural birthmark of the long-gone days of the emerging ghost cults."[23] For more than two hundred thousand years, Lucifer and his followers were able to influence and dominate weaker-minded human beings. Their activities on Earth became known as demoniacal possessions and the perpetrators, devils.

By Pentecost, most arch-rebels and their followers were in celestial custody and demoniacal possession ended. "The supposed casting out of devils since the arrival of the Spirit of Truth has been a matter of confounding a belief in demoniacal possession with hysteria, insanity, and feeble-mindedness."[24] A normal human mind cannot be influenced against its will. "The doctrine of a personal devil on Urantia, though it had some foundation in the planetary presence of the traitorous and iniquitous Caligastia, was nevertheless wholly fictitious in its teachings that such a 'devil' could influence the normal human mind against its free and natural choosing."[25]

Satan and Caligastia were last together on Earth during the time of their unsuccessful combined assault upon the Son of Man during his six-week sojourn on the slopes of Mount Hermon.[26] As the fifth epochal revelation was being transmitted, Lucifer, Satan, and the fallen angels were awaiting judgment (2 Peter 2:4; Jude 1:6). Caligastia (the devil) and his assistant, Daligastia, remained free on Earth, having rejected Jesus' offer of mercy.

Although Caligastia and Daligastia are still able to promote their rebellious philosophy on Earth, they cannot corrupt the human mind without willful consent. Both are servile before the majesty of the Indwelling Spirit and the protective Spirit of Truth. "In general, when weak and dissolute mortals are supposed to be under the influence of devils and demons, they are merely being dominated by their own inherent and debased tendencies, being led away by their own natural propensities. The devil has been given a great deal of credit for evil which does not belong to him. Caligastia has been comparatively impotent since the cross of Christ."[27]

Length of the Rebellion

One may wonder why the Lucifer rebellion lasted two hundred thousand years and was not immediately terminated by superuniverse administrators. The first reason for the long delay of justice is that sufficient time must be given to ensure that the moral values and spiritual realities of the creature who has consciously chosen evil are truly extinct—evil and sin must be allowed if an individual so chooses, if that person is to be truly free. "The free will of evolving man . . . is not a mere philosophic concept, a symbolic ideal. Man's ability to choose good or evil is a universe reality."[28] There must always be an adequate amount of time between the moment an individual willfully rejects God and the moment the cosmic results of that choice are harvested, so that even that individual will realize the justice of the divine judgment.

The second reason for the delay of justice lies in the recognition that through patience, good comes of evil. This recognition is the exact reason for the "mercy delays of time" mandated by the Creators. "While it is all too true that good cannot come of evil to the one who contemplates and performs evil, it is equally true that all things (including evil, potential and manifest) work together for good to all beings who know God, love to do his will, and are ascending Paradiseward according to his eternal plan and divine purpose."[29] Enough time must, therefore, be given to allow for the possibility of repentance and rehabilitation.

Gabriel had been informed that three times the amount of beings would be influenced by the rebels if there had been an immediate suppression of the rebellion. "The angelic hosts were directed to work for full disclosure and unlimited opportunity for sin-expression as the quickest technique of achieving the perfect and final cure of the plague of evil and sin."[30]

Lucifer's Doctrine of Self-Determination

From a human perspective, self-determination (or free will) may be defined as the freedom to determine how to act, what to believe, and how to express oneself as one chooses. Lucifer's doctrine of "self-assertion and liberty" may at first glance seem to be a principle well worth rebelling for. To understand the limitations and implications inherent in this doctrine, however, it is helpful to explore the concept of freedom in the context of epochal revelation.

The Divine Plan of Creation provides for the human being to survive physical death, grow in perfection as we ascend through the multilevel universe, and personally find and recognize the Universal Father in Paradise as perfected spirits. To achieve this purpose, we are endowed with the gift of free will and are indwelt by the spirit of the Father. While the spirit nucleus in every human constitutes the potential of eternal personality, every person has the freedom of spiritual choice and action—they can accept or reject God (the source of love) and the gift of eternal life.

The gift of eternal life, and the capacity to love and be loved, comes with the responsibility of harmoniously developing cosmic insight, moral awareness, and spiritual perception (God-consciousness). As God-consciousness is developed, the factual and philosophical accuracy of the individual's worldview is enhanced. Reasoning becomes increasingly more objective, inclusive, moral, loving, and selfless. Decision-making becomes more effective, socially progressive and peace enhancing. A mind that chooses to grow in God-consciousness becomes progressively identified with the Universal Father and attuned to the Indwelling Spirit. It recognizes the involvement of the universe in the individual's progressive spiritual experience, and the cosmic responsibility of every child of God to master the human nature—the true measure of human liberty. Such an accurate worldview is reflected in a peaceful and altruistic society.

Lucifer's doctrine of self-assertion rested on his charge that the Universal Father does not really exist—that physical gravity and space-energy are inherent in the universe; that immortality is innate in human personalities, and that resurrection is natural and automatic. His plan to usurp the universe administration was doomed to fail because it was based on delusion and his self-deception led him to crave power over others for the purpose of depriving them of their natural liberties.

On mortal worlds, humans may be subjected to tyrants and oppressors, but such injustice is precluded in the morontia and spirit realms. Individuals have the right and privilege to create their own destinies and the destiny of their world. "No being in all the universe has the rightful liberty to deprive any other being of true liberty, the right to love and be loved, the privilege of worshiping God and of serving his fellows."[31]

At the time of the rebellion, Michael was not yet a sovereign ruler over the realm of his creation. Lucifer and his chief rebels were therefore permitted to freely roam the worlds in the Satania system, planting seeds of doubt and confusion as they spread their doctrines of discontent and self-assertion.[32] Deprived of the usual superhuman guidance that normally fosters a well-ordered society, their influence on an increasingly self-willful race contributed to the distortions found in our worldview today. An incomplete and inaccurate worldview is reflected in the religious conflicts that continue to plague us, in growing indifference toward others, the violence in our schools and society, and much of the faulty decision-making of our leaders. "True liberty is the associate of genuine self-respect; false liberty is the consort of self-admiration. True liberty is the fruit of self-control; false liberty, the assumption of self-assertion. Self-control leads to altruistic service; self-admiration tends toward the exploitation of others for the selfish aggrandizement of such a mistaken individual as is willing to sacrifice righteous attainment for the sake of possessing unjust power over his fellow beings."[33]

> *The free will of evolving man . . . is not a mere philosophic concept, a symbolic ideal. Man's ability to choose good or evil is a universe reality.*
>
> The Urantia Book

9.

Adam and Eve:
Biologic Uplifters

Adam and Eve are like imaginary numbers, like the square root
of minus one . . . If you include it in your equation, you can calculate all
manners of things, which cannot be imagined without it.

Phillip Pullman

Cultures across the globe have stories about the creation of the first humans, although the names in each may differ. As noted in chapter 8, the oldest recorded story is the Mesopotamian myth of *Enuma Elish*, the *Epic of Creation*, in which the victorious god Marduk not only reestablishes order among the gods but also creates the human race. According to *The Urantia Book*, "In Babylon the god Marduk was a perpetuation of the Adam legend, the son-of-God idea, the connecting link between man and God. Following the appearance of Adam on earth, so-called sons of God were common among the world races."[1]

Adam and Eve first appear as the parents of all humanity in the texts that make up the Old Testament. "Jewish tradition became crystallized about Moses, and because he endeavored to trace the lineage of Abraham back to Adam, the Jews assumed that Adam was the first of all mankind."[2] Below is the biblical perspective of Adam and Eve:

It should be apparent that, when an Adam and Eve arrive on an evolutionary world, the task of achieving racial harmony and social cooperation among its diverse races is one of considerable proportions.

The Urantia Book

- In Hebrew, "Adam" is both a personal name (cf. Genesis 2:20; 3:17, 21; 4:25; 5:2–3; and I Chronicles 1:1) and a general noun meaning "mankind" (found more than five hundred times in the Old Testament). In the Old Testament, Adam is represented as the first man made in God's image.

He is provided with a garden and a wife, and given work to do (Genesis 1–2). The Bible tells of Adam's rejection of God's authority and how this led to the breaking of communion with God, Adam's expulsion from the Garden, and his life of toil (Genesis 3). It is implied that the human race emerged from the physical descendants of Adam and Eve. Adam is mentioned nine times in the New Testament (Luke 3:38; Romans 5:14 [twice]; 1 Corinthians 15:22, 45 [twice]; 1 Timothy 2:13–14; and Jude 14).[3]

- Eve is represented in Genesis as the first woman. While the scriptures uniformly trace the fall of the race to Adam's sin, the part Eve played in this tragedy is vividly portrayed in Genesis 3. Her weakness and susceptibility to temptation are contrasted with Adam's willful act of disobedience. Deceived by Satan, she ate of the fruit. Enamored of his wife, Adam chose to leave God for Eve (2 Corinthians 11:3 and 1 Timothy 2:13).[4]

While the biblical story of Adam and Eve holds timeless insights, most philosophers treat these passages as allegory and fashion them as morality tales. Scholars concede that most legends have a core of truth; the difficulty lies in finding it. To dispel the myths born in ancient times, it behooves us to search deeper into the origin and mission of Adam and Eve in light of the epochal revelation.

Origin and Mission

Adam and Eve are the offspring of the Creator Son of a local universe (refer to illustration 10). They are a reproducing order of descending Sons of God, created male and female, who volunteer to serve on the evolutionary worlds. These superhuman examples of physical strength and spiritual ideals are the literal blueprint for the final stages of human evolution. They supply the superior DNA designed to evolve the human species to its highest potential.

"During the dispensation of a Planetary Prince, primitive man reaches the limit of natural evolutionary development, and this biologic attainment signals the System Sovereign to dispatch to such a world the second order of sonship, the biologic uplifters. These Sons, for there are two of them—the Material Son and Daughter—are usually known on a planet as Adam and Eve."[5]

Unlike other created Sons serving mortal worlds, the Material Sons and Daughters of God are visible to human beings. These descending volunteer beings live among the indigenous population and function as intermediaries to the invisible Planetary Prince, contributing their "super life plasm" for the augmentation of a higher level of humankind. Adam and Eve's primary task is to produce a race of their own, numbering a million of their pure-line progeny; the new race grows due to their own mating and the intermarrying of their children. During this reproductive phase they also educate and spiritually elevate the native population. Eventually their children will intermarry with superior mortals and go on to build up an advanced civilization. For many good reasons developed over numerous planetary assignments, this prolonged sequence is a key directive of the Divine Plan.

A successful Adam and Eve share in the evolving destiny of the inhabitants of their world. Eventually, when the planet is spiritually settled and the couple is liberated from all planetary duties, Adams and Eves become "perfected" Material Sons—they actually become Ascending Sons of God, and along with mortals, begin the long journey of ascent to Paradise. When they fail in their mission as biological accelerators, as happened on our world, they must pass through physical death and continue their ascending journey to the Universal Father.

The First Garden of Eden

In the Old Testament, the Garden of Eden is described as being planted by God for the newly created man, Adam. Every tree that was beautiful to the eye and had fruit to eat grew in the garden, including the tree of life and knowledge of good and evil. Those who ate its fruit (Genesis 2:17 and 3:3) succumbed to death. Adam and Eve lived in the Garden of Eden until they ate the forbidden fruit and were expelled (Genesis 3:6–24).

Epochal revelation confirms that the planetary headquarters of Adam and Eve is usually referred to as the Garden of Eden; the Divine Plan intends the Garden to serve as a permanent center of advanced culture. In the middle of the garden a shrub is planted that renders the antidote to the aging process of superhuman beings. This shrub, imported from Jerusem, is known in biblical texts as "the tree of the knowledge of good and evil" (Genesis 2:9, 17). During their mission on a planet Adam and Eve maintain their physical bodies by eating native foods, but their immortal existence is sustained by the intake of cosmic energies inherent in the "tree of life." The life-extending properties of the shrub are of no value to the natives of a planet, but are essential for the immortality of Adam and Eve during their planetary stay. Myths surrounding this unique shrub have survived in numerous legends and artifacts.

On Earth, the First Garden was located on ". . . a long narrow peninsula— almost an island—projecting westward from the eastern shores of the Mediterranean Sea."[6] "The coast line of this land mass was considerably elevated, and the neck connecting with the mainland was only twenty-seven miles wide at the narrowest point."[7] Eden became a paradise of botanic expression, where the cream of civilization gathered to learn. Outside of Eden, the world lay in darkness, ignorance, and savagery—Eden was the one bright spot on Earth. From there, the Adamic pair served to educate and inspire the races for more than a hundred years before defaulting in the Divine Plan.

Adam and Eve had been gone from the First Garden for almost four thousand years when ". . . in connection with the violent activity of the surrounding volcanoes and the submergence of the Sicilian land bridge to Africa, the eastern floor of the Mediterranean Sea sank, carrying down beneath the waters the whole of the Edenic peninsula. Concomitant with this vast submergence the coast line of the eastern Mediterranean was greatly elevated."[8]

With the passage of time, the geographical location of the First Garden was forgotten and its factual history relegated to legend and myth. In the field of "alternative archaeology," the ill-fated settlement has been linked with the myth of the lost civilization of Atlantis, first promulgated in Plato's ancient dialogues *Timaeus* and *Critias*. Robert Sarmast's book, *Discovery of Atlantis*, claims to provide ". . . unmistakable evidence that almost every clue in Plato's description of the legendary continent perfectly correlates with the recent discovery of a site on the sea floor of the Eastern Mediterranean region, stretching between Cyprus and Syria that matches Plato's famed account of Atlantis with astonishing accuracy. The book goes on to provide a stunning link between this hard scientific data and the biblical legend of the Garden of Eden . . ."[9]

A few of the many similarities between Plato's *Critias* and *The Urantia Book* are presented in illustration 18.[10] The detailed description of the lost island of Atlantis outlined in the *Critias* has been assigned to almost every possible place on Earth. However, *The Urantia Book* places Eden on a peninsula stretching westward from the eastern shores of the Mediterranean Sea connecting to the mainland by a land-bridge that was ". . . twenty-seven miles wide at the narrowest point."[11] It was this information missing from Plato's account but provided in *The Urantia Book*, that provided the vital clues that led to the discovery of the seafloor site.

To date, results from modern technology have failed to either prove or disprove the theory that the island of Cyprus is the mountaintop of a submerged Eden/Atlantis. For Sarmast, one thing is certain: "The dozens upon dozens of perfect matches with the ancient world's detailed descriptions cannot be ignored, nor can they be coincidental. There is no other Atlantis theory which even remotely comes close to matching these descriptions, much less matching practically every one of them. It is unprecedented."[12]

Until the strong evidence pointing to Cyprus is eventually verified using accepted scientific facts and academic proposals, the search for Atlantis continues.

The Sojourn of Adam and Eve on Earth

The plans for genetic improvement on a planet are normally prepared by the Planetary Prince and his staff and carried out by the planetary Adam and Eve. Our material pair was placed at a great disadvantage when they arrived on Earth in the midst of the Lucifer rebellion. They came to a planet that was groping in spiritual darkness and blighted by Caligastia's betrayal.

From the time of their arrival, Adam and Eve were challenged by Caligastia, who offered cunning and effective opposition to their mission. The disloyal Planetary Prince did succeed in compromising the mission of Adam and Eve, but he failed to involve them in the Lucifer rebellion. A summary of their adventure on Earth and their default is outlined below, as it is presented in *The Urantia Book*.

Adam and Eve were materialized on Earth approximately thirty-seven thousand years ago through a special process, their "constructed bodies" having been attuned to the life patterns of the planet. The story of creating Eve from Adam's rib resulted from confusion regarding their unique construction and the interchange of living substances associated with Caligastia's assistants eons ago. But "[t]he majority of the world's peoples have been influenced by the

Illustration 18
PLATO'S *CRITIAS* AND *THE URANTIA BOOK*

Plato's *Critias*	*The Urantia Book*
Poseidon descended from the heavens to his island/peninsula home [the original Greek word is *nesos*, which can mean either "island" or "peninsula"], Atlantis. Plato's story of Atlantis was imported from Egypt, and the legend centers on events taking place primarily in the eastern Mediterranean.	Adam and Eve materialized on Eden peninsula "[Eden was] a long narrow peninsula—almost an island—projecting westward from the eastern shores of the Mediterranean Sea . . . This area was virtually an island in an inland sea."
"To begin with the region as a whole [whole island of Atlantis] was said to be high above the level of the sea, from which it rose precipitously."	"The coast line of this land mass [whole island of Eden] was considerably elevated."
Atlantis island/peninsula had a "greatest length."	The Eden peninsula was "long and narrow."
Atlantis proper was in a valley, surrounded by mountains which "came right down to the sea." This would deprive it of rain, which is why the Atlanteans had to collect water from mountain streams.	While it rained copiously on the surrounding highlands, it seldom rained in Eden proper. Eden proper was sheltered from the sea by "coastal hills."
Midway along the greatest length of Atlantis and "near the sea, was a plain, said to be the most beautiful and fertile of all plains."	"The site chosen for the Garden was probably the most beautiful spot of its kind in all the world, and the climate was then ideal. Nowhere else was there a location which could have lent itself so perfectly to becoming such a paradise of botanic expression."
Atlantis had precious gems, gold, silver, copper, and tin.	"The mountains surrounding the Garden abounded in precious stones and metals . . ."
"They [the Atlanteans] had two harvests a year . . . for which the channels, fed by the rivers, provided irrigation." The irrigation reportedly covered thousands of miles.	"[Eden] had thousands of miles of irrigation ditches."
"[Poseidon] equipped the central island with godlike lavishness . . . he caused the earth to grow abundant produce of every kind."	"[D]uring the early days of his [Adam's] sojourn in Eden the whole Garden took on new form and assumed new proportions of beauty and grandeur."
"In the center was a shrine sacred to Poseidon and Cleito [temple of Zeus], surrounded by a golden wall through which entry was forbidden." At a later time there were earthquakes and floods of extraordinary violence and "in a single dreadful day and night all your fighting men [in the eastern Mediterranean area] were swallowed up by the earth, and the island of Atlantis was similarly swallowed up by the sea and vanished . . ."	"At the center of the Edenic peninsula [central sector] was the exquisite stone temple of the Universal Father, the sacred shrine of the Garden." "[I]n connection with the violent activity of the surrounding volcanoes and the submergence of the Sicilian land bridge to Africa, the eastern floor of the Mediterranean Sea sank, carrying down beneath the waters the whole of the Edenic peninsula."

tradition that Adam and Eve had physical forms created for them upon their arrival on Urantia. The belief in man's having been created from clay was well-nigh universal in the Eastern Hemisphere; this tradition can be traced from the Philippine Islands around the world to Africa. And many groups accepted this story of man's clay origin by some form of special creation in the place of the earlier beliefs in progressive creation—evolution."[13]

To understand the origin of the universal belief that humans were created from clay it is helpful to explore how this concept evolved. The *Encyclopedia of Apocalypticism* explains: "The concept of creation in the ancient Near East differs from the modern Western view, shaped as the latter is by evolutionary and scientific concerns (Clifford 1994, chapter 1). Ancient accounts usually imagine creation on the model of human activity (molding clay, building a house, fighting a battle) or natural processes (life forms left by the ebbing Nile flood). What emerged from the process for the ancients was a *populated* universe, a human society organized for the service of the gods with a king and a culture; not as with modern accounts of a physical world (often the planet Earth in its solar and stellar system)."[14]

1. Adam and Eve spent their first six days on Earth inspecting the Garden and preparing plans to carry out their assignment. The story of the creation of Earth in six days was based on the tradition that Adam and Eve spent six days in their initial survey of the Garden. "The legend of the making of the world in six days was an afterthought, in fact, more than thirty thousand years afterwards."[15]

2. On the evening of the sixth day, while Adam and Eve slept, the local inhabitants concluded that these Sons of God were far too modest and deserved to be worshiped. On hearing this in the early morning of the seventh day, Adam explained to the well-meaning Garden dwellers that only the Universal Father should be worshiped. He directed all to go to the Father's temple and worship. "And this was the origin of the Sabbath-day tradition. Always in Eden the seventh day was devoted to the noontide assembly at the temple; long it was the custom to devote this day to self-culture. The forenoon was devoted to physical improvement, the noontime to spiritual worship, the afternoon to mind culture, while the evening was spent in social rejoicing. This was never the law in Eden, but it was the custom as long as the Adamic administration held sway on earth."[16]

3. For more than one hundred years, while their pure-blood family grew, Adam and Eve educated and inspired those promising natives who were recruited to the Edenic paradise. But despite their best efforts, the realization of race improvement seemed hopelessly distant. Caligastia knew the challenges that Adam and Eve faced and made many attempts to encourage them to derail the Divine Plan. However, Adam and Eve were not influenced by his suggestions; they refused to rebel against the righteous rule of the Universal Father and Creator Son. So Caligastia decided to entrap Eve.

4. After one hundred and seventeen years of adherence to the mission plan, Eve became impatient with the slow progress of breeding and interbreeding so many children to uplift the races on the planet. During secret meetings with Serapatatia, a native who was an unknowing pawn of Caligastia, Eve was convinced that world improvement could be accelerated if she deviated from the Divine Plan. Influenced by flattery, enthusiasm, and great personal persuasion, Eve finally agreed and mated with Cano, a splendid leader from a nearby tribe.

5. In the moonlit Garden, as Adam and Eve were discussing what had happened, they were admonished by "the voice in the Garden" for disobeying instructions and defaulting in their implementation of the Divine Plan. The reprimanding "voice in the Garden" was the chief of the planetary helpers then on duty. "The fifth order of angels, the planetary helpers, are attached to the Adamic mission, always accompanying the Planetary Adams on their world adventures. The corps of initial assignment is usually about one hundred thousand."[17]

6. Adam was aware that Eve's transgression meant he would have to continue his vigil on Earth without her. Unable to bear that option, Adam decided to share in her fate and sought out a brilliant native named Laotta, who worked as a teacher in the Garden. With premeditation, he committed Eve's same recklessness. It was Adam and Eve's deviation from the Divine Plan that Paul interpreted in the scriptures as the origin of sin in the human race.

7. When the inhabitants of the Garden learned what had happened, they became enraged and declared war on the settlement of the native with whom Eve had mated. Everything and everyone in the settlement was destroyed. Thus began a long and bitter feud.

8. Some seventy days later, Adam and Eve were officially informed that they would become as natives of Earth and be subject to the mortality of the physical body. They abandoned the First Garden and traveled to Mesopotamia, where the Second Garden was built between the Tigris and Euphrates Rivers. Only a third of their children over twenty years of age stayed with them, the rest being remanded by seraphic transport to Jerusem. The First Garden was submerged due to geologic activity approximately four thousand years later.

9. Before reaching Mesopotamia, Eve gave birth to Cain, the offspring of her union with Cano. Adam's mistress, Laotta, died giving birth to a baby girl. Two years after Cain's birth, Abel arrived, the first child of Adam and Eve to be born in the Second Garden.

10. Abel's continuous reminders to Cain that Adam was not his father nourished a simmering hatred for his younger brother, leading finally to sibling murder. Cain was shamed and, knowing that his presence in the Second Garden was symbolic of the default, he traveled to the land of Nod (cf. Genesis 4:15–16), where he became a great leader among those people. The revelations explain this reference to the land of Nod in

Genesis: "In his early teachings, Moses very wisely did not attempt to go back of Adam's time, and since Moses was the supreme teacher of the Hebrews, the stories of Adam became intimately associated with those of creation. That the earlier traditions recognized pre-Adamic civilization is clearly shown by the fact that later editors, intending to eradicate all reference to human affairs before Adam's time, neglected to remove the telltale reference to Cain's emigration to the 'land of Nod,' where he took himself a wife."[18]

11.   Adam and Eve remained in the Second Garden until they died of old age.

12.   The religious priesthood originated with Seth, the eldest surviving son of Adam and Eve born in the Second Garden. He was born one hundred and twenty-nine years after Adam's arrival on Earth. It was Seth's purpose to improve the spiritual status of his father's people, and he became the head of the new priesthood of the Second Garden. His son, Enos, founded the new order of worship and his grandson, Kenan, instituted the first foreign missionary service known as the Sethites. The Sethite priests spread Adam's teachings to tribes near and far. Thousands of years later, the Salem missionaries would be organized by Machiventa Melchizedek according to the missionary system established by the Sethites. Illustration 19 presents a limited genealogy of Adam and Eve.

13.   Approximately 5000 BC, continuous floods throughout the Euphrates Valley submerged the Second Garden and neighboring cities.

"Adam's bestowal improved the brain power of the races, thereby greatly hastening the processes of natural evolution."[19] This contribution of superior genetics may be evident in recent results obtained by researchers at the Howard Hughes Medical Institute analyzing the sequence variations in two genes that regulate brain size in human populations. Analysis was focused on the *Microcephalin* and *ASPM* genes involved in brain evolution. Their statistical findings indicated that a genetic variation occurred about thirty-seven thousand years ago. "In the case of *Microcephalin*, the origin of the new variant coincides with the emergence of culturally modern humans."[20]

Sin and Evil

Primitive people observed taboos to keep from offending the spirit ghosts. "Every primitive tribe had its tree of forbidden fruit, literally the apple but figuratively consisting of a thousand branches hanging heavy with all sorts of taboos. And the forbidden tree always said, 'Thou shall not.'"[21] The concept of sin as a transgression of taboos emerged as good and bad spirits were envisaged. The idea of sin, therefore, ". . . was universally established in the world before revealed religion ever made its entry. It was only by the concept of sin that natural death became logical to the primitive mind. Sin was the transgression of taboo, and death was the penalty of sin."

Illustration 19
LIMITED GENEALOGY OF ADAM AND EVE

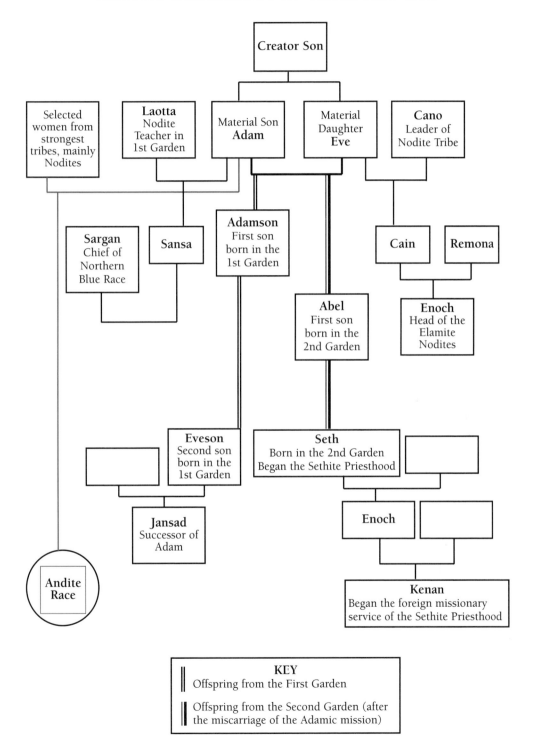

Creator Son

Selected women from strongest tribes, mainly Nodites

Laotta
Nodite Teacher in 1st Garden

Material Son
Adam

Material Daughter
Eve

Cano
Leader of Nodite Tribe

Sargan
Chief of Northern Blue Race

Sansa

Adamson
First son born in the 1st Garden

Cain

Remona

Abel
First son born in the 2nd Garden

Enoch
Head of the Elamite Nodites

Eveson
Second son born in the 1st Garden

Seth
Born in the 2nd Garden
Began the Sethite Priesthood

Jansad
Successor of Adam

Enoch

Andite Race

Kenan
Began the foreign missionary service of the Sethite Priesthood

KEY
‖ Offspring from the First Garden

▌ Offspring from the Second Garden (after the miscarriage of the Adamic mission)

In the Abrahamic and Christian traditions, Adam and Eve have long had the infamous reputation for being the originators of sin as a result of their transgression: disobeying God. In Genesis 3, the fall of the human race is narrated within a context of historical facts. Paul's theology expressed in Romans 5:12–13, 1 Corinthians 15:22, and 1 Timothy 2:14 reinforces the fall of Adam and Eve as the origin of sin in the human race. Epochal revelation explains the origin of such theories: "Sin was ritual, not rational; an act, not a thought. And this entire concept of sin was fostered by the lingering traditions of Dilmun and the days of a little paradise on earth. The tradition of Adam and the Garden of Eden also lent substance to the dream of a onetime 'golden age' of the dawn of the races. And all this confirmed the ideas later expressed in the belief that man had his origin in a special creation, that he started his career in perfection, and that transgression of the taboos—sin—brought him down to his later sorry plight."[22]

Adam and Eve were sent to Earth as part of the Divine Plan to biologically uplift the human race and to foster moral and spiritual ideals. Their failure to follow the original plan for the advancement of the world family resulted in their fall, reducing them from the rank of Material Son and Daughter of God to the status of mortals. This, however, was not the fall of humanity, and their disobedience was not the origin of sin. Epochal revelation explains: ". . . Paul's theory of original sin, the doctrines of hereditary guilt and innate evil and redemption therefrom, was partially Mithraic in origin, having little in common with Hebrew theology, Philo's philosophy, or Jesus' teachings. Some phases of Paul's teachings regarding original sin and the atonement were original with himself."[23]

According to Christian theology, the fall of Adam and Eve brought both sin and death upon all humanity. The teachings in *The Urantia Book* clarify the dynamics of the fall: "Caligastia rebelled, Adam and Eve did default, but no mortal subsequently born on Urantia has suffered in his personal spiritual experience because of these blunders. Every moral born on Urantia since Caligastia's rebellion has been in some manner time-penalized, but the future welfare of such souls has never been in the least eternity-jeopardized. No person is ever made to suffer vital spiritual deprivation because of the sin of another. Sin is wholly personal as to moral guilt or spiritual consequences, notwithstanding its far-flung repercussions in administrative, intellectual, and social domains."[24]

Sin, therefore, did not originate in the behavior of Adam and Eve; rather it is in the swing between imperfection and perfection that error, evil, sin, and iniquity take hold. "Man is slow to perceive that contrastive perfection and imperfection produce potential evil; that conflicting truth and falsehood create confusing error; that the divine endowment of freewill choice eventuates in the divergent realms of sin and righteousness; that the persistent pursuit of divinity leads to the kingdom of God as contrasted with its continuous rejection, which leads to the domains of iniquity."[25]

Human beings have been given free will to either pursue or reject divine ideals. Both our mental faculties and our state of mind at any given time influence the freewill choices we make. From a cosmic perspective, the development of our spiritual nature is reflected in the quality of our decisions and actions, and the fruits of the spirit they yield. The choice between good and evil accompanies us every day of our lives. Actions that are good—increasingly wise, ethical, caring, and selfless—reflect harmonious development of the three mind endowments: cosmic insight, moral awareness, and spiritual perception. Imbalance in the development of these endowments results in unwise judgment and acts that are harmful to others.

Epochal revelation, however, reveals that the nature and cause of "evil" as we generally define it can be better understood when we discover that there are different aspects of the misuse of our free will. These are distinguished as error, evil, sin, and iniquity:

- **Error**—unwise judgment—arises from mistaken or incomplete beliefs, misinterpretation, or misunderstanding.

- **Evil** arises from erroneous judgment coupled with harmful thinking—a selfish and vengeful consciousness potentially causing an evil act—harm to others.

- **Sin** is the result of deliberately rejecting divine ideals and willfully embracing evil. Sin is therefore the *intentional* disloyalty to God, with the following degrees of disloyalty:

  - **Indecision**: partial loyalty
  - **Conflict**: divided loyalty
  - **Indifference**: dying loyalty
  - **Devotion to Godless ideals**: death of loyalty[26]

  Sin is not transmitted from parent to child, though the tendency toward evildoing may be hereditary. Violation of social mores may give a feeling of guilt but is not necessarily sin. There is no real sin in the unintentional disloyalty to Deity.

- **Iniquity** is the deliberate and habitual rejection of the ideals of divinity, the open and persistent expression of an unmitigated, selfish consciousness. Iniquitous acts deprive an individual from attaining the moral and spiritual qualities necessary to cultivate the soul-connection with the Universal Father and achieve eternal survival. Unmitigated iniquity leads to eventual soul death.

From a cosmic perspective, the consequences of confusion, evildoing, and sinful planning are experienced on both a group and personal level:

- **On a group level**, as is often in the case of families, the consequences of individual evil and sinful acts are to a certain extent shared by all; they seriously slow down intellectual development, moral growth, and the spiritual attainment of society as a whole. Nonetheless, when we do good in the face of evil, good ultimately prevails.

- **On a personal level**, the full consequences of evil and sinful acts are experienced only on the level of actual performance and are dependent on whether there was a deliberate disloyal attitude toward God. "The transgression of universe law may be fatal in the physical realm without seriously involving the mind or impairing the spiritual experience. Sin is fraught with fatal consequences to personality survival only when it is the attitude of the whole being, when it stands for the choosing of the mind and the willing of the soul."[27] Evildoers, therefore, may or may not experience social justice, but whether or not personality survival is jeopardized is dependent on the presence and level of deliberate rebellion against God.

Summary

The planetary rebellion precipitated worldwide confusion and robbed subsequent generations of the moral assistance provided by a well-ordered society. Cumulatively more disastrous was the default of Adam and Eve, in that it deprived the races of a full complement of superior genes, such as would produce an improved physical nature and foster higher spiritual aspirations. Humanity is compelled to undergo a more contentious struggle between the spirit and the flesh because our remote ancestors did not receive the full measure of the Adamic life plasm bestowal. It was the Divine Plan that the human races should have had physical natures more responsive to spiritual impulses along with a permanent center of advanced culture. A less-than-optimum resistance to physical disease and a tendency to harbor emotional fears, selfishness, and greed, are but some of the unfortunate legacies of the Adamic default that plague humanity to this day. Although the Divine Plan of fully uplifting the human race miscarried and delayed the realization of the brotherhood of man, the human race did profit from the limited contribution that the Edenic pair and their descendants made to the races. In addition, "Adam and Eve also contributed much that was of value to the social, moral, and intellectual progress of mankind; civilization was immensely quickened by the presence of their offspring."[28]

10.

The Evolution of the Monotheistic Concept

The Hebrew religion encompasses the philosophic transition from polytheism to monotheism; it is an evolutionary link between the religions of evolution and the religions of revelation.

The Urantia Book

The evolution of worship from many gods to one God can be directly attributed to Machiventa Melchizedek, a Local Universe Son of God, who materialized on Earth at a time when the sublime concept of God had devolved in the minds of mortals.

Ages after Caligastia's staff lifted the mind and culture of primitive people to higher levels, and long after Adam and Eve had advanced the worship of one God, this emergency bestowal Son incarnated on a crucial mission. "And thus did Melchizedek prepare the way and set the monotheistic stage of world tendency for the bestowal of an actual Paradise Son of the one God, whom he so vividly portrayed as the Father of all, and whom he represented to Abraham as a God who would accept man on the simple terms of personal faith."[1]

Melchizedek was considered to be a priest and king; he is mentioned twice in the Old Testament. In Genesis 14:18 we read: "And Melchizedek king of Salem brought forth bread and wine: and he [was] the priest of the most high God." The second time in the messianic Psalm 110:4: ". . . Thou [art] a priest for ever after the order of Melchizedek." It was generally agreed that the ideal ruler of the Hebrew nation would be one who combined in his person the role of both priest and king. Melchizedek's divine origin is recognized in Hebrews 7:3: "Without father, without mother, without descent, having neither beginning of days, nor end of life; but made like unto the Son of God; abideth a priest continually."

In *Melchizedek* 11Q13, a first century AD text from the Dead Sea Scrolls, Melchizedek is depicted as a major figure in the eschatological drama, functioning in the role of judge, a teacher bearing good news, and a priest effecting atonement. He is exalted over all angels and is identified as one of the *Elohim* (gods, sons of God, or divine beings) of Psalm 82:1.

The teachings in *The Urantia Book* expand and reconcile the scant historical references to Melchizedek's origin and mission, including the evolution of his teachings after his departure.

The Origin of Machiventa Melchizedek

Melchizedeks are the first order of Local Universe Sons created to assist in governing the local universe. They are created by the Creator Son and the Local Universe Mother Spirit in collaboration with their original offspring, the Father Melchizedek (see illustration 10).

Melchizedek Sons function directly in the ministry of mortal spiritualization—teaching, training, counseling, acting as unprejudiced observers, and serving as advisory commissioners on inhabited worlds. Melchizedeks are the first to take action in emergencies and serve in various unique capacities when there is a planetary crisis. During Earth's planetary rebellion, they assumed the functions of the deposed ruler of our planet.

Interrelation with Humanity

After the default of Adam and Eve, the status of revealed truth slowly declined. The human races were making intellectual progress but losing ground spiritually. By 3000 BC, an exalted concept of God had grown dim. In an effort to preserve the light of truth, the governing Melchizedeks agreed to allow one Machiventa, a trustworthy volunteer, ". . . to personalize on earth as a temporary man of the realm, to bestow himself as an emergency Son of world ministry."[2]

At the time, Palestine was centrally located and a hub of trade and travel. This locale was favorable both for Machiventa's mission and Michael of Nebadon's subsequent appearance as Jesus of Nazareth. One of the proposed contact families that the Melchizedek receivers had been observing was that of Terah, the father of Abram. They confidently expected Terah's offspring to be characterized by intelligence, initiative, sagacity, and sincerity. "It was this possibility of contact with these versatile children of Terah that had considerable to do with the appearance of Machiventa at Salem, rather than in Egypt, China, India, or among the northern tribes."[3] Salem was subsequently called Jebus and then Jerusalem.

Machiventa Melchizedek materialized on Earth one thousand nine hundred and seventy-three years before the birth of Jesus, and no one witnessed his appearance. He was first observed when he entered the tent of a Chaldean herder and proclaimed: "'I am Melchizedek, priest of El Elyon, the Most High, the one and only God.'"[4] Within ten years of his arrival, Machiventa Melchizedek organized his schools at Salem to teach basic revealed truth and had a following of pupils, disciples, and believers. Some of his teachings included:

- The concept of one God, taught according to each follower's capacity to understand. He allowed the people to associate this teaching with the Constellation Father, whom he termed El Elyon, the Most High.

- The concept of the Trinity as "the three Most Highs who functioned as one."

- The concept of God's acceptance of all people and salvation through personal faith, rather than through sacrifices and offerings. He offered ". . . the substitute of a sacrament of bread and wine for the older sacrifice of flesh and blood."[5] This is recorded in Genesis 14:18.

- Many modern religious ideas about heaven and Earth, of humankind, God, and angels, are not far removed from Melchizedek teachings. Only to some of his disciples did Machiventa teach about the organization of the local universe, the superuniverse, and central universe. One such group was the family of Katro, with whom Machiventa lived for more than thirty years. Many of these higher truths lingered in the family, even to the days of their well-known descendant Moses.

- Melchizedek prepared the people for the appearance of Jesus. "Melchizedek taught that at some future time another Son of God would come in the flesh as he had come, but that he would be born of a woman; and that is why numerous later teachers held that Jesus was a priest, or minister, 'forever after the order of Melchizedek.'"[6]

Melchizedek and Abraham

Shortly after the death of Abram's father, Machiventa Melchizedek sent for Abram (cf. Genesis 14:18–20) who had already moved from Ur to Salem. Abram (later called Abraham) attended the Salem school three different times and finally became a convert to the Salem teachings, becoming one of Melchizedek's most brilliant pupils and chief supporters. "Although it may be an error to speak of 'chosen people,' it is not a mistake to refer to Abraham as a chosen individual. Melchizedek did lay upon Abraham the responsibility of keeping alive the truth of one God as distinguished from the prevailing belief in plural deities."[7]

Melchizedek maintained peaceful relations with all the surrounding tribes, allowing a defense policy only for Salem, which Abram put into effect. When Melchizedek would not approve Abram's increasing aspirations to conquer Canaan, they severed their relationship peacefully and Abram went to Hebron to establish a military capital.

Abram was well on his way to establishing a powerful state in Palestine when he began to worry that he had no son to succeed him. He met with Melchizedek, who persuaded him to let go of his plans to conquer Canaan, in favor of the spiritual concept of the kingdom of heaven. It was at this time that Melchizedek told him the story of the future occupation of Canaan by Abram's progeny after their enslavement in Egypt as recorded in Genesis 15:18. Abram believed Melchizedek and made a formal covenant that represented the agreement between God and humanity: ". . . God agrees to do *everything*; man only agrees to *believe* God's promises and follow his instructions."[8]

After the birth of his son Isaac, Abram publicly formalized his covenant with Melchizedek and changed his name from Abram to Abraham. "It was following this real and public surrender of his personal ambitions in behalf of the larger plans of Melchizedek that the three celestial beings appeared to him on the plains of Mamre [Genesis 18:1–15]. This was an appearance of fact, notwithstanding its association with the subsequently fabricated narratives relating to the natural destruction of Sodom and Gomorrah."[9]

Abraham regained civil and military leadership of Salem. He improved the Salem temple, provided new tents for the entire Salem school, and reorganized and expanded the dairy operation. Melchizedek also continued for some years to instruct and train the Salem missionaries who were able to penetrate all the surrounding tribes, especially those in Egypt, Mesopotamia, Asia Minor, and later, the remote regions of both Europe and Asia, reaching even the British Isles, Iceland, China, and Japan. "But the task was so great and the tribes were so backward that . . . except in Palestine, never was the idea of one God able to claim the continued allegiance of a whole tribe or race."[10]

"It was shortly after the destruction of Sodom and Gomorrah that Machiventa decided to end his emergency bestowal on Urantia. Melchizedek's decision to terminate his sojourn in the flesh was influenced by numerous conditions, chief of which was the growing tendency of the surrounding tribes, and even of his immediate associates, to regard him as a demigod, to look upon him as a supernatural being, which indeed he was; but they were beginning to reverence him unduly and with a highly superstitious fear."[11] He also wanted to depart before Abraham's death to insure that the truth of the one God would become established strongly in the minds of his followers.

Melchizedek's followers were not prepared for his departure, even though he had warned them that he would leave as he had come. On the night of his departure he went to his tent after saying good night, and by morning was gone. Machiventa Melchizedek resumed his spiritual career as planetary adviser in the administrative headquarters of our local universe. For nineteen centuries he also spiritually influenced many prophets in an effort to keep the truths of Salem alive until the bestowal of Michael as Jesus of Nazareth.

Abraham never fully overcame the loss of Melchizedek; but as his successor, Abraham became a greatly respected spiritual leader in Palestine, albeit contaminated by the superstitions of his converts, particularly the practice of sacrificing firstborn sons. Abraham died confident in his faith in God, which had been inspired by Melchizedek.

Although replete, Melchizedek's teachings seemed impossible and even fantastic to the Hebrew priests who discovered them during their captivity in Babylon. Subsequent massive editing of the Old Testament records resulted in many distortions: "What the Old Testament records describe as conversations between Abraham and God were in reality conferences between Abraham and Melchizedek. Later scribes regarded the term Melchizedek as synonymous with God. The record of so many contacts of Abraham and Sarah with 'the angel of the Lord' refers to their numerous visits with Melchizedek . . . Abraham was not so old as the records indicate, and his wife was much younger. These ages were deliberately altered in order to provide for the subsequent alleged miraculous birth of Isaac."[12]

Conserving Belief in One God

It was hard for the generation after Abraham to comprehend the story of Melchizedek and, within five hundred years, many regarded the whole episode as a myth. Abraham's son, Isaac, held fairly well to the teachings of his father and nourished the gospel of the Salem colony, although it was harder for Jacob to grasp the significance of these traditions. Joseph, like his great-grandfather Abraham, was able to exert great influence throughout Egypt on behalf of the Salem teachings of one God. The progeny of Abraham through Isaac as intermarried with the Kenites became the only line that long continued to nourish any clear concept of the Salem teachings. "The Hebrew narratives of Isaac, Jacob, and Joseph are far more reliable than those about Abraham, although they also contain many diversions from the facts, alterations made intentionally and unintentionally at the time of the compilation of these records by the Hebrew priests during the Babylonian captivity."[13]

The original Melchizedek teachings took their deepest root in Egypt. The strong social and moral ideals of the Egyptians provided fertile ground for the doctrines of the Salem religion to flourish. The ancient Egyptian seer and author Amenemope functioned to conserve the ethics of evolution and the morals of revelation, and in his writings, passed these on to the later Hebrews and the Greeks. "In the Book of Hebrew Proverbs, chapters fifteen, seventeen, twenty, and chapter twenty-two, verse seventeen, to chapter twenty-four, verse twenty-two, are taken almost verbatim from Amenemope's Book of Wisdom. The first psalm of the Hebrew Book of Psalms was written by Amenemope and is the heart of the teachings of Ikhnaton."[14]

"The teachings of Amenemope were slowly losing their hold on the Egyptian mind when, through the influence of an Egyptian Salemite physician, a woman of the royal family espoused the Melchizedek teachings. This woman prevailed upon her son, Ikhnaton, Pharaoh of Egypt, to accept these doctrines of One God."[15] During this time of increasing spiritual decline in Mesopotamia, Ikhnaton kept alive the doctrine of El Elyon ". . . under the guise of the sun-god. Ikhnaton took the generalized doctrines of the then existent Aton faith regarding the fatherhood and motherhood of Deity and created a religion which recognized an intimate worshipful relation between man and God."[16] In so doing, Ikhnaton maintained the monotheistic channel that was important to the religious landscape for the future bestowal of Michael. "The glory of this great era of moral development and spiritual growth in the Nile Valley was rapidly passing at about the time the national life of the Hebrews was beginning, and consequent upon their sojourn in Egypt these Bedouins carried away much of these teachings and perpetuated many of Ikhnaton's doctrines in their racial religion."[17]

The concept of the personality of God, essential to the mission of the coming Son of God, was taught at Salem in the days of Melchizedek. It gradually evolved in the Hebraic mind from generation to generation in response to the teaching of the spiritual leaders.

Evolution of the Monotheistic Concept: From Moses to Jeremiah

The evolution of the Hebraic ideal of a Supreme Creator dates from the departure of the Bedouin Semites from Egypt under the great leader, teacher, and organizer, Moses.

Due to a severe famine, the Levantine Bedouins entered Egypt as contract laborers on the Egyptian public works and eventually became enslaved. In clarifying their relationship to Abraham, epochal revelation explains: "It was only after the days of Machiventa Melchizedek and Abraham that certain tribes of Semites, because of their peculiar religious beliefs, were called the children of Israel and later on Hebrews, Jews, and the 'chosen people.' Abraham was not the racial father of all the Hebrews; he was not even the progenitor of all the Bedouin Semites who were held captive in Egypt. True, his offspring, coming up out of Egypt, did form the nucleus of the later Jewish people, but the vast majority of the men and women who became incorporated into the clans of Israel had never sojourned in Egypt. They were merely fellow nomads who chose to follow the leadership of Moses as the children of Abraham and their Semite associates from Egypt journeyed through northern Arabia."[18]

Moses

Moses was the most important individual world teacher and leader between the times of Machiventa and Jesus. According to the Bible, Moses was adopted as an infant after being found in a basket in the Nile, close to the Pharaoh's palace. But according to epochal revelation, "[h]is mother was of the royal family of Egypt; his father was a Semitic liaison officer between the government and the Bedouin captives."[19] Moses had heard of the teachings of Machiventa Melchizedek from both his parents. His father-in-law was a Kenite worshiper of El Elyon and, through his influence, Moses became an El Elyonist.

"Many of the advances which Moses made over and above the religion of the Egyptians and the surrounding Levantine tribes were due to the Kenite traditions of the time of Melchizedek. Without the teaching of Machiventa to Abraham and his contemporaries, the Hebrews would have come out of Egypt in hopeless darkness. Moses and his father-in-law, Jethro, gathered up the residue of the traditions of the days of Melchizedek, and these teachings, joined to the learning of the Egyptians, guided Moses in the creation of the improved religion and ritual of the Israelites. Moses was an organizer; he selected the best in the religion and mores of Egypt and Palestine and, associating these practices with the traditions of the Melchizedek teachings, organized the Hebrew ceremonial system of worship."[20]

Moses tried unsuccessfully to free the Bedouin captives but did not give up; ". . . he bided his time, and in less than a year, when the Egyptian military forces were fully occupied in resisting the simultaneous onslaughts of a strong Libyan thrust from the south and a Greek naval invasion from the north, this intrepid organizer led his compatriots out of Egypt in a spectacular night flight."[21]

At the Hebrew camp in the area of Mount Sinai, Moses decided to present to his people his new and enlarged concept of Deity as an expanded concept of their old tribal god, Yahweh. Under his teachings, Yahweh became the Lord

God of Israel. "Moses made a heroic effort to uplift Yahweh to the dignity of a supreme Deity when he presented him as the 'God of truth and without iniquity, just and right in all his ways.' And yet, despite this exalted teaching, the limited understanding of his followers made it necessary to speak of God as being in man's image, as being subject to fits of anger, wrath, and severity, even that he was vengeful and easily influenced by man's conduct."[22]

"It does not appear that Moses would ever have succeeded in the establishment of his somewhat advanced ceremonial worship and in keeping his followers intact for a quarter of a century had it not been for the violent eruption of Horeb during the third week of their worshipful sojourn at its base. 'The mountain of Yahweh was consumed in fire, and the smoke ascended like the smoke of a furnace, and the whole mountain quaked greatly.' In view of this cataclysm it is not surprising that Moses could impress upon his brethren the teaching that their God was 'mighty, terrible, a devouring fire, fearful, and all-powerful.'"[23] It was amidst the roar and fire of Sinai that Moses gave the Hebrews the Ten Commandments to accompany the enlarging Yahweh concepts of Deity.

Moses eventually turned over the leadership of the Hebrews to his son Joshua. Despite Joshua's efforts, the superior concept of Yahweh rapidly deteriorated after the death of Moses. Back in Palestine, the Hebrews soon drifted back into the primitive beliefs of the desert and became contaminated with the less advanced Canaanite religious practices. "They came near losing all concept of monotheism; they nearly lost their opportunity of becoming the people who would serve as a vital link in the spiritual evolution of Urantia, the group who would conserve the Melchizedek teaching of one God until the times of the incarnation of a bestowal Son of that Father of all."[24]

Teachers of Israel

"Hostile pressure of the surrounding peoples in Palestine soon taught the Hebrew sheiks they could not hope to survive unless they confederated their tribal organizations into a centralized government. And this centralization of administrative authority afforded a better opportunity for Samuel to function as a teacher and reformer."[25]

Samuel came from a long line of Salem teachers who had maintained the truths of Melchizedek as a part of their faith. He restated the Melchizedek covenant with Abraham and declared that the Lord God of Israel was the source of all truth, stability, and constancy. "Only his great devotion, coupled with his extraordinary determination, enabled him to withstand the almost universal opposition which he encountered when he started out to turn all Israel back to the worship of the supreme Yahweh of Mosaic times. And even then he was only partially successful; he won back to the service of the higher concept of Yahweh only the more intelligent half of the Hebrews; the other half continued in the worship of the tribal gods of the country and in the baser conception of Yahweh."[26]

In the tenth century before Christ, the Hebrew nation became divided into two kingdoms. The northern kingdom included the followers of the god Baal (the Canaanites) and the southern kingdom those of Yahweh.

The Canaanites believed in the right to buy and sell land; the Yahwehites believed that land was a gift of Deity to the clan and was not to be sold. "Out of this basic difference in the regard for land, there evolved the bitter antagonisms of social, economic, moral, and religious attitudes exhibited by the Canaanites and the Hebrews. This socioeconomic controversy did not become a definite religious issue until the times of Elijah."[27]

The Hebraic religion did not advance until Elijah began to teach. Elijah restored Samuel's concept of God to the northern kingdom but was not able to advance the Hebrews' understanding much further. He was kept busy, as Samuel had been before him, overthrowing the altars of Baal and demolishing the idols of false gods. Elisha, Elijah's successor, was able to keep the drive toward monotheism alive in Palestine with the assistance of the little-known Micaiah.

Amos and Hosea furthered the evolution of the Melchizedek revelation. Amos denounced the double standard of national justice and morality. He quickened the national conscience of the Hebrews to the recognition that Yahweh would not condone crime and sin among them simply because they were supposed to be his chosen people. Hosea continued the moral warnings of Amos, but also proclaimed hope and forgiveness. "Hosea followed Amos and his doctrine of a universal God of justice by the resurrection of the Mosaic concept of a God of love. Hosea preached forgiveness through repentance, not by sacrifice. He proclaimed a gospel of loving-kindness and divine mercy . . ."[28]

The first Isaiah arrived when the Hebrew nation was experiencing an awakening of scruples and awareness. "Isaiah went on to preach the eternal nature of God, his infinite wisdom, his unchanging perfection of reliability."[29]

"This Isaiah was followed by Micah and Obadiah, who confirmed and embellished his gospel. And these two brave messengers boldly denounced the priest-ridden ritual of the Hebrews and fearlessly attacked the whole sacrificial system."[30] "And but for the stubborn resistance of the priests, these teachers would have overthrown the whole bloody ceremonial of the Hebrew ritual of worship."[31]

The Sixth Century before Christ: The Mysterious Renaissance of Melchizedek's Gospel

By the sixth century before Christ, the monotheistic God concept was becoming submerged in the older and more widespread superstitions and beliefs. Social progress was threatened.

According to epochal revelation, "About six hundred years before the arrival of Michael, it seemed to Melchizedek, long since departed from the flesh, that the purity of his teaching on earth was being unduly jeopardized by general absorption into the older Urantia beliefs. It appeared for a time that his mission as a forerunner of Michael might be in danger of failing. And in the sixth century before Christ, through an unusual coordination of spiritual agencies, not all of which are understood even by the planetary supervisors, Urantia witnessed a most unusual presentation of manifold religious truth. Through the agency of several human teachers the Salem gospel was restated and revitalized, and as it was then presented, much has persisted to the times of this writing."[32] The spiritual awakening of this century was experienced in many parts of the globe and is briefly described below:

- **In Jerusalem**, where several teachers continued to preach the gospel of Isaiah, it remained for Jeremiah to take the next bold step in the evolution of the Hebrew religion. "He asserted that Yahweh was God of all the earth, of all nations and of all peoples. Jeremiah's teaching was the crescendo of the rising wave of the internationalization of the God of Israel; finally and forever did this intrepid preacher proclaim that Yahweh was God of all nations, and there was no Osiris for the Egyptians, Bel for the Babylonians, Ashur for the Assyrians, or Dagon for the Philistines. And thus did the religion of the Hebrews share in that renaissance of monotheism throughout the world at about and following this time; at last the concept of Yahweh had ascended to a Deity level of planetary and even cosmic dignity. But many of Jeremiah's associates found it difficult to conceive of Yahweh apart from the Hebrew nation."[33]

- **In Babylon**, during the time of the Hebrew captivity, the second Isaiah eclipsed the nationalistic Yahweh by his inspiring portrayal of the majesty and universal omnipotence of the supreme Yahweh, God of love, ruler of the universe, and affectionate Father of all humankind. His writings were subsequently folded into the writings of the earlier Isaiah by the Hebrew priests. "I have made the earth, and created man upon it . . ." [Isaiah 45:12]. ". . . he created it not in vain . . . he formed it to be inhabited . . ." [Isaiah 45:18]. "I the LORD, the first, and with the last; I [am] he." [Isaiah 41:4]. ". . . there is no God beside me . . ." [Isaiah 45:5]. "Had the priests not dedicated themselves to the work of building up a misconceived nationalism, the teachings of the two Isaiahs would have prepared the way for the recognition and reception of the promised Messiah."[34]

- **In India**, Siddhartha Gautama, the founder of Buddhism, challenged Brahmin supremacy and the caste system. "According to the original teachings of Gautama, salvation is achieved by human effort, apart from divine help; there is no place for saving faith or prayers to superhuman powers. Gautama, in his attempt to minimize the superstitions of India, endeavored to turn men away from the blatant claims of magical salvation. And in making this effort, he left the door wide open for his successors to misinterpret his teaching and to proclaim that all human striving for attainment is distasteful and painful. His followers overlooked the fact that the highest happiness is linked with the intelligent and enthusiastic pursuit of worthy goals, and that such achievements constitute true progress in cosmic self-realization."[35] Although Gautama failed to perceive the personality of God, "Buddhism prospered because it offered salvation through belief in the Buddha, the enlightened one."[36]

- **In China**, Lao Tzu built directly upon the concepts of the Salem traditions when he declared Tao to be the One First Cause of all creation. "He taught the return of the creature to the Creator and pictured life as the emergence of a personality from the cosmic potentials, while death was like the returning home of this creature personality. His concept of true faith was unusual, and he too likened it to the 'attitude of a little child.'"[37] Confucius, a younger contemporary of Lao Tzu, compiled wise sayings of ancient philosophers that helped replace magic with morality and establish a respect for ancestral conduct that is still venerated today. "Confucius based his doctrines upon the better moral traditions of the long history of the yellow race, and he was also somewhat influenced by the lingering traditions of the Salem missionaries."[38]

- **In Iran (Persia)**, Zoroaster emerged to revive the smoldering embers of the Salem gospel. "He had imbibed the Hebraic idea of a God of justice, the Mosaic concept of divinity. The idea of a supreme God was clear in his mind, and he set down all other gods as devils, consigned them to the ranks of the demons of which he had heard in Mesopotamia."[39] Zoroaster was intent on reforming the ancient Indo-Iranian religious practices, some of which were parallel to the Vedic religion of ancient India. The doctrine of the one God became a central teaching in the religion that he founded, as did the concept of resurrection and the Day of Judgment.

"This was the situation when, during the sixth century before Christ, the Orient and the Levant experienced a revival of spiritual consciousness and a new awakening to the recognition of monotheism. But the West did not share in this new development; neither Europe nor northern Africa extensively participated in this religious renaissance. The Greeks, however, did engage in a magnificent intellectual advancement. They had begun to master fear and no longer sought religion as an antidote therefor, but they did not perceive that true religion is the cure for soul hunger, spiritual disquiet, and moral despair. They sought for the solace of the soul in deep thinking—philosophy and metaphysics. They turned from the contemplation of self-preservation— salvation—to self-realization and self-understanding."[40]

The Babylonian Captivity and the Writing of the Old Testament

When the Neo-Babylonian Chaldeans conquered Jerusalem six centuries before the birth of Jesus, thousands of prominent Hebrews, including professionals, priests, craftsmen, and the wealthy, were forced to relocate to the city of Babylon.

The Jews, as the Hebrews became known during their Babylonian captivity, found themselves without a homeland. It was in this atmosphere of depression and hopelessness that the Hebrew priests, anxious to restore the Jews as the chosen people, began to revise the Jewish religion of the Old Testament by rewriting the history of the Hebrew people and completely destroying many of the original records of Hebrew affairs, preserving only those narratives that reflected great honor. But epochal revelation warns against passing judgment: "If there is resentment of the fact that these priests have fastened their erroneous ideas upon such a large part of the Occidental world, it should be remembered that they did not intentionally do this; they did not claim to be writing by inspiration; they made no profession to be writing a sacred book. They were merely preparing a textbook designed to bolster up the dwindling courage of their fellows in captivity. They were definitely aiming at improving the national spirit and morale of their compatriots. It remained for later-day men to assemble these and other writings into a guide book of supposedly infallible teachings."[41]

While some of the distortions in the Old Testament have already been mentioned, it is not within the context of this book to reconcile Hebrew secular history with the altered version depicted in the texts that make up the Old Testament. For more information on this matter, readers may reference *The Urantia Book*, which includes a brief recital of the high points in Hebrew history (Paper 97, Section 9). What deserves compassion is the unfortunate result: In forgetting about Melchizedek, the Hebrews ". . . also lost sight of the teaching of this emergency Son regarding the spiritual mission of the promised bestowal Son; lost sight of the nature of this mission so fully and completely that very few of their progeny were able or willing to recognize and receive Michael when he appeared on earth and in the flesh as Machiventa had foretold."[42]

11.

Jesus of Nazareth:
Son of God and Son of Man

*Jesus revealed God as the Father of each human being.
The entire mortal concept of God is transcendently
illuminated by the life of Jesus.*

The Urantia Book

The declaration by Jesus that he was a Son of God is recorded in the New Testament, our main historical source. Validation of this declaration was found in the Dead Sea Scrolls, specifically the scroll discovered in Cave Four known as 4Q246, which contains specific phrases considered unique to the Hellenistic New Testament writings, including "Son of God" and "Son of the most High," found in the Gospel of Luke (1:32, 35).[1]

In reconciling our understanding of these appellations with epochal revelation, we can finally place Jesus and his matchless teachings in their rightful spiritual context.

Christian theology holds to the belief that Jesus' declaration that he is "Son of God" means that he is God the Son, a member of the Trinity. Jesus, however, never claimed to be a member of the Trinity. *The Urantia Book* explains:

1. "Except when quoting the Hebrew Scriptures, Jesus referred to Deity by only two names: God and Father. And when the Master made reference to his Father as God, he usually employed the Hebrew word [*Elohim*] signifying the plural God (the Trinity) and not the word Yahweh, which stood for the progressive conception of the tribal God of the Jews."[2]

2. "Jesus never claimed to be the manifestation of Elohim (God) in the flesh. He never declared that he was a revelation of Elohim (God) to the worlds. He never taught that he who had seen him had seen Elohim (God). But he did proclaim himself as the revelation of the Father in the flesh, and he did say that whoso had seen him had seen the Father. As the divine Son he claimed to represent only the Father."[3]

3. "He was, indeed, the Son of even the Elohim God; but in the likeness of mortal flesh and to the mortal sons of God, he chose to limit his life revelation to the portrayal of his Father's character in so far as such a revelation might be comprehensible to mortal man."[4]

According to epochal revelation, Jesus explained to the apostles the truth about the Trinity, but they were never able to reconcile the persons of the Paradise Trinity with the dominant Hebrew concept of Yahweh—"The Lord our God, the Lord is One." Paul, the organizer of Christianity, shared their dilemma. "Paul knew of the Paradise Trinity of Father, Son, and Spirit, but he seldom preached about it and made mention thereof in only a few of his letters to the newly forming churches [cf. 2 Corinthians 13–14, 1 Thessalonians 1:3–5]."[5] As a result, the belief that Jesus was God the Son continued to gain recognition by Christians toward the end of the first century, making it ". . . increasingly difficult for Jews, [Muslims], Hindus, and other Eastern religionists to accept the teachings of Jesus."[6]

Section one of this book described the personalization of Deity as the Paradise relationships of Father, Son, and Spirit. It also explained how this association enables personal Deity to be revealed to the creatures of the evolving universes through the self-distribution technique of the Father. Thus, the personalities of the Trinity, functioning together or in their individual capacities, create associate spirits beings to assist in manifesting the Divine Purpose and Plan. God the Son, therefore, does not function in the physical realm except through his Sons who possess creative attributes.

Jesus was misidentified as a member of the Trinity due to human confusion, though the spiritual elements in this doctrine hold truth. Jesus, as the incarnated Paradise Creator Son, was the personification of the Universal Father and the Eternal Son: "But though the Christian concept of the Trinity erred in fact, it was practically true with respect to spiritual relationships. Only in its philosophic implications and cosmological consequences did this concept suffer embarrassment: It has been difficult for many who are cosmic minded to believe that the Second Person of Deity, the second member of an infinite Trinity, once dwelt on Urantia; and while in spirit this is true, in actuality it is not a fact. The Michael Creators fully embody the divinity of the Eternal Son, but they are not the absolute personality."[7]

Thus, God the Son (the Eternal Son, or the Second Person of the Trinity), in essence, came to humanity when the Creator Son Michael of Nebadon incarnated as the human person, Jesus of Nazareth.

With the passage of time during his earthly life, Jesus advanced in the task of mastering the human challenges we all face, all the while retaining his divinity. "Christ Michael did not progressively become God. God did not, at some vital moment in the earth life of Jesus, become man. Jesus was God *and* man—always and even forevermore. And this God and this man were, and are now, *one* even as the Paradise Trinity of three beings is in reality *one* Deity."[8] Thus "Urantia belongs to a local universe whose sovereign is the God-man of Nebadon, Jesus of Nazareth and Michael of Salvington."[9]

Jesus' Mission

There are important reasons why a Michael Son of God came to Earth, but being killed to atone for the sins of the human race was not one of them. "Jesus did not die to ransom man from the clutch of the apostate rulers and fallen princes of the spheres. The Father in heaven never conceived of such crass injustice as damning a mortal soul because of the evildoing of his ancestors. Neither was the Master's death on the cross a sacrifice which consisted in an effort to pay God a debt which the race of mankind had come to owe him."[10]

When Michael of Nebadon was planning his seventh and final bestowal as a being of his own creation, there were many planets in his realm that had been formally isolated due to their participation in the rebellion of Lucifer. He decided that part of his mission was to restore their spiritual status. "Never lose sight of the fact that the prime mission of Jesus in his seventh bestowal was the acquirement of creature experience, the achievement of the sovereignty of Nebadon. And in the gathering of this very experience he made the supreme revelation of the Paradise Father to Urantia and to his entire local universe. Incidental to these purposes he also undertook to untangle the complicated affairs of this planet as they were related to the Lucifer rebellion."[11]

There was long and deliberate preparation involved in this once-in-a-universe occurrence. From the thirty-seven planets involved in the rebellion, Michael chose Earth as the place to enact his final bestowal. Earth became the mortal bestowal planet of the Creator Son, who would be known as Jesus of Nazareth. The Hebrew race was selected as the bestowal race because it possessed the ". . . spiritual, intellectual, racial, and geographic . . ."[12] advantages relative to other human groups and locations at that time. From three equally favorable couples, Mary and Joseph were chosen to be the parents of the bestowal child. The final bestowal of Michael, here on planet Earth as Jesus, ushered in an age that was to be characterized by the pursuit of moral culture and spiritual truth.

Virgin Birth

The Christian doctrine of the virgin birth asserts that Jesus was conceived in the womb of his mother by the action of the Holy Spirit, without the participation of a human father. Despite the lack of scientific or historical evidence, and despite the doubts expressed by biblical scholars, the doctrine is widely accepted among Christians. A 2005 survey of *Church of England* members and clergy found that sixty-two percent of the laity and sixty percent of the clergy believe in the virgin birth of Jesus.[13] In the United States, according to the findings of a Harris poll conducted in November 2008, sixty-one percent of Americans believe that Jesus Christ was born of Mary, without a human father.[14]

As we explore the historical origin of this doctrine in light of epochal revelation, it may appear to contradict current Christian teachings about Jesus and Mary; however, objective discernment shows that it only eliminates superstition, corrects certain physical and cosmological information and assumptions, and expands the entire life and teachings of Jesus. The essential spiritual truths are found to remain the same.

Where did the doctrine of the virgin birth originate? Long before the Christian era, supernatural conception was a belief that explained the arrival of gods on Earth in human guise. It was also the characteristic method by which the divine origin of prophets and leaders was determined. Many ancient cultures worshiped "virgin mothers" and their divine children. According to epochal revelation, the practice of mother worship originated in Elam (Persia), with the descendants of Cain, who worshiped Eve as the Great Mother. "Images of Eve were everywhere. Thousands of public shrines were erected throughout Crete and Asia Minor. And this mother cult persisted on down to the times of Christ, becoming later incorporated in the early Christian religion under the guise of the glorification and worship of Mary the earth mother of Jesus."[15] Creative artifacts dating from as early as the Upper Paleolithic period (the era broadly dating between forty thousand and ten thousand years ago) offer confirmation on this point.

Professor Cesar Vidal, author of *The Myth of Mary*, writes: "The mother goddess received different names and external appearances, but, in substance, she was always the same. In Egypt, she was called Isis. In Crete, she was represented as a mother who made friendly contact with snakes. In Greece, she was known as Demeter, and in Rome she was worshiped as Cybele, the Magna Mater (Great Mother), a mother goddess of Phrygian origin. There is practically no ancient culture that did not worship this type of deity."[16]

While Christian theologians generally affirm that Jesus was both human and divine, many biblical scholars have long recognized that the glorification of Mary evolved with time to make the divine nature of Jesus more believable to the people. In the Bible, Mary is presented as a regular wife and mother who had no other children. The importance of the virginity of Mary took on a life of its own in postapostolic times. Initially, the early church taught that Mary was born without sin and was a virgin at the time of the conception of Jesus. By 392, Pope Siricius declared Mary a "perpetual virgin"—a virgin before, during, and after the birth of Jesus. By August 7, 1555, this threefold belief was affirmed by Pope Paul IV at the Council of Trent in the ecclesiastical constitution *Cum Quorundam*. This dogma was then reaffirmed in the twentieth century.

Neither Paul, in his letters to the Galatians, nor Mark and John in their gospels, mention the virgin birth. The story of the virgin birth only appears in the Gospels of Luke and Matthew. Epochal revelation clears any misunderstanding regarding the virginity of Mary. With these revelatory insights, the life of Jesus is expanded so that the true meaning of his life and message can emerge and be discovered by all humanity.

1. **Virgin conception—fact or myth?** "Joshua ben Joseph, the Jewish baby, was conceived and was born into the world just as all other babies before and since *except* that this particular baby was the incarnation of Michael of Nebadon, a divine Son of Paradise and the creator of all this local universe of things and beings. And this mystery of the incarnation

of Deity within the human form of Jesus, otherwise of natural origin on the world, will forever remain unsolved. Even in eternity you will never know the technique and method of the incarnation of the Creator in the form and likeness of his creatures."[17]

2. **Mary and Joseph**: Contrary to current teachings, Mary and Joseph had been married for months before the conception of Jesus and the visit from Gabriel. "It was late in the month of June, 8 B.C., about three months after the marriage of Joseph and Mary, that Gabriel appeared to Elizabeth at noontide one day, just as he later made his presence known to Mary."[18]

3. **Announcement to Mary**: "Gabriel appeared to Mary about the middle of November, 8 B.C., . . ."[19] "Gabriel's announcement to Mary was made the day following the conception of Jesus and was the only event of supernatural occurrence connected with her entire experience of carrying and bearing the child of promise."[20] In his announcement, Gabriel made no mention of the house of David nor did he intimate that Jesus was to be a "deliverer of the Jews" or that he was to be the long-expected Messiah. His words to Mary were: "I come at the bidding of one who is my Master and whom you shall love and nurture. To you, Mary, I bring glad tidings when I announce that the conception within you is ordained by heaven, and that in due time you will become the mother of a son; you shall call him Joshua, and he shall inaugurate the kingdom of heaven on earth and among men. Speak not of this matter save to Joseph and to Elizabeth, your kinswoman, to whom I have also appeared, and who shall presently also bear a son, whose name shall be John, and who will prepare the way for the message of deliverance which your son shall proclaim to men with great power and deep conviction. And doubt not my word, Mary, for this home has been chosen as the mortal habitat of the child of destiny. My benediction rests upon you, the power of the Most Highs will strengthen you, and the Lord of all the earth shall overshadow you."[21] Mary waited for weeks until she was certain that she was pregnant before disclosing the events to her husband, Joseph.

4. **Announcement to Joseph**: Joseph found it difficult to believe the events disclosed by Mary—until he had a memorable dream. "In this dream a brilliant celestial messenger appeared to him and, among other things, said: 'Joseph, I appear by command of Him who now reigns on high, and I am directed to instruct you concerning the son whom Mary shall bear, and who shall become a great light in the world. In him will be life, and his life shall become the light of mankind. He shall first come to his own people, but they will hardly receive him; but to as many as shall receive him to them will he reveal that they are the children of God.' After this experience Joseph never again wholly doubted Mary's story of Gabriel's visit and of the promise that the unborn child was to become a divine messenger to the world."[22]

5. **Brothers and sisters**: According to epochal revelation, Mary and Joseph had nine children—six sons and three daughters—with Jesus being the eldest. Joseph never saw his last child. He died (September 25, AD 8) before his youngest daughter, Ruth, was born (April 17, AD 9).[23]

6. **Mary's death**: "After the Passover, Mary returned to Bethsaida, where she lived at John's home for the rest of her natural life. Mary did not live quite one year after the death of Jesus."[24]

The doctrine of the virgin birth underestimates the Father's power to bestow divinity through the natural process of conception and birth. It undermines the significance to humanity of the fact that Jesus was a human *and* a divine being functioning on Earth as a single personality. Jesus was indeed a Son of Man and a Son of God, a human being who attained his full spirit potential in human experience, revealing to all of humanity the personality of God. His human life serves as an inspirational and spiritual ideal to humankind. "The Son of Man was a splendidly unified human personality; he was a perfectly endowed divine being; he was also magnificently coordinated as a combined human and divine being functioning on earth as a single personality. Always did the Master coordinate the faith of the soul with the wisdom-appraisals of seasoned experience. Personal faith, spiritual hope, and moral devotion were always correlated in a matchless religious unity of harmonious association with the keen realization of the reality and sacredness of all human loyalties—personal honor, family love, religious obligation, social duty, and economic necessity."[25] The myth of a miraculous conception may inspire awe, but modern minds understand his majestic unity.

Birth Date

According to the *Catholic Encyclopedia*, Jesus' exact birth date is unknown and there is no reference to his birth date in the Gospels. Most scholars have accepted the theory that the celebrated birthday of Jesus on December 25 was given ". . . because on this day, as the sun began its return to northern skies, the pagan devotees of Mithra celebrated the *dies natalis Solis Invicti* (birthday of the invincible sun). On Dec. 25, 274, [Roman Emperor] Aurelian had proclaimed the sun god principal patron of the empire and dedicated a temple to him . . ."[26]

At that time, Christians were still being persecuted by the Roman authorities, although Christianity was blossoming throughout the Roman Empire. Pagans and pagan converts to Christianity celebrated December 25. Christian worship incorporated the deep traditions of Mithraism to gain widespread support, and by the end of the fourth century the mystery cult succumbed to Christianity. In AD 529, Emperor Justinian declared Christmas a civic holiday; but December 25 was neither the *day* nor *month* of Jesus' birth.

The year Jesus was born has been extensively analyzed. In AD 525, the monk Dionysius Exiguus abandoned the pagan calendar to start a new one using the data he had available, including the Gospel of Luke (3:1 and 3:23). He calculated the probable year of the birth of Jesus as year 1; this erroneous method of dating the year is universally adopted today. The passage of time and the reconciliation of various biblical events with historical records and scientific facts has brought greater accuracy, repeatedly pointing to 6 or 7 BC as the most probable year for the birth of Jesus.

The Gospel of Luke chapter one places the announcement of the birth of John the Baptist ". . . in the days of Herod, the king of Judea." There is scholarly consensus based on the Jewish historian Josephus' *Antiquities of the Jews* that Herod died in the early months of 4 BC.[27] Therefore Jesus would have been born prior to 4 BC.

Similarly, according to Luke 2:1–5, Joseph and Mary went to Bethlehem to be registered for a census when "Cyrenius was governor of Syria" during the reign of "Caesar Augustus." Josephus recorded that Quirinius (in Greek, Cyrenius) was governor of Syria and conducted a tax census (*Ant.* XVII, xiii, 5, and XVIII, i, 1) which is said to have occurred in 6 or 7 AD.[28] This date poses a problem when assigning to Jesus a birth prior to 4 BC. "In 1912, however, the discovery by W. M. Ramsay of a fragmentary inscription at Antioch of Pisidia arguably established that Quirinius was in Syria on a previous occasion. (1) His role was more military to lead a campaign against the Homanadenses, a tribe in the Taurus Mountains. This is confirmed by Tacitus. This means that Quirinius would have established a seat of government in Syria, including Palestine, from the years 10 to 7 BCE. In this position he would have been responsible for the census mentioned by Luke. This census of 7 BCE would therefore have been the 'first' census taken when Cyrenius was governor (Luke 2:2) and the historically documented census [by Josephus] of 6/7 CE was really the second."[29]

Epochal revelation clarifies: "In the month of March, 8 B.C. (the month Joseph and Mary were married), Caesar Augustus decreed that all inhabitants of the Roman Empire should be numbered, that a census should be made which could be used for effecting better taxation. The Jews had always been greatly prejudiced against any attempt to 'number the people,' and this, in connection with the serious domestic difficulties of Herod, King of Judea, had conspired to cause the postponement of the taking of this census in the Jewish kingdom for one year. Throughout all the Roman Empire this census was registered in the year 8 B.C., except in the Palestinian kingdom of Herod, where it was taken in 7 B.C., one year later."[30]

The Urantia Book states that on August 19, 7 BC, Mary and Joseph left the city of Judah and traveled to Bethlehem to enroll in the census decreed by Caesar Augustus. They arrived in Bethlehem on August 20. On August 21 at noon, 7 BC, Michael of Nebadon, Creator Son and ruler of our local universe, was born as Jesus of Nazareth in Bethlehem, Palestine. All of this clarification in no way diminishes the stature of Jesus. In the sifting of ancient accounts with new information, we affirm his divinity while reconciling the fanciful stories of a distant era.

The Star of Bethlehem

The Star of Bethlehem has been a source of particular interest in scientific attempts to set the timing of Jesus' birth. Astronomers have included supernovae, comets, and planets in their search for the bright star in the East that dominated the heavens that year. In the early seventeenth century, the German mathematician, astronomer, and astrologer Johannes Kepler observed a triple conjunction of Saturn and Jupiter and calculated that a similar event happened in 7 BC. In the twentieth century, British astronomer David Hughes suggested in *The Star of Bethlehem* (Walker and Co., New York, 1979), that Kepler's theory might explain the Star of Bethlehem, particularly as it happened in the constellation of Pisces often associated with the Jews.

The Saturn/Jupiter triple conjunction theory, it turns out, is a factor in reconciling the heavenly events to biblical accounts of a "star" that led the three wise men to Bethlehem. Epochal revelation sheds light on how the "star in the east" (cf. Matthew 2:2) and astronomical history are related: "Jesus was born August 21 at noon, 7 B.C. On May 29, 7 B.C., there occurred an extraordinary conjunction of Jupiter and Saturn in the constellation of Pisces. And it is a remarkable astronomic fact that similar conjunctions occurred on September 29 and December 5 of the same year. Upon the basis of these extraordinary but wholly natural events the well-meaning zealots of the succeeding generation constructed the appealing legend of the star of Bethlehem and the adoring Magi led thereby to the manger, where they beheld and worshiped the newborn babe . . . In the absence of printing, when most human knowledge was passed by word of mouth from one generation to another, it was very easy for myths to become traditions and for traditions eventually to become accepted as facts."[31] Note: This particular astronomic statement was published in *The Urantia Book* long before computer modeling software had confirmed these planetary movements.

The Magi

It is generally accepted that the three visitors to the infant Jesus were magi, men who used their astrological knowledge to lead them to the predicted king in the Land of Israel. In separating fact from myth, epochal revelation explains that the magi were priests searching for the newborn "light of life" and not for the new "King of the Jews." It also makes clear that they reached the babe not because they were led by a star but rather because they were given directions by a human envoy. "These wise men saw no star to guide them to Bethlehem."[32] "No shepherds nor any other mortal creatures came to pay homage to the babe of Bethlehem until the day of the arrival of certain priests from Ur, who were sent down from Jerusalem by Zacharias [the father of John the Baptist]. These priests from Mesopotamia had been told sometime before by a strange religious teacher of their country that he had had a dream in which he was informed that 'the light of life' was about to appear on earth as a babe and among the Jews. And thither went these three teachers looking for this 'light of life.' After many weeks of futile search in Jerusalem, they were about to return to Ur when Zacharias met them and disclosed his belief that Jesus was the object of their quest and sent them on to Bethlehem, where they found the babe and left their gifts with Mary, his earth mother. The babe was almost three weeks old at the time of their visit."[33] Thus the charming legend retains its inspirational power— we have only to acknowledge minor discrepancies in the tale.

Massacre of the Innocents

The Gospel of Matthew 2:16–18 attests to the massacre of male children two years old and under ordered by Herod to avoid the loss of his throne to a newborn "King of the Jews," whose birth had been related to him by the magi. This episode of infanticide is not mentioned in other gospels nor in most of the early accounts of the time. As a result, many scholars do not consider this and other nativity stories as historical fact.

Epochal revelation confirms and clarifies the massacre. Herod was informed of the priests of Ur's visit to Bethlehem. Aware of the Jewish prophecies about a Messiah who would arrive in the future, he summoned a meeting with these priests but was unsatisfied with their answers to his questions about the new "King of the Jews." He instructed them to look for the child so that he too could worship him. The wise men sensed the real motive of Herod and did not return. Herod grew more suspicious when told by his informants of Jesus' presentation at the Temple, where a song identifying him as the Messiah had been sung by Simeon, a Judean singer (cf. Luke 2:22–40). Zacharias had confided in Simeon and Anna, the Galilean poetess who wrote the song, that Jesus was the expected deliverer of the Jewish people, and informed them of the upcoming Temple visit.

Herod immediately organized a search for Jesus that lasted more than a year. Unable to find him and apprehensive that the baby was still hidden in Bethlehem, Herod ordered that all male babies under the age of two be killed.

How did Jesus escape? Luke 2:39 reports that after the birth of Jesus, the family went to Nazareth, while in Matthew 2:14, we are told that the family went to Egypt. Epochal revelation clears up this scriptural dilemma and explains the escape: "The massacre of these infants took place about the middle of October, 6 B.C., when Jesus was a little over one year of age. But there were believers in the coming Messiah even among Herod's court attachés, and one of these, learning of the order to slaughter the Bethlehem boy babies, communicated with Zacharias, who in turn dispatched a messenger to Joseph; and the night before the massacre Joseph and Mary departed from Bethlehem with the babe for Alexandria in Egypt. In order to avoid attracting attention, they journeyed alone to Egypt with Jesus. They went to Alexandria on funds provided by Zacharias, and there Joseph worked at his trade while Mary and Jesus lodged with well-to-do relatives of Joseph's family. They sojourned in Alexandria two full years, not returning to Bethlehem until after the death of Herod [in 4 BC]."[34]

The Title "Son of Man"

During his fifteenth year, Jesus formulated the prayer he subsequently taught to his apostles and which has become known as The Lord's Prayer. The prayer originated in Jesus' desire to teach his siblings, after the death of his father, how to express themselves individually in prayer.

At age fifteen, Jesus was well aware of his mission on Earth as a world teacher; he was unsure what to call himself or what claim he should make concerning his mission. He wondered how he would be called by the people who would become believers in his teachings. "While turning all these problems over in his mind, he found in the synagogue library at Nazareth, among the apocalyptic books which he had been studying, this manuscript called 'The Book of Enoch'; and though he was certain that it had not been written by Enoch of old, it proved very intriguing to him, and he read and reread it many times. There was one passage which particularly impressed him, a passage in which this term 'Son of Man' appeared. The writer of this so-called Book of Enoch went on to tell about this Son of Man, describing the work he would do on earth and explaining that this Son of Man, before coming down on this earth to bring salvation to mankind, had walked through the courts of heavenly glory with his Father, the Father of all; and that he had turned his back upon all this grandeur and glory to come down on earth to proclaim salvation to needy mortals. As Jesus would read these passages (well understanding that much of the Eastern mysticism which had become admixed with these teachings was erroneous), he responded in his heart and recognized in his mind that of all the Messianic predictions of the Hebrew Scriptures and of all the theories about the Jewish deliverer, none was so near the truth as this story tucked away in this only partially accredited Book of Enoch; and he then and there decided to adopt as his inaugural title 'the Son of Man.' And this he did when he subsequently began his public work. Jesus had an unerring ability for the recognition of truth, and truth he never hesitated to embrace, no matter from what source it appeared to emanate."[35]

The Messiah

The Old Testament is the main source of prophecy foretelling the coming of a messiah, the expected deliverer of the Jews, with the writers of the New Testament attempting to record its fulfillment. "Most of the so-called Messianic prophecies of the Old Testament were made to apply to Jesus long after his life had been lived on earth. For centuries the Hebrew prophets had proclaimed the coming of a deliverer, and these promises had been construed by successive generations as referring to a new Jewish ruler who would sit upon the throne of David and, by the reputed miraculous methods of Moses, proceed to establish the Jews in Palestine as a powerful nation, free from all foreign domination. Again, many figurative passages found throughout the Hebrew scriptures were subsequently misapplied to the life mission of Jesus. Many Old Testament sayings were so distorted as to appear to fit some episode of the Master's earth life. Jesus himself onetime publicly denied any connection with the royal house of David . . . The early followers of Jesus all too often succumbed to the temptation to make all the olden prophetic utterances appear to find fulfillment in the life of their Lord and Master."[36]

For almost two thousand years these human documents have had a twofold effect: (1) The truth in the documents has guided the course of history and been an inspiration in the lives of the faithful and (2) the inaccuracies in the documents have been a source of great dissension. Now it is possible to clarify these records so that religious thought and historical study may rise above the controversy generated by them.

According to epochal revelation, the Israelites had been taught by their leaders that they were the people chosen to carry the truth of the one God to every nation. They were also promised that if they fulfilled this destiny, they would become the spiritual leaders of all people, and that the coming Messiah would reign over them and the entire world as the Prince of Peace. To many Jews, the Messiah would be the new king in Palestine, a successor of King David, who would regenerate the Jewish nation and deliver it from its enemies. The Jewish Messiah would quickly be acknowledged as the rightful and righteous ruler of the entire world.

The authentic Messiah, however, was to be much more than the deliverer of the Jews or the Savior of those who believed in him. The Messiah was to be the deliverer of the world; his mission was to all races and peoples, not to any one group. He was also the revelation of the union of both the human and divine natures. "There was one feature of the bestowal of Michael which was utterly foreign to the Jewish conception of the Messiah, and that was the *union* of the two natures, the human and the divine. The Jews had variously conceived of the Messiah as perfected human, superhuman, and even as divine, but they never entertained the concept of the *union* of the human and the divine. And this was the great stumbling block of Jesus' early disciples. They grasped the human concept of the Messiah as the son of David, as presented by the earlier prophets; as the Son of Man, the superhuman idea of Daniel and some of the later prophets; and even as the Son of God, as depicted by the author of the Book of Enoch and by certain of his contemporaries; but never had they for a single moment entertained the true concept of the union in one earth personality of the two natures, the human and the divine. The incarnation of the Creator in the form of the creature had not been revealed beforehand. It was revealed only in Jesus; the world knew nothing of such things until the Creator Son was made flesh and dwelt among the mortals of the realm."[37]

According to epochal revelation, the one and only direct, positive, and undisguised pronouncement by Jesus of Nazareth that he was the Messiah was made to the woman from Sychar recorded in John 4:1–26: "The woman saith unto Him, I know that Messias cometh, which is called Christ; when He is come, He will tell us all things . . . Jesus saith unto her, I that speak unto thee am He."

The Title "Prince of Peace"

To the Jews in Palestine, the coming Messiah was to reign over the entire world as the Prince of Peace (Isaiah 9:6). Later, followers of Jesus saw in him the fulfillment of Isaiah's prophecy and called Jesus the "Prince of Peace."

With a title such as the Prince of Peace, questions arise as to what Jesus meant when he said during the Sermon on the Mount (cf. Mathew 10:34): "Think not that I am come to send peace on earth: I came not to send peace, but a sword." And in the gospel of Thomas, "Men think, perhaps, that it is peace which I have come to cast upon the world. They do not know that it is dissension which I have come to cast upon the earth: fire, sword, and war. For there will be five in a house: three will be against two, and two against three, the father against the son, and the son against the father. And they will stand solitary."[38]

Not surprising, the words of Jesus in Luke 12:49 have been used to equate Jesus to Lucifer: "I am come to send fire on the earth; and what will I, if it be already kindled?" To understand these words, which appear to conflict with the message of love that Jesus professed, one must understand the context in which they were said. Epochal revelation provides clarification:

When a bestowal Son arrives on a planet, angels announce his arrival with the message "Glory to God in the highest, and on earth peace, good will toward men." (cf. Luke 2:10–14). On normal worlds, the arrival of a bestowal Son starts a dispensation during which nations no longer participate in war and enjoy worldwide peace. Therefore a bestowal Son is generally referred to as a Prince of Peace.

On Earth, the planetary rebellion and the consequent spiritual isolation ensured that progress did not proceed in the normal sequence. The usual peace influence that follows a bestowal Son's arrival on a planet was, therefore, not present when Michael of Nebadon (as Jesus of Nazareth) lived on Earth.

Jesus warned the disciples that his advent would not bring the usual reign of peace that the arrival of a bestowal Son usually presaged. He distinctly told them that there would be "wars and rumours of wars" and that "nation shall rise against nation" (cf. Matthew 24:6–8). He emphasized his point during the Sermon on the Mount. Jesus knew that humanity would have to develop a greater capacity to love and pass through many tribulations before achieving worldwide peace.

The Missing Years

The Bible has an eighteen-year gap in the account of the life of Jesus. Much speculation has arisen as to what he did during those missing years. Epochal revelation tells us that Jesus spent his childhood and early adolescent years in a normal family environment, growing and learning about life. But Joseph died when he was fourteen and Jesus became the breadwinner of the family, working as a carpenter and taking on the role of father for his brothers and sisters. After his eldest brother James was mature enough to take over his responsibilities, Jesus began a series of work and travel adventures both near and far from his Nazareth home. During most of his twenty-eighth year and the whole of his twenty-nineth year, Jesus traveled the Roman Empire with an Indian merchant and his son. After this Mediterranean tour, he conducted a camel caravan to the Caspian Sea region. Throughout this period, he ministered truth to many souls on a personal level and prepared the way for a better reception of his future apostles' message.

The Concept of "the Kingdom"

The Melchizedek teaching about the coming of a Son of God became distorted with the passage of time. About one hundred years before the days of Jesus and John the Baptist, this prophecy became associated with the establishment of an earthly kingdom of God. The Hebrew prophets presented this kingdom both as a present reality and later as a future fulfillment that would occur with the appearance of the Messiah and after the destruction of unbelievers. This was the kingdom concept that John the Baptist taught and that Jesus of Nazareth tried to modify in conveying the father–child relationship between God and every individual. "To the Jews of Palestine the phrase "kingdom of heaven" had but one meaning: an absolutely righteous state in which God (the Messiah) would rule the nations of earth in perfection of power just as he ruled in heaven . . ."[39]

In the New Testament, the kingdom of God is sometimes referred to as a future event, while at other times as an ongoing one. The confusion about the meaning of the kingdom was compounded when Christianity became a religion centered on Jesus; the gospel of the kingdom became more and more about *Jesus* than about his unparalleled teachings. The Jewish idea of a future earthly kingdom became supplanted by the Christian concept of Jesus as king upon his return to Earth.

To capture the true essence of Jesus' gospel of the kingdom, we can seek clarification of the kingdom concept by turning to epochal revelation. Although Jesus appears to be presenting numerous concepts of the "kingdom" in the New Testament, they can be incorporated into the two phases of the kingdom that Jesus portrayed:

1. The kingdom of God in this world represents the personal realization of the spiritual brotherhood of the sons and daughters of God on Earth; the establishment of the brotherhood of man through every individual's commitment to doing the will of the Father—becoming Godlike.

2. The kingdom of God in heaven is the vast expanse traversed by the ascending personality on its journey to Paradise. It represents ". . . the goal of believers, the estate wherein the love for God is perfected, and wherein the will of God is done more divinely."[40]

The Kingdom of God in This World

To enter the kingdom of God in this world is to believe in God as Father of all, and yourself as a son or daughter of God. Belief in Jesus is not a prerequisite to enter the kingdom. "Jesus does not require his disciples to believe in him but rather to believe *with* him, believe in the reality of the love of God and in full confidence accept the security of the assurance of sonship with the heavenly Father. The Master desires that all his followers should fully share his transcendent faith. Jesus most touchingly challenged his followers, not only to believe *what* he believed, but also to believe *as* he believed. This is the full significance of his one supreme requirement, 'Follow me.'"[41]

"To Jesus the kingdom was the sum of those *individuals* who had confessed their faith in the fatherhood of God, thereby declaring their wholehearted dedication to the doing of the will of God, thus becoming members of the spiritual brotherhood of man."[42] In an attempt to impart this understanding, Jesus tried to substitute many terms for "the kingdom" that would more accurately portray his message about the relationship between God and mortals. "Jesus often spoke of it as the 'kingdom of life.' He also frequently referred to "the kingdom of God within you." He once spoke of such an experience as 'family fellowship with God the Father' . . . Among others, he used: the family of God, the Father's will, the friends of God, the fellowship of believers, the brotherhood of man, the Father's fold, the children of God, the fellowship of the faithful, the Father's service, and the liberated sons of God."[43] Jesus, however, could not escape the use of the word "kingdom." Resigning himself to using the term "kingdom of heaven" (which he used interchangeably with the expression "kingdom of God"), Jesus explained to his disciples that the kingdom of God in this world is not an earthly kingdom but an individual's *inner experience* centered in the dual concept of the father-child relationship between God and mortals. This dual concept was to set a new standard of moral values and provide the ideal of a new order of human society.

To enter this spiritual kingdom, Jesus taught, there are three essentials: The first is the recognition of the sovereignty/fatherhood of God. The second is the belief in the truth of sonship with God. A third essential is the desire to do the will of God. Once these essentials are in place, to do the will of God requires the development of an unshakable growing attitude of loyalty to God and cultivation of the qualities of divinity to live the golden rule from its highest level of interpretation. "Though Jesus taught that faith, simple childlike belief, is the key to the door of the kingdom, he also taught that, having entered the door, there are the progressive steps of righteousness which every believing child must ascend in order to grow up to the full stature of the robust sons of God."[44] Living in the kingdom while on Earth is, therefore, living a life of growing faith, consciously choosing to be Godlike, and striving toward the highest expression of love, truth, beauty, and goodness.

This understanding of the kingdom became hazy as the Christian church was organized. Jesus' ideals of a brotherhood based on the father–child relationship between God and every individual with faith as its only admittance requirement, was replaced with a social fellowship between a group of believers in Jesus—the church. As the early organizers made Christ the head of the church rather than the elder brother of each individual believer in the Father's family, ". . . they struck a deathblow to Jesus' concept of the divine kingdom in the heart of the individual believer."[45] Membership in the church must, therefore, not be considered synonymous with fellowship in the kingdom; one is spiritual, the other mostly social.

Misconceptions about the Kingdom and the Second Coming of Christ

As the church grew, it strayed from the spiritual concept of the kingdom as Jesus taught and lived it. Not only did its meaning and structure change, but the spiritual kingdom in the hearts of all people was set into the future, associated with the Second Coming of Christ and even with the end of the world. Epochal revelation explains how these three misconceptions came about:

1. **Projection of the kingdom into the future**: "When Jesus' immediate followers recognized their partial failure to realize his ideal of the establishment of the kingdom in the hearts of men by the spirit's

domination and guidance of the individual believer, they set about to save his teaching from being wholly lost by substituting for the Master's ideal of the kingdom the gradual creation of a visible social organization, the Christian church. And when they had accomplished this program of substitution, in order to maintain consistency and to provide for the recognition of the Master's teaching regarding the fact of the kingdom, they proceeded to set the kingdom off into the future. The church, just as soon as it was well established, began to teach that the kingdom was in reality to appear at the culmination of the Christian age, at the second coming of Christ."[46]

2. **The Second Coming of Jesus**: The Christian doctrine of the Second Coming of Christ was incorporated early into their teachings. Despite Jesus' warning to his apostles that no one knows when he will come again (cf. Mark 13:32–33), the past two thousand years have seen never-ending speculation—mostly interpretation of current events based on cryptic verses in the Book of Revelation.

   According to *The Urantia Book*, Jesus made two promises. "He promised a new revelation of the kingdom on earth and at some future time; he also promised sometime to come back to this world in person; but he did not say that these two events were synonymous."[47] By "a new revelation of the kingdom on earth," Jesus was probably referring to the next dispensation of knowledge following his, which may or may not usher in a new planetary epoch; his second coming is not necessarily linked to that future dispensation.

   The revelations explain how this misconception came about: "His apostles and disciples most certainly linked these two teachings together. When the kingdom failed to materialize as they had expected, recalling the Master's teaching concerning a future kingdom and remembering his promise to come again, they jumped to the conclusion that these promises referred to an identical event; and therefore they lived in hope of his immediate second coming to establish the kingdom in its fullness and with power and glory."[48] This inspiring but disappointing hope became the concept of an age, the idea of a future visitation, and the ideal of the final redemption.

   Jesus' promise to come again *will* be fulfilled, but the exact time is not revealed. However, prior to his coming, humanity must have attained a unity in the ideal of the fatherhood of God and be *living* the brotherhood of man. Epochal revelation explains: ". . . the times of the reappearing of the Son of Man are known only in the councils of Paradise; not even the angels of heaven know when this will occur."[49]

3. **Second Coming linked with the end of the world**. The concept of the end of the world linked with the Second Coming of Christ originated out of the apostles' inability to understand Jesus' explanation of the coming destruction of the Holy Temple in Jerusalem, along with their stubbornness in holding to their mistaken beliefs. To the apostles, no event short of the end of the world could occasion the destruction of the Temple.

When Jesus and his disciples were one day observing and commenting on the structure of the Temple, Jesus predicted: "In the days soon to come there shall not be left one stone upon another."[50] As he responded to the concerns of the apostles, Jesus pondered over the reason for such destruction: "The Master realized that the rejection of the spiritual concept of the Messiah, the determination to cling persistently and blindly to the material mission of the expected deliverer, would presently bring the Jews in direct conflict with the powerful Roman armies, and that such a contest could only result in the final and complete overthrow of the Jewish nation. When his people rejected his spiritual bestowal and refused to receive the light of heaven as it so mercifully shone upon them, they thereby sealed their doom as an independent people with a special spiritual mission on earth. Even the Jewish leaders subsequently recognized that it was this secular idea of the Messiah which directly led to the turbulence which eventually brought about their destruction."[51]

Knowing that Jerusalem was to become the cradle of the early gospel movement, Jesus did not want its teachers and preachers to perish in the overthrow of the Jewish people in connection with the destruction of Jerusalem. He urged his disciples to avoid the great tribulation by fleeing Jerusalem when the Roman armies arrived.

"As his followers awakened to the fact that their Master was not going to function as a temporal deliverer, and as they listened to his predictions of the overthrow of Jerusalem and the downfall of the Jewish nation, they most naturally began to associate his promised return with these catastrophic events. But when the Roman armies leveled the walls of Jerusalem, destroyed the temple, and dispersed the Judean Jews, and still the Master did not reveal himself in power and glory, his followers began the formulation of that belief which eventually associated the second coming of Christ with the end of the age, even with the end of the world."[52]

Many of Jesus' followers interpreted these predictions as referring to the changes that would occur when the expected Messiah established the New Jerusalem. In their minds, the Jews were determined to connect the destruction of the Temple with the end of the world. Believing that the end of the world would be followed by the immediate appearance of the new heavens and the new Earth—the coming of the Messiah—they attached a new teaching to an old one; both contained misunderstandings.

Thus there was little agreement between the subsequent written accounts, based on memories of what Jesus had said. Much was left blank on the records. This opened the door to confusion for future generations. ". . . very early in the second century a Jewish apocalyptic about the Messiah written by one Selta, who was attached to the court of the Emperor Caligula, was bodily copied into the Matthew Gospel [24–25] and subsequently added (in part) to the Mark [13] and Luke [17] records. It was in these writings of Selta that the parable of the ten virgins appeared. No part of the gospel record ever suffered such confusing misconstruction . . ."[53] The parable of the ten virgins became mistakenly associated with the return of Jesus Christ and survival of the Great Tribulation.

The Great Temptation (AD 25)

The unsuccessful assault of Satan and Caligastia upon the Son of Man (cf. Matthew 4:1–11) during his six-week sojourn on the slopes of Mount Hermon marked the termination of the Lucifer rebellion. Epochal revelation documents this event as having occurred some months before Jesus' baptism. The forty days of isolation after his baptism marked the beginning of the more divine phase of his bestowal.

The Urantia Book describes and clarifies the misconceptions surrounding the great temptation: "During the last week on Mount Hermon the great temptation, the universe trial, occurred. Satan (representing Lucifer) and the rebellious Planetary Prince, Caligastia, were present with Jesus and were made fully visible to him. And this 'temptation,' this final trial of human loyalty in the face of the misrepresentations of rebel personalities, had not to do with food, temple pinnacles, or presumptuous acts. It had not to do with the kingdoms of this world but with the sovereignty of a mighty and glorious universe. The symbolism of your records was intended for the backward ages of the world's childlike thought. And subsequent generations should understand what a great struggle the Son of Man passed through that eventful day on Mount Hermon."[54]

The words from Jesus, "Get thee hence, Satan" (Matthew 4:10) signaled the real end of the Lucifer rebellion, with final adjudication of the rebels resting with the tribunals of the superuniverse government. On Mount Hermon, Jesus removed Caligastia as the prince of this world and, on the universe records, Jesus of Nazareth became the Planetary Prince of Urantia.

Caligastia was recognized by Jesus of Nazareth as the technical sovereign of Earth almost until the time of the Master's death, as indicated in his words: "Now is the judgment of this world; now shall the prince of this world be cast out." (John 12:31). And then still nearer the completion of his lifework he announced: ". . . the prince of this world is judged" (John 16:11). It is indeed this same dethroned and discredited Prince—Caligastia–who was once termed "the god of this world." (2 Corinthians 4:4).

The Baptism (AD 26)

Jesus was baptized in AD 26 at the age of thirty-one and a half, the same year that Pontius Pilate became governor of Judea and John the Baptist was preaching his message "the kingdom of God is at hand" to hopeful crowds.

The baptismal ceremony was the final act of Jesus' strictly human life. He had attained the pinnacle of human development in matters relating to the mastery of mind and self-identification with the Indwelling Spirit. "The divine Son has found his Father, the Universal Father has found his incarnated Son, and they speak the one to the other."[55] Jesus accepted baptism at the hands of John just as many pious Israelites had done before him. In no sense did he receive baptism as a rite of repentance or for the remission of sins. "His was the baptism of consecration to the performance of the will of the heavenly Father."[56]

Normally, when a human being attains such high levels of personality perfection, the soul and the Indwelling Spirit fuse to become as one. In the case of Jesus, something unexpected happened. As John baptized him, Jesus' Indwelling Spirit departed, only to return moments later and speak on behalf of the Universal Father those words that have been immortalized in the Bible: "This is my beloved Son in whom I am well pleased." John and Jesus' two brothers heard these words, but only Jesus beheld the apparition of the Spirit. As Jesus looked up, praying, the "heavens were opened" and he saw a vision of himself as he was before he had come to Earth, a Son of God.[57]

At the time of his baptism, Christ Michael achieved sovereignty of his universe. Though he could have ended his bestowal mission at that time, he chose to continue with his revelation of the Father to humanity, leading mortals to become conscious of themselves as children of God.

The Forty Days after His Baptism

After his baptism, Jesus retreated to the mountain wilderness of the Perean hills to formulate plans for the remainder of his bestowal and to determine a method of proclaiming the new kingdom of God in the people's hearts. He was now fully aware of himself as the sovereign of his universe and had to decide how to conduct his world ministry. There were two ways he could do this:

"1. His own way—the way that might seem most pleasant and profitable from the standpoint of the immediate needs of this world and the present edification of his own universe.

2. The Father's way—the exemplification of a farseeing ideal of creature life visualized by the high personalities of the Paradise administration of the universe of universes."[58]

Should he conduct his world ministry as Creator Son of God using his creator prerogatives, or as the Son of Man, a mortal man doing his Father's will? These forty days marked the beginning of the more divine phase of Jesus' bestowal; it was the period of six great decisions:

1. Jesus had been granted a vision of the twelve legions of seraphim and other orders of universe intelligence at his disposal. Should he make use of these mighty personalities during his public work on Earth? Jesus' first decision was to not utilize a single celestial personality to assist him in his mission unless it should become evident that this was his Father's will.

2. Jesus' second great decision addressed his personal needs. Three days of meditation made him hungry. "Should he go in quest of food as any

ordinary man would, or should he merely exercise his normal creative powers and produce suitable bodily nourishment ready at hand? And this great decision of the Master has been portrayed to you as a temptation—as a challenge by supposed enemies that he 'command that these stones become loaves of bread.'"[59] Jesus decided that he would pursue the path of normal earthly existence as far as his personal necessities were concerned and in general, even in his relations with other personalities. He would not deliberately transcend or violate his own established natural laws. However, he could not promise himself that these natural laws might not, in certain conceivable circumstances, be greatly accelerated.[60]

In accordance with his mission to instruct and inspire the creatures of his far-flung universe, he decided to not seek self-preservation; that his superhuman power might possibly be used for others, but not for himself. "This great decision of Jesus portrays dramatically the truth that selfish satisfaction and sensuous gratification, alone and of themselves, are not able to confer happiness upon evolving human beings. There are higher values in mortal existence—intellectual mastery and spiritual achievement—which far transcend the necessary gratification of man's purely physical appetites and urges. Man's natural endowment of talent and ability should be chiefly devoted to the development and ennoblement of his higher powers of mind and spirit."[61]

3. Jesus' third decision revolved around how he would react in the face of danger. Jesus decided that if confronted with personal danger, he would refrain from all superhuman intervention and refuse to defend himself. He would, however, exercise normal vigilance over his human safety and take reasonable precaution to prevent an untimely termination of his human career. Jesus knew his people were expecting a Messiah who would be above natural law. He also knew that while miracles would please the Jews seeking signs of the coming Messiah, miracles would not reveal his Father to his people.

4. The next decision that Jesus had to make was whether he should use his superhuman powers to attract the attention of others and win them over. Jesus generally decided against it. His task was to establish the kingdom of heaven and not to be a wonder-worker. The working of miracles would only call forth an outward allegiance and would not necessarily reveal God nor save anyone.

5. Jesus' next dilemma was how to continue the work that John the Baptist began and how best to organize his followers. Jesus could have inaugurated the spiritual kingdom "with a brilliant and dazzling display of power" as the Jews expected their deliverer to do. Although Jesus had the power to do it, he decided against it. "He had won the world in potential by submission to the Father's will, and he proposed to finish his work as he had begun it, and as the Son of Man."[62] He would quietly return to Galilee after his forty days in isolation to begin the proclamation of the kingdom and trust his Father through his associates to work out the details of procedure day by day.

6. Jesus' last declaration was that during his world ministry his will would be subject to the will of his Father in heaven.

The Relation of Jesus to Women

The twelve apostles of Jesus were surprised when one evening he proposed to admit women into the ministry. The apostles were even more stunned when he announced that the selected women would be traveling with them. Jesus required from his apostles equal treatment toward women, an attitude that perhaps was the most radical characteristic of his mission on Earth. "In a day and generation when a man was not supposed to salute even his own wife in a public place, Jesus dared to take women along as teachers of the gospel in connection with his third tour of Galilee. And he had the consummate courage to do this in the face of the rabbinic teaching which declared that it was 'better that the words of the law should be burned than delivered to women.'"[63]

The admittance of women as preachers received mixed reactions in the community. Jesus' enemies questioned his judgment while women believers everywhere ". . . stood staunchly behind their chosen sisters . . ."[64] Eight women were chosen first, and the last two, Mary Magdalene and Rebecca (the daughter of Joseph of Arimathea), were selected at a later date.

When Jesus departed from Earth, his apostles continued the practice of equality toward women, but with the passage of time old habits returned. "Throughout the early days of the Christian church women teachers and ministers were called deaconesses and were accorded general recognition. But Paul, despite the fact that he conceded all this in theory, never really incorporated it into his own attitude and personally found it difficult to carry out in practice."[65] According to epochal revelation, a planet is not considered to have emerged from barbarism so long as one sex seeks to tyrannize the other.

Much speculation has arisen about the relationship between Jesus and Mary Magdalene. In the New Testament, Mary Magdalene becomes a follower of Jesus after he rescues her from being stoned to death. The apocryphal Gospel of Mary Magdalene attests to the important role she played in early Christianity.

Epochal revelation clarifies that Mary Magdalene became a follower of Jesus, not as a result of Jesus rescuing her from being stoned to death, but rather because of the ministry of the ten women evangelists. "It was Martha and Rachel who made plain to Mary that the doors of the kingdom were open to even such as she."[66] The ten women had been allowed by Andrew to work with women of dubious character. As the party preached in areas of ill repute in the town of Magdala, they came across Mary, who eagerly welcomed the good news—knowing God as Father and self as a son or daughter of God. She was baptized by Peter the next day and became the most effective teacher of the gospel of Jesus and the public spokesperson of the women evangelists. This clarifying revelation in our religious history highlights Mary Magdalene's role in the early development of Christianity.

The Gospel according to John, also known as the Fourth Gospel, is yet another document that promotes speculation, with some claiming that Mary Magdalene is the disciple whom Jesus loved. According to epochal revelation, the First Epistle of John was written by the apostle John Zebedee as a cover letter for the work [the Gospel of John] that Nathan, a Greek Jew from Caesarea, executed under John's direction. John liked to refer to himself as "the disciple whom Jesus loved," especially as he got older. This was not surprising, considering that John had had a long association with Jesus and was probably the disciple most trusted by Jesus. "When this record was made, John had the other Gospels, and he saw that much had been omitted; accordingly, in the year A.D. 101, he encouraged his associate Nathan . . . to begin the writing."[67] John was ninety-nine years old.

Some modern writers speculate that Mary Magdalene was the wife of Jesus, citing noncanonical and Gnostic references to support their theories, and fueling the belief that Jesus sired a child with Mary Magdalene. *The Urantia Book* explains that while bestowal Sons are permitted to marry, ". . . the leaving of human offspring behind on any planet by a bestowal Son of Paradise origin . . ."[68] is strictly forbidden. Although Jesus was "tested in all points," he was ". . . too much occupied with the pressing problems of practical earthly affairs and the intriguing contemplation of his eventual career 'about his Father's business' ever to have given serious consideration to the consummation of personal love in human marriage."[69] When a young woman named Rebecca (not Mary Magdalene), the daughter of Ezra, professed her love for Jesus, "[h]e made it clear that his first and paramount duty was the rearing of his father's family . . ."[70] For many years, whenever the story of Jesus was told, the devotion of Rebecca was narrated and even confused with Mary Magdalene's devotion to Jesus.[71]

Miracles

While Christians profess that the divinity of Jesus is established by the miracles he performed, some biblical scholars question the authenticity of the miracles. Since the nineteenth century, scholars have examined the credibility of Jesus' life as depicted in the Gospels. Some argue that it is more rational to assume a scientific explanation or false reporting than it is to assume the existence of miraculous events. Others argue that miracles cannot be historically proven. The discovery of the apocryphal books in the middle of the twentieth century heralded a new period of biblical scholarship, especially concerning the New Testament.

In 1985, a group of theological scholars created The Jesus Seminar and set out to determine the degree of authenticity of Jesus' words and deeds. The result of their deliberations held ". . . that while the various cures for diseases are probably true, since there were many others in the ancient world credited with healing power, most of the other miracles of Jesus are unfactual, at least in their *literal* interpretation from the Bible."[72] Scholars particularly question the authenticity of the exorcisms carried out by Jesus, as well as Jesus walking on water. A study published in the *National Post* in April 2006 suggested that the miracle of Jesus walking on water could have been the result of a freak ice formation that is thought by climatologists to have occurred on the Sea of Galilee during that time.[73]

The light of epochal revelation dissolves the myths embedded within our scriptural religion and reconciles the scientific with the nonscientific perspectives.

According to *The Urantia Book*, the quest for miracles dates back to the primitive religion of magic. Nevertheless, "True religion has nothing to do with alleged miracles, and never does revealed religion point to miracles as proof of authority. Religion is ever and always rooted and grounded in personal experience. And your highest religion, the life of Jesus, was just such a personal experience: man, mortal man, seeking God and finding him to the fullness during one short life in the flesh, while in the same human experience there appeared God seeking man and finding him to the full satisfaction of the perfect soul of infinite supremacy."[74]

In the time of Jesus, there was widespread belief in miracles as commonplace occurrences. Jesus knew that the Jews expected a Messiah who would usher in an era of miraculous plenty. He nevertheless understood that the working of miracles would neither reveal God nor save mortals. Miracles would only impress the mind and create a superficial allegiance to him. After his baptism, when Jesus went into isolation in the Perean hills to determine a strategy for his public ministry, he resolved to live as a mortal. Only on specific occasions did Jesus exert his creator prerogatives and perform miracles, always appealing to his Father in heaven.

The New Testament reports the many miracles attributed to Jesus. Which are true miracles? What explanations may there be to explain some of the reported happenings? Revelations help to alleviate confusion from the reported events and shed light into the actual circumstances surrounding the so-called miracles of Jesus. Some clarifications are presented below:

1. **Nature Miracles**

   a. **Feeding the five thousand** AD 29 (cf. Matthew 14:13, Mark 6:30, and Luke 9:10): According to epochal revelation, ". . . this is the first and only nature miracle which Jesus performed as a result of his conscious preplanning."[75]

   b. **Walking on water** (cf. Matthew 14:25, Mark 6:48, and John 6:19): This famous event occurred only in Simon Peter's mind; it was a night vision he had during a stormy boat ride while Jesus was alone in the Perean hills. "To Peter this experience was always real. He sincerely believed that Jesus came to them that night. He only partially convinced John Mark, which explains why Mark left a portion of the story out of his narrative. Luke, the physician, who made careful search into these matters, concluded that the episode was a vision of Peter's and therefore refused to give place to this story in the preparation of his narrative."[76]

   c. **Turning water into wine** AD 26 (cf. John 2:1–11). This event demonstrates the deep affection of Jesus for his mother, but it was not a miracle in the strict definition of epochal revelation. It was an unintentional event that surprised even Jesus, having occurred as a result of his expressing to Mary his wish to help: "On this occasion power transformers, midwayers, and all other required personalities were assembled near the water and other necessary elements, and in the face of the expressed wish of the Universe Creator Sovereign, there was no escaping the instantaneous appearance of *wine*."[77]

d. **Draught of fish** AD 28 (cf. Luke 5:1): This is another event that was not miraculous, though it represented preknowledge on the part of Jesus: "Jesus was a close student of nature; he was an experienced fisherman and knew the habits of the fish in the Sea of Galilee. On this occasion he merely directed these men to the place where the fish were usually to be found at this time of day. But Jesus' followers always regarded this as a miracle."[78]

e. **Stilling the storm** AD 29 (cf. Matthew 8:23, Mark 4:35, Luke 8:22). This event was a case of coincidence that occurred when Jesus and his disciples were crossing the Sea of Galilee. Half way across the sea, their boats encountered high winds and the sail was torn from the boat that carried Jesus and Peter. When Jesus was awakened from sleep by a frightened Peter, Jesus questioned Peter's faith and told him to be at peace. Coincidentally, at almost that precise moment, the winds and waters calmed. ". . . but the apostles, particularly Simon Peter, never ceased to regard the episode as a nature miracle."[79]

2. **Resurrections**

a. **Lazarus** AD 30 (cf. John 11:43). The resurrection of Lazarus was Jesus' last effort to win the Jewish rulers on their own terms of the miraculous. He performed the greatest of all demonstrations of the divine power of the Son of Man—the resurrection of the dead. "When Jesus spoke those words of command, 'Take away the stone,' the assembled celestial hosts made ready to enact the drama of the resurrection of Lazarus in the likeness of his mortal flesh."[80] With this miracle, Jesus demonstrated that he was indeed "the resurrection and the life."

b. **The widow's son** AD 28 (cf. Luke 7:11–17). According to epochal revelation, this young man was not dead but in a prolonged comatose state. During the funeral procession, the miracle-minded mother requested Jesus to bring her son back to life. Though he tried to explain that her son was not dead, neither the mother nor the disciples believed Jesus. "Never was Jesus able to make even all his apostles fully understand that the widow's son was not really dead when he bade him awake and arise. But he did impress them sufficiently to keep it out of all subsequent records except that of Luke, who recorded it as the episode had been related to him."[81]

c. **The ruler's daughter** AD 29 (cf. Matthew 9:18, 23, Mark 5:22, 35, and Luke 8:40, 49). Like the widow's son, the ruler's daughter was comatose, not dead, when Jesus ". . . took her by the hand and said, 'Daughter, I say to you, awake and arise!'"[82] Jesus explained to the family and his apostles that the young girl had awakened from a coma, but to no avail. Everyone insisted that another miracle had been performed.

3. **Casting Out Demons**

a. **Casting out the unclean spirit** AD 29 (cf. Matthew 12:22–28, Luke 11:14–18). This was the first case of casting out devils—a case of an unstable mind possessed by a celestial rebel. Jesus performed this miracle in response to a challenge from a Pharisee and out of compassion for the young man. The pouring of the Spirit of Truth at Pentecost made it ". . . forever impossible for these few celestial rebels to take such advantage of certain unstable types of human beings."[83]

b. **The Kheresa lunatic** AD 29 (cf. Matthew 8:28–34, Mark 5:1–20, Luke 8:26–39). Amos, the man said to be possessed by demons, suffered from emotional problems. The words of assurance from Jesus enabled him to rise above his troubles. This event was a case of Amos responding to psychological treatment even though Amos and observers, including the men minding the herd of swine, considered it a miracle. The swine rushing over the cliff to their death was an incidental occurrence that was interpreted as a second miracle. "As the swine herders rushed into the village to spread the news of the taming of the lunatic, the dogs charged upon a small and untended herd of about thirty swine and drove most of them over a precipice into the sea. And it was this incidental occurrence, in connection with the presence of Jesus and the supposed miraculous curing of the lunatic, that gave origin to the legend that Jesus had cured Amos by casting a legion of devils out of him, and that these devils had entered into the herd of swine, causing them forthwith to rush headlong to their destruction in the sea below . . . It is equally true that all of Jesus' apostles (save Thomas) believed that the episode of the swine was directly connected with the cure of Amos."[84]

c. **Healing the epileptic** AD 28 (cf. Mark 1:21–28, Luke 4:31–37). The young man in the synagogue suffered from epilepsy, but had been taught that his suffering was caused by demoniac possession. As he was coming out of a seizure, "Jesus bade the people be quiet and, taking the young man by the hand, said, 'Come out of it'—and he was immediately awakened."[85] This incident is included as a miracle because on the evening of that same day, the young man was actually cured. Rumors spread rapidly that Jesus had cast a demon out of a man and miraculously healed him. "Long after the day of Pentecost the Apostle John, who was the last to write of Jesus' doings, avoided all reference to these so-called acts of "casting out devils," and this he did in view of the fact that such cases of demon possession never occurred after Pentecost."[86]

d. **The Syrian woman's daughter** AD 29 (cf. Matthew 15:21–28, Mark 7:24–30). Although epochal revelation does not diagnose this case, the daughter most likely suffered from epileptic seizures. Her mother regarded her episodes as demoniacal possession. The mother's faith was so strong, pure, and persistent that Jesus honored it by healing her daughter. Through this gesture, Jesus taught the apostles that even Gentiles had rights to the privileges of the kingdom.[87]

4. **Healing Miracles**

   a. **Cleansing of the leper at Iron** AD 28 (cf. Matthew 8:1–4, Mark 1:40–45, and Luke 5:12–15). This cleansing of the leper at Iron was the first miracle that Jesus intentionally and deliberately performed up to this time. "And this was a case of real leprosy."[88] Although Jesus performed this miracle in private and told the leper to tell no one of what he had done, the leper did not comply with Jesus' instructions.[89]

   b. **Healing the son (of fever) of the nobleman Titus** AD 28 (cf. John 4:46–54). Although this event has been included among the miracles, it was not a miracle of healing. It was a case of Jesus' understanding the working of natural law ". . . just such knowledge as Jesus frequently resorted to subsequent to his baptism."[90] Jesus wanted to honor the father's faith, and although he did not explain what was taking place, he sent the nobleman home with the assurance that his son was well.

   c. **The man with the withered hand** AD 28 (cf. Matthew 12:9–14, Mark 3:1–6, and Luke 6:6–11). "This is the first case of a miracle to be wrought by Jesus in response to the challenge of his enemies. And the Master performed this so-called miracle, not as a demonstration of his healing power, but as an effective protest against making the Sabbath rest of religion a veritable bondage of meaningless restrictions upon all humankind."[91]

   d. **Healing the paralytic** AD 28 (cf. Matthew 9:2–8, Mark 2: 1–12, and Luke 5:17–26). This is another genuine miracle that Jesus intentionally performed in response to sincere faith and as a challenge to his enemies so that those ". . . who witness all this may finally know that the Son of Man has authority and power on earth to forgive sins . . ."[92]

   e. **Healing the hemorrhaging woman (on the way to the ruler's house)** AD 29 (cf. Matthew 9:18–26, Mark 5:21–43, and Luke 8:40–56). This incident was a good illustration of many apparently miraculous cures that happened while Jesus was on Earth but which he did not consciously will. "The passing of time demonstrated that this woman was really cured of her malady. Her faith was of the sort that laid direct hold upon the creative power resident in the Master's person. With the faith she had, it was only necessary to approach the Master's person. It was not at all necessary to touch his garment; that was merely the superstitious part of her belief."[93]

   f. **Healing the blind beggar** AD 29 (cf. John 9:1); and **the man with dropsy** AD 30 (cf. Luke 14:1–6). Both of these healings were deliberate and performed for the purpose of once more bringing ". . . his mission on earth to the notice of the Sanhedrin and the other Jewish leaders and religious teachers."[94] The healings challenged the rulers to accept

Jesus on their own terms with regard to his miracles. Jesus also wanted to correct the wrong ideas of his apostles and others about the cause of congenital blindness.

g. **Healing Peter's mother-in-law** AD 28 (cf. Matthew 8:14, Mark 1:29–31, and Luke 4:38–39). According to revelations, the healing of Peter's mother-in-law was not a miracle. She had been suffering from malarial fever for a few days when the fever happened to break just as Jesus was comforting her. This coincidence was seized upon by the apostles as yet another miracle, especially since the incident at the synagogue and the changing of water into wine at Cana were still fresh in their minds.[95]

Scholars may speculate about the life of Jesus of Nazareth, but epochal revelation reconciles the happenings in his life: "Jesus' apostles, let alone the common people, could not understand the nature and attributes of this God-man. Neither has any subsequent generation been able to evaluate what took place on earth in the person of Jesus of Nazareth. And there can never occur an opportunity for either science or religion to check up on these remarkable events for the simple reason that such an extraordinary situation can never again occur, either on this world or on any other world in Nebadon. Never again, on any world in this entire universe, will a being appear in the likeness of mortal flesh, at the same time embodying all the attributes of creative energy combined with spiritual endowments which transcend time and most other material limitations."[96]

The Death on the Cross and the Atonement Doctrine

It may be accurate to say that Jesus lived and died for the spiritual uplift of the human race. However, he did not die on the cross to atone for the sins of mortals or to appease the wrath of God. The atonement doctrine is quite simply a remnant of primitive beliefs—a God who requires blood to bestow his graces.

In the time of Jesus, pagan cults, emperor worship, astrology, and mystery religions abounded. The mystery religions, in particular, prepared the way for Christianity in several ways. First, their emphasis shifted adherents away from religion as a collective national experience and more toward the promise of individual salvation, that is, ". . . deliverance from evil, survival after death, and enduring life in blissful realms beyond this world of sorrow and slavery."[97] Second, the mystery religions were built on myths with a strong theme of the life, death, and resurrection of a god, as illustrated by the teachings of Mithraism. Third, their more majestic concept of Deity moved people away from the revering of nature and mere human beings.

In contrast to the mystery religions, Paul's Christianity was founded upon a historic fact: the bestowal upon humanity of Michael, the Son of God, as Jesus of Nazareth. To make the gospel of Jesus more acceptable to a larger number of prospective converts, Paul blended Jesus' teachings with:

"1. The philosophic reasoning of the Greek proselytes to Judaism, including some of their concepts of the eternal life.

2. The appealing teachings of the prevailing mystery cults, especially the Mithraic doctrines of redemption, atonement, and salvation by the sacrifice made by some god.

3. The sturdy morality of the established Jewish religion."[98]

Christian belief early centered around the death of Jesus as well as the truth of his life. It is no surprise that one of Christianity's key doctrines is that God sent his Son to Earth to shed his blood and die for our sins as the fulfillment of the Old Testament scriptures. The teaching that Jesus was a sacrificial Son who would satisfy the Father's stern justice and appease the divine wrath was incorporated into Christian theology in an effort to make the gospel of the kingdom more acceptable to disbelieving Jews. "Though these efforts failed as far as winning the Jews was concerned, they did not fail to confuse and alienate many honest souls in all subsequent generations."[99] According to epochal revelation, "The erroneous supposition that the righteousness of God was irreconcilable with the selfless love of the heavenly Father, presupposed absence of unity in the nature of Deity and led directly to the elaboration of the atonement doctrine, which is a philosophic assault upon both the unity and the free-willness of God."[100]

The freedom to *choose* salvation is a gift of God that cannot be coerced. Bestowal Sons live and die for the spiritual uplift of the mortals in the world in which they incarnate, but dying on a cross is not a prerequisite. Jesus died not as a sacrifice to atone for humanity's sins but because he was selfishly betrayed and subjected to an unjust system—he was sentenced to die even though innocent of all crime. The decision to not use his creator prerogatives to save himself *was* a willful decision that Jesus made: "Jesus had purposed to live without resort to his supernatural power, and he likewise elected to die as an ordinary mortal upon the cross. He had lived as a man, and he would die as a man—doing the Father's will."[101] Jesus knew that he had the authority to lay down his life and restore it again.

Although Jesus did not die to atone for the sins of mortals or to appease the wrath of God, his death was significant:

- The crucifixion was the supreme and final expression of his love and the completed revelation of his mercy. "The triumph of the death on the cross is all summed up in the spirit of Jesus' attitude toward those who assailed him. He made the cross an eternal symbol of the triumph of love over hate and the victory of truth over evil when he prayed, 'Father, forgive them, for they know not what they do.'"[102]

- Jesus lived and died for a whole universe, not just for the people of Earth. The technique of salvation—the evolution of the human mind from matter up to spirit status—existed before Jesus lived and died on Earth. His bestowal, however, shed light on the way of salvation; his death and resurrection confirmed the certainty of personality survival after death. Jesus showed that salvation is the gift of God, and righteousness is the natural result of living a spirit-led life as a son or daughter of God.

- Though it is not accurate to refer to Jesus as a sacrificer, a ransomer, or a redeemer, Jesus may be referred to as a *savior*. "He forever made the way of salvation (survival) more clear and certain; he did better and more surely show the way of salvation for all the mortals of all the worlds . . ."[103]

- "The great thing about the death of Jesus, as it is related to the enrichment of human experience and the enlargement of the way of salvation, is not the fact of his death but rather the superb manner and the matchless spirit in which he met death."[104]

- Jesus' ". . . death on the cross was not to effect man's reconciliation to God but to stimulate man's *realization* of the Father's eternal love and his Son's unending mercy, and to broadcast these universal truths to a whole universe."[105]

The Resurrection of Jesus

For almost two thousand years, the Christian church has taught that Jesus was crucified, died, and was bodily resurrected (that is, returned to life in his original body) three days later. The claim that Jesus resurrected in the flesh has led to many attempts throughout the centuries to disprove the events in the Bible: "'No doctrine of the Christian Faith,' says St. Augustine, 'is so vehemently and so obstinately opposed as the doctrine of the resurrection of the flesh' (In Ps. lxxxviii, sermo ii, n. 5)."[106] Of course, many have presented what they postulate as historical evidence for the bodily resurrection of Jesus Christ.

Jesus did resurrect from the dead, but not in his physical body. *The Urantia Book* explains: "The Christian belief in the resurrection of Jesus has been based on the fact of the 'empty tomb.' It was indeed a *fact* that the tomb was empty, but this is not the *truth* of the resurrection. The tomb was truly empty when the first believers arrived, and this fact, associated with that of the undoubted resurrection of the Master, led to the formulation of a belief which was not true: the teaching that the material and mortal body of Jesus was raised from the grave. Truth having to do with spiritual realities and eternal values cannot always be built up by a combination of apparent facts. Although individual facts may be materially true, it does not follow that the association of a group of facts must necessarily lead to truthful spiritual conclusions."[107]

While reconciliation of the resurrection with epochal revelation will present one of the biggest challenges to Christianity, it will nevertheless present the greatest opportunity to strengthen and augment faith. The truth of the resurrection is a significant spiritual belief; clarifying *how* it happened does not detract from the spiritual experience of the believer.

To begin reconciling the events surrounding the resurrection of Jesus, the word "resurrection" first has to be redefined in general to mean "awakening from death" and not "return to life in the physical body." The process of resurrection is discussed at length in section three.

If Jesus did not return after his death in his physical body, what were the witnesses seeing? Epochal revelation introduces the term "morontia," used to designate a vast realm between the material and spiritual dimensions. After death of the physical body, the surviving soul continues to experience spiritual growth in a morontia form. The many appearances of Jesus after his resurrection and before his ascension were in this form: "By the aid of certain morontia auxiliary personalities, the morontia form can be made at one time as of the spirit so that it can become indifferent to ordinary matter, while at another time it can become discernible and contactable to material beings, such as the mortals of the realm."[108] Human eyes were able to see the morontia form of Jesus because of the ministry of special beings and morontia personalities then accompanying Jesus.

With regard to his resurrection, epochal revelation clarifies and explains:

- Jesus as Creator Son effected his own morontia resurrection: "As far as we can judge, no creature of this universe nor any personality from another universe had anything to do with this morontia resurrection of Jesus of Nazareth. On Friday he laid down his life as a mortal of the realm; on Sunday morning he took it up again as a morontia being . . ."[109] The morontia resurrection occurred in the tomb where the physical body of Jesus lay wrapped in burial clothes: ". . . at two minutes past three o'clock, this Sunday morning, April 9, A.D. 30, the resurrected morontia form and personality of Jesus of Nazareth came forth from the tomb."[110]

- When Jesus emerged from the tomb in his morontia form, his physical body remained undisturbed in the tomb. "He emerged from the burial tomb without moving the stones before the entrance and without disturbing the seals of Pilate."[111] The soldiers were still on guard.

- "He did not emerge from the tomb as a spirit nor as Michael of Nebadon; he did not appear in the form of the Creator Sovereign, such as he had had before his incarnation in the likeness of mortal flesh on Urantia."[112] He did emerge from the tomb in the likeness of morontia personalities that resurrect after mortal death.

But if Jesus did not resurrect in his physical body and his body remained in the cave after his resurrection, why was the tomb empty and how was the stone moved?

The Urantia Book reveals: "The tomb of Joseph was empty, not because the body of Jesus had been rehabilitated or resurrected, but because the celestial hosts had been granted their request to afford it a special and unique dissolution, a return of the 'dust to dust,' without the intervention of the delays of time and without the operation of the ordinary and visible processes of mortal decay and material corruption. The mortal remains of Jesus underwent the same natural processes of elemental disintegration as characterizes all human bodies on earth except that, in point of time, this natural mode of dissolution was greatly accelerated, hasted to that point where it became well-nigh instantaneous."[113]

Regarding the stones that sealed the tomb, the revelation explains that as the celestial hosts prepared to perform the dissolution of the body, they assigned secondary midwayers to roll away the stones from the entrance of the tomb (midwayers and their place in the celestial hierarchy are discussed in section one; their function on Earth is addressed later in this section). The opening of the tomb did not go unnoticed: "When the watching Jewish guards and the Roman soldiers, in the dim light of the morning, saw this huge stone begin to roll away from the entrance of the tomb, apparently of its own accord—without any visible means to account for such motion—they were seized with fear and panic, and they fled in haste from the scene."[114] The Roman soldiers reported what they saw to the Jewish leaders and ". . . instead of thinking of punishing the guards who deserted their post, they resorted to bribing these guards and the Roman soldiers. They paid each of these twenty men a sum of money and instructed them to say to all: 'While we slept during the nighttime, his disciples came upon us and took away the body.'"[115]

Jesus remained on Earth in his morontia form for a short time in order to more fully know the life of his ascendant creatures and further reveal the will of his Father in Paradise. "The true evidences of the resurrection of Michael are spiritual in nature, albeit this teaching is corroborated by the testimony of many mortals of the realm who met, recognized, and communed with the resurrected morontia Master. He became a part of the personal experience of almost one thousand human beings before he finally took leave of Urantia."[116] He made nineteen separate appearances in visible form to his believers on Earth.

The Ascension

In Christian teachings, Jesus' ascension refers to the ". . . movement of the eternal Son, in his assumed and glorified humanity, from earth to heaven in order to sit at the right hand of the Father as coregent."[117] In Christianity, ascension presupposes bodily resurrection; ". . . this same Jesus, which is taken up from you into heaven, shall so come in like manner as ye have seen him go into heaven." (Acts 1:11)

However, while the final disappearance of Jesus from the apostles' mortal vision did indicate his ascent from Earth to the right hand of his Father, it was not a physical ascent. "This so-called ascension of Jesus was in no way different from his other disappearances from mortal vision during the forty days of his morontia career on Urantia."[118] By the aid of special morontia personalities, the morontia form of Jesus was sometimes made visible and at other times, invisible. At seven forty-five on the morning of May 18, AD 30, the morontia form of Jesus was not discernible to the eleven apostles as he began his ascent to the right hand of his Father to accept complete sovereignty of his universe.[119]

The Significance of Pentecost and the Spirit of Truth

Pentecost, which occurs at the beginning of summer, is one of three feasts established by Moses. The other two feasts are Passover, held seven weeks before Pentecost, and the feast of the harvest, otherwise known as the feast of tabernacles, held in October.

"Pentecost was the great festival of baptism, the time for fellowshipping . . . those gentiles who desired to serve Yahweh."[120] It was during Pentecost, after Jesus had ascended to the Father, that he kept his promise to send into the world another teacher, the Spirit of Truth—the spiritual "comforter." In John 14:16–18,

Jesus says: "And I will pray the Father, and he shall give you another Comforter, that he may abide with you for ever; [Even] the Spirit of truth; whom the world cannot receive, because it seeth him not, neither knoweth him: but ye know him; for he dwelleth with you and shall be in you. I will not leave you comfortless: I will come to you."

The apostles were not sure how Jesus would keep his promise, but on that day of Pentecost, "About one o'clock, as the one hundred and twenty believers were engaged in prayer, they all became aware of a strange presence in the room. At the same time these disciples all became conscious of a new and profound sense of spiritual joy, security, and confidence. This new consciousness of spiritual strength was immediately followed by a strong urge to go out and publicly proclaim the gospel of the kingdom and the good news that Jesus had risen from the dead."[121]

"These men had been trained and instructed that the gospel which they should preach was the fatherhood of God and the sonship of man, but at just this moment of spiritual ecstasy and personal triumph, the best tidings, the greatest news, these men could think of was the fact of the risen Master. And so they went forth, endowed with power from on high, preaching glad tidings to the people—even salvation through Jesus—but they unintentionally stumbled into the error of substituting some of the facts associated with the gospel for the gospel message itself. Peter unwittingly led off in this mistake, and others followed after him on down to Paul, who created a new religion out of the new version of the good news."[122]

"Christianity, as it developed from that day is: the fact of God as the Father of the Lord Jesus Christ, in association with the experience of believer-fellowship with the risen and glorified Christ."[123] The overemphasis of the personality of Jesus in the theology of Christianity worked to obscure his teachings, and made it increasingly difficult for Jews, Moslems, Hindus, and other Eastern religionists to accept the teachings of Jesus. Despite the distortions, the new message carried many of the fundamental truths and teachings of the earlier gospel; it rapidly spread, reflecting the universality of the teachings of Jesus.

Jesus lived a life that can be called the revelation of a mortal submitting to the will of the Father. His religion, founded on faith, hope, and love, fosters in humanity the highest type of civilized being and the highest type of spiritual personality—a religion that serves all humankind and proclaims the sacredness in all. "On the day of Pentecost the religion of Jesus broke all national restrictions and racial fetters . . . On this day the Spirit of Truth became the personal gift from the Master to every mortal."[124]

The epochal revelators caution us: "Do not make the mistake of expecting to become strongly intellectually conscious of the outpoured Spirit of Truth. The spirit never creates a consciousness of himself, only a consciousness of Michael, the Son . . . The proof, therefore, of your fellowship with the Spirit of Truth is not to be found in your consciousness of this spirit but rather in your experience of enhanced fellowship with Michael."[125]

The Spirit of Truth came to reveal the Father's spirit nature and the Son's moral character, to help humanity recall and understand the words of Jesus as well as to illuminate and reinterpret his life on Earth. The bestowal of the Spirit of Truth prepared all normal human minds for the subsequent universal bestowal of the spirit of the Father (the Indwelling Spirit) upon all humanity. While the Spirit of Truth enables the human mind to grasp the *wisdom* of spirit realities, the Indwelling Spirit attaches the *feeling* of reality to our spiritual insights into the universe.

There is further significance to the event at Pentecost:

- Pentecost was the call to spiritual unity among those who believe in the fatherhood of God and the brotherhood of men.[126]

- "Pentecost, with its spiritual endowment, was designed forever to loose the religion of the Master from all dependence upon physical force; the teachers of this new religion are now equipped with spiritual weapons. They are to go out to conquer the world with unfailing forgiveness, matchless good will, and abounding love. They are equipped to overcome evil with good, to vanquish hate by love, to destroy fear with a courageous and living faith in truth."[127]

- "Pentecost endowed mortal man with the power to forgive personal injuries, to keep sweet in the midst of the gravest injustice, to remain unmoved in the face of appalling danger, and to challenge the evils of hate and anger by the fearless acts of love and forbearance . . . The secret of a better civilization is bound up in the Master's teachings of the brotherhood of man, the good will of love and mutual trust."[128]

- "Pentecost was designed to lessen the self-assertiveness of individuals, groups, nations, and races. It is this spirit of self-assertiveness which so increases in tension that it periodically breaks loose in destructive wars. Mankind can be unified only by the spiritual approach, and the Spirit of Truth is a world influence which is universal."[129]

- "Up to Pentecost, religion had revealed only man seeking for God; since Pentecost, man is still searching for God, but there shines out over the world the spectacle of God also seeking for man and sending his spirit to dwell within him when he has found him."[130]

Summary

"Jesus lived his earth life on Urantia, not to set a personal example of mortal living for the men and women of this world, but rather to create *a high spiritual and inspirational ideal* for all mortal beings on all worlds."[131] The life of Jesus depicts humanity at its best and serves as an inspiration to achieve higher levels of personal righteousness and loving service.

While the person of Jesus of Nazareth may not be part of all religions and beliefs, his message of the fatherhood of God and the brotherhood of man is universal and as pertinent to Hindus, Buddhists, Muslims, and other religionists as it is to Christians. His message is one that is realized through progressive personality development, including loving ministry and social service. "'Feed my sheep. Do not forsake the flock. Be an example and an inspiration to all your fellow shepherds. Love the flock as I have loved you and devote yourself to their welfare even as I have devoted my life to your welfare. And follow after me even to the end.'"[132]

"To 'follow Jesus' means to personally share his religious faith and to enter into the spirit of the Master's life of unselfish service. One of the most important things in human living is to find out what Jesus believed, to discover his ideals, and to strive for the achievement of his exalted life purpose. Of all human knowledge, that which is of greatest value is to know the religious life of Jesus and how he lived it."[133]

Michael of Nebadon is both a father and a brother to every human being. He is our local universe Creator Son. His message is relevant to everyone, regardless of whether or not the person of Jesus of Nazareth fits into our individual cultural or religious beliefs and heritage.

When Jesus said, "I am the way, the truth, and the life: no man cometh unto the Father, but by me" (John 14:6), he spoke as the representative of the Universal Father and as the Creator Son of our local universe. His words were directed to every human being in his vast creation, then and now. And as we begin to understand and appreciate our location in the universe, we will recognize that it is impossible to proceed to our Paradise destination without first living in and passing through the local universe of Nebadon, where Michael—Son of Man and Son of God—tenderly pours forth his love and mercy.

12.

The Human Races and Their Global Migration

That question is not the rise of Kingdoms, but the Origin of Races . . . When and how did they begin? And in this feature of color it is remarkable that we have every possible variety of tint from the fairest to the blackest races, so that the one extreme passes into the other by small and insensible gradations.

Duke of Argyll, in his ethnological enquiry, *Primeval Man*

Biblical accounts of Adam and Eve as God's first human beings, with all of humankind as their descendants, are not supported by scientific findings on the origin of our species. The scriptural story is problematic in light of the diversity of humans as evidenced by differing skin colors and other physical characteristics.

There are two preeminent theories about the origin of Homo sapiens. The first, the Out of Africa Model, posits that humans originated in Africa. The second, the Multi-Regional Hypothesis, states that premodern humans migrated from Africa and evolved to become modern humans in other parts of the world. Stone tools and fossilized bones of modernlike humans found at archaeological digs in Africa support the theory that the human race originated in Africa. However, stone tools found in recent years at an archaeological site in southern India are very similar to those found in Africa. "Whoever was living in India was doing things identical to modern humans living in Africa."[1] Science is slowly recognizing, and epochal revelation confirms, that human culture is a great deal more ancient than its suggested origin in the Middle and Upper Paleolithic eras.

The discovery of Neanderthal man in the nineteenth century[2] gave evidence to the so-called cavemen and laid the foundation for the field of paleoanthropology. Neanderthals are considered an older subspecies, and even a separate species, of humans that cohabited with modern humans for thousands of years before becoming extinct. Genetic anthropology has found that Neanderthal DNA sequences are ". . . about 99.5% similar to the modern human genome, indicating that modern humans and Neanderthals had a common ancestor about 700,000 years ago."[3] Epochal revelation confirms the genetic ties that exist between Neanderthals and modern humans and reveals their common ancestry with the birth of Andon and Fonta approximately one million years ago (cf. chapter 7).

Regarding the origin of different skin colors and physical characteristics, genetic anthropology can identify different genes for physical traits such as skin and hair color between individuals, but ". . . no consistent patterns of genes across the human genome exist to distinguish one race from another. There also is no genetic basis for divisions of human ethnicity."[4]

The races of color had their origin in a unique phenomenon, which—like the missing link in the evolution process—would remain a mystery without the insights of epochal revelation. In this chapter, we will explore the sudden appearance of the six colored races a half million years ago, an unusual episode that marked the beginning of an extraordinary chapter in humanity's evolutionary progress. From one area of our planet, these protoracial humans eventually migrated throughout most of the globe. In addition, we will explore how the gene pool was enhanced by semispirit beings, recorded in myth as the "Sons of God who went with the daughters of men,"[5] and the further uplift of our human DNA by the descendants of Adam and Eve approximately thirty-seven thousand years ago. Following is a brief chronicle of the origin and migration history of the human races, along with some highlights of the periods.

1,000,000 to 500,000 BC: The Andonites (Andonic Aborigines)

Almost one million years ago, Andon and Fonta, the first human beings, were born in what is now known as Afghanistan. At the approximate age of twelve, they migrated to the northwestern highlands of India, where the human race began.

- Descendants of Andon and Fonta are called Andonites.

- The Andonites eventually established a language and the rudiments of human culture.

- Because of tribal conflicts, the Andonites dispersed from their homeland in the northern Indian highlands to the following areas:

  - Europe, including England (connected at the time by land with France).

  - Iceland, Greenland, and arctic regions of North America, surviving as present-day Eskimos.

  - Java, Tasmania, and the Caspian Sea.

  - Tibet, China, and throughout India.

  - Northern Africa when it was joined to Europe by the Sicilian land bridge.

- Approximately nine hundred and eighty thousand years ago, the most advanced Andonites lived in the region of the present-day Caspian Sea. These tribes developed an efficient government and a spiritual culture. Within eighty thousand years, their numbers were greatly diminished.

- By nine hundred and fifty thousand years ago, the descendants of Andon and Fonta had migrated far. To the west they passed over Europe to France and England. In later years, they penetrated eastward as far as Java, and then journeyed on to Tasmania.

- The Foxhall peoples were mongrel groups that arrived in England from Southern France about nine hundred thousand years ago. "These tribes were so largely mixed with the forest apelike creatures that they were scarcely human. They had no religion but were crude flintworkers and possessed sufficient intelligence to kindle fire."[6] "Many of the more intelligent and spiritual of the Foxhall peoples maintained their racial superiority and perpetuated their primitive religious customs. And these people, as they were later admixed with subsequent stocks, journeyed on west from England after a later ice visitation and have survived as the present-day Eskimos."[7] "They were followed in Europe by a some-what superior and prolific people, whose descendants soon spread over the entire continent from the ice in the north to the Alps and Mediter-ranean in the south. These tribes are the so-called Heidelberg race."[8]

- The best genetic stock of Andonites persevered in the foothills of the northwestern Indian highlands among the Badonan tribes; Badonan was a distant relative of Andon. "850,000 years ago the superior Badonan tribes began a warfare of extermination directed against their inferior and animalistic neighbors. In less than one thousand years most of the borderland animal groups of these regions had been either destroyed or driven back to the southern forests. This campaign . . . brought about a slight improvement in the hill tribes of that age. And the mixed descendants of this improved Badonite stock appeared on the stage of action as an apparently new people—the Neanderthal race."[9] The Neanderthalers gradually spread from India to France on the west, China on the east, and down into northern Africa, dominating the world for almost half a million years.

- The mingling of the later blue people with the Neanderthalers led to the immediate improvement of the older race. Eventually this new blue-Neanderthal race extended from England to India. The Cro-Magnon peoples, a blending of the later Adamites with the best of the blue race, finally exterminated the lingering strains of Neanderthal stock.

The timing of the appearance of the Andonites was unique. On no other world in the local system had such a race of creatures with will emerged in advance of the evolutionary races of color and evolved without the usual corresponding administrative and spiritual planetary guidance. The early emergence of free will resulting from the experimental modifications to the life plasm inaugurated by the Life Carriers had far-reaching consequences. The intervening five hundred thousand years before the first revelatory dispatch permitted self-will to ingrain itself deeply into the disposition of the evolving race.

500,000 BC: The Colored Races

Concurrent with the arrival of the Planetary Prince and his volunteer staff (cf. chapter 8), a man and a woman from the Badonan tribe of India *suddenly* began to produce a family of remarkable mutant children, nineteen in number, who were not only more intelligent than their tribesmen but whose skin was tinted various colors. There were five red, two orange, four yellow, two green, four blue, and two indigo.[10] This was the Sangik family, the ancestors of the six colored races. "On an average evolutionary planet the six evolutionary races of color appear one by one; the red man is the first to evolve, and for ages he roams the world before the succeeding colored races make their appearance. The simultaneous emergence of all six races on Urantia, and in one family, was most unusual."[11]

For almost one hundred thousand years, the Sangik peoples mingled together and spread out around the foothills of the northwestern Indian highlands, until population expansion forced them to migrate.

- The primary Sangiks—red, yellow, and blue—sought the colder north.

  - **RED**: The red people were the most advanced of the Sangik. They developed a tribal civilization and government and were monogamous. They occupied eastern Asia four hundred thousand years ago, until their yellow brethren came to establish themselves one hundred thousand years later. "For over two hundred thousand years these two superior races waged bitter and unremitting warfare."[12] Eighty-five thousand years ago, defeated by the yellow race, the remaining tribes of the red race left the Asiatic continent for western North America when the Bering land isthmus became passable. The red people left behind their genetic imprint in Siberia, northern China, central Asia, India, and Europe.

    When the Andonite Eskimos in Greenland were forced by the freezing over of the north seas to move in a westerly direction, they reached the northeastern land mass of North America soon after the red people arrived in what is now called Alaska. "About five thousand years ago a chance meeting occurred between an Indian tribe and a lone Eskimo group on the southeastern shores of Hudson Bay. These two tribes found it difficult to communicate with each other, but very soon they intermarried with the result that these Eskimos were eventually absorbed by the more numerous red men. And this represents the only contact of the North American red man with any other human stock down to about one thousand years ago, when the white man first chanced to land on the Atlantic coast."[13]

  - **RED, YELLOW, ORANGE, and BLUE**: Three small groups of mixed origin, a combination of the orange and blue races, accompanied the red tribes across the Bering Strait. "These three groups never fully fraternized with the red man and early journeyed southward to Mexico and Central America, where they were later joined by a small group of mixed yellows and reds. These peoples all intermarried and founded a new and amalgamated race, one which was much less warlike than the pure-line red men. Within five thousand years this amalgamated race broke up into three groups, establishing the civilizations respectively of Mexico, Central America, and South America."[14] The great civilizations of the Olmec, Maya, Aztec, and Inca were predominantly red but contained a considerable admixture of yellow, orange, and blue.

- **YELLOW**: The yellow people were skilled in the art of warfare and were the first to learn that in union there is strength. Having a fraternal spirit, the yellow people fostered racial civilization and were the most successful at living together in relative peace. They entered China over three hundred thousand years ago, eventually infringing on the red people's territory. After two hundred thousand years of struggle for control of Asia, the yellow race defeated the red race, driving them away. The yellow race advanced by the later infusion of Adamic blood.

- **BLUE**: The blue race had the brain power of the red and the outlook of the yellow. They invented the spear and subsequently worked out the rudiments of many of the arts of modern civilization. The blue people chiefly migrated from their Indian highland to Europe around 200,000 BC, where they persisted until recent times. The race was first modified by a slight mixture with yellow and red, and was greatly invigorated when it commingled with the violet blood of Adam around 25,000 BC to produce progressive groups of superior blue people, now known as Cro-Magnons. The Cro-Magnon blue people constituted the biologic foundation for modern-day Europeans, but have survived only as absorbed by their white conquerors, the Aryans, who were a commingling of the blue race with the much thoroughly mixed Andites no earlier than 15,000 BC. The Andite race resulted from Adam's post-default sex relations with superior females, primarily Nodite, in an effort to spread his gene pool. "The Andite races were the primary blends of the pure-line violet race and the Nodites plus the evolutionary peoples."[15]

- The secondary Sangiks—orange, green, and indigo—preferred the warmer south.

  - **ORANGE**: The orange race loved to build. They moved from their birthplace southward along the coast, establishing headquarters in Palestine around 298,000 BC. The orange people were the first to follow the coastline southward toward Egypt and Africa as the Mediterranean Sea withdrew to the west. But they never secured a favorable footing in Africa and were wiped out of existence by the later-arriving green race. The orange people, as a race, ceased to exist approximately one hundred thousand years ago.

- **GREEN**: From their homeland, the green race split into three groups. The eastern group amalgamated with the peoples of those days. The northern tribes were enslaved and assimilated by the yellow and blue races. The southern group entered Africa where they destroyed their orange cousins. The green race spread throughout the African continent and was subsequently absorbed by the indigo race.

- **INDIGO**: The physically strong indigo people were the last of the Sangik to migrate from their homeland. They traveled southward along the coast to Palestine and then into Egypt, where they absorbed the remnants of the orange people and much of the stock of the green race. Long before Adam arrived, the blue people of Europe and the mixed races of Arabia—a blending of the indigo, blue, and modified green people—drove the indigo race out of Egypt to the south, onto the African continent, where they have been the dominant racial group ever since.

Varying mixtures of the Sangik races formed cultures in Burma, Indo-China, and the islands of the Pacific. Of all human stocks, it was the red and yellow races that achieved the highest degree of civilization apart from the influences of the later Andites. "As the Sangik migrations draw to a close, the green and orange races are gone, the red man holds North America, the yellow man eastern Asia, the blue man Europe, and the indigo race has gravitated to Africa. India harbors a blend of the secondary Sangik races, and the brown man, a blend of the red and yellow, holds the islands off the Asiatic coast. An amalgamated race of rather superior potential occupies the highlands of South America. The purer Andonites live in the extreme northern regions of Europe and in Iceland, Greenland, and northeastern North America."[16]

200,000 BC: The Nodites (The Hybrid Race)

Three hundred thousand years into the rule of the Planetary Prince, Caligastia, the work of his staff was diverted by the planetary rebellion. Sixty members of the Prince's staff joined the rebellion while forty members remained loyal to the Universal Father. When the rebel staff members led by Nod elected to mate with the local Andonite tribe, their children were far superior to the Andonites and the Sangiks—physically, intellectually, and spiritually.

About fifty years after the rebellion, the Prince's planetary headquarters in Dalamatia was plagued by the lowest types of the Sangik races, and the Nodites were forced to move north and east. Their place of dwelling became known as "the land of Nod." Soon after, Dalamatia was submerged by a tsunami, which gave rise to many legends that were further confused with the race mixtures of the later-appearing Adamites in the Second Garden. Some of the legends, as they relate to the Nodite generations and their forebears, are reconciled below:

- Caligastia's rebel staff equate to the "sons of god" who "went to the daughters of men and had children by them" mentioned in Genesis 6:4;

their children were the Nephilim, the "mighty men of old," the "men of renown"—the early Nodite descendants.[17] These "sons of god" could perhaps be the source of the concept of polytheism that spread throughout the ancient world and is still evident today.

- The rebel staff may also be identified with the Anunnaki, described on clay tablets by the ancient Sumerians as being the founders of their civilization who brought them great knowledge and technology and who created a hybrid race (the Nodites)—a fusion between the genes of "the gods" and mortals.

- The rebel staff may also equate to the "authorities of the darkness" who started the human race in the *Hypostasis of the Archons* (The Reality of the Rulers), part of the ancient Nag Hammedi texts.[18]

- The apocryphal *Book of Enoch* describes the fall of the Watchers, who fathered the Nephilim. The Watchers may equate to the members of the Prince's staff who joined the Lucifer rebellion and the Nephilim to the Nodites, the progeny of the rebellious staff and members of the Andonic tribes.

- With regard to the Prince's headquarters in Dalamatia, some of the recovered Sumerian tablets tell of the earthly paradise "where the gods first blessed humankind with the example of civilized and cultured life," while others describe the site of a remarkable settlement that was located on the Persian Gulf near the earlier city of Dilmun, "a land that is 'pure,' 'lean,' and 'bright'—a 'land of the living,' which knows neither sickness nor death."[19]

  In 1912, Dr. Stephen Lagdon of Oxford University identified Dilmun "with a strip of land from about the twenty-ninth degree of latitude southward along the eastern cost of the Persian Gulf, including the islands off the coast perhaps as far as the Strait of Ormuz and the Arabian Sea."[20] He equated Dilmun with the Sumerian Paradise, or Eden. Epochal revelation explains: "The Egyptians called this city of ancient glory Dilmat, while the later Adamized Sumerians [who perhaps wrote these tablets] confused both the first [land of Nod] and second [Dilmun] Nodite cities with Dalamatia [the original] and called all three Dilmun."[21]

- A tablet depicting the Sumerian Family Tree (The Grand Assembly of the Anunnaki) distinguishes between those gods and goddesses who came from the heavens (the Planetary Prince's staff) and those who were born on Earth (their progeny, the Nodites).

- The Book of Genesis parallels the Babylonian tablet depicting the *Epic of Creation (Enuma Elish)*, which evolved from Sumerian myths. During their captivity in Babylon, the Jews were greatly influenced by the Babylonian traditions and legends. The Hebrew priests and compilers of the Old Testament probably had access to these tablets.

Worldwide Flood

Many civilizations have harbored the story of a worldwide flood occurring at some time in the past. Perhaps the most well known is the biblical story in Genesis 5:28–9:17 where God commands Noah, "a righteous man, blameless among the people of his time," to build an ark to save himself, his family, and pairs of animals and birds of all species from a flood that would destroy all life on Earth. The oldest account of a worldwide flood, estimated to be written in the first centuries of the second millennium BC, is the eleventh tablet of the Babylonian *Epic of Gilgamesh*, which depicts a flood brought on by an angry God for the purpose of destroying all living creatures. In this eleventh tablet of the epic, Utnapishtim, like Noah in the Bible, is forewarned by the gods of the great flood and builds a boat that he loads with everything he can find. In a second legend, the Akkadian Atrahasis epic, also from the first half of the second millennium BC, the god Enki warns Atrahasis to build a boat to escape the flood.[22]

While geologic and fossil records prove that there have been extensive regional floods in the past, there is no conclusive scientific evidence of a worldwide flood. With the understanding that in every legend there is truth, epochal revelation sheds light onto the historical events that gave origin to the legends of a worldwide flood and clarifies the version presented in the Bible. In this chapter, we have already reconciled the identity of "the gods," the Anunnakki described in the epics.

As to a worldwide flood: "One hundred and sixty-two years after the rebellion a tidal wave swept up over Dalamatia, and the planetary headquarters sank beneath the waters of the sea, and this land did not again emerge until almost every vestige of the noble culture of those splendid ages had been obliterated."[23] The Prince's staff (the Anunnakki) and their associates had migrated northward prior to the submergence. With the passage of time, this event became hazy in the minds of their progeny, the Nodites, who verbally passed their recollections from one generation to another.

To add to the confusion, over one hundred and fifty thousand years after the submergence of the city of Dalamatia, the First Garden was submerged under the eastern end of the Mediterranean Sea. "For thousands of years after the submergence of the first Eden the mountains about the eastern coast of the Mediterranean and those to the northwest and northeast of Mesopotamia continued to rise. This elevation of the highlands was greatly accelerated about 5000 B.C., and this, together with greatly increased snowfall on the northern mountains, caused unprecedented floods each spring throughout the Euphrates valley. These spring floods grew increasingly worse so that eventually the inhabitants of the river regions were driven to the eastern highlands. For almost a thousand years scores of cities were practically deserted because of these extensive deluges."[24]

As to the authenticity of a worldwide flood, epochal revelation asserts that "[t]here has never been a universal flood since life was established on Urantia. The only time the surface of the earth was completely covered by water was during those Archeozoic ages before the land had begun to appear."[25] With the passage of time, memories of the submergence of Dalamatia and the First

Garden of Eden were eternalized as legends throughout the globe and became inscribed in cuneiform on pottery, clay cylinder seals, and clay tablets. The eleventh tablet of the Babylonian *Epic of Gilgamesh*, discovered in Nippur, is very likely a creative version of the submergence of the ancient Nodite city of Dalamatia.

The Hebrew priests, during their exile in Babylon, had access to these ancient records. Was the Old Testament version of the flood derived from the Gilgamesh version? And did Noah, who according to Genesis 9 was "a man of the soil" who planted "a vineyard," really exist? In the Sumerian *Epic of Paradise* the person of Tagtug is "a gardener," and the "hero" who escaped the flood that destroyed the world. Identification of Tagtug with Noah could be assumed upon the obvious resemblances of their adventures during the flood. An unproven but interesting theory, presented by the late Sumerian scholar Dr. Stephen Langdon, proposed that the Hebrew word "Noah" was derived from the Semitic word nu-hu, which was in turn derived from the Sumerian word tag-tug.[26]

Epochal revelation confirms the authenticity of Noah "the gardener" and explains his participation in a local flood about 5000 BC: ". . . Noah really lived; he was a wine maker of Aram, a river settlement near Erech. He kept a written record of the days of the river's rise from year to year. He brought much ridicule upon himself by going up and down the river valley advocating that all houses be built of wood, boat fashion, and that the family animals be put on board each night as the flood season approached. He would go to the neighboring river settlements every year and warn them that in so many days the floods would come. Finally a year came in which the annual floods were greatly augmented by unusually heavy rainfall so that the sudden rise of the waters wiped out the entire village; only Noah and his immediate family were saved in their houseboat."[27] .

Whether the Old Testament version of the flood was inspired by stories and legends or was an invention of the Hebrew priesthood during the Babylonian captivity, the tale of a worldwide flood proved useful in glorifying the history of the Jewish race. "[A]s the Hebrew priests in Babylonian captivity sought to trace the Jewish people back to Adam, they found great difficulty in piecing the story together; and it occurred to one of them to abandon the effort, to let the whole world drown in its wickedness at the time of Noah's flood, and thus to be in a better position to trace Abraham right back to one of the three surviving sons of Noah."[28]

The Tower of Babel and the Dispersion of the Nodites

About fifty thousand years after the death of Nod, the leaders of the various Nodite tribes in the land of Nod decided that something should be done to preserve their racial unity. Bablot, a descendant of Nod and member of the council of the tribes ". . . proposed to erect a pretentious temple of racial glorification at the center of their then occupied territory. This temple was to have a tower the like of which the world had never seen. It was to be a monumental memorial to their passing greatness."[29] Bablot was an architect and builder, and the tower was to be built according to his plans in a city named after him. "This location later became known as Bablod and eventually as Babel."[30]

Work on the tower stopped after four and a half years of construction because of a disagreement among the Nodites as to the plans and usage of the building after its completion. Some believed the tower should be a memorial of Nodite history and racial superiority, while others wanted the tower to be a great center of commerce, art, and manufacture. Still others believed the tower presented an opportunity for making atonement for the recklessness of their ancestors in participating in the planetary rebellion. The dispute was never settled, and work on the tower was abandoned as fighting broke out amongst themselves. The religious and noncombatant Nodites spilled over into the adjoining lands and eventually intermarried with the Andonic and Sangik tribes.

"About twelve thousand years ago, a second attempt to erect the tower of Babel was made. The mixed races of the Andites (Nodites and Adamites) undertook to raise a new temple on the ruins of the first structure, but there was not sufficient support for the enterprise; it fell of its own pretentious weight. This region was long known as the land of Babel."[31]

The unfinished tower of the Nodites is the Tower of Babel referenced in Genesis 11:1–9.

Dispersion of the Nodites

The dispersion of the Nodites was a direct result of the unresolved conflict over the Tower of Babel. One great Nodite center was established before the Bablot conflict and three afterwards:

- **The northern Nodites and Amadonites—the Vanites.** Prior to the Bablot conflict, Van (the leader of the loyal members of the Planetary Prince's staff) and his followers withdrew to the highlands west of India. They were accompanied by Amadon (". . . the outstanding human hero of the Lucifer rebellion"[32]), and loyal members of his Andonite tribe who became known as the Amadonites. Amadon was a male descendant of Andon and Fonta who contributed life plasm to the Prince's staff and had since been attached to Van as his associate and human assistant. The Amadonites represented the best of the Andonic culture. Great Vanite-Nodite centers were later established in the Lake Van and Caspian Sea regions, which furnished leadership for the world through the long dark ages of the post-rebellion era. Van and Amadon stayed on Earth for over one hundred and fifty thousand years until the arrival of Adam, sustained by the tree of life.[33]

- **The western (Syrian) Nodites** journeyed from Mesopotamia northward to Syria where they contributed much to the forthcoming Assyrian stock.

- **The eastern (Elamite) Nodites** migrated from Mesopotamia eastward into Elam, Persia (now Iran). They mixed with the Sangik tribes and became largely Sangik in nature, maintaining a civilization superior to that of the surrounding barbarians. Enoch, the son of Cain, eventually became the head of the Elamite Nodites. Cain had migrated from the Second Garden to the land of Nod, where he became a great leader among one group of his father's people, promoting peace between the Elamites and the Adamites throughout his lifetime. He married a distant cousin, Remona. It was these early descendants of Cain that began the mother cult—the worship of Eve as the Great Mother—that, in time, spread throughout Asia Minor, Europe, and Crete. In the early 1960s, shrines dedicated to what has been called the Mother Goddess were discovered by British archaeologist James Mellaart in the ruins of the ancient city of Çatalhöyük, in the Konya region of what was then Anatolia (now Turkey).[34] The discovery of this Neolithic city supports the existence of civilizations older than those in recorded history and confirms the early proliferation of the worship of the "mother and child" that later appeared in many countries, in many forms, and in many languages.

- **The central (pre-Sumerian) Nodites** were a small group that lived at the mouth of the Tigris and Euphrates rivers. They maintained most of their racial integrity. For thousands of years, they remained in Mesopotamia, eventually blending with the later Adamites to found the Sumerian peoples of historic times. "And all this explains how the Sumerians appeared so suddenly and mysteriously on the stage of action in Mesopotamia. Investigators will never be able to trace out and follow these tribes back to the beginning of the Sumerians, who had their origin two hundred thousand years ago after the submergence of Dalamatia. Without a trace of origin elsewhere in the world, these ancient tribes suddenly loom upon the horizon of civilization with a full-grown and superior culture, embracing temples, metalwork, agriculture, animals, pottery, weaving, commercial law, civil codes, religious ceremonial, and an old system of writing. At the beginning of the historical era they had long since lost the alphabet of Dalamatia, having adopted the peculiar writing system originating in Dilmun. The Sumerian language, though virtually lost to the world, was not Semitic; it had much in common with the so-called Aryan tongues."[35]

35,800 BC: The Adamites

Adam and Eve founded the imaginative and spiritually progressive violet race. "Material Sons vary in height from eight to ten feet, and their bodies glow with the brilliance of radiant light of a violet hue."[36] The Divine Plan called for Adam and Eve's progeny in the Garden of Eden to build up a large reserve of pure-line Adamites before mating with selected members of the human race. By the time Adam and Eve left the First Garden, their family consisted of four generations numbering 1,647 pure-line descendants. Two-thirds chose to leave the planet after the default.

After establishing the Second Garden in Mesopotamia, Adam and Eve had forty-two additional children plus the two offspring of joint parentage with humans. Adam also elected to leave behind as much of his life plasm as possible to benefit the world after his death. Accordingly, Adam impregnated select women that were chosen by Eve from the surrounding tribes and the Nodite race. In this way, the world benefited from an additional 1,570 superior men and women who constituted the ancestry of the later-appearing mighty Andite race.

A secondary and northern center of the violet race was established by Adamson (the eldest son of Adam and Eve) and his second wife, Ratta, a pure-line descendant of Prince Caligastia's staff. This Adamite center was situated east of the southern shore of the Caspian Sea near the Kopet Mountains, Turkestan. The Andonites maintained settlements to the north and east of the Adamson headquarters and were also scattered throughout Turkestan.

"For about thirty-five thousand years after the days of Adam, the cradle of civilization was in southwestern Asia, extending from the Nile valley eastward and slightly to the north across northern Arabia, through Mesopotamia, and on into Turkestan."[37]

25,000–15,000 BC: The Adamic Migrations

When population pressures forced the Adamites to expand, around 25,000 BC, they began sending forth teachers, traders, and explorers to the surrounding lands. In the Second Garden, it had long been the custom for the sons of God to mate with human females, finding wives in the nearby land of Nod. The Sumerian peoples of historic times were the progeny of this blending of the Adamites from the Second Garden and the Nodites. They settled along the southern portions of the valley of the Euphrates and Tigris Rivers in Mesopotamia.

By 19,000 BC, the Adamites of the Second Garden were a real nation, numbering four and a half million, and had poured forth millions of their progeny into the surrounding lands where they mixed with many of the existing races to eventually form the Andite race.

15,000–2000 BC: The Andites

By 15,000 BC, the Adamites had become so blended with the Nodites and the better strains of the yellow, blue, and green races, that they could no longer be considered Adamites. This racial mix created a new race called the Andites, which was neither an Occidental nor an Oriental race.

Mesopotamia

- With the terminal Andite migrations between 8000 and 6000 BC, culture declined in the Euphrates Valley and shifted to the Nile.

- The biologic backbone of Mesopotamian civilization was broken around 6000 BC. However, a small minority of Sumerians remained near the mouths of the Euphrates and Tigris Rivers. "These Sumerians were able to defend themselves because of superior intelligence, better weapons, and their extensive system of military canals, which were an adjunct to their irrigation scheme of interconnecting pools. They were a united people because they had a uniform group religion. They were thus able to maintain their racial and national integrity long after their neighbors to the northwest were broken up into isolated city-states . . . They were greatly respected and sought after as teachers of art and industry, as directors of commerce, and as civil rulers by all peoples to the north and from Egypt in the west to India in the east."[38]

- With the passage of time, the city-states became ". . . ruled by the apostate descendants of the Sethite priests [missionary priests of the Second Garden—named after Seth, son of Adam and Eve]. Only when these priests made conquests of the neighboring cities did they call themselves kings."[39]

- Sargon, "the priest of Kish, who proclaimed himself king,"[40] terminated the long weak rule of the city priests when he conquered the whole of Mesopotamia and adjoining lands. Sargon unified the Sumerian city-states and built the Akkadian empire, including Assyria, based in the city of Akkad, that was later to become Babylon. The Akkadians absorbed vast amounts of Sumerian culture until their defeat, followed by a long period of constant warfare.

- One of the dominant rebellious forces in the area were the Gutians, a seminomadic people of Aryan descent from the Mesopotamian plains and the Zagros Mountains in what is now northern Iran. According to Sumerian and Akkadian texts, the Gutians were "[n]ot classed among people . . . With human instinct but canine intelligence and monkey's features . . ."[41] It was at the hands of the Gutians that the Sumerians suffered severe losses.

- The third dynasty of Ur was established after the defeat of the Gutians, at which time there was a short-lived revival of Sumerian culture and literature. With the overthrow of Ur by the Elamites, the Sumerian influence ended. By the time Hammurabi established the greatness of Babylonia in 1795 BC, the Sumerians had become absorbed into the ranks of the Amorites—the northern Semites. The Mesopotamian Andites finally passed from the pages of history.

- By the time the Salem teachers of Melchizedek arrived in Mesopotamia, the religions of Mesopotamia had lost the teachings of the Sethites, and were under the influence of the primitive beliefs of the invading Semites. Although the arrival of the Salem teachers did much to refine and uplift the religions of Mesopotamia, they did not succeed in bringing the various peoples to the permanent recognition of one God.

Egypt

"For more than thirty thousand years Egypt received a steady stream of Mesopotamians, who brought along their art and culture to enrich that of the Nile valley. But the ingress of large numbers of the Sahara peoples greatly deteriorated the early civilization along the Nile so that Egypt reached its lowest cultural level some fifteen thousand years ago."[42]

However, the strong Sumerian influence remained evident throughout Egyptian culture. In *The Quest for Sumer*, Leonard Cottrell states: ". . . there are certain elements in Egypt's Early Dynastic Period which seem to betray unmistakable Sumerian influence. Egyptian hieroglyphic writing may be one. Another is the so-called 'panelled-façade' type of architecture found in Egyptian tombs from the First to the Third Dynasties (3200 to 2800 BC) . . . But the most remarkable evidence of cultural connection is that shown in the architecture of the Early Dynastic tombs of Egypt and Mesopotamian seal-impressions showing almost exactly similar buildings."[43]

- Between 8000 and 6000 BC, the culture in the Euphrates valley suffered ". . . and the immediate center of civilization shifted to the valley of the Nile. Egypt became the successor of Mesopotamia as the headquarters of the most advanced group on earth."[44]

- In the epoch when India harbored the greatest mixture of the world races, Egypt fostered the most thoroughly blended religious philosophy to be found on Earth. From the Nile Valley, it spread to many parts of the world.

- Egyptian culture, as understood by modern scholars, had its roots in the period between 5000 and 3100 BC, but it was the later Egyptian theories of a future life and the burial customs of the Old, Middle, and New Kingdoms that made ancient Egypt famous. The *Papyrus of Ani*, otherwise known as the Egyptian *Book of the Dead*, is ". . . an ancient Egyptian collection of mortuary texts made up of spells or magic formulas, placed in tombs and believed to protect and aid the deceased in the hereafter. Probably compiled and reedited during the 16th century BC, the collection included Coffin Texts dating from c. 2000 BC, Pyramid Texts dating from c. 2400 BC, and other writings."[45]

- With the decline of the Old Kingdom, many of the more cultured families fled to Crete.

- When the Salem missionaries first entered Egypt, they encountered a highly ethical culture blended with the modified moral standards of Mesopotamian immigrants. It was in Egypt that the original Melchizedek teachings took their deepest root, and from there, they subsequently spread to Europe. According to epochal revelation, "The Jews received much of their idea of the creation of the world from the Babylonians, but they derived the concept of divine Providence from the Egyptians."[46] "Although the culture and religion of Egypt were chiefly derived from Andite Mesopotamia and largely transmitted to subsequent civilizations through the Hebrews and Greeks, much, very much, of the social and ethical idealism of the Egyptians arose in the valley of the Nile as a purely evolutionary development."[47]

- When the Greek king Alexander the Great delivered the Egyptians from Persian rule in the third century before Christ, he founded the city of Alexandria, which received a great influx of Greeks and quickly flourished into a prominent cultural, intellectual, political, and economic metropolis.

Crete

While archaeological evidence testifies to Crete's habitation since approximately the seventh millennium BC, epochal revelation attests to an earlier occupancy: "About 12,000 B.C. a brilliant tribe of Andites migrated to Crete. This was the only island settled so early by such a superior group, and it was almost two thousand years before the descendants of these mariners spread to the neighboring isles. This group was the narrow-headed, smaller-statured Andites who had intermarried with the Vanite division of the northern Nodites. They were all under six feet in height and had been literally driven off the mainland by their larger and inferior fellows. These emigrants to Crete were highly skilled in textiles, metals, pottery, plumbing, and the use of stone for building material. They engaged in writing and carried on as herders and agriculturists."[48]

These skills, passed on through many generations, are evident in the Knossos archaeological discoveries led by Sir Arthur Evans in the early twentieth century (1900–1905). The excavations uncovered elaborate systems of sewage disposal and drainage that resemble those of today; multistoried houses and labyrinth constructions; and artistic works that indicate great advances in gem engraving, stoneworking (especially vases), metalworking, and pottery. The sophisticated civilization that emerged from the excavation has been linked with the lost continent of Atlantis.

- In Crete, the worship of the Great Mother attained its greatest vogue during the cultural decline of the Aegean region.

- When Egypt followed Mesopotamia in cultural decline, many of the more able and advanced families fled to Crete, greatly augmenting the already advanced civilization.

- When the arrival of inferior groups from Egypt later threatened the civilization of Crete, the more educated families moved westward to Greece.

Greece

Two thousand years after the settlement of Crete, Greece was populated by a group of the tall descendants of Adamson, three hundred and seventy five in number. They left their highland home near the Caspian Sea and crossed by way of the northern islands to Greece. "These later sons of Adamson [and progenitors of the Greeks] carried the then most valuable strains of the emerging white races. They were of a high intellectual order and, physically regarded, the most beautiful of men since the days of the first Eden."[49]

- By 5000 BC, the three purest strains of Adam's descendants were in Sumeria, northern Europe, and Greece. During this period, the Aryans began to conquer and integrate with the existing occupants of the region.

- "Presently Greece and the Aegean Islands region succeeded Mesopotamia and Egypt as the Occidental center of trade, art, and culture. But as it was in Egypt, so again practically all of the art and science of the Aegean world was derived from Mesopotamia except for the culture of the Adamsonite forerunners of the Greeks. All the art and genius of these latter people is a direct legacy of the posterity of Adamson, the first son of Adam and Eve, and his extraordinary second wife, a daughter descended in an unbroken line from the pure Nodite staff of Prince Caligastia. No wonder the Greeks had mythological traditions that they were directly descended from gods and superhuman beings."[50]

- The religion of Egypt greatly influenced the thinking of Greek philosophers, who elevated many Egyptian doctrines and ethical concepts. Their teachings subsequently influenced the Hebrews and, later, the Christians.

Turkestan

Around twenty thousand years ago, when the migrating Adamites and Nodites from Mesopotamia entered the Turkestan region, they soon blended with the superior inhabitants (Adamsonites and advanced tribes of Andonites) to form the Turkestan Andites, the pre-Aryan peoples. The parent language of Sanskrit, the Aryan mother tongue, developed in the highlands of Turkestan. It was a combination of the regional Andonic dialect and the language of the Adamsonites. The Andites spread Sanskrit into the lands that they later conquered—the Middle East, India, Europe, and the borderlands of China.

- "About 15,000 B.C. [and for at least fifteen centuries] increasing population pressure throughout Turkestan and Iran occasioned the first really extensive Andite movement toward India."[51]

- By 10,000 BC, the final exodus of the Andites from Mesopotamia entered Central Asia.

- Around 8000 BC, as a result of the increasing aridity of the highland regions of Central Asia, hunting became unprofitable for the migrating Andites. Traders began to arrive, driving many Andites to the valleys of the Nile, Euphrates, Indus, and Yellow rivers. From Egypt through Mesopotamia and Turkestan to the rivers of China and India, the more highly civilized tribes began to congregate in cities devoted to manufacture; thus trade between these regions progressed. Adonia, near the present city of Ashkhabad in Turkestan, became the central Asian commercial metropolis.

- From 7500 BC, the increasing aridity in the region brought about a great exodus of the Aryans, the now thoroughly blended Andites. They migrated into Assyria, the northern part of Mesopotamia, and into the Levant region (Jordan, Lebanon, and Syria). It was around 2500 BC that the Aryans from Turkestan began their invasion of India, which lasted almost five hundred years.

India

"About 15,000 BC increasing population pressure throughout Turkestan and Iran occasioned the first really extensive Andite movement [preAryan] toward India. For over fifteen centuries these superior peoples poured in through the highlands of Baluchistan, spreading out over the valleys of the Indus and Ganges and slowly moving southward into the Deccan."[52] By 10,000 BC, they had become subsumed into the native stock; the resultant people were called Dravidians. The earlier and purer Dravidians possessed a great capacity for cultural achievement, which was continuously weakened as their Andite inheritance became progressively reduced. The Dravidian civilization has survived into modern times in the Deccan, in southern India.

- The final Andite migration from Turkestan to India began approximately 2500 BC—the Aryan invasion. The Aryans brought with them their own Vedic religion and by 2000 BC, India was under the political and religious dominance of the Aryan-Andite invaders. At this time, only the northern and western portions of the peninsula had been extensively permeated by the Aryans.

- As they moved southward, the Aryans instituted the social caste system that has been preserved to the present time. "Of the four great castes, all but the first were established in the futile effort to prevent racial amalgamation of the Aryan conquerors with their inferior subjects. But the premier caste, the teacher-priests, stems from the Sethites; the Brahmans of the twentieth century after Christ are the lineal cultural descendants of the priests of the second garden, albeit their teachings differ greatly from those of their illustrious predecessors."[53]

- The Aryan invaders never completed their conquest of the country. By 1000 BC, they had been totally absorbed by the Dravidians of the south, who subsequently overran the entire peninsula except the Himalayan provinces. "[The] caste system failed to save the Aryan race, but it did succeed in perpetuating the Brahmans, who, in turn, have maintained their religious hegemony in India to the present time."[54]

- These priests never accepted the teaching of salvation through faith taught by the migrating Salem missionaries. "The Brahmans culled the sacred writings of their day in an effort to combat the Salem teachers, and this compilation, as later revised, has come on down to modern times as the Rig-Veda, one of the most ancient of sacred books."[55] "The superior culture and religious leanings of the peoples of India date from the early times of Dravidian domination and are due, in part, to the fact that so many of the Sethite priesthood entered India, both in the earlier Andite and in the later Aryan invasions. The thread of monotheism running through the religious history of India thus stems from the teachings of the Adamites in the second garden."[56]

Europe

By 8000 BC, Mesopotamian Andites had entered Europe via the Caspian Sea to conquer and integrate with the Aryans—the newly appearing white races who were a blend of the blue people with the earlier Andites. "As they moved westward across the Russian plains, absorbing the best of the blue man and exterminating the worst, they became blended into one people. These were the ancestors of the so-called Nordic race, the forefathers of the Scandinavian, German, and Anglo-Saxon peoples."[57] The Nordic aggressors met their biggest challenge from the Cro-Magnons in southern France, where the older race successfully defended their territories for five hundred years before succumbing to the white invaders. By 5000 BC, the evolving white races were dominant throughout all of northern Europe, including northern Germany, northern France, and the British Isles.

Mixed Races of Today

The races of today have resulted from a blending and reblending of the five basic human stocks of Earth:

1. Andonic—Earth aborigines
2. Primary Sangik—red, yellow, and blue
3. Secondary Sangik—orange, green, and indigo
4. Nodites—descendants of the staff of the Planetary Prince
5. Adamites—the violet race, descendants of Adam and Eve

The Lapps and Eskimos are blends of Andonite and Sangik-blue races, their skeletal structures coming nearest to preserving the aboriginal Andonic type.

"The so-called *white races* of Urantia are the descendants of these blue men as they were first modified by slight mixture with yellow and red, and as they were later greatly upstepped by assimilating the greater portion of the violet race."[58]

The Adamites and the Nodites became so admixed with other races throughout the ages that they can only be detected as a generalized Caucasoid order. In general, therefore, as the human remains of the last twenty thousand years become unearthed, it will be impossible to clearly distinguish the five original types. Study of such skeletal structure discloses that humankind is now divided into approximately three classes, as expressed in illustration 20.

Illustration 20
THE HUMAN RACE

Racial Types as Defined by Epochal Revelation*	Racial Types as Generally Defined Today*
THE CAUCASOID: the Andite blend of the Nodite and Adamic stocks, further modified by primary and (some) secondary Sangik admixture and by considerable Andonic crossing.	CAUCASOID: 1,000 million people with varied skin color, white to dark brown. Hair variable, never woolly, body hair often thick. Lips tend to be thin. Three subdivisions exist: Nordic, Mediterranean, and Alpine.
1. The Occidental white races, together with some Indian and Turanian peoples, are included in this group.	1. Nordic: Often tall, blonde, narrow-headed (Scandinavia, Baltic countries, Germany, France, Britain).
2. The unifying factor in this division is the greater or lesser proportion of Andite inheritance. It is Andite inheritance that gives to the polyglot mixture of the so-called white races that generalized homogeneity that has been called Caucasoid.	2. Mediterranean: Lighter in body build, darker skin, narrow-headed (southern France, Spain, Italy, Wales. Also Egyptians, Semites, Persians, Afghans, and some Indians).
	3. Alpine: Broad heads, square jaws, olive skin, brown hair (extends from the Mediterranean to Asia).
THE MONGOLOID: The primary Sangik type, including the original red, yellow, and blue races.	MONGOLOIDS: Most numerous of the present-day populations, split into three groups:
• The Chinese and Amerinds belong to this group.	1. The Eastern Siberians, Eskimos and the Northern American Indians.
• In Europe the Mongoloid type has been modified by secondary Sangik and Andonic mixture; still more by Andite infusion.	2. The Japanese, Koreans, Chinese.
• The Malayan and other Indonesian peoples are included in this classification, though they contain a high percentage of secondary Sangik blood.	3. The Indonesians and Malays.
THE NEGROID: The secondary Sangik type, which originally included the orange, green, and indigo races. This is the type best illustrated by the Negro, and it will be found throughout Africa, India, and Indonesia wherever the secondary Sangik races located.	NEGROIDS: 100 million from Africa south of the Sahara and Melanesians of the South Pacific.
The Urantia Book, Paper 81:4, p. 905: 1–4.	* "The Human Races" by Dr. D. R. Johnson; http://www.cartage.org.lb /en/themes/Sciences/LifeScience/Human Races/RacesMan/RacesMan.htm.

The Urantia Book explains that cultures such as the Central African pygmies and the Bushmen are "... remnants of the nonsocial peoples of ancient times [who] bear eloquent testimony to the fact that the natural individualistic tendency of man cannot successfully compete with the more potent and powerful organizations and associations of social progression. These backward and suspicious antisocial races that speak a different dialect every forty or fifty miles illustrate what a world you might now be living in but for the combined teaching of the corporeal staff of the Planetary Prince and the later labors of the Adamic group of racial uplifters."[59]

The Midwayers

Midwayers are the permanent citizens of a planet and are the primary assistants of angels. While angels cannot generally interact in the material realm, midwayers can and do. They are the material arm of a planet's spiritual protectors and they account for many paranormal or scientifically unexplained phenomena.

There are of two types of midwayers:

1. The primary midwayers are the more spiritual order of beings and normally number no more than fifty thousand on any one planet. Primary midwayers are derived from the modified ascendant-mortal staffs of the Planetary Princes.[60]

2. The secondary midwayers have a more physical nature, and their numbers differ in every world. Secondary midwayers are derived from the planetary biologic uplifters, the Adams and Eves, or from their offspring.[61]

The Urantia Book explains that midwayers do not require food or energy intake, and are able to enjoy and follow our humor as well as our worship. They do not sleep or possess powers of procreation. Primary midwayers resemble angels more than mortals, while the secondary orders are much more like human beings. Secondary midwayers are able to make, at will, physical contact with material things. It is likely that midwayers seen by humans have been mistaken to be deceased mortals, angels, or spirits. The core secondary midwayers now number 1111.

Midwayers on Earth

On Earth, primary midwayers came into being in the days of Dalamatia, as progeny of Caligastia's volunteer staff. They constituted the intelligence corps of the Prince's administration and provided invaluable services to the Prince and his staff in the work of influencing human society far from the planetary headquarters. Over four-fifths of the original fifty thousand joined the planetary rebellion, leaving a loyal corps of less than ten thousand to the service of the emergency Melchizedeks. They functioned under the leadership of Van until Adam arrived.[62]

The original secondary midwayers were the progeny of sixteen direct descendants of Adamson and Ratta, the first son of Adam and Eve and the human descendant of two of the rebel staff. After the death of Adamson, a loyal grouping of secondary midwayers went over to the service of the Melchizedeks who had been administering the affairs of the planet since the rebellion.

On the day of Pentecost, both groups of loyal midwayers came together voluntarily and now function as a single corps under the title of the United Midwayers.

Midwayers have impeccable memories. "Thus does the culture of a planet remain ever present on that planet, and in proper circumstances such treasured memories of past events are made available, even as the story of the life and teachings of Jesus has been given by the midwayers of Urantia to their cousins in the flesh."[63] It was through their organizing efforts that the teachings in *The Urantia Book* were presented to the world.

Midwayers are very understanding in their contact with human beings. They are invaluable to the seraphim in their multifaceted work for and with humanity. In fact, "Many of the more literal phenomena ascribed to angels have been performed by the secondary midway creatures. When the early teachers of the gospel of Jesus were thrown into prison by the ignorant religious leaders of that day, an actual 'angel of the Lord' 'by night opened the prison doors and brought them forth.' But in the case of Peter's deliverance after the killing of James by Herod's order [cf. Acts: 12:3–19], it was a secondary midwayer who performed the work ascribed to an angel."[64]

Midwayers are classified as:

- Permanent citizens of evolutionary worlds. Midwayers *live* on the planet, unlike the various orders of celestial beings who are assigned to *minister* on a world. "Such permanent citizens are encountered at various points in the Paradise ascent."[65]

- Ministering spirits of time. They work in intimate and useful association with the angelic hosts in the work of serving humanity.

- Ascending Sons of God. Once the midway creatures are relieved from planetary duty, they are registered in the local universe as Ascending Sons of God and immediately start the progressive Paradise ascent.

As our planetary cousins, midwayers perform special services that include:

- Serving as liaisons between the celestial and physical realms and working with the planetary seraphim.

- Serving as guardians of the worlds of space.

- Safeguarding, even rescuing from physical jeopardy, mortals who are key to the planetary spiritual economy.

- Keeping records of planetary history to share with humanity when appropriate.

- Choosing, training, organizing, and supervising cosmically aware mortals for service in one of twelve divisions of the Reserve Corps of Destiny, utilizing them for numerous crucial positions on Earth and keeping them in readiness to act in possible planetary emergencies.

- Working to elevate planetary civilization on Earth.
- Keeping active records of physical and mental facts that are contrary to the idea of a purely mechanistic, unplanned universe.

Rebel Midwayers

Over two hundred thousand years ago, the planetary rebellion played itself out in the headquarters of Caligastia in Mesopotamia. Cuneiform texts confirm that the Mesopotamian Valley was rich in demon lore, and this tradition was similarly exhibited in other ancient cultures, including Egypt, the successor of Mesopotamia.

Most of the primary midwayers went into rebellion with Caligastia and were later joined by a group of secondary midwayers. Together they did many strange things on Earth, until the days of Machiventa Melchizedek. Although Melchizedek partially brought these rebels under control, they still did much mischief up to the days of Christ Michael, when many chose to enlist under the leadership of the loyal primary midwayers.

Up until the time of the bestowal of Michael as Jesus of Nazareth, these rebel midwayers were able to influence the weak-minded and somewhat to control their actions. "It is no mere figure of speech when the record states: 'And they brought to Him all sorts of sick peoples, those who were possessed by devils and those who were lunatics.' Jesus knew and recognized the difference between insanity and demoniacal possession, although these states were greatly confused in the minds of those who lived in his day and generation."[66]

"These disloyal midwayers were able to reveal themselves to mortal eyes under certain circumstances, and especially was this true of the associates of Beelzebub, the leader of the apostate secondary midwayers. But these unique creatures must not be confused with certain of the rebel cherubim and seraphim who also were on Earth up to the time of Christ's death and resurrection. Some of the older writers designated these rebellious midway creatures as evil spirits and demons, and the apostate seraphim as evil angels."[67]

Michael's bestowal forever liberated all humans from the possibility of demoniacal influence and possession without their willful consent. The entire group of rebel midwayers is now in custody awaiting judgment. According to a 2005 Gallup poll, forty-two percent of Americans still believe in demonic possession. As to the real nature of such hideous phenomena attributed to the devil and/or evil spirits, the question remains unresolved.

13.

The Cosmic Human Being

*Cosmically moral and divinely spiritual character represents the
creature's capital accumulation of personal decisions which have
been illuminated by sincere worship, glorified by intelligent love,
and consummated in brotherly service.*

The Urantia Book

The human being is a wonder of creation, having evolved into the most
complex living organism on Earth. Two characteristics separate humans
from other species: a highly developed mind that allows for cumulative
knowledge and the contemplative power of wisdom, and the spiritual
inclination to acknowledge God in the form of worship. Wisdom and worship
are extraordinary aspects of humanity, but how do these characteristics surface
and function? A "cosmic human being" operates with a cosmic perspective,
fully aware of being a faith son or daughter of God and recognizing that every
human is part of the same universal family.

A cosmic human has developed a God-knowing personality, consecrated to
the loyal service of loving God and serving humanity. Her daily life is lived in
tune with the spirit that indwells the mind, developing the soul that is the
vehicle for transcending death. The cosmic human recognizes that mind
facilitates the development of the spiritual nature and that the human body is
the mechanism for living. The cosmic human understands that mortal life is
only a small but significant period of time in an eternal adventure.

From a cosmic perspective four attributes of universal reality operate in
human beings, and are unified by personality:

1. Form
2. Mind/Intelligence
3. Spirit
4. Soul

1. Form

According to epochal revelation, the human body is the soul's first vehicle of expression. After awakening from physical death, the cosmic human functions with a morontia body—neither physical nor spiritual. "As the mortal body is personal and characteristic for every human being, so will the morontia form be highly individual and adequately characteristic of the creative mind which dominates it. No two morontia forms are any more alike than any two human bodies."[1] As the surviving soul-personality ascends through the universe, it experiences five hundred and seventy progressive morontia transformations and then enters the first of seven spirit stages, eventually to appear on Paradise as a perfected spirit. Progress from Earth to Paradise, therefore, is a process, a journey in which the body or form continuously undergoes transformation.

The Human Body

The mortal body is a structured container of personalized electrochemical, mental, and spiritual energies—the mechanism of creature existence animated by the vital spark of life. The material composition of the human being—with its inner organs, skeletal frame, and neurological system, functioning together as a physical body—is the wonder of God's creation.

It is becoming more accepted within mainstream medicine that the human body exhibits subtle energy signatures. For thousands of years, this has been recognized in metaphysical and religious cultures; individuals who have higher sense perception (HSP) have been able to detect and manipulate the human energy field. Often, these individuals were able to diagnose, and even heal diseases. Ongoing scientific research is now validating these accounts. "Sensitive instruments have been developed that can detect the minute energy fields around the human body. Of particular importance is the SQUID [Superconducting Quantum Interference Device] magnetometer which is capable of detecting tiny biomagnetic fields associated with physiological activities in the body . . . Scientists are using SQUID instruments to map the ways diseases alter biomagnetic fields around the body. Others are applying pulsating magnetic fields to stimulate healing"[2]

In her books *Hands of Light* and *Light Emerging*, American author and spiritual healer Barbara Brennan, PhD, describes how the human energy field, powered by seven energy centers called chakras in the Eastern traditions, relates to health, disease, and even to moral and spiritual development. As mentioned in section one, all evolving forms are encircuited to respond to and accommodate the differential urges of the seven adjutant mind-spirits. It may be that the centers for adjutant interaction, through which the mind-spirits are able to influence our inner world, are related to the seven energy centers or chakras.

As medical science expands its research and holistic practice evolves, the art of medicine—allopathic and alternative—is slowly becoming one again. As we reconcile our growing understanding of human development with epochal revelation, and gain a deeper appreciation of the vast spirit/mind ministry contributing to the evolution of consciousness, we will increasingly acknowledge the mind as the temple of divinity and the body as the vehicle that sustains our soul journey on the physical plane. This realization will foster a more respectful and discerning attitude toward our bodies and what we entertain with our mind and senses.

2. Mind

Brain and mind, although intimately entwined, are two separate entities. If we were to use a computer as a crude analogy, the brain would be analogous to the central processing system hardware and the mind corresponds to the operating system software.

Brain

The *American Heritage Dictionary* defines "brain" as "the portion of the vertebrate central nervous system that is enclosed within the cranium, continuous with the spinal cord, and composed of gray matter and white matter. It is the primary center for the regulation and control of bodily activities, receiving and interpreting sensory impulses, and transmitting information to the muscles and body organs. It is also the seat of consciousness, thought, memory, and emotion."[3]

The origin of the brain is physical. Our brain developed to accommodate increasing mind potential, an essential part of the evolutionary process. However, our complex brain has not been the result of random gene transmutation—complexity was inherent in the life plasm designed by the Life Carriers. These life patterns were a crucial component of the universal plan for the creation and evolution of will creatures. The brain, in association with both its known and as yet undiscovered functions, possesses innate capacity for response to spirit/mind ministry.

Human Mind

According to epochal revelation, mind is "[o]rganized consciousness which is not wholly subject to material gravity, and which becomes truly liberated when modified by spirit."[4] More broadly defined, mind is "[t]he thinking, perceiving, and feeling mechanism of the human organism. The total conscious and unconscious experience. The intelligence associated with the emotional life reaching upward through worship and wisdom to the spirit level."[5] "Material mind is the arena in which human personalities live, are self-conscious, make decisions, choose God or forsake him, eternalize or destroy themselves."[6]

From a cosmic perspective, "[m]ind is a phenomenon connoting the presence-activity of *living ministry* in addition to varied energy systems; and this is true on all levels of intelligence"[7] "The unique feature of mind is that it can be bestowed upon such a wide range of life. Through his creative associates, the Third Source and Center ministers to all minds on all spheres. He ministers to human and subhuman intellect through the adjutants of the local universes and, through the agency of the physical controllers, ministers even to the lowest nonexperiencing entities of the most primitive types of living things."[8]

The human mind is an individual circuit of the cosmic mind with the Infinite Spirit as its source. "The mind is a personal-energy system existing around a divine spirit nucleus [the Indwelling Spirit] and functioning in a material environment [the brain]. Such a living relationship of personal mind and spirit constitutes the universe potential of eternal personality. Real trouble, lasting disappointment, serious defeat, or inescapable death can come only after self-concepts presume fully to displace the governing power of the central spirit nucleus, thereby disrupting the cosmic scheme of personality identity."9

In human personality, mind is continually trying to harmonize the human with the divine. "Man experiences matter in his mind; he experiences spiritual reality in the soul but becomes conscious of this experience in his mind. The intellect is the harmonizer and the ever-present conditioner and qualifier of the sum total of mortal experience. Both energy-things and spirit values are colored by their interpretation through the mind media of consciousness."10

The human mind is cosmically endowed: "These scientific, moral, and spiritual insights, these cosmic responses, are innate in the cosmic mind, which endows all will creatures. The experience of living never fails to develop these three cosmic intuitions; they are constitutive in the self-consciousness of reflective thinking."11 But without a clear understanding of their relation to personality survival and spiritual progress, their development is often haphazard and disproportionate, resulting in inconsistent moral behavior and attitudes such as indifference, intolerance, and self-righteousness. The balanced and progressive development of these three responses and their unification in human personality produces the cosmic insight essential to harmonious and selfless living. "It is the purpose of education to develop and sharpen these innate endowments of the human mind; of civilization to express them; of life experience to realize them; of religion to ennoble them; and of personality to unify them."12

Upon death, the mind circuit is interrupted. The consciousness of that individual cannot reappear unless the soul survives death. In order to ensure the survival of mortal identity, the human personality must consent to develop the soul by spiritualizing the mind. In living experience, we progress along this path by constantly elevating our thoughts from matter association to spirit union.

3. Spirit

The human mind intuitively senses the indwelling presence of a divine, immortal spirit—priests and philosophers have long professed it to be synonymous with the soul. A major departure from traditional theology and modern spiritual models is the revelation in *The Urantia Book* that soul and spirit are two separate realities. This key distinction is pivotal to expanding the Big Picture of Existence.

The Father indeed abides on Paradise, but his divine presence also dwells in the minds of men.

The Urantia Book

The closest comprehension of the nature and presence of the Indwelling Spirit was described by Hindu philosophers in their concept of the atman. However, they did not distinguish the copresence of the evolving soul. The human mind finds it easier to

Illustration 21
ORIGIN AND FUNCTION OF MIND-SPIRIT
ENTITIES MINISTERING TO THE HUMAN MIND

	Adjutant Mind-spirits	Holy Spirit	Indwelling Spirit	Spirit of Truth	Seraphim
Origin	The Local Universe Mother Spirit.	The Holy Spirit is the spiritual circuit of the Local Universe Mother Spirit.	Prepersonal fragment of the Universal Father indwelling man.	The Spirit of Truth is the bestowal spirit of the Creator Son and the Universal Father.	The Local Universe Mother Spirit.
Function	The circuit of the adjutant mind-spirits functions in the minds of primitive animals up to the highest types in the evolutionary scale. They assist life to adapt to its environment. Their influence is experienced as: intuition, understanding, courage, knowledge, and counsel—and in humans, includes worship and wisdom.	All minds are included in the spiritual circuits of the Holy Spirit. 1. Provides the inspirational ministry for accepting the spiritual presence of the Universal Father. 2. Functions to enlarge man's viewpoint of ethics, religion and spirituality. 3. Provides the ministry to recognize and understand spiritual insights.	The mission of the Indwelling Spirit: 1. To represent the Universal Father. 2. To bring into existence the soul. 3. To elevate the mind and soul to the spiritual levels of perfection. 4. To work with the human mind to foster new spiritual insights.	Every soul receives the Spirit of Truth "in accordance with the love for truth and the capacity to grasp and comprehend spiritual realities." 1. Is concerned primarily with the revelation of the Father's spirit nature and the Son's moral character. 2. Works in conjunction with the Holy Spirit to foster, and personalize truth; to interpret and reconcile spiritual insights.	The Seraphim seek to promote spiritual decisions in the human mind by working through the social, ethical, and moral environment of human beings.

sense an immortal indwelling presence than to grasp the fact that it cocreates a soul with the *potential* for immortality. Epochal revelation explains that without enhancement of spiritual insight and growth in the God concept, the presence of the Indwelling Spirit in the human mind makes it impossible for either science or philosophy to attain a satisfactory comprehension of the evolving soul.

Bestowal of the Indwelling Spirit

The Indwelling Spirit is the immortal aspect of the human being. Like the atman of the Hindus, the "Thought Adjuster," as referred to in *The Urantia Book*, is a prepersonal fragment of God that resides in the superconscious domain of the mind. The Indwelling Spirit ministers to the human mind in conjunction with other spirit entities. Illustration 21 clarifies their origin and function as they relate to humankind.

The bestowal of Indwelling Spirits on *all* humans began on Pentecost, when the Spirit of Truth was poured out upon our planet. Since Pentecost, Indwelling Spirits are bestowed upon all normal-minded human beings at the moment they make their first moral decision.

A key revelation is the process by which mortals come to be indwelt by a fragment of God. The various spirit influences that operate within all minds progressively nurture the ideals of duty and altruism in young humans, aided by parental reinforcement of personal and social ethics. The Indwelling Spirit does not arrive until the young mind ". . . has been duly prepared by the indwelling ministry of the adjutant mind-spirits and encircuited in the Holy Spirit. And it requires the coordinate function of all seven adjutants to thus qualify the human mind for the reception of an Adjuster. Creature mind must exhibit the worship outreach and indicate wisdom function by exhibiting the ability to choose between the emerging values of good and evil—moral choice."[13] Bestowal of the Indwelling Spirit occurs on the average just prior to the sixth birthday. Illustration 22 shows the chain of events that leads to the arrival of the Indwelling Spirit, subsequent to the first moral choice.

Only personal beings receive Indwelling Spirits. Animals do have feelings; they can express emotions, but not ideas and ideals. It is the factual presence of the Indwelling Spirit in the human mind that forever distinguishes a human being from an animal.

Mission of the Indwelling Spirit

The mission of Indwelling Spirit is to represent the Universal Father in humankind and to foster the birth and growth of the soul, the necessary vehicle for the human personality to survive physical death. Indwelling Spirits help develop the soul by spiritualizing our thinking and fostering in us an unselfish interest in the welfare of others that goes beyond the sense of duty. Indwelling Spirits are the essence of our eternal nature—the perfect guide toiling tirelessly for our spiritual growth.

Epochal revelation explains that Indwelling Spirits begin a planetary assignment with a definite and predetermined plan for the intellectual and spiritual development of their human subjects, who have full liberty to reject any part or the entire divine program. While it is the goal of Indwelling Spirits to influence human thinking and to make spiritual adjustments as a person may willingly and intelligently authorize, under no circumstances can they arbitrarily influence the choices and decisions of their human subjects. "The free will of man is supreme in moral affairs; even the indwelling Thought Adjuster refuses to compel man to think a single thought or to perform a single act against the choosing of man's own will."[14]

The presence of the Indwelling Spirit does not mean an easy life and freedom from deep thinking; rather it acts in harmony with the intellect to stimulate meaningful decisions and augment personal well-being. "When my

Illustration 22
BESTOWAL PROCESS OF THE INDWELLING SPIRIT

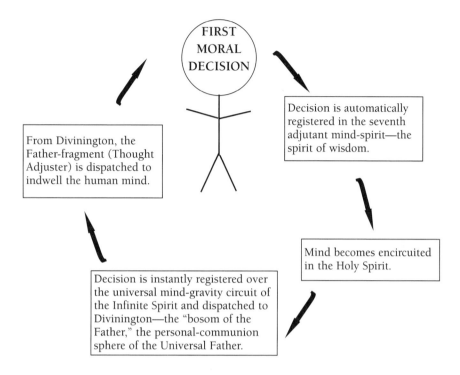

FIRST MORAL DECISION

From Divinington, the Father-fragment (Thought Adjuster) is dispatched to indwell the human mind.

Decision is automatically registered in the seventh adjutant mind-spirit—the spirit of wisdom.

Mind becomes encircuited in the Holy Spirit.

Decision is instantly registered over the universal mind-gravity circuit of the Infinite Spirit and dispatched to Divinington—the "bosom of the Father," the personal-communion sphere of the Universal Father.

children once become self-conscious of the assurance of the divine presence, such a faith will expand the mind, ennoble the soul, reinforce the personality, augment the happiness, deepen the spirit perception, and enhance the power to love and be loved."[15]

Our words and actions reflect our level of receptivity to the guidance of the Indwelling Spirit; they indicate whether our thinking is ascending toward the superconscious level of mind, the zone of immediate contact with the Indwelling Spirit.[16] When we are in tune with our Indwelling Spirit, our words and actions become saturated with love and wisdom, creating an influence that is sincere, beautiful, and good. Illustration 23,[17] adapted for this book, provides a comparison between the influence of those thoughts, words, and actions that spring from love and those that reflect blocked love.

4. The Soul

"The evolving soul of a human being is difficult of description and more difficult of demonstration because it is not discoverable by the methods of either material investigation or spiritual proving. Material science cannot demonstrate the existence of a soul, neither can pure spirit-testing.

Illustration 23
INFLUENCE OF SPIRIT GUIDANCE

Influence of Egocentric Information	Influence of Spirit Guidance
Creates conflict with personal ethics	Creates no conflict with personal ethics
Creates fear, negativity	Creates more love, inspiration, empowerment
Demands obedience or surrender	Suggests, advises, enables independent decisions
Includes generalities, avoids content	Is relevant, intelligent, logical
Is conditional	Is unconditional, appropriate, natural
Appeals to curiosity, self-image	Appeals to goodwill, beauty, unity
Originates from disingenuous sources	Originates from still, single inner-knowing voice
Affirms ultimate authority for itself	Counsels, acquiesces to higher power
Requires little if any personal effort	Requires personal effort and commitment
Promotes emotional desires, glamour	Promotes higher spiritual guidance
Benefits the receiver of information	Benefits the common good
Has fixed interpretation	Has flexible interpretation
Creates dependencies	Creates interdependence
Promotes separation	Promotes unity
Is self-focused	Is outgoing, socially responsive
Affirms mediocrity	Promotes development, making a difference
Reflects partial picture	Reflects the whole picture
Overly emotional or rational	Is intuitive
Results in self-delusion	Results in self-discovery
Focuses on self-service	Focuses on meanings and values
Addresses myopic needs	Addresses community needs
Creates illusion	Reveals truth

Notwithstanding the failure of both material science and spiritual standards to discover the existence of the human soul, every morally conscious mortal knows of the existence of *his* soul as a *real* and actual personal experience."[18]

Since primitive times, people believed there was something inside of them destined to survive the short span of terrestrial life. At first this something, eventually called soul, ". . . was thought to reside in different physical organs— the eye, liver, kidney, heart, and later, the brain. The savage associated the soul with blood, breath, shadows and with reflections of the self in water."[19]

The ancient monistic Hindu theory of creation suggests that creation began when the individual immortal souls (atmans) become separated from Brahm, the "undifferentiated One." Each individual soul is indestructible, immortal, each identical with Brahm. A soul enters into many bodies, assumes many forms and passes through many births and deaths, with the ego, or individual identity, being but a passing state that can be dismissed in meditation or shunned in action.

To the ancient Egyptians, the *ba* (soul) made it possible for the deceased to leave his tomb and rejoin his *ka* (spirit). The *akh* was the result of the union between the ba and the ka. The Chinese distinguished between a lower, sensitive soul that disappears upon death and a rational principle, the *hun*, that survives death and is the object of ancestor worship.

Know ye not that ye are the temple of God and that the spirit of God dwelleth in you?
1 Corinthians 3:16

The early Hebrews could not conceive of the body and soul as being separate entities; thus many scriptural references to the soul are tied to the concepts of breath, blood, the seat of emotions, and the origin of moral feelings. Despite the wide variation of definitions, in the Old Testament, soul is ". . . a united and unifying entity, the carrier of individual psychological and spiritual life in all its various manifestations. It is also the *nephesh* that is that part of God's creation that knows the Creator most intimately."[20]

In the Western world, the concept of soul emerged slowly and blossomed in the mythological thinking of Plato. "For Socrates and Plato the soul was clearly a definite entity that could exist apart from the body. It was far more than merely a personification of the life of the body, for, Plato said, it was a 'self-moving' power, which could produce its own motion and could also set the body into motion. As such it existed before the body and could survive the death of the body. It was also the carrier of individual personality and . . . could be reincarnated in other existences."[21]

In the New Testament, the soul is a living reality; it survives mortal death and continues to live a vital life in heaven.

Concepts of the relation between body and soul originated with the ancient Greeks and were introduced into Christian theology in the fourth century after Christ by the Cappadocian father St. Gregory of Nyssa, and by the Christian Neoplatonist and North African bishop Aurelius Augustinus, more commonly known as St. Augustine. In Christian traditions, the soul enlivens the body. It is the carrier of identity and the seat of consciousness, individual choice, and action. While some traditions hold that souls may be saved or destroyed, others maintain that souls may be saved or eternally separated from God. If salvation is understood to require some human effort, then emphasis is placed on prayer, belief in Jesus, service work, scripture reading, and other activities.

From the Middle Ages onward, the existence and nature of the soul and its relationship to the body has been a source of debate in Western philosophy. Regardless of how much discussion the topic elicits, there is no scientific evidence for a soul; its existence may be accepted on the basis of one or more of the following:

- Faith
- Intuitive knowledge supported by the wisdom of ancient sacred texts

- The words of Jesus of Nazareth, who mentions the soul in the Gospels
- Epochal revelation

Some scholars deny the immortality of the soul; others affirm it. Some debate its essence and others its form. A perennial question remains: Is the soul created or is it preexistent?

Illustration 24 outlines concepts associated with the soul, including reconciled function based on the teachings in *The Urantia Book*.

We can now address some questions: What is the soul? What is the soul's origin, purpose, and destination? Do animals have souls?

According to epochal revelation, "The soul is the self-reflective, truth-discerning, and spirit-perceiving part of man which forever elevates the human being above the level of the animal world . . . Moral choice and spiritual attainment, the ability to know God and the urge to be like him, are the characteristics of the soul."[22]

The Divine Plan of Progress provides for the human personality to survive physical death and attain eternal life. To enable this, the Indwelling Spirit, the immortal aspect of mortals, is bestowed by the Universal Father on every human personality. The presence of the Indwelling Spirit gives birth to the soul, the evolving entity that has the capacity for spiritual growth and immortality.

The first moral *activity* of the human mind triggers the arrival of the Indwelling Spirit and subsequent birth of the soul. The soul is therefore not preexistent; it is a joint creation of the Indwelling Spirit and the mind early in the life of a human being. Once created, this embryonic soul, neither material

Illustration 24
SOUL CONCEPTS

Common Concepts	Revealed Concepts
Vital spark that animates the body; breath	The soul is not the "vital spark." The vital spark is the essential factor of the living plasm that turns inert physical patterns into living matter. It is *imparted* by the Life Carriers but is *supplied* by the Local Universe Mother Spirit. When the energy of the vital spark is spent, the physical body dies.
Spirit	The soul is not the indwelling immortal spirit.
	The Indwelling Spirit is the aspect of mortals that is eternal and immortal.
	The indwelling immortal spirit is a prepersonal, fully conscious fragment of the Universal Father.
	The Indwelling Spirit is the potential of the human personality's next order of existence. Its attainment of personality is dependent on the survival of the soul.
The Mind	The soul is not the human mind. The mind is an individualized "circuit" of the cosmic mind.
Human Identity	The soul is not the human personality. Survival after death of mortal identity is dependent on the survival of the soul.

nor spiritual (morontia), is destined to grow and evolve relative to the individual's increasing attunement of the human will with the will of God as it resides in the Indwelling Spirit.

Soul survival, in union with the human personality, is neither automatic nor imminent. The human personality must develop the soul deliberately and progressively through free-will choices. Recognition of the relationships between the soul, the Indwelling Spirit, and the human personality engenders a life of love and service and assures us of the real possibilities of personality survival—advancement, growth, experience, and adventure after death.

The Urantia Book explains that animals do not have souls, for they lack the ministry of the mind adjutants of worship and wisdom and are not indwelt by the spirit of the Father, the parent of the soul. When asked whether dogs have a soul and a will, Jesus presented the following eloquent response: "'The dog has a mind which can know material man, his master, but cannot know God, who is spirit; therefore the dog does not possess a spiritual nature and cannot enjoy a spiritual experience. The dog may have a will derived from nature and augmented by training, but such a power of mind is not a spiritual force, neither is it comparable to the human will, inasmuch as it is not *reflective*—it is not the result of discriminating higher and moral meanings or choosing spiritual and eternal values. It is the possession of such powers of spiritual discrimination and truth choosing that makes mortal man a moral being, a creature endowed with the attributes of spiritual responsibility and the potential of eternal survival.'"[23]

Jesus went on to explain that it is the absence of such mental powers in the animal that makes it forever impossible for the animal world to experience anything equivalent to personality survival in eternity. "The departing life of such a living thing possesses neither identity nor personality; it does not individually survive death. During its existence and the time of its sojourn in the body of matter, it has undergone a change; it has undergone energy evolution and survives only as a part of the cosmic forces of the universe; it does not survive as individual life."[24]

Personality

Human personality is usually considered synonymous with identity, the character traits that distinguish one living being from another, including a variety of physical characteristics as well as temperamental and emotional expressions. Scholars agree that personality is the complex of characteristics that include both the external appearance one presents to the world and the inner qualities more representative of the "true, spiritual self." Epochal revelation provides stunning new insights into this intriguing subject.

The Universal Father has been defined as the divine personality of the I AM, and the Eternal Son the pattern, the exemplar of divine personality. God is characterized as personal in that ". . . he exercises a sovereign will, experiences self-consciousness of divinity, executes the mandates of a creative mind, pursues the satisfaction of the realization of an eternal purpose, and manifests a Father's love and affection for his universe children."[25]

Each human is gifted by the Universal Father with an individualized pattern of divine personality. Every one of us is a unique child of the universe. Just as an oak tree exists in an acorn as potential, so do divine potentials exist at the core of human personality. The will and self-consciousness inherent in personality enable the individual to carry out the dictates of the creative mind—to find and recognize the Father in Paradise and manifest a father's love and affection for fellow human beings. "Truth is coherent, beauty attractive, goodness stabilizing. And when these values of that which is real are coordinated in personality experience, the result is a high order of love conditioned by wisdom and qualified by loyalty."[26]

> *The Universal Father is the secret of the reality of personality, the bestowal of personality, and the destiny of personality.*
>
> The Urantia Book

The personalization of mortals by the Universal Father is augmented by an extraordinary gift: the bestowal of his immortal spirit devoted to realizing the spiritual potential of the human mind and immortalizing the soul. These unique bestowals by the Father constitute a personal ministry to his universe children and are his exclusive domain. A human personality therefore is a personal mind-energy system with a spirit nucleus—it has identity and is endowed with self-consciousness and liberty of choice.[27]

"Self-consciousness is in essence a communal consciousness: God and man, Father and son, Creator and creature."[28] A person not only is able to be intellectually aware of other human personalities, but is also able to sense the indwelling divine presence and choose to follow its leadings. The endowment of self-consciousness indicates the capacity for personal experience with cosmic realities;[29] a person therefore has the inherent potential to recognize mind/spirit ministry and to eventually personally recognize the Universal Father in eternity.

"In human self-consciousness four universe-reality realizations are latent and inherent:

1. The quest for knowledge, the logic of science.

2. The quest for moral values, the sense of duty.

3. The quest for spiritual values, the religious experience.

4. The quest for personality values, the ability to recognize the reality of God as a personality and the concurrent realization of our fraternal relationship with fellow personalities."[30]

Developing the spiritual capacity inherent in self-consciousness is up to the individual. This is most effectively done when we consecrate our will to doing the will of the Father—to grow in God-consciousness and Godlikeness.

Will is more than the power to choose a purpose and to act upon it. "Will is that manifestation of the human mind which enables the subjective consciousness to express itself objectively and to experience the phenomenon of aspiring to be Godlike."[31] When a person is reflective and spiritually minded, she can thus become creative. "That which the enlightened and reflective human imagination of spiritual teaching and leading wholeheartedly and unselfishly wants to do and be, becomes measurably creative in accordance with the degree of mortal dedication to the divine doing of the Father's will. When man goes in partnership with God, great things may, and do, happen."[32]

The power of choice constitutes our greatest opportunity and our supreme cosmic responsibility—the eternal destiny of the human personality depends upon the integrity of the human will.[33] "The relative free will which characterizes the self-consciousness of human personality is involved in:

1. Moral decision, highest wisdom.
2. Spiritual choice, truth discernment.
3. Unselfish love, brotherhood service.
4. Purposeful cooperation, group loyalty.
5. Cosmic insight, the grasp of universe meanings.
6. Personality dedication, wholehearted devotion to doing the Father's will.
7. Worship, the sincere pursuit of divine values and the wholehearted love of the divine Value-Giver."[34]

The character traits of a human personality are transient achievements without development of the soul, the vehicle for identity survival, via progressive attunement to the immortal Indwelling Spirit. The Indwelling Spirit tutors the growth of the immortal soul, and the soul in turn frees the human personality from ". . . the fetters of causation response, at least as pertains to eternal destiny . . ."[35] However, survival is a choice, and it is left to the human personality to will or inhibit the growth of the soul, the immortal self. When the God-seeking human personality discovers higher moral meanings and chooses spiritual and eternal values, she effects the potential transfer of the seat of human identity from the intellect to the more enduring and immortal nature of the soul.[36]

The will is simply the extension of a purpose and since Spirit is absolute, there can be nothing to deny its will. Choice, volition, and will are necessary attributes of self-existent power, for without them, there would be no channel through which the ideas of God could be expressed.

Ernest Holmes, *Science of Mind Glossary*

Through the power of choice, the human personality develops the soul, and in union with the soul, survives physical death. This is the difference between a personal and a nonpersonal energy system; the latter has no choice. An animal or plant undergoes energy evolution but cannot survive as an individual without the immortal spirit to originate the soul. It is this powerful entity of the soul, the offspring of the human mind and Indwelling Spirit, which offers the human personality the potential to transcend the experience of death.

14.

Morality, the Golden Rule, and the Family

Only moral beings will ever seek for that spiritual insight
which is essential to living the golden rule.

The Urantia Book

Morality means different things to different people but is generally defined as righteous behavior based upon the discrimination between right and wrong. A higher level of interpretation perceives it to be a pattern of conduct informed by spiritual insight; a discipline of self-action guided by divine ideals.

Values of a moral nature have developed through the ages as expressions of conscience, adopted socially as ethics. Unfortunately, civil mores haven't evolved evenly across world cultures; differences in class, status, and gender—often defined by stagnant beliefs—inhibit moral growth. Nevertheless, morality has generally advanced worldwide, even independent of belief in God. Morality, as practiced today, embraces ethical reasoning, religious beliefs, moral understanding, and social mores. What may be considered moral in the West, however, may not always reflect the same values in other cultures. In time, our world will grow in cosmic awareness, and humanity will increasingly live the golden rule from its highest level of interpretation.

What is the springboard for the moral impulses that push civilization toward higher ideals of living? *The Urantia Book* reveals moral insights of epochal import—new understanding with the potential to reshape the very foundation of religion and philosophy.

The human mind is endowed with three cosmic responses: scientific, moral, and spiritual insight. "Intelligence alone cannot explain the moral nature. Morality, virtue, is indigenous to human personality. Moral intuition, the realization of duty, is a component of human mind endowment and is associated with the other inalienables of human nature: scientific curiosity and spiritual insight."[1] These innate endowments of the human mind are developed with education, expressed by culture, and appreciated through life experiences; they are ennobled by religion and unified by personality.[2]

Balanced development of scientific, moral, and spiritual insight cultivates a noble character of spiritual endowments—a wise, loving, and unselfish character. In this effort, we are not alone. According to epochal revelation, God has endowed every normal-minded human with the gift of direct lines to divine righteousness. What is accepted as a reasoning process, the determination of right and wrong, is in essence a conspiracy of spirit influences operating within the human mind. "The physical brain with its associated nervous system possesses innate capacity for response to mind ministry just as the developing mind of a personality possesses a certain innate capacity for spirit receptivity and therefore contains the potentials of spiritual progress and attainment. Intellectual, social, moral, and spiritual evolution is dependent on the mind ministry of the seven adjutant spirits and their superphysical associates."[3]

The human urge to serve others and the ideal of altruism are the direct result of the collaboration of spiritual ministries that include the adjutant mind-spirits, the Holy Spirit, the Spirit of Truth, and the Indwelling Spirit. These spiritual influences are always present, but it rests upon the evolving human personality to choose and act on them. Our free will is the wild card in moral and spiritual evolution. The reality of spirit intuition is evidenced by the certainty of knowing right from wrong; choosing to act in accordance with divine guidance is righteousness. "Moral evaluation with a religious meaning—spiritual insight—connotes the individual's choice between good and evil, truth and error, material and spiritual, human and divine, time and eternity."[4]

With the first moral decision of a child (indicating response to the adjutant spirits of worship and wisdom) the mind is in full attunement with the ministry of the Holy Spirit, and the Father responds with a bestowal of divinity: the Indwelling Spirit. This achievement of moral status is momentous, for it signals the birth of the soul. "'. . . and the soul is that part of man which represents the potential survival value of human experience. Moral choice and spiritual attainment, the ability to know God and the urge to be like him, are the characteristics of the soul. The soul of man cannot exist apart from moral thinking and spiritual activity . . . But the soul of man is distinct from the divine spirit which dwells within the mind. The divine spirit arrives simultaneously with the first moral activity of the human mind, and that is the occasion of the birth of the soul.'"[5]

The endowment of the Indwelling Spirit enables the meta-meaning of morality to evolve, informing our recognition of universal right and wrong and igniting our realization of the inner presence of the spirit of the Father. Choosing to obey the divinity within promotes consistent moral behavior and enlivens spiritual activity—essentials in developing the soul and living the golden rule. Jesus of Nazareth made this truth the centerpiece of his revelation: "'The kingdom of God is within you' was probably the greatest pronouncement Jesus ever made, next to the declaration that his Father is a living and loving spirit."[6]

This new and enlarged perspective of morality is further clarified by revelation. Our moral nature is but the initial stage in our celestial evolution, the ascent of personality perfection. The choosing between good and evil, though influenced by the moral motivation of the individual, is also colored by relative ignorance, immaturity, and stubborn self-will. Likewise, our emerging moral nature is hampered without the willingness to explore deeper meanings and discover higher spiritual values. "Religion cannot be bestowed, received, loaned, learned, or lost. It is a personal experience which grows proportionally to the growing quest for final values. Cosmic growth thus attends on the accumulation of meanings and the ever-expanding elevation of values. But nobility itself is always an unconscious growth."[7]

The human personality ascends from the expression of inconsistent morality to supermorality. "Moral will embraces decisions based on reasoned knowledge, augmented by wisdom, and sanctioned by religious faith. Such choices are acts of moral nature and evidence the existence of moral personality, the forerunner of morontia personality and eventually of true spirit status.[8]

The recognition of the presence of the Indwelling Spirit widens our understanding of morality in profound ways. As we explore the evolution of social mores and codes of conduct, we realize that every impulse to righteous action and every moral law handed down had origin in *spirit*, even a team of spiritual helpers that speak to us in "a still small voice" (1 Kings 19:11–12) and guide us with visions, dreams, and creative imagination. The process of evolving the soul is possible because the human mind is personal (it experiences self-consciousness and free will) and is endowed with spirit ministry. These properties promote the evolution of a moral nature capable of choosing God, emulating his nature, and perfecting the soul. "Every time man makes a reflective moral choice, he immediately experiences a new divine invasion of his soul."[9]

This expanded awareness of ever-present moral guidance is a potent kernel of truth, the seed of a developing paradigm shift in the scheme of advancing civilization. Epochal revelation projects that as humankind attunes and responds to divine ideals, it will progressively personify altruism and cooperation—the practical and spiritual impulses that will inaugurate the universal brotherhood of man.

The Emergence of Morality

The evolution of moral law parallels the development of humankind, starting with the religious impulse in primitive peoples. The inability to understand the unseen forces of nature cultivated superstition, which gave rise to the earliest codes of conduct. The ancients believed that their taboos, or prohibitions, had been given to their ancestors by the gods, an understanding informed by a degree of truth. Religious rituals evolved, designed to appease the unseen forces; sacrifice was introduced to ward off calamities wrought by angry spirits, and to please the gods. "The intention and will of the spirits were studied by means of omens, oracles, and signs. And these spirit messages were interpreted by divination, soothsaying, magic, ordeals, and astrology. The whole cult was a scheme designed to placate, satisfy, and buy off the spirits through this disguised bribery."[10] In this environment of emotional fear, early notions of social duty and moral obligation took root. "And thus there grew up a new and expanded world philosophy consisting in:

1. Duty—those things which must be done to keep the spirits favorably disposed, at least neutral.

2. Right—the correct conduct and ceremonies designed to win the spirits actively to one's interests.

3. Truth—the correct understanding of, and attitude toward, spirits, and hence toward life and death."[11]

Humans passed these civilizing principles from generation to generation, influencing and building greater societies. As formalized language developed, the moral imperative became crystallized into the maxims, proverbs, and rules that became society's mores and laws. "But in all of this religious evolution the moral element was never wholly absent . . . notwithstanding it [religion] was so often threatened with extinction by a thousand subversive tendencies and hostile antagonisms."[12]

Religion's Influence on Morality

True religion references God and spirit realities. Society can reach a fair level of moral refinement without religion, but "[m]orality without religion fails to reveal ultimate goodness, and it also fails to provide for the survival of even its own moral values. Religion provides for the enhancement, glorification, and assured survival of everything morality recognizes and approves."[13] Without faith and growth in the God concept, the higher values of religion remain undiscovered; the quality of selflessness in moral behavior does not flourish in a nonreligious society, stunting the full expression of goodness that builds the brotherhood of man. "A lasting social system without a morality predicated on spiritual realities can no more be maintained than could the solar system without gravity."[14]

Human curiosity leads to growth in scientific insight, and human experience gives birth to the consciousness of duty for the sake of others. But it is religion, living faith, that vaults the sense of duty up to the affectionate level of intimate family morality, the parent-child relationship, and inspires individuals to live unselfishly. True religion flourishes and moral behavior blossoms to great heights of expression when individuals are engaged in continued efforts at self-improvement for the purpose of growing in their love for God as Father and their fellow human beings as brothers and sisters. Loving service for humanity is manifested by the heartfelt relationship with God the

> *The germs of true religion originate in the domain of man's moral consciousness, and they are revealed in the growth of man's spiritual insight, that faculty of human personality which accrues as a consequence of the presence of the God-revealing Thought Adjuster in the God-hungry mortal mind.*
>
> The Urantia Book

Father. True religion ". . . is a genuine personal experience which no man can contain within himself . . . the consciousness of being a member of the family of believers leads inevitably to the practice of the precepts of the family conduct, the service of one's brothers and sisters in the effort to enhance and enlarge the brotherhood."[15]

The evolving human mind fashions codes of ethics and moral law, but the Indwelling Spirit reveals the Father-source of all that is true, beautiful, and good. Morality embraces values, and growth in spiritual insight conserves, exalts, and spiritualizes those values. The spiritual choices and moral decisions of the human personality determine individual survival and social progress.

There is a pattern by which civilizations evolve in greatness over time: genuine religion embodies spiritual intuition, which promotes higher expressions of morality; laws are enacted that reflect an enhanced sense of personal and social duty, raising the standards and achievements of that civilization. Religion, morality, and law march in step for the advancement of humanity. The evolution of the golden rule demonstrates how higher understanding of this universal moral code is in keeping with the enlarging concepts of divinity.

The Evolution of the Golden Rule

The golden rule, also called the "ethic of reciprocity," is found in nearly all religions and philosophies. In the modern era, it is usually expressed as "Love others as oneself" and "Do unto others as you would have them do unto you."

The impulse to selflessly do good to others, though limited in past eras, grows as religious civilization advances. Five hundred thousand years after the appearance of human will, fear and ignorance prevailed. The Planetary Prince Caligastia and his staff arrived on Earth to launch the long program of guiding primitive tribes of people toward a human civilization. One of the greatest obstacles to the positive influence of these extraplanetary teachers was the tendency of the primitive people to regard them as gods, a theme that became cemented in the later combat myths. For the first thousand years, the superhuman staff worked to instill an awareness of God the Creator, upgrading human animal fear and superstitious worship of the unknown. They provided the early races with a moral system known as "the Father's Way," which included the following seven guidelines expressed in negative form:

"1. You shall not fear nor serve any God but the Father of all.

2. You shall not disobey the Father's Son, the world's ruler, nor show disrespect to his superhuman associates.

3. You shall not speak a lie when called before the judges of the people.

4. You shall not kill men, women, or children.

5. You shall not steal your neighbor's goods or cattle.

6. You shall not touch your friend's wife.

7. You shall not show disrespect to your parents or to the elders of the tribe.

This was the law of Dalamatia for almost three hundred thousand years. And many of the stones on which this law was inscribed now lie beneath the waters off the shores of Mesopotamia and Persia. It became the custom to hold one of these commands in mind for each day of the week, using it for salutations and mealtime thanksgiving."[16] The laws of Dalamatia were practiced by humans until the Lucifer rebellion. Henceforth, Earth's civilization morally regressed due to the promotion of self-assertion. Between the start of the Lucifer rebellion and the ten commandments of Moses, other laws of morality were taught by Adam and Eve and Machiventa Melchizedek.

Adam and Eve, the material son and daughter, arrived on Earth over thirty-seven thousand years ago to begin the process of moral and biologic uplift. They reintroduced knowledge of the Father and orders of divine sonship and taught that only the Father was to be worshiped. Adam and Eve introduced the moral law of Eden, which was similar to the seven commandments of Dalamatia. Although Adam and Eve aided the biological progress of the human race and contributed many artistic and practical gifts to civilization, their default sentenced our world to long ages of confusion and struggle.

During the millennia that followed, revealed truth was threatened with extinction; the human races were making progress intellectually but losing ground spiritually. The concept of God had grown hazy in the minds of mortals. About two thousand years before the birth of Jesus, Machiventa Melchizedek materialized on Earth and taught the concept of one God, a universal Deity. The Salem religion, as presented by Melchizedek, was based on faith: believing in the one God, Creator, and Universal Father. Melchizedek taught that God's favor was earned by faith rather than by sacrifices and burnt offerings. His teachings also included obeying a moral code presented in the seven commandments. "The seven commandments promulgated by Melchizedek were patterned along the lines of the ancient Dalamatian supreme law and very much resembled the seven commands taught in the first and second Edens. These commands of the Salem religion were:

1. You shall not serve any God but the Most High Creator of heaven and earth.

2. You shall not doubt that faith is the only requirement for eternal salvation.

3. You shall not bear false witness.

4. You shall not kill.

5. You shall not steal.

6. You shall not commit adultery.

7. You shall not show disrespect for your parents and elders."[17]

The concept of faith, however, was too advanced for the people of those days. "They simply could not grasp the idea of getting divine favor for nothing—by faith. They were too deeply confirmed in the belief that man was born under forfeit to the gods."[18] Abraham, Melchizedek's prize pupil, wholeheartedly believed in him and promulgated the covenant of divine favor through faith. But by the time the Semite peoples were enslaved in Egypt,

Melchizedek's teachings were submerged in the older and more prevalent superstitions and beliefs of the many existing cults. When Moses led the Bedouin Semites into the Promised Land, they had their moral rules, which served as law right up to the time this Semitic group were encamped before Sinai. "And these ten commandments were:

1. You shall worship no other god, for the Lord is a jealous God.
2. You shall not make molten gods.
3. You shall not neglect to keep the feast of unleavened bread.
4. Of all the males of men or cattle, the first-born are mine, says the Lord.
5. Six days you may work, but on the seventh day you shall rest.
6. You shall not fail to observe the feast of the first fruits and the feast of the ingathering at the end of the year.
7. You shall not offer the blood of any sacrifice with leavened bread.
8. The sacrifice of the feast of the Passover shall not be left until morning.
9. The first of the first fruits of the ground you shall bring to the house of the Lord your God.
10. You shall not seethe a kid in its mother's milk."[19]

"The seven commandments of Dalamatia and Eden, as well as the ten injunctions of the Hebrews, were definite taboos, all expressed in the same negative form as were the most ancient prohibitions. But these newer codes were truly emancipating in that they took the place of thousands of preexistent taboos. And more than this, these later commandments definitely promised something in return for obedience."[20]

Moses, the emancipator of the Semite people, had been greatly influenced by the teachings of Machiventa as they had been perpetuated in his family. ". . . and by the time of the Hebrew encampment about Mount Sinai after the flight from Egypt, he had formulated a new and enlarged concept of Deity (derived from all his former beliefs), which he wisely decided to proclaim to his people as an expanded concept of their olden tribal god, Yahweh."[21] When Sinai erupted, Moses used the opportunity to present his people with the new ten commandments (cf. Deuteronomy 5:6–21 and Exodus 20:2–17):

1. Have no other gods before me.
2. Make no images of anything in heaven, earth or the sea, and do not worship or labor for them.
3. Do not vainly use the name of your God.
4. Do not work on the seventh day of the week.
5. Honor your parents.
6. Do not kill.
7. Do not commit adultery.
8. Do not steal.
9. Do not give false testimony against another.
10. Do not desire another's wife or anything that belongs to another.

"Moses, in the addition of the second commandment to the ancient Dalamatian moral code, made an effort to control fetish worship among the Hebrews. He carefully directed that they should make no sort of image that might become consecrated as a fetish. He made it plain, 'You shall not make a graven image or any likeness of anything that is in heaven above, or on the earth beneath, or in the waters of the earth.' While this commandment did much to retard art among the Jews, it did lessen fetish worship."[22]

The commandments of Moses are recorded twice in the Scriptures, and the reason for keeping the Sabbath day (fourth commandment) is different in each passage. In Deuteronomy 5:15, deliverance from Egypt is assigned as the reason for Sabbath keeping, while in Exodus 20:11, the advancing religious beliefs of the Jewish forefathers demanded that this be changed to recognize the fact of creation as the reason for observing the Sabbath.[23]

"Words eventually became fetishes, more especially those which were regarded as God's words; in this way the sacred books of many religions have become fetishistic prisons incarcerating the spiritual imagination of man. Moses' very effort against fetishes became a supreme fetish; his commandment was later used to stultify art and to retard the enjoyment and adoration of the beautiful."[24]

During the Babylonian exile, the young prophet Isaiah the second presented to the Jews an enlarged and sublime portrayal of the magnificence of the supreme Yahweh. He condensed the ten negative commandments ". . . into the great and positive law of love, the injunction to love God supremely and your neighbor as yourself."[25] As religious civilization and human interaction advanced, the concept of one's neighbor expanded to embrace the tribe and the homeland. With this evolution of the golden rule, humans began to express sympathetic understanding and eventually arrived at the recognition of one's personal duty toward the welfare of others.

Two thousand years ago, Jesus of Nazareth enlarged the scope of neighbor to embrace the whole of humanity, including enemies, and declared that this supreme law of love for God and for others constitutes our whole duty. With his personal revelation of the nature of the Father, he elevated the meaning of the golden rule: ". . . Jesus taught his followers to manifest fatherly love rather than *brotherly* love. Brotherly love would love your neighbor as you love yourself, and that would be adequate fulfillment of the 'golden rule.' But fatherly affection would require that you should love your fellow mortals as Jesus loves you."[26]

The Urantia Book clarifies and expands the concept of God and provides unparalleled information on the nature and mission of the Indwelling Spirit, which greatly enhances our ability to grasp the cosmic relatedness between God and mortals and among human beings. This enlarged perspective bears higher awareness of our sonship status and deeper appreciation for the familial relationship between all personalities, inspiring us to treat each other with brotherly, even fatherly, love.

Spiritual growth demands progress in meanings. The way we interpret a teaching depends upon how appreciative we are of ideals, morals, ethics, standards, and principles. Interpretations have many levels of meaning; the highest level is produced by a cultivated spiritual insight. How we treat others reflects our interpretation of the golden rule; it indicates our level of understanding of God and his relation to humanity, as well as the level of spiritual meaning we have been able to discover through our efforts at cultivating a balanced God-knowing personality:

1. **The level of self-interest**: At this basic level of interpretation, a person functions from a purely selfish perspective. "The golden rule, when divested of the superhuman insight of the Spirit of Truth, becomes nothing more than a rule of high ethical conduct. The golden rule, when literally interpreted, may become the instrument of great offense to one's fellows. Without a spiritual discernment of the golden rule of wisdom you might reason that, since you are desirous that all men speak the full and frank truth of their minds to you, you should therefore fully and frankly speak the full thought of your mind to your fellow beings. Such an unspiritual interpretation of the golden rule might result in untold unhappiness and no end of sorrow."[27]

2. **The level of the emotions**: At this level of interpretation, a person's behavior demonstrates fairness and sympathy or pity.

3. **The level of mind**: As the mind is cultivated, a person learns from experience and grows in patience, self-respect, and ethical awareness. This is reflected in good judgment when we interact with others.

4. **The level of brotherly/sisterly understanding**: As we enhance spiritual insight, sibling affection for others grows out of the consciousness of the fatherhood of God and the consequent recognition of the brotherhood of man. A genuine concern for the good of others, including those outside our circle of family and friends, is carved into our interpretation of the golden rule.

5. **The moral level**: When people are able to attain true philosophic levels of interpretation, they gain real insight into the rightness and wrongness of actions and are merciful. They apply the golden rule to personal problems as would a high-minded, idealistic, wise, and impartial third person.

6. **The spiritual level**: The level of heightened spiritual insight and spiritual interpretation impels us to recognize in the golden rule the divine command to look upon every person as God looks upon his creatures. We treat everyone with the unselfish attitude of a wise and loving parent and are moved by that love to provide unconditional service to humanity. This is the universe ideal of human relationships. "And when such spirit-led mortals realize the true meaning of this golden rule, they are filled to overflowing with the assurance of citizenship in a friendly universe, and their ideals of spirit reality are satisfied only when they love their fellows as Jesus loved us all, and that is the reality of the realization of the love of God."[28]

"The present can be truly interpreted only in the light of the correlated past and future."[29] Our consideration of the six levels of meanings of the golden rule enables us to gauge where we are in our spiritual development and gives us an indication of how much we have yet to grow. To elevate our functioning from the level of self-interest, we must increase the *quality* and *consistency* of our expression of love by developing our thinking skills, striving for emotional maturity, and strengthening our moral values, specifically trustworthiness. To function from the level of brotherly/sisterly love, we must simultaneously increase our *capacity* to love by enhancing spiritual insight—growing in the revelatory knowledge of God and increasing our understanding of God's relation to the universe. As we grow in recognition of the indwelling presence of the spirit of the Father and become attuned to its guidance, we are empowered to worship God by living the golden rule from its highest level of interpretation. In the expression of the highest ideals of parental love toward one another, humanity will achieve the highest possible demonstration of goodness in our world.

"You can psychologize evolutionary religion but not the personal-experience religion of spiritual origin. Human morality may recognize values, but only religion can conserve, exalt, and spiritualize such values. But notwithstanding such actions, religion is something more than emotionalized morality. Religion is to morality as love is to duty, as sonship is to servitude, as essence is to substance. Morality discloses an almighty Controller, a Deity to be served; religion discloses an all-loving Father, a God to be worshiped and loved. And again this is because the spiritual potentiality of religion is dominant over the duty actuality of the morality of evolution."[30]

Marriage and Family

Growing up, I did not give much thought to the institution of marriage outside of my preteen dreams of falling in love, having babies, and living happily ever after. I believed that marriage was part of the natural sequence of events after finding my "other half." Two weeks after my wedding, I realized that being in love was not enough to make a marriage work. It took two decades of self-development and a second failed marriage to realize that the success of a marriage relationship invariably hinges upon:

1. the quality of the intent and vision that we bring into the marriage

2. our capacity to trust

3. our capacity to give and receive

When I explored the concept of marriage in the light of epochal revelation and realized the function of marriage in the cosmic scheme of evolution, I gained a renewed sense of respect, humility, and commitment to my family.

Most people are born into less than ideal family relationships. Whatever the quality of our family life, our experience of these relationships sets the pattern of our interactions with others. When higher spiritual meanings and values are missing, dysfunctional behavior becomes generational, and the prospects for the marriage institution grow dimmer. This trend is reflected in current statistics. (Although our discussion here focuses mainly on the United States, data about other countries is included for context and comparison.)

In our society today there is an increasing inclination in the younger generation to extend childhood—to play video games every night, hang out with and text friends, and live a life free of responsibility. The cosmic importance of marriage is undervalued; life revolves around self, the tendency toward self-indulgence grows, and the value of unselfishness is ignored.

A study conducted in 2000 by Rutgers University's National Marriage Project showed that among adults aged 20–29, marriage does not represent the grand social, economic, religious, and public ideals it once did. Ninety-four percent said that finding their soul mate is more important to them than matters of religion, finances, and the ability to be a good parent. According to the study, young Americans are more interested in having fun than in developing lasting relationships that lead to marriage. Marriage is now often seen less as a necessary institution and more as a celebration that brings together family and friends. More marriages are being built on the concept of materialism and romance instead of ". . . a life-long partnership of self-effacement, compromise, devotion, and unselfish dedication to child culture."[31]

Troubling statistics and other documented trends reflect a breakdown of traditional marriage mores that have served to stabilize society for millennia.

- About one in three Americans will be divorced at least once.[32]

- In 2008, 67 percent of American children ages 0 through 17 lived with two parents, down from 77 percent in 1980.[33]

- Out-of-wedlock births have kept pace with the rise of civil unions. In France, Sweden, Norway, Estonia, and Bulgaria, for example, out-of-wedlock births have passed the 50 percent mark. In the United Kingdom, it is over 40 percent.[34] Unmarried childbearing in the United States reached historic levels in 2007, accounting for 39.7 percent of all births. In Catholic countries while births to married couples are still the norm, the percentage of out-of-wedlock births has doubled in the past decade.[35]

- In the United States, more than one million children each year experience the breakup of their families.

Caitlin Flanagan, author of the *Time* article "Why Marriage Matters," comments on the current health of the American marriage: "An increasingly fragile construct depending less and less on notions of sacrifice and obligation than on the ephemera of romance and happiness as defined by and for its adult principals, the intact, two-parent family remains our cultural ideal, but it exists under constant assault. It is buffeted by affairs and ennui, subject to the eternal American hope for greater happiness, for changing the hand you dealt yourself. Getting married for life, having children and raising them with your partner—this is still the way most Americans are conducting adult life, but the numbers who are moving in a different direction continue to rise . . ."[36]

Flanagan's article goes on to explain how much the American family has changed in the past forty years. "As sociologist Andrew J. Cherling observes in a landmark new book called *The Marriage Go-Round: The State of Marriage and the Family in America Today*, what is significant about contemporary American families, compared with those of other nations, is their combination of 'frequent marriage, frequent divorce' and the high number of 'short-term cohabiting relationships.' Taken together, these forces 'create a great turbulence in American family life, a family flux, a coming and going of partners on a scale seen nowhere else. There are more partners in the personal lives of Americans than in the lives of people of any other Western country.'"[37]

The lack of commitment between parents is taking a serious toll on children. Children are witnessing their parents drift in and out of their lives and experiencing the parents' half-hearted interest in their education and upbringing. The percentage of parents who work together at the significant job of rearing healthy children who have a love for wisdom and a righteous character is decreasing. Too many children lack a healthy parental role model to emulate for a higher understanding of love and selflessness, trust and respect. Organized religions understand the social implications of such a trend, but crystallized dogmas hinder their ability to successfully address this social crisis.

Epochal revelation explains that monogamy is the idealistic goal of human sex evolution; it is also indispensable to the development of social civilization. This is because "[i]t favors and fosters that intimate understanding and effective cooperation which is best for parental happiness, child welfare, and social efficiency." Because monogamy is not a natural human tendency, it requires development of self-control, moral awareness, and spiritual growth to make a success of marriage and home building.

Marriage is what gave humanity the home ". . . and the home is the crowning glory of the whole long and arduous evolutionary struggle. While religious, social, and educational institutions are all essential to the survival of cultural civilization, *the family is the master civilizer*. A child learns most of the essentials of life from his family and the neighbors."[38]

The amount of loving care and consideration that men and women are willing to bestow upon one another and their children is directly related to their attainment of higher levels of creative and spiritual consciousness. Selfless affection between two people is the spiritual connection that sustains a marriage.

Men and women are partners with God in their creation of children who, like themselves, have the potential for immortality. Parents fully share in the divine experience of creating sons and daughters of God. If parents develop their capacity to love selflessly, they will love and cherish each other "'. . . as the Father in heaven honors and exalts the Infinite Spirit, the mother of all the spirit children of a vast universe.'"[39]

According to epochal revelation, "[a]lmost everything of lasting value in civilization has its roots in the family. The family was the first successful peace group, the man and woman learning how to adjust their antagonisms while at the same time teaching the pursuits of peace to their children."[40] The home as an institution dates from the days of Dalamatia, about one-half million years ago. The stability of marriage has always shifted with fluctuations of the religious, moral, and ethical mores of the time. Earlier man protected his woman because she was his property, and she obeyed for the same reason. The relative merit of this system aside, it did provide stability.

As women and men finally emerge as peers, new mores will also emerge to stabilize the marriage/home institution, and they will address the following issues:

- "The new role of religion—the teaching that parental experience is essential, the idea of procreating cosmic citizens, the enlarged understanding of the privilege of procreation—giving sons to the Father."[41] According to epochal revelation, every human being must experience rearing children—their own or others—either on their planet of origin or in the aferlife. "Fathers must pass through this essential experience just as certainly as mothers. It is an unfortunate and mistaken notion of modern peoples on Urantia that child culture is largely the task of mothers. Children need fathers as well as mothers, and fathers need this parental experience as much as do mothers."[42] As humans grow in their appreciation of the Universal Father, they will recognize the privilege of bearing God's children and its inherent responsibility— to care for, train, and love their children so as to assist them in their development not only as wise, socially responsible and productive citizens, but as God-knowing individuals with the capacity to selflessly love and serve others.

- "The new role of science—procreation is becoming more and more voluntary, subject to man's control. In ancient times lack of understanding insured the appearance of children in the absence of all desire therefor."[43] Today, education and science have come a long way in enabling individuals to make intelligent choices about methods of conceiving children. The challenge lies in making wise and ethical choices that take into consideration the greater good. The default of Adam and Eve wrecked the Divine Plan of race improvement, leaving the challenge solely to the ingenuity of the human race. With scientific advancement in DNA modification comes the promise of less disease and more control over inherited disorders. Sometime in the future, reproduction will be wisely regulated in accord with planetary requirements, consensual compliance, and innate hereditary endowments; it will lead to a healthy population of citizens who contribute to the steady evolution of racial, political, economic, and religious harmony.

- The enjoyment of sex solely as a pleasure—marriage cannot survive when based purely on romantic chemistry and self-centered love. The true purposes of marriage are endangered when self-indulgence trumps family values: "Let man enjoy himself; let the human race find pleasure in a thousand and one ways; let evolutionary mankind explore all forms of legitimate self-gratification, the fruits of the long upward biologic struggle. Man has well earned some of his present-day joys and pleasures. But look you well to the goal of destiny! Pleasures are indeed suicidal if they succeed in destroying property, which has become the institution of self-maintenance; and self-gratifications have indeed cost a fatal price if they bring about the collapse of marriage, the decadence of family life, and the destruction of the home—man's supreme evolutionary acquirement and civilization's only hope of survival."[44]

- The enhancement of parental instinct[45]—parental love is instinctive because of the mind presence of the adjutant spirits, but it can stagnate when the capacity to love is not expanded.

The value of family in today's world of turmoil cannot be overemphasized: civilization is directly dependent on the effective functioning of the family unit. Family life is the ancestor of true morality, of the consciousness of loyalty to duty. "The enforced associations of family life stabilize personality and stimulate its growth. But even more, a true family—a good family—reveals to the parental procreators the attitude of the Creator to his children, while at the same time such true parents portray to their children . . . the love of the Paradise parent of all universe children."[46] A child best relates to its surroundings by first mastering the child–parent relationship and then by enlarging this concept to embrace the family as a whole. As the mind of the child grows, it is able to adjust to the concept of family relations, relationships of the community and the world, and then to those of the universe, the superuniverse, and even Paradise.[47] With the experience of a healthy, stable, and loving parent-child relationship, a child has the framework from which to relate to others lovingly as members of a family.

> *The only rock I know that stays steady, the only institution I know that works, is the family.*
>
> Lee Iacocca

Marriage is the enterprise of home building, offspring-rearing, mutual culture, and self-improvement. When we expand our cosmic perspective, build character, and grow in our receptivity to spirit guidance, we discover higher spiritual meanings and values in marriage and family and halt the current negative trend in the moral health of society. "Marriage, with children and consequent family life, is simulative of the highest potentials in human nature and simultaneously provides the ideal avenue for the expression of these quickened attributes of mortal personality. The family provides for the biologic perpetuation of the human species. The home is the natural social arena wherein the ethics of blood brotherhood may be grasped by the growing children. The family is the fundamental unit of fraternity in which parents and children learn those lessons of patience, altruism, tolerance, and forbearance which are so essential to the realization of brotherhood among all men."[48]

Section Two Summary

In our study thus far of humanity's spiritual history, vital information has advanced our knowledge of the past and increased our understanding of the present. When we approach this information with an objective and searching attitude, our study promotes self-inquiry and reflection while inviting critical assessments and dialogue.

The spiritual panorama presented in this section builds upon—and then eclipses—previous philosophical attempts to unite faith with reason; as with all new knowledge, it is gainful only to the degree that one is willing to objectively consider and test it. The following is a review of the history and administration of our planet. Along with the revelations in section one, these revelations add to the clarity of the Big Picture of Existence, raising the standard in our effort to reconcile science with religion, God, and the universe:

- Local Universe Sons are involved in the establishment and elevation of humanity and in the administration of the local systems and planets.

- Life does not spontaneously appear on a planet that can support and accommodate physical progress. Life Carriers, an order of Local Universe Sons, are the transporters, disseminators, and guardians of life.

- From the perspective of universal government, a planet is considered to be humanly inhabited when biological evolution attains the level of intelligent moral choice. At this point, the work of the Life Carriers terminates.

- The seven adjutant mind-spirits influence life in its evolution and adaptation to the environment.

- On Earth, Andon and Fonta were the first creatures to acquire the human standard of moral choice. They spawned the first human race, the Andonites, roughly one million years ago. The six colored races emerged from descendants of Andon and Fonta living in the north of India, over five hundred thousand years ago.

- When the protohumans of a planet have evolved to the point where they choose to worship and make moral decisions, the System Sovereign assigns a Planetary Prince to inaugurate human civilization. These spiritual rulers work to promote advancing levels of social functioning among primitive people, ushering in the emergence of family life.

- The Planetary Prince assigned to Earth more than five hundred thousand years ago was Caligastia, a Local Universe Son. He arrived

with a staff of one hundred volunteers, planetary missionaries from
other worlds who were provided with humanlike forms so as to interact
with Earth's inhabitants.

- Lucifer was the System Sovereign who assigned Caligastia as planetary
  ruler and whose rebellion later hindered the spiritual and social
  development of our planet.

- About two hundred thousand years ago, Lucifer instigated a system-
  wide revolt against the Universal Father, assisted by his first lieutenant,
  Satan. Earth's planetary ruler and sixty members of his staff joined the
  rebellion. The planet was quarantined when the spiritual circuits to all
  rebellious spheres in the local system were severed.

- The activities of the disloyal Caligastia earned him the title of "devil."
  Demoniacal possessions began at the onset of the planetary rebellion
  and ended at Pentecost when the Spirit of Truth was poured out upon
  all humanity.

- Although the Lucifer rebellion was not a physical battie on this or other
  worlds, it precipitated worldwide confusion—racial pandemonium—
  and the long delay in achieving a universal language and fraternal
  culture. The influence of Caligastia on Earth to this day promotes
  narcissistic tendencies and the perils of unrestrained self-will.

- Members of the rebellious staff became portrayed in myths and legends
  as the gods and rulers who came to Earth to create humanity.

- The rebel staff mated with local inhabitants, and their offspring
  demonstrated superior physical, intellectual, and spiritual capacities.
  This new eighth race on Earth was known as the Nodites.

- Adam and Eve were the Material Son and Daughter responsible for the
  biological uplift of humanity. They arrived on our planet over thirty-
  seven thousand years ago with the difficult task of reclaiming our world
  from a chotic state of affairs.

- Although Adam and Eve's genetic contribution increased human brain
  power, the pair's deviation from the Divine Plan deprived the races of a
  full complement of superior genes that would have improved the
  physical nature and spiritual potential of humanity.

- Three thousand years ago, Machiventa, a Melchizedek Son, materialized
  in Palestine to rekindle spiritual truth and prepare the world for the
  appearance of Jesus. He taught the Semitic tribes to worship one God
  and foretold of another Son of God who would come to teach them
  more.

- Abraham was one of Melchizedek's most brilliant pupils and chief
  supporters. He united the Bedouin tribes and sponsored the new
  Hebrew religion.

- Moses was the most important individual teacher and leader between
  the times of Machiventa and Jesus.

- Michael of Nebadon is the Creator Son of our local universe who bestowed himself on Earth as Jesus of Nazareth to attain full sovereignty of his creation and end the upheaval of a planetary rebellion. Though a Creator Son of God, he is not the second person of the Trinity, the Eternal Son.

- Jesus of Nazareth officially terminated the campaign of supreme self-assertion when he met face to face with Satan (representing Lucifer) and Caligastia on Mount Hermon.

- The greatest revelation of the Father's love is discovered in the life of Jesus of Nazareth. He was the rarest of the rare: a divine human. "[H]is life of achieving the Father's will becomes man's most real and ideal revelation of the personality of God."[1]

- From a cosmic perspective, a human being consists of form, mind, spirit, and soul, unified by personality. The Indwelling Spirit partners with the mind to originate and foster the growth of the soul and the immortality of the human personality.

- The endowment of the Indwelling Spirit enables the meta-meaning of morality to evolve, informing our recognition of universal right and wrong and igniting our realization of the inner presence of the spirit of the Father.

- Men and women are cocreators with God, producing children who likewise have the potential for immortality. Parents must share in the responsibility of educating their sons and daughters about the reality of God and his universe.

- Civilization is directly dependent on the effective functioning of the family unit. The family is where parents and children learn to exercise self-control and be patient, altruistic, and tolerant.

In this section, we have learned that humanity was placed at a disadvantage by three events in the "superphysical" history of our experimental planet:

1. The early emergence of free will engendered a self-willfulness that ingrained itself into the disposition of the human race. This was aggravated by the absence of a normal spiritual regime, the much-delayed assignment of a Planetary Prince.

2. The planetary rebellion robbed all subsequent generations of the moral and spiritual assistance—that superhuman guidance—that normally fosters a well-ordered society.

3. The Adam and Eve default deprived humans of a superior physical nature that would have contributed vitality to all the races and a disposition toward higher spiritual living.

The Melchizedek incarnation helped maintain the light of truth on the planet, but it was not until the bestowal of the Creator Son Michael as Jesus of Nazareth that our universe witnessed the perfect demonstration of the personality of God in a truly human experience. In the life of Jesus we see a portrayal of humanity at its best—a server of all, obedient to the Father's will.

The above revelations provide a broad perspective of our universe, the celestial hierarchy, and the part humanity plays in relation to God's Divine Plan. A significant conceptual shift in our human understanding of the relation between personality, the mind, the soul, and the Indwelling Spirit bring an enhanced perspective of the interior makeup of individuals. Knowledge of how celestial events affected humankind broadens our minds to embrace the fact that we are participants in God's Divine Plan. Understanding the commonalities in our origin and history provides us with the opportunity to unite in devotion to the Universal Father of all.

Illustration 25 provides a timetable of events that depict our common ancestry. It reveals the scope of our interconnectedness, enabling us to transcend concepts that do not support individual spiritual growth and collective unity. As we examine the information, we are reminded that science is ever in the process of discovering the full expanse of the cosmos, ever redefining its existing terms in light of new findings. We must patiently develop our efforts to understand the physical structure of our immense creation, but we must not wait to embark upon the spiritual journey that will ensure the eventual realization of world amity and peace.

Illustration 25
A BIGGER PICTURE OF EXISTENCE:
DENOTING SPIRITUAL AND PHYSICAL
RELATIONSHIPS IN HUMANITY'S ANCESTRY

The I AM Paradise/The Trinity All three Paradise Deities: The Father, Son, and Spirit	In the beginning, the I AM is static, motionless, timeless, and spaceless. The I AM releases itself from its static bonds of infinity. By becoming the Isle of Paradise, it establishes the center of all creation and the source and origin of all energies—material, mindal and spiritual. By simultaneously becoming the Father, Son, and Spirit, it establishes the associative relationships of eternity collectively known as *The Paradise Trinity*. The birth of Havona, the central universe, concurrently with the eternalizing of the Infinite Spirit, marks the traditional starting point of the history of the universe of universes. The Universal Father "eventuates" spirit beings such as: • The Architects of the Master Universe • The Master Force Organizers • The Architects of Being Master Force Organizers are nebulae creators. They instigate, organize, and direct these gigantic energy cyclones of space destined to become physical systems.	Existed before time began. Potentials enlivened. The vast stage of space is set for the stupendous drama of creation.
All three Paradise Deities: The Father, Son, and Spirit	Create triune-origin beings that include: • The Supreme Spirits (Seven Master Spirits, Seven Supreme Executives, Seven Reflective Spirits) • Supreme Trinity Personalities (Eternals of Days, Ancients of Days, Perfections of Days, etc.) • Trinitized beings: (Trinity Teacher Sons, Havona Natives, Paradise Citizens, etc.)	
Any two Paradise Deities or any two of their descendants	Create dual-origin beings that include: • Descending Sons of God (including Creator Sons)	
Any one of the Paradise Deities or any one of their descendants	Create single-origin beings that include: • The Supreme Spirits (Gravity Messengers, Reflective Image Aids, Universe Mother Spirit) • The family of the Infinite Spirit, which includes: Solitary Messengers, supernaphim, seconaphim, tertiaphim, omniaphim, Seven Supreme Power Directors, the Supreme Power Centers, the Master Physical Controllers	
	Early in the materialization of the universal creation, the sevenfold scheme of the superuniverse organization and government was formulated. The first post-Havona creation was divided into seven segments and the headquarter worlds of these superuniverse governments were designed and constructed. Space force and primordial energies are continually regulated and manipulated by force organizers.	

Illustration 25 *(continued)*

CREATION OF EARTH'S LOCAL UNIVERSE—NEBADON		
	An associate force organizer reported to the Ancients of Days that in an easterly segment of Superuniverse #7 (Orvonton), conditions were favorable for the emergence of a new physical creation.	987 billion years ago
	Force Organizers initiated the nebula named Andronover after receiving the mandate from the Ancients of Days, inaugurating the energy whirl that would ensure the progressive and orderly evolution of a new physical system. At this point, the Force Organizers withdrew, having prepared space-energy conditions for the action of the Power Directors and Physical Controllers of the superuniverse.	875 billion years ago
Power Directors and Physical Controllers	Power Directors and Physical Controllers support and supply cooperation to the power centers of this rapidly evolving new material system.	700 billion years ago
All evolutionary material creations are born of circular and gaseous nebulae, becoming spiral as they grow older. Forming suns, they develop as clusters of stars of various sizes, each surrounded by varying numbers of planets or satellites or smaller groups of matter, such as Earth's diminutive solar system.		
	The first Andronover sun is born. This particular nebula eventually gives birth to our solar system (Monmatia).	500 billion years ago
Creator Son Michael of Nebadon accompanied by Creative Daughter of the Infinite Spirit, who is destined to become the Mother Spirit of the new local universe	Andronover solar circuits are well established. Mobilization of the space-energies has been effected sufficiently to provide a material foundation for the emerging local universe. Power Directors and Physical Controllers continue to regulate and stabilize the physical energies of the evolving system.

Michael of Nebadon, a Creator Son of Paradise origin, selects the disintegrating Andronover nebula as the site of his adventure to build his local universe of Nebadon. Almost immediately, the spirit administrative capital worlds of Salvington, the universe headquarters, are created. Local universe creation continues evolving, suns become stabilized, planets form and swing into their orbits, while the work of creating the spirit architectural worlds that are to serve as constellation headquarters and system capitals continues.

When life is ready to be projected, the Creative Spirit is individualized as the Mother Spirit. | 400–300 billion years ago |
| Creator Son and the Local Universe Mother Spirit | The Creator Son and Local Universe Mother Spirit bring into existence the staff that will help administer and govern their local universe: Brilliant Morning Star (Gabriel), archangels, Brilliant Evening Stars, and Local Universe Sons of God (Melchizedeks, Vorondadeks, and Lanonandeks).

When the local universe is completed and staffed, the Creator Son, the Local Universe Mother Spirit, and the Ancients of Days participate in the creation of the Life Carriers, who are entrusted with establishing physical life on the evolving worlds. | |

Illustration 25 *(continued)*

Creator Son	Creates Material Sons and Daughters (Adams & Eves), whose function is to biologically uplift the mortal races.	
Local Universe Mother Spirit	Creates the seven adjutant mind-spirits. Creates seraphim and cherubim.	
CREATION OF PLANET EARTH		
	The final eruption of the Andronover nebular nucleus gives birth to our sun. The total number of suns and sun systems having origin in the Andronover nebula was 1,013,628.	6 billion years ago
	Earth is a well-developed sphere and cooling rapidly.	2½ billion years ago
	Date of actual beginning of Earth's history. Name "Urantia" (Earth) given and registered in local universe of Nebadon.	1 billion years ago
	First scouting party consisting of Life Carriers, Lanonandek Sons, Melchizedeks, seraphim, and other orders of celestial life arrive to examine the planet.	900 million years ago
	Waters are rapidly attaining the degree of saltiness essential to life on Earth.	650 million years ago
Life Carriers	Arrive from Salvington to begin studying the physical conditions preparatory to launch life on Earth.	600 million years ago
LIFE ESTABLISHMENT		
Life Carriers	Returns and plants a sodium chloride pattern of life in the planet's ocean waters.	550 million years ago
	Primitive marine vegetable life is well established.	500 million years ago
SPIRITUAL INFLUENCE	**BIOLOGICAL EVOLUTION**	
Of the seven adjutant mind-spirits, only the spirit of intuition could function in the instinctive and reflex behavior of the primordial animal life.	Transition from vegetable to the higher protozoan type of animal life (amoeba) occurs suddenly and evolves progressively.	450 million years ago
	The progressive evolution of the single-celled animal sets the stage for the appearance of the first backboned animals, the fish. The appearance of the fish family, the vertebrates, one of the most important steps in all pre-human evolution.	250 million years ago
	From the fish family springs two unique modifications: the frog and the salamander. Soon after, insects, spiders, cockroaches, scorpions, snails, crickets, and locusts appear.	210 million years ago
	The frogs give rise to the reptilian dinosaurs: ". . . *suddenly* . . . the reptiles appeared in full-fledged form. They developed rapidly, soon yielding crocodiles, scaled reptiles, and eventually both sea serpents and flying reptiles."[2]	140 million years ago

Illustration 25 *(continued)*

Gradually evolving life becomes responsive to the influence of the mind-spirits of understanding, courage, and knowledge.	Before passing out of existence, these reptilia give origin to the whole bird family and the numerous orders of placental mammals, which give rise to the common modern varieties and also the evolving marine types, such as whales and seals, and air navigators such as the bat family. The greatest single leap of all prehuman evolution was probably when the reptile became a bird.	55 million years ago
	The modern types of mammals begin to make their appearance. Formerly they had lived in the hills; now suddenly begins the evolution of the hoofed type, the grazing species.	30 million years ago
	The first deer appear.	20 million years ago
The spirit of counsel begins to function with the resulting growth of the herd instinct and the beginnings of primitive social development.	As the first great glacier retreats northward, the Mesopotamian dawn mammals (the direct descendants of the North American lemur-type of placental mammal) *suddenly* appear. They did not habitually walk on their hind legs, but they could easily stand erect. They possessed large brains in proportion to their size. For thousands of years, these animals multiply, constantly improving in physical type and general intelligence. A sudden differentiation gives rise to the first of the new species of primates, constituting the next vital step in prehuman evolution. In the same tribe and around the same time, a much retarded pair bear twins whose offspring found the modern simian tribes.	A little more than 1 million years ago
HUMAN SPECIES		

HUMAN SPECIES: EVOLUTION OF RACES AND RELIGIONS

The five adjutant mind-spirits increasingly function. The spirit of worship makes contact with the minds of the twins, indicating the appearance of the human mind. About a year later, the spirit of wisdom begins to function.	A mutation within the stock of the progressing primates suddenly produces twins destined to become the first true human beings (named Andon and Fonta) born around the area of Afghanistan. At ten years of age, the twins experienced a new group of worshipful feelings that included respect, veneration, modesty, and gratefulness. When the twins were eleven years old, they resolved as a result of moral thought and purposeful decision to flee from home and journey north toward India. Descendants of Andon and Fonta are called Andonites, referred to as Andonic Aborigines, the first race of humanity established in the northern hills of India, from where they migrated to other parts of the world. The ministry of the sixth and seventh adjutants indicates mind evolution crossing the threshold of spiritual ministry. The twins become recipients of the Indwelling Spirit. Earth is formally recognized as an inhabited planet.	A little less than 1 million years ago

Illustration 25 *(continued)*

Caligastia, Local Universe Son and Planetary Prince, arrives on Earth with materialized staff to develop humanity.	The world center of culture, Dalamatia, is established in the Persian Gulf region. First Epochal Revelation about the First Source and Center and the transition worlds after death are introduced by the Prince's staff. Nonsexual union between staff members creates the Primary Midwayers, permanent citizens of Earth, who are outside normal human vision range. "Concurrent with the arrival of the Planetary Prince, superior descendants of Andon and Fonta began *suddenly* to produce a family of mutant children, nineteen in number, who were not only more intelligent than their fellows but whose skins had a tint of various colors when exposed to sunlight. There were five red, two orange, four yellow, two green, four blue, and two indigo. This was the Sangik family, the ancestors of the colored races."[3]	Approx. 500,000 years ago
The Lucifer rebellion. The system of Satania is isolated and quarantined from other systems.	Planetary rebellion. Thirty-seven planets, including Earth, join the rebellion. Union between Andonites and rebellious members of the Prince's staff results in the Nodite Race. Their centers were referred to as "the land of Nod" north of the Persian Gulf area. Descendants migrate north, east, and west.	200,000 years ago
	Extinction of orange race.	100,000 years ago
	Migration of red race across Bering land bridge to North America.	83,000 years ago
	Civilizations established in Mexico, Central America, and South America.	78,000 years ago
		YEARS BC (approx.)
	Material Son and Daughter (Adam and Eve) arrive at First Garden of Eden, located on a Mediterranean peninsula. Second Epochal Revelation introduces spiritual truths about the One God of all and the concept of the Trinity. Universal Truths were once again introduced. Adam and Eve begin to establish the first branch of the violet race called Adamites. More than 120 years after the arrival of Adam and Eve, Edenic regime collapses and Adam and Eve migrate to Mesopotamia.	37,000 BC

Illustration 25 *(continued)*

	Second Garden is established between the Tigris and Euphrates rivers in Mesopotamia.	
	Birth of Seth and subsequent development of Sethite priesthood.	
	511 years after Adam and Eve's arrival, Eve dies.	
	530 years after Adam and Eve's arrival, Adam dies.	
	Adamson, firstborn of Adam and Eve in First Garden, founds Adamson center near Lake Van. Adamson marries Ratta, and their descendants are called Adamsonites, the second branch of the violet race.	
	Adamson and Ratta produce offspring that constitute the Secondary Midwayers. Within 100 years, almost two thousand are brought into being. The sixteen original children live and die as mortals of the realm, but their electrically energized offspring live on and on, not being subject to the limitations of mortal flesh.	
	Beginning of primary Adamite migrations.	23,000 BC
	Continuing blend of Adamites and Nodites in Mesopotamia (Sumerian civilization) and other regions in the world.	
	Sethite missionaries disseminate the teachings of Adam in India. Their teachings commingle with existing beliefs of the time.	16,000 BC
	End of Adamite migrations.	15,000 BC
	Complete blend of the Adamites and Nodites, with a later addition of yellow, blue, and green races, make up the Andite race.	
	Deterioration of Sethite teachings in India.	11,000 BC
	Descendants of Adamson settle in Greece.	
	Final dispersion of Andites.	8000–6000 BC
	Period of severe flooding in Mesopotamia. City of Susa greatly prospers during this time.	5000 BC
	Evolving white races dominant in northern Europe.	
	The purest strains of Adam's descendants live in Sumeria, northern Europe, and Greece.	
	Refugees from Mesopotamia floods settle in Cyprus.	
	Complex city-states emerge in Mesopotamia.	3500 BC
Melchizedek receivers petition Most Highs of Edentia for help.	Concept of God has grown hazy in the human mind.	3000 BC

Illustration 25 *(continued)*

	Akkadian domination of Mesopotamia. Deterioration of culture in Egypt.	2350 BC
	Estimated dates of Egyptian *Papyrus of Ani* scrolls, later collectively referred to as the Egyptian *Book of the Dead*, containing concepts of judgment, heaven, hell, and resurrection of the soul.	2300–1240 BC
	Aryan-Andites from the north and west invade India. Vedism is their religion—a polytheistic system in which Indra is the highest-ranked god. The Aryans institute the caste system in an effort to perpetuate racial identity. The Brahmanic priest caste, stemming from the Sethite priests, is the very essence of this system. It is this social order that greatly retards the progress of the later Salem teachers.	2300 BC
	First intermediate period: 7th-11th Egyptian Dynasties.	2258–2134 BC
	Suite and Gutians assault Mesopotamia. Lagash, the Sumerian capital, falls. Final collapse of Second Garden culture.	2193 BC
	The Ur III State restores the Akkadian Empire and brings unification and peace to Mesopotamia. It establishes Sumerian as the official language, to promote its use and also to promote Sumerian culture.	2113 BC
	With the fall of Ur, the Sumerian influence ends. Sumerians become totally absorbed into the ranks of the invading northern Semites and the Amorites. Thus the Mesopotamian Andites pass from the pages of history. *Epic of Gilgamesh* and *Epic of Creation*. By 2000 BC, the teachings of the Sethites are largely under the influence of the primitive beliefs of the Semite invaders, paving the way for the eventual elevation of the Babylonian god Marduk to the head of the pantheon.	2004 BC
Machiventa Melchizedek	Machiventa Melchizedek, a Local Universe Melchizedek Son, materializes in Salem, Palestine. Third Epochal Revelation. He introduces the concept of salvation through *faith* and once again introduces teachings about the One Universal God. Covenant with Abraham. Machiventa trains Salem missionaries who are to travel from Salem into Mesopotamia and remote regions of both Europe and Asia, reaching even the British Isles, Iceland, and Japan. 12th Egyptian Dynasty.	2000–1906 BC

Illustration 25 *(continued)*

	Salem missionaries compose many of the Old Testament psalms, inscribing them on stone, later found by Hebrew priests during the Babylon captivity in 586 BC.	1800 BC
	Hammurabi reunites Sumerian city-states and establishes Babylonia, the ancient empire of Mesopotamia, with Babylon as its capital.	1795 BC
START OF FORMALIZED RELIGION		
	Aryans have been absorbed by Dravidians. Vedism evolves to Brahmanism.	1500 BC
	Brahmanism evolves to Hinduism. Birth of Judaism.	1000 BC
	Approximate birth of Jainism, Zoroastrianism, Taoism/Shintoism, Buddhism, and Confucianism.	600 BC
	Hebrew priests during captivity in Babylon find psalms composed by Salem missionaries as well as the Babylonian Tablets, which are then edited and incorporated into what is now known as the Old Testament.	586 BC
Michael of Nebadon, Creator Son	Michael of Nebadon, the Creator Son of our universe, bestows himself on Earth as Jesus of Nazareth. His message is one of love and service. Fourth Epochal Revelation. End of Lucifer rebellion.	2000 years ago (approx.)
Assorted group of celestial beings	Birth of Christianity, Islam, Sikhisim, Jehovah's Witnesses, Baha'i Faith, Mormonism, Christian Science, etc.	AD 30 to present day
	Fifth Epochal Revelation compiled as and published in *The Urantia Book*.	AD 1955

SECTION THREE

Our Individual and Collective Destiny

Destiny is not a matter of chance, it is a matter of choice.
It is not a thing to be waited for, it is a thing to be achieved.

WILLIAM JENNINGS BRYAN

Introduction

It is in your moments of decision that your destiny is shaped.
Anthony Robbins

Distorted concepts of heaven and hell have long been used as tools for the manipulation of followers. Religious seekers are susceptible to visions of a self-gratifying heaven and they can be persuaded to do the most unholy things to attain illusory rewards. The human craving for heavenly comfort is universal, not unlike the need for love. In contrast, the fear of a miserable hell has also been effectively exploited throughout the ages by religious institutions and fanatics. Without a clear and expanded perspective of our common destiny after death, we are easy prey for those who promise eternal ecstasy or damnation in exchange for faithful submission or evil behavior.

The origin and history of humanity have been reconciled by epochal revelation in the previous two sections; matters of individual and collective destiny are addressed and reconciled in this section. Escalating social disunity and cultural decline reflect a world operating on erroneous beliefs that support economic and political tyrannies. When we explore newly revealed knowledge and dispel confusion in our religious beliefs, we cultivate faith and become increasingly committed to self-improvement and spiritual transformation. As we integrate new insights and apply them in daily living, we grow in wisdom and increase our capacity to serve others lovingly, enlivening the spirit of unity in our hearts. Individually we secure eternal survival, and collectively each generation moves the world closer to an age of light and life popularly depicted as "heaven on Earth."

This journey toward greater understanding of our glorious personal and planetary destiny requires us to embrace the process and dramatically expand our vision of the Big Picture of Existence. We can then move beyond philosophical speculation to construct a new and appealing philosophy of living. "Such a new and righteous vision of morality will attract all that is good in the mind of man and challenge that which is best in the human soul."[1]

Epochal revelation confirms this eternal religious wisdom: the goal of personal survival and peace on Earth rests upon each mortal. It also sheds light on the mechanics of immortality, which allows us to reinterpret emerging evidence and rethink assumptions that are no longer valid. Epochal revelation powerfully illuminates our individual destiny and confirms the truth of our deepest longings:

- There is a God whom we can find and recognize in eternity, ". . . a perfect Creator personality, a person who can 'know and be known,' who can 'love and be loved,' and one who can befriend us."[2]

- The heavenly realms and Paradise are real, an integral part of our eternal career of perfection ascent.

- We are evolving beings with much to learn; our personal voyage through the vast multilevel universe begins here on Earth.

15.

Reincarnation

I do not believe in the return of the soul to another life on this plane. The spiral of life is upward. Evolution carries us forward, not backward. Eternal and progressive expansion is its law and there are no breaks in its continuity.

Ernest Holmes, *The Science of Mind*

Reincarnation is popularly defined as the rebirth of the soul in a new human body. This idea formed around the ancient theory of transmigration which postulates the cyclical rebirth of the soul in a physical vehicle whether human, animal, or inanimate.

The concept of reincarnation is a basic tenet in Hinduism, Buddhism, and Jainism. It is an essential part of the mystic teachings of Theosophy, the New Age movement, the Society for Krishna Consciousness (commonly known as Hare Krishna), the Unity School of Christianity, Gnosticism, Rosicrucianism, and Spiritualism. And many of the Eastern practices of yoga and mental techniques such as Transcendental Meditation base their quest for higher consciousness on the reincarnation theory.

Reincarnation is linked with the doctrine of karma, which teaches that the consequences of thoughts and deeds (both good and bad) are experienced from one life to the next on Earth. This belief gives credence to such modern practices as Scientology's "auditing," which claims to remove the traumas of past lives by using a device called an E-meter, and past-life therapy, which claims to access prior existences and resolve traumas from those lives.

Statistics based on the number of adherents of major religions have indicated that more than forty percent of the world population believes in reincarnation: Hinduism (14 percent), Buddhism (6 percent), Chinese traditional (6 percent) and nonreligious/agnostic, etc. (approximately 15 percent).[1] These figures do not include Christians who have incorporated the belief into their faith.

To gain a wider perspective of human destiny, it is important to explore the history of reincarnation and its impact on religious beliefs in the light of epochal revelation.

Primitive Origins

Family resemblance is easy to recognize and led primitive peoples to believe that deceased ancestors reincarnated in infants. This was the origin of the custom of naming children after past relatives. The prehistoric mind found it easy to believe that at death, the breath, and later the soul, entered another body. The soul could leave the body if a person fainted, was sleeping or dreaming, was in an unconscious state, or was dead. The soul could enter humans, animals, or even inanimate objects. Unable to imagine anything beyond the concept of the soul, the vivid and simplistic idea of rebirth into a new physical body (transmigration) blossomed in the primitive mind. Independent versions eventually emerged in locations widely separated from each other both geographically and historically. The primordial concept of survival after death was not necessarily a belief in immortality; to early mortals hardly able to count, the concept of eternity was unimaginable.

Resurrection versus Reincarnation

Resurrection is the awakening after death in a nonphysical body. The Sethite missionaries taught the advanced concept of repersonalization on successive worlds in our cosmic evolution (detailed in chapter 17). But as this superhuman knowledge was passed down it was confused with the human belief in reincarnation, which was rooted in natural genetics but misunderstood by the primitive mind: "This idea of reincarnation originated in the observance of hereditary and trait resemblance of offspring to ancestors . . . Some later-day races believed that man died from three to seven times."[2] Many such ancient beliefs, commingled with remnants of revealed truth, became the doctrines still found among modern cults and religions.

The desire for eternal life (immortality) was a driving force in the lives of the Sumerian people, a mix of Nodites and Adamites, descendants of Caligastia's staff and Adam and Eve. The Sumerian myth of Inanna's Descent to the Nether World is perhaps the first historical tale of resurrection, predating both the Babylonian myth of Ishtar and Tammuz, and the Greek myth of Persephone's kidnapping by Hades, which underlies many of the Greek mystery cults.

Egypt was greatly influenced by Sumerian thinking. The Egyptians' quest for eternal life became the driving force behind their funeral practices and embraced the revealed concepts of salvation, resurrection, and individual moral judgment. The *Pyramid Texts*, dating back to approximately 2350 BC, are the oldest known collection of religious spells from ancient Egypt. The main theme in these texts is the king's resurrection and ascension to the afterworld. But in the Old Kingdom, "[t]he teaching of immortality for all men was too advanced for the Egyptians. Only kings and the rich were promised a resurrection; therefore did they so carefully embalm and preserve their bodies in tombs against the day of judgment."[3] During the eighteenth dynasty of the New Kingdom, the pharaoh Ikhnaton (1372–1354 BC), inspired by the Salem teachings of Melchizedek and the writings of Amenemope, kept alive the doctrine of the One God and taught the concepts of salvation and resurrection for all. This led to later misconceptions, such as the Egyptians believing in the survival of animals.

Even though there is no evidence that suggests such a belief, some people are of the opinion that the ancient Egyptians taught transmigration. This postulate is partly based on references to Egyptian theories of the future life made by Herodotus, the fifth-century BC Greek historian. The Egyptian *Book of the Dead* provides the chief source of information concerning the future life as believed by the Egyptians. This great collection of texts and magical spells describes the travel of the soul into a next world without coming back to Earth, and speaks of the soul being able to change itself into various life forms after death. The American Egyptologist James Henry Breasted (1865–1935) explains: "It was this notion which led Herodotus to conclude that the Egyptians believed in what we now call transmigration of souls, but this was a mistaken impression on his part."[4] Most Egyptologists perceive these transformations or rebirths as a spiritual evolution in heaven.

A Doctrine Evolves

The Brahmins in India formulated the oldest doctrinal version of reincarnation around 800 BC. To understand how the belief in reincarnation evolved, we can turn to epochal revelation for its religious history of India.

The secondary Sangik races that originated in India over five hundred thousand years ago were particularly prone to the belief that the souls of dead family members were reborn in grandchildren or great grandchildren. The early Andites, the pre-Aryans, encountered these people when they first migrated from the Turkestan region into northern India around 15,000 BC.

The pre-Aryans were a superior and adventurous people of predominant Adamite and Nodite ancestry. As they migrated into the valleys of the Indus and Ganges, they mixed with the Sangik races to produce the people called Dravidian. The Dravidians founded the leading cultural, religious, philosophic, and commercial civilization at the time, engaging in extensive land and sea trade. Sethite missionaries inhabited India during the Dravidian period, but they only partially succeeded in introducing the teachings about one God. "Within five thousand years their doctrines of the Paradise Trinity had degenerated into the triune symbol of the fire god."[5] Nevertheless, the thread of one-God monotheism had already been established.

The history of traditional Indian religion begins in the period known as the Vedic era, which corresponds with the Aryan invasion—the second Andite penetration of India. By 2000 BC, India was under the political and religious authority of these Vedic invaders. As they traveled south, however, they were absorbed by large numbers of Dravidians. In an effort to perpetuate their racial identity, the Aryans set up a caste system.

At the time of the Aryan invasion, the Vedic newcomers had long lost their monotheistic religion. Instead, they brought their many tribal deities and other forms of worship. Under the direction of the Brahmin caste and the lingering influence of the Sethite missionaries, the many Vedic deities were organized into a pantheon with Agni, the three-headed fire god, as the father-head. With the passage of time, "The deity-father principle, sometimes called Prajapati [Lord of the people], sometimes termed Brahma, was submerged in the theologic battle which the Brahman priests later fought with the Salem teachers. *The Brahman* was conceived as the energy-divinity principle activating the entire Vedic pantheon."[6]

The one-God concept of the arriving Salem missionaries did not at first clash with the emerging concept of the Father-Brahma. However, the nonritualistic nature of the Salem doctrine did conflict with the dogmas, traditions, and teachings of the Brahmin priesthood. While the Salem missionaries advocated trust in one God and personal salvation through faith, the Brahmin priests favored ritualistic observances and sacrificial ceremonials, a rigid stance that would later greatly hamper cultural progress.

To combat the teachings of the Salem missionaries, the Brahmins revised their sacred writings, known in modern times as the Rig-Veda. As they sought to formalize their rituals of worship and sacrifice upon the peoples of those days, they formulated what are now known as the second, third, and fourth Vedas (the Sama, Yajur, and Atharva Vedas). These early Vedas portray the Aryan views of the afterlife: an individual continues to exist after death as a whole person; mortals and gods exist separately; immortality constitutes celestial abodes for the good, and hellish abodes for the bad. The concept of *moksha*, union with God, was far from their capacity to conceive. In these early writings, there is no mention of either karma or reincarnation.

By 1000 BC, the Aryans had been absorbed by the Dravidians and society was dominated by the Brahmins. Every aspect of life became subject to the control of priestly rituals and spells. The inferior cults of the south, however, overpowered the Brahmins, who sank beneath a flood of apathy and pessimism. It was in this state of despair that the Brahmanas (900–700 BC) and the Upanishads (800–400 BC) were written. These scriptures came to be perceived and venerated as divine revelation and reflected a dual change in the Vedic religion.

On the practical side, there was a vigorous growth of complex religious rites, elaborate sacrificial ceremonies, and social restrictions and duties. The caste system became more rigid with more laws and regulations per caste. The Brahmins placed themselves at the top of the caste system, proclaiming it a divine principle of the universe, exalted above even their gods. Meanwhile, the lower castes and untouchables lost any hope of personal growth beyond the limits of their caste.

On the theoretical side, dual lines of thought developed that merged into the primary beliefs and metaphysical speculations existing in India today. One line of thought embraced the concepts of karma and reincarnation; the other, the concepts of an impersonal God, Brahm, and an immortal and preexistent soul, the *atman*.

According to Hinduism, souls do not differ from each other in their nature and exist in all forms of life. From the Brihadaranyaka Upanishad: "[S]ouls live forever and are reborn into this world in endless cycles." The reincarnating soul may be reborn in human or animal form. The Chandogya Upanishad (5:10:7) says, "Those who are of pleasant conduct here . . . they will enter a pleasant womb, either the womb of a Brahmin, or the womb of a *Kshatriya* [the warrior caste], or the womb of a *Vaishya* [the caste of ordinaries]. But those who are of perfidious conduct here . . . they will enter a contemptible womb, either the womb of a dog, or the womb of a swine or the womb of an outcast (*Chandala*) . . ."[7]

In the Upanishads, karma differs from "one reaps what one sows" by postponing into the next earthly life what one sows in this one. This doctrine of transmigration and karma lacked a concept of salvation. The endless cycle of rebirth was first broken with the advent of the metaphysical philosophy of Brahm-Atman.

"In the concept of Brahman the minds of those days truly grasped at the idea of some all-pervading Absolute, for this postulate was at one and the same time identified as creative energy and cosmic reaction. Brahman was conceived to be beyond all definition, capable of being comprehended only by the successive negation of all finite qualities. It was definitely a belief in an absolute, even an infinite, being, but this concept was largely devoid of personality attributes and was therefore not experiencible by individual religionists."[8]

To end the cycle of rebirth, the Brahmins equated the soul with Brahm. With the conception of the atman as a spark of Brahm, the Indian mind demonstrated an appreciation of the nature and presence of the Indwelling Spirit. However, in crystallizing their beliefs about Brahm, no room was left to consider the soul as a separate entity from spirit. The synonymous identification of Brahm with the soul had its implications: (1) the soul was perceived as already immortal rather than having a mortal origin with the potential for immortality; (2) the soul was perceived as already divine rather than evolving toward divinity; and (3) the immortal soul was to be liberated by the removal of all personality traits, not by the survival of personal identity through soul evolution.

These teachings had negative personal and social repercussions: certain immortality meant less mortal ambition and human appreciation, inhibiting cultural progress. Life's experience was not perceived as an opportunity to personally evolve toward God in readiness for the next life. Instead, life was a time for the immortal soul to awaken to its divinity and gain union with God. In Hinduism, the soul that attains union with God ceases to function. It becomes a formless part of God's energy as depicted in Brihadaranyaka Upanishad 4.2: ". . . as a lump of salt dropped into water becomes dissolved in water and cannot be taken out again."

Epochal revelation addresses this deflation of our unique value: "Man attains divine union by progressive reciprocal spiritual communion, by personality intercourse with the personal God, by increasingly attaining the divine nature through wholehearted and intelligent conformity to the divine will."[9] This process begins on Earth and continues throughout the ascending path to Paradise. It is during this journey that the soul in union with personality generally fuses with the Indwelling Spirit to become as one with the Creator.

Progressive Reform: Buddhism and Hinduism (600 BC–AD 1000)

In the sixth century before Christ, two religions, Buddhism and Jainism, emerged in India in response to the hegemony of Brahmanic religious traditions. Siddhartha, the founder of Buddhism, stood up against the growing caste system. He denounced gods and priests, and rejected sacrifices and rituals as a means to attain salvation. Not believing in the existence of individual human souls, Siddhartha tried to replace the belief in transmigration of the soul with salvation through faith in righteousness and justice. His doctrine of nirvana implied a condition of supreme enlightenment and supernal bliss that could be experienced during mortal existence. Enlightenment would break all fetters binding us to the material world, free us from the desires of mortal life, and deliver us from all danger of ever again experiencing reincarnation.

According to epochal revelation, Siddhartha never grasped a clear concept of the Universal Father nor the way to God. His teachings therefore lacked the spiritual power to transform society. "The great weakness in the original gospel of Buddhism was that it did not produce a religion of unselfish social service."[10] However, by taking a stand on salvation through faith in the tradition of the Salem missionaries, Siddhartha ensured the perpetuation of his teachings. Buddhism prospered because it offered salvation through belief in the Buddha and because it succeeded in conserving many of the highest moral values.

The farther Buddhism spread from India, the more it grew to be like the religions it supplanted. The Indian Buddhist missionaries who arrived in China toward the second century after Christ altered the principles of Buddhism to make them compatible with ancestor worship and China's hierarchical system.

In India, the growing need for the experience of devotion between humans and a superior being brought the unknowable and distant Brahm closer to the masses, awakening the spirit of service. "The period from roughly 500 BC to AD 1000 is sometimes spoken of as that of classical Hinduism. It was during this period that the major literature was composed, the great philosophical systems developed, and the basic Vaishnava and Shaiva sects organized. After AD 1000 (beginning somewhat earlier in south India), a spirit of devotional fervor, coupled with social reform, swept through India. The period from that time until the near present is known as the bhakti period. During this era, the forms of religious worship changed and diversified. Singing of devotional songs and poems in the vernacular rather than in Sanskrit, the language in which practically all classical Hindu literature was written, is one example. Direct approach to the god was emphasized, and the mediating role of the priest was somewhat curtailed. Love, a sentiment common to all but particularly to the most ordinary villager, is now celebrated as the way to the highest end; some bhakti philosophies hold that liberation is not the supreme goal and that loving service to God is a higher one."[11]

"Hinduism has survived because it is essentially an integral part of the basic social fabric of India. It has no great hierarchy which can be disturbed or destroyed; it is interwoven into the life pattern of the people. It has an adaptability to changing conditions that excels all other cults, and it displays a tolerant attitude of adoption toward many other religions, Gautama Buddha and even Christ himself being claimed as incarnations of Vishnu."[12]

Transmigration and Western Philosophy

The ancient Greek (Olympian) religion failed to provide a concept of salvation that quenched the spiritual thirst of its believers. By the sixth century before Christ, the Greeks were without a national religion. Morals, ethics, and philosophy quickly advanced far beyond the Greeks' God concept, and this imbalance between the cultivation of intellectual and spiritual insight was to be as hazardous to Greece as it had proved to be in India.

As a substitute for the belief in survival, the Greeks attempted to attain security through rigorous thinking. ". . . in Greece, human thought became so abstract that the concept of God resolved itself into a misty vapor of pantheistic speculation not at all unlike the impersonal Infinity of the Brahman philosophers."[13] The doctrine of reincarnation found fertile ground in this environment and was first disseminated through the teachings of the Ionian mathematician and philosopher Pythagoras (580–500 BC). Pythagoras founded a philosophical and religious school first in his homeland Samos,[14] and then in Croton, southern Italy, where he taught and disseminated the knowledge, customs, and beliefs he had gathered during his many years in foreign lands. It is not known where Pythagoras came into contact with the doctrine of transmigration. What is known is that in his schools, he taught that souls "reincarnated into other forms of existence," and this presupposed a continuity of a soul's experience from "one incarnation to another."[15]

The concept of transmigration developed independently after Pythagoras, but it was especially Plato (427–347 BC) who expanded upon Pythagoras's teachings in the *Phaedrus* and *Phaedo*. Plato never pinned down the details of reincarnation or the experiences of the soul after death, but he did develop valuable new and progressive insights about the soul that would later influence Christianity. Unlike the Hindu concept in which the soul loses personal identity in union with Brahm, Plato advocated that the soul retains its individuality and is "self-moving," having an "essential life all its own." From Socrates, he brought forth the idea of paying careful attention to the inner principle of one's being, and spoke of caring for the soul above all else to ensure growth toward perfection.[16]

Eastern philosophy continued to combine with Greek thought to become part of the great Hellenistic civilization that influenced the Jews and gave Christianity an opportunity to flourish. Influenced by Christian thinking, the traditional doctrine of reincarnation was adapted to Western thought:

- Disintegration of personal identity was replaced with continuity of individual consciousness from one life to another.

- Rather than reincarnation being a torment out of which we have to escape by eradicating ego (personality), reincarnation was reinterpreted to constitute a progression of the "higher self" toward increasing levels of self-awareness.

Various concepts of reincarnation were adopted by the emerging European esoteric traditions, including Neo-Platonism, Gnosticism, Kabbalah, and Catharism.

Historical Influence on the Jews

During the period of Greek domination, the Hellenized Jews were greatly influenced by the teachings of Plato. Under the rule of Ptolemy II Philadelphus (309–246 BC), the Jews began to learn both Egyptian and Oriental theology and appropriated some of these foreign scriptures into their own ancient creed. *The Urantia Book* explains that the Jews found it easy to conform Hebrew theology with Aristotelian philosophy. "But this all led to disastrous confusion until these problems were taken in hand by Philo of Alexandria [20 BC–AD 50], who proceeded to harmonize and systemize Greek philosophy and Hebrew theology into a compact and fairly consistent system of religious belief and practice. And it was this later teaching of combined Greek philosophy and Hebrew theology that prevailed in Palestine when Jesus lived and taught, and which Paul utilized as the foundation on which to build his more advanced and enlightening cult of Christianity."[17]

During the time of Jesus of Nazareth, there was a lingering belief in reincarnation. "The older Jewish teachers, together with Plato, Philo, and many of the Essenes, tolerated the theory that men may reap in one incarnation what they have sown in a previous existence; thus in one life they were believed to be expiating the sins committed in preceding lives. The Master found it difficult to make men believe that their souls had not had previous existences."[18]

Throughout Jewish history, Jews have compared contemporary events to passages from their scriptures, searching for signs of their Messiah's arrival. The belief that Elijah would return before the arrival of the Messiah rested on the words of Malachi 4:5 written approximately 435 BC: "Behold, I will send you Elijah the prophet before the coming of the great and dreadful day of the Lord."

The intriguing and semiaccurate biblical account of Elijah's unusual departure—he was engulfed in a chariot of fire (2 Kings 2:7–12)—gave rise to the speculation that Elijah did not really die and that he would return to Earth, his arrival signalling the dawn of the Messianic era. The increasingly popular theory of reincarnation in the Levantine region provided a convenient modus operandi for his return.

John the Baptist's belief in Malachi's prophecy, along with his belief that Jesus was the Messiah, caused him great distress. "And it was only this promise of Malachi that Elijah would return that deterred John from going forth to preach about the coming kingdom and to exhort his fellow Jews to flee from the wrath to come. John was ripe for the proclamation of the message of the coming kingdom, but this expectation of the coming of Elijah held him back for more than two years. He knew he was not Elijah."[19] His resolve was in evidence when the Pharisees in Jerusalem asked the Baptizer if he was Elijah or the prophet that Moses promised and John replied, "I am not" (John 1:21).

"It was the influence of Elijah that caused John to adopt his methods of direct and blunt assault upon the sins and vices of his contemporaries. He sought to dress like Elijah, and he endeavored to talk like Elijah; in every outward aspect he was like the olden prophet. He was just such a stalwart and picturesque child of nature, just such a fearless and daring preacher of righteousness."[20] With such similarities between the Elijah in the sacred writings and the prophet who preached "in the spirit of Elijah," there was wide speculation that John was a reincarnation of Elijah. In an environment of excited expectation for the fulfillment of Malachi's prophecy, this sentiment flourished and became a staple of debate recorded as early as the second century AD by the Alexandrian philosopher and Gnostic teacher Carpocrates.[21]

On one occasion (cf. Matthew 17:10–13) after the death of John the Baptist, the apostle Peter asked Jesus why is it that the scribes say that Elijah must first come before the Messiah shall appear. Jesus responded, "But I say unto you, [t]hat Elias is come already, and they knew him not, but have done unto him whatsoever they listed [willed]." The three apostles perceived that he referred to John the Baptist as Elijah. "Jesus knew that, if they insisted on regarding him as the Messiah, then must John be the Elijah of the prophecy."[22]

Jesus did not fit the scriptural requirements regarding the Messiah; therefore the belief that Jesus was the incarnation of one of the prophets was also convenient for the metaphysically minded. In Matthew 16:13–14, when Jesus asked his disciples, "Whom do men say that I the Son of man, am?" they told him that he was regarded by some as John the Baptist risen from the dead while others compared him with Moses, Elijah, Isaiah, or Jeremiah.

So fixed had been the Jews on their expectations of the Messiah, that most could hardly accept Jesus in that role. "The Jews devoutly believed that, as Moses had delivered their fathers from Egyptian bondage by miraculous wonders, so would the coming Messiah deliver the Jewish people from Roman domination by even greater miracles of power and marvels of racial triumph. The rabbis had gathered together almost five hundred passages from the scriptures which, notwithstanding their apparent contradictions, they averred were prophetic of the coming Messiah. And amidst all these details of time, technique, and function, they almost completely lost sight of the *personality* of the promised Messiah. They were looking for a restoration of Jewish national glory—Israel's temporal exaltation—rather than for the salvation of the world. It therefore becomes evident that Jesus of Nazareth could never satisfy this materialistic Messianic concept of the Jewish mind. Many of their reputed Messianic predictions, had they but viewed these prophetic utterances in a different light, would have very naturally prepared their minds for a recognition of Jesus as the terminator of one age and the inaugurator of a new and better dispensation of mercy and salvation for all nations."[23]

Cultural Effects in India, China, and the West

The theory of reincarnation postulates multiple deaths and rebirths into multiple physical bodies, thereby resolving accumulated karma. The practical application of this philosophy can have a detrimental effect on the people and cultures that embrace it. Belief in reincarnation negates the uniqueness of the human personality; it denies the personal deliverance and spiritual evolution found in resurrection. When karma is viewed as circumstances and events that cannot be changed, it can promote procrastination and evasion of responsibility. When reincarnation is ingrained in a Godless religion, it stifles the spiritual power necessary to truly advance civilization.

Peace is the standard by which society is measured, built on the continuous efforts of individuals to progress spiritually. To attain peace in our world, there is great need to superimpose higher spiritual meanings and values on our thoughts and actions. A further step is to see each other as brothers and sisters in the common realization of God as father. These simple yet profound truths hold the power to increase our capacity to cooperate with one another on the basis of unity of ideals. These dynamics will now be explored in cultural context in the light of epochal revelation.

India

Hinduism remains an integral part of the basic social fabric of India. Its adaptability has allowed for growth; thus Hinduism's monotheistic theology and concept of God have slowly been evolving. The Dvaita or "dualist" school of Hindu Vedanta philosophy, which originated in the thirteenth century, teaches that the universe is a real creation of Brahman and provides a strict distinction between God and souls. This doctrine contrasts sharply with the oldest and most influential Hindu philosophy, Advaita Vedanta, which teaches the nonduality of the individual soul and God and declares that the world has no separate existence apart from Brahman.

While the concept of Deity is slowly expanding, the understanding of God's relation to humanity lags behind. Survival of personality isn't part of the doctrine of reincarnation. "This belief in the weary and monotonous round of repeated transmigrations robbed struggling mortals of their long-cherished hope of finding that deliverance and spiritual advancement in death which had been a part of the earlier Vedic faith."[24]

When the pain and suffering of today are blamed on actions in a previous life, it is easy to understand how despondency has plagued many generations. Karma and reincarnation entrenched in a caste system bury ambition, weakening the personal and social fabric of hope that is so essential for cultural transformation. With the majority demoralized by discrimination, social cooperation is brought to a standstill and self-destructive behavior to the point of suicide takes hold. In April 2004, *The Lancet*, a respected British medical journal, declared that South India was the world's suicide capital, with the average suicide rate for women as high as 148 per 100,000, and for young men 58 per 100,000. Worldwide, this rate was 14.5 per 100,000.[25]

Growth of social consciousness in a progressive Indian religious society may lead to an expanded God concept inclusive of Brahman as associative and creative—as a personality approachable by created and evolving beings. It might also include newly revealed relationships between Atman (the Indwelling Spirit), the soul, the mind, and the human personality.

Increased understanding of God's complex and intimate relation to humanity will inevitably promote a fresh assessment of the futile theory of reincarnation. Growth in spiritual insight will augment the individual's capacity to live the golden rule and move society forward.

As India makes the transition into a nation of professional services, its spiritual philosophies are challenged to remain open to critical interpretation.

The ability of Hinduism to remain flexible in the quest for God will ensure that it develops the moral energy and the spiritual driving power necessary to progressively transform the people and exalt the nation.

China

China presents a different dynamic than that of India—the Godless religion of Buddhism nourishes the moral authority of Marxism.

Although contemporary Chinese metaphysics include concepts of a sacred and sometimes spiritual world, they do not invoke a concept of God as a personal supreme being. According to *The Cambridge Companion to Atheism*, China is the country with the largest number of atheists, agnostics, and non-believers in God.[26] China also has the largest national Buddhist population.[27] While Buddhism does not concern itself with refuting God, it nevertheless reserves no place for a supreme personal deity.

But this has not always been the case. According to epochal revelation, about one hundred thousand years ago a tribal chief in the yellow race named Singlangton led his people in the devotion of one God instead of the many. "Long adherence to the worship of the One Truth proclaimed by Singlangton kept them ahead of most of the other races . . . The Chinese of even six thousand years ago were still keen students and aggressive in their pursuit of truth."[28]

"The belief in, and worship of, the 'One Truth' as taught by Singlangton never entirely died out; but as time passed, the search for new and higher truth became overshadowed by a growing tendency to venerate that which was already established. Slowly the genius of the yellow race became diverted from the pursuit of the unknown to the preservation of the known. And this is the reason for the stagnation of what had been the world's most rapidly progressing civilization."[29]

"The religious development of ancestor veneration became further complicated by a flood of superstitions involving nature worship, but lingering vestiges of a real concept of God remained preserved in the imperial worship of Shang-ti."[30] Shang-ti was the supreme god of the Shang dynasty (1766–1050 BC) depersonalized in the later Chou dynasty (1111–255 BC): "This deity eventually evolved into the concept of T'ien, or 'Heaven,' which, as an abstract and impersonal concept, became synonymous with Shang-ti. For the ancient Chinese, Heaven ruled the physical universe through ming, or 'destiny,' which was beyond human understanding and control, and ruled the moral universe, the universe of human behavior, through T'ien ming, or 'The Mandate of Heaven.'"[31] The Mandate of Heaven gave Chinese emperors the right to rule, similar to the "divine right of kings" in western civilization. The Chou Dynasty used the Mandate of Heaven to justify the ousting of the tyrannical Shang Dynasty.

The sixth century BC saw a great ethical, moral, and semireligious awakening with the teachings of Lao Tzu and Confucius. It was Lao who, building directly upon the concepts of the Salem traditions, declared Tao to be the One First Cause of all creation, Supreme God and Universal King, replacing T'ien as the source of all there is. Lao also taught the return of the creature to the Creator. With the passage of time, Lao became deified by his followers and his finest teachings were lost or corrupted. Prevailing Taoism "... has very little in common with the lofty sentiments and cosmic concepts of the old philosopher who taught the truth as he perceived it, which was: That faith in the Absolute God is the source of that divine energy which will remake the world, and by which man ascends to spiritual union with Tao, the Eternal Deity and Creator Absolute of the universes."[32]

Confucius, a younger contemporary of Lao, "... based his doctrines upon the better moral traditions of the long history of the yellow race, and he was also somewhat influenced by the lingering traditions of the Salem missionaries."[33] He compiled wise sayings of ancient philosophers that helped replace magic with morality. His writings, however, made a new fetish out of order and established a veneration for ancestral conduct that is still upheld today. His compilation of sayings played a part in stifling the investigative spirit of the Chinese people. "These Confucian precepts, while perpetuating the best of the past, were somewhat inimical to the very Chinese spirit of investigation that had produced those achievements which were so venerated. The influence of these doctrines was unsuccessfully combated both by the imperial efforts of Ch'in Shih Huang-ti [259–210 BC] and by the teachings of Mo Ti [472–391 BC], who proclaimed a brotherhood founded not on ethical duty but on the love of God. He sought to rekindle the ancient quest for new truth, but his teachings failed before the vigorous opposition of the disciples of Confucius."[34] Like Lao, Confucius eventually became deified and his teachings altered. Confucius' genuine concern for aesthetic, moral, and social order and for the formation of hierarchies so as to provide the greatest benefit for the people was in time manipulated by his followers to form rigid bureaucracies.

Throughout the period of the deterioration of the Taoist faith and the coming of the Buddhist missionaries from India toward the second century after Christ, Chinese religion continued its decline. "During these spiritually decadent centuries the religion of the yellow race degenerated into a pitiful theology wherein swarmed devils, dragons, and evil spirits, all betokening the returning fears of the unenlightened mortal mind. And China, once at the head of human society because of an advanced religion, then fell behind because of temporary failure to progress in the true path of the development of that God-consciousness which is indispensable to the true progress, not only of the individual mortal, but also of the intricate and complex civilizations which characterize the advance of culture and society on an evolutionary planet of time and space."[35]

"Buddhism entered China in the first millennium after Christ, and it fitted well into the religious customs of the yellow race. In ancestor worship they had long prayed to the dead; now they could also pray for them. Buddhism soon amalgamated with the lingering ritualistic practices of disintegrating Taoism. This new synthetic religion with its temples of worship and definite religious ceremonial soon became the generally accepted cult of the peoples of China, Korea, and Japan."[36] Buddhism became the national religion of China, and continues to grow today because it conserves many of the highest moral values of its adherents. It promotes calmness and self-control, augments serenity and happiness, and does much to prevent sorrow. From an individual perspective, therefore, those who follow this philosophy live better lives than many who do not follow it.[37]

From a universal perspective, however, "[y]ou cannot have a genuine spiritual religion without the supreme and supernal ideal of an eternal God. A religion without this God is an invention of man, a human institution of lifeless intellectual beliefs and meaningless emotional ceremonies."[38] It lacks the moral energy and the spiritual driving power that a religion must have if it is to transform a race and exalt a nation.

The social history of China, especially as it pertains to human rights and ethics, is an unfortunate indicator of how seriously hampered the development of unselfishness can be in a society that lacks a concept of God. In the middle of the nineteenth century, as China and the West began extensive contacts, the idea of human rights began to gain ground in the Chinese intellectual scene and in the Chinese consciousness. But a review of history shows human rights dwindling, with semifeudalism, despotic rulers, and the imperialism of Japan in the twentieth century.

The Chinese Civil War ended in 1949, with Mao Zedong's communist army defeating Chiang Kai-shek's nationalists, who were in control of China after Japan's World War II defeat and exit in 1945. Mao's Communist Party of China recruited peasants and the poor, using human rights language to win their loyalty and to condemn the Kuomintang—Chiang's Chinese Nationalist Party, which withdrew with its supporters to the island of Taiwan, where it resides today.

Soon after the Communist victory, public discourse about human rights was squelched on the mainland. It was inconsistent with the socialist project and considered to be a political/ideological strategy of the bourgeoisie. For nearly four decades, the topic of human rights was a "forbidden zone" for Chinese scholars. During that time, the People's Republic of China, under the leadership of Mao Zedong, maintained the same bureaucratic spirit of corrupted Confucianism. During his Cultural Revolution that began in 1966, Mao's Red Guards purged old intellectual leaders and their followers and ordered young intellectuals living in cities to work in the fields. Under the latter half of Mao's rule, every Chinese citizen had to own, read, and carry Mao's *Little Red Book* of quotations under threat of punishment. After Mao's death in 1976, China emerged from the quagmire of anti-intellectualism and started its progress toward phenomenal urban and economic development.

More than twenty years later, in 1997, the Gallup Research Co. Ltd. (China) conducted a national survey of Chinese consumers and found that the most commonly held attitude toward life was "work hard and get rich" (57 percent), while the least popular was "never think of yourself, give everything in service to society" (3 percent).[39] A Gallup poll conducted in 2006 indicated little change in the work-hard attitude.[40]

By 2007, China had ". . . the first generation in the world's history in which a majority are single children, a group whose solipsistic [egocentric] tendencies have been further encouraged by a growing obsession with consumerism, the Internet and video games."[41] Today, unlike the time of the Cultural Revolution

(1966–1976), the prevalent urban attitude that one's own future comes first will continue amidst the battle for human rights.

Throughout the second half of the twentieth century, human rights violations in China remained systematic and widespread, with the government suppressing dissenting opinions and maintaining political control over the legal system.[42] In the twenty-first century, human rights violations continue to be prevalent. In 2004, "[t]ens of thousands of people continued to be detained or imprisoned in violation of their fundamental human rights and were at high risk of torture or ill-treatment. Thousands of people were sentenced to death or executed, many after unfair trials."[43] Stories of widespread corruption of government and party officials persist, but urbanites are mainly concerned that political demands will bring reprisal and interfere with their material pursuits.

Despite the human degradation, by the first decade of the twenty-first century, China was "... already the world's second largest economy (measured by purchasing power), and the second largest holder of foreign exchange reserves, mainly U.S. dollars. It has the world's largest army (2.5 million men), and the fourth largest defense budget, which is rising over 10 percent annually."[44] China's growing economic might, however, parallels a global environmental plight with no clear end in sight. China has overtaken the United States as the world's leading producer of greenhouse gases, with Beijing being one of the worst-polluted capital cities in the world.

China's burgeoning urban middle class has forced its leaders to support the perspective of steady growth, with more emphasis and money going to protection of the environment. But without growth in the cosmic insight necessary to live as true members of God's family, solutions remain self-serving. Economic development will accelerate as social and political ethics lag behind, while self-interest continues to forestall meaningful reform. The political and economic chasm existing between urban and rural China only invites disaster.

Widespread problems are the harvest of a nation whose material achievement has surpassed the growth of worship and wisdom. "No social system or political regime which denies the reality of God can contribute in any constructive and lasting manner to the advancement of human civilization."[45] An imbalance between intellectual and spiritual growth could prove as hazardous to China as it proved to be in Greece and India.

China's current religious awakening promises to be the impetus for much-needed reform—China's Christian population has climbed to an estimated seventy million. "The government is confronting an uncertain new player: a vast movement for change in the name of God ... The Christian current rippling through China's human-rights circles is an important part of the rise of Christian activism in China."[46]

The West

In the late nineteenth century, Christian fragmentation was on the rise. Liberal Christians sought freedom to construct individual perspectives of God and desired broader views of salvation. Willing to consider and adopt viewpoints that had their roots outside of traditional Christianity, many were drawn to the philosophies found in Eastern scriptures as well as diverse European occult and esoteric traditions. While this pick-and-choose approach to religion was a relief from Christian dogmatism and promoted spiritual diversity, it also served to weaken faith as it exalted the sovereignty of the individual. The once-shared cultural belief in God as Father held the spiritual driving power to usher in the family of God and the universal unity that many sought. Instead, opting for a plurality of beliefs, liberal Christians found themselves in a fractured world of increasing competitiveness and uncertainty.

Esotericism and occultism became fashionable in the West largely through the Theosophical Society cofounded by Helena Blavatsky in 1875. Disheartened by Christianity and having lost faith in the Russian Orthodox God after the death of her son, Blavatsky provided a coherent system of teachings that drew mainly from Indian, Tibetan, and Buddhist religions; she also drew from European esoteric traditions such as Platonism, Neoplatonism, and Kabbala.

Blavatsky presented a revolutionary concept of life in the universe that included a complex cosmology of planes and subplanes and the universal processes by which everything is brought into being, including the human birth, death, and rebirth experiences. She presented and popularized the version of reincarnation wherein the soul, as the permanent ego or self, is not reborn as an animal once it has reached the level of complexity of a human being. This modification to the doctrine of transmigration was readily accepted in the West and it became a pillar of belief in the New Age Movement of the twentieth century.

> *Always, in the absence of revelation or in the failure to accept or grasp it, has mortal man resorted to his futile gesture of metaphysics, that being the only human substitute for the revelation of truth . . .*
> The Urantia Book

The belief in reincarnation provided escape from a final judgment and the possibility of eternal damnation in hell, a comforting panacea for those facing illness and death. To others, it offered a good explanation for the injustices in human life and the differences between people. Reincarnation offered an acceptable solution for the punishing or rewarding of one's deeds without the ministry and obligation of a personal God. In short, it was a convenient *deus ex machina* for a variety of unknown realities and unexplainable phenomena.

The teachings of the Indian philosophers Swami Vivekananda and Sri Aurobindo advanced the view of God as an impersonal force and the self as divine. Both paved the way for an influx of original Indian mysticism that turned to a flood in the late 1960s.

Influenced by the teachings of Vivekananda and motivated by the writings of the American transcendentalist Ralph Waldo Emerson (1803–1882), the New Thought Movement emerged. It consciously incorporated Eastern and Western insights, producing sects such as Divine Science, Religious Science, the Japanese Seicho-No-le, and Unity.

Aurobindo envisaged the evolution of the human mind from the material to the spiritual and even perceived the evolution of God the Supreme; he grasped the concept of Deity expanding outward and downward toward humanity. But because he didn't recognize the soul as a separate entity from spirit or its relation to human personality, he could not conceive of the journey inward and upward of the human soul/personality in union with spirit, from life on Earth to Paradise, and its significance to God the Supreme. He merged the cosmic approach of Theosophy and the evolutionary findings of science with ancient Indian philosophy to produce a vision that appealed to the twentieth-century "spiritual seeker" mindset—an upward spiral that reclaims self-perfection through reincarnation.

The New Age Movement blossomed as an idealistic generation sought refuge from its disillusion with mainstream faith. Followers could shape their spiritual lives and practices according to their own understanding of spiritual development. The New Age Movement in the United States found traction with the counterculture of the 1960s and expanded into popular culture in the 1970s and onward.

"The higher a civilization climbs, the more necessitous becomes the duty to 'seek first the realities of heaven' in all of man's efforts to stabilize society and facilitate the solution of its material problems."[47] By the 1990s, however, forty percent of the American population either had no affiliation with an organized religion—embracing instead concepts from the religions of the East—or were church members but not faithful and active participants, fond of picking and choosing what they wanted from their traditions. Professor Karel Dobbelaere, a sociologist of religion at the time, made the following observation: ". . . the successful removal by science of all kinds of anthropomorphisms from our thinking has transformed the traditional concept of 'God as a person' into a belief in a life-force, a power of spirit and this has also gradually promoted agnosticism and atheism—which explains the long-term decline of religious practices."[48] Epochal revelation explains: "Man's greatest spiritual jeopardy consists in partial progress, the predicament of unfinished growth: forsaking the evolutionary religions of fear without immediately grasping the revelatory religion of love. Modern science, particularly psychology, has weakened only those religions which are so largely dependent upon fear, superstition, and emotion."

The growing belief in an all-pervasive conscious force reinforced the belief in solipsism ("My mind is all that there is"), with humans as divine and the process of reincarnation as the means to regain our inherent perfection. These beliefs, with their pervasive focus on the self, became woven into the spiritual tapestry of many New Age doctrines, and their influence persists. The outcome of this religious drift is revealed in stunning statistics:

1. Two European Values Surveys conducted in 1981 and in 1990 reported that between 1968 and 1990 in Western Europe, there was a steady increase in the acceptance of reincarnation. For example, in 1968, 23 percent of people in France believed in reincarnation; in 1990, that figure had risen to 28 percent. In Britain, it rose during the same period from 18 percent to 30 percent; and in the Netherlands, from 10 percent to 18 percent.[49] A third survey between 1999 and 2002 reported that the concept of reincarnation continues to be a major belief among the inhabitants of Western Europe, with a mean of 22.2 percent.[50] In the United States, a Gallup poll in 2005 showed that 20 percent of American adults believe in reincarnation.[51]

2. Most significant is the influence that the belief in reincarnation appears to have on the belief in God: Statistics in the European Values Systems Study showed that as the belief in reincarnation *increased*, the belief in God *declined*.[52]

3. A 2004 study published in the *Washington Times* indicated that twenty-three percent of Generation Y (born between 1980 and 2000), like Generation X (born between 1960 and 1980), do not identify with a religious denomination or believe in God—more than twice the number of nonbelieving baby boomers born between 1946 and 1965.[53]

The evidence seems to suggest that there is a connection between indifference toward God and a social decline in ethics. Epochal revelation tells us that the brotherhood of man cannot be created while ignoring or denying the fatherhood of God. It warns us that "[w]ithout God, without religion, scientific secularism can never coordinate its forces, harmonize its divergent and rivalrous interests, races, and nationalisms."[54] If this counsel is accurate, the repercussions of the personal waning interest in God will be reflected in society. "Ethics is the eternal social or racial mirror which faithfully reflects the otherwise unobservable progress of internal spiritual and religious developments."[55]

By the end of the twentieth century, the West witnessed increased technological sophistication, a growing diversity of organized religions, increased volunteerism, and the creation of a wide range of secular groups that cut across religious lines. But moral and higher intelligence declined. The Russian historian Alexander Solzhenitsyn expressed his concern: "The West . . . has been undergoing erosion and obscuring of high moral and ethical ideals. The spiritual axis of life has grown dim."[56]

Statistics in America reflected that claim. Between 1960 and 1990, there was "a 560% increase in violent crime, a 419% increase in illegitimate births; a quadrupling in divorce rates; a tripling of the percentage of children living in single-parent homes; more than a 200% increase in the teenage suicide rate; and a drop of almost 80 points in SAT scores."[57] By 1991, the crime rate was 313% the 1960 crime rate.[58]

Cultural decline has continued into the twenty-first century. Individuals continue to place more value on self-expression than self-control. There is less worth placed on social respectability and moral responsibility, on sacrifice of pride, selflessness as a moral good, and on restraint in matters of sexual indulgence. There is a weakening of family life and a pervasiveness of violence in schools, homes, and society.

- In 2007, a study conducted by Jean Twenge, SDSU, psychology professor and author of *Generation Me: Why Today's Young Americans Are More Confident, Assertive, Entitled—and More Miserable Than Ever Before,* found that Generation Y (born between 1980 and 2000) is the most narcissistic generation in recent history. "Narcissism is defined as having an inflated sense of entitlement, low empathy toward others, fantasies of personal greatness, a belief that ordinary people cannot understand."[59] Narcissists have a propensity to exploit others and to express hostility and sexual aggression. Tom Huston, in his article "The Dumbest Generation?" refers to Generation Y as "sophisticatedly narcissistic;" bright and authentically idealistic but ". . . glued to a world of pure virtuality . . . floating freely—within millions of bubbles of self-reflecting opacity . . . "[60]

- In 2008, the United States experienced an increase in violent crimes such as murder, forcible rape, and robberies in cities with fewer than 10,000 residents (murder up 5.5 percent, forcible rape up 1.4 percent, robbery up 3.9 percent)."[61] In 2005, the country had the largest annual increase in violent crime since 1991 (an 8.3 percent rise).[62]

- Sex crimes on children and by children are growing at an alarming rate.

Once the shining worldwide example of moral and social justice, America in recent years has flexed its imperial muscle and operated on questionable moral ground with the exercise of preemptive military action, condoned torture in military prisons, increased government corruption, and a curtailment of many individual rights in the name of security. This cultural skid has evoked the ultimate challenge to reverse the declining ethics not only in America and the West, but worldwide.

Beyond Reincarnation

In God's natural order, the pupa evolves into a caterpillar, which then transforms into a butterfly; the magnificent little creature does not return to its cocoon stage. "Can you not advance in your concept of God's dealing with man to that level where you recognize that the watchword of the universe is *progress*?"[63]

For thirty years, my framework of understanding about the nature of spiritual development included a cyclic pattern of mortal incarnations. My Christian training held aloft a personal God and an immortal soul that maintained its personal individuality after death. While I resonated with this teaching, I still questioned the resurrection of the physical body and the concept of eternal suffering after a life on Earth; these questions seemed to be addressed by the concepts of reincarnation and karma, which I then embraced without reservation. Meditation awakened an interest in the Hindu concept of *Paramatma*, God as indwelling spirit/soul. However, I could not reconcile my Christian beliefs with the concept of *moksha*—the soul's release from the bonds of reincarnation. While I could identify with the New Age concept of "the higher self." I found it difficult to identify with the concept that God is an impersonal force or consciousness and the proclamation, "All is One."

For decades, these blended beliefs (and the resulting unresolved conflicts) coexisted in my spiritual repertoire until I began to question the effectiveness of my spiritual practices; despite many years of meditation and prayer, I still yearned for a more lively connection with God. My spirituality seemed to be self-centered and focused on personal enlightenment, which was the main goal of the community in which I lived. Why did I not feel any closer to God now than I did before beginning to meditate? As a community of spiritual people, why were we not more oriented toward selfless and loving service?

When I began to explore my beliefs, I had no idea that I would question the validity of reincarnation. Through my first years of research into *The Urantia Book*, I remained a firm believer despite the clear statement that reincarnation is a human concept. I was convinced that information about it was being withheld and I was determined to find the hidden clues that validated its existence.

My research and reflection continued, and I finally started to write this book. As I approached the section on destiny, I noticed that I was experiencing an inner turmoil whose origin I could not identify. I decided to skip that section and advance to the last one. Try as I might, I could not move forward—I was experiencing writer's block! I also developed digestive problems. Friends suggested that I was struggling with unresolved conflict. Deep down, I knew that fear was keeping me from objectively exploring the concept of reincarnation, which had to precede any other topic on destiny. What if I discovered flaws in my cherished belief? I decided to face my inward struggle. I hesitantly began to deepen my understanding of the doctrine of reincarnation, and then to reconcile my findings with epochal revelation.

At the time I was a student of Theosophy, and I was familiar with a book written by Geoffrey A. Barborka, called *The Divine Plan*. The book had a diagram that represented the mechanics of reincarnation, shown below, which helped me explore this Eastern concept.

The doctrine of reincarnation involves the evolution of an immortal Self, represented as the top circle of the diagram. According to Barborka, for us to

Illustration 26
THE IMMORTAL SELF AND THE EGO

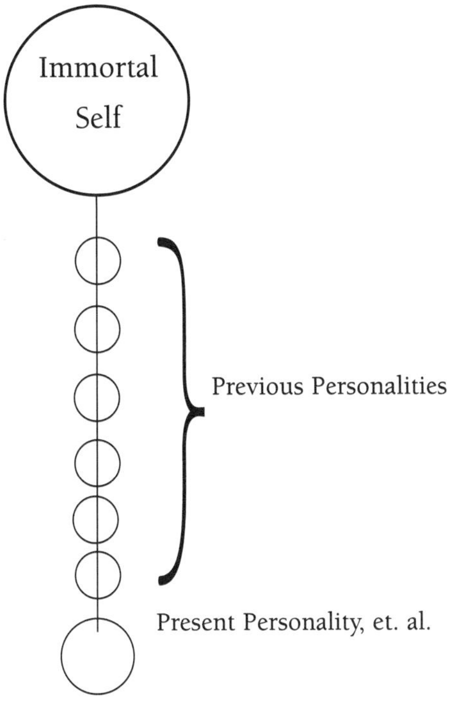

Immortal Self

Previous Personalities

Present Personality, et. al.

experience a life cycle on Earth, a ray is extended from the immortal Self, or *atman*, into the material realm, where it links to a newborn personality or ego. "When death occurs, this personality, represented as a small sphere, is left as a bead upon the Thread-Self. Then a passive cycle is undergone. At the conclusion of this period of rest, another ray is sent forth and another personality is brought into being, which manifests in the world for another period of activity. This in turn is followed by another period of rest, and another personality is left on the thread . . . The lowest sphere depicts the present personality."[64] Barborka explains that the bottom sphere represents the collection of all the previous personalities combined or blended into the present personality, creating a new thought pattern and causes. In this process, the purpose of each personality is to grow in receptivity to the immortal Self, so that eventually the latter can effect its liberation from the cycle of reincarnation and merge with its source.

When I began to explore the mechanics of reincarnation in the light of epochal revelation, no amount of logical new knowledge dissuaded me from my belief until I began to recognize new cosmic relations and appreciate their implications on the technique of survival. Although a cherished and traditional spiritual premise was being challenged, I realized that it was not so much a matter of letting go of my long-held belief in reincarnation, but of allowing a natural transformation to evolve through the discovery of higher meanings and values in my collective beliefs. In the process of reconciliation, I was constructing a more logical philosophy of the universe and arriving at a more satisfying understanding of my place in that universe.

How then did my belief in reincarnation evolve to embrace cosmic truths from each discipline to arrive at a vision that was more personally fulfilling and intellectually complete?

The most compelling factors in my evolution beyond reincarnation were the recognition of the multilevel universe, the uniqueness and significance of personality, the distinction between spirit and soul, and the implications of these relationships on survival after physical death. As I discovered new meaning in these concepts, along with greater clarity in the process of spiritual evolution and divine attainment, a larger framework of understanding began to compete with the concept of reincarnation. "The personality is the unique bestowal which the Universal Father makes upon the living and associated energies of matter, mind, and spirit, and which survives with the survival of the morontial soul."[65] Human personality *is* unique. We are indwelt by divinity, able to discern the indwelling divine presence, and choose or reject its guidance; a person can even choose or reject eternal life. The human personality therefore exists not to liberate an immortal Self, but to choose and realize God, and in the process, give God ascending sons and daughters. By actively developing the soul and attaining immortality through union of the soul and spirit, the human personality can eventually, as a perfected spirit being, behold the spirit person of God in Paradise.

Personality *is* much more than an "evanescent Ego," left after death as a bead on a cosmic thread. Our efforts to find God and emulate his nature have their own personal and eternal rewards. As the implications of this understanding came to full realization, I burst into tears. God was closer to me than I could have ever imagined and his fragment indwelling me would lead me to his presence!

The rewriting began, almost from scratch. This time, I approached the destiny section without hesitation. My behavior seemed unchanged to me, but judging by the response of others, my interactions with them seemed much more empathetic. In the discovery of new meaning, I gained an expanded perspective of life that simultaneously increased my love and appreciation of God, infusing that love into my interactions with others. I began to experience hints of the quality and depth of love that transforms lives.

As Eastern, New Age, and Christian perspectives became clarified by epochal revelation, they were unified into a broader worldview—clearer, brighter, and more compelling. I was inspired to rethink what was necessary to become a better person in the service of others. I began to identify *with* spirit rather than *as* spirit, developing an unexpected intellectual and spiritual humility and gratefulness to God that was even more self-empowering and socially productive.

Conceptual Expansion

Aside from religious belief, the theory of reincarnation hinges on "past-life recall." Below are three plausible explanations for this mind phenomenon:

1. Scientific study of DNA function has just begun. It is too soon to know whether DNA may carry and transmit ancestor experience. But stories of people who have received donated organs and report memories that are verified to be from the life of the organ donor point to a strong possibility of DNA memory transfer.

2. Conscious or unconscious transference can occur, especially in hypnotic regressions, including suggestive give-and-take between mediator and subject.

3. Dormant memories could be planted via personal experience or media exposure of any sort.

As a spiritual person who wholly embraced the phenomenon of "past-life recall," I discovered the most convincing and comprehensive explanations of these types of memories in *The Urantia Book*: the human mind's encircuitment in the cosmic mind and the mind-presence of an Indwelling Spirit.

The study of consciousness is in its infancy, but most of us know that minds are capable of nonlocal activities such as clairvoyance, telepathy, remote viewing, and so on. These activities are not fully scientifically understood but when we accept that the human mind is connected to the cosmic mind—a repository of infinite thought and experience—unusual memory phenomena as well as paranormal affinities between personalities are no longer mysterious. "The fact of the cosmic mind explains the kinship of various types of human and superhuman minds. Not only are kindred spirits attracted to each other, but kindred minds are also very fraternal and inclined toward cooperation the one with the other. Human minds are sometimes observed to be running in channels of astonishing similarity and inexplicable agreement."[66] Also, "[t]hat mind which can affect a partial abridgment of time and space, by this very act proves itself possessed of the seeds of wisdom which can effectively serve in lieu of the transcended barrier of restraint."[67]

The fact of the human mind's superconscious contact with the cosmic mind also explains the dreams that sometimes carry us beyond real life experiences, those fleeting glimpses into higher realities that affirm mind transcendence over the merely material.

Given the relation between the human and cosmic mind, the *memory* phenomenon of "past-life recall" should be considered a *mind experience*, even an unexplainable phenomenon of supermind capture, rather than a confirmation of previous physical incarnation. Such intriguing recollections may also have another cosmic explanation. Since every normal-minded individual is indwelt by a fragment of the infinite and eternal, it is spiritually unsound to set limits on what the human partner may sometimes tap into as part of the Indwelling Spirit's efforts to spiritualize the mind. Access to an unlimited "memory bank" of experiences has been historically misunderstood, though the concept of Akashic Records bears witness to cosmic mind—the "living libraries" that are the angelic recorders of the Infinite Spirit's family.[68]

The value of any experience lies in whether or not our souls are evolving through our expanded capacity to know God and love one another. Regardless of the interpretation of the "recall" experience, there is value if it motivates the individual to develop into a proactive, cosmic-minded, selfless, and loving individual. Nevertheless, the ability to objectively utilize information for spiritual growth depends on a broad perspective and a balanced personality.

How easy it is to remain passive, dodging personal responsibility for our actions! We seek answers to rationalize our shortcomings without a proportionate effort to improve. We venerate the indefinable realm of memory to explain our progress (or lack thereof) and excuse our irresponsible behavior; we empower mediums and hypnotists as intermediaries between ourselves and our divine potential. All this focus on *regression* hinders personal and collective *progression*.

As we develop a well-balanced, God-knowing personality and a cosmic perspective illuminated by epochal revelation, we discover a higher value in the life we are living *now*. As our knowledge of human mind potential grows and we evolve in our understanding of cosmic relations, the theory of reincarnation will be recognized as a metaphysical construct born of human fears and confusion about death and the next level of life.

16.

Salvation and Death

Three things are necessary for the salvation of man: to know what he ought to believe; to know what he ought to desire; and to know what he ought to do.

St. Thomas Aquinas

D own through time, the conflict between selfish desire and the urge to be altruistic prompted belief in the need to be saved. It was assumed that the soul had value and can be redeemed or ransomed. It remains true today that the majority of people crave ". . . promises of salvation—religious consolation for today and assurances of hope for immortality after death."[1]

Religions teach doctrines of salvation that reflect their understanding of the relationships that exist between God and mortal: In Hinduism, soul and spirit are one and the same. Salvation therefore is the soul's liberation from the cycle of death and rebirth through the practice of meditation. Most forms of Buddhism emphasize the doctrine of no soul and no self; therefore does it promise salvation (end of suffering and complete happiness) in this life through self-reliance, belief in the Buddha, and the practice of meditation. The Jewish religion promises salvation (prosperity and eternal reward) through the practice of righteousness. Christian doctrine limits salvation (eternal life, entrance into heaven) to those who believe in Jesus Christ as Lord and Savior. According to a 2009 national survey conducted by Barna Research, fifty-five percent of adults agree (strongly 35%, somewhat 20%) that it is possible for someone to earn their way into heaven through good behavior.[2]

The New Thought movement blends psychology and religion, proposing that we are transformed, if not saved, by attuning with the Divine Mind. New Age spirituality encompasses an eclectic approach, including the recognition of

Salvation is a matter of clean hearts rather than of clean hands.

The Urantia Book

self as divine; salvation, therefore, is the attainment of enlightenment and liberation from the reincarnation cycle. For humanists whose lives are guided primarily by reason and science, with ambivalent or no belief in God or survival after death, salvation is active problem-solving and their reward lies in leaving the world a better place for all.

To reconcile and expand these perspectives in the light of epochal revelation, we must explore salvation within the context of the Divine Plan, specifically the Plan of Progressive Attainment and the Bestowal Plan as described in *The Urantia Book*, which sets the stage for exploration of personality survival (addressed in the following chapter).

The Plan of Progressive Attainment provides for personal survival after physical death, spiritual advancement through the multilevel universe, and perfection in eternity. When individuals complement the assuredness of personal religious experience with an attitude of faith toward the highest realms of universe objective reality, it enables them to depend without any reservations upon the absolute love of the Universal Father. "Such a genuine religious experience far transcends the philosophic objectification of idealistic desire; it actually takes salvation for granted and concerns itself only with learning and doing the will of the Father in Paradise."[3]

Salvation is the result of our ongoing journey of progressive spiritual growth that begins with the first flicker of faith in God. "Faith acts to release the superhuman activities of the divine spark, the immortal germ, that lives within the mind of man, and which is the potential of eternal survival."[4]

The Bestowal Plan provides for the missions of the Sons of God who visit evolutionary worlds to reveal the love of the Father, the mercy of the Son, and also the way of salvation. Four thousand years ago, Machiventa Melchizedek proclaimed salvation through faith, reforming the olden practice of sacrifice and other offerings to attain favor with God.

Jesus of Nazareth expanded upon Machiventa's teachings and shed significant light on the technique of salvation. He revealed that just as we look for God, God is likewise looking for us. Jesus' favorite way of teaching about the Father's love was through the parables of the lost sheep (Luke 15:3–7), the lost coin (Luke 15:8–10), and the lost son (Luke 15:11–32). Through the parable of the lost sheep, Jesus showed that the Father is mindful of any person who unintentionally strays. God uses all his powers to find that lost soul. Through the parable of the lost coin, he illustrated how thorough is the divine searching for all who are confused or spiritually blinded by materialism and physical cares. With the parable of the lost son, Jesus showed how complete is the restoration of the lost son into his Father's house and heart.[5]

The teaching of the fatherhood of God and the brotherhood of man dominated Jesus' ministry and encapsulated the love of the Father and the way of salvation. "The teachings of Jesus constituted the first Urantian religion which so fully embraced a harmonious coordination of knowledge, wisdom, faith, truth, and love as completely and simultaneously to provide temporal tranquility, intellectual certainty, moral enlightenment, philosophic stability, ethical sensitivity, God-consciousness, and the positive assurance of personal survival."[6] Jesus' faith and the way he lived his life illuminates the way to the ultimate of human universe attainment, since it provided for:

- Salvation from physical restrictions, through the realization that every human being is a son or daughter of the eternal Father-God.

- Salvation from intellectual bondage, by seeking and recognizing truth when we find it: "The truth shall make you free."

- Salvation from spiritual isolation, by personally striving to live the brotherhood of man.

- Salvation from imperfect human nature, through soul development and continual progress on the ascending path to Paradise in the service to God.

- Salvation from a myopic perspective of the universe, through increased understanding of cosmic relationships and the interrelatedness between universal facts and spiritual values.

- Salvation from time/space limitations, through discovery of the transcendental possibilities in Paradise and beyond.[7]

Such a sevenfold salvation is tantamount to the maximum of Godlikeness and exists in potential in the attitude of faith. "And all this, in potential, is contained within the reality of the faith of the human experience of religion. And it can be so contained since the faith of Jesus was nourished by, and was revelatory of, even realities beyond the ultimate . . ."[8]

The fifth epochal revelation presented in *The Urantia Book* brings new clarity and meaning to the mechanics of salvation by illuminating relationships between soul, spirit, and human personality.

"The soul is the self-reflective, truth-discerning, and spirit-perceiving part of man which forever elevates the human being above the level of the animal world. Self-consciousness, in and of itself, is not the soul. Moral self-consciousness is true human self-realization and constitutes the foundation of the human soul, and the soul is that part of man which represents the potential survival value of human experience. Moral choice and spiritual attainment, the ability to know God and the urge to be like him, are the characteristics of the soul. The soul of man cannot exist apart from moral thinking and spiritual activity. A stagnant soul is a dying soul. But the soul of man is distinct from the divine spirit which dwells within the mind. The divine spirit arrives simultaneously with the first moral activity of the human mind, and that is the occasion of the birth of the soul."[9]

The soul is the morontia seed of personal identification that has the *potential* to survive physical death. Human logic and reasoning develop within our intellect—but it is the growth of spiritual insight superimposed upon this human reasoning that not only enhances moral expression but also cultivates the spiritual vision and understanding that assures development of the soul and survival of the human personality beyond death.

The soul grows through our intentional efforts to detect higher spiritual meanings and values and apply such insight discoveries in daily living.

Intellectual and moral growth without faith engenders greater consistency in ethical behavior but it is faith that attunes us to the guidance of the Indwelling Spirit and ensures life eternal; living faith develops the spiritual reverence and fraternal love that transforms civilization.

Living faith merges the faculty of reason with growing spiritual insight to develop the soul and the spiritual humility that assures progress. "Reason, through the study of science, may lead back through nature to a First Cause, but it requires religious faith to transform the First Cause of science into a God of salvation; and revelation is further required for the validation of such a faith, such spiritual insight."[10] Conscious soul development enables believers to become, in deed and in truth, the everlasting sons and daughters of the eternal God.

The exercise of living faith and the cultivation of universal intelligence give spiritual depth to the concept of salvation. Our understanding of the relationship between God and mortals is personified with the fatherhood of God ideal, as our relationships with each other are glorified by the ideal that we are all sons and daughters of the same God. With sincere devotion to the development of God-consciousness, we supplant the self-centered desire for personal salvation with the unselfish urge to love and serve others, just as Jesus loved and served humanity. "This concept of love generates in the soul of man that superanimal effort to find truth, beauty, and goodness; and when he does find them, he is glorified in their embrace; he is consumed with the desire to live them, to do righteousness."[11]

Salvation is truly personality progress in the service of God, now and in the afterlife. As we consent to the spiritualization of the mind and actively engage in developing the soul, we joyfully adopt the concept of divine attunement with the Indwelling Spirit as our philosophy of salvation. This is the spiritually progressive attitude of living faith that Jesus lived and modeled for all humanity. The way of salvation is thus open to every motivated seeker.

The evolving morontia soul provides for the continuity of identity in the afterlife, and the Indwelling Spirit provides for its immortality. The achievement of eternal life is, nevertheless, tied to the self-consciousness of salvation through faith and sincere effort to develop the soul. "The saving or losing of a soul has to do with whether or not the moral consciousness attains survival status through eternal alliance with its associated immortal spirit endowment [the Indwelling Spirit]. Salvation is the spiritualization of the self-realization of the moral consciousness, which thereby becomes possessed of survival value. All forms of soul conflict consist in the lack of harmony between the moral, or spiritual, self-consciousness and the purely intellectual self-consciousness."[12]

Great achievements require a steadfast commitment to excellence. When we choose salvation, we accept responsibility to grow in godliness, that we may improve our ability to serve others lovingly and unselfishly in God's service. This means that regardless of the quality and depth of our faith, we consent to expanding our concept of God and his relation to us and the universe; we master the ability to make moral choices in the spiritual realms of reason, being attentive to our innate guidance. Thus, we progressively develop the soul and grow in harmony with the Indwelling Spirit, a self-consciousness of salvation that truly gains favor with God. "Human salvation is *real*; it is based on two realities which may be grasped by the creature's faith and thereby become incorporated into individual human experience: the fact of the fatherhood of God and its correlated truth, the brotherhood of man."[13]

Death

The subject of death runs an emotional gamut from fright to relief, and even to anticipation of a coming adventure. Death means different things to different people, but for the spiritual and the religious, death means survival, a continuation of existence. Most of our beliefs have been qualified by ancient teachings carried forward by tradition.

Medical advances have necessitated a refined definition of death. In modern society, physical death is strictly defined in order to facilitate various legal actions, including disconnection from body-maintaining machines and the enactment of predetermined wishes via wills and trusts.

In America, the National Conference of Commissioners on Uniform State Laws formulated in 1980 the Uniform Determination of Death Act, which states that an individual is considered dead if he or she has sustained either (1) "irreversible cessation of circulatory and respiratory functions," or (2) if irrespective of the continuing function of the physical body, there is "irreversible cessation of all functions of the entire brain, including the brain stem."[14]

On Earth, death is determined by physical criteria; from a cosmic perspective, it occurs when the last act of personal will takes place. According to epochal revelation, an individual's last such act is confirmed and registered by a celestial Census Director. Census Directors are the creation of the Infinite Spirit and are responsive to nothing but will function. "Census Directors register the existence of a new will creature when the first act of will is performed; they indicate the death of a will creature when the last act of will takes place."[15]

For the materialist, death means the end of existence. For the religionist, death brings the possibility of survival and immortality—a continuation of existence and the beginning of eternal life. From a human perspective, the process of physical death is inevitable, despite the growing trend of biological and mechanical replacement technologies. But the cosmic perspective reveals that the experience of physical death is not inevitable. "Natural, physical death is not a mortal inevitability. The majority of advanced evolutionary beings, citizens on worlds existing in the final era of light and life, do not die; they are translated directly from the life in the flesh to the morontia existence."[16]

There are seen and unseen activities that simultaneously occur when physical death overtakes a person who has chosen survival during life:

1. On the physical level, the circulatory, respiratory, and brain functions cease. The material body slowly returns to the elemental world from which it was derived.

2. Behind the scenes:

    a. The circuit of the human mind ceases to function.

    b. The preexistent Indwelling Spirit, with the memory transcription of the mortal career, takes leave of the vanishing mind. In the case of brain or intellectual death, the Indwelling Spirit is immediately released, irrespective of the continuing function of the physical body.

    c. The mind pattern and inert potentialities of the human personality remain with the soul, entrusted to the safekeeping of seraphic guardians. The deceased individual temporarily loses identity and consciousness but not personality.[17]

There is yet another death that may occur even while the person is still alive. Spiritual (soul) death, one of the two types of deaths mentioned in the Bible, results when survival has been deliberately rejected (see chapter 18).

17.

Survival, Resurrection, and Eternal Life

*I would rather live my life as if there is a God and die to find out there isn't,
than live my life as if there isn't and die to find out there is.*
Albert Camus

Some form of life after death has always been a staple of human beliefs, with as many variations as the number of faithful. Personal artifacts found in ancient burial grounds attest to our fascination with the journey of the afterlife. A poll conducted in February–March 2006 by the Scripps Survey Research Center at Ohio University found that seventy-two percent of Americans believe in an afterlife with "some sort of consciousness."[1]

To some believers, the highest goal of spiritual attainment is the release of the soul from the bonds of reincarnation to join with its source; for others, it is the survival of the soul—to be in heaven in the presence of God and with loved ones. All afterlife scenarios have common elements as well as subtle differences that can now be reconciled with the revealed mechanics of personality survival.

As pertains to eternal survival, God has decreed the sovereignty of the material and mortal will, and that decree is absolute.
The Urantia Book

During physical life, the human personality is dependent on the continuing function of the human body. To transcend the experience of death, however, the human mind must increasingly identify itself with the Indwelling Spirit. "The technique of survival is embraced in those adjustments of the human will and those transformations in the mortal mind whereby such a God-conscious intellect gradually becomes spirit taught and eventually spirit led."[2] Sincerity, persistence, and steadfastness in making God-conscious decisions is essential to increasingly attune to the Indwelling Spirit and survive physical death. Human survival constitutes the continued existence of the human soul/personality in a new form in association with the Indwelling Spirit, the essence of our eternal nature.

Survival, in the context of awakening from death, is assured for those with even the faintest flicker of faith in higher realities, provided one has engaged in moral activities that yield love, joy, peace, goodness, and kindness. The presence of these moral and spiritual values indicates responsiveness to the spirit of the Father resident in the mind, and denotes the potential for eternal existence that can be cultivated in the afterlife. "As to the chances of mortal survival, let it be made forever clear: All souls of every possible phase of mortal existence will survive provided they manifest willingness to cooperate with their indwelling Adjusters and exhibit a desire to find God and to attain divine perfection, even though these desires be but the first faint flickers of the primitive comprehension of that 'true light which lights every man who comes into the world.'"[3] "Only conscious resistance to the Adjuster's leading can prevent the survival of the evolving immortal soul."[4]

Survival in death does not imply uninterrupted consciousness. According to epochal revelation, there is a period of unconsciousness between death and awakening. How long we have to wait before awakening and in which celestial world we will begin our Paradise adventure depends on how deeply we have developed and integrated our physical and spiritual natures and capacities during the mortal life. Steadfast and growing faith becomes the connecting fabric between moral awareness and the spiritual realization of eternal life. With such faith-trust engaged, an individual is naturally drawn to do the will of God: to develop the God-awareness, cosmic insight, and balanced character necessary to live the golden rule from its highest level of interpretation.

Sleeping Survivors

A person who survives death generally starts the journey to eternity by joining the ranks of sleeping survivors. Sleeping survivors are those individuals of "survival status" who have passed through the portals of death, and their souls, mind matrixes, and inert characteristics are either in the custody of personal guardians or group custodians.

The concept of sleeping survivors is found in Ecclesiastes 9:5: "The dead know not anything" and in I Thessalonians 4:13 where Paul refers to the dead as "those who fall asleep." In addition, the captives that Christ led in Ephesians 4:8 were sleeping survivors. Epochal revelation clarifies: "And these captives were the sleeping survivors from the days of Adam to the day of the Master's resurrection on Urantia."[5]

Sleeping survivors are not conscious (aware) during the interim between death and awakening. "At death the functional identity associated with the human personality is disrupted through the cessation of vital motion. Human personality, while transcending its constituent parts, is dependent on them for functional identity. The stoppage of life destroys the physical brain patterns for mind endowment, and the disruption of mind terminates mortal consciousness. The consciousness of that creature cannot subsequently reappear until a cosmic situation has been arranged which will permit the same human personality again to function in relationship with living energy."[6]

This universal process may be termed resurrection.

Resurrection

Teachings of the resurrection of the dead are found in biblical passages, such as John 5:28–29; 6:39–40; 11:25 and Luke 14:14. In Christianity, resurrection has been interpreted to mean the act of rising from the dead in the same body of flesh and blood, as Jesus was believed to have risen. A poll conducted in February–March 2006 by the Scripps Survey Research Center at Ohio University found that thirty-six percent of those surveyed, mostly churchgoing people, believe in the resurrection of the body after death.[7]

Long before the time of Christ, many cultures celebrated the death and resurrection of various gods. The ancient Sumerian tale "Inanna's Descent to the Nether World" is perhaps the earliest story of resurrection. The text describes the descent of the goddess Inanna into the underworld, where she was turned into a corpse and hung on a stake. After three days and three nights, she was brought back to life.

The subsequent stories of Ishtar and the biblical Tammuz; Isis and Osiris; Venus and Adonis; and Cybele, the early Asiatic goddess who loved Attis, are all variations on the resurrection theme. According to epochal revelation, "The Phrygian and Egyptian mysteries taught that the divine son (respectively Attis and Osiris) had experienced death and had been resurrected by divine power, and further that all who were properly initiated into the mystery, and who reverently celebrated the anniversary of the god's death and resurrection, would thereby become partakers of his divine nature and his immortality."[8]

Spiritual resurrection of the human personality is depicted in the Pyramid Texts of Egypt, dating back to approximately 2350 BC. These texts are the oldest known collection of religious spells, the main theme being the king's resurrection and ascension to the afterworld.

The Egyptian and Phrygian mysteries eventually gave way to Mithraism, a Persian mystery cult. By the time of its influence on early Christianity, Mithraism had absorbed many of the teachings of Zoroaster, including the resurrection of the human body.

Among Hebrews, the belief in the bodily resurrection of the dead was adopted by the Pharisees, although it is not clearly found in the Hebrew scriptures. According to epochal revelation, in his discussions about survival and resurrection, Jesus confirmed the resurrection of the human personality but not in a physical body: "The Master in his answer, though positively affirming the fact of the survival of mortal creatures by the technique of the resurrection, did not in any sense speak approvingly of the Pharisaic beliefs in the resurrection of the literal human body."[9]

Although most Christian churches subscribe to the dust-to-dust principle, many continue to believe there will be a physical resurrection of the dead at the end of time. Jesus' post-crucifixion appearances firmly established this belief.

Let us reconcile and redefine the common understanding of resurrection as the awakening from death and, more specifically, as repersonalization or reassembly of the constituent parts of the once-human personality.

Repersonalization

A new term, "repersonalization," is used in epochal revelation to more accurately describe our awakening from death—the process wherein the human personality regains identity consciousness and function in a new body. Repersonalization does not involve the mortal body of flesh and blood; it is the reunion of the immortal Indwelling Spirit and the evolving human soul/personality in a morontia body—the next and higher level of evolutionary reality. The steps in this process include:

1. The creation of a new life vehicle, within which the morontia variant of the cosmic mind can be encircuited. "As the mortal body is personal and characteristic for every human being, so will the morontia form be highly individual and adequately characteristic of the creative mind which dominates it."[10] The surviving human personality will undergo hundreds of progressive transformations and refinements on the path to Paradise, from the lowest morontia to the higher spirit forms. On Earth, one is a creature of flesh and blood. During the local universe experience, one is a morontia being; at the superuniverse level, the surviving personality is an evolving spirit. "From the time of leaving the material worlds until you are constituted a first-stage spirit on Salvington, you will undergo just 570 separate and ascending morontia changes. Eight of these occur in the system, seventy-one in the constellation, and 491 during the sojourn on the spheres of Salvington."[11]

2. The return of the Indwelling Spirit, with the memory transcription of the mortal career to the waiting morontia being.

3. The bestowal of the inert mortal identity, in union with the soul, upon the created morontia mind-body form.

When the soul and the spirit are reunited in a morontia form, this constitutes personality resurrection. The survivor is given possession of a morontia body; the mortal body has been left behind on the world of its origin. This resurrection body is the form that followers of Jesus beheld during his many appearances after Calvary. That phenomenon was unique to the experience of the Creator Son—mortals do not repersonalize on Earth.

Mortal survivors will pass through the adjustment sleep and resurrection awakening seven times in their ascension career. In subsequent transitions, they will experience no break in the continuity of personal memory. Each new resurrection enables the perception of an additional family of spirit beings without altering the ability to recognize friends and colleagues of previous experiences.

Interim between Physical Death and Morontia Resurrection

The timing of individual repersonalization is linked with human self-mastery and spiritual progress. "All mortals of survival status, in the custody of personal guardians of destiny, pass through the portals of natural death and, on the third period [day], personalize on the mansion worlds. Those accredited beings who have, for any reason, been unable to attain that level of intelligence mastery and endowment of spirituality which would entitle them to personal guardians cannot thus immediately and directly go to the mansion worlds. Such surviving souls must rest in unconscious sleep until the judgment day of a new epoch, a new dispensation, the coming of a Son of God to call the rolls of the age and adjudicate the realm, and this is the general practice throughout all Nebadon."[12] Those who have slept for three days or for thousands of years will react no differently upon awakening. Children who have not been indwelt by an Indwelling Spirit and have died before choosing a Paradise career will remain in custody of the guardians of destiny until the exact time that one or both of the child's parents awaken after death.

"Special resurrections occur . . . at least every millennium of planetary time, when not all but 'many of those who sleep in the dust awake.' These special resurrections are the occasion for mobilizing special groups of ascenders for specific service in the local universe plan of mortal ascension. There are both practical reasons and sentimental associations connected with these special resurrections."[13] Most survivors, however, are repersonalized at the inauguration of a new epoch associated with the arrival of a Divine Son. Illustration 26 reconciles individual destiny after physical death.

Communication with the Dead

A 2001 Gallup poll on paranormal beliefs showed that between 1990 and 2001, there was a 10 percent increase in Americans who believe in communication with the dead. A similar poll in 2005 showed a decline from 28 to 21 percent since 2001. There was, however, only a three percent decrease in the overall percentage of people with at least one paranormal belief—from 76 percent in 2001 to 73 percent in 2005.

Alleged communication with the dead dates to the first shamans—medicine men and women who presumed to place themselves between humanity and the spirit world as mediators and interpreters. "Since in olden times anything abnormal was ascribed to spirit possession, any striking mental or physical abnormality constituted qualification for being a medicine man. Many of these men were epileptic, many of the women hysteric, and these two types accounted for a good deal of ancient inspiration as well as spirit and devil possession. Quite a few of these earliest of priests were of a class which has since been denominated paranoiac."[14] "Women who were able to throw themselves into a trance or a cataleptic fit became powerful shamanesses; later, such women became prophets and spirit mediums. Their cataleptic trances usually involved alleged communications with the ghosts of the dead."[15]

In the twenty-first century, mediums continue to flourish.

Illustration 27
PERSONAL PROGRESS AT DEATH

As Presented in Christian Theology (Note: Denominational variations may exist.)		As Presented in Epochal Revelation
Most Christian and non-Christian thinking asserts that the souls of infants and children, baptized or not, are entrusted into the hands of a loving God. In 2007 Pope Benedict XVI reversed centuries of traditional Roman Catholic teaching on limbo, approving a Vatican report that says there were "serious" grounds to hope that children who die without being baptized can go to heaven. ("Vatican revises limbo view, hope for unbaptized babies," *USA Today*, April 22, 2007.)	Children from birth to approximately 5 years, who did not have the opportunity before death to make a moral conscious choice.	The *potential* identity of these children remains in custody of guardians of destiny until awakening of one of the parents, at which time it is delivered into the hands of the Mansion World Teachers in the probationary nurseries of the morontia worlds, where surviving parent(s) will be involved in their upbringing. These children will receive the Indwelling Spirit after attaining the requisite age of moral choice, but by age 16 must make a final choice for or against the path to Paradise.
	Children and youths 5 to 16 years of age who have made a moral choice but have not, at the time of death, chosen to find, know, and love God.	These children, who received the Indwelling Spirit at the time of their first moral choice, are repersonalized in the probationary nursery and join an age-appropriate group. At approximately age 16, if final choice for the Paradise path has been made, they are transferred to the first mansion world, where they may join parent(s) and begin their ascent to Paradise. Upon reaching Paradise, they remain there as permanent ascendant citizens. Having been deprived of the essential evolutionary experience on Earth, they will not be mustered into the Corps of the Finality. If by age 16 no choice has been made for the ascendant life, or if these children definitely decide against the path to Paradise, death automatically terminates their probationary careers. "There is no adjudication of such cases; there is no resurrection from such a second death. They simply become as though they had not been."
Those who reject God's love by mortal sin and die without repenting are condemned to everlasting suffering.	Adults 16+ who unequivocally reject survival and are consciously and willingly opposed to growing in cosmic insight and spiritual perception.	These iniquitous personalities cease to exist after being pronounced spiritually insolvent in the high courts of the Ancients of Days. They become as though they had not been.

Illustration 27 *(continued)*

As Presented in Christian Theology (Note: Denominational variations may exist.)	As Presented in Epochal Revelation	
Those who must undergo purification prior to entering heaven do so in an intermediary state or place of purgatory.	Adults 16+ who believe in an ultimate reality and have intentions and desires for survival prior to death but who for any reason have been unable to attain the self-mastery and spiritual progress that would entitle them to personal guardians.	These individuals must rest in unconscious sleep until the judgment day of a new epoch or a special resurrection. These are the sleeping survivors. Upon awakening, if they so choose, they will continue qualifying for eternal life in their ascending path to Paradise.
Those who die at peace with the church and have perfected their love for God in this life go straight to heaven, where they enjoy endless happiness in the presence of God.	Adults 16+ of survival status who have developed the cosmic insight and spiritual perception to achieve the third cycle of psychic development and merit assignment of a personal guardian.	These personalities are resurrected in the mansion worlds on the third day after death. They are given every opportunity to continue growing in love and service of God to qualify for eternal life.
	Adults 16+ who have completed the seven circles of cosmic achievement and have made the irrevocable choice for God and the Paradise career.	These personalities experience fusion of their souls with their immortal Indwelling Spirits, thereby ensuring eternal life. In our present age, fusion rarely happens during physical life, usually occurring during the ascending path to Paradise. These personalities continue their ascending journey to God, growing in love and service of God. They may be mustered into the Corps of Finality.

A complex web of rationalization underlies the belief that the deceased can communicate with the living: the immortality of the soul and the continuity of consciousness, the fascination with the unknown, and the desire, curiosity, or emotional need to communicate with a loved one. And, without insight into the survival process, we are limited in our interpretation of the unexplainable.

Epochal revelation reveals that upon death, the mind circuit is severed and the Indwelling Spirit takes leave with the memory transcript of life. Prior to awakening after death, the human personality is inert and unable to communicate. Furthermore, once the personality awakens in the resurrection halls of the mansion worlds, the ascending pilgrims are not permitted to communicate with the living. "Never does a departed Thought Adjuster return to earth as the being of former indwelling; never is personality manifested without the human will; and never does a dis-Adjustered human being after death manifest active identity or in any manner establish communication with the living beings of earth. Such dis-Adjustered souls are wholly and absolutely unconscious during the long or short sleep of death. There can be no exhibition of any sort of personality or ability to engage in communications with other personalities until after completion of survival. Those who go to the mansion worlds are not permitted to send messages back to their loved ones. It is the policy throughout the universes to forbid such communication during the period of a current dispensation."[16]

This revelation is significant because it forces us to question the interpretation of our personal experiences and the validity of the information given to us by mediums. It is more interesting and dramatic to recount an experience of unexplained paranormal phenomena than to explain it rationally.

The mind, however, interprets its surroundings through a variety of senses or a combination of them. These impressions are recorded in a way that each person finds easiest to understand. For example, some people are visual, others are auditory, while still others seem to be kinesthetic. When a surreal event happens, the mind interprets it based on past experiences, knowledge, and belief. Information stored in the subconscious can be used by the mind to interpret an event.

According to Susan Blackmore, author of *The Adventures of a Parapsychologist* and *Beyond the Body*, recalling past events can create psychic illusions. "Memory does not bring back a perfect copy of the past. It couldn't. Rather we reconstruct what happened and how." Often when we retell an event, ". . . we contract, expand, simplify and distort to produce a convincing and coherent account. We remember the things that fit in and forget those we would rather not accept. We fill in missing details to cover the bits we never paid attention to—often filling them in correctly, but also often not."[17] Highlights good and bad are remembered as if they just occurred, but details between highlights are often muddled.

Many explanations exist for what has been termed paranormal phenomena. Some explanations are physical, others are psychological. A great many examples are hoaxes, while still others may include genuine spiritual experiences that are misunderstood or misinterpreted. Epochal revelation confirms that there are actual spirit and ascendant beings that function outside humanity's range of vision. These beings, which include midwayers, are not the dead but are part of the invisible celestial family, and many are charged with assisting ascending mortals individually and collectively. Without an accurate cosmic perspective, human beings with extraordinary perceptive ability are likely to translate experiences in terms of prior knowledge and intuition. For example, communication by midwayers to mortals on behalf of a guardian angel may be construed as direct communication from the dead, or from Buddha, Jesus, or even God himself.

The idea that those who have passed over can make contact with the living is perpetuated in Hollywood productions. Well-known mediums have produced volumes of teachings that the public embraces as truth, even though many have been publicly debunked. For example, James Randi, a magician and skeptic, conducted a critique of television psychic John Edward and found that Edward had an accuracy rate of a mere 13 percent. "In one 45-second interrogation of a TV guest, Randi counted 23 questions by Edward with three correct answers."[18] Nevertheless, people who want to believe or need to believe will embrace the accuracies and deny or ignore the inaccuracies.

Mediums fulfill an emotional need to communicate with the departed, often out of guilt, fear, or grief. As long as that need is not supplanted with greater cosmic awareness, mediums will continue their practices that may provide short-term comfort. Nonetheless, it is also important to remain uncynical and humble—it is not given us to understand fully the laws and transactions of the spirit realm. We do better to stand in tolerant awe of the unexplainable than to critically dismiss all episodes.

Eternal Life

Eternal life is not generally synonymous with survival. "Even after survival the ascending mortal still retains this prerogative of choosing to reject eternal life . . ."[19] The choice of eternal life, like the choice of salvation, comes with the responsibility to develop the soul by progressing in God-recognition and God-service. Immortality is assured when the soul has been developed to such a degree that it can fuse with the Indwelling Spirit, signaling complete attunement of the personal will with the will of God.

Fusion, which can be likened to the concept of union with God, confirms that the ascending mortal has eternally and wholeheartedly chosen to do the Father's will. At any time prior to fusion, the evolving and ascending being can choose to reject eternal life. Fusion imparts to the human personality eternal qualities that were previously only potential, and elevates the ascending mortal from morontia status to the spirit level. Spirit ascenders advance in spirit status, eventually finding the Father in Paradise and achieve their glorious final destiny—joining the ranks of the Corps of the Finality.

Fusion normally occurs during the ascending journey through the heavens, but can also happen during mortal life, though this is rare. Fusion during life on Earth instantly consumes the physical body; human beings witnessing such a spectacle would only observe the person disappear as if "in chariots of fire." "*Enoch*, [son of Cain] [was] the first of the mortals of Urantia to fuse with the Thought Adjuster during the mortal life in the flesh."[20] Elijah, too, experienced such an escape. In 2 Kings: 2:11, the event is recorded: "And it came to pass, as they still went on, and talked, that, behold, [there appeared] a chariot of fire, and horses of fire, and parted them both asunder; and Elijah went up by a whirlwind into heaven." This mode of terrestrial escape during physical life, bypassing the death experience, becomes increasingly common in the advanced planetary eras. When fusion occurs, there is never a lapse in consciousness.

There are surviving mortals who are unable to fuse with their Indwelling Spirit: "While practically all surviving mortals are fused with their Adjusters on one of the mansion worlds or immediately upon their arrival on the higher morontia spheres, there are certain cases of delayed fusion, some not experiencing this final surety of survival until they reach the last educational worlds of the universe headquarters; and a few of these mortal candidates for never-ending life utterly fail to attain identity fusion with their faithful Adjusters."[21] After it becomes evident that there is something inhibiting fusion with the Father fragment, and when it is determined that the ascending mortal is not at fault, these individuals achieve the security of survival through fusion with an individualized gift of the spirit of the Creator Son.[22] These Son-fused mortals normally remain in the eternal service of the local and superuniverse governments.

While the inability to fuse with the Indwelling Spirit may at first appear as a flaw in the ascension scheme, it is purposeful. It enables the local and superuniverse governments to have a permanent group of ascendant citizens who are able to gain intimate knowledge of one universe and develop authoritative wisdom vital in the settling of any local universe.

Summary

We live in a universe where personality survival is a reality, as is the attainment of eternal life. For those who recognize that there is life after death, it may be a challenging shift in perspective to grasp that survival after death does not mean uninterrupted consciousness. In fact, throughout our journey to Paradise, we are subject to periods of complete unconsciousness as we attain increasing levels of spirit progression.

Another challenging shift in perspective reveals that resurrection is a cosmic process, not just part of a religious belief. Resurrection is the means by which the human personality regains consciousness and function in a new body each time—not one of flesh and blood but one that is suitable for the next level of evolutionary development.

For thousands of years, the concept of union with God has been associated with the attainment of divinity, with merging oneself into the source of Creation, and with personal closeness with the divine. Epochal revelation now sheds light upon this important concept, clarifying and expanding its meaning. Union with God is synonymous with fusion, the cosmic process whereby the soul and the Indwelling Spirit become as one with the Universal Father. Fusion guarantees eternal life—but eternal life is not synonymous with mortal survival, which is attained with the slightest hint of faith in a higher reality. Eternal life requires growth in attunement with the Indwelling Spirit through the development of the intellectual, moral, and spiritual capacities in the human mind.

The human confusion about destiny and the process of survival lends itself to divisiveness, superstition, and manipulation of followers. The acquisition of new knowledge does not immediately overwrite existing worldviews, but it does help us elevate them; and this recognition of shared ideals can increase cooperation and harmony.

18.

Hell versus Soul Death

Death is more universal than life; everyone dies but not everyone lives.

A. Sachs

The rewards for noble living, not always gained during our short life on Earth, are generally understood to be harvested in heaven. What about the results of iniquitous living? If development of the soul ensures survival after death, what is the outcome of consciously neglecting to nurture one's soul? Is it a fiery afterlife of eternal punishment in hell? Is it an eternal state of separation from God? Or is it a cessation of existence as professed by annihilationists? The first two options are based on the belief that the soul is immortal, a Christian doctrine that was cemented by the Italian theologian Thomas Aquinas in his *Summa Theologica*. The last option, first defended by the Christian apologist Arnobius, is based on the belief that the soul is not innately immortal.[1]

Of all the teachings of Christianity, the doctrine of hell as a fiery place of eternal punishment is one of the most disconcerting. For most of their history, Christians have been taught that hell is the consequence of a life of iniquity and denial of God. According to a 2007 Gallup report, 69% of Americans believe in hell.[2] While the concept of hell from the early church has been a strong incentive to lead a righteous life, it has also been a major stumbling block to the acceptance of Christianity today.

Early people had no thoughts of future punishment. They hoped their future life would be much like their current one, only without bad luck. Heaven and hell, as separate destinies for the good and the bad, developed with the passage of time and the appearance of organized religion.[3] The traditions of heaven and hell presented in Judaism, Christianity, and Islam can be traced to the teachings of Zoroaster, when Jews were under the dominance of the Persians.

As Christianity developed, the conception of hell as a fiery place of eternal torment became official, although some early Christian thinkers, such as Origen of Alexandria (AD 185–254) and Gregory of Nyssa (approximately AD 385), had their doubts about the literal interpretation of hell as a flaming afterlife. Catholicism's version of hell was associated with mortal sin as part of the *Decretum Gratiani*, a collection of texts touching on all areas of church discipline and regulation, compiled about AD 1140 by the Benedictine monk John Gratian. Hell was declared to be inhabited not only by the heathen, but also by Christian heretics and the excommunicated who had died without obtaining forgiveness from the church.

For many centuries, Christianity preached hellfire and brimstone to enforce piety, striking fear into the masses. Even today, some Christian denominations teach that unsaved sinners—those who don't repent for their sins and accept Jesus Christ as their Lord and Savior—will suffer for all eternity in a fiery hell. But alongside these are many that do not believe in hell. A definite shift away from the literal interpretation of the doctrine has even occurred in the Catholic Church. At the General Audience of Wednesday July 28, 1999, Pope John Paul II reflected on hell as a state of being, the result of definitive rejection of God. In his catechesis, the pope said that care should be taken to correctly interpret the images of hell in sacred scripture, and explained that ". . . hell is the ultimate consequence of sin itself . . . Rather than a place, hell indicates the state of those who freely and definitively separate themselves from God, the source of all life and joy."[4]

With this papal pronouncement, the concept of hell as a place of eternal torment was officially put to rest for the Catholic faithful. Its replacement, an eternal state of separation from God, still provided a befitting punishment for unrighteous immortal souls.

Annihilationists argue that belief in eternal torture is incompatible with God's love and results from misunderstanding particular verses of the Bible. They also argue that the idea of hell as traditionally understood in Christianity is virtually absent in the Hebrew Bible (the Old Testament). Instead, "Sheol" and "Hades" are used to refer to "the grave" or "death." No reference to eternal torment in hell is found in the Old Testament. While mentions of fire and everlasting condemnation exist in Isaiah 66:24 and Daniel 12:2, other passages, such as Ecclesiastes 9:10, indicate extinction or destruction of the soul after death.

Similarly, in the New Testament, the word "hell" never appears in the Gospel of John or in any of the letters of Paul. Paul and John were more inclined to believe that the fury or judgment of God was expressed as a denial of eternal life. The idea of hell being a place of everlasting torment comes primarily from the Book of Revelation, a work originating with John, but according to epochal revelation, greatly condensed and distorted.

It is generally recognized among scholars that the Greek word *gehenna*, which appears in the original Latin Vulgate twelve times,[5] was mistakenly translated as "hell" in the early seventeenth century during the Bible's translation into English from the original Hebrew and Greek and from the Latin Vulgate. According to the *Encyclopedia Britannica*, "Gehenna originally was a valley west and south of Jerusalem where children were burned as sacrifices to the Ammonite god Moloch. This practice was carried out by the Israelites during the reigns of King Solomon in the 10th century BC and King Manasseh in the 7th century BC and continued until the Babylonian Exile in the 6th century BC. Gehenna later was made a garbage centre to discourage a reintroduction of such sacrifices. The imagery of the burning of humans supplied the concept of 'hellfire' to Jewish and Christian eschatology."[6] The concept of hell as a place of torment can be easily associated with Gehenna, a place where the "worm does not die and the fire is not quenched" (Mark 9:48). But a refuse dump recalls degradation more than unending torment.

Epochal revelation offers holistic reconciliation: survival is a choice and the soul possesses the *potential* for immortality. Eternal survival is part of the Divine Plan of Progress and a gift that, when accepted, bestows upon the individual the responsibility to maintain an unshakable attitude of loyalty to God and to live the golden rule from its highest level of interpretation.

An attitude of conscious rebellion toward God is one that includes the persistent choice of immoral decisions, fully understanding that the will of God demands righteousness and increasing progress toward perfection for the benefit of all. Epochal revelation clarifies that the attitude of disrespect toward God is not one of the imperfections innate in human behavior. Such an attitude of iniquity was brought to this world by the disloyal Local Universe Sons of God: Caligastia, Satan, and Lucifer. Deliberate rebellion against the will of God—sin—is a choice. Unchecked, it can lead to unmitigated wrongdoing, which reflects escalating disloyalty to God.

Belief in God and commitment to doing his will spiritualize the mind and develop the soul, thereby ensuring personality survival and the possibility of eternal existence. Disloyalty to God results in the tendency of mind to move away from spirit reality, which stunts the growth of the soul and leads to the domains of iniquity. When sin becomes a habit, a wedge grows between creature and Creator. When the separation builds between mortal and God, the individual becomes less likely to experience sincere sorrow for his or her misdeeds or accept forgiveness for his or her actions. When the human mind does not experience a progressive enhancement of meanings and elevation of values, the soul tends to remain embryonic. By identifying with evildoing, an individual inhibits the transfer of personal identity from the mortal intellect to the more enduring nature of the morontia soul and risks self-destruction. Thus, the inner reaping of a person with an iniquitous will is a soul-destroying harvest.[7] "The greatest punishment (in reality an inevitable consequence) for wrongdoing and deliberate rebellion against the government of God is loss of existence as an individual subject of that government. The final result of wholehearted sin is annihilation. In the last analysis, such sin-identified individuals have destroyed themselves by becoming wholly unreal through their embrace of iniquity."[8] Everlasting extinction of the personal self is therefore not the will of God but the self-imposed consequence of the iniquitous individual.

The Urantia Book confirms what the scriptures have always implied: the opposite of eternal survival is the extinction of the soul—the result of a Godless existence and the deliberate rejection of God.

Identification with evil is the precursor to nonexistence. However, divine justice is always tempered with mercy. "Mercy is . . . justice tempered by that wisdom which grows out of perfection of knowledge and the full recognition of the natural weaknesses and environmental handicaps of finite creatures."[9] Actual extinction, therefore, is not immediate. Before cessation of existence is executed, all moral and spiritual values must be extinct. "Supreme justice can act instantly when not restrained by divine mercy. But the ministry of mercy to the children of time and space always provides for this time lag, this saving interval between seedtime and harvest. If the seed sowing is good, this interval provides for the testing and upbuilding of character; if the seed sowing is evil, this merciful delay provides time for repentance and rectification. This time delay in the adjudication and execution of evildoers is inherent in the mercy ministry of the seven superuniverses. This restraint of justice by mercy proves that God is love, and that such a God of love dominates the universes and in mercy controls the fate and judgment of all his creatures."[10]

Soul death is final and can occur while a person is still physically alive. When a human personality willfully rejects survival and is pronounced morontially and spiritually ruined, the Ancients of Days order immediate release of the Indwelling Spirit irrespective of the continuous function of the physical and mind mechanisms.

With the departure of the Indwelling Spirit, the human soul loses its immortal potential, forsaking individual survival after physical death. "When the continued embrace of sin by the associated mind culminates in complete self-identification with iniquity, then upon the cessation of life, upon cosmic dissolution, such an isolated personality is absorbed into the oversoul of creation, becoming a part of the evolving experience of the Supreme Being. Never again does it appear as a personality; its identity becomes as though it had never been."[11] These nonsurvivors are referred to in Acts 24:15 as the "unjust." Any experiential spiritual values developed during the human life survive in the learning experience of the Indwelling Spirit.

In the new paradigm of salvation, faith pilgrims will not concern themselves about future punishment. They will take survival into their own hands. They will take personal responsibility for their relationship with God and focus on the development of a well-balanced God-knowing personality for the benefit of humanity. Their progress will be measured by their response to questions like: "Am I growing in my knowledge, love, and worship of God?"[12] "Am I learning to understand and to love one more human being each day?"[13] The increasing spiritual progress of the individual will be reflected in a growing harmonious society that builds the brotherhood of man.

19.

The Process of
Moral Judgment

Mercy among the virtues is like the moon among the stars.
It is the light that hovers above the judgment seat.
Edwin Hubbel Chapin

The stereotypical Christian images of divine judgment—a guilty person standing nervously at the Pearly Gates, or cowering before the Judgment Seat—breed a fearful uncertainty in believers. Partial truth is a sure prescription for anxiety. The notion of a wrathful God meting out painful justice is at odds with the concept of a merciful God of love, and causes many to be confused. The knowledge of the true workings of the Divine Plan of eternal progress has been largely lost and replaced with perilous speculation.

Conceptual truths regarding the nature of divine judgment spread to many parts of the world due to the work of the Sethite and Salem missionaries. With the passage of time, however, the original teachings were distorted as they became blended into a multitude of beliefs.

In Egypt, toward the end of the Old Kingdom, the afterlife was no longer considered exclusive to royal bloodlines. Faced with the increasing desecration of tombs, reference to the moral judgment of the deceased first appeared in the *Coffin Texts* during the Middle Kingdom Period. This concept of individual moral judgment found its most complete expression in the Egyptian New Kingdom *Book of the Dead*, a collection of spells, texts, and vignettes (small illustrative sketches) that were placed with the dead in order to help them pass through the dangers of the underworld and attain an afterlife of bliss. In India's Vedic writings, a judgment after death, using a scale to weigh good against evil, is described in the *Satapatha-Brahmana*. In the New Testament, the concept of individual moral judgment is clearly evident in Hebrews 9:27, where the author declares: "Men only die once, and after that the judgment."

As long as we believe our destiny is out of our control, judgment will continue to be misunderstood and feared. Catholic doctrine asserts ". . . that *immediately* after death the *eternal destiny of each separated soul is decided by the just judgment of God.*"[1] Other Christians believe that souls sleep until the last judgment, at which time they are rewarded or punished according to how they lived their lives. Still others believe that all souls, good and bad, are annihilated at death only to be recreated on Judgment Day, when their fates are decided by God.

Does survival depend on judgment? Does divine judgment reflect an individual's intent and spiritual progress? Can the concepts of individual judgment and Last Judgment be reconciled? When we explore the relation between the Divine Plan of Progress and the concepts of divine mercy and justice in the light of epochal revelation, we find a context where moral judgment can be understood.

The Divine Plan of Progress embraces the creation of intelligent creatures with the power of moral decision and spiritual choice. It provides for their evolution, survival, and ascension through the universes of time and space and the celebration of their attainment of Paradise perfection. The Divine Plan was set in motion to fulfill the Universal Father's eternal purpose—that of elevating free-will creatures to the destiny of sharing in his perfection, righteousness, and love. Fulfilling this purpose is central to the complex scheme of life and education throughout the universes of time and space.

In the Divine Plan, individual progress is measured by soul development, which is dependent on conscious efforts at becoming Godlike. Spiritual progress requires discovery of higher meanings and values in the divine command to love one another. Their ongoing discovery and integration on the ascending path to Paradise enables the human personality eventually to see God.

In the Divine Plan, survival provides for eternal life. But survival is always a choice; it must be desired and accepted by faith. "Eternal survival of personality is wholly dependent on the choosing of the mortal mind, whose decisions determine the survival potential of the immortal soul. When the mind believes God and the soul knows God, and when, with the fostering Adjuster, they all *desire* God, then is survival assured."[2] In our physical world, the highest achievement of personality development is limited to the successive mastery of seven levels of human potential, each reflecting the level of mind and soul development and degree of receptivity to and attunement with the Indwelling Spirit. Progress is monitored, assessed, and judged throughout the journey to Paradise. Positive growth is rewarded with advancement, while stasis and regression are met justly and mercifully. The symbol of the Scales of Justice is a true representation of divine judgment but ". . . your survival depends not so much on the theories of your beliefs as upon your decisions, determinations, and steadfast *faith.*"[3]

Divine righteousness demands that every error in judgment, moral infraction, and disloyalty to God in the journey to Paradise be dealt with swiftly. On the other hand, the goodness and love of the Father makes it inevitable that supreme justice is fairly implemented. "Divine mercy represents a fairness technique of adjustment between the universe levels of perfection and imperfection."[4] In essence, this denotes either consecrated dedication to doing the will of the Father or deliberate rejection thereof. In the post-mortal realm, justice *and* mercy are always ministered simultaneously.

Mandates for judgments originate in the local universe courts, but the sovereign Creator Sons never sit in judgment of their creatures; only the Ancients of Days may sit in executive judgment on the issues of eternal life and death.

The Sons of the local universes can decree the survival of mortals—the spiritually advanced who have been assigned a seraphic guardian may proceed within three days to the mansion worlds. "Other mortals may be detained until such time as the adjudication of their affairs has been completed, after which they may proceed to the mansion worlds, or they may be assigned to the ranks of the sleeping survivors who will be repersonalized en masse at the end of the current planetary dispensation."[5] The following must be noted:

- If there are reservations as to the survival qualities of the individual, the ruling is always for advancing the soul so as to observe and evaluate the emerging intent and spiritual purpose.

- If a person dies because of an accident or if a handicap prevented mastering the seven circles of human development—but the person's intentions and desires are of survival value—the ruling provides for survival so that these intentions may be proved. [See chapter 24 for more on the seven circles.]

- Survival provisions are made for children who die prior to attainment of an Indwelling Spirit, or youngsters who die under the age of sixteen who have an Indwelling Spirit but have not made a conscious decision for survival.

Questions regarding the right of continued existence are referred to the tribunals of the Ancients of Days for adjudication.[6] This process provides for the defense of the individual and the presentation of evidence prior to a final decision or judgment. In the administration of justice, evidence is the basis of fairness. In the high courts of the superuniverse, evidence is submitted by angels who have reflective capabilities. These reflective personalities function like a living mirror, able to see and hear the responses of another being regardless of the distance between them. In human courts, evidence may be biased, incomplete, inaccurate, and even fraudulent. In the celestial courts, the reflective spirits are living evidence; they accurately reflect the true character and intentions of ascending personalities as well as the qualities of divinity they have developed. Some of the reflective angels that submit living evidence in the celestial courts include:

1. **The Significance of Origins** are able to instantly portray anything that is required about the nature and circumstances of origin of any individual, race, or world throughout the superuniverse. "They are always ready to supply their superiors with an up-to-date, replete, and trustworthy estimate of the ancestral factors and the current actual status of any individual on any world of their respective superuniverses;

and their computation of possessed facts is always up to the minute."[7] All God–creature relationships and the application of ethics grow out of the fundamental facts of origin.

2. **The Memories of Mercy** ". . . are the actual, full and replete, living records of the mercy which has been extended to individuals and races . . ."[8] They disclose "the moral debt," that is, "the spiritual liabilities" of the individual in relation to the saving grace established by the Sons of God. "In revealing the Father's preexistent mercy, the Sons of God establish the necessary credit to insure the survival of all. And then, in accordance with the findings of the Significance of Origins, a mercy credit is established for the survival of each rational creature, a credit of lavish proportions and one of sufficient grace to insure the survival of every soul who really desires divine citizenship."[9] "The Memory of Mercy is a living trial balance, a current statement of your account with the supernatural forces of the realms. These are the living records of mercy ministration which are read into the testimony of the courts of Uversa when each individual's right to unending life comes up for adjudication . . ."[10]

The Memory of Mercy might be the collection of books referenced in Daniel 7:10: "A fiery stream issued and came forth from before him: thousand thousands ministered unto him, and ten thousand times ten thousand stood before him: the judgment was set, and the books were opened." According to epochal revelation, "The Memory of Mercy must show that the saving credit established by the Sons of God has been fully and faithfully paid out in the loving ministry of the patient personalities of the Third Source and Center."[11] However, "[w]hen the provisions of endless mercy and nameless patience have been exhausted in an effort to win the loyalty and devotion of the will creatures of the realms, justice and righteousness will prevail. That which mercy cannot rehabilitate justice will eventually annihilate."[12]

3. **The Imports of Time** reflect how individuals have utilized or squandered their time. "Time is the one universal endowment of all will creatures; it is the 'one talent' intrusted to all intelligent beings. You all have time in which to insure your survival; and time is fatally squandered only when it is buried in neglect, when you fail so to utilize it as to make certain the survival of your soul. Failure to improve one's time to the fullest extent possible does not impose fatal penalties; it merely retards the pilgrim of time in his journey of ascent. If survival is gained, all other losses can be retrieved . . . In the final judgment before the Ancients of Days, time is an element of evidence. The Imports of Time must always afford testimony to show that every defendant has had ample time for making decisions, achieving choice."[13]

4. **The Solemnities of Trust** unerringly reflect to the governing authorities the exact trustworthiness of any candidate for confidence or trust. "Trust is the crucial test of will creatures. Trustworthiness is the true measure of self-mastery, character."[14] "These seconaphim weigh trustworthiness

in the living scales of unerring character appraisal, and when they have looked at you, we have only to look at them to know the limitations of your ability to discharge responsibility, execute trust, and fulfill missions. Your assets of trustworthiness are clearly set forth alongside your liabilities of possible default or betrayal."[15] In our ascending journey, only our lack of trustworthiness can keep us from opportunities to serve. Trust is one of the moral elements of greatness.

5. **The Sanctities of Service** reveal the real nature of any service, be it rendered by human or angel. They reveal the true and hidden motives behind every action. "These angels are indeed the mind readers, heart searchers, and soul revealers of the universe. Mortals may employ words to conceal their thoughts, but these high seconaphim lay bare the deep motives of the human heart and of the angelic mind."[16] The appreciation of the sanctity of service is another moral element of greatness.

6. **The Reflectors of Greatness and Goodness.** The manifestation of greatness is found in the exhibition of self-control, and the quality of greatness is wholly determined by the content of goodness.[17] "*Greatness and goodness simply cannot be divorced* . . . Hence, on any world, in any universe, must these reflectors of greatness and of goodness work together, always showing a dual and mutually dependent report of every being upon whom they focalize. Greatness cannot be estimated without knowing the content of goodness, while goodness cannot be portrayed without exhibiting its inherent and divine greatness."[18]

7. **The Discerners of Spirits** reflect the actual moral and spiritual character of any individual and the true intent and spiritual purpose behind every choice and action.[19]

In addition, the following evidence is available:

- A final report is prepared and filed in the high courts of the Ancients of Days by the Indwelling Spirit. This account details the survival character of the individual, specifically the spiritual values and morontia meanings gained during his or her lifetime.

- The assessment of a deceased human's survival character and spiritual qualities is communicated by the Indwelling Spirit to a Universal Censor in a way that is not fully understood. If the question of eternal life and death comes up for adjudication, this data, together with the seraphic records, is available for presentation. This information is also used to confirm those mandates that make it possible for certain ascenders to immediately proceed to the mansion worlds ahead of the formal termination of a planetary dispensation.

The defense of individuals in the tribunals of the Ancients of Days is offered by Mighty Messengers, perfected mortals who have been rebellion-tested or have stood firm and loyal in the face of the disloyalty of their superiors, have been embraced by the Paradise Trinity, and have been assigned to the government of the Ancients of Days.[20]

Judgment, the final application of law or justice, falls within the province of the Paradise Trinity and is carried out by Sons of the Trinity who participate in the government and judicial system of the Ancients of Days. They are privy to the history of all wrongdoing, as well as its motivation. Depending on the nature and gravity of the case, an Ancients of Days, a Perfector of Wisdom, or a Divine Counselor presides over judicial proceedings. The evidence for or against an individual, a planet, system, constellation, or universe is presented and interpreted by the Universal Censors. These Sons of the Trinity represent the collective attitude of Deity in the domains of justice and work hand in hand with a Discerner of Spirits. Censors always render their verdicts in liaison with Perfectors of Wisdom and Divine Counselors; such decisions embrace the united wisdom, counsel, and judgment of the Paradise Trinity.

On the issues of eternal life and death, it is the Ancients of Days that sit in executive judgment. Rulings for continued survival are carried out by the tribunals of the local universe. Sentences of extinction are meted out by those judges who reside and operate from the headquarters of the superuniverse.

Thus we see that legions of personalities and immense celestial resources are given over to the matter of mortal survival. Our existing beliefs are vague and misconstrued, offering hope yet mired in speculation and fear of retribution— all this owing to our disordered history and isolation status. But to the confusion of this world and our single most important question, epochal revelation brings clarity and comfort: there is life beyond this life for those who believe. "Mercy is the natural and inevitable offspring of goodness and love. The good nature of a loving Father could not possibly withhold the wise ministry of mercy to each member of every group of his universe children. Eternal justice and divine mercy together constitute what in human experience would be called *fairness*."[21]

20.

The Destiny of Humanity

Thoughts lead on to purposes; purposes go forth in action; actions form habits; habits decide character; and character fixes our destiny.
Tyron Edwards, American theologian (1809–1894)

It took thousands of years for humanity to reach the point where scientific advancement propelled civilization to comfortable levels. In the last one hundred years—a millisecond in cosmic time—a relatively small but significant percentage of the population has progressed to a middle class. The leading edge of Western civilization has evolved from harsh living and working conditions to the relative luxury of today. In a historically short time, humanity has progressed from serfdom and domination by religious institutions to law-based governments and international law, witnessed by the Geneva Convention, the United Nations, and other humanitarian and watchdog agencies.

The ultimate goal of human progress is the reverent recognition of the fatherhood of God and the loving materialization of the brotherhood of man.
The Urantia Book

Material progress, however, has not come without harm to the precious sphere on which we live. Though aware of the intricate web of nature that sustains life, we continue to upset that balance and flirt with self-destruction. Air pollution, the greenhouse effect, holes in the ozone layer, the destruction of rainforests, and polluted waterways all threaten our fragile existence. Without a major expansion of cosmic awareness, indifference, economic greed, and the pursuit of a materialistic lifestyle will continue to threaten the ecological balance in our world for future generations.

Along with an environmental crisis, we face the menace of competitive weapons development and stockpiles of weapons of mass destruction. Instead of helping the faithful to awaken their personal connection with the God of justice *and* love, radical religious factions have been tutoring believers in mass murder. With a possible holy war engulfing half the world's population, all of the above calamitous situations bring to mind the age-old question, "Is the end near?"

The end of a civilization as we know it does not imply the destruction of humanity; rather it reflects the derailment of organized religion, the curtailment of spiritual insight, and our stubborn resistance to learning from the mistakes of our ancestors. Many spiritual and religious folks have reframed this dilemma, believing that a selfish humanity is destined to destroy civilization but the wicked will go down and God will uplift the righteous, dawning a new age of peace everlasting.

Is our current world shifting from the end of one age to the beginning of a new one? That question begs another: Has the development of human civilization been self-driven, spiritually guided, or both? The surprising answers are found in epochal revelation.

A high planetary destiny is inherent in God's purpose of creation and is characterized by a world unity of ideals: physical security, intellectual expansion, social progress, and spiritual accomplishment. Epochal revelation regales us with descriptions of the truly utopian ages of light and life, when governments of every nation faithfully reflect the intellectual keenness, economic wisdom, social awareness, and moral stamina of their citizens. This exalted fate of our species is a prime purpose of planetary evolution. The question is not whether it will be achieved but how far and how smoothly each generation will progress toward that destiny of "light and life."

The distant outlook for humanity is indeed bright, but we must have a clear understanding of the factors in human development that will progressively draw civilization forward and upward.

Culture and the Factors in Human Development

Culture is defined by the *Encyclopedia Britannica* as "behaviour peculiar to *Homo sapiens*, together with material objects used as an integral part of this behaviour. Thus, culture includes language, ideas, beliefs, customs, codes, institutions, tools, techniques, works of art, rituals, and ceremonies, among other elements. The existence and use of culture depends upon an ability possessed by humans alone. This ability has been called variously the capacity for rational or abstract thought . . ."[1]

Various theories based on the study of human history and the development of consciousness aim to explain the dynamics of human development. Spiral Dynamics, an extension of the human development theory of psychology professor Clare W. Graves, purports that adaptive value codes emerge in individual and collective minds in response to the stress forged by life conditions. Some call these value codes "paradigms" or "levels of psychological existence." According to the theory, new and more complex paradigms ("conceptual value models of the world") emerge when conditions warrant. Each new model includes and transcends all previous models, forming themselves into new value systems, which reshape organizational productivity, national prosperity, and global transformation. Don Beck, PhD, the codeveloper of Spiral Dynamics, points out that humanity now faces the challenge of creating an integrated train of reasoning that would shape the dynamics of social transformation worldwide. Dr. Beck suggests that these emerging values must be recognized, correlated, and their expression globally facilitated.

Integral philosopher Ken Wilber proposes that stages of social development addressed in Spiral Dynamics are correlated with higher stages of consciousness. According to Wilber, the advancement of culture is the result of the evolution of consciousness through three developmental stages, or tiers, characterized by changing perceptions of self.

The first tier has three major perspectives: egocentric, ethnocentric, and worldcentric. An *egocentric* (me) perspective expresses selfish personal needs and wants, not caring about others or their viewpoints. An *ethnocentric* (us) perspective is regional, expanding self-identity to include one's family, interest or faith groups, nationalism and political parties. The *worldcentric* (all of us) perspective embraces all people, and those who have developed it tend to be social activists, multicultural, and environmentally conscious.

The second is the *integral* tier, a leap in perspective that begins "to remake the planet as we know it." In the integral tier, there is a growing concern for the "global village" and peaceful operation of world affairs.

The third is the *kosmocentric* tier, which embraces a worldview that fosters an individual sense of "responsibility for the evolutionary process as a whole."

Wilber suggests that regular practice of meditation is key to accelerating movement through those stages.[2]

Religious practices that promote God-consciousness are an important part of a balanced approach to self-mastery and spiritual growth—the keys to ever-ascending human progress. Understanding the epochs of human development as outlined in epochal revelation also adds valuable insight to our understanding of how far we've come and how far we have to go; bridging these gaps is the challenge of today. The concept of divine dispensations (discussed in this chapter) and the development of consciousness, when explored in a new light, will help us discover new meaning in cultural progress. With all this in mind, it is helpful to explore the following three factors of human development in the light of epochal revelation.

1. **History**: "History alone fails adequately to reveal future development . . . The present can be truly interpreted only in the light of the correlated past and future."[3] Epochal revelation unifies fragmented history. It reduces confusion by eliminating error, fills in vital gaps, and restores lost knowledge. As revelations of truth, each succeeding epochal revelation has been successively more enlightening. Humanity now stands at the crossroads between the fourth and fifth epochal revelation. Will our commitment to human progress motivate us to gain historical insights from this planetary revelation, or will skepticism and fear relegate this responsibility to the next generation?

2. **Development of consciousness**: "Culture presupposes quality of mind; culture cannot be enhanced unless mind is elevated . . . Inferior minds will spurn the highest culture even when presented to them ready-made."[4] Elevation of mind requires the coordinated development of

rational thinking, moral awareness, and spiritual perception. Social progress is impeded by crystallized doctrines and interpretations based on dogmatic understandings of God. Similarly, "[a] human being can find truth in this inner experience, but he needs a clear knowledge of acts to apply his personal discovery of truth to the ruthlessly practical demands of everyday life."[5] Epochal revelation expands the truth in existing beliefs and adds new meaning to spiritual experiences, thereby providing humanity with added insights into the development of consciousness.

3. **Dispensations of divine Sons**: Humanity evolves through the development of consciousness. But in this journey we are never alone. The advancement of culture greatly depends ". . . upon the successive missions of the divine Sons and upon the extent to which enlightenment is received by the ages of their respective dispensations."[6] When we illuminate existing wisdom with divine revelation, we increase our capacity for partnership with God.[7] Epochal revelation is humanity's most precious gift, dispensed successively throughout the ages by divine Sons, those descending beings who are heaven-trained for service to mortal will creatures. To the extent that these dispensations of divine wisdom are assimilated, so does human culture progress.

With the above understanding, the definition of "culture" can be elevated: Culture is the collective expression of human wisdom, defined as knowledge directed by reason and experience and illuminated by divine revelation. The quality and speed of cultural progress is dependent upon the individual receptivity and response to wisdom reaching critical mass within society.

Human progress is always aided by spirit mind-ministry and fostered by superhuman (divine) visitations to the planet. Following is a brief description of the planetary epochs of human development and their relation to the dispensations of the divine Sons; it is also interesting to learn how they relate to the last judgment. A strategy for the development of universal intelligence—a creative plan for the realization of world peace—is outlined in section four.

Epochs and Dispensations

According to epochal revelation, "[t]he social, economic, and governmental problems of the inhabited worlds vary in accordance with the age of the planets and the degree to which they have been influenced by the successive sojourns of the divine Sons."[8]

After a planet evolves habitable conditions, Life Carriers are dispatched to initiate life. As modern science has now discovered, the bulk of cosmic, atmospheric, and terrestrial conditions for life support (as we know it here) are exceedingly precise. But interestingly, although *The Urantia Book* gives prolific details on the planting and fostering of planetary life, it is vague on the manipulation of our extraterrestrial environment.

The period from life implantation to the appearance of humans is the prehuman era. From a cosmic perspective, human epochs begin with the appearance of will and continue to progress through successive planetary missions by divine Sons of various orders. The arrival of a Son of God on a planet terminates a dispensation and inaugurates a new era of planetary progression. "Under the benign rule of a Planetary Prince, augmented by the Material Sons and punctuated by the periodic missions of the Paradise Sons, the mortal races on an average world of time and space will successively pass through the following seven developmental epochs:"[9]

- **First Epoch—nutrition.** Evolving beings are chiefly concerned with seeking food or fighting.

- **Second Epoch—security.** The primitive hunter can now spare time from the search for food. Attention turns toward security in the home and clans.

- **Third Epoch—material comfort.** Additional leisure time is utilized to promote personal comfort. Such an age is often characterized by oppression, intolerance, greed, and overindulgence, but is gradually liberated by the stronger and truth-loving elements of an advancing civilization.

- **Fourth Epoch—quest for knowledge and wisdom.** Food, security, and material comfort still dominate society, but there are many who hunger for knowledge and thirst for wisdom. Education becomes the watchword of this era. Civilization arrives as people gain wisdom by implementing knowledge and learn how to profit and improve by experience.

- **Fifth Epoch—philosophy and brotherhood.** Greater reasoning and discriminative judgment is being exercised. Society becomes more ethical as individuals grow morally, thereby establishing the foundation for living the brotherhood of man. People begin to treat others as they are willing to be treated in the same circumstances.

- **Sixth Epoch—spiritual striving.** The physical, intellectual, and social stages of development have been experienced, and greater spiritual satisfactions and cosmic understandings are sought. Religion rises from the domains of fear and superstition to high levels of cosmic wisdom and personal spiritual experience.

- **Seventh Epoch—light and life.** The physical, intellectual, social, and spiritual achievements of the past epochs come to fruition. These accomplishments are unified in personality and expressed and coordinated in unselfish service.[10]

The above outline of human development levels finds parallels in the current theories already noted. But their progressive manifestation on our world was hindered by the planetary rebellion and by the default of Adam and Eve more than thirty-seven thousand years ago. Social and spiritual development was handicapped to the extent that Earth is more than a full dispensation behind the average planetary schedule, as shown in illustration 28.

Nonetheless, Adam and Eve did biologically uplift the human races through the infusion of the lifeblood of their descendants: ". . . the Adamic blood did augment the inherent ability of the races and did accelerate the pace of economic development and industrial progression. Adam's bestowal improved the brain power of the races, thereby greatly hastening the processes of natural evolution."[11] Science now recognizes that specific genes experience selection and mutation, which propels a rapid increase of brain size and complexity. In a compelling confirmation of revelation, it has recently been discovered that a new variant class of this gene suddenly appeared about thirty-seven thousand years ago and now shows up in about seventy percent of the population.[12]

Adamic culture spread in waves from the Second Garden in the Euphrates Valley until the whole of the pure-line Adamic heritage enriched the civilizations of Asia and Europe. Although the races did not fully blend, their civilizations mixed to a considerable extent. No new sources of culture exist today, no Adamites or Andites to invigorate and stimulate the slow progress of the evolution of civilization. It is up to each generation to maintain and push civilization in an upward spiral toward the glorious destiny that awaits it. And due to a highly unusual deviation in the dispensational scheme, this can now be done wisely by guiding human development strategies with our fifth epochal revelation.

The belief that God's purpose for humanity unfolds during a series of succeeding dispensations is embraced by some branches of Christianity. Current dispensation theories revolve around the impending return of Christ, an "any-moment" rapture of the church that will be followed by Jerusalem once again taking center stage in God's plan, and a millennium of peace.

Epochal revelation expands and clarifies dispensationalist theories. Although there may be a succession of dispensations by various orders of Sons of God, only epochal dispensations modify the course of planetary events and culminate in a "judgment of the realm." Illustration 28 describes the successive planetary dispensations on a planet that has not been sidetracked by rebellion; the dispensations that Earth has experienced are highlighted.

Illustration 29 shows in gradual shading the level of human development that has been achieved in relation to dispensations and planetary epochs. When the true teachings of Jesus of Nazareth are widely embraced and the revelations in *The Urantia Book* are integrated into the mainstream body of religious wisdom, humanity will have taken bold steps toward developing the God-consciousness and cosmic insight that presages the brotherhood of man.

As shown by models of human development and the charts of epochal evolution, human progress on our planet has suffered and we are epochs behind culturally. The dearth of spiritual idealism in modern culture contributes to selfishness. And the zealous competitiveness and territorial posturing result in disharmony, indifference, procrastination, envy, and war. Humanity can no longer afford to lag in the development of the cosmic perspective that elevates every personal, business and socioeconomic decision to foster social harmony and a world unity of ideals. If the ideals of the religious life of Jesus of Nazareth were widely adopted, civilization would progressively advance and enjoy more harmony one generation at a time. In his life we find the inspiration to become righteous, caring, and loving toward our fellow humans—to live a life as a beloved son or daughter of God.

As prophecies become reconciled by epochal revelation, we can dispense with the doomsday predictions and see that our individual and collective efforts will lift human civilization toward living the ideals befitting a world that has been blessed with the bestowal mission of a Creator Son.

Judgment of the Realm

The official termination of a planetary dispensation by a Son of God marks the end of an epoch and the beginning of a new one, and constitutes a "judgment of the realm."

The concept of a last judgment was probably introduced into religious tenets in Persia (present-day Iran). Around 600 BC, the prophet Zoroaster revived the smoldering embers of the Salem gospel, and his teachings are now embodied in Zoroastrianism. Like the Egyptians, he taught the doctrine of individual judgment. But he also originated the concepts of the future resurrection of the body and a final judgment, connecting these events with the end of time, when evil is defeated and the world is restored to goodness. The teachings of Zoroaster greatly influenced the Jews. Early Christianity, along with the Mithraic cult, followed many of the doctrines of Zoroaster, as did Islam.

And have hope toward God, which they themselves also allow, that there shall be a resurrection of the dead, both of the just and unjust.
Acts 24:15

With the passage of time, the concept that came to be known as the Last Judgment was incorporated into Judeo-Christian eschatology—the theology of the so-called end times. The doctrines include the coming kingdom, either as the Old Testament messianism, which awaits the kingdom within a political/historical framework, or the New Testament apocalypticism, which expects the total end of the world at the Last Judgment, when all the dead are resurrected. Epochal revelation places this final judgment and resurrection in context.

Each planetary epoch ends with a "judgment of the realm" by an assigned Son of God and includes planetary roll calls. The judgment and roll calls that occur as one epoch ends and another begins is similar to the Christian notion of the Last Judgment at the end of time, in that it includes the resurrection of both of the just and the unjust. These planetary roll calls represent the roll calls of justice and mercy and are not physical events.

- The roll calls of mercy (for the just) pertain to the resurrection of sleeping survivors, those who were not awakened at individual, special, or millennial resurrections during an epoch. These resurrections take place in the first mansion world, where the survivors' personal guardians and Indwelling Spirits are in attendance. When the soul/personality and the spirit are reunited in a morontia form, this constitutes repersonalization, the true resurrection.

- Immediately following the roll calls of mercy are the roll calls of justice, which constitute the formal recognitions of the cessation of creature existence of all human personalities who unequivocally rejected

Illustration 28
PLANETARY DISPENSATIONS

Dispensations	Sons of God	Mission	Earth's Divergence from Regular Cycle	Duration of Dispensation
Pre-Planetary Prince (is not a dispensation)	Life Carriers.	Life Carriers initiate and monitor evolving life.	Early emergence of ethical judgment and moral will.	Life Carriers function until evolutionary appearance of primitive people.
Planetary Prince	Local universe Lanonandek Son arrives on the planet with a full quota of helpers, usually within 100,000 years from the time evolving humans acquire erect posture and will has emerged.	The Planetary Prince initiates revealed religion, inaugurates human civilization and focalizes human society.	On Earth, the Planetary Prince and staff arrived 500,000 years after the emergence of "humans." Earth isolated because of rebellion after 300,000 years.	Usually 100,000 years.
Adamic	Adam and Eve: Material Son and Daughter. Adam and Eve usually arrive when highest possible level of evolutionary life has been attained.	Adam and Eve elevate the physical, moral, intellectual, and spiritual aspects of humankind. New dispensation of ministry and grace.	The default of Adam and Eve complicated Earth's planetary history; it slowed the world's social and spiritual development. Toward the end of this defaulted Adamic dispensation, the emergency dispensation of Machiventa Melchizedek was effected.	10,000 to 25,000 years on average.
Magisterial Son	Paradise Avonal Son arrives on a magisterial mission when the intellectual and ethical progress of a human race has reached the limits of evolutionary development. They incarnate on their initial mission but never experience birth or death. They may or may not incarnate in subsequent missions during the epoch.	Avonal Sons prepare mortals for the arrival of the bestowal Son. There may be various magisterial missions prior to the arrival of the bestowal Son.	Earth has never had a Magisterial mission.	25,000 to 50,000 years on average.

Illustration 28 *(continued)*

Dispensations	Sons of God	Mission	Earth's Divergence from Regular Cycle	Duration of Dispensation
Bestowal Son	Bestowal Sons usually incarnate on a planet when the highest levels of intellectual development and ethical attainment have been attained. Bestowal Sons are usually a Paradise Son that belongs to the Avonal or Magisterial order except in one case in each local universe, when the Creator Son, a Michael Paradise Son, makes his terminal bestowal on some evolutionary world.	Bestowal Sons reveal God as Father to the mortals of the realm and inaugurate the brotherhood of man. The bestowal Son releases the Spirit of Truth, and makes possible the universal bestowal of the Indwelling Spirits.	On Earth, the bestowal Son, a Paradise Son of the Michael order, appeared at the close of the Adamic dispensation, the Third Planetary Epoch. Earth enjoys the honor of being the mortal bestowal planet of the Sovereign Paradise Creator Son, Michael of Nebadon, born as Jesus of Nazareth.	10,000 to 100,000 years. Because Earth skipped the Magisterial Son dispensation, it may take many more thousands of years to complete this present dispensation.
Teacher Son	Paradise Trinity Teacher Sons arrive when the advancing races begin to approach the apex of planetary evolution.	The Teacher Sons usher in the spiritual age—the age of light and life.		1,000+ years. Continues through era of light and life.

survival during an epoch. These roll calls are formalities and do not result in resurrections or awakenings, although they are probably related to the biblical concept of the resurrection of the unjust in Acts 24:15. When a person rejects survival and the rejection has been formally accepted in the celestial courts, cessation of existence is immediate; it is not deferred until the last judgment or the end of an age. The Indwelling Spirits of those personalities who rejected survival during an epoch do not respond to the dispensational roll calls. Only the personal or group guardians respond to "the voice of the archangel" on behalf of the nonsurviving personalities. Without the presence of the Indwelling Spirit there is no awakening, no resurrection.

On Earth there have been three judgments of the realm, with their corresponding rolls calls. The first planetary roll call, or complete dispensational resurrection of the sleeping survivors of the first dispensation, occurred at the time of the arrival of the Planetary Prince over five hundred thousand years ago, as he began the second planetary epoch.

Illustration 29
HUMAN DEVELOPMENT IN RELATION TO
DISPENSATIONS AND PLANETARY EPOCHS

Human Development	Pre-Planetary Prince (primitive mortals)[14] The Nutrition Epoch	Planetary Prince Dispensation The Security Age	Adamic Dispensation The Material Comfort Era
Social organization	Cave dwellers; tribes.	Racial groupings. National life begins.	Internationalism.
Group relationships	Brutal struggles.	Decreasing racial struggles and tribal wars.	Worldwide peace is a social goal.
Government	Tribal government.	Advanced tribal epoch.	Monarchial or paternal form of rulership, later replaced by representative government.
Ethics	Ethics of the jungle.	Dawning awareness.	Growing ethical advancement.
Art	Hunting tools developed.	Appearance of crafts, pottery and weaving.	Awakening of the interest in art, music, and literature.
Races	Unique to Earth: the Andonite race.	Six colored races. On Earth, also the Nodite race (offspring of rebellious staff and Andonites). Racial dispersion.	Race improvement by Adamic "violet" blood infusion. Races well blended at end of dispensation.
Intellectual capacity	Creative imagination begins to be exercised.	Planning, building, and communication skills are developed. Formal education begins.	As a result of blending with the violet race, an enhancement of intellectual and spiritual capacity. Interest in true philosophy. Worldwide educational system.
Language	Simple language is developed.	Tribes develop separate languages.	Gradually the languages of the races give way to one world language.

Illustration 29 *(continued)*

Magisterial Son Dispensation **The Quest for Knowledge and Wisdom**	Bestowal Son Dispensation **The Epoch of Philosophy and Brotherhood**	Teacher Son Dispensation **The Age of Spiritual Striving**	The Era of Light and Life
Humans are learning to live more naturally and effectively.	International harmony arrives.	Society approaches the ideals of social brotherhood and spiritual equality.	The Era of Light and Life continues indefinitely.
Brotherhood and worldwide peace.	Planetary peaceful coexistence.	Brotherhood of man under the Fatherhood of God.	
Highest type of representative government—only those leaders and rulers who are most fit to bear social and political responsibilities.	The military passes away. Gradual lessening of governmental supervision; fewer and fewer restrictive laws are necessary.	Representative government vanishes and world is under the rule of individual self-control. The function of government is chiefly directed to collective tasks of social administration and economic coordination.	
Ethical basis for world economy.	Worldwide pursuit of moral culture and spiritual truth; great ethical and spiritual progress.	Focus on local universe ethics.	
Flowering of art, music, and higher learning.	Higher levels of art, music, and philosophy.	Art, music, and higher learning fully expressed.	
One race.	One race.	One race.	
A great intellectual advancement is initiated.	Philosophic integration leads to wisdom. Educational systems are becoming, idealistic, self-realizing, and able to grasp cosmic realities.	New functioning of mind circuit. Understanding of cosmic citizenship.	
One world language.	World language improved.	Local universe language learned.	

Illustration 29 (continued)

Human Development	Pre-Planetary Prince (primitive mortals)[14] The Nutrition Epoch	Planetary Prince Dispensation The Security Age	Adamic Dispensation The Material Comfort Era
Sex Equality	No equality.	Sex needs lead to cooperation.	Adam and Eve provide a living example of equality.
Family Life	No family life.	Emergence of home and family life.	Home life established.
Material progress	Basic tools, hunting, and herding.	Agriculture makes its appearance. Domestication of animals and development of home arts begin.	Age of invention, mechanical development, and energy control. Agriculture and horticulture expanded. Exploration and the advancement of science.
Religion	Evolutional: animal fear, ignorance, and superstition.	A blend of evolutional and revelational.	Planetary presentation of Paradise Trinity.
Cosmology: Revelation of Truth		The local system.	The constellation.
Indwelling Spirit's bestowal	Limited bestowal; some receptivity to the Indwelling Spirit.	Limited bestowal; increased receptivity to the Indwelling Spirit.	Increased bestowal and receptivity to the Indwelling Spirit; increased capacity for fusion.
Terrestrial escape	By death.	By death; some by fusion during life.	By death; some by fusion during life.
Eugenics	Survival of the fittest.	Racial sorting starts.	Apex of purification of racial strains. Physical improvement.
Length of epoch	Usually 100,000 years until appearance of free-will creatures.	500,000 years on average. On Earth, 300,000 years because of rebellion.	10,000 to 25,000 years.

Illustration 29 (continued)

Magisterial Son Dispensation The Quest for Knowledge and Wisdom	Bestowal Son Dispensation The Epoch of Philosophy and Brotherhood	Teacher Son Dispensation The Age of Spiritual Striving	The Era of Light and Life
Men and women are equal.	Men and women are equal.	Men and women are equal.	The Era of Light and Life continues indefinitely
Family becomes the foundation of society.	Family life harmonized.	Family life perfected.	
Economic liberation. The daily work required to sustain one's independence down to two and one-half hours per day. Leisure time used for self-improvement. Height of development of physical sciences.	Economic liberation continues.	Economic and administrative systems of the planet undergo radical transformations. The daily work required to sustain one's independence down to one hour per day per individual. Earth is in close touch with universe affairs.	
Worldwide religious awakening.	One religion.	One religion. Paradise Trinity awareness.	
The local universe	The superuniverse	The central universe and Paradise	
Majority of humans are indwelt by the Indwelling Spirit.	Spirit of Truth arrives and bestowal of Indwelling Spirits becomes universal.	Individuals consciously aware of communion with Indwelling Spirit.	
By death. Increasing potential for fusion with Indwelling Spirit while on Earth.	By death. Fusion more common.	Many are translated from among the living. Death becomes less frequent.	
Further purification of the racial stocks by the restriction of reproduction.	Degeneracy has already been largely eliminated by selective reproduction. Problems of disease and delinquency are virtually solved. Average length of life climbs well above three hundred years.	Degeneracy has been virtually obliterated. Reproductive rate of racial increase is intelligently controlled. The length of life approaches five hundred years.	
25,000 to 50,000 years.	10,000 to 100,000 years. (more in the case of Earth because of irregular sequence)	1,000+ years.	

The arrival of Adam and Eve, over thirty-seven thousand years ago, marked the beginning of the third planetary epoch. The second planetary roll call of the sleeping survivors of the second dispensation occurred at that time.

The third planetary roll call occurred nineteen hundred years ago and signaled the mortal transit or resurrection of Jesus of Nazareth. This third judgment roll call formally terminated the third planetary epoch and Adamic dispensation on Earth. Those personalities of survival status who had fallen asleep since the days of Adam and who had not already gone on to judgment by means of a special or millennial resurrection were resurrected at that time. In Catholicism, these sleeping survivors may equate to the souls of good persons in the "Limbo of the Fathers" who died before the resurrection of Jesus.

A judgment of the world at the end of a planetary epoch does not constitute the end of the world. Rather it marks the beginning of a new age that brings humanity closer to its highest possible evolutionary achievement.

End of the World

Since the beginning of time, people have conjectured about the final events in the history of the world. Sacred texts and folklore predict the end of the world as we know it. Buddhists and Hindus believe in cycles of creation and destruction of the universe. To the Native American Hopis, the coming of the white man signaled the beginning of the end. Since the 1980's, erroneous ideas about the Mayan culture and calendars have spread easily throughout the world, resulting in a great number of people believing that the world will end in 2012. Many Christians hold the belief that the end of the world follows the golden age when Christ will reign.

The destruction of the world is commonly linked with the word "apocalypse," although this word technically refers to the revealing of God as the Messiah. The apocalyptic literature of Jews and early Christians references events such as the coming kingdom, the resurrection of the dead, and judgment day. These prophetic writings were mostly written between the periods of the Jewish oppression under the Syrian king Antiochus Epiphanes in 168 BC, the destruction of the Jerusalem Temple in AD 70, and the failed Bar Kokhba revolt in AD 135.

Perhaps the origin of apocalyptic thought can be found in the Persian prophet Zoroaster, who in the sixth century BC connected the resurrection of the entire human race and the final judgment with the end of the world, when individuals would be rewarded or punished. In due course, Zoroaster's teachings came to Christians via the Jews.

The Babylonian exile of the Hebrews in 587 BC left the national ego of the Jews at an all-time low. There was a great need to explain why God's people were suffering and why the establishment of the kingdom was delayed. Under the Persian rule beginning in 539 BC, the Hebrew people became exposed to the Zoroastrian teachings. The concept of a final judgment offered a way of facing the injustices that had been so apparent in their life. The apocalyptic mindset of doom and destruction began to emerge as the Hebrews perceived the end of prophecy. This was seen as a time when godly intervention would destroy their enemies and their loyalty would be rewarded, which gave the Hebrews hope and motivation to persevere.

History informs us that the apocalyptic movement grew stronger after Antiochus Epiphanes desecrated the Jewish Temple during his defiant occupation of Jerusalem in 168 BC. Epochal revelation confirms: "About one hundred years before the days of Jesus and John a new school of religious teachers arose in Palestine, the apocalyptists. These new teachers evolved a system of belief that accounted for the sufferings and humiliation of the Jews on the ground that they were paying the penalty for the nation's sins. They fell back onto the well-known reasons assigned to explain the Babylonian and other captivities of former times. But, so taught the apocalyptists, Israel should take heart; the days of their affliction were almost over; the discipline of God's chosen people was about finished; God's patience with the gentile foreigners was about exhausted. The end of Roman rule was synonymous with the end of the age and, in a certain sense, with the end of the world. These new teachers leaned heavily on the predictions of Daniel, and they consistently taught that creation was about to pass into its final stage; the kingdoms of this world were about to become the kingdom of God."[13]

Perhaps the most influential apocalyptic writing is the Book of Revelation. While there are various systems of approach to the study of John's revelation, the most popular is the prophetic approach that addresses events that will take place at the close of the age, such as the second coming of Christ, the millennial age, the general judgment, and the resurrection of the dead.

For many Christians, the Book of Revelation has become the text by which every event is measured to end-of-the-world prophecies. The father of modern Christian apocalyptism is, perhaps, the best-selling author Hal Lindsey, who created the modern interpretation of the Book of Revelation in his 1970 book *The Late Great Planet Earth*. Despite the fact that none of the catastrophic predictions in his book for the 1980s came true,[14] Lindsey is still regarded by some as an expert on prophecy.

Hal Lindsey's apocalyptic best-sellers were surpassed in 1995 by the *Left Behind* series. The *Left Behind* novels, by Tim LaHaye and Jerry B. Jenkins, use the literal translations of biblical prophecies to develop a drama that deals with the physical disappearance of true believers (the Rapture), the ruling of the world by an Antichrist, the rebuilding of the Temple in Jerusalem, and the adventures of the Tribulation Force that is "left behind" after the Rapture and dedicated to fight the seven-year-war with the Antichrist. A 2002 *Time*/CNN poll found that fifty-nine percent of Americans believe that the events in the Book of Revelation will become reality and almost a quarter think the Bible predicted the 9/11 attacks.

The Book of Revelation, written by John Zebedee when he was banished to the Isle of Patmos for a period of four years, is incomplete and has been edited. "When in temporary exile on Patmos, John wrote the Book of Revelation, which you now have in greatly abridged and distorted form. This Book of Revelation contains the surviving fragments of a great revelation, large portions of which were lost, other portions of which were removed, subsequent to John's writing. It is preserved in only fragmentary and adulterated form."[15]

Furthermore, epochal revelation has clarified the following aspects of the Book of Revelation that deal with the perceived end of the world and the age preceding it:

- There will be a second coming of Christ, but the timing is unknown. It could correspond with the end of a mortal epoch and the beginning of a new one, but it does not involve the destruction of the planet.

- There is a future age of light and life, a golden age when peace will reign on Earth. This destiny of humanity is a result of growth in spiritual ideals and wisdom, culminating in cultural and spiritual progress.

- There is a "judgment of the realm" at the end of every mortal epoch, but it is not linked to the destruction of the planet. It marks the end of an era and the beginning of a new dispensation. The judgment of the realm is not a public or physical event.

- The general resurrection of the dead does not mean that all the dead will awaken with their previous flesh and blood bodies made immortal. Rather, only the just—the sleeping survivors who have not resurrected during the epoch—will awaken in mansion world number one, in a morontia body, to continue their pursuit of God. The unjust, those who rejected survival throughout the epoch, will not experience resurrection. They will, instead, be represented by their personal or group guardians at the roll calls of justice, which constitutes the formal recognition of their cessation of existence.

Trials and tribulations are germane to living on an imperfect planet where the population is evolving toward perfection. But our disrespect of Earth, along with worldwide conflict, does not indicate a coming age of light or enlightenment; rather it reflects the collective resistance to living the brotherhood of man. "The good effort of each man benefits all men; the error or evil of each man augments the tribulation of all men."[16] The degree of tribulation that humanity experiences during each mortal epoch is, therefore, dependent on the spiritual progress achieved by previous generations.

Until the brotherhood of man is established, peace and progress will be delayed. This harmony among people cannot be achieved if ethics and religion are discarded for politics and power and if the fatherhood of God is ignored or denied. "The complete secularization of science, education, industry, and society can lead only to disaster. During the first third of the twentieth century, Urantians killed more human beings than were killed during the whole of the Christian dispensation up to that time. And this is only the beginning of the dire harvest of materialism and secularism; still more terrible destruction is yet to come."[17] Indeed, the violent harvest continues into the twenty-first century, across the globe. Scientific progress without moral and spiritual advancement only yields failed policies among nations and global wars. Moral and spiritual progress is requisite to establishing an effective government of humanity, to the enjoyment of permanent peace, and to the blessed tranquility of worldwide goodwill among all people.

It is natural to imagine the destruction of our planet as a result of some conflagration, perhaps a physical disaster such as the demise of the sun. Scientists predict that the sun's end will happen in five billion years; but "[i]t will shine on as of present efficiency for more than twenty-five billion years."[18] In either event, the demise of our planet and solar system by the sun presents no urgency to humanity. Nevertheless, in the scheme of progression, contingencies are always made for the continuation of life in the event of a catastrophe. "If some physical catastrophe should doom the planetary residence of an evolving race, the Melchizedeks and the Life Carriers would install the technique of dematerialization for all survivors, and by seraphic transport these beings would be carried away to the new world prepared for their continuing existence. The evolution of a human race, once initiated on a world of space, must proceed quite independently of the physical survival of that planet . . ."[19] While this thought-provoking news provides comfort, it also lends itself to much speculation.

Without the aid of epochal revelation, we are relegated to the status quo of ". . . either extrapolating past progress and foretelling more of the same or extrapolating one's present conception of the world and foretelling the end of progress."[20] To reconcile our beliefs with epochal revelation is to expand our perspective and to harness the power to break inhibiting patterns. We are able to shift our attention from doom and uncertainty to gain greater insight of the truth behind the written word. We elevate meanings and values and develop our capacity to love selflessly and live in peace. We recognize that *progress* is the principle of the universe that leads humanity to its final destiny and that the *quality* of our transition from one epoch to another is dependent on the cosmic perspective and spiritual perception developed by the individuals of successive eras.

Humanity's Ultimate Challenge

Cultural decline is relatively easier to gauge in the West, with social scientists and the media constantly measuring the pulse of politics and social mores. For every published statistic there are more explanations to rationalize the decay: economics, government legislation, religious indifference, and complacency. But spiritual stagnation is a root cause, stunting the growth of higher values and compromising the morality of modern societies.

Christianity, the primary religion of the West, is hampered by spiritual confusion. Christians have adopted a plurality of beliefs, which has resulted in a range of attitudes from indifference to God to stifling fanaticism. When God is deemed unnecessary, culture slides into cheap values and situational morality. Furthermore, the tyranny of religious fundamentalism resists innovation and compromise, which results in stark yes-or-no and black-or-white reasoning. Such polarization derails moral and spiritual growth, with liberal materialism and narcissistic self-glorification on one side and self-righteous fundamentalism on the other.

An unfortunate consequence of this spiritual confusion is delay in the collective recognition of the fatherhood of God, and the brotherhood of all humanity without which the religious ideals of Jesus are lost in the narcissism and fanaticism so prevalent today.

In the West, religious divisiveness permits the fear of the fundamentalist, the indifference of the religious liberal, and the self-aggrandizement of individual spirituality. Popular self-centered tenets such as, "We've chosen to enter this world of particles and form," "We knew what we were coming here to accomplish," and "We participated in setting this life process in motion" are a direct affront to God, the Universal Father and author of each individual. When self-absorbed beliefs direct our lives, the fruits of our actions are likewise distorted and our humanitarian efforts do not have the spiritual driving power to change the world.

How can the world escape the spiritual stasis that now envelops it? Organized religions are the cocoon in which the concept of divine brotherhood is evolving. The challenge facing all humanity: to increase the capacity to love so as to awaken the spirit of brotherhood in every individual.

Increasing the capacity to love requires the discovery of new and higher spiritual meanings and values. When individuals and religious institutions connect with the uncompromised teachings of Jesus and reconcile their beliefs and doctrines with epochal revelation, a spiritual unity will emerge that will supplant the current organizations of diverse believers. This spiritual brotherhood will be characterized by unity of ideals and puposes, not necessarily theological uniformity. In rediscovering the true and universal teachings of Jesus, humankind will find the inspiration to grow in the ability to live, love, and serve as Jesus taught his disciples to do, thereby facilitating the religious, social, moral, economic, and political reorganization—not only of the West, but of the whole world.

Socialized religion serves a vital role as the caretaker of moral ideals—despite historical abuses—and civilization benefited progressively until reaching moral crisis in the twentieth century. In the West, looser mores (tolerating drug use, corruption, sexual indiscretion, and so on) parallel decreasing God-awareness. Militant fundamentalism in the Middle East brings terror and power-play; in China and India, religious stagnation parallels indiscriminate economic growth. This is the status at the beginning of the twenty-first century, as moral decline reflects a growing belief in reincarnation and indifference to a personal God.

The Western world, despite its liberal spirituality and Christian base, has discarded many of its values and traded ethics and religion for politics and power. Religious zealotry often rides with global politics. Religious extremists promote mass murder in the name of God. Others respond with self-righteous fundamentalism and some claim territory by scriptural mandate. As this extremism intensifies, the world stage is set for escalating religious wars.

Is there a way out of this mind-boggling display of worldwide religious zealotry? The answer lies in the simple faith of a far greater religious majority—the moderate religious faithful who are willing to recognize that in the family of God ". . . there is no place for sectarian rivalry, group bitterness, nor assertions of moral superiority and spiritual infallibility."[21]

The alternative to religious zealotry is a spiritual humility that casts out dogma and seeks greater knowledge and understanding of the Father. The cure for religious divisiveness is a spiritual unity driven by a living faith that sees the spirit of love in the teachings of all scriptures and applies this ideal in a personal philosophy of living.

Spirit unity can be won by moderate believers of all religious faiths who have the courage to relinquish the ancient past as the exclusive source of truth and recognize that truth is ever expanding, living always in the present and achieving new expression of higher spiritual values in each generation. Organized religions can profitably expand their philosophies and theologies in light of epochal revelation so that their members truly experience the unifying message from the spiritual realm. Are we willing to elevate our ideals above human greed, war-madness, and the lust for power? Can our hearts be inspired by the beauty and sublimity, the humanity and divinity, the simplicity and uniqueness of the life of Jesus? The answer must be a resounding YES!

[N]o mystic has to tell us that God is our "father." Every one of us has that intuition already.

Amit Goswami, *God Is Not Dead*

Identification with God as Universal Father, appreciation of the indwelling presence of the Father fragment, and recognition of the potential immortality of the human soul in union with personality will revitalize belief systems across the world. True understanding of their significance and relationship with each other holds the key to steering humanity toward collective spiritual growth and world peace.

Our planet has a glorious destiny, a golden age, when contentious expansion and development is exhausted and the spiritual status of its citizens has been stabilized. But it will take the effort of enlightened and farsighted generations to embrace the ultimate challenge and emerge from the troubles of a dysfunctional past.

21.

The Golden Age

The golden age is before us, not behind us.
William Shakespeare

As we glimpse the promise of a glorious destiny, it is inspiring to imagine how our personal, social, and civic relationships will transform once we have developed a strong altruistic character. With insight from *The Urantia Book*, here is a brief preview of how our world might someday function. Some of these ideals may take generations to achieve, while others could see fruition sooner.

- The highest honor conferred upon a citizen is the order of "supreme service." This recognition is bestowed upon those who distinguish themselves in some phase of spiritual discovery or planetary social service.

- The planet slowly evolves toward having one philosophy and one religion.

- There is due recognition of sex equality and coordinated functioning of men and women in society.

- Poverty is erased worldwide; corruption and delinquency diminish with advancing social mores and values. Mental illness is practically nonexistent; feeble-mindedness has a cure and is rare.

- Political and economic life are grounded in sound morality and ethics. Society is increasingly proactive in providing peaceful solutions to domestic and international problems.

- Competition is gradually replaced by intelligent cooperation, understanding alliances, and spiritual unity for more efficient worldwide problem solving. Workers increasingly become shareholders in all business and industrial concerns.

- War gradually becomes historical memory. Nations maintain their armed forces ". . . without yielding to the temptation to employ this military strength in offensive operations against other peoples for purposes of selfish gain or national aggrandizement."[1] With the passage of time, armies and police forces become minimally necessary.

- The profit motive is replaced by ". . . superior types of nonprofit motives for economic striving and social serving—the transcendent urges of superlative wisdom, intriguing brotherhood, and excellency of spiritual attainment."[2]

- The extent of civil government and statutory regulation is in inverse proportion to the morality and spirituality of the citizenship. The greater the spiritual quality of morality (selflessness), the fewer regulations.

- Competitive play, humor, and other phases of personal and group achievement are viewed as essential for personal balance and provided for accordingly.

- Biologic and physical fitness of the human race is a science and has increased to a high level. Population becomes stationary in numbers, reproduction being guided in accordance with planetary stability and innate hereditary endowments. Vision and hearing are extended. Changes in the range of human vision enable people to recognize midwayers, their invisible cousins. "This is made possible by the final discoveries of physical science in liaison with the enlarged planetary functions of the Master Physical Controllers."[3]

- Diseases have been reduced after determining their causes, finding means of prevention, and making cures available to citizens worldwide.

- Nations are defined by the high ideals of spiritual unity and motivated by service.

- Compulsory education includes the acquirement of skills, the pursuit of wisdom, and attainment of spiritual values. Education continues throughout life, with science and philosophy becoming the major pursuits of citizens.

- Every nation has a threefold representative government of executive, legislative, and judicial branches, with reliable and efficient checks and balances in place.

- Every nation enjoys the freedom of social, political, and religious activities.

- All forms of slavery and human bondage have been abolished worldwide.

- Citizens control the raising of taxes through vastly improved information-distribution and voting techniques.

- There is equitable distribution of research, development, and manufacturing for an optimal employment rate worldwide. Natural resources are developed to supply these needs.

- A global standard of measurement is used by all.

- A universal language is spoken worldwide.

- The home/family is the basic and most respected institution of civilization. Religion, the progressive experience of knowing and finding God and becoming Godlike, is an integral part of home life.

22.

The Ascending Path
to Paradise

*The Paradise ascent is the supreme adventure of all time,
the rugged achievement of eternity.*
The Urantia Book

The afterlife goal of all universal beings of faith is to comprehend the divine nature and to find and personally recognize the Universal Father. Ascendant beings indwelt by the spirit of the Father can find God in Paradise, but without adequate spiritual comprehension of the Father, they would be oblivious to his presence.

To compensate for our conceptual limitations, the Universal Father established a sevenfold approach to God. Growth in God-awareness during our life on Earth expands our spiritual vision so that in the afterlife, we can increasingly recognize and contact the seven successive levels of Deity as personal beings.

The sevenfold approach to God begins in our local universe with the personal recognition of the Creator Son and continues through the superuniverse with the identification of the Ancients of Days. In Havona, we identify the Master Spirit of our superuniverse and gain an expanded comprehension of God the Supreme.[1] Only through this experiential and progressive journey can an ascender personally discover and recognize in Paradise the divine personalities of the Infinite Spirit, the Eternal Son, and finally, the Universal Father.

The goal of eternity is ahead! The adventure of divinity attainment lies before you!
The Urantia Book

To acquire the spiritual vision that enables an ascending being to see the Father requires factual, intellectual, and spiritual progress, along with selfless service on Earth and "heaven." The teachings presented in *The Urantia Book* offer a profound upgrade to human knowledge by clarifying our diverse notions about the afterlife and providing a clear description of the adventure that awaits every surviving personality. Indeed, the ascending path to Paradise is an eternal voyage of discovery that awaits those who choose it.

Moral personality is the forerunner of morontia personality and of true spirit status—the highest personal reality.[2] Life in the morontia and spirit realms may be full of adventure—but it is not one of relaxation. Human character traits such as procrastination, evasion, insincerity, problem avoidance, unfairness, and seeking ease must first be eradicated. Dodging situations or circumventing disagreeable obligations are no longer options. Life in the celestial abode requires *progress*, continuous growth in the technique of doing the Father's will.

In the heavens, spheres that function as educational and training grounds are material creations of varying levels of density. "The material universe is always the arena wherein take place all spiritual activities; spirit beings and spirit ascenders live and work on physical spheres of material reality."[3] The system capitals of the local universe are specifically unique in that they are the only worlds able to accommodate material, morontia, and spirit personalities.

Ascending mortals are classified according to their level of progress through the heavens. From the mansion worlds up through the spheres of the local system, constellations, and the universe, they traverse the spheres of mortal ascension and are classed as morontia progressors. As they leave the local universe, Father-fused ascenders are classified as young spirits. There are seven levels of spirit classification that can be achieved, and these are determined by actual advancement from one realm of universe service to another, and even from one universe to another.

Morontia Progression

Ascending mortals progress from the mansion worlds to the local universe headquarters and satellites. They study, work, and serve on countless assignments in association with and under the guidance of teachers and more-advanced colleagues. Through the morontia experience, ascending personalities continue to rest, drink, eat, and partake of living energy "food" unknown to humanity. They are progressively introduced to a new range of vision and experience, to increasing levels of mind and spirit development.

During the morontia experience, attainment of morontia mota—post-mortal wisdom—is actively pursued. "Increasingly in the morontia progression the truths of revealed religion are expanded; more and more you will know the truth of supreme values, divine goodness, universal relationships, eternal realities, and ultimate destinies."[4] After acquiring mota insight, ascending mortals will have every opportunity to satisfy any latent or lingering intellectual, artistic, and social longing or true ambition they had while on Earth.

An ascending personality who is sufficiently gifted may apply for admission to the artisan corps for a period of no less than one thousand years of superuniverse time. Celestial artisans are the thought recorders, energy manipulators, musicians, artists, designers, and builders of the morontia and spirit worlds. Although celestial artisans do not personally work on inhabited planets (like Earth), they are sometimes recruited to assist and inspire human artists who are innately skilled and possess Indwelling Spirits.[5]

If the universe had a motto, it would be PROGRESS. From the time of awakening in the mansion worlds there are continuous opportunities for personal development.

Mansion Worlds and the Local System

The mansion worlds are the seven satellites circling the first of fifty-six worlds that orbit Jerusem, the capital of the system to which Earth belongs. These are the worlds that Jesus was referring to when he said, "In my Father's house are many mansions" (John 14:2). The mansion worlds are training spheres that offer a transition experience between one's native planet and the advanced spiritual worlds where the unification of the evolving mortal personality is completed. The resurrected resume their intellectual training and spiritual development at the exact level they were when interrupted by death. On the mansion worlds, ascenders begin to learn self-government for the benefit of all beings. The mind learns cooperation, how to work with wiser beings, and how to quicken appreciation of the interactions between liberty and loyalty. The tongue of the system of Satania and the language of the local universe of Nebadon are mastered on the mansion worlds.

Mansion World Number One

- The resurrection hall is the center of all activities. The only difference between resurrecting in the first mansion world compared with subsequent mansion worlds is that in the latter, the Indwelling Spirit does not leave during the transit sleep. A newly developed morontia body is received at the time of each advancement from one mansion world to another.

- If a guardian angel was assigned during life on Earth, this personal guardian of destiny will greet you upon your resurrection.

- Permanent residence is assigned. Resurrected individuals are given ten days of personal liberty.

- Relatives and friends who have passed before may be contacted. "You also have time to gratify your desire to consult the registry and call upon your loved ones and other earth friends who may have preceded you to these worlds."[6]

- "No ascending mortal can escape the experience of rearing children— their own or others."[7] All survivors, male and female, must meet the criteria that satisfy this requirement. If parenting is not experienced while on Earth, this crucial role is taken up in the probationary nurseries.

- In the first mansion world, the focus is on correcting biological deficiencies and defects of character pertaining to sex life, family association, and parental function. Such problems are either corrected there or earmarked for future remedy.

- Efforts to master the significance of morontia mota are begun.

- "If you are not to be detained on mansion world number one, at the end of ten days you will enter the translation sleep and proceed to world number two, and every ten days thereafter you will thus advance until you arrive on the world of your assignment."[8]

Mansion World Number Two

Mansion World number two provides for the removal of all phases of intellectual conflict and for the cure of all varieties of mental disharmony. Earnest efforts to master the significance of morontia wisdom continue.

Mansion World Number Three

- Ascenders experience great personal and social achievement.

- More positive educational work is begun. "The chief purpose of this training is to enhance the understanding of the correlation of morontia mota and mortal logic, the coordination of morontia mota and human philosophy. Survival mortals now gain practical insight into true metaphysics. This is the real introduction to the intelligent comprehension of cosmic meanings and universe interrelationships."[9]

Mansion World Number Four

- Increased appreciation of local universe culture and progress.

- Introduction to the social life of morontia creatures, predicated neither on personal aggrandizement nor on self-seeking conquest. "A new social order is being introduced, one based on the understanding sympathy of mutual appreciation, the unselfish love of mutual service, and the overmastering motivation of the realization of a common and supreme destiny—the Paradise goal of worshipful and divine perfection."[10]

- Local universe language is mastered.

Mansion World Number Five

- Time is devoted to the perfection of the superuniverse tongue.

- Knowledge of the constellation worlds is gained.

- Time is spent preparing for the subsequent constellation sojourn.

- A real birth of cosmic consciousness takes place. Ascenders become more universe minded.

- "Study is becoming voluntary, unselfish service natural, and worship spontaneous."[11]

Mansion World Number Six

- First lessons in the prospective spirit career are given.
- Initial instruction in the technique of universe administration is received, including lessons on embracing the affairs of a whole universe.
- Ascending mortals usually witness the perfect fusion of the human mind and the Indwelling Spirit. (It is on the fifth mansion world that working synchrony is usually achieved between the two.)
- Newly Father-fused mortals are introduced to their fellows for the first time by a new name. "Human subjects are often known by the numbers of their Adjusters; mortals do not receive real universe names until after Adjuster fusion, which union is signalized by the bestowal of the new name upon the new creature by the destiny guardian."[12]
- Forty days of spiritual retirement from all routine activities are granted post-fusion, for the purpose of communing with self and choosing one of the optional routes to Edentia, Salvington, Uversa, and Havona.

Mansion World Number Seven

- Preparation for life in Jerusem, the capital of the local system.
- New and more spiritual worship of the unseen Father.
- Graduation from morontia training and formation of groups to travel to Jerusem. Ascenders may delay their transfer to Jerusem if they wish to wait for a friend, family member, or morontia ascender to catch up.

Jerusem

- Attain Jerusem citizenship.
- Observe local system administrator at work.
- Achieve the ability to voluntarily submit to the disciplines of group activities and coordinated undertakings.

Constellation Training

The experience throughout the seventy worlds of Edentia constitutes the prespirit socialization training of the morontia ascenders. Ascendant beings are "... chiefly occupied with the mastery of group ethics, the secret of pleasant and profitable interrelationship between the various universe and superuniverse orders of intelligent personalities."[13] This cultural acquirement includes learning various skills:

- Function socially and vocationally with ten ascending beings of similar likeness. Work as a group with other groups of similar structure.

- Function socially and vocationally with ten permanent citizens of Edentia who differ in every way with yourself except intellectually. Work as a group with other groups of similar organization.

- Achieve the ability to voluntarily and effectively cooperate with beings of similar likeness in close working association with a dissimilar group of intelligent creatures.

- Achieve intellectual harmony with both groups of associates.

- Further perfect the ability to live in intimate contact with similar and slightly dissimilar beings with ever-increasing friendliness and contentment.

- Augment universe insight by grasping the eternal goals of the above socialization practices.

- Augment spiritual insight and personal growth through group spiritual association and morontia coordination. Two participants working together, actually quadruple not double, the personal potential of universe achievement intellectually, socially, and spiritually.

In addition, ascenders will:

- Hear the story of their awaiting career as it is depicted by the Faithful of Days, the first of the Supreme Trinity–origin personalities that they meet.

- Observe the functioning of legislative assemblies.

- Serve in varied capacities in constellation programs concerned with group, racial, national, and planetary welfare.

- Achieve Edentia citizenship.

Local Universe Training

- Attend review of life on Earth. "Those from Urantia pursue such an experiential review together."[14]

- Participate in review of experiences obtained while passing through the mansion worlds and the capitals and training spheres of the local system and constellations. Correlate these experiences.

- Receive training for advancing service. Ascenders are assigned tasks and then afforded the opportunity to receive instruction as to the ideal and divine method of best performing those tasks.

- Receive instruction in local universe supervision.

- Participate in the enactment of the general legislation of the local universe.

- Participate in the actual coordination of the administrative pronouncements of local systems.

- Come face to face with the Creator Son and receive confirmation of spirit status from the Creator Son and the Local Universe Mother Spirit.

Spirit Progression

Mortal ascenders begin their journeys through the superuniverse system of training and culture at the receiving spheres of the minor sectors. They continue their training and service through the worlds of the ten major sectors, the higher cultural spheres of the superuniverse headquarters, and on to Havona and Paradise.

Minor and Major Sectors

Ascenders master new worlds while they practice teaching others that which they have so far assimilated. On the worlds surrounding the headquarters of a major sector, instruction is chiefly of an intellectual nature, in contrast with the more physical character of the training in a minor sector and the spiritual activities on the university worlds of a superuniverse headquarters.[15] During their sojourn in the minor sectors, Father-fused mortals are classified as first-stage spirits and advance to second-stage spirits in the major sectors.

Superuniverse Training

Father-fused mortals are classified as third-stage spirits when they advance to the training worlds of the superuniverse. The superuniverse routine is not the same for all ascending mortals. While certain groups receive exclusive and specific courses of instruction and training, all receive the same general education:

- Increased capacity to detect the presence of the Eternal Son.
- Mastery of local and superuniverse administration.
- Ability to recognize and communicate with the high spiritual rulers and directors of the advanced realms, including the Ancients of Days.
- Father-fused mortals are prepared for eventual transit to Havona.
- Perfection of purpose is developed through steadfastness of faith.

Havona Training

"The billion worlds of Havona are arranged in seven concentric circuits immediately surrounding the three circuits of Paradise satellites."[16] Personal training begins in Havona. Father-fused ascenders land on the receiving planet of the seventh Havona circuit having achieved only one aspect of perfection: perfection of purpose. They develop perfection of understanding as they achieve higher levels of intellectual, spiritual, and experiential values through the seven circles of Havona. These are not the seven circles of human achievement referred to on pages 289 and 352, which are traversed much earlier in the mortal journey. In Havona, the ambition to reach God now overshadows the previous curiosity for the adventure of time and space.

- **Seventh circle:** Ascenders further their understanding of the Paradise Trinity, the Father-Son partnership, and strengthen their intellectual recognition of the Infinite Spirit. They attain recognition of and commune with the Master Spirit of their superuniverse.

- **Sixth circle:** After reaching the sixth circle, Father-fused ascenders are classified as fourth-stage spirits. As "spiritual graduates" they achieve a new spiritualization of purpose and sensitivity for divinity that enables them to attain an enlightened realization of God the Supreme.

- **Fifth circle:** The goal in this circle is to recognize the Infinite Spirit. As candidates for the Deity adventure, ascenders receive advanced instruction concerning the divine Trinity in preparation to achieve the personality recognition of the Infinite Spirit.

- **Fourth circle:** The goal in this circle is to recognize the Eternal Son. Ascending pilgrims achieve a new comprehension of the nature and mission of Creator Sons. In this circle, they arrive at their first truly mutual understanding of one another. Ascenders are instructed on the adequate spiritual comprehension of the Son, the satisfactory personality recognition of the Son, and the proper method for differentiating the Son from the personality of the Infinite Spirit.

- **Third circle:** The goal in this circle is to recognize the Universal Father. Ascenders are classified as fifth-stage spirits when they succeed.

- **Second circle:** Successful ascenders become familiar with the Paradise hosts. They are instructed on the career of eternity and the transition slumber of the last resurrection.

- **First circle:** Acceptance into the service of Paradise. Much time is devoted to the study of the impending problems of Paradise residence, including the issues of adjustment to the many diverse groups of beings encountered in Paradise. Ascenders are further prepared for the last transit sleep.

Paradise

In general, perfected mortals in Paradise:

- Receive instruction in the ethics of Paradise relationships.
- Receive instruction on the use of perfect conduct.
- Achieve comprehension of the nature and function of more than one thousand groups of the transcendental supercitizens of Paradise.

- Use living automatic libraries for reference and verification of knowledge.
- Solve universe problems.
- Achieve fullness of worship.

Corps of Mortal Finaliters

After the attainment of the fullness of worship, the perfected Father-fused mortals are qualified for admission to the Corps of the Finality.[17] The Corps of Mortal Finaliters represents the presently known destiny of ascending mortals who have fused with their Indwelling Spirits and attained Paradise. Mortals attain the sixth stage of spirit existence upon taking the oath that musters them forever into the Corps of the Mortal Finality. While perfected mortals make up the bulk of the corps, other glorified celestial beings are also members.

The Corps of Mortal Finaliters currently ministers to those worlds that are settled in light and life. In their work in the universes of time and space, there is no domain of universe service to which finaliters are not assigned; they function universally and with alternating, equal periods of assigned duty and free service. They minister in their native superuniverses only after they have served in the other six supercreations.

The future function of the Mortal Finaliters is not revealed in *The Urantia Book*, for it has not been fully determined: "While the Corps of the Mortal Finality is mobilizing on Paradise, and while they now so extensively minister to the universes of space and administer the worlds settled in light and life, their future destination must be the now-organizing universes of outer space. At least that is the conjecture of Uversa."[18] It is also speculated that mortal finaliters may be destined to provide this future service under the leadership of the Creator Son of their universe.

Mortal finaliters are classified as sixth-stage spirits. "Such beings have attained the present limit of spirit progression but not *finality of ultimate spirit status*. They have achieved the present limit of creature perfection but not *finality of creature service*. They have experienced the fullness of Deity worship but not *finality of experiential Deity attainment*."[19]

Seventh-spirit classification may, therefore, be achieved when and if mortal finaliters are advanced to the eternal assignment of service in the unrecorded and unrevealed spheres of outer space, at which time they may also find God the Supreme. Hence, the title of this book, *Heaven Is Not the Last Stop*, takes on a new dimension of meaning!

Section Three Summary

When our understanding of human origin and history is inaccurate, it follows that our conception of human destiny is flawed as well, hindering the development of a worldview that can increasingly support the advancement of peace and social progress. In this section, our limited ideas of afterlife and collective destiny have been reconciled with epochal revelation. The new concepts presented will no doubt elicit mixed responses. A rational dose of skepticism is warranted, but our fears and doubts must not paralyze reasoned questioning and active probing.

The following summary of significant disclosures offers unprecedented knowledge upon which to build the foundation of higher universal meanings and values:

- Salvation is the technique of evolving the human mind from matter association to spirit union.

- World peace *and* eternal survival rest directly with each human being.

- Human souls have not had previous existences.

- Survival in death is possible for those who harbor the faintest flicker of faith in a higher reality and participate in moral activities that yield relative love, joy, peace, goodness, and kindness.

- Survival in death is the continued existence of the soul-personality in a new form, in association with the Indwelling Spirit, through the transfer of the seat of individual identity from the material intellect to the morontia-soul system.

- Survival in death does not imply uninterrupted consciousness. There is a period of unconsciousness between death and resurrection.

- The time lapse before resurrection and our arrival on the particular celestial world in which we begin our Paradise adventure depends on the degree of self-mastery and spiritual progress we have attained on Earth.

- Resurrection is synonymous with repersonalization or reassembly of the constituent parts of the once-human personality. It is the higher level of universe existence that we are reborn into that we generally refer to as heaven.

- Resurrected mortals are not ordinarily permitted to visit their native planet or communicate in that realm until after the current dispensation.

- There is no hell. The deliberate final rejection of God is literally suicidal for the soul and, therefore, the human personality.

- Eternal life is not synonymous with survival after death. Eternal life is dependent on the progressive development of the soul and is achieved through fusion of the human soul with the immortal Indwelling Spirit.

- The central plan for life and the administration of the universes of time and space involves elevating free-will creatures to the destiny of the Father's Paradise perfection.

- Divine judgment is accurately represented in the symbol of the Scales of Justice. Progress for perfection is rewarded with advancement, while resistance is dealt with justly and mercifully.

- Collective progress is linked to individual progress—developing and integrating intellectual, moral, and spiritual insight—while attaining wisdom by learning from mistakes, choices, and decisions.

- The destiny of humanity is characterized by a world unity of ideals: physical security, intellectual expansion, social progress, and spiritual accomplishment. The question is not whether it will be achieved but how smoothly each generation will progress toward that destiny of light and life.

- The progress of civilization on every planet is dependent on the physical and intellectual attributes of its evolving creatures, aided by spiritual ministry.

- Each planet's mortal epochs are determined by the planetary dispensations of Divine Sons.

- Each planetary epoch ends with a judgment of the realm by an assigned Son of God and includes planetary roll calls depicted in Christian doctrine as the resurrection of the living and the dead, the judgment of the just and unjust. The general resurrection of the dead does not mean that the dead will awaken with their previous flesh and blood bodies made immortal.

- The roll calls of mercy (for the just) constitute the resurrection of sleeping survivors apart from those awakened during the individual, special, or millennial resurrections of an epoch.

- The roll calls of justice (for the unjust) constitute the formal recognition of the cessation of creature existence for those human personalities who have unequivocally rejected survival by willfully rejecting God during an epoch.

- There will be a second coming of Christ, but its timing is unknown. It may correspond with the end of a mortal epoch and the beginning of a new one, but it is not connected with the destruction of the planet.

- Peace and progress—the brotherhood of man—cannot be established if ethics and religion are discarded for politics and power and if the fatherhood of God is ignored or denied.

- The complete secularization of major elements of society, such as science, education, and industry, can only lead to disaster. Moral and spiritual progress on personal and cultural levels are requisite to establishing an effective government of humanity, to enjoying the blessings of permanent peace, and to thriving on the tranquility of worldwide goodwill among all people.

- Humankind's disrespect of Earth, along with pervasive violence, does not indicate a coming age of enlightenment or an apocalypse; rather it reflects the collective resistance to living the brotherhood of man.

- The ascending path to Paradise is an eternal universe voyage of discovery that awaits those who choose it.

- Life after death continues to focus on progress, mandating an increased growth and perfection in the technique of doing the Father's will.

- The Corps of Mortal Finaliters represents the present known destination of ascending mortals who have fused with their Indwelling Spirits and attained Paradise.

SECTION FOUR

Living the
Religion of the Spirit

*Few will have the greatness to bend history itself;
but each of us can work to change a small portion of
events, and in the total of all those acts
will be written the history of this generation.*

ROBERT F. KENNEDY

Introduction

As a spiritual adventurer, include in your spiritual practice a willingness to
stay on the razor's edge, not to become so comfortable that you become
lethargic or mechanical in your spiritual practices.

Rev. Michael Bernard Beckwith, *Spiritual Liberation*

Once *Heaven Is Not the Last Stop* was completed, I came to the realization that from a cosmic perspective, we are all students of the universe, and Earth is our first learning institution. Every student is also a teacher. "In the universal regime you are not reckoned as having possessed yourself of knowledge and truth until you have demonstrated your ability and your willingness to impart this knowledge and truth to others."[1]

As evolving spiritual students and teachers, we need a comprehensive and rational framework that identifies common objectives and outcomes. Such a tool would offer guidance for living and flexibility for learning. It would support the student of faith in wise decision-making, in the empowerment to effectively teach what has been learned, and in the progressive achievement of doing the will of the Father—becoming Godlike. A universal framework would satisfy the intellectual, moral, and spiritual aspirations of all who embrace it, regardless of nationality, religious belief, culture, or race. It can do this because it is based on shared ideals: the deepening of the heartfelt connection to God and others. Such a framework will enhance all philosophies of living and provides an effective path to personal and collective progress.

This section outlines the universal framework that I call "Living the Religion of the Spirit," a guidance system of knowledge, concepts, values, and practices associated with personal and spiritual growth. The framework is then supercharged with the insights from epochal revelation to accelerate the growth of cosmic wisdom and increase the capacity to love. Illustration 30 provides the essential elements in the framework. Each will be detailed in its own chapter.

Illustration 30
LIVING THE RELIGION OF THE SPIRIT

Concept or Practice	Qualities/Capacities Enhanced
Cultivating Universal Intelligence	Describes the framework for living the religion of the spirit. Places life in the context of living as a cosmic citizen.
Advancing the Meaning of Spiritual Growth	Expands understanding of spiritual growth. Redefines familiar terms and concepts.
Understanding the Relation of Love to the Mind	Illuminates the vital relationship between love and the development of human consciousness.
Exploring Beliefs	Develops faith, courage, commitment, steadfastness, and spiritual insight. Increases ability to discern true relations between physical and spiritual realities. Increases ability to grasp and apply in daily living higher meanings, moral values, and advanced wisdom. Develops spiritual reverence. Increases capacity to love. Elevates understanding and expression of worship.
Elevating the Quality of Thinking	Cultivates scientific and moral insight. Develops intellectual integrity and perseverance, confidence in reason, fair-mindness, intellectual humility and courage, intellectual empathy and autonomy, improved decision-making, greater ability to reflect.
Acquiring Sound Taste	Increases comprehension of the meaning of life and appreciation of beauty, precision, discernment, joy, peace, clarity, patience, and gratefulness. Strengthens and develops the ability to analyze and think critically. Cultivates the imagination. Develops powers of observation and strengthens listening skills. Promotes excellence.
Developing Emotional Maturity	Builds courage, hope, patience, balance, self-control, humility, gentleness, determination, emotional strength, self-worth, reliability, confidence, self-understanding, responsibility. Increases quality of love.
Sharpening Moral Awareness	Develops moral consistency, trustworthiness, compassion, empathy, patience, tolerance. Helps increase quality of behavior.
Nourishing a Consecrated Attitude	Cultivates loyalty, faith, spiritual strength, devotion, consecration, steadfastness.
Attuning to Spirit Guidance	Promotes peace, creativity, clarity of thinking, discipline, and mastery over emotions. Develops discernment of spirit presence and receptivity to its guidance. Expands spiritual vision and humility.

We cannot leapfrog into Paradise or into world peace; we must progressively develop the consciousness that will support a growing spiritual nature. This framework for living the religion of the spirit is wholly based on human experience, and to embrace it ". . . means effort, struggle, conflict, faith, determination, love, loyalty, and progress."[2] It ". . . consists in progressive revelation and ever beckons you on toward higher and holier achievements in spiritual ideals and eternal realities."[3]

Each activity in this framework is essential to balanced development and conscious living; knowledge and practice go hand in hand. Every activity, as applicable, may be tailored to address individual needs, preferences, resources, and capabilities. The process is ideally started in childhood, but *it is never too late to begin*. Many will have reached a certain level of mastery in one or more of these activities, but excellence is characterized not only by physical and intellectual qualities but also by moral and spiritual capacities. Progress in building a divine character entails expansion of spiritual meanings and exaltation of values—an ongoing, even eternal, process.

The activities in this framework can be simultaneously addressed in varying degrees of intensity. Various qualities may be enlivened or strengthened by each action taken. Long-term focus and commitment are important for overcoming personal challenges, such as doubt and lack of self-esteem. As with learning a new language, we will have frustrating times, but also times when we know that we are moving in the right direction. Challenges deepen the meaning of life! With inspired purpose, our motivation is strengthened and we grow in connection with God and our fellow humans.

All belief systems have a framework for developing spirituality and all are based on expanding or deepening consciousness through various means such as prayer, meditation, and service. But the ability of a particular framework to progressively foster social progress and collective peace is entirely dependent on the accuracy and depth of the information on which its practices are based. The framework for living the religion of the spirit is unique: it is laced with the teachings of the latest epochal revelation, which add depth, breadth, and perspective to everything known today—all existing knowledge. When actions and practices are reset based on this knowledge, more spiritual power is released, and all decisions and actions are increasingly more effective and far-reaching.

The path of spiritual courage winds through the back alleys of self-discovery and reminds us to focus on the beckoning light of self-mastery. There are no shortcuts to soul development, and it is spiritual humility that converts the work into a joyful exercise! This section offers suggestions for energizing your spiritual life—not as something separate from the activities of daily life but as an integral part of it. It also unveils valuable new insights into spiritual terms and practices that challenge us to consider how a cosmic perspective enhances our personal and global quest for elevated human consciousness—lifting our world into a new era of spiritual vitality.

23.

Cultivating Universal Intelligence

It is the nature of revelation to be shocking and startling because when it hits up against our cherished beliefs, we become conscious of the degree to which our minds have been conditioned by the opinions and theories current in human thinking, and suddenly realize the extent of our unenlightenment.

Joel Goldsmith, *The Thunder of Silence*

In 1988, I left my Caribbean island home and moved to an Iowa town where more than four thousand people were committed to a lifestyle that was centered on the practice of Transcendental Meditation. A moral upbringing, together with prayer, had helped me through many difficult times. But the regular practice of meditation instilled calmness in my life. Subjective experiences during meditation cemented my dedication and commitment to spiritual growth.

Progress demands development of individuality; mediocrity seeks perpetuation in standardization.

The Urantia Book

After a few years, I noticed community behavior that was not in keeping with my ideal concepts of spirituality, despite the community's dedication to world peace through regular meditation practice. For example, some people basked in their extended meditations and unique subjective experiences but took no responsibility for the chaos in their personal lives. Others considered their problems as karmic experiences necessary for growth in detachment. When I started an adopt-a-grandparent program, many of those I approached for volunteer work excused themselves on the grounds that the practice of meditation was sufficient social service. The philosophy of the teachings underlying the meditation practice focused on the goal of enlightenment—living life in "bliss consciousness." It was the general understanding that "the values of pure awareness" (joy, peace, and love) would surface through regular meditation rather than by actively cultivating them in daily life. I questioned whether my notions of spirituality were wrong or if the teachings were faulty.

I now believe that my expectations were valid, and that the spiritual guidance enacted in the community was incomplete. Spiritual teachings are only as accurate as the information on which they are based; their capacity to foster peace is directly proportional to the truth content in the teachings.

To grow in selflessness requires living a life with intention, commitment, and the full enlistment of the faculties of the human personality—to expand our concept of God and strive to emulate the divine nature. This entails a willingness to challenge our habitual ways of thinking. "[I]t requires courage to invade new levels of experience and to attempt the exploration of unknown realms of intellectual living."[1] The narrow perspective held even in the social culture beyond our TM community became evident when I approached local churches to present the adopt-a-grandparent program to their congregations. Church ministers were mainly interested in adopting grandparents of their own denomination. The focus on shared theology rather than human need was witness to their priorities.

This experience showed me that even a sincere quest for spiritual attainment can be ineffective; that insular, incomplete, or biased foundations of spiritual practice can curb progress by sabotaging our passion for the discovery of new and higher spiritual meanings and values—the seeds for cultivating the wise devotion and unconditional love necessary to transform societies.

So what is needed to avoid this type of limited vision? How does one go about cultivating universal intelligence in order to become empowered to live an authentic religion of the spirit?

During his sermon at Tyre, Jesus made use of his first and only parable having to do with his own trade—carpentry. In the course of his admonition to "[b]uild well the foundations for the growth of a noble character of spiritual endowments," he said, "In order to yield the fruits of the spirit, you must be born of the spirit. You must be taught by the spirit and be led by the spirit if you would live the spirit-filled life among your fellows. But do not make the mistake of the foolish carpenter who wastes valuable time squaring, measuring, and smoothing his worm-eaten and inwardly rotting timber and then, when he has thus bestowed all of his labor upon the unsound beam, must reject it as unfit to enter into the foundations of the building which he would construct to withstand the assaults of time and storm. Let every man make sure that the intellectual and moral foundations of character are such as will adequately support the superstructure of the enlarging and ennobling spiritual nature, which is thus to transform the mortal mind and then, in association with that recreated mind, is to achieve the evolvement of the soul of immortal destiny."[2]

> *Evolutionary religion creates its gods in the image and likeness of mortal man; revelatory religion seeks to evolve and transform mortal man into the image and likeness of God.*
>
> The Urantia Book

What Universal Intelligence Is—and Is Not

In exploring the factors that go into such an achievement, we must first realize that universal intelligence is not to be confused with other faculties that we have. Firstly, it is not the same as cultivating the intellect—human reasoning limited to our five senses and interpretation of our surroundings. To cultivate the intellect alone is to live a life of perception only, to embrace the shortsighted attitude that seeing is believing. In *The Book of Life*, Jiddu Krishnamurti says: "Training the intellect does not result in intelligence. Rather, intelligence comes into being when one acts in perfect harmony, both intellectually and emotionally. There is a vast distinction between intellect and intelligence. Intellect is merely thought functioning independently of emotion. When intellect, irrespective of emotion, is trained in any particular direction, one may have great intellect, but one does not have intelligence, because in intelligence there is the inherent capacity to feel as well as to reason; in intelligence both capacities are equally present, intensely and harmoniously."[3] The cultivation of universal intelligence embraces the development of an emotionally balanced, God-knowing, moral, and selfless personality.

Secondly, universal intelligence must not be confused with conscience. At every level of spiritual understanding, conscience constitutes those thoughts and actions a person conceives as the highest moral or ethical potentials regarding any given situation. "Conscience is not a divine voice speaking to the human soul. It is merely the sum total of the moral and ethical content of the mores of any current stage of existence; it simply represents the humanly conceived ideal of reaction in any given set of circumstances."[4]

That is why "[c]onscience, untaught by experience and unaided by reason, never has been, and never can be, a safe and unerring guide to human conduct." Sociopaths, for example, are disordered individuals who disregard social rules and norms and are indifferent to the rights and feelings of others. But even among those who function normally in society, or those who seem to operate with a high degree of ethical clarity, one can never say that the voice of conscience is the prompting of the divine, as so many have claimed. When we cultivate universal intelligence, we progressively cultivate the quality of our decision-making and our ability to discriminate wisely in any given situation.

Although universal intelligence is neither intellect nor conscience, we do need to discover how to upgrade our consciousness by the harmonious and progressive development of the three endowments of the human mind—cosmic insight, moral awareness and spiritual perception. Through this comprehensive development, we progressively attain God-consciousness, reflected in reasoning that is always objective, inclusive, moral, loving, and selfless.

1. To develop *cosmic insight* is to expand our understanding of the personality of Deity and recognize the multilevel universe as being involved in our progressive spiritual experience. New and higher spiritual meanings emerge as our knowledge of the infinite character of God is expanded by epochal revelation. Some of the activities that can help us develop cosmic insight include improving the quality of our thinking, acquiring sound taste, and exploring beliefs in the light of epochal revelation.

2. To develop *moral awareness* is to master our human nature and cultivate our divine nature. It involves continual choices that are guided by our highest spiritual ideals. To strengthen this capacity, we can engage in activities that help us to develop emotional maturity, acquire sound taste, and sharpen moral awareness.

3. To develop *spiritual perception* is to enhance sensitivity to spiritual realities, including our indwelling guidance. Spiritual perception allows us to be grounded in faith, raises the quality of our emotions, and empowers us to recognize true revelations. Development of spiritual perception is limited only by the individual's capacity to *receive* and *discern* spirit realities. The experience of divine presence, and its related concept of God-realization, will be explored further in the chapter "Attuning to Spirit Guidance." Some of the activities that help us cultivate spiritual perception include prayer, worship, and meditation.

When we commit to the harmonious development of the three endowments of the human mind, we gradually come to the realization that the purpose of developing human consciousness is not to become enlightened or survive physical death; those are fringe benefits. *The true purpose of developing human consciousness is to be fully empowered to contribute one's best to the advancement of civilization.* This is the responsibility, challenge, and privilege of every generation.

An imbalance in the development of God-consciousness—within any of these areas or in the harmonization of all three—can foster dysfunctional attitudes and behaviors that hinder the very progress the individual may be seeking:

1. **Spiritual indigestion:** Absorbing a mixed menu from spiritual books or advisers without testing the principles in one's own practical experience. Spiritual indigestion dilutes the real hunger for truth; it impairs the ability to discriminate between progressive teachings and misleading guidance and places dependence on spiritual mentor(s) rather than on trusting authentic inner guidance.

2. **Spiritual arrogance:** Assuming that one is divine and spiritually superior to everyone else; that personal views and opinions are the only truth and one's path is the only way. A spiritually arrogant person often has a narrow devotion to a sacred text believed to be infallible.

3. **Fanaticism:** Misguided enthusiasm or overzealous behavior—obsessing about religious and spiritual ideas. This disorder narrowly focuses on particular beliefs or a particular issue or "truth" assumed to preclude all other spiritual truths. This creates an imbalance in the personality that may border on mental instability and even result in dominating or harming others.

4. **Apathy:** Indifference; lack of awareness or concern for the responsibilities of everyday life, including avoidance of socially responsible action. Apathy is often confused with equanimity, a calm mind that is not easily elated or depressed. Apathy is actually a

negative, uncaring state that can serve as a refuge, especially during life's downturns. Apathy is ultimately deadening.

When cosmic insight, moral awareness, and spiritual perception are cultivated and integrated in a balanced way, the realization of the *personality* of God increasingly permeates all levels of human consciousness. This realization fosters a deeper identification with the Universal Father and a consecrated commitment to doing God's will. As our appreciation and love for the Universal Father gains depth and breadth, we grow in familial love for our fellow human beings, invariably manifesting unselfish service.

The cultivation of universal intelligence aligns with the Divine Plan of Progress; it has the potential to progressively accomplish the following:

- Enhance those religious/spiritual habits of thought and action that contribute to spiritual growth and righteous living.

- Promote intellectual growth.

- Foster emotional maturity.

- Cultivate moral insight—a sense of duty promoting moral values and their expression.

- Cultivate true spiritual insight—the ability to recognize and embrace the reality of God as a Father/personality and the fraternity of all personalities.

- Strengthen one's familiarity with God through better attunement with the Indwelling Spirit.

- Deepen appreciation for the beauty of natural creation.

- Foster the quality of selflessness, the capacity to love, and the ability to live the brotherhood of man.

- Cultivate the cosmic perspective that contributes to religious unity and cultural progress.

- Self-empower each individual to blossom with cosmic insight.

With this in mind, let us now examine some of the elements that comprise the framework for living the religion of the spirit presented in the introduction. Illustration 31 reveals a program of activities; each strengthens or enlivens a particular aspect of human consciousness. When these endowments are harmoniously developed, our actions become increasingly more effective and socially far-reaching.

Building the Framework from the Ground Up

Every framework must be built on a strong foundation that includes nonnegotiable elements. In the framework for living the religion of the spirit, these are faith and purpose. In the context of a clear universal purpose, our framework must also provide standards that will build trust and cooperation among all people as well as sound criteria for assessing our attitudes and behaviors and measuring our progress.

Illustration 31
LIVING THE RELIGION OF THE SPIRIT BY CULTIVATING UNIVERSAL INTELLIGENCE

PROGRAM: To Develop God-consciousness Through Personality		
Cosmic Insight	**Moral Choice and Soul Development**	**Spiritual Perception**
Cultivating Universal Intelligence (appreciating the scope of the framework) Advancing the Meaning of Spiritual Growth (developing consistency of concepts) Understanding the Relation of Love to the Mind Exploring Beliefs (our own & others, in light of epochal revelation) Elevating the Quality of Thinking Acquiring Sound Taste (through art, music, and maintaining a healthy body)	Sharpening Moral Awareness (through service opportunities and upliftment of attitudes) Developing Emotional Maturity	Nourishing a Consecrated Attitude (through prayer and worship) Attuning to Spirit Guidance (through worshipful meditation)

STANDARDS:

To treat everyone with the selfless attitude of a wise and loving parent
When functioning as a teacher, to always maintain the attitude of a student

ASSESSMENT:

To assess every thought, word, and action by the unvarying test: What does it do for my soul? Does it bring God to me and others? Does it bring me and others to God?

MEASUREMENT:

Indicators of individual progress in spiritual development:

- the quality and extent of the manifested fruits of the spirit

- the growing commitment to continued personal growth

Reflected in society as:

- religious unity and cooperation among all people

- peaceful coexistence and social progress among all nations

THE FOUNDATION: FAITH AND PURPOSE

With living faith, we steadfastly pursue our purpose of cultivating a well-balanced God-knowing personality for the purpose of expressing the qualities of divinity and living the brotherhood of man.

Purpose

The process of developing our consciousness must be powered by an unequivocal purpose, a supreme goal toward which all our efforts, labor, and organization are directed. A universal purpose that pervades all goals and actions becomes the inspiration for living, the core of our personal roadmap of life. "Given all the thought and all the intellect in the world and no fixity of purpose, no steadiness of mental attention, a man may be a good encyclopedia but he will never be a creator."[5]

Humans evolve through life experiences, yet many activities are undertaken by habit or simply from desire. We often fail to identify and carry out purposeful value-actions. The result is minor goals achieved but failure in defining and engaging the major ones.

The process of cultivating universal intelligence is centered on the ". . . divine purpose of elevating all will creatures to the high destiny of the experience of sharing the Father's Paradise perfection."[6] Doing the will of God, therefore, is the progressive experience of becoming Godlike (developing our spiritual nature). This goal is ". . . the pivotal factor in human development, indicating the direction in which we travel and the type of being we wish ultimately to become."[7] These personal goals, combined with the social goal to serve humanity, can become a realistic purpose specific for our lives on Earth, and the purpose that can unite our turbulent world.

My own quest for purpose started with the ideal to express the divinity within. My actions were always preceded by the words, "It is my desire to express the divinity within." But it was not until I gained a deeper understanding of the Indwelling Spirit and expanded recognition of the spirit personality of the Universal Father that I discovered greater meaning in my purpose, and was moved to add a second part—to live the brotherhood of man. This second part invoked in my mind a vision of universal harmony through personal efforts to increase my love, trust, and respect for others.

> *Evolutionary religion creates its gods in the image and likeness of mortal man; revelatory religion seeks to evolve and transform mortal man into the image and likeness of God.*
>
> The Urantia Book

A mission statement for living emerged that combined my personal goal of becoming more spiritual with the social goal of advancing peace, and it fits perfectly within all other purposes and goals. Below I share with you the mission statement that now drives my life:

To develop a well-balanced, God-knowing personality for the purpose of expressing the qualities of divinity and living the brotherhood of man.

This mission statement communicates the essence of living as a proactive student of the universe consecrated to doing the will of the Father; it promotes unity of ideals and nourishes a peaceful culture. As our quest for true reality unfolds, a spiraling pattern of personality evolution leads us Godward; meaningful actions are fueled by devotion to purpose, spurring inner development that helps align our growing principles and values with our daily activities.

Faith

Purpose must be supported by faith. Growth in perfection is a mysterious adventure; we can only ponder what it is like to be perfect. Allegiance to our purpose, however, inspires consecration—solemn commitment to becoming Godlike. While we may understand the term "brotherhood of man," most of us have yet to master the experience of truly living as sons and daughters of God. We have the power to create what we intend, but we must believe in our purpose without knowing how it will manifest or how it feels once we get there. We must have faith, living faith.

Personally, I always associated faith with the belief that God exists. In writing *Heaven Is Not the Last Stop*, I realized that faith is much more than an intellectual commitment; it is an attitude that overcomes all obstacles to the discovery of higher meanings and values, and then it surprises us with the experience of greater love and appreciation for God and our fellow human beings.

Thus I discovered that growth in the personal experience of living faith not only validates our belief in God as Universal Father, but also in ourselves as the sons and daughters of God. Even more, it opens our feelings to the brotherhood of all humankind and invokes the commitment to grow in our capacity to wisely and lovingly serve others. "Belief has attained the level of faith when it motivates life and shapes the mode of living. The acceptance of a teaching as true is not faith; that is mere belief. Neither is certainty nor conviction faith. A state of mind attains to faith levels only when it actually dominates the mode of living."[8]

Faith is reflected in our reactions when faced with adverse circumstances:

- Despite all opposing logical arguments, we sustain an unswerving belief in God and the soul's survival.

- When we face disappointment and defeat, we maintain sublime trust in the goodness of God.

- Despite natural adversity and physical calamity, we find profound courage and confidence.

- Despite a physical problem, we maintain emotional stability.

- In the face of an injustice, we uphold our composure.

- In spite of human selfishness, social hostility, industrial greed, or political instability, we answer the call to service.

- As we face any of the above adversities, we continue to worship God.[9]

The truth of God ". . . can never become man's possession without the exercise of faith. This is true because man's thoughts, wisdom, ethics, and ideals will never rise higher than his faith, his sublime hope. And all such true faith is predicated on profound reflection, sincere self-criticism, and uncompromising moral consciousness. Faith is the inspiration of the spiritized creative imagination."[10] The practice of cultivating universal intelligence, fueled by faith, consecration, and purpose, ensures individual and social progress. It expands our perspective of the Big Picture of Existence, as it develops the soul, elevates the quality of our moral character, and expands our capacity to love one another.

Standards of Good

To commit to cultivating universal intelligence is to commit to expressing a standard of good not yet firmly established in our world: to treat everyone with the unselfish attitude of a wise and loving parent, in keeping with the highest interpretation of the golden rule to love one another even as the Father loves us. This is the only standard that aligns with divine will. Jesus explained: "If you are ethically lazy and socially indifferent, you can take as your standard of good the current social usages. If you are spiritually indolent and morally unprogressive, you may take as your standards of good the religious practices and traditions of your contemporaries. But the soul that survives time and emerges into eternity must make a personal choice between good and evil as they are determined by the true values of the spiritual standards established by the divine spirit which the Father in heaven has sent to dwell within the heart of man. This indwelling spirit is the standard of personality survival."[11]

The extent to which we live by this high standard is determined by our consecrated commitment to actively engage in developing God-consciousness. The mind thus engaged has no time or space for self-aggrandizement, pride, or willfulness, no idle time for the machinations and sophistry of evil intent.

When a student begins to function as a teacher, maintaining the attitude of a student becomes a necessary standard. "The true teacher maintains his intellectual integrity by ever remaining a learner."[12]

Measurement and Assessment

As we have already noted, actual spiritual growth can be judged only in the celestial realm, where the true intent of the individual is always known and considered. However, a good indicator is ". . . the nature and extent of the fruits of the spirit which are yielded in the life experience of the individual believer. 'By their fruits you shall know them.'"[13] "The evidence of true spiritual development consists in the exhibition of a human personality motivated by love, activated by unselfish ministry, and dominated by the wholehearted worship of the perfection ideals of divinity."[14]

We can follow the example of Jesus of Nazareth and increasingly measure everything we think, do, and say by the unvarying test: What does it do for the human soul? Does it bring God to mortals? Does it bring mortals to God?[15]

True personal spiritual development is reflected in society and among nations as peaceful coexistence. Peace will reign as individuals of all faiths live the religion of the spirit guided by a coherent framework that is informed by revelation.

Our determined efforts to develop a unified personality through increasing spirit dominance do not preclude joyful living. "The great goal of human existence is to attune to the divinity of the indwelling Adjuster; the great achievement of mortal life is the attainment of a true and understanding consecration to the eternal aims of the divine spirit who waits and works within your mind. But a devoted and determined effort to realize eternal destiny is wholly compatible with a lighthearted and joyous life and with a successful and honorable career on earth. Cooperation with the Thought Adjuster does not entail self-torture, mock piety, or hypocritical and ostentatious self-abasement; the ideal life is one of loving service rather than an existence of fearful apprehension."[16]

What are the behavior traits of a well-balanced God-conscious character? *The Urantia Book* provides us with insight as it describes why the apostle Thomas admired Jesus: "Increasingly, Thomas admired and honored one who was so lovingly merciful yet so inflexibly just and fair; so firm but never obstinate; so calm but never indifferent; so helpful and so sympathetic but never meddlesome or dictatorial; so strong but at the same time so gentle; so positive but never rough or rude; so tender but never vacillating; so pure and innocent but at the same time so virile, aggressive, and forceful; so truly courageous but never rash or foolhardy; such a lover of nature but so free from all tendency to revere nature; so humorous and so playful, but so free from levity and frivolity. It was this matchless symmetry of personality that so charmed Thomas. He probably enjoyed the highest intellectual understanding and personality appreciation of Jesus of any of the twelve."[17]

As we grow in cosmic understanding, love will not remain confined to that which is near to us, but will spread extensively and gain strength and depth by practice until it embraces all human beings, regardless of ethnic background or religious identity. We will come to regard everyone's welfare as our own, and that of our family and friends. We will joyfully and actively participate in making the world a better place.

Summary

From a universal perspective, perfection is a process; its full attainment is achieved only in Paradise. However, when we daily engage in developing aspects of consciousness, we progressively attain relative levels of perfection. "When man consecrates his will to the doing of the Father's will, when man gives God all that he *has*, then does God make that man more than he is."[18] Such a commitment, however, constantly competes with selfish human nature. "Evolutionary man does not naturally relish hard work. To keep pace in his life experience with the impelling demands and the compelling urges of a growing religious experience means incessant activity in spiritual growth, intellectual expansion, factual enlargement, and social service. There is no real religion apart from a highly active personality."[19] How focused we are on our own selves as we work toward spiritual attainment and even self-transformation! Our efforts may satisfy us personally, but are they socially transforming? A "highly active personality" is the key in cultivating universal intelligence. "It requires time for men and women to effect radical and extensive changes in their basic and fundamental concepts of social conduct, philosophic attitudes, and religious convictions."[20]

The external results may include a positive outlook on life, improved health, better relationships, enhanced career opportunities, a harmonic rhythm to everyday events, and a stable life environment. However, these are merely the icing on the cake. Genuine happiness is a natural outgrowth of a universally intelligent life beyond even those laudable achievements.

When we cultivate universal intelligence, we free faith, elevate wisdom, and live truth. Faith is the fuel for true religious growth; wisdom is elevated when new and higher spiritual meanings are invited to live and reign in the human soul.

The cultivation of universal intelligence requires a dynamic, comprehensive, and ongoing positive approach to life. It is a voluntary lifestyle that is powered by fearless faith, moral resolve, and commitment to high spiritual ideals—all supported by decisive action. In order for a tree to realize its full potential, it must have water, sun, light, and air; it must work its roots through soil and around any rocks and weeds that hinder its growth. Similarly, to achieve our highest potential, we must take steps to strengthen our own efforts toward excellence and also address the factors that hinder our progress. The commitment required for an individual can be daunting and sometimes overwhelming, but the benefit to self and society will give impetus to such consecration.

In this chapter, we examined the scope of the framework and identified its foundation—faith and purpose—as well as the standards and methods of assessing progress. In the following chapters, we will examine the activities in the program essential to increasing our capacity to live the religion of the spirit and realizing cosmic citizenship.

24.

Advancing the Meaning of Spiritual Growth

If we're not willing to be led through our fears and anxieties, we will never see or grow. We must always move from one level to a level we don't completely understand yet. Every move up the ladder of moral development is taken in semidarkness, by the light of faith. The greatest barrier to the next level of conscience development is our comfort and control at the one we are at now.

Fr. Richard Rohr, *Everything Belongs*

As a young adult, I craved to know the meaning of my childhood near-death experiences, which drew me to the investigation of parapsychology (psychic phenomena). Years into my studies, a friend suggested that meditation would enhance my efforts to develop intuitive abilities. As a Catholic, I had been told by the local priest to stay away from Transcendental Meditation (TM), but his reasoning did not convince me; still, I approached my TM initiation with a mixture of anticipation and trepidation. Within two weeks I was having experiences of great inner peace, light, and unity. My instructor told me that I was connecting with the "pure field of consciousness" and that regular meditation was the one activity that would raise the collective consciousness and bring personal enlightenment—liberation of the Self from the cycles of death and rebirth.

I had been entertaining the concept of reincarnation for a long time. My activities for the next fifteen years revolved around the goal of enlightenment. I measured spiritual growth by the calm I felt during stressful situations, my experiences of "higher states of consciousness" during meditation, and the growing sense of interconnectedness with everything. Then, a series of events, including my involvement with the Liberal Catholic Church, awakened new feelings—the desire for a relationship with God. I wanted to experience devotion, a life dominated by the worshipful attitude of love. Unknowingly, my quest had begun: to reconcile the concept of a personal God with the meditative states of consciousness I was experiencing.

At that time I did not know that I had a fragment of God guiding me in my spiritual journey, enlivening my curiosity about God and continuously leading me toward greater understanding of my place in the universe. I also did not know that through the influence of this ministering spirit, I was retaining—with each exposure to increasingly higher levels of truth—that which is eternal in what I learned and explored. Far from needing to jettison everything from within a particular teaching or path, I was beginning to see how I could incorporate the wisdom from each to forge an expanded and more complete worldview. Part of that process included the redefinition of terms that will be familiar to every reader of this book.

Spiritual Terms

As I explored my connection with God and my Indwelling Spirit in the light of epochal revelation, I examined this new understanding in relation to the terms and phrases that I had been using to describe various aspects of spiritual experience. Within the array of paths I had been involved in, I had been exposed to multiple definitions for terms such as "spiritual transformation," "self-mastery," "God-consciousness," "self-realization," and "enlightenment," which now seemed incomplete. The insights I gained in my reconciliation process brought new meaning to these terms, revealing a clearer picture of my journey in the pursuit of God. I had to begin with the most basic redefinition, which I did by answering a question that I believe every seeker of truth would do well to consider.

Spiritual Experiences

Spiritual experiences are usually considered hallmarks of spiritual growth, but what classifies an experience as spiritual? We tend to call an experience spiritual when it is unexplainable, especially when it is associated with a spiritual or religious practice. Spiritual practices bridge the gap between acquired theoretical knowledge and direct experience. For example, the inner experience of light or feeling of universal love during the practice of meditation or prayer may be associated with an acquired knowledge of God or spirit, and therefore is considered to be a spiritual experience.

From a cosmic perspective, however, every experience has the *potential* to be spiritual—to be influenced by spirit. But the spiritual power in an experience remains latent until it is activated by the response of the individual. In other words, a particular experience *is not* spiritual because it is perceived as such; *it is* spiritual because the subsequent decisions and actions reflect an expanding worldview and increasing sensitivity to spiritual guidance.

True spiritual experiences emanate from the inner ministry of the spirit, usually reflected in a great outward calm and almost perfect emotional control. "The divine spirit makes contact with mortal man, not by feelings or emotions, but in the realm of the highest and most spiritualized thinking. It is your *thoughts*, not your feelings, that lead you Godward."[1]

True spiritual experiences foster humility, balance, growth, and progress, and they empower the individual to:

- Enjoy more complete physical health.

- Mentally function more efficiently.

- Socialize the spiritual/religious experience more fully and joyfully.

- Spiritualize daily living more completely while faithfully performing the routine duties of human existence.

- Enhance life with a deeper appreciation of truth, beauty, and goodness.

- Conserve important social, moral, ethical, and spiritual values.

- Increase spiritual perception (awareness).

Spiritual experiences are usually driven by the personal desire and effort to find and know God, and are often encountered during prayer and meditation. However, if our concept of God is not evolving or if personal identification with the Father is lacking, spiritual practices can lead to a preoccupation with oneself and one's own level of attainment. It can also distort our perception of the experiences we are having. The static and blissful peace of mind experienced in mystic communion, for example, may be resonating from the subconscious mind rather than the superconscious realm of the Indwelling Spirit—a result of physical fatigue, psychic dissociation, profound aesthetic experiences, or other interior impulses.[2]

Likewise, a vivid and intense emotional experience is not necessarily a divine revelation or a spiritual insight. "Scientists assemble facts, philosophers coordinate ideas, while prophets exalt ideals. Feeling and emotion are invariable concomitants of religion, but they are not religion. Religion may be the feeling of experience, but it is hardly the experience of feeling. Neither logic (rationalization) nor emotion (feeling) is essentially a part of religious experience, although both may variously be associated with the exercise of faith in the furtherance of spiritual insight into reality, all according to the status and temperamental tendency of the individual mind."[3]

This is perhaps not difficult to understand intellectually, but many seekers become easily attached to the feelings associated with the meditative state, especially if they identify these experiences with a growing spirituality. This understanding helps us to redefine the broad term "spirituality" in a manner that reflects a more precise meaning than is generally used.

Spirituality

Spirituality is the progressive revelation of the qualities of divinity in everything we think, say, and do. A growing spirituality is reflected when we consistently treat others as we would like to be treated in the same circumstances, and ultimately when our decisions and actions reflect the selfless attitude of a wise and loving parent. This spirituality is the goal of the ongoing process of spiritual growth on Earth.

Spiritual Growth

To better understand spiritual growth, we must refine our concept of God and our understanding of universe relationships. God is spirit personality—perfect and complete; human beings are *potential* spirit personalities with a high capacity for growth.

As explained previously, humans have a spirit nucleus—the Indwelling Spirit. Because the human mind is a personal energy system existing around this spirit nucleus, the mind has the potential for eternal personality. To the degree that the human mind identifies with spiritual realities and is attuned to the presence and guidance of its spirit nucleus, to that degree is the soul developed—the evolving vehicle for the continuity of selfhood. It is this eventual union of soul and spirit, of human will with divine will, which marks the attainment of eternal personality, with the ultimate achievement in Paradise of perfect spirit status.

Spiritual growth may therefore be defined as ". . . those adjustments of the human will and transformations in the human mind whereby the God-conscious intellect gradually becomes spirit taught and eventually spirit led. This evolution of the human mind from matter association to spirit union results in the transmutation of the potentially spirit phases of the mortal mind into the morontia realities of the immortal soul. Mortal mind subservient to matter is destined to become increasingly material and consequently to suffer eventual personality extinction; mind yielded to spirit is destined to become increasingly spiritual and ultimately to achieve oneness with the surviving and guiding divine spirit and in this way to attain survival and eternity of personality existence."[4]

Spiritual growth is generally unconscious though it is nurtured when we willingly adopt a commitment to personal transformation; our progress becomes evident in the increasing quality of our decisions and our behavior toward others. "The evidence of true spiritual development consists in the exhibition of a human personality motivated by love, activated by unselfish ministry, and dominated by the wholehearted worship of the perfection ideals of divinity."[5]

Spiritual Transformation

Spiritual transformation is the process by which the human personality achieves immortality and attains spirit perfection. From a cosmic perspective, spiritual transformation begins with the first inkling of faith in spiritual realities and progresses steadily with the balanced cultivation of cosmic insight, moral awareness, and spiritual perception (God-consciousness). Every decision we make that is in attunement with the Indwelling Spirit spiritualizes the mind—this is true spiritual transformation. In a cooperative cycle, these decisions further enable the Indwelling Spirit to uplift and advance our illumination.

This process of continual Godly decision-making—which includes acting on our highest choices—accelerates our growth toward fusion of the evolving soul with the Indwelling Spirit, an event that reflects the complete attunement of personal will with the will of God. This achievement is very rare during mortal life, usually occurring, as we have said, in the mansion worlds. But even this event does not signal the end of the process of our spiritual transformation. Ascending personalities continue to grow in cosmic insight and spirit vision, experiencing new levels of mind and spirit development throughout all the realms we traverse on our journey to Paradise.

God-consciousness

God-consciousness is the capacity to think, reason, and make decisions with the mind of God. Growth in the capacity for God-consciousness is the result of the harmonious development of the three endowments of the human mind: cosmic insight, moral awareness, and spiritual perception. God-consciousness is reflected in reasoning and behavior that is increasingly objective, inclusive, loving, moral, and selfless, and in decisions that are progressively more effective in advancing peace and social progress. Development of God-consciousness is a process that begins on Earth and continues during our journey through the multilevel universe.

God-realization

God-realization is the progressive experience of discovering higher levels of Deity. The ultimate achievement is to stand in the presence of the Universal Father in Paradise as a perfected spirit. Progress in God-realization is directly linked to the development of God-consciousness and is explained further in the chapter "Attuning to Spirit Guidance."

Self-mastery

Self-mastery is the conscious control of one's attitudes and behavior. The mastery of human nature and its integration into the developing divine nature (as we conform our will to the divine will) is evident in the consistent expression of wise judgment, joy, peace, kindness, tolerance, trustworthiness, love, and peace. Self-mastery is inherent in the development of God-consciousness.

Enlightenment

Enlightenment refers to the intellectual, moral, and spiritual wisdom that affords clarity and depth of perception. Enlightenment is growth in understanding that stretches from life on Earth through eternity as the individual grows in God-consciousness and Godlikeness.

Self-realization

Self-realization is the progressive attainment of increasing levels of Godlikeness, beginning with the mastery of human nature and progressing through the development of God-consciousness. Relative to the soul, self-realization fosters increasing levels of communion with the Indwelling Spirit, culminating in fusion.

Thus the journey we are on is an eternal one. However, is it possible to understand how our growth is measured and assessed, beginning with the early stages of growth here on Earth as we evolve toward this Adjuster fusion?

Measuring Spiritual Growth/Spirituality

The motive behind every action determines its moral value. Therefore, actual spiritual growth can be judged only in the celestial realm, where the true intent of the individual is always known and considered. From a cosmic perspective, spiritual growth is measured according to progress within seven successive circles or stages of human development. "The individual progress of human beings is measured by their successive attainment and traversal (mastery) of the seven cosmic circles. These circles of mortal progression are levels of associated intellectual, social, spiritual, and cosmic-insight values."[6] As we move through these circles, we increasingly grow in our recognition, realization, and appreciation that we are all universe citizens and sons and daughters of God.

The circle we inhabit at any given time mirrors our current capacity for God-consciousness. According to epochal revelation, the first moral choice ushers an individual into the outer, or seventh, circle as a potential citizen of the local universe. From there we continue in the tasks of self-understanding, self-conquest, and self-mastery. Circle by circle we advance.[7] Attainment of the third circle prompts the bestowal of a seraphic guardian, a personal angel of guidance, watchcase, and other ministerial benefits. The first circle represents the highest possible mind-spirit connection in the terrestrial experience.

The traversal of these seven circles of cosmic growth does not guarantee immortality—fusion of the soul with the Indwelling Spirit—but their mastery marks the attainment that is preliminary to fusion. While it is impossible to determine the circle in which a person is functioning, steadfast effort in the balanced development of the personality ensures soul growth according to individual capacity.

Jesus of Nazareth: Perfect Example of Spiritual Growth

The chronicle of Jesus' life provides us with valuable insights into the process of spiritual development, which embraces the mastery of human nature and its integration with the developing divine nature. We have seen how the first moral act of an individual triggers the arrival of the Indwelling Spirit and initiates the spiritual ascent of the human personality. This occurred in Jesus' life just before he was five years old. "In something more than a year after the return to Nazareth the boy Jesus arrived at the age of his first personal and wholehearted moral decision; and there came to abide with him a Thought Adjuster, a divine gift of the Paradise Father . . . Jesus was no more aware of the coming of the divine Monitor than are the millions upon millions of other children who, before and since that day, have likewise received these Thought Adjusters to indwell their minds and work for the ultimate spiritualization of these minds and the eternal survival of their evolving immortal souls."[8]

Progress continues as the evolving human strives to bring erratic emotions under control in his or her interactions with others. "While inherited urges cannot be fundamentally modified, emotional responses to such urges can be changed; therefore the moral nature can be modified, character can be improved. In the strong character emotional responses are integrated and coordinated, and thus is produced a unified personality."[9] During his sixth year, ". . . Jesus made great progress in adjusting his strong feelings and vigorous impulses to the demands of family cooperation and home discipline."[10] At the age of seven, Jesus received his intellectual and theological education at the Nazareth synagogue and his moral training at home, "[b]ut his real education— that equipment of mind and heart for the actual test of grappling with the difficult problems of life—he obtained by mingling with his fellow men."[11]

It is the human intellect that gives meaning to sensations and determines the quality and intensity of corresponding emotions. Progress continues as the evolving individual accumulates knowledge and mentally sorts, classifies, and correlates this knowledge while integrating these growing perspectives with family and social responsibilities. This was a constant challenge for Jesus during the adolescent years twelve through fourteen. "Throughout this and the two following years Jesus suffered great mental distress as the result of his constant effort to adjust his personal views of religious practices and social amenities to the established beliefs of his parents. He was distraught by the conflict between the urge to be loyal to his own convictions and the conscientious admonition of dutiful submission to his parents . . . However, he never shirked the responsibility of making the necessary daily adjustments between these realms of loyalty to one's personal convictions and duty toward one's family, and he achieved the satisfaction of effecting an increasingly harmonious blending of personal convictions and family obligations into a masterful concept of group solidarity based upon loyalty, fairness, tolerance, and love.[12]

According to Carolyn Myss, PhD, author of *Anatomy of the Spirit*, "A spiritual adult inconspicuously involves his or her inner spiritual qualities in everyday decisions. One's 'spiritual' thoughts and activities are inseparable from other aspects of life: all becomes one."[13] Jesus became a spiritual adult at an early age by living this truth. "As the years passed, this young carpenter of Nazareth increasingly measured every institution of society and every usage of religion by the unvarying test: What does it do for the human soul? does it bring God to man? does it bring man to God?"[14]

Our moral and spiritual capacities grow in response to our decisions, enabling us to maintain composure and a compassionate heart regardless of the events in our lives. We experience increasing devotion to the welfare of others, remain loyal to our responsibilities, and pursue active social service. Jesus' father died when Jesus was only fourteen, and the lad was faced with the responsibility of supporting and protecting his mother and siblings. He had to make many emotional adjustments in his relationships and duties. During his seventeenth year, for example, Jesus refused to become associated with the

Zealots' movement. At eighteen, he made a final decision regarding marriage: despite the desirability of marriage, he chose to pursue his earth mission without a wife. By his twentieth year ". . . he now stands on the threshold of full manhood, rich in the experience of human living, replete in the understanding of human nature, and full of sympathy for the frailties of human nature."[15]

As the mind is increasingly developed and spiritized and our ability to love wisely and selflessly grows, we become increasingly attuned to divine guidance. Jesus was conscious of "being about the Father's business" from a very young age and he trusted the guidance of his Indwelling Spirit. As he grew up, Jesus continued to cultivate moral status and spiritual understanding and to effectively integrate his human and divine natures. By the age of twenty, "[h]e has learned well to bear responsibility. He knows how to carry on in the face of disappointment. He bears up bravely when his plans are thwarted and his purposes temporarily defeated. He has learned how to be fair and just even in the face of injustice. He is learning how to adjust his ideals of spiritual living to the practical demands of earthly existence. He is learning how to plan for the achievement of a higher and distant goal of idealism while he toils earnestly for the attainment of a nearer and immediate goal of necessity. He is steadily acquiring the art of adjusting his aspirations to the commonplace demands of the human occasion. He has very nearly mastered the technique of utilizing the energy of the spiritual drive to turn the mechanism of material achievement. He is slowly learning how to live the heavenly life while he continues on with the earthly existence. More and more he depends upon the ultimate guidance of his heavenly Father while he assumes the fatherly role of guiding and directing the children of his earth family. He is becoming experienced in the skillful wresting of victory from the very jaws of defeat; he is learning how to transform the difficulties of time into the triumphs of eternity."[16]

As we increase our capacity for God-consciousness, our expression of unconditional love becomes more expanded and our decisions reflect greater understanding and wisdom; as we grow in attunement with the Indwelling Spirit we become increasingly aware of its guidance. The Urantia Book highlights Jesus' thirtieth year of life as one in which ". . . great progress was made in effecting working harmony between his human mind and the indwelling Adjuster. The Adjuster had been actively engaged in reorganizing the thinking and in rehearsing the mind for the great events which were in the not then distant future. The personality of Jesus was preparing for his great change in attitude toward the world. These were the in-between times, the transition stage of that being who began life as God appearing as man, and who was now making ready to complete his earth career as man appearing as God."[17]

God-conscious individuals know themselves as sons and daughters of God. The decisions they make are increasingly in harmony with the will of their indwelling divine presence, and this is reflected in the quality and extent of the fruits of their actions. During his thirty-first year, ". . . Jesus became absolutely assured of his nature and of the certainty of his triumph over the material levels of time-space personality manifestation. He fully believed in, and did not hesitate to assert, the ascendancy of his divine nature over his human nature."[18] During his six weeks alone on Mount Hermon before his baptism, Jesus finished

". . . the mortal task of achieving the circles of mind-understanding and personality-control . . . The mortal goal of this earth creature was there attained. Only the final phase of mind and Adjuster attunement remained to be consummated."[19] At the time of his baptism, Jesus experienced a unique union of his human and divine natures.

Jesus trained his disciples so that they were able to triumph over doubt and assert full-fledged faith in his gospel of the kingdom. The disciples' stringent training and consequent attainment of unity of comprehension influenced the rapid spread of Jesus' message of salvation throughout Rome and the rest of Europe. Similarly, as one individual at a time begins to grasp the true message of Jesus as it is clarified by epochal revelation, the uplifting effects will ripple throughout societies, and ultimately the world. These dynamics are explored in the following section.

The Connection between Individual and Collective Growth

All religions teach that spiritual growth is essential to individual progress and collective peace. They recognize the wisdom of the golden rule that urges us to "do unto others as you would have them do unto you." So how can we best understand the relationship between our individual spiritual growth and the advancement of Godly ideas and ideals for all of humanity?

As we have already noted, the peak of human spirituality is equivalent to attaining the maximum blend of cosmic insight, moral awareness, and spiritual perception; in practical terms this implies developing consciousness through building character, discovering new and higher spiritual meanings and values, and growing in attunement with spirit guidance

To build character is to increase our reasoning ability, emotional maturity, self-control, and moral standards. Humankind is prone to egotism, prejudice, self-justification, and self-deception, but these attitude flaws are simply the rough edges that call out for self-development. Our active and deliberate efforts to build a noble character lead to improved interactions with others through enhancement of positive traits such as kindness, honesty, reliability, loyalty, empathy, fairness, tolerance, respect, generosity, and forgiveness.

What does it mean to discover new and higher spiritual meanings and values? It means that we refine our worldview, factually and philosophically. This results in reasoning and behavior that can create and support useful, durable, and sustainable transformation. Our worldview represents our general outlook on life—our personal perspective and interpretation of society, the world, and our place in it. It answers questions such as: Who are we? Why is the world the way it is? Where do we come from? Where are we going?

As we reflect on the answers to these questions, we gain insight into cosmic relationships that can transform our lives. The power to transform societies, however, is directly related to the truth content in our conclusions. To the degree that our worldview is accurate, factually and philosophically, so are our decisions and behavior likely to be effective at advancing spiritual unity and social progress. "And this intense striving for the attainment of supermortal ideals is always characterized by increasing patience, forbearance, fortitude, and tolerance."[20]

Every spiritual path has a plan for growth based on a concept of God and an understanding of humanity's relationship to God and the universe. Most traditions elevate the social ideals of love and service, and the disciplines of prayer and reflection. Yet despite the piety of the world's religionists and the active involvement of many governments in promoting purposeful interdependence for peace, indifference and greed still plague the world. Intolerance, violence, and war still impact a large portion of our world's population.

We tend to blame this trend on the failure of organized religion, or on terrorism, ideology, or power struggles—but critique comes easily. Only after exploring my own beliefs and reconciling them with epochal revelation did I find new meaning in personal spiritual growth. I finally understood the reason why we seem to take one step forward and two backward in our efforts to establish world peace. The reason:

Our human philosophies are yet to achieve unity in the intelligent comprehension of the universe.

Epochal revelation explains: "There is unity in the cosmic universe if you could only discern its workings in actuality. The real universe is friendly to every child of the eternal God. The real problem is: How can the finite mind of man achieve a logical, true, and corresponding unity of thought?"[21] It goes on to say that unity of comprehension can only be achieved by understanding that all facts and values originate in the Paradise Father, revealing the spiritual goal of progressive personality achievement.

We live in a multireligious world where it seems that unity of spritual comprehension is impossible. However, a hopeful step toward the goal of unity can be found in the growing number of interfaith groups seeking to build communities where people of different traditions learn from each other and work together for the common good. Interfaith dialogue and cooperation provide an interim step that allows us to explore spiritual unity without intellectual uniformity.

The realization of global world peace will require an even bolder next step. Practicing spirituality without the expansion of meanings is like exploring new lands using old navigational charts; we may locate the coastline but fail to find the precious calm of the harbor. As epochal revelation begins to illuminate current religious thinking, an expanded perspective will bring renewed passion into spiritual development and the pursuit of truth. Such concerted focus on spiritual growth by religious groups everywhere will multiply the potentials of achieving peace exponentially. "Intellectually, socially, and spiritually two moral creatures do not merely double their personal potentials of universe achievement by partnership technique; they more nearly quadruple their attainment and accomplishment possibilities."[22] If that is true of only two people, what are the potentials when entire groups work together across the globe?

When the realization that each person is indwelt and guided by the spirit of the Universal Father reaches a critical mass, there will be a blossoming of spiritual unity. This will happen because such collective awareness is grounded on the fact that we share a spirit goal identical in origin, nature, and destiny. This unity of comprehension implies two things. First, that we possess a common motive for serving others—the desire above everything else to do the will of the Father. And second, that we share a common goal of existence—to find the Father in heaven—validating that we have become Godlike.[23]

In my own life, these valuable insights brought a greater awareness of my responsibility to become the best that I could be so that my service to others could reap the maximum benefits for all. They also motivated me to rethink my concept of spiritual development and what that meant in practice. If I was to improve the yield of my spiritual development efforts, I needed to embrace a universal framework that was based on the recognition that all of us share a common goal of existence, even though we have not yet agreed on what that may be. To this end, I garnered some very meaningful realizations from my process of exploration and personal reconciliation:

- Religion is not a belief or an institution but the experience of finding and knowing God with the goal of becoming Godlike.

- Growth in the capacity for God-consciousness is the promise of religion.

- Spiritual humility is essential to break free from the comfort of one's long-held beliefs.

- Growth in the experience of love and empathy are a more accurate indication of spirituality than the inner experiences one may have during prayer or meditation.

- The knowledge of God that one may possess, no matter how comprehensive, is yet a fraction of what is yet to be discovered.

- True spiritual growth is driven by the desire to worship God through a higher expression of goodness.

Summary

The concept of spiritual growth is laden with misunderstanding; hence, despite thousands of years of religious guidance, our world lags behind in the attainment of peace and social progress. True spiritual growth is the result of the balanced development of cosmic insight, moral awareness, and spiritual perception, reflected in balanced living, wise, objective, and selfless decision-making, loving relationships, and a deepening relationship with God.

Jesus lived his short but full life committed to doing the will of God the Father, progressively developing his intellectual, emotional, moral, and spiritual capacities and integrating them into daily living. This authentic process has the power to transform all sincere seekers. Spiritual growth requires that we move from indifference, through conflict, to harmony, and from uncertainty to undoubting faith in the liberating recognition that we are all sons and daughters of the Universal Father, cosmic citizens evolving in a multilevel universe who share the same goal of progressive spiritual attainment. As the whole self grows, the accompanying growth in cosmic understanding leads to an increased capacity to wisely and selflessly love and serve others—true spirituality.

Our progress toward global spiritual unity is in peril if we cling to beliefs that are rigid, incomplete, or outright flawed. Decisions and actions based on such beliefs are likely to manifest flawed results. We may *feel* spiritual, but are we *growing* spiritually? Are we more tolerant and forgiving than we were five years ago? We profess love, but are we growing in our love for God and our fellow human beings? Is our main motivation in life to become enlightened or to worship God by lovingly serving others?

If we truly want to grow spiritually and advance our civilization, we must discover new meanings in our philosophic concepts and theological definitions. We must also be willing to subject our beliefs to intelligent criticism and reasonable philosophic assessment.

"The evidence of true spiritual development consists in the exhibition of a human personality motivated by love, activated by unselfish ministry, and dominated by the wholehearted worship of the perfection ideals of divinity."[24] On Earth, this is the reference by which to measure the effectiveness of a spiritual practice or philosophy of living. It follows that we can gauge our collective spirituality by the level of love and peace we find in the world. Harmony in a nation progresses in direct proportion to the morality and spirituality of its citizenship.

Adversity often serves as a catalyst to propel us forward, but troubles are not necessary to expand our spiritual insight. We can choose to start the journey anytime. Our consecration to spiritual growth will determine the boundaries we challenge and the perseverance we maintain as we progress in the adventure of cultivating universal intelligence.

25.

Understanding the Relation of Love to the Mind

You will learn to love your brethren more when you first learn to love their Father in heaven more, and after you have become truly more interested in their welfare in time and in eternity.

The Urantia Book

In *The Spirit and the Forms of Love*, Daniel Day Williams writes: "Love does not solve every problem, but without growth in love and in the capacity to receive love, the kind of knowledge of the world and of other persons which requires objectivity, dependability, and insight does not come . . . Without love the mind becomes the weapon of sophisticated violence. The love of wisdom becomes self-serving pride. Tradition becomes frozen dogma and descends into triviality and dishonesty. Scientific research into human problems becomes a wasteland of abstractions which never reach the human, or science may serve a demonic and inhuman evil as in the Nazi medical experiments. The intellect can serve love only when it is given its power and direction by love. This truth rests on no theological special-pleading, but on the evidence of human experience"[1]

What characterizes love? Is love a sensation, a bond, or a way of being? For the first thirty-five years of my life, I associated love with caring but also with its dark emotional shadows of rejection, abuse, and deceit. Though my Puerto Rican mother and English father were caring and loving parents, I often internalized my feelings, including the sadness I felt when on occasions my mother would casually push me aside if I tried to hug her.

When I was seven, I enjoyed the attention of my eighteen-year-old cousin, with whom I was occasionally left. When he started to fondle me inappropriately, I had difficulty reconciling why I felt as bad then as I did when my mother dismissed my displays of affection. During my first confession at the age of nine, the priest asked me to tell him every detail of what had happened with my cousin—and then he told me to say twenty Hail Mary's as penance.

That experience validated feelings of guilt and unworthiness and surely weakened my self-esteem. When I was a teenager, familiar feelings of discomfort surfaced when I was in the presence of my father and his secretary. Why did he visit her at home or buy her gifts unbeknown to my mother? When I married, I experienced the familiar feelings of rejection, abuse, and dishonesty and associated them with love. By the time I was thirty-five, I was emotionally numb and confused. Only with my children did I feel emotionally safe; yet my feelings remained guarded.

In 1990, I asked Ammachi, an Indian guru, if I would ever feel devotion in my lifetime. Her reply, "Love God because only God truly loves you," catapulted me into a spiritual roller-coaster ride that eventually led me to write this book.

Later, a series of providential happenings changed the course of my life by giving me the direct experience of God's love that eventually opened my heart to humanity. The increasing recognition of God's indwelling presence and a deepening appreciation of God became the portal through which I could expand my expression and ability to receive love. In this section, I share the insights that were gained in the exploration of my beliefs. Epochal revelation was a powerful source of light that melted my misinterpretations of love and clarified its transcendent meaning in human experience.

Are we Pure Divine Love, able to love and serve others selflessly at will, or do we have to cultivate our capacity to be unselfish? Can we grow love as we grow flowers in a garden? What is the connection between God, love, and the mind?

The answers to these questions will come after we fully recognize the relationship between love and unselfishness *and* differentiate love from our expressions of human affection that are so often misunderstood.

Unselfishness versus Self-Negation

Unselfishness is not a natural human characteristic. "It requires the enlightenment of reason, morality, and the urge of religion, God-knowingness, to generate an unselfish and altruistic social order."[2] Unselfishness is born of an increasing brotherhood consciousness and love that come with the recognition of God as Father of all.

Unselfishness—being selfless—isn't a masochistic tendency rooted in self-denial and suppression of desire. "The meaningless and menial practices of an ostentatious and false humility are incompatible with the appreciation of the source of your salvation and the recognition of the destiny of your spirit-born souls. Humility before God is altogether appropriate in the depths of your hearts; meekness before men is commendable; but the hypocrisy of self-conscious and attention-craving humility is childish and unworthy of the enlightened sons of the kingdom."[3] Well-intentioned acts of convenience or actions with expectation of reward may be benevolent, but still fall into the human realm of self-interest.

As we grow in our understanding of God, we grow in our appreciation of his selfless nature and the desire to emulate his nature in our relations with others—not from a sense of duty but from the inspiration of love. As we grow in awareness of our Indwelling Spirit, we increasingly recognize that godliness is the destiny of humanity. A spiritual reverence and deep conviction evolve within our soul, reflected in the declaration: "It is *my* will that *your* will be done."[4] In other words, I choose to show my love and appreciation for God by striving to be Godlike, thereby deepening the capacity to lovingly serve my fellow human beings.

A healthy family unit provides the best setting for learning unselfishness. Ideally, parents embrace the supreme responsibility of assisting the child in the battles of life by caring and through training the child to become a self-supporting, wise, loving, and honest individual who can contribute to the progress of civilization. The young adult attains respect and trust for her parents, not from obligations but as a result of the quality of care, training, and affection that the parents display. "The true parent is engaged in a continuous service-ministry which the wise child comes to recognize and appreciate."[5] Young adults are thus trained to expand their perception of a loving family to include their neighbors, their country, and the world.

This quality of unselfishness is the real measure of human greatness. To nurture the selfless element in moral behavior is to nurture the capacity to love, trust, and respect—capacities that thrive on knowledge of God and enhanced spiritual insight. We may have high moral standards and be idealistic, but growth in spiritual insight transforms morality into a driving force of enlightened change for societies and nations.

Love Defined

"Love is the outworking of the divine and inner urge of life. It is founded on understanding, nurtured by unselfish service, and perfected in wisdom."[6] Pure love activates the highest expression of trust, respect, and devotion, and rises above conditional feelings and circumstances. Known to the ancient Greeks as agape, it is the force that holds the various conditional expressions of human affection in place. "Agape has to do with the mind: it is not simply an emotion which rises unbidden in our hearts; it is a principle by which we deliberately live. Agape has supremely to do with the will."[7]

The personal attitude of love springs from loyalty to both divine duty and human need. It activates the unconditional and beneficial concern for the good of others and is expressed in respectful and unselfish behavior. Our depth of love and the quality of its expression is proportional to our comprehension of Deity, our efforts to cultivate the qualities of divinity, and our receptivity to the guidance of the Indwelling Spirit.

Unlike the instability of emotions or fickleness of affection, pure love is loyal, forgiving, reliable, compassionate, and truthful. A profound and poetic description of love is found in 1 Corinthians 13:4–7 (*New American Standard Bible*): "Love is patient, love is kind and is not jealous; love does not brag and is not arrogant, does not act unbecomingly; it does not seek its own, is not provoked, does not take into account a wrong suffered, does not rejoice in unrighteousness, but rejoices with the truth; bears all things, believes all things, hopes all things, endures all things." Without love, the other virtues lose their vigor.

Love and unselfishness go hand in hand. Selfishness is an inherent characteristic of human behavior; people outside the immediate family are not naturally loved or socially served. Therefore, unconditional love must be cultivated. "Love, unselfishness, must undergo a constant and living readaptative interpretation of relationships in accordance with the leading of the Spirit of Truth. Love must thereby grasp the ever-changing and enlarging concepts of the highest cosmic good of the individual who is loved. And then love goes on to strike this same attitude concerning all other individuals who could possibly be influenced by the growing and living relationship of one spirit-led mortal's love for other citizens of the universe. And this entire living adaptation of love must be effected in the light of both the environment of present evil and the eternal goal of the perfection of divine destiny."[8]

Conditional Expressions of Love

There are several expressions of human affection that are instinctive and, unless cultivated, often remain conditional:

- The natural liking or admiration people have for one another was known by the ancient Greeks as *phileo* and arises out of benevolence or common interests. Most friendships are built on phileo. It is the type of affection that says: "I like you *if* . . ."

- Familial love, which includes parental love, was labeled by the Greeks as *storge*. Storge is a strong, bonding, and protective love toward an animal, object, or person. A living being with storge feels a strong sense of duty and is often willing to die to protect this love. Storge is a conditional love that says: "I love you because I should." The strength and devotion of storge is often proportional to the need of the loved one and may be thwarted by influences such as ambition, selfishness, or religious conviction.

- Physical attraction, called *eros* by the ancient Greeks, is the chemical reaction, the sex urge, the infatuation between two people. "Notwithstanding the personality gulf between men and women, the sex urge is sufficient to insure their coming together for the reproduction of the species. This instinct operated effectively long before humans experienced much of what was later called love, devotion, and marital loyalty."[9] Eros is often mistaken for love and therefore easily abused. Without phileo and storge, eros is passion, the sex urge that, when unbridled, can devastate personal lives, its effect radiating into families and society. But the sex impulse is the catalyst that eventually leads to love. Eros gets beyond the romance stage with the support of phileo, storge, and agape, which helps sustain the friendship and spirituality that long-term relationships require.

The Heart and the Human Mind

After starting my journey into devotion, the most common expressions I heard were, "Follow your heart" and "Listen to your heart, not your mind." I knew that in spiritual circles, the heart had long been considered the energy center from which feelings of love emanated. While my friends kept insisting that love grows through the practice of meditation, I instinctively knew that a greater understanding of God was my path to loving more deeply.

Meditation is generally considered to be a technique for opening the heart to spirit, yet the spirituality I witnessed in the meditating community was not the vibrant and selfless spirituality that I truly desired. After years of meditation and deep subjective experiences, my connection to God remained impersonal and lacked devotion. Likewise, my relationships with others were friendly but guarded and often judgmental. I even found myself indulging in an "enlightened" self-image, the shadow of spiritual ego.

It wasn't until I allowed my mind to explore the *personality* of God through the cosmic lens of epochal revelation that I began to feel spiritual humility and sense a change in the quality and depth of my love for others. Reconciling these experiences with news from the emerging science of neurocardiology served to deepen my understanding of the subtle ties between the mind, heart, and spirit.

While the mind is "[t]he thinking, perceiving, and feeling mechanism of the human organism,"[10] scientists are offering new insight into the intimate connection between the heart and the brain: "Groundbreaking research in the field of neurocardiology has established that the heart is a sensory organ and a sophisticated information encoding and processing center, with an extensive intrinsic nervous system sufficiently sophisticated to qualify as a 'heart brain.'"[11] In fact, ". . . about sixty to sixty-five percent of all the cells in the heart are neural cells which are precisely the same as in the brain, functioning in precisely the same way, monitoring and maintaining control of the entire mind/brain/body physical process as well as direct unmediated connections between the heart and the emotional, cognitive structures of the brain."[12]

Humans were created and wired to know God and experience his love. The heart is where we "feel" love, and the mind is where the Indwelling Spirit fosters the love of God and individualizes the Father's love in each human soul. It is through the mind that we can know and love God and know and love our neighbors. Through the cultivation of universal intelligence and the application of those associated insights in our daily lives, we can experience the full and undiminished impact of the Father's love in our hearts.

The *quality* of our experience of the Father's love is always varied and unlimited. And though we can share human affection without developing our consciousness, that affection remains conditional, selective, and incomplete; it pales in comparison to the human reflection of divine and enduring love. The *quantity* of the Father's love that we experience is precisely measured by our spiritual receptivity and capacity to return the love of our Father. The more we know and love God as our Father, the better we can understand and live the familial relationship that we share with each human being. When we act with love toward our fellow humans, the Father's love becomes increasingly reflected in our experience, and that love is replete, compassionate, trusting, reverent, and unconditional.

The mind is the key to attaining new and higher spiritual meanings and values—and to expressing and experiencing greater love in our hearts. The cultivation of universal intelligence forges the gap between basic human affection and living agape love. "While the mind is not the seat of the spiritual nature, it is indeed the gateway thereto."[13]

Cultivating the Capacity to Love

The yearning for love is the most basic desire in a human being. Yet, to experience great depths of love, we must commit to an active and expanded understanding of its *source*; otherwise, we do not discover love's profound depth. This was my experience when learning how to play an instrument.

As a young teenager, my greatest desire was to play the guitar like my father. I loved the old songs he sang at social gatherings, many from his days courting my mother. In less than six months, I was playing all the songs I set out to learn and a few extra ones. Today I still play the same songs. If anyone asks me if I play guitar, I will certainly say yes; but I chose not to progress, not to find the joy of mastering the instrument. Instead, my choice was for comfortable mediocrity.

Let us look at some underpinnings of these personality dynamics.

Adults often relate to God as they did when they were children, that is, based on an immature understanding of God and the everyday needs in our lives. The years go by and, if we are attentive to spirit leading, we might think of ourselves as very spiritual and deeply connected with God. Yet promoting peace, studying scripture, talking about God, or feeling a strong connection with the divine is not an objective indicator of our understanding of God. Our capacity to love others is how a mature and holistic understanding expresses itself.

Our collective convergence with God is reflected in the health of our society. Peace confirms that we are in attunement with the spiritual realities of our universe. War, immorality, violence, and intolerance reflect a shallow and misguided understanding of God.

The mental activity of our mind forms thoughts. Some of these thoughts turn to desire. As a result of desire, choices are made. As we make choices to cultivate and harmonize our emotional and mental energies, we experience clarity of thought and develop emotional maturity. This enables us to express feelings and still remain calm under stress. Internal balance allows freedom of expression, depending on what is appropriate to the situation. We grow in self-confidence and self-control.

With the continued development of the intellect, we grow in ethical awareness and understanding of what behavior best serves our fellows. Such moral insight evolves as we make choices that take into consideration the welfare of others. As moral insight matures, we progress in social awareness and consistency of moral behavior, thereby improving the quality of our interactions with others.

When we critically examine our philosophies and expand our understanding of God and his relation to humankind and the universe, we enhance spiritual insight, we progress in spiritual meanings, and human wisdom advances. Such growth does not come without conflict. "New meanings only emerge amid conflict; and conflict persists only in the face of refusal to espouse the higher values connoted in superior meanings."[14]

As enhanced spiritual insight is infused into our intellectual, moral, and religious thinking, we develop a stereoscopic vision of higher spiritual meanings and values. As this vision comes into focus, a heightened cosmic perspective feeds our feeling of interconnectedness with each other and increases our capacity to love and develop a more selfless attitude. Making positive choices empowers us to change our lives and positively impact the lives of others, ultimately spinning a web of connective love that embraces all of humanity.

Growth in this cosmic perspective is in harmony with the will of God and reflects a growing response to our Indwelling Spirit. With this inner consecration, we profess: "It is my will that your will be done."[15] The moral qualities that we develop are further spiritualized to attain the fruits of the divine spirit, expressed in human behavior as:

- Loving service
- Unselfish devotion
- Courageous loyalty
- Sincere fairness
- Enlightened honesty
- Undying hope
- Confiding trust
- Merciful ministry
- Unfailing goodness
- Forgiving tolerance
- Enduring peace[16]

These personal habits are reflected in practical application by a harmonious and balanced person of faith attuned with the Indwelling Spirit. Such an integrated personality not only senses the presence of God but also understands the personality of God and becomes a catalyst for change—a living expression of loving kindness. Words and actions that are saturated with love create an influence that is sincere and good. We cannot observe the Indwelling Spirit at work, but by the degree of love, trust, and respect we feel toward our fellow humans, our brothers and sisters, it becomes obvious how much we have yielded to its teaching and leading.

26.

Exploring Beliefs

*Although survival may not depend
on the possession of knowledge and wisdom,
progression most certainly does.*

The Urantia Book

Discovering new and higher spiritual meaning in our religious understanding is one of the most important activities spiritual seekers can engage in today. Why? Because it is our responsibility, as evolving spiritual beings, to increasingly develop the cosmic perspective that will sustain peace and progress—in our personal lives and in our world.

This chapter stresses the importance of advancing human wisdom by upgrading beliefs, a goal that is driven by a strong commitment to cultivate the capacity to love, which is essential to that peace and progress we seek. With the aid of the latest epochal revelation, we can clarify our philosophies and reframe our beliefs. And as we improve the quality of spiritual knowledge, we will enhance our expression of goodness.

The greatest obstacles to acquiring an expanded perspective are fear and arrogance—fear of the unknown, and the certitude that our beliefs hold the exclusive truth. Many of us find our current set of beliefs adequate and see no value in critically investigating them. Even if we are interested in looking a little more deeply, time is a precious commodity, and there are always many other things we would rather be doing. The effort it takes to upgrade the quality of our thinking doesn't seem worth it, even if we don't have an aversion to change. But once we are willing to consider that becoming permeable to new ideas and diverse viewpoints is not only vital for our inner growth but essential to the peaceful advancement of civilization, the desire to follow truth flourishes.

In order to begin such an exploration, it is helpful to consider *how* the beliefs and perspectives we currently hold were formed. Much of the information on which our religious worldview is based has its origin in ancient teachings—revealed truth and historical events that were lost or subverted as they became absorbed into the teachings and ritual practices of the time. "In the absence of printing, when most human knowledge was passed by word of mouth from one generation to another, it was very easy for myths to become traditions and for traditions eventually to become accepted as facts."[1]

Religious beliefs have varied through the ages and from culture to culture. Where freedom of religion is practiced today, beliefs can be as transient as fads while dogmatic differences enflame disunity. But now an epic text, a new revelation, has been given to humankind at a time when philosophies are in dire need of greater clarity, and extreme religious zeal threatens global stability.

Since 1955, humanity has had access to the printed form of the fifth epochal revelation, which has the potential to uplift all gospels, resolve the greatest mysteries of human existence, and in the process, create universal harmony. Epochal revelation expands the truth in our beliefs by restoring important bits of lost knowledge and filling in vital gaps. It synthesizes science and religion into a consistent and logical universe philosophy that can be explored and evaluated in light of existing knowledge to attain an enlarged cosmic perspective.[2]

Without progressive revelation, we struggle to generate in our decisions and actions the spiritual power necessary to transform societies. Global conditions confirm that current worldviews are unable to sustain a growing spiritual nature or foster the reasoning that is increasingly more objective, inclusive, moral, loving, and selfless.

The Adventure of Reflection

Both aversion to religious confusion and commitment to accuracy energized my search for an orderly universe; resolving the inconsistencies and inaccuracies in my beliefs became the compelling drive that resulted in *Heaven Is Not the Last Stop*. The insights that I share were gained after many years of intellectual effort and spiritual struggle.

An unexpected but welcomed development during this process was a deeper heartfelt connection with God. In the interest of spiritual unity, I also felt a strong commitment to help others rediscover the true meaning of religion. Courage, one of the teachings of Jesus, is a virtue that has blossomed in me—it overcomes all anxieties that stand in the way of the journey into joyful service.

Exploring beliefs in the light of the latest epochal revelation and reflecting on cosmic relations is not an easy task. Forming questions, musing on implications, and welcoming debate takes faith, motivation, and courage. It is easier to rationalize an inconsistency than to resolve it. As I engaged in exploration, I wrestled with uncomfortable questions such as, "Am I being disloyal to God if I critically assess my current beliefs?" and "Will I lose my faith?"

The path to growth is never easy, and this is most evident in our spiritual lives. Confusion, frustration, and despair are common encounters. But persevere! The cosmic perspective that builds greater understanding and advances wisdom will emerge . . . with patience.

Your process of exploration might begin with a question that has been percolating in the back of your mind, just waiting to be challenged. Opening your mind to new understanding never threatens your faith; in fact, it ultimately enhances it. Your current framework of beliefs orients you toward particular behaviors and religious habits, and toward interpreting your experiences in a specific way. When you explore your beliefs in the light of epochal revelation, you expand your framework of understanding in new and unexpected ways.

Epochal revelation informs us that "[t]ruth can be *acted out*; it can be lived."[3] You will know that you have synthesized genuine revealed knowledge and expanded the truth in your beliefs when you are spending less time judging others and more time developing a noble and selfless character, and when you witness an increase in the quality of your decisions and actions.

An online survey sponsored by the nonprofit organization Reaching Common Ground, conducted by Harris Interactive in May 2004, determined that the majority of adult Americans (69%) believe that religious differences are the biggest barrier to global peace.[4] But this need not be the case.

Breaching the religious barriers to world peace is a process that begins with the recognition that unity of spirit is not dependent on uniformity of beliefs. It is possible for people of all faiths to effect cooperation on the basis of *unity of ideals and purposes*. Love, respect, tolerance, forgiveness, mercy, human rights, peace, brotherhood, and freedom are the fundamental ideals exalted by all religions.

The process continues when we recognize that religious dissension arises not because our beliefs are different but because we have closed the circuits of expanding truth. The motivation to open to ever new understanding and experiences will strengthen our capacity to arrive at valid conclusions, discriminate between sound and unsound points of view, and still have respect and compassionate understanding for those who perceive spirit realities differently than we do. Any prior conflicts can be converted into reasonable and friendly discussion; tense debates about who is wrong and who is right can be replaced by a shared adventure of exploring points of connection and points of divergence.

To achieve collective peace requires that we understand where each religious perspective fits into the Big Picture of Existence. The fifth and latest epochal revelation found in *The Urantia Book* validates the truths in all religions; it then synthesizes and expands them, bringing to humanity a more logical and consistent philosophic concept of the universe. This integration of science and religion harmonizes the mind and reveals a personal spiritual goal of progressive personality achievement. When individuals appreciate their shared origin and destiny, this transforms faith into a living experience that expresses increasing wisdom and goodness, magnifying the effects of collaborative cooperation.

And this understanding must embrace the domain of science as well in order to be effective at addressing today's problems: "When both science and religion become less dogmatic and more tolerant of criticism, philosophy will then begin to achieve unity in the intelligent comprehension of the universe."[5]

In Conclusion

The ideas, ideals, and loyalties that you personally discover when you explore beliefs in light of epochal revelation will enrich your spiritual affiliations and aid the movement of all religions towards spiritual unity. "The old cults were too egocentric; the new must be the outgrowth of applied love. The new cult must, like the old, foster sentiment, satisfy emotion, and promote loyalty; but it must do more: It must facilitate spiritual progress, enhance cosmic meanings, augment moral values, encourage social development, and stimulate a high type of personal religious living. The new cult must provide supreme goals of living which are both temporal and eternal—social and spiritual."[6]

The conflicting emotions experienced during this sifting process are relieved by reaffirming personal faith and having an overarching, supreme purpose that defines all our goals. As spiritual discernment is activated and fresh insights are applied, we grow in completeness of knowledge and in fullness of personal experience.

27.

Elevating the Quality of Thinking

We can't solve problems by using the same kind
of thinking we used when we created them.
Albert Einstein

Thinking is a mental process that most of us take for granted. We rarely consider the intricacies and complexities of thinking. Yet, without training, the mind is limited in what it does. To improve the quality of thinking, therefore, is to develop objective and reflective mind skills.

Like most people, I learned the rudiments of thinking in school, where I was coached in memory work but challenged little to think analytically. A life of stubborn inquiry and deep reflection was initiated by some unexplainable experiences I had at a young age. I was drawn to abstract learning and solving mysteries. I often questioned what others said, and discovered that their answers often raised more questions.

I now realize that one's passion for deep thinking is sparked by personal curiosity and the desire to search for elusive answers. Without personal motivation or ideals to inspire us, and without proper training, the ability to reflect and critically analyze remains largely undeveloped and/or declines from atrophy. It remains, therefore, the joint responsibility of parents and teachers to cultivate critical-thinking skills and habits in children.

[R]ealize that culling out thought and strengthening the mind are an entirely different and higher process from the putting in of knowledge and the heaping up of facts.
John Ruskin (1819–1900)

The National Council for Excellence in Critical Thinking offers this definition: "Critical thinking is the intellectually disciplined process of actively and skillfully conceptualizing, applying, analyzing, synthesizing and/or evaluating information gathered from or generated by observation, experience, reflection, reasoning, or communication as a guide to belief or action. In its exemplary form, it is based on universal intellectual values that transcend subject matter divisions: clarity, accuracy, precision, consistency, relevance, sound evidence, good reasons, depth, breadth, and fairness."[1] The ability to recognize gaps in knowledge and construct an appropriate path of exploration by which to address and fill those gaps is one of the most important skills we can learn.

If a populace is never taught the basics of analytical inquiry, there are serious consequences: intellectual apathy and a lazy acquiescence to indoctrination. Without objective and reflective mind skills, we are easy prey for those who pander immorality, greed, violence, and other selfish vices that blunt our compassion for one another.

As a volunteer mediator working with youth, I witnessed the failure of the educational system to incorporate thoughtful deliberation as part of the learning cycle. There are too many young adults who act without thinking and once in trouble, cannot understand the impact of their actions. They often have no remorse for their choices and the injuries these have caused. Their only regret is that they were caught.

The crisis that our educational system faces is reflected in a phone call I received from a former special-education student who had relocated. She was a slow reader and found it hard to listen with comprehension and to use correct grammar. Four years earlier, I had taught her basic Spanish and privately tutored her twice a week so she could stay abreast of the class. Within a few months, she surpassed her classmates in the subject, and in two years she was conversing fluently at her level and was comfortable with Spanish grammar. In her new school, without the necessary support and encouragement, she gave up on Spanish and failed many of her tenth-grade classes, yet had been passed through to the eleventh grade. She felt as if she were just a number, automatically advanced without anyone caring or addressing her educational needs and learning challenges. She was afraid of leaving high school unprepared for the workforce or college.

"Unprepared" describes many high school students at the end of their senior year. National surveys have found that the average high school and college graduate lacks academic skills and advanced applied skills such as critical thinking, problem solving, creativity, and innovation—essential for effective citizenship. This is not surprising since rigorous intellectual standards have been squeezed out of classrooms in favor of memorization. Far too many students are being taught how to pass tests to raise collective scores rather than how to think and learn. "Peter, James, and Andrew were the committee designated by Jesus to pass upon applicants for admission to the school of evangelists . . . This school was conducted on the plan of learning and doing."[2]

Without enlightened education, individuals lose respect for knowledge, experience, and the opinions of others. The pursuit of wisdom gets sidetracked. A system that lowers standards to accommodate the masses is a social disaster in the making. If we want a more responsible and less apathetic society, we should implement creative methods of developing our students.

Critical thinking requires self-reliance of thought. Intelligent action becomes possible only when we are able to systematically and objectively evaluate the merit of our knowledge, skills, attitudes, and actions. The process is explained by Ruth A. Rosenbaum, TC, PhD, in her article titled "Factoids, Facts, Information, Knowledge, Wisdom": "We only approach wisdom when we can sort through different perspectives and see how the pieces of facts come together. Patterns, rather than a disarray of information, allow greater understanding of the dynamics of the interplay between the facts. Patterns allow us to see the flow of knowledge and/or power within a situation or a system. Often the willingness and ability to look at the facts in a new alignment will provide an insight into the systems at work. The pieces of mosaic now become a kaleidoscope. As we turn the kaleidoscope and hold it up to new light, the pieces come together in different patterns, enabling us to see different associations of color, or facts. We see new realities, and become aware of what sources are missing from which we have yet to receive factual information."[3]

When people lack advanced thinking skills, they hesitate to reflectively question—but questioning is the fulcrum of progressive life-examination and the basis of all personal growth. Reflection is an important aspect of critical thinking because it evokes meaningful questions: What went well? What didn't? Why? How do I feel about it?

We reflect to evaluate our experiences and learn from our mistakes, to identify what worked and to repeat our successes. Effective inquiry promotes growth in understanding by creating opportunities to explain, clarify, explore, make connections, and identify problems and issues. When an answer generates another question, the life of a thought continues.

In an article titled "The Critical Mind is a Questioning Mind," the authors explain that, as a species, "[t]here are too many domains of our thinking that we, collectively, do not want questioned. We have too many prejudices that we do not want challenged. We are committed to having our vested interests served. We are not in fact typically concerned to protect the rights of others. We are not typically willing to sacrifice our own desires to meet someone else's basic needs. We do not want to discover that beliefs which we have taken to be 'obvious' and 'sacred' might be neither. We will ignore any number of basic principles, if in doing so, we can maintain or gain power and advantage."[4]

As a result, the article continues, ". . . the standards that humans instinctively use to assess thinking are not only intellectually flawed but actually intellectually absurd." The authors provide examples of psychological reasoning that inhibits most people from questioning:

1. **"It's true because I believe it."** (Innate egocentrism: continually assuming a belief is true without questioning the basis for the belief.)

2. **"It's true because we believe it."** (Innate sociocentrism: continually assuming that the dominant beliefs of one's group are true without questioning the basis for the beliefs.)

3. **"It's true because I want to believe it."** (Innate wish fulfillment: behavior that creates a positive rather than a negative self- or group image without considering contrary evidence. Belief in feel-good,

supportive statements that do not require a change in thinking or require self-exoneration.)

4. **"It's true because I have always believed it."** (Innate self-validation: feeling a strong ego-attraction to long-held beliefs without seriously considering the evidence for the critique of those traditional beliefs.)

5. **"It's true because it is my vested interest to believe it."** (Innate selfishness: gravitating to beliefs that would justify power, money, or personal advantage without questioning the substance of those beliefs.)

Recognizing flawed reasoning in oneself or in others is an essential step to breaking free from chronic patterns of self-deception and narcissism—which are the bonds of intellectual and spiritual unreality.

To develop better reasoning skills:

• Read nonfiction books and persuasive essays and articles.

• Practice writing, especially persuasive essays.

• Engage in understanding more science.

• Attend specialized critical-thinking courses.

• Engage in activities that require active use of the mind. These may include solving anagrams, puzzles, and brain teasers; researching and responsibly debating or discussing current issues and controversies; questioning authority and probing into alternatives to the status quo, when there is good reason to do so.

• Watch less television. Avoid mindless discussion, arguing without a point, listening passively (without participating), and accepting the status quo without question.

As we develop our reasoning skills, we begin to entertain alternative ideas and think from alternative perspectives. We develop a healthy objectivity that may detect and correct exaggerations or distortions. And, as we simultaneously grow in moral insight, we develop a greater sense of duty toward the welfare of others and cultivate moral virtues such as fair-mindedness, honesty, and integrity, which further elevates our thinking and the quality of our actions.

While it is true that you can be moral without much intellectual training, development of ethical awareness enables you to improve the quality of your interactions with others by increasing your capacity to put yourself in their place. "Critical thinking varies according to the motivation underlying it. When grounded in selfish motives, it is often manifested in the skillful manipulation of ideas in service of one's own, or one's groups' vested interest. As such it is typically intellectually flawed, however pragmatically successful it might be. When grounded in fair-mindedness and intellectual integrity, it is typically of a higher order intellectually, though subject to the charge of 'idealism' by those habituated to its selfish use."[5]

We can become critical and ethical thinkers without religion, but without growth in spiritual insight, we do not develop the enlarged consciousness of the fatherhood of God and the brotherhood of man—which has the driving power to make a better society. "As religion evolves, ethics becomes the philosophy of morals, and morality becomes the discipline of self by the standards of highest meanings and supreme values—divine and spiritual ideals. And thus religion becomes a spontaneous and exquisite devotion, the living experience of the loyalty of love."[6] This brings to the forefront a great challenge, for without living faith, growth in spiritual insight—the highest order of thinking—does not occur.

If new and higher meanings and values require the development of spiritual insight, then this challenge will be taken up by a critical thinker regardless of religious orientation or lack thereof. To a believer, the challenge lies in questioning the tenets of religion without losing faith in God or spiritual ideals. For a nonbeliever the challenge is being open to the possibility of the reality of God, with personal experience being the only positive proof of God's existence. While physical and moral truths can be validated by others, the certainty of spirit realities is only validated within.

Clarity and expansion of truth in religious beliefs is as essential to the advancement of civilization as is the development of thoughtful deliberation. The ability to critically reflect and think enhances the integration of the facts of science with the values of religion—but logic without faith will not harmonize them.

A personality who sincerely desires to follow the truth will think about both the scientific and religious aspects of any issue, wherever it may lead. When we are guided by faith to explore beliefs in the light of epochal revelation and reflect on our findings, we validate the harmony that exists between science and religion, thereby advancing human wisdom and reducing religious speculation.

28.

Developing Emotional Maturity

The Inside-Out approach to personal and interpersonal effectiveness means
to start first with self; even more fundamentally, to start with the most inside
part of self—with your paradigms, your character, and your motives.
Stephen Covey, *The 7 Habits of Highly Effective People*

Development of emotional maturity is a complex topic addressed by many experts in the field of psychospiritual health. This chapter briefly touches on various wisdom teachings that have been useful to me in the ongoing process of self-transformation, including insights gleaned from revelation.

To develop emotional maturity is to recognize and address our character weaknesses and to reinforce our strengths. Author, I. K. Taimni, in the book *Gâyatrî*, expresses the importance of this process: "Before any spiritual light from the innermost recesses of our being can break through into the realms of our mind, much has to be accomplished. Impurities have to be removed, distortions have to be straightened out, and the vehicles have to be harmonized. It is only in such a prepared mind, freed from these ordinary defects that the light of higher knowledge can manifest."[1]

What is emotional maturity? After years of testing and research, sociologist Dwight G. Dean compiled a list of emotional maturity attributes that can be used as goals or guidelines, adapted below:

Stress. Maintains a sense of balance and equanimity in dealing with stress; knows personal boundaries; takes responsibility for personal feelings, actions, and emotions.

Anger. Handles frustration and anger constructively and as catalysts for social improvement.

Authority. Accepts the laws of the land and hierarchies.

Integration. Is integrated in personal "philosophy of life." Perseveres despite doubt or obstacles. Is patient, decisive, and firm in commitments.

Self-control. Exercises self-control in difficult situations; thinks before acting. Experiences emotions more fully, and their control is expressed more deliberately. Stops negative thoughts from becoming destructive. Controls speech.

Intellectual maturity. Is fair minded. Is prudent (farsighted and sensible) in making judgments. Habitually seeks facts before making decisions. Is inquisitive (curious, questioning). Is open minded (unbiased, flexible). Is able to evaluate new ideas rather than accepting or rejecting them blindly.

Relationships. Sustains an intimate relationship with a significant other, progressing from an undeveloped potential toward a deeply and mutually satisfying relationship. Values and nourishes personal relationships. Is able to establish positive connections with others.

Attitude toward learning. Is mentally alert and eager to learn. Learns from experience. Relates positively to life experiences.

Responsibility. Is trustworthy and reliable. Faces challenges and deals with them constructively. Keeps commitments.

Ego/Sociocenteredness. Is generous and can be emotionally present for others.

Communication. Communicates effectively on various levels from superficial conversation to deep intimacy. Builds stronger ties with family, colleagues, and friends through empathy and compassion.

Emotional security/self esteem. Readily admits when he/she is wrong. Is open to honest feedback. Has self-confidence, healthy self-worth, and self-respect. [2]

We develop emotional maturity to the extent that we empower ourselves to wisely and appropriately respond to events in our lives. The characteristics of emotional excellence are eloquently exemplified in the life of Jesus: "He lived in the midst of stress and storm, but he never wavered. His enemies continually laid snares for him, but they never entrapped him. The wise and learned endeavored to trip him, but he did not stumble. They sought to embroil him in debate, but his answers were always enlightening, dignified, and final. When he was interrupted in his discourses with multitudinous questions, his answers were always significant and conclusive. Never did he resort to ignoble tactics in meeting the continuous pressure of his enemies, who did not hesitate to employ every sort of false, unfair, and unrighteous mode of attack upon him."[3]

The first step in developing emotional maturity is perhaps the most difficult: recognizing dysfunctional habits—negative attitudes, emotions, and behaviors that hinder the development of our higher potentials. Once these are identified, we can outline a corrective course and bring balance to our character. Some elements of emotional maturity are addressed elsewhere in this section, but this chapter focuses on three major challenges: self-esteem, anger, and self-control.

Recognizing Dysfunctional Habits

There are varieties of detrimental attitudes, emotions, and behaviors that become habitual and negatively program our minds: intolerance, hypocrisy, suspicion, envy, jealousy, cheating, fault-finding, codependency, lying, pessimism, counterproductive work/school habits, hostility, avarice, cruelty, backbiting, selfishness, addictions (smoking, drinking, drugs, food, etc.), compulsions, and obsessions. Other impediments to growth include shyness, tardiness, procrastination, circumventing obligations, dishonesty, problem avoidance, unfairness, and laziness.

Sometimes we are able to derail a dysfunctional habit simply by increased awareness, easily accommodating the corrective action. But many times the reasons are hidden or challenging and result in:

- Unintentional self-deception and rationalizations, such as the smoker who believes smoking calms the nerves, a benefit greater than its deadly long-term effects. Irrational beliefs such as, "I am not good enough," "I am never going to grow up," "This is the way I am," "I am addicted," "I enjoy what I am doing," and "I can't change" can keep individuals on a roller coaster of uncontrolled emotions and in dysfunctional patterns and/or relationships.

- Unconscious motives (the "social" drink that masks self-doubt or lack of self-esteem)

- Emotional reactions that overpower our best intentions.

Effective and corrective action to foster psychospiritual health becomes possible only when we overcome the reluctance to face ourselves and take responsibility for our lives. Human nature leads us to believe what we want to believe, and to see only things that confirm those beliefs, especially about ourselves. Such attitudes keep us from seeking and discovering higher values that enhance our lives and relationships. "When men shut off the appeal to the spirit that dwells within them, there is little that can be done to modify their attitude."[4]

To grow in emotional maturity is to choose an area that needs improvement and then take steps to reprogram ourselves and develop positive habits—the mental and behavioral patterns that open us to greater possibilities. "Successful living is nothing more or less than the art of the mastery of dependable techniques for solving common problems. The first step in the solution of any problem is to locate the difficulty, to isolate the problem, and frankly to recognize its nature and gravity. The great mistake is that, when life problems excite our profound fears, we refuse to recognize them. Likewise, when the acknowledgment of our difficulties entails the reduction of our long-cherished conceit, the admission of envy, or the abandonment of deep-seated prejudices, the average person prefers to cling to the old illusions of safety and to the long-cherished false feelings of security. Only a brave person is willing honestly to admit, and fearlessly to face, what a sincere and logical mind discovers."[5]

Some of the ways that we can identify dysfunctional behavior patterns include the following:

1. **Self-observation**: Think about your thoughts, speech, and behavior—
   you will discover and determine where there is room for improvement.
   Through self-observation, we can recognize a behavior pattern that is
   producing less than desired results and then take steps to transform it.
   "Universe progress is characterized by increasing personality freedom
   because it is associated with the progressive attainment of higher and
   higher levels of self-understanding and consequent voluntary self-
   restraint."[6] Self-observation doesn't equate to punishing ourselves for
   not being perfect; it identifies opportunities for growth and
   improvement.

2. **Getting Feedback from Our Surroundings**: We can learn volumes about
   ourselves by observing the effect our behavior has on others. Are we
   surprised that our aggressive behavior provokes a defensive response?
   Are we aware that a lie breeds distrust? Do we accept that sexual
   irresponsibility leads to disease, sorrow, and broken relationships, that it
   weakens the family unit? How often do we find ourselves in
   circumstances that are inharmonious, and then blame others for the
   disharmony? We may even relocate or change relationships, home, or
   jobs to get away from the discord, only to find ourselves in chronic self-
   sabotage. Recurring disharmony and lack of success may be signs that
   some facet of our behavior is not serving us and must be addressed.
   Being sensitive to the effect of our behavior on our surroundings makes
   us more open to honest self-analysis and healthy adjustment.

3. **Requesting Feedback from Others**: In his book *The Success Principles*,
   Jack Canfield suggests that one of the best ways to improve personal
   and business relationships is to make a habit of asking two questions of
   the important people in our lives: "On a scale of 1 to 10, how would you
   rate the quality of our relationship?" This question may be asked
   concerning any situation, for example, our sex life, my cooking, or my
   parenting. Any answer less than 10 informs us of dissatisfaction. A
   second question provides the most useful information: "What would it
   take to make it a 10?" This is a request for positive suggestions for
   improvement rather than criticism. With corrective feedback, we can
   take the steps to improve any situation, including behavior modification.

4. **Giving and Receiving Constructive Criticism**: Criticism can be a bitter
   pill. Many people haven't learned the art of tactfully and
   compassionately giving constructive feedback. Common defensive
   reactions may well block opportunities to learn and grow and also
   invoke distrust born of the feeling that honesty invites an unkind
   response. Welcoming criticism with the mindset that we are collecting
   information will do the opposite; it will build confidence and trust while
   it fosters humility. Making an effort to understand the facts behind the
   criticism is a big step in the right direction. As we develop an
   empathetic attitude, we allow that the criticism may have been valid.
   The emotions aroused by criticism can be translated into motivation to

take corrective action, if necessary, and to delight in discovering the route to a more balanced and fulfilling behavior.

5. **Journaling**. Keeping a journal is an effective way to develop and practice thinking skills and increase self-understanding. Daily entries may include day-to-day experiences, specifically noting any challenging interactions with others. By recording our thoughts, feelings, and responses, we can begin to understand and unravel our behavior patterns. I started keeping a journal at the age of eighteen. My journal was the one place where I could express my innermost desires, goals, and fears. It was in rereading journal entries that I was able to identify recurring negative patterns of behavior. Once I acknowledged the behaviors, I was able to explore their root cause. This gave me the impetus to seek professional help and read self-development books. As I understood myself better, I was able to make life-altering changes. As improvement is an ongoing process, I still keep a journal.

Recognition of a particular unwanted attitude or behavior is the first step toward resolving it. This creative activity of the mind, when directed toward appropriate action, will eventually lead to balanced emotions and more intimate communion with the Indwelling Spirit. To overcome dysfunctional habits, a *deliberate plan of corrective action* must be undertaken individually, as part of a group, or both. Medical plans or twelve-step programs for help in overcoming addictions are commonly available. Attitude problems that are not addiction-based can be improved when a conscious effort produces better choices. For example, instead of being critical or sarcastic, we simply decide to either say nothing at all, or to responsibly express *how we feel in response to* another person rather than *what we think about* that person.

These new behaviors must be consciously repeated until a positive attitude becomes natural. It requires a methodical process of willful and directed thought and action, with commitment to train and develop the mind, thereby bringing the negative emotions underlying our dysfunctional behavior under control.

Self-Esteem

The way we perceive ourselves has much to do with how we interact with others. According to the National Association for Self-Esteem (NASE), individuals with healthy self-esteem are tolerant and respectful toward others and themselves. "They accept responsibility for their actions, have integrity, take pride in their accomplishments, are self-motivated, willing to take risks, are capable of handling criticism, are loving and lovable, seek the challenge and stimulation of worthwhile and demanding goals, and take command and control of their lives."[7] A healthy self-esteem finds balance between an equal sense of self-worth and self-respect supported by appropriate ethical behavior. "Self-respect is always coordinate with the love and service of one's fellows. It is not possible to respect yourself more than you love your neighbor; the one is the measure of the capacity for the other."[8] People with healthy self-esteem take responsibility for their lives and learn from feedback. They are always open to opportunities for self-improvement and for social service.

Low self-esteem is one of the major roadblocks to developing emotional maturity. It presents itself in many ways, and recognizing it is sometimes difficult. For example, I always thought I was self-motivated, a risk-taker, and a confident and tolerant person; yet, with honest reflection, I recognized that my boisterous behavior and tendency to monopolize conversations were just cover-ups for my low self-esteem. Balancing self-esteem with true humility is a lifelong project—I always need to consider low self-estem as a possible factor in behavior that I am trying to improve.

Low self-esteem favors a nagging internal voice of self-disapproval that transforms everyday issues into confrontations and obstacles. This subversive component of stunted emotional maturity often results in destructive behavior that colors all our interactions, such as repressed anger, arising from the belief that we are being treated unfairly. Low self-esteem breeds irrational thoughts and is characterized by self-criticism, self-rejection, and self-contempt. Depression, anxiety, obsessive-compulsive tendencies, phobias, and related personality disorders reflect emotional distress and unconscious conflict that may be rooted in low self-esteem. Some of humanity's worst mental health problems, such as suicide, alcoholism, and drug abuse, may also reflect low self-esteem. People with low self-esteem tend to lack self-confidence and attribute their successes to luck rather than to their own abilities. "Low self-esteem is kind of the spark plug for self-destructive behaviors, and drug use is one of these."[9]

On the other hand, egocentric self-esteem and narcissism instill feelings of superiority, entitlement, and vanity that also serve as catalysts for socially destructive behaviors. This imbalance is personified in obsessive self-admiration, a strong sense of personal grandeur, seductive and manipulative behavior, unscrupulous striving for gratification and power, willingness to sacrifice personal integrity for self-centered needs, and insensitivity to the needs of others. Excessive self-admiration tends toward exploitation for personal aggrandizement and possession of unjust power over others and is not synonymous with self-respect. Self-absorption, self-centeredness, and selfishness characterize a narcissistic personality. Arrogance, insolence, hostility, and anger are central to the emotional life of the narcissist, triggered by perceived threats to personal and social images. Jesus had profound words of balance on this topic, still relevant today: "While overmuch self-respect may destroy proper humility and end in pride, conceit, and arrogance, the loss of self-respect often ends in paralysis of the will. It is the purpose of this gospel to restore self-respect to those who have lost it and to restrain it in those who have it."[10]

Researchers in the past have reported a close relationship between low self-esteem and problems such as violence. However, recent studies on violence, aggression, and antisocial behavior have yielded mixed results. According to a group of psychologists led by Florida State University Francis Eppes Professor Roy Baumeister, ". . . neither high self-esteem nor low self-esteem is a direct cause of violence, although narcissism leads to increased aggression in retaliation for wounded pride. Certain subcategories of high self-esteem also yield both the highest and the lowest rates of antisocial behavior such as cheating or bullying. On the other hand, low self-esteem may be a contributing factor to delinquency."[11]

According to Baumeister, "Raising self-esteem will not by itself make young people perform better in school, obey the law, stay out of trouble, get along better with their fellows or respect the rights of others . . . A better approach . . . would be to boost self-esteem as a reward for ethical behavior and worthy achievements."[12]

Self-esteem becomes balanced as we engage in true spiritual living. Whether a person has low self-esteem or a narcissistic attitude, cultivation of spiritual insight promotes ethical behavior and the cosmic perspective that builds an awareness that we are sons and daughters of God—cosmic citizens, brothers and sisters all, indwelt by a fragment of the Universal Father of all. "The marks of human response to the religious impulse embrace the qualities of nobility and grandeur. The sincere religionist is conscious of universe citizenship and is aware of making contact with sources of superhuman power. He is thrilled and energized with the assurance of belonging to a superior and ennobled fellowship of the sons of God. The consciousness of self-worth has become augmented by the stimulus of the quest for the highest universe objectives—supreme goals."[13]

This realization of the familial connection with God and one another is a motivator for greater altruistic service and provides the highest inspiration to transform our lives. Without growth in spiritual insight, our full potential goes unachieved.

As we actively develop a cosmic perspective, the use of practical exercises and activities that encourage increased personal understanding of others may help to bring balance to our self-esteem. I have personally found the following to be helpful:

- Recite the following affirmation several times during the day, before going to bed at night, and when you get up in the morning: "I am a beloved son (daughter) of God." Feel the words when you say them.

- Volunteer. Teach another a skill you know well.

- Surround yourself with positive, supportive, and respectful people.

- Make a list of your present and past accomplishments, such as graduating from high school or college, receiving a promotion, and learning a new language. Include your social service accomplishments. Strive to enter into new activities that bring balance to your list.

- Refrain from comparing yourself to other people or repeating negative phrases about yourself and your abilities. Become aware when you are whining, boasting, demanding, or putting yourself down. Awareness can be an incentive for change.

- Make a list of your positive qualities and virtues. Review it often.

- Surround yourself with uplifting music and spend more time in nature.

- Take time each day for reflection and personal development activities. Attend workshops, read books, or listen to audio programs on self-development. Put into practice what you learn.

- Develop or strengthen your communication and conflict-resolution skills.

- Perform one action daily that benefits the well-being of another.

- Commit to doing your best at everything you try. When you feel that you have done your best, everyone benefits and there are no regrets.

- Reward yourself when you succeed through honest efforts and not at the expense of others.

- Practice self-forgiveness. This act of self-love enables us to accept ourselves as humans who have faults and make mistakes. When we forgive ourselves, we calm self-rejection, quiet the sense of failure, and lighten the burden of guilt. The practice of self-forgiveness empowers us to let go of all inward-directed negativity.

- Talk with a counselor or therapist to learn more about your self-esteem issues. If you are suffering from characterological depression, a result of low self-esteem, or have a narcissistic personality disorder, a professional can help you balance your self-image, using proven therapeutic approaches.

Self-Control

The exercise of self-control is essential to develop emotional maturity. Self-control may be defined as the ability to make decisions about how and when to express feelings, and on which impulses to act. In *Tools for Coping with Life's Stressors*, the authors define self-control as a set of behaviors that:

" 1. Accepts the reality that the only thing in life which you can successfully change and control is yourself.

2. Keeps in check all self-destructive, addictive, obsessive, compulsive, irrational, and unacceptable behaviors.

3. Gives you a sense of personal mastery, autonomy, and competency over your own life.

4. Is under your control and power to direct and orchestrate with no need for interference or manipulation from others.

5. Makes you the master of your own destiny because it keeps in check those barriers and obstacles which are a threat to your overall success in life.

6. Is a middle ground between perfectionism and laxity in self care.

7. Results in your life having a balance and focus by helping you to cope with new challenges in life as they come.

8. Helps you to keep your over-emotional responses in check or moderation.

9. Helps you to open yourself up from nonfeeling or pulled-in emotions so that you can have a healthy emotional life.

10. Is the foundation for healthy coping and contributes to your accepting personal responsibility for your life.

11. Keeps your life in moderation, helping you to avoid extremes in any direction.

12. Is the focus of the efforts to let go of the uncontrollables and unchangeables in your life so that you can concentrate on yourself.

13. Eliminates the need for you to be manipulative, helpless, fixing others, intimidating, overdependent or a caretaker of others.

14. Helps you to be detached from others and to keep your relationships in a healthy balance of give and take.

15. Reflects your inner desire to grow up into a mature, responsible adult."[14]

Emotions such as boredom, anger, guilt, depression, resentment, loneliness, wounded pride, and fear are common triggers for lack of self-control. To achieve self-control, therefore, requires awareness of our attitudes and behaviors and constant corrective actions. "Self-denial and self-control were two of the greatest social gains from early evolutionary religion. Self-control gave man a new philosophy of life . . ."[15] This is the art of increasing self-control by lowering personal demands instead of increasing the demand for selfish gratification. As spiritual insight is developed, we cultivate our capacity to love so that our behavior increasingly reflects wise and loving goodness.

> *Activity in a certain thing gives a man that character—dispositions are attained through actually doing things.*
>
> *Ethics*, Book III
> *The Philosophy of Aristotle*

We can have the best intentions to improve ourselves, but unless we are clear about our goals, intentions, standards, and action steps, it is unlikely that we will maintain a successful momentum. Planned action steps, with professional assistance when needed, help convert destructive thought, speech, and action into more constructive forms. Through the conscious and directed use of the mind, we develop the functional habits that assist us in mastering our emotions, enhancing our spirit connection, and improving our relations with others.

As we pursue self-control, it helps to be aware of the common pitfalls so that we may identify them in our evaluation process. In the e-book *Psychological Self-Help*, Dr. Clayton E. Tucker-Ladd illustrates how we often stunt our progress:

" 1. We set no goals or set impossible goals;

2. We lose control or don't pay attention to our goals or to our behavior;

3. We quit because we get tired or stressed and weakened;

4. We attend to our immediate situation and needs, overlooking long-range goals;

5. We misjudge what is important to do;

6. We focus on calming our emotions but lose focus on doing our tasks or solving our problems;

7. We become obsessed with protecting our egos and neglect getting the job done;

8. We let the initial failure lead to a 'snowballing' of many failures;

9. We believe in venting our feelings rather than in eliminating the emotions;

10. We decide we are helpless or bad and stop trying in order to avoid further failure."[16]

According to Dr. Tucker-Ladd, when effecting change, the first attempt is usually the most difficult. If you haven't exercised in months or have smoked for years, the first day is the toughest. You must use willpower, motivation, or self-talk. Dr. Sidney Simon, author of *Getting Unstuck: Breaking Through Your Barriers to Change*, suggests building willpower by:

" 1. Practicing in [increasingly] difficult self-control situations;

2. Taking small successful steps followed by rewards;

3. Planning alternatives to use when major temptations threaten."[17]

To counter negative behavior, we need to set goals, carefully monitor progress, reward desired behavior, and practice self-control. In the process, learn as much as possible about the self-help methods that work for you.

"As Baumeister, Heatherton & Tice [authors of *Losing Control: How and Why People Fail at Self-Regulation*] explain, one barrier to gaining this self-knowledge is that most people don't really want to know too much information about themselves. Human beings prefer to be told positive things or, at most, be told negative things they already know, avoiding accurate self-knowledge about weaknesses. The more we can overcome this 'I-don't-want-to-know-the-truth' trait, the better we can gain self-control."[18]

Anger

Anger is the antithesis of calmness, happiness, peace, enjoyment, and agreeability. It summons a range of feelings from irritation and determination to rage and affront. When you are angry ". . . you have a palpable sense of:

1. Injustice: A rule of conduct, a cherished belief or instrumental goal is being threatened or abused; you see yourself (also others with whom you are psychologically dependent or connected) as a victim of an injustice, unfairness or disloyalty.

2. Injury. You feel disrespected, discarded or ignored; there's a sense of insult and humiliation along with injury—often psychological, at times also physical.

3. Invasion. Your freedom, autonomy, boundary and personal space are perceived to be constricted, disrupted or violated; your identity and bodily and/or psychological integrity are being threatened or attacked.

4. Intention. There is an energy and determination to do something about the above injustices, injuries and invasions; you are ready—reflexively and/or purposefully—to challenge the status quo."[19]

Our attitudes shape the way we perceive the world—they determine its breadth, depth, intensity, and interactive potential. Uncontrolled anger has been responsible for inestimable human damage. "Impatience is a spirit poison; anger is like a stone hurled into a hornet's nest."[20] Jesus taught his apostles a powerful spiritual lesson on emotional maturity: "'Anger is a material manifestation which represents, in a general way, the measure of the failure of the spiritual nature to gain control of the combined intellectual and physical natures. Anger indicates your lack of tolerant brotherly love plus your lack of self-respect and self-control. Anger depletes the health, debases the mind, and handicaps the spirit teacher of man's soul . . . Let your hearts be so dominated by love that your spirit guide will have little trouble in delivering you from the tendency to give vent to those outbursts of animal anger which are inconsistent with the status of divine sonship.'"[21]

The advice to think before you act is easier said than done, especially during a fit of anger, but it is possible to heed it. Viktor Frankl, the psychologist and survivor of Nazi concentration camps, gives us a glimpse of decisive opportunity: "Between stimulus and response, there is a space. In that space is our power to choose our response. In our response lies our growth and our freedom."[22] When we summon self-control in a moment of truth, we open ourselves to divine insight. The Greek philosopher Aristotle said: "[A]nyone can get angry—that is easy . . . but to do this to the right person, to the right extent, at the right time, with the right motive, and in the right way, *that* is not for everyone, nor is it easy . . ."[23]

When we open ourselves to feedback and inner guidance, and consciously take steps to develop emotional maturity, we find avenues to deal with volatile feelings in a deliberate and constructive way. We learn to appropriately express anger, with consideration and self-control, and maintain our integrity by observing salient personal boundaries.

Unbridled Sex

Since the sexual revolution of the 1960s, there is no escaping the overt presence of sex in our culture. The motion picture industry, marketers, and music mavens know that sex sells—and they take their profits where they can. Nowadays many young people have a casual attitude toward sex—it is easier than talking! This attitude may be a masquerade for the emotional anxiety they feel as a result of conflicting messages coming from parents, teachers, peers, and the media, as well as the lack of morally wise role models and the absence of cultural consensus about morality and sexual behavior.

Such was my experience. In her effort to protect me when I was a young girl, my Catholic mother cautioned me to stay away from boys but did not explain why. My more liberal father advised me to use the pill to avoid unwanted pregnancies. This parental dissonance confused me. Neither of my parents spoke to me about sex or its connection to love, commitment, communication, and mutual respect. I became pregnant at eighteen, with no memory of how it happened. I was so fearful and uninformed that the experience became blocked from my memory.

Early in my marriage I learned to use sex as a manipulative tool, not realizing how desensitized to my husband I was becoming. One time my husband was violently sick after a night out drinking. Instead of being concerned or wanting to help him, I just felt hollow. Then the thought came: "How easy it would be to watch him die." I was shocked at my indifference toward him. It was this moment of self-reflective providence that changed my direction and my life. I thought of my children and realized that I could teach them nothing about love, commitment, communication, or respect. How could I teach my children what I didn't know? These realizations foreshadowed a new phase in my quest for wholeness.

In his book *The Rise and Fall of the American Teenager*, Thomas Hine makes the uncomfortable observation that the baby boomers ". . . seem to have moved, without skipping a beat, from blaming our parents for the ills of society to blaming our children. We want them to embody virtues we only rarely practice. We want them to eschew habits we've never managed to break. Their transgressions aren't their own. They send us the unwelcome, rarely voiced message that we, the adults, have failed."[24] Unless we take responsibility for elevating our own expressions of love, trust, and commitment, we cannot expect better from our children and grandchildren, and society will continue its downward trend. Neither religion nor morals can be elevated if we are not willing to do what it takes—elevate the choices we make.

The growing crisis of unbridled sex begs attention. The United States has ambiguous sexual mores with a puritanical legacy of repression and a cultural ethos of indulgence. It also has one of the highest sex-offense rates in the world. Rape, child pornography, Internet sex scams involving minors, and sex trafficking of even very young children, are a growing concern. "No human emotion or impulse, when unbridled and overindulged, can produce so much harm and sorrow as this powerful sex urge. Intelligent submission of this impulse to the regulations of society is the supreme test of the actuality of any civilization. Self-control, more and more self-control, is the ever-increasing demand of advancing mankind. Secrecy, insincerity, and hypocrisy may obscure sex problems, but they do not provide solutions, nor do they advance ethics."[25]

Unbridled self-expression is the height of selfishness and ungodliness. The Indian political and spiritual leader Mohandas Gandhi once said, "We must become the change we want to see in the world." Without growth in devotion and individual selflessness, marriages cannot thrive, children are emotionally scarred, the family unit is disrupted, and ultimately our world cannot taste the freedom of peace. True freedom is founded in the joy of serving others with a wise and compassionate attitude. "Liberty without the associated and ever-increasing conquest of self is a figment of egoistic mortal imagination. Self-motivated liberty is a conceptual illusion, a cruel deception. License masquerading in the garments of liberty is the forerunner of abject bondage."[26]

Social regulations and laws serve as a deterrent to those individuals hesitant to exercise self-control and provide consequences for those unable or unwilling to cultivate it. For the effects of developing emotional maturity to be far-reaching, however, they must include efforts to spiritualize the mind. "The spiritually blind individual who logically follows scientific dictation, social usage, and religious dogma stands in grave danger of sacrificing his moral freedom and losing his spiritual liberty. Such a soul is destined to become an intellectual parrot, a social automaton, and a slave to religious authority."[27]

Control of Speech

Control of speech is crucial in the process of developing character. It demands patience, awareness, and a certain level of humility. This is never easy, but the rewards are worth the effort. I was twenty-four years old when my brother-in-law informed me, in no uncertain terms, that I was a complainer. I was shocked at his outburst because I did not perceive myself that way.

Rather than brush off his judgment, I set out to prove him wrong. I made a commitment at that very moment to observe my words objectively— and soon noticed that I *did* complain—about everything! I didn't like my own whining, so I began to assess my thoughts before expressing them. Before long, this discipline led to progress— growth in acceptance, tolerance, and tact. As a learning process, it encouraged me to accept healthy criticism as a stimulus for growth.

> *The great man is not he who "takes a city" or "overthrows a nation," but rather "he who subdues his own tongue."*
>
> The Urantia Book

Thoughts generate speech. The inaudible sound of the harmony or disharmony of our thoughts is expressed to the world through our speech. As we cultivate universal intelligence, it is important to start the habit of mentally considering what we are going to say before we vocalize it, to organize our thoughts for more logic and harmony. Making this mental exercise a habit is an important step in creating harmony, both internally and externally.

Personally, I found this exercise rewarding, although extremely challenging. As I began to work on being more positive, it took a while for me to be aware of what I was going to say before I said it. Initially I realized my negativity *after* the fact. Then I started to catch myself in the middle of a thought or statement. On these occasions, I followed the negative statement with a positive one. After a while, I was able to rephrase a statement in mid-sentence so that it had a positive tone.

Being gentle with yourself is important. It is easy to be disappointed when you make a slip and feel that you are not moving forward. On those occasions, rather than focus on your failure, assess the response of others and follow with some positive or clarifying remarks to offset your previous statements. Practice makes perfect, and mastery of this art is an ongoing affair.

Words are the first expression of manifestation; negative thoughts are reinforced by voicing them. For example, if you are discontented with some part of your life and reinforce that feeling by saying, "I work too much" or "I don't have enough money" or "I can never pay my bills" or "I never have time" or "There are not enough hours in the day," chances are you are living that discontented reality and bringing negativity ever deeper into your future. The power of thought is reinforced by the spoken word.

The real art of conversation is not only to say the right thing at the right place but to leave unsaid the wrong thing at the tempting moment.

Dorothy Neville

Catching yourself in the process of forming a negative thought is a precursor to spiritual living. Negativity is reinforced by speaking the words and serves to deepen the conviction. It is also easier on the emotions to catch negativity in its tracks and to turn it into something positive. For example, mentally criticizing the person driving slowly in front of you can be turned around by a positive thought such as, "Maybe he is getting ready to turn" or "The driver may be unsure of her next move," thereby abating the internal negative emotions and building emotional balance.

What we say and how we say it oftentimes do not depend on our intellectual understanding but rather on the emotions that become charged when a particular situation occurs. Changing old habits and accepting unsolicited advice can be bitter pills, but the will to grow makes them easier to swallow. A follow-up dose of tenacity—staying the course—always helps.

It has been said that to rule speech is to rule the whole of human nature. Therefore, it is a good plan for us to deliberately check our speech until:

1. We are clear about what we are going to say.

2. We are sure that the words are true.

3. We have adapted what we are going to say to the person whom we are addressing, choosing words wisely and sparing the quantity of words for their quality.

4. We are sure that what is about to be said should be said.

Raising awareness of how our words may be interpreted is crucial because they are extremely effective in filling our surroundings with the qualities of our personal intentions. I find the following prayer for harmonious and honest speech to be both beautiful and inspiring:

"Aware of the suffering caused by wrongful speech, I vow to cultivate a practice of holy speech in which my words are directed to increasing the love and caring in the world. I vow to avoid words that are misleading or manipulative, and avoid spreading stories that I do not know to be true, or which might cause unnecessary divisiveness or harm, and instead will use my speech to increase harmony, social justice, kindness, hopefulness, trust and solidarity. I will be generous in praise and support for others. To heighten my awareness of this commitment, I will dedicate one day a week to full and total holiness of words, refraining from any speech that day which does not hallow God's name or bring joy to others."[28]

Summary

Negative emotions have been shown to be closely associated with blame. When we have unresolved anger, fear, or resentment or feel emotionally threatened and experience self-doubt, we tend to blame others for our emotional status. Quickly offended, we are barely aware of how we hurt others.

We perceive aggressiveness and meet it with defensiveness; the interaction becomes confrontational and lacks constructive expression. Outbursts of anger can never be taken back, and the emotional wounds they inflict can be as damaging as physical ones.

Pausing to reflect, evaluate, and reassess our reasoning is a good habit to cultivate—even after the fact—so we can guard against such actions in the future. The truth is that we bear complete responsibility for our lives and the quality of our interactions with others. We are responsible for understanding and controlling our personal responses.

The expression of greatness is found in the exhibition of self-control. "Self-control, more and more self-control, is the ever-increasing demand of advancing mankind."[29] To build true character is to transform unbridled emotions into the higher loyalties of mind and the experiences of the spirit.

The path to enlightened social culture begins with balanced individuals. When we embark on the process of personal transformation with living faith, our narrow views fade. Living faith infuses our interactions with love, directed by higher wisdom.

To uplift society, individuals must first discover the value of expressing the divinity within, and then, as faith sons and daughters of God, embark on building character and developing a cosmic perspective. As we become consecrated to this purpose and process, our self-respect begins to balance while dysfunctional behaviors are rooted out; life becomes more focused and meaningful. As we grow in God-consciousness, we increase spiritual reverence and the capacity to understand each other, anticipating what effect our actions might have on the lives of others. "Being sensitive and responsive to human need creates genuine and lasting happiness, while such kindly attitudes safeguard the soul from the destructive influences of anger, hate, and suspicion."[30]

Emotional maturity means taking responsibility for our lives, adopting better attitudes that are harmonious, peaceful, and life enhancing. Emotional maturity, informed with a cosmic perspective, effectively guides us in the progressive and harmonious direction of familial love, which is essential to living as members of the family of God.

29.

Acquiring Sound Taste

*The search for beauty is a part of religion only in so far as it is
ethical and to the extent that it enriches the concept of the moral.
Art is only religious when it becomes diffused with purpose
which has been derived from high spiritual motivation.*

The Urantia Book

The word "sound," as used in the expression "sound taste," is defined as being free of error or defect, solid or firm; based on thorough knowledge or experience and having true premises. "Taste" in this context is the aesthetic quality related to discernment and/or appreciation. To cultivate sound taste, then, is to develop an aesthetic sense that expresses discernment and appreciation of things that reflect perfection.

When I realized that progressive growth in the discernment and appreciation of beauty is an important step in cultivating universal intelligence, I was mystified as to how I would express it. Beauty is such a subjective descriptor and we've cast a wide frame of reference embodied in the maxim "Beauty is in the eye of the beholder." Naturally, I had my own concepts of beauty, from scenes of nature to certain characterstics of human appearance, to pieces of literature and poems and the sounds of certain music. But beauty, like truth and goodness, is actually a quality of the divine—magnificence higher than anything earthly.

While I could acknowledge and appreciate the magnificence of God in creation, it was not something that I felt deeply. In my reconciliation of beliefs in the light of epochal revelation, I discovered new depths of God. I felt, however, that to bring this understanding into everyday life, I had to experience it through my senses. I had to broaden my personal taste—enrich my senses to enliven the imagination and create a new universe of emotions that would further stimulate the soul and fill it with pure enjoyment.

Researching the concept of beauty was part of my process of deepening personal taste. I came upon the following definition of "taste," which clarified the distinction between personal and sound taste: "Some consider *taste* as a mere *sensibility* and others as a simple exercise of *judgment*; but a union of both is requisite to the existence of anything which deserves the name. An original sense of the beautiful is just as necessary to aesthetic judgments as a sense of right and wrong is to the formation of moral subjects. But this 'sense of the beautiful' is not an arbitrary principle. It is under the guidance of reason; it grows in delicacy and correctness with the progress of the individual and of society at large; it has its laws, which are seated in the nature of man; and it is in the development of these laws that we find the true 'standard of taste.'"[1]

As Mark Akenside, the famous British poet and author of *The Pleasure of Imagination*, expressed: "What then is taste, but those internal powers, active and strong and feelingly alive to each fine impulse?"[2]

Personal taste, therefore, differs from sound taste, which has a more cultured connotation, informed by reason, progress, and law. Expressing personal taste has become a modern pastime, exemplified by the comic's line, "Everybody's a critic these days." Everyone is expected to have an opinion—appreciation or disapproval about movies, music, art, social mores, and so on. Emotions and peer identification play a large role in the expression of personal taste.

Sound taste, on the other hand, is based upon a thorough grasp of truthful knowledge, not necessarily devoid of emotion but certainly achieved with an open and rational mind. As sound taste develops, it refines our ability to communicate, enables us to delight in excellence, and helps us appreciate the good and beautiful whenever found.

My determination to develop sound taste lead me to a subject I had neglected—art. How could authentic intelligence be cultivated without a deeper knowledge of humankind's greatest works and what drove the artists to create?

I attended a class that examined the connection between architecture and Sacred Geometry, which attributes a spiritual value to the many patterns, designs, and structures found throughout space and in nature. In Sacred Geometry, a mathematical constant known as the Golden Ratio equals the number 1.618 and is symbolized by the Greek letter *Phi*. This Divine Proportion is based on three lines whose length ratios are 1.618: the middle line is 1.618 times the length of the short line, and the long line is 1.618 the length of the middle line. In combination, these three lines make the perfect proportion, aesthetically pleasing in everything from architecture and art to the physical features of human beings. Our perception of beauty, balance, and harmony, is directly related to this Divine Proportion.

The Golden Ratio is found universally in mollusk and conch shells, sunflower florets, crystals, snowflakes, rose petals, and even the shape of galaxies. It can also be found in the rectangular design of the Greek Parthenon, one of the primary examples of aesthetic architecture. The Divine Proportion can also be seen in the warm smile of the Mona Lisa, from the center to each corner of her lips.

Illustration 32
THE PARTHENON

Being exposed to Sacred Geometry was more than inspiring. I was fascinated by the passionate and poetic discourse and the revealing demonstrations. Mere listening evoked an incredible feeling of awe. Most importantly, it gave me a different perspective: what were once uninteresting buildings with doors and windows now had new meaning. I had a greater appreciation for the design behind virtually all material structures. I began taking art appreciation classes and, to this day, my aesthetic sense is keener when viewing a simple painting, a masterpiece, or the masterwork of nature.

This chapter points to what inspired and guided my discoveries. It is an attempt to shed light on the value of cultivating a sense of beauty and on how to cultivate it.

A commitment to seek deeper levels of awareness challenges us to learn the difference between personal taste and discerning ability. In *Learning About Art*, Professor Ronald Silverman states: "We need to cultivate abilities that enable going beyond such limited reports of one's personal state of mind. We need to develop the skills and knowledge required to make sense of the visual qualities that permeate everyday experience as well as the vast world of art; for example, being able to engage in making informed and objective critical responses."[3]

To evolve from "I like/don't like" to interpreting our world with a trained and refined approach means to develop a sense of beauty, to articulate the reasons for our preferences, and to observe and listen with greater attention.

The study of art is a profound way to develop these skills, and the level of refinement is dependent upon the level of commitment to opening your mind to the different cultures of humanity:

- The visual arts, such as sculpture, drawing, painting, and photography

- The literary arts, such as poetry and literature

- The performance arts, such as music, theater, ballet, drama, film, and opera

- The decorative arts, such as woodworking, pottery, ceramics, jewelry making, metal crafting, textiles, furniture, and interior design—which become fine art when they achieve an aesthetic value beyond their utility

The arts are universal expressions of human personality and evolved with humanity as an integral part of all cultures. The arts are intrinsic to the ideals, values, and events of each era, and provide meaning, pleasure, and emotional stimulation—benefits inherent in the art experience.

A study conducted by the RAND Corporation addresses the widely perceived need to articulate the private and public benefits of involvement in the arts: "A work of art is a bit of 'frozen' potential communication (Taylor, 1989, p. 526) that can be received only through direct personal experience of it. Unlike most communication which takes place through discourse, art communicates through felt experience, and it is the personal, subjective response to a work of art that imparts intrinsic benefits."[4]

According to the RAND report, in American society the value of art as a personal experience has ceded to a more practical philosophy—measuring the benefits of art as a means of achieving desirable social and economic goals that can justify funding. This approach refers to benefits as "instrumental" and includes:

- Cognitive benefits, such as improved academic performance and test scores; improved basic skills, such as reading and mathematical skills and the capacity for creative thinking; improved attitudes and skills that promote the learning process itself, particularly the ability of learning how to learn.

- Attitudinal and behavioral benefits, such as increased self-confidence, self-discipline, self-efficacy, self-criticism, and development of critical-thinking skills, tolerance, and a healthy self-image that can promote school performance, support success in life, enhance economic growth, and encourage the spirit of brotherhood within local and global communities.

- Health benefits, such as stress reduction and increased quality of life.

These instrumental benefits are not necessarily obtainable through the arts but are being used to promote involvement in the arts. Yet "[w]hat draws people to the arts is not the hope that the experience will make them smarter or more self-disciplined. Instead, it is the expectation that encountering a work of art can be a rewarding experience, one that offers them pleasure and emotional stimulation and meaning."[5]

The arts open us up to a wider appreciation of life—emotionally, intellectually, and spiritually. They remind us of our innate human talents and arouse in us a passion for excellence. As we expand our concept of beauty beyond the level of the senses, we become more empathetic and understanding of human concerns and frailties and their inseparable link to the spiritual interpretation of life.

Visual-aesthetic Education

Visual-aesthetic education, as defined by Professor Silverman, is ". . . the process whereby one learns how to produce art, engage in the aesthetic and critical analysis of art, and to talk, read and write about art."[6] Through visual-aesthetic education we develop a sense of beauty; beyond that, it promotes keener judgments, stimulates the mind and heart, uplifts the soul, and ennobles the personality.

Some of the activities that we can engage in to develop our aesthetic sense include:

1. Learning how to do a selected form of art.

2. Learning how to critique. By discovering how to react to the visual and auditory world with an artist's sensibilities, we stimulate our imagination and sharpen our abilities to observe and listen carefully. We also develop skills to identify, analyze, and evaluate what we experience from an artistic perspective.

3. Studying art history, which includes exploring how and why art forms develop in specific cultural contexts and how the cultural period influences the artist.

4. Developing the ability to define the nature of beauty and art, and the principles governing its production and evaluation.

5. Building a vocabulary relevant to particular forms of art to increase levels of art-aesthetic literacy.

Educating ourselves in this way fosters a refinement of artistic sensibilities that increasingly attune us to the beauties of creation—both our own and God's. Developing our sensitivity to beauty nurtures a mind and spirit appreciation of excellence that exceeds the senses alone. These are the effects that ". . . open people to life and create the fabric of shared values and meanings that improves the public sphere."[7]

Sharing meaning and value has been a primary pursuit of artists throughout the ages. Experiencing beauty through the eyes and ears of the soul is to perceive fresh meanings that could well enhance our gratitude for life. Many have learned to experience beauty, but only those who develop an educated eye or ear discover a deep and meaningful appreciation.

Art-aesthetics education should be a lifelong endeavor, beginning at an early age and continued throughout adulthood. Curtailing art education in schools does our children a great disservice by removing opportunities to cultivate the imagination and creativity, sharpen the abilities to observe and listen carefully, develop a heightened appreciation of beauty, and develop the abilities to identify, analyze, and evaluate life's experiences. Unexposed to the more aesthetic qualities in our world, children migrate to the pervasive culture of banal TV and music, violent video games, and other uninspired pastimes. It is essential to promote counterbalancing, visual-aesthetic education to stimulate uplifting awareness in our children's lives.

The Human Body: A Temple of Divinity

In the matter of sickness and health, you should know that these bodily states are the result of material causes; health is not the smile of heaven, neither is affliction the frown of God.

The Urantia Book

The magnificence of God is evidenced by the complexity of the human body's functioning and composition. When we simultaneously cultivate sound taste and expand our understanding of God and his relation to humanity, we attain a higher spiritual meaning for the maxim "The human body is a temple of divinity," and gain a deeper appreciation for the majesty of God.

As a youngster, I heard that the body is a temple of God. But those words never meant much to me. How could God be inside of me? I took care of my body because I knew it was good for me. However, when I grasped the significance of the Indwelling Spirit and acquired a fuller understanding of the relation of God to humanity, there emerged a new and deeper appreciation for the body. There was a heightened sense of humility in the recognition that my body housed the spirit of God that guides me. I felt a new urgency in the duty to treat my body with respect.

As I continued to explore the concept of beauty in connection with the human body, the awesomeness of God's creation was further revealed.

Mathematicians, architects, and artists down the ages have demonstrated that our human body is virtually a temple of divinity. Pythagoras (560–480 BC), the Greek geometer, was especially interested in the Golden Ratio and proved that it was the basis for the proportions of the human figure. He showed that the human body is built with each part in a definite proportion to all the other parts.

Leonardo da Vinci's (1451–1519) rendition of the human form in the drawing *Vitruvian Man* (illustration 33) gave us the most accurate depiction of the perfect proportions of the human body. For example, the length of the leg to the hip is 1.618 times the length of the arm to the torso (the nearer to this proportion, the more perfect); the ratio of the hand to the forearm, and each of the three sections of the finger from the tip to the knuckle, is also 1.618.

In religion, the circle often symbolizes the spiritual, and the square, the physical. In Leonardo's *Vitruvian Man*, the human form is embedded in a square and circle, popularly considered to be indicative that the human form is both spiritual and physical, with the physical housing the spiritual.

The human body is a universal and profound symbol that represents perfection. The Book of Genesis declares that humanity was created "in the

Illustration 33
VITRUVIAN MAN

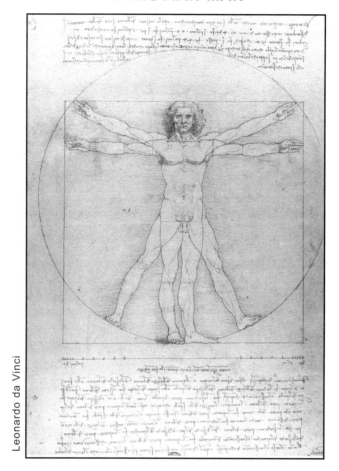

Leonardo da Vinci

image and likeness of God." The New Testament refers to the body as the temple of God. "What? know ye not that your body is the temple of the Holy Ghost [which is] in you, which ye have of God, and ye are not your own?" (1 Corinthians 6:19) In Hinduism, the soul is considered to be a fragment of God, the Supreme Soul, and all living beings are therefore his manifestations.

The sanctity of the human body is recognized by many cultures and religions, at least in theory. The Indian greeting and parting phrase "Namaste," which means "I bow to you," has been popularly adopted in the West as recognition of the divinity that indwells each human being.

A true recognition of the divinity within, however, is reflected in the efforts to develop a well-balanced, God-knowing personality. Desecration of the body—disrespect—shows a low appreciation and shallow understanding of the complex relationships between the soul, spirit, and personality. A greater awareness of the Father-fragment indwelling every individual and its relation to the soul and personality helps us truly appreciate our bodies as temples of divinity and act accordingly. "It is not enough that this spirit be poured out upon you; the divine Spirit must dominate and control every phase of human experience."[8]

Such conscious and meaningful realization brings a benevolent attitude upgrade in the way we view ourselves and others. We access higher insight into the sacred duty to respect each other and keep our physical bodies healthy. Vibrant health contributes to the intrinsic value of life and allows us to appreciate the beauty around us and taste the joys of life, which in turn expands the arena of our life experience.

Knowing the reality of the Indwelling Spirit invigorates our relationships and motivates us to be of greater service by engaging the enthusiastic pursuit of worthy goals. *The Urantia Book* reminds us that "[h]ealth, sanity, and happiness are integrations of truth, beauty, and goodness as they are blended in human experience. Such levels of efficient living come about through the unification of energy systems, idea systems, and spirit systems."[9]

To truly honor God, we must be mindful of his indwelling representative and respectful of what we do with our bodies, from food consumption to emotional expression and physical actions. "The Adjuster remains with you in all disaster and through every sickness which does not wholly destroy the mentality. But how unkind knowingly to defile or otherwise deliberately to pollute the physical body, which must serve as the earthly tabernacle of this marvelous gift from God. All physical poisons greatly retard the efforts of the Adjuster to exalt the material mind, while the mental poisons of fear, anger, envy, jealousy, suspicion, and intolerance likewise tremendously interfere with the spiritual progress of the evolving soul."[10]

Section four of this book addresses human emotions, thinking, and behavior and provides suggestions to strengthen your connection with God. It offers progressive steps intended to unify your energy systems, idea systems, and spirit systems. But health is key to progress and balance is key to health.

There are many physical and environmental factors that influence your state of balance, including diet, activities, lifestyle, emotions, stress, attitude, age, pollution, and even weather. It is your responsibility to understand how these factors affect you and to develop a plan that contributes to the maintenance of a temple fit for the indwelling God-presence. Some steps that can be taken in this regard include:

- Maintain a healthy attitude toward food.
- Be cognizant of the proper combination of proteins, fats, and carbohydrates.
- Favor organic foods.
- Sustain a healthy weight.
- Be cognizant of the nutritional requirements that may help you fight illness and disease.
- Maintain a sensible exercise plan.

- Occasionally detoxify the body to revitalize the tissues and organs.

- Stop smoking and curb alcohol consumption.

- Avoid recreational drugs.

- Maintain an effective dental hygiene protocol.

- Develop a healthy and respectful sense of humor and a positive attitude.

- Substitute herbs for pharmaceuticals whenever possible or as guided by a health practitioner.

Your commitment to excellence is reflected by an increased mastery of the art of living. Vitality of body, mind, and spirit support this quest, and rest on a foundation of personal health that radiates out to home and workplace, building a balance of wholesomeness, sanity, and happiness. "[W]hat stands in the way is partly our apathy and indifference, partly our incontinent appetites, partly the unwholesome and deadening social influences in which we find ourselves enmeshed."[11]

Summary

Through the arts, you can intensify your appreciation for beauty, sharpen your communication skills, and enhance your ability to interpret the meanings and values in your surroundings, even in the midst of routine tasks. When your search for beauty is imbued with spiritual insight, you ennoble the soul, enhance the power to love and be loved, and augment happiness in yourself and others. The pursuit of beauty inspires the highest possible expression of goodness, which is the ultimate reflection of the divinity within.

When looking at the human body through the eyes of an artist, you see the beauty, order, and perfection that is God—a sentiment that Anthony Blunt, the well-known British art historian affirmed: "Nowhere does God, in his grace, reveal himself to me more clearly than in some lovely human form, which I love solely because it is a mirrored image of himself . . ."[12]

In his book *The Nude: A Study in Ideal Form*, Kenneth Clark states: "'The Greeks perfected the nude in order that man might feel like a god, and in a sense this is still its function, for although we no longer suppose that God is like a beautiful man, we still feel close to divinity in those flashes of self-identification when, through our own bodies, we seem to be aware of a universal order."[13]

When you develop sound taste and infuse it with spiritual insight, you expand your perspective of existence to unify the cosmic extremes of God and his creation. "Beauty, art, is largely a matter of the unification of contrasts. Variety is essential to the concept of beauty. The supreme beauty, the height of finite art, is the drama of the unification of the vastness of the cosmic extremes of Creator and creature. Man finding God and God finding man—the creature becoming perfect as is the Creator—that is the supernal achievement of the supremely beautiful, the attainment of the apex of cosmic art."[14]

30.

Sharpening Moral Awareness

A man is truly ethical only when he obeys the compulsion to help
all life which he is able to assist, and shrinks from injuring anything that lives.
Albert Schweitzer

The mind and morality of the individual are the soil from which faith grows and spiritual nature evolves. Of all the activities necessary to cultivate universal intelligence, the development of moral awareness can be the most challenging. We often consider ourselves to be responsible citizens, loving parents, conscientious workers, and caring friends. How, then, can we improve upon something that is already good? As I delved deeper into the concept of God, I began to recognize that to express a higher standard of good, we must first elevate our attitudes and our motives.

Wherever we live, we see moral inconsistency or confusion in families, business, politics, civic life, and religion. Selective morality has become the accepted norm. Public outcries against unfairness in levying property taxes are common, but the plight of abused and undernourished children in that same neighborhood goes unaddressed. Similarly, we jail a juvenile for petty theft, but those responsible for the plague of dishonesty and outright fraud in business

Ethical obligations are innate, divine, and universal.
The Urantia Book

and government are only selectively prosecuted. Affronts to sound ethics and morals are endless—the mutilations of war, inequalities in gender and education, and rampant materialism, to name a few.

Selective morality will continue as long as our moral and ethical choices are not laced with the loving, objective, inclusive, and selfless reasoning that recognizes our place in the universe and is centered on a growing understanding of God.

Rigid perceptions, biased judgment, and uncaring attitudes do not build an ethical society. Moral evaluation, to be consistent and spiritually progressive, entails growth in spiritual insight. This in turn requires that we recognize the indwelling interpreter and unifier—the Indwelling Spirit—and grow in attunement to its guidance.

An ethical society, therefore, is built by the moral and ethical decisions from citizens who are actively engaged in "revelational evolution," that is, in developing God-consciousness. Adopting this bottom-up approach to morality has not been easy for me. While I thrive on expanding my knowledge of cosmic wisdom and also meditating, practicing unselfishness does not come easy. My own self-centeredness becomes painfully obvious when I fail to see the needs of others, hurt a loved one, or hold a grudge. I am however, through self-evaluation, becoming more mindful of poor choices and when my honesty wanes. Moral and ethical habits build upon our commitment to matters, such as returning too much change to a clerk who has miscounted, helping someone when you are busy, speaking up for goodness when you know you should, and refusing to voice even small tales of untruth. When we achieve a balanced development of cosmic, moral, and spiritual insight, our decisions and actions become saturated with love and wisdom.

"Morality is about being transparent and wholly trustworthy—to family and friends, in the workplace and in all of life. It is about integrity, 'walking the talk' day in and day out, in matters great and small, in private and public life. While we may be called to take a stand on issues we believe are important, we need less moral grandstanding, which is political and selective, and more serious study and dialogue about the pressing ethical issues we face—trying to get at the multi-faceted truth. We need to recognize that moral people can honestly differ on such things as stem cell research, or capital punishment, or legal recognition of homosexual relationships."[1]

Overcoming temptation is part of the process of cultivating moral awareness. The temptation of self-pride is perhaps one of the most difficult to conquer because it leads to further temptations in a spiral of rationalized unrighteousness. We are not led to temptation by God to be tested, punished, or strengthened; we are led to temptation by our own pride and arrogance. Temptation cannot be overcome by suppressing human desires or willfully supplanting one desire by another supposedly superior desire. To triumph over temptation requires progressive spiritual transformation—developing an actual interest and love for superior ideals of conduct and substituting them for lower habits of behavior that spring from temptation.

We develop moral awareness by thinking before we act and making more intelligent moral choices. Moral behavior is always preceded by a decision between actions that are respectful and righteous versus those that are self-serving and perhaps malicious. Such choices are always informed by our Indwelling Spirit, the true and ever-present moral compass. Our foremost obstacle is stubborn self-will—resistance to inner guidance and to doing the will of God. The whisper of exemplary morality, the highest choice in any situation, ever echoes in the human mind. Evolving the eternal soul requires that we attune to the Indwelling Spirit and follow its spiritual leadings.

Morality becomes a quality of character when it is allied with ethical reasoning and mature social skills, such as:

- Attentive listening
- Respect for the opinions of others
- Tolerance despite differences
- Non-prejudicial and humble attitudes
- Empathy and forgiveness

To be respectful requires an acceptance of personal differences; treating everyone with courtesy and dignity; never intentionally ridiculing, embarrassing, or hurting others; and solving problems with intelligence and tact. "Morality can never be advanced by law or by force. It is a personal and freewill matter and must be disseminated by the contagion of the contact of morally fragrant persons with those who are less morally responsive, but who are also in some measure desirous of doing the Father's will."[2]

Cultivating morality includes assessing our beliefs and actions to root out inconsistencies, and keeping open minds, searching hearts, and spiritual humility. Moral consistency reveals itself in a growing sense of duty toward the well-being of others and the habit of behaving ethically in all situations. True morality is inseparable from true spirituality, evidenced by an enhanced vision of righteousness that breeds new levels of love and devotion, of service and fellowship.

This evolving social awareness is intimately associated with an expanding consciousness of the fatherhood of God and the brotherhood of man. "The enlightened spiritual consciousness of civilized man is not concerned so much with some specific intellectual belief or with any one particular mode of living as with discovering the truth of living, the good and right technique of reacting to the ever-recurring situations of mortal existence. Moral consciousness is just a name applied to the human recognition and awareness of those ethical and emerging morontial values which duty demands that man shall abide by in the day-by-day control and guidance of conduct."[3]

In the progressive scheme of advancing civilization, an awareness of and response to ever-present spirit guidance has world-changing implications. Epochal revelation informs us that as mortals become attuned and responsive to divine ideals received via moral and spiritual insight, we become less dependent upon our human constructs of justice and enforcement. Self-control, the fruit of spiritual discipline, eventually negates the need for police and military institutions. What a day it will be when righteousness is the norm—the hallmark of a God-conscious civilization!

There are many noble traits that help us cultivate moral character, but these three are transformative: trustworthiness, forgiveness, and altruistic service.

Trustworthiness

According to epochal revelation, trustworthiness is the crucial test of personality, the true measure of self-mastery. Trustworthiness denotes human integrity, honesty, reliability, and loyalty, the foundational moral traits that elicit personal trust.

- To have *integrity* is to live by your principles despite opposition, and to have moral courage in the face of difficult choices.

- To be *honest* is to be compassionately truthful at all times. "You shall know the truth, and the truth shall make you free."[4]

- To be *reliable* is to act upon your promises and commitments and be accountable for personal actions.

- To be *loyal* is to stand by your family, friends, and faithful convictions; to keep the trust of those who trust you.

"A person of integrity is open and honest. He doesn't have any hidden agendas or ulterior motives. A person of integrity is true to his word. He keeps his commitments. He doesn't need a legal contract; his word is his bond. People of integrity are the same in private as they are in public. They don't go out and treat their friends and coworkers kindly and then go home and treat their family rudely or disrespectfully. No, when you have integrity, you'll do what's right whether anybody is watching or not."[5]

> *To be trusted is a greater compliment than being loved.*
> George MacDonald

Primitive people were not inherently trustful, since suspicion of predators and enemies was a key survival instinct. Trust is a relatively recent human acquisition that was fostered by the ministry of planetary seraphim at the time of the Adamic regime more than thirty-seven thousand years ago. Growth in the ability to trust and be trusted promotes familiarity, a sense of personal connection that can blossom into the affection necessary to live the brotherhood of man. Trust allows us to:

- Establish ties

- Maintain consistency and fairness in our relations

- Respond appropriately to individual differences

- Be faithful to personal bonds

- Maintain high personal and moral standards

Trustworthiness is the basis of all good relationships—disloyalty is the most dishonorable character flaw. "And of all forms of evil, none are more destructive of personality status than betrayal of trust and disloyalty to one's confiding friends."[6] Trust is the most meaningful of characteristics, but it is also one of the most vulnerable to the quirks, needs, and desires of human nature. Without personal evaluation and growth in spiritual insight, collective trustworthiness is constantly eroded by white lies, by spin and misinformation in the media, and by corruption and a lack of credibility among many in the civic and business sectors. Every individual breach of trust adds to the collective growth of suspicion. As the national mood of distrust and insecurity grows, the maxim "Trust only yourself" dominates individual thinking and narcissism blooms.

To trust and be trusted, we must question, explore, and improve our own trustworthiness: "Do I keep my promises?" "How am I at keeping my commitments?" "Am I honest without exceptions?" "Do I rate high in truth and loyalty?" "How well do I respond to trust-adverse temptation?"

We must be willing to monitor ourselves morally. Keeping a journal that focused on personal relationships and trustworthiness helped me become aware of habits that were not in alignment with my ideals. Through this process I discovered that my honesty and reliability had many shades of gray. Recognizing these shortcomings forced a review of my intentions and a new perspective on opportunities to grow.

It is not always an easy exercise and, on many occasions, I have not made the best decisions. I discovered that sometimes it was better to hold my peace instead of blurting out some fact or what I perceived to be the truth. Did that compromise my integrity? In the area of human relations, we walk a fine line— a constant balancing act—between diplomacy on one side and forthrightness on the other. Loyal and trustworthy motives function to improve the results of such efforts. A benefit of this exercise has been growth in empathy and consideration for others, as well as reflecting on my commitments before I make them known.

We promote consistency in trustworthiness as we gain spiritual insight. "Consistency demands the recognition of the activities of a purposive Creator."[7] When we recognize the faithfulness of the Father toward his universe children and the constancy of his efforts in the loving ministry and ceaseless service of our spirit guardians on Earth and beyond, it stimulates our enthusiasm and commitment to cultivate the qualities of divinity.

Personal choices constitute our greatest opportunity and supreme cosmic responsibility. Our eternal destiny and peace on Earth depend upon the integrity of our decisions. When our choices are consciously focused on developing a well-balanced God-knowing personality, we grow in grace and the willingness to reliably and faithfully serve others. "Faithfulness is the unerring measure of human trustworthiness. He who is faithful in little things is also likely to exhibit faithfulness in everything consistent with his endowments."[8]

Forgiveness

"Pentecost endowed mortal man with the power to forgive personal injuries, to keep sweet in the midst of the gravest injustice, to remain unmoved in the face of appalling danger, and to challenge the evils of hate and anger by the fearless acts of love and forbearance."[9] With such an endowment, forbearance stands out as a truly courageous ideal. Learning to genuinely say "I am sorry" or "I forgive you"—without residual resentment—has been one of the most challenging experiences of my life. I may take responsibility for my part in a conflict, but it certainly does not guarantee similar action from the other party, nor does it mean that the emotional pain from unresolved hurt will be released.

Until recently, I thought that forgiveness was the ability to be cordial, even loving, toward the person who hurt you. But the greatest challenge of forgiving is preempting the personal grievance and its associated resentment that feeds the sense of separation. Jesus demonstrated a new standard of forgiving: "By showing mercy, he meant to portray spiritual deliverance from all grudges, grievances, anger, and the lust for selfish power and revenge."[10] There are often many layers to an emotional injury. You may forgive one layer and not recognize the one that holds the resentment. The result is incomplete forgiveness.

> *You will know that forgiveness has begun when you recall those who hurt you and feel the power to wish them well.*
>
> Lewis B. Smedes

Much has been written on the subject of forgiveness, with varying perceptions of what exactly it means to forgive someone. According to Robert D. Enright, PhD, board member of the International Forgiveness Institute, all religions and most modern philosophical writings ". . . place forgiveness within morality or the quest for the good."[11] Enright explains that forgiveness exhibits two moral characteristics:

- Giving up of resentment. "Giving up resentment in this context is moral (and paradoxical) precisely because I am giving a gift to the one who injured me (the gift is that I no longer resent the injurer even though I have a right to resentment)."[12] This step in the process of forgiveness is easier to intellectualize than it is to practice. You can't transcend resentment without first identifying the feeling and behavior it provokes in yourself. I know I am holding resentment toward someone when I go out of my way to avoid them, or I guard my affections, feel angry, impatient, or irritable when they are around me. Denial, dislike, bitterness, or hatred toward someone are sure signs that we are holding resentment. Once we recognize the resentment, then we can explore its source by doing much soul-searching to find the answers. Only by going through this process, alone or with professional help if needed, can we slowly begin to release resentment.

- Reaching out to the injurer with merciful restraint, generosity, and/or moral love. "By merciful restraint, we mean that the forgiver refrains from deserved punishment. By generosity, we mean that the forgiver actually begins to give good things to the injurer, such as attention, time, favorable judgments, and so forth. By moral love, we mean that the forgiver gives of oneself toward the rehabilitation and betterment of the injurer."[13] This step can be practiced even when resentment is present.

Forgiveness is not complete without letting go of resentment. We may think we are forgiving when what we are really doing is trying to accept what happened, move on, or cope with the injury. Forgiveness is complete when we feel peacefully and lovingly connected to the person who injured us.

A few years ago, my eldest son provided me with an opportunity that challenged my ability to forgive. I had been deeply hurt on several occasions by statements that threatened to ruin our mother–son relationship. Although there was an apology and forgiveness, uneasiness lingered. It took quite some time before I recognized and understood my underlying resentment.

During the estrangement from my son, I learned about the content of an effective apology: A statement of regret (example: "I'm sorry I used those words."); recognition of responsibility (example: "I could have chosen other words."); and giving an indication of future intentions (example: "In the future, I will try to think about the impact of my words before speaking.") or even asking, "What can I do to make things right?" This three-step apology from the heart has the potential to repair, even enrich, torn relationships. In my case, excuses and rationalizations made my son's apology feel incomplete. Resentment continued to surface until I expanded my understanding of forgiveness and realized that from my son's perspective, he had apologized appropriately. Only then was I able to release the grievance and reconcile with my son. The choice to reconnect with him despite a partial apology empowered me to genuinely and lovingly share in his life without expectations.

Sometimes guilt and fear keep us from the healing therapy of forgiveness. A cousin sexually molested me at the age of eight, but I only became emotionally aware of the consequences of self-inflicted guilt decades later. A lack of self-respect, coupled with denial, bred further guilt. When a workshop facilitator suggested that I call my cousin to forgive him, I did so despite my fear to confront him. My cousin answered the phone as if we were long-lost friends. Though my tendency was to go with false civility, I told him how I had been affected by his actions and that I forgave him for what he did. I was expecting a denial—instead he acknowledged what he had done and told me how grateful he was for my phone call and that not a day went by that he did not feel remorseful. For the next four hours after putting down the phone, I was conscious only of my head and my lower legs. The space in between felt hollow. As the sensation in that area returned, I felt a new clarity and emotional lightness. I was empowered by my cousin's remorse and acceptance of responsibility. It dissolved my misplaced sense of guilt and resentment.

Such breakthroughs in assimilating and appreciating the significance of forgiveness are facilitated when we are actively committed to cultivating universal intelligence.

When we engage in building character, while simultaneously enlarging our concept of God, we absorb new spiritual meanings and higher values that challenge us to elevate the quality of our interactions with others, which gives us courage to venture into new levels of participation and to explore higher realms of intellectual living.

A milestone achievement in the modern "science" of spiritual healing is the Forgiveness Project of Stanford University, created by Dr. Fred Luskin, author of the best-seller *Forgive for Good*. In this practical book, Luskin brings a researcher's mind and minister's heart to the subject: "I define forgiveness as the experience of peace and understanding that can be felt in the present moment. You forgive by challenging the rigid rules you have for other people's behavior and by focusing your attention on the good things in your life as opposed to the bad. Forgiveness does not mean forgetting or denying that painful things occurred. Forgiveness is the powerful assertion that bad things will not ruin your today even though they may have spoiled your past."[14]

Along with dramatic findings on the wide-ranging health benefits to forgiveness, Dr. Luskin discovered that there are three core components that underlie the creation of any long-standing hurt and grievance:

- The exaggerated taking of personal offense
- The blaming of the offender for how you feel
- The creation of a grievance story

Forgive for Good offers a proven and practical methodology to detect the formation of grievances—those inner conflicts that sap our physical, mental, and spiritual health. The recognition of our grievance patterns helps us realize we have a choice to forego them; we can choose to not let other people's behavior dictate our internal responses.

Understanding these psychospiritual dynamics makes forgiving sensible, if not always easy. Of course, life brings us upsets we don't expect or want, so forgiving is an ongoing practice. "Forgiveness is the decision to free ourselves from the personal offense and blame that have us stuck in a cycle of suffering." According to Dr. Luskin, "The most important benefit of forgiveness is our assertion that we are not victims of the past . . . The second benefit of learning to forgive is how much help we can offer to others . . . The third benefit from forgiveness emerges as we give more love and care to the important people in our lives."[15]

Epochal revelation affirms the latest good news about forgiveness when Jesus says: "'Your inability or unwillingness to forgive your fellows is the measure of your immaturity, your failure to attain adult sympathy, understanding, and love. You hold grudges and nurse vengefulness in direct proportion to your ignorance of the inner nature and true longings of your children and your fellow beings. Love is the outworking of the divine and inner urge of life. It is founded on understanding, nurtured by unselfish service, and perfected in wisdom.'"[16]

When we forgive without letting go of grievance and resentment, we practice *merciful forgiveness*. We intellectually set the hurt to one side and may even be cordial to the one who injured us, but we hold on to the pain. In offering merciful forgiveness, we sell ourselves short. We may be satisfied that we have managed to forgive, but we never experience true emotional deliverance from resentment, hostility, anger, and, sometimes, even the lust for retribution, for these may remain unconscious. When we offer merciful forgiveness, we feel justified in maintaining a stance of separation from the one who hurt us, and the relationship remains superficial

When we cultivate our capacity to love, we empower ourselves to practice forgiveness as a wise and compassionate parent. "A compassionate father is freely forgiving; fathers do not hold vengeful memories against their children. Fathers are not like judges, enemies, or creditors. Real families are built upon tolerance, patience, and forgiveness."[17] A wise and compassionate parent practices *loving forgiveness*; she understands the inner motives and sentiments of her children, and loving them unconditionally, forgives them for all wrongdoings. She remains emotionally connected to her children despite the sense of guilt that the children may harbor. "This capacity to understand man's nature and forgive his apparent wrongdoing is Godlike. If you are wise parents, this is the way you will love and understand your children, even forgive them when transient misunderstanding has apparently separated you. The child, being immature and lacking in the fuller understanding of the depth of the child–father relationship, must frequently feel a sense of guilty separation from a father's full approval, but the true father is never conscious of any such separation. Sin is an experience of creature consciousness; it is not a part of God's consciousness."[18] When we develop our capacity to love, we remain connected with those who have wronged us no matter what.

As we express more appreciation of God as Father, it becomes natural to cast aside the misdeed and the resentment. The transgressor is lovingly, emotionally, and unconditionally accepted, even when these feelings are not reciprocated. According to epochal revelation, you cannot truly forgive your fellows unless you love that person as you love yourself. Loving forgiveness always transcends merciful forgiveness.

When we become aware of these differences, we can elevate our expression of forgiveness. Such courageous personal adjustment can be an inspiring example of growth and progress for others.

What Forgiveness Is and Is Not

In *The Freedom and Power of Forgiveness*, John F. MacArthur offers these insights: "Genuine forgiveness is not feigned or grudging, but is given as freely as we ourselves desire to be forgiven. It involves a deliberate refusal to hold the guilt over the head of the offender. It means ending the bitterness, laying aside anger, and refusing to dwell on the offense that has been forgiven. It is a complete letting go of any thought of retaliation or reprisal."[19]

Loving forgiveness dispels the negativity of hatred, anger, guilt, and resentment, and opens the path to peace—peace within and peace with others. Growth in spiritual insight and in our understanding of the motives and sentiments of others increases our ability to begin the journey to loving forgiveness. "If you could only fathom the motives of your associates, how much better you would understand them. If you could only know your fellows, you would eventually fall in love with them."[20]

There are volumes of information available on the subject of forgiveness, but increasing our understanding of what forgiveness is and is not can help us in our goal of spiritual living. Forgiveness is not:

- Admitting defeat
- Doing the offender a favor
- Forgetting the offense (A person may always remember the wrongdoing and choose to forgive and let go of resentment.)
- Ignoring the effects of the wrongdoing
- Excusing or giving permission to continue the hurtful behavior
- Absolving the offender or yourself of responsibility
- Condoning the wrongdoing
- A sign of weakness

- Reconciliation (Once forgiveness is extended, a choice must still be made about the relationship. Forgiveness is one person's moral response to another's injustice. Healthy reconciliation requires mutual respect.)

Forgiveness is a conscious choice to:

- Be courageous
- Do yourself a favor
- Relinquish the right to punish, to harbor resentment, and to hold grudges
- Move on with life without the burdens from the past
- Give up blame and faultfinding
- Strengthen positive self-esteem and not be a victim
- Improve the depth and quality of your relationships with others
- Favor peace of mind over negative thinking

Forgiveness is a gift that we give ourselves, freeing us from the past and deepening the love and joy in our lives. There are a number of additional things we can do to develop our ability to genuinely ask for forgiveness and to forgive without resentment: keep a personal journal and read inspiring and courageous stories of forgiveness; seek professional help; attend workshops; and practice what we learn.

We can write a forgiveness letter, such as the one described in the book *Men Are from Mars, Women Are from Venus* by John Gray, PhD, and we can also pray. The "Prayers of Life" by Howard Wills, available on his website (www.howardwills.org/prayers.html) encourage humility, heightened awareness, healing release, and peacemaking. I personally found these prayers extremely powerful, and they can, in a very short time, release much of the negative emotion that chains us to pain from the past.

Forgiveness from God

The topic of forgiveness would not be complete without expanding our understanding of the relationship between forgiveness and God. Many people are motivated to forgive others out of fear that they will lose divine favor. The following statements reflect orthodox beliefs:

- Without forgiveness there is no salvation.
- If I am unwilling to forgive, then God will be unwilling to forgive me.
- Our sins and iniquities separate us from God.
- Refusing to forgive welcomes in the demons.
- To be forgiven by God, one must believe in Christ.

When you forgive out of fear, grievance and resentment remain unresolved. But there is liberation in reconnecting to the one who has wronged you.

Epochal revelation reminds us that divine forgiveness is inherent in God's nature. "The affectionate heavenly Father, whose spirit indwells his children on earth, is not a divided personality—one of justice and one of mercy—neither does it require a mediator to secure the Father's favor or forgiveness. Divine righteousness is not dominated by strict retributive justice; God as a father transcends God as a judge."[21]

Forgiveness from God the Father is freely given regardless of our own forgiveness quotient. "With the earthly child and the heavenly Father, the divine parent possesses infinity and divinity of sympathy and capacity for loving understanding. Divine forgiveness is inevitable; it is inherent and inalienable in God's infinite understanding, in his perfect knowledge of all that concerns the mistaken judgment and erroneous choosing of the child."[22] However, "God's forgiveness is made actually available and is personally experienced by man just in so far as he forgives his fellows."[23]

Thus, unless we are willing to forgive those who have wronged us and go through the process of forgiveness, we perpetuate the feelings of separation and cannot experience the sense of connection that comes with forgiveness. When we acknowledge our wrongs and forgive others, we renew our loyalty and connection to the heavenly Father, who always rewards us with a greater experience of love.

Service

To engage in social service is one of the most effective ways to develop and practice the virtues of trustworthiness, patience, tolerance, and forgiveness, and to cultivate unselfishness. If goodness is an attribute of God, service is the moral component of goodness; unselfishness is its spiritual coordinate. Too often, we fail to discern between the call of duty (*doing* righteousness) and the attitude of spiritual reverence (*being* righteous). Understanding the difference and expressing these service and faith ideals require sincere devotion to personal develop-ment and spiritual growth.

Doing service is an excellent way of developing a selfless attitude. When I first arrived in the United States, with my three sons and meager finances, there were many months when I struggled to meet monthly obligations. At times, my worries resulted in anxiety attacks that would literally render me unconscious. Recognizing that worrying wasn't solving any problems—in fact, it was making me dysfunctional—I shifted my attention from worry to helping others. I became a volunteer at a nearby nursing home, occasionally playing the guitar and helping to serve coffee. I would enter the facility feeling miserable and come out feeling renewed and grateful for my many blessings. With time, the anxieties lifted and I found myself enjoying these visits with the residents, getting to know them and making a small difference in their lives. My experience at the nursing home taught me patience, tolerance, and a deeper appreciation for others. I was moved and inspired by the joyful attitude of many severely disabled individuals. Since those early days, service has

> *Teach this triple truth to all: A generous heart, kind speech, and a life of service and compassion are the things which renew humanity.*
>
> Buddha

become an integral part of my life, a moral uplift and a spiritual activity that constantly challenges me to express a higher level of goodness.

My positive service experiences are not unique. Documented studies have proven a scientific link between altruism, serving others, and a wide range of physical and psychological benefits. Dr. Stephen Post, head of the Institute for Research on Unlimited Love, reveals some amazing findings in his book *Why Good Things Happen to Good People*. Following is a sample of the research news: "Giving in high school predicts good physical and mental health all the way into adulthood, a time period of over fifty years; Giving reduces mortality significantly in later life, even when you start late; Giving reduces adolescent depression and suicide risk; Giving is more powerful than receiving in its ability to reduce mortality; Giving to others helps us forgive ourselves for our own mistakes, which is key to a sense of well-being; Helping friends, relatives, and neighbors, along with providing emotional support to a spouse, reduces mortality, although receiving the same kind of help does not."[24]

> *Life's most urgent question is: What are you doing for others?*
> Martin Luther King, Jr.

Service work is an activity that can reshape or even reform us, transforming our character from self-indulgence to that of a loving, caring individual. So many human beings have basic, unfulfilled needs. They are alone and feel uncared for, perhaps due to age, illness, or disability, or for other reasons have become emotionally withdrawn or isolated. All are in need of human warmth, support, and companionship.

The fulfillment we experience when serving our fellow humans adds greater meaning to our lives, irrespective of our degree of spiritual reverence. However, when the attitude of respect for God evolves to one of appreciation and love for God as Father, the opportunity to give to our brothers and sisters becomes more than a moral duty—it becomes a worship experience. "The new loyalties of enlarged spiritual vision create new levels of love and devotion, of service and fellowship; and all this enhanced social outlook produces an enlarged consciousness of the fatherhood of God and the brotherhood of man."[25]

Sathya Sai Baba, in a discourse entitled *Be and Be Blessed*, states: "Worship of God in temples and shrines has its place . . . But, activity in the shape of service charged with love fulfills the aims of all paths of Godhead." True service is imbued with purpose and heightened spiritual reverence. It radiates with the love and gratefulness we feel for God and those we serve. Loving service adds to the growth of universal goodness and the value of life of the giver and the receiver. The intrinsic love in true service is transferred to others as we perform a good deed or give encouragement through our words. True service purifies the heart, broadens one's sense of morality, and expands the compassion in our attitude, enabling us to radiate an inner joy and love.

Altruism was rare in past ages; a lack of personal conveniences was the order of the day, and serving others was often a hardship. It took dedication and a strong moral attitude, driven by a Good Samaritan's strong belief in God, to help a fellow human being. In today's world, our indifference to God and the stay-at-home convenience of donating money instead of self, threatens growth in moral values and the transforming love of service. Service is spiritually productive and socially transforming as it inspires a higher expression of goodness in those we serve.

When we serve each other with the increasing recognition of the father–child relation between God and every individual it ". . . leads inevitably to the practice of the precepts of the family conduct, the service of one's brothers and sisters in the effort to enhance and enlarge the brotherhood"[26] Those around us are stimulated by the growing depth of our love and the service rendered is more fulfilling and beneficial to both the giver and the receiver.

Today there are many opportunities to express awakened compassion and loving service:

1. Engage in service activities. Volunteer. Join a service club. Teach a skill. According to former president Bill Clinton in his book, *Giving: How Each of Us Can Change the World*, "One of the greatest gifts anyone can give is a useful skill. Most of us know how to do something not everyone can do as well as we can. Transferring that knowledge and the ability to use it can empower others in amazing ways."[27]

2. Actively cultivate universal intelligence so that higher meanings and values motivate our service, increasing its quality and scope.

3. Monitor behavior and attitude toward others: "Am I readily available to assist or only when scheduled or in the mood?" "Am I giving others presence of mind or does my mind wander?" "Am I being judgmental and self-righteous when serving?" "Am I feeling impatient or indifferent toward those I serve?" "Am I serving lovingly or am I serving out of personal need?" Checking our behavior and attitude develops our reasoning abilities and serves as a compass for further growth.

Perform random acts of kindness. These may not feel meaningful to us immediately, but the experience awakens joy, acceptance, patience, empathy, and compassion—feelings that spring from emerging love.

An open heart connects us with those we serve, elevating the expression of goodness in our lives. Love redoubles our generosity of spirit and raises service to an expression of spiritual reverence. We become beacons of light for others along the path.

Summary

The only true end of love is spiritual growth or human evolution.

M. Scott Peck, MD
The Road Less Traveled

Metamorphosis is the path to moral development and spiritual progress. "Ethics and morals become truly human when they are dynamic and progressive, alive with universe reality."[28] When we discover new spiritual meanings in trustworthiness, forgiveness, and service, we elevate our sense of morality and discover higher ideals that lift us beyond our present boundaries.

With the guidance of revelation, moral law has evolved from the ancient prohibitions, which were all negative injunctions, to a mixture of "Thou shalt's" and "Thou shalt not's" in Hebrew culture, to finally becoming ". . . the great and positive law of love, the injunction to love God supremely and your neighbor as yourself."

This supreme law of love for God and all people constitutes the whole duty of every individual.[29] Jesus of Nazareth prophesied: "I declare that in the coming kingdom . . . no longer shall they concern themselves with commands to refrain from this and take care not to do that, but rather shall all be concerned with one supreme duty. And this duty of man is expressed in two great privileges: sincere worship of the infinite Creator, the Paradise Father, and loving service bestowed upon one's fellow men. If you love your neighbor as you love yourself, you really know that you are a son of God."[30]

31.

Nourishing a Consecrated Attitude

As you ascend the personality scale, first you learn to be loyal, then to love,
then to be filial, and then may you be free . . .

The Urantia Book

To have a consecrated attitude is to have steadfast devotion to doing the will of God—knowing God and becoming Godlike. Such a consecration of will carries the potential for union of the spirit of God and the nature of mortals in the everlasting service of the children of God. A consecrated attitude emerges and intensifies as a result of unwavering efforts to expand the God concept, cultivate the qualities of divinity, and commune with God.

What is loyalty? It is the fruit of an intelligent appreciation of universe brotherhood . . .

The Urantia Book

Devotion flourishes when we make a habit of confiding in God while expanding our concepts of prayer, attunement, and worship. Progress in meanings safeguards devotion from the perils of prejudice or the dead end of ritualistic habit. Genuine devotion to God is socially effective and spiritually progressive, instilling the wise and selfless love that is essential to living the brotherhood of man.

When the Indian guru Ammachi told me to love God because only God truly loves you, her words gave me great pause. I was not thinking of God when asking her about devotion; my inquiry was spurred by frustration in my marital relationship. Her response ignited my search for a deeper meaning of devotion. For months, no day went by without a brief encounter with the concept of devotion: a definition by a friend, an article at a doctor's office, a movie, or a song.

Soon after my encounter with Ammachi, I began to attend weekly rosary meetings at the invitation of a friend. I was fascinated by the tangible sense of devotion. Although wishing such devotional sanctity would rub off on me, the structure of the prayer meetings bored me and I often found myself daydreaming.

One day I had a vision while thinking that I would rather be dancing than praying: I was in the presence of a beautiful, long-robed woman who towered over me and radiated love and serenity as she beckoned me to come closer. Initially hesitant, I drew near, and then suddenly I threw myself at her feet, crying, and confessed that I was afraid. The next six months were an emotional roller coaster—a mixture of spiritual ecstasy and intellectual confusion. Drawn to attend weekly services at the local Liberal Catholic Church, I became an altar server and eventually a deaconess. I looked forward to participating in the group prayer meetings that once bored me. I joined hospice, attended retreats, and read books—seeking ways to comprehend and deepen the unfamiliar feelings of appreciation and love for God that were slowly becoming my constant companion.

When we first commit to cultivating devotion, it can be a mental exercise; we intellectually commit our will to the service of God and might take action in faith without feeling a strong connection with God. However, when we sincerely admit that God is much more than we perceive him to be and willingly pursue growth in our concept of God, despite fear and doubt, our conviction grows and service becomes the means of sharing the love that is blazing in our hearts.

One of the most humbling and powerful moments in my life was when I recognized the love and devotion that the Father has toward his children, as witnessed by the spirit ministry that he has made available for our guidance and evolution. Another was the understanding that this Divine Indweller cannot spiritualize our minds without our consent. What a realization it is when we fully grasp that the Father desires us to willingly accept his invitation to perfect ourselves so we can meet him face to face! Arriving at such a simple yet profound truth inspires consecration to the Father's will. Our joy in service then flows not from obligation but from our acknowledgement and gratitude for the care, training, and affection we receive on our journey to Paradise.

Consecration, the faith response of the soul, engages the heart and focuses the guidance system of the supermind so that devotion does not deviate due to doubt or emerging obstacles. Consecration firmly fixes our plan in the superconscious and renders a straight pathway to the achievement of our purpose. "The affectionate dedication of the human will to the doing of the Father's will is man's choicest gift to God; in fact, such a consecration of creature will constitutes man's only possible gift of true value to the Paradise Father."[1]

A halfhearted or partial commitment to God leads to a life of spiritual ambivalence and indifference. Such attitudes sow the seeds of disregard and disrespect that breed tyranny and terrorism—serious barriers to the brotherhood of man. Self-will and denial of God's will are obstacles that threaten the consolidation of peace and democracy, both nationally and internationally.

Likewise, when devotion springs from misguided beliefs and erroneous interpretations, it often leads to prejudicial actions:

1. **Fanatic devotion to causes**, as exhibited by extremist cults, militant religious orders, corrupt evangelists, and those who harm or kill for their beliefs.

2. **Extreme religious devotion**, as revealed by those who retreat from all social interaction, especially when characterized by extreme self-denial and self-mortification.

"Prejudice blinds the soul to the recognition of truth, and prejudice can be removed only by the sincere devotion of the soul to the adoration of a cause that is all-embracing and all-inclusive of one's fellow men. Prejudice is inseparably linked to selfishness. Prejudice can be eliminated only by the abandonment of self-seeking and by substituting therefore the quest of the satisfaction of the service of a cause that is not only greater than self, but one that is even greater than all humanity—the search for God, the attainment of divinity. The evidence of maturity of personality consists in the transformation of human desire so that it constantly seeks for the realization of those values which are highest and most divinely real."[2]

Genuine devotion is a consecration of self to the service of meaningful and supreme values. It is unbiased, tolerant, and compassionate. Genuine devotion is expressed in wholehearted, intelligent, and selfless social service that grows out of the consciousness of God as Father and the consequent recognition of the brotherhood of man. While devotion to duty promotes service to humanity, consecration to supreme ideals (based on living faith) develops the genuinely unselfish love that is contagious and unifying. "If each mortal could only become a focus of dynamic affection, this benign virus of love would soon pervade the sentimental emotion-stream of humanity to such an extent that all civilization would be encompassed by love, and that would be the realization of the brotherhood of man."[3]

Prayer

"Prayer" is defined in the *Britannica Concise Encyclopedia* as a "silent or spoken petition made to God or a god." The entry continues, "Prayer has been practiced in all religions throughout history. Its characteristic postures (bowing the head, kneeling, prostration) and position of the hands (raised, outstretched, clasped) signify an attitude of submission and devotion. Prayer may involve confessions of sin, requests, thanks, praise, offerings of sacrifice, or promises of future acts of devotion. In addition to spontaneous private prayer, most religions have fixed formulas of prayer (for example, the Lord's Prayer), often recited in group worship."[4] Prayers function to keep us connected to God in our daily lives.

Consistent and sincere prayer connects the believer in a growing fellowship with the divine. This experience is best understood and elevated when we recognize not only an external and personal God but also an internal and impersonal divinity, the Indwelling Spirit that guides us.

Prayer is the most fundamental, most widespread, and most comforting of all spiritual practices. The sincere prayer of faith has been a mighty force throughout the ages in promoting personal happiness, individual self-control, social courage, harmony, fair-mindedness, moral progress, and spiritual attainment.[5]

Prayer is also the most widespread form of therapy when a person is confronted with illness. This perspective is reflected in a survey released in May 2004 by the National Center for Complementary and Alternative Medicine, which found that 43 percent of Americans prayed for their own health, 24.4 percent had others pray for them, and 9.6 percent participated in a prayer group for their own health. Prayer is not a recognized medical technique for curing sickness, but the inner peace it affords certainly contributes to the health of the body. "Prayer is not a technique for curing real and organic diseases, but it has contributed enormously to the enjoyment of abundant health and to the cure of numerous mental, emotional, and nervous ailments. And even in actual bacterial disease, prayer has many times added to the efficacy of other remedial procedures. Prayer has turned many an irritable and complaining invalid into a paragon of patience and made him an inspiration to all other human sufferers."[6]

Some people pray just to pray and some people pray to know God.

Andrew Murray

The motive and content of prayer usually reflect the quotient of personal spirit attainment. Some prayers are centered upon the self and include confessions, petitions, or requests for material favors. Altruistic prayer offers strength, uplift, and comfort and includes petitions on behalf of others and forgiveness prayers. Prayers that request better understanding for improved self-control, that seek to understand God's universe and to attain higher meanings and values, become true spiritual prayers. "Jesus taught that the prayer for divine guidance over the pathway of earthly life was next in importance to the petition for a knowledge of the Father's will. In reality this means a prayer for divine wisdom. Jesus never taught that human knowledge and special skill could be gained by prayer. But he did teach that prayer is a factor in the enlargement of one's capacity to receive the presence of the divine spirit."[7] Sincere prayer assists the individual in attuning to the guidance of the Indwelling Spirit.

Praying out of helplessness or distress is natural, but we are destined to disappointment when placing requests before God. Prayer is only effective relative to our own personal efforts to achieve the answers to such prayers. Indeed, prayer best serves as a stimulus to action to solve our own problems and difficulties, albeit with the guidance of our Indwelling Spirit. According to epochal revelation, it is not the mission of the Indwelling Spirit to lessen the hardships of life but to face them with you. "You could be so comforted and inspired, so enthralled and intrigued, if you would only allow the Adjuster constantly to bring forth the pictures of the real motive, the final aim, and the eternal purpose of all this difficult, uphill struggle with the commonplace problems of your present material world."[8]

When we grow in our understanding of God, we consciously open ourselves to the inspiration and guidance of our Indwelling Spirit and to taking responsibility for dealing constructively with our problems. We realize that God is, indeed, the beckoning spirit but that we must do the work. When we fully grasp the truth of the factual presence of the Indwelling Spirit as the representative of the Universal Father, then we are essentially speaking with God through prayer as if face to face with him. "There is no other technique whereby every man, regardless of all other mortal accomplishments, can so effectively and immediately approach the threshold of that realm wherein he can communicate with his Maker, where the creature contacts with the reality of the Creator, with the indwelling Thought Adjuster."[9] Indeed, the practice of living faith, supported by sincere, wholehearted, and unselfish prayer, guarantees contact with God.

Prayer involves both our greeting to God and our attention to his guidance in all matters. "Jesus taught his followers that, when they had made their prayers to the Father, they should remain for a time in silent receptivity to afford the indwelling spirit the better opportunity to speak to the listening soul."[10] This process of attunement to spirit guidance enriches the prayer experience and culminates in decision/action in consecrated obedience to the will of the Father. For example, thanking God in prayer may indicate authentic gratefulness, but this is a passive form of gratitude. Spiritual gratitude in its highest expression is active; it *chooses* to see the best even during the worst of times. We *choose* to keep silent when we feel like complaining. We *choose* to share when we feel like hoarding. Genuine gratitude is personal work that leads us one step closer to living the golden rule.

As a child, I never cared to recite from a prayer book, nor did I enjoy praying in groups; it all felt too impersonal. The standard words failed to evoke the

1. Ángel de mi guardia, dulce compañía.	My guardian angel, sweet companion.
No me desampares, ni de noche ni de día.	Do not forsake me in the night nor during the day.
Si me desamparas, "¿Qué será de mí?"	If you forsake me, "What will become of me?"
Ángel de mi guardia, ruega a Dios por mí.	My guardian angel, pray to God for me.
2. Al acostarme en mi cama tres ángeles encontré.	As I went to bed, I found three angels.
Uno en el cabecero y dos a los pies.	One by the headboard and two at my feet.
Y a Jesucristo en el medio diciendo: "Descansa, reposa, no le tengas miedo a ninguna cosa."	And Jesus Christ at the center saying: "Rest, sleep, and fear not."

peace I felt in two simple prayers that my mother taught me in Spanish. I loved to say them at night as I was falling asleep or if I was awakened by a nightmare. They always gave me solace and the assurance that I was safe.

The first prayer was recited as if I were speaking directly with my guardian angel. The second prayer I vividly visualized—on two occasions while in bed I had a superconscious experience of the sacred heart of Jesus looking over me. I now share these prayers with you, although as in most translations, the English version lost its rhyme.

There is but one form of prayer which is appropriate for all God's children, and that is: 'Nevertheless, your will be done.

The Urantia Book

As I got older, I abandoned these simple yet profound prayers. I prayed when in need, but my prayers were often trite and lacking in spirit conviction.

After my encounter with the guru Ammachi, I found myself once again attending church services, and surprisingly, enjoying the formal group prayers that I had once disliked. I also developed a strong desire to connect with God on a personal level. I decided to pray as if I were speaking personally to God, just as I had done with my guardian angel as a child. I would mentally address God everywhere—in the car, at work, at business meetings, even in workshops. I addressed him as a friend. When I grasped the significance of the Indwelling Spirit and its relation to God and the soul, my experience of prayer shifted. The realization of the actual indwelling presence of a fragment of God evoked immense reverence and gratefulness. My petitions for help with everyday problems faded, and cultivating the capacity to express God's divine nature became the compelling purpose of my life.

Quite unexpectedly, I started to feel connected to God all the time whether in prayer or not. The feeling of gratitude and reverence was so overwhelming that on one such occasion, I wrote this poem to capture it:

Oh God, my Beloved.
In the eternity of life I feel the comfort of Thy Love.
I feel Thy bright light like a bubbling volcano erupting in its entire splendor.
In the intense heat of Thy Love,
I feel the cooling, soothing waters of Thy Presence;
Forever in my heart;
Forever present along the path that leads to eternal bliss.
My Beloved,
Never leave my side.
Continue to pour Thy Light
Immersing me deeper and deeper in the ocean of Thy Love.
What ecstasy to feel Thee so close, so near!
Thy presence deep inside like a burning coal;
Yet soothing and comforting like the early morning sun.
What longing!!! My soul in such rapture enveloped by Thy Love!

The words of the sixteenth-century Spanish mystic Saint Teresa of Avila began to resonate within me: ". . . mental prayer in my opinion is nothing else than an intimate sharing between friends; it means taking time frequently to be alone with him who we know loves us."[11] Prayer became the heartfelt and trusting communion between the creature and Creator, the child and the loving Father, ranging from an active petition to the Father to silent adoration. As I practiced listening for the Father's guidance, the experience of prayer took on new meaning. It was not only a technique for developing devotion, but also for accessing the spiritual vision that enables the faithful to personally find God in eternity. Such cosmic insight has the spiritual potency to spark consecrated self-transformation and ignite the brotherhood of man.

Mechanics of Prayer

We may sometimes wonder about the mechanics of prayer. Are our prayers heard? Epochal revelation informs us that bona fide adoration and worship always goes directly to the Universal Father via the Indwelling Spirit.

All prayers for personal requests no matter to whom they are addressed, rise to the Creator Son to be interpreted for spiritual value; prayers of selfish intent or for material enrichment go unanswered. "If anything originates in your consciousness that is fraught with supreme spiritual value, when once you give it expression, no power in the universe can prevent its flashing directly to the Absolute Spirit Personality of all creation. Conversely, if your supplications are purely material and wholly self-centered, there exists no plan whereby such unworthy prayers can find lodgment in the spirit circuit of the Eternal Son . . . such purely selfish and material requests fall dead; they do not ascend in the circuits of true spirit values. Such words are as 'sounding brass and a tinkling cymbal.'"[12]

True praying is the sincere attitude of reaching heavenward for the attainment of your ideals.

The Urantia Book

Our willingness and capacity to receive the guidance of the Indwelling Spirit are determining factors in the heavenly blessings we can realize as an answer to prayer. When we actively cultivate universal intelligence and courageously take steps to face our challenges, we are acting in accordance with the will of the Father and setting the stage for our prayers to be answered. However, being creatures of time and space, we may never understand the divine response to our diverse prayers, hence the colloquialism, "God works in mysterious ways."

An urge to pray may stem from personal desire or the influence of angelic ministry. Guardian angels are constantly seeking ways to help their God-knowing charges expand their cosmic perspectives and recognize the presence of the Indwelling Spirit. Likewise, in the divine symmetry of mind and spirit, when we become receptive to our indwelling Father-fragment, we can better cooperate with all the spiritual presences at our disposal.

We can pray on our own or we can pray collectively with groups who gather to enhance their connection with God. "Group or congregational praying is very effective in that it is highly socializing in its repercussions. When a group engages in community prayer for moral enhancement and spiritual uplift, such devotions are reactive upon the individuals composing the group; they are all made better because of participation. Even a whole city or an entire nation can be helped by such prayer devotions. Confession, repentance, and prayer have led individuals, cities, nations, and whole races to mighty efforts of reform and courageous deeds of valorous achievement."[13]

Worship

Worship is generally defined as reverence or devotion to a divine being or supernatural power, embracing activities such as prayer, formal liturgies, rituals, pilgrimages, singing of hymns and psalms, and dance.

Personally, the act of worship harbors mystery and uncertainty for me—my mind can grasp the familiar concepts, but I know in my soul that there is more than I could ever understand or express in this lifetime. Is it worship if my heart feels full of love and gratitude for God? Or when I am doing the will of the Father by sincere efforts to cultivate and express the qualities of divinity? It seems that both go hand in hand. Perhaps worship is the reaction to the deep appreciation of the Father's loving and giving personality, a giving of oneself. If that is the case, then worship is love in motion; the greater the appreciation and reverence, the greater the selflessness and the deeper the worship.

> *The spirit of the Father speaks best to man when the human mind is in an attitude of true worship.*
>
> The Urantia Book

Earlier in my life, I believed that worship was the same as praying—alone or with others—attending church services, or chanting. I spent some time worshiping, and then I was finished for a while. This now rings hollow to me. Religious activities *can* lead to true worship through a humble attitude of appreciation and reverence. But without greater Deity understanding, relations with God remain shallow and our devotional practices ritualistic, devoid of the spiritual driving power that progressively augments the quality of our love for God and of our dedication to serve others selflessly in his name.

"Worship is the highest privilege and the first duty of all created intelligences. Worship is the conscious and joyous act of recognizing and acknowledging the truth and fact of the intimate and personal relationships of the Creators with their creatures. The quality of worship is determined by the depth of creature perception; and as the knowledge of the infinite character of the Gods progresses, the act of worship becomes increasingly all-encompassing until it eventually attains the glory of the highest experiential delight and the most exquisite pleasure known to created beings."[14]

We elevate the worship experience when we recognize two concepts of deity: the transcendence of God and the immanence of God. In the former, we encounter a personal God whom we can strive to emulate and personally find in eternity, giving greater meaning to our devotional practices. In the latter, we embrace the indwelling presence of a fragment of that same God that spiritualizes our thinking and communicates to the divine Father the inexpressible yearning of our soul for union with God. "Worship is, therefore, the act of the material mind's assenting to the attempt of its spiritualizing self, under the guidance of the associated spirit, to communicate with God as a faith son of the Universal Father. The mortal mind consents to worship; the immortal soul craves and initiates worship; the divine Adjuster presence conducts such worship in behalf of the mortal mind and the evolving immortal soul."[15] This understanding gave me great comfort. I may feel inept at worshiping God, but I do feel the craving of my soul for God and I trust my Indwelling Spirit to communicate the love I have cultivated for God directly to him.

Jesus taught many great insights about the worship experience that can help us gain a greater perspective of worship. In particular, he placed emphasis on the following:

- Worship is the technique of looking to the *One* for the inspiration of service to the *many*.

- Worship is the yardstick that measures the extent of the soul's detachment from the material universe and its simultaneous and secure attachment to the spiritual realities of all creation.

- Worship is effortless attention, true and ideal soul rest, a form of restful spiritual exertion.

- Worship is the act of a part identifying itself with the Whole; the finite with the Infinite; the son with the Father; time in the act of striking step with eternity.

- Worship is the act of the son's personal communion with the divine Father, the assumption of refreshing, creative, fraternal, and romantic attitudes by the human soul-spirit. [16]

The major distinction between worship and prayer is that worship requests nothing and demands nothing in return. We simply worship God for what we comprehend him to be. When our prayer finally seeks nothing, either for self or other; when the attitude is solely one of giving praise and reverence to God; it is then that such attitudes of the soul attain to the levels of true worship.

We are truly worshiping when our hearts are filled with love and appreciation for God as we increasingly do the will of the Father. "[T]here is nothing which man can give to God except this choosing to abide by the Father's will, and such decisions, effected by the intelligent will creatures of the universes, constitute the reality of that true worship which is so satisfying to the love-dominated nature of the Creator Father."[17] We grow in the experience of worship as we become love in motion.

Jesus taught that worship brings one nearer to God, and the worshiper becomes more Godlike. "Worship is a transforming experience whereby the finite [human] gradually approaches and ultimately attains the presence of the Infinite [God]."[18] Individual worship will be addressed in greater depth in the chapter on spirit attunement.

Group Worship

True worship is the expression of genuine reverence, sending praise to God. Just as the quality and depth of our personal worship experience reflects our status of communion with God, so does the quality of collective worship reflect the group's relationship to God. True worship in group settings lifts the individual closer to God while it nourishes spiritual camaraderie among the participants. "There is a real purpose in the socialization of religion. It is the purpose of group religious activities to dramatize the loyalties of religion; to magnify the lures of truth, beauty, and goodness; to foster the attractions of supreme values; to enhance the service of unselfish fellowship; to glorify the potentials of family life; to promote religious education; to provide wise counsel and spiritual guidance; and to encourage group worship."[19]

Group worship, typically in organized religious settings, has become an experience in which the individual is all too often the focus. Religious services are often judged by whether or not the worshiper was "spiritually massaged."

Congregational worship, as well as personal worship, can become rote and uninspired. In an article titled *Worship: Definition and Purpose of Worship*, Jimmy Cutter states: "Misunderstandings about the real purpose of worship have contributed to sterile congregational worship and have devastated the potential for growth in many churches."[20] Below, Cutter describes three factors that account for our misunderstandings: our culture, personal imbalance, and a lack of private worship.

" 1. **Our culture.** We live at a frantic pace. We live in an 'instant' age. Television has taught us to expect instant gratification of our every desire and need. Patience in our society is a scarce commodity. It is hard to be patient even in fast food restaurants; somehow they are not fast enough. This characteristic of our culture has carried over into our spiritual lives and particularly in our worship, and in insidious ways.

   . . . Many times we rush into our congregational worship services. Worship by its very nature demands a preparation of heart. It involves refocusing our mind and heart from self, others, and cares of this life to God.

   Physically we may be quiet, but our minds are still racing. They are occupied with life outside of the service.

   When we do mentally adjust to a quieter atmosphere, we may not focus upon God. We may look around us to see who is attending the service or we determine whether or not the singing is 'on' or 'off,' or we fight drowsiness . . . We look approvingly or disapprovingly at our watches. We walk out. We greet people. We get in our cars and discuss the merits or demerits of the sermon.

   How tragic! We have gone and been sung to, preached at, and informed about coming events, but we have not worshiped because God did not receive anything from us. We were in a hurry. We were not prepared. We evaluated our experience by how much we received.

2. **An Imbalance.** Worship involves a balance of our intellect, emotion and will.

   a. **Intellectual response**. Worship involves knowledge. We must know about God. We must know something about who He is and what He has done, before we can ascribe worth to Him. Unfortunately many often concentrate on an intellectual response. It is important but it is not the whole of it.

b. **Emotional response.** Emotional excess in some quarters has made many wary of any emotional expression. However, when we focus on the greatness, power, majesty, wisdom, and love of God it creates joy, exuberance, a liveliness that is the opposite of dead, ritualistic services.

c. **Volitional response.** Worship also involves our will. We must constantly submit our will to His will.

3. **A lack of private worship.** Our daily relationship to God in worship is to be characterized by an attitude and practice of thanksgiving. If we are not thankful of people in our private lives, we probably will not engage in meaningful congregational worship."

The declining quality of group worship will continue unless we reflect on our understanding of personal prayer and worship and elevate their meanings; unless we seek a balance of our physical, emotional, mental, and spiritual energies; unless we integrate reason and love. As we strive to attain these things, the motivation for true worship will blossom in our hearts. For a congregation, this will translate to a genuine, fulfilling, and effective worship experience that will be reflected in the quality of our service and in our ability to treat others with a wise, loving, and selfless attitude.

In these troubled times, there is an increasing need to expand our relationship with God. Many people are hungry for a deeper meaning in life, for a God connection. We like our religious music to enliven our souls, a sermon that is relevant to our lives, and a worship service that energizes us. These spiritual needs are being increasingly filled by nondenominational and community religious groups. Many are breaking from the rituals of tradition and providing a slate of programs, including seminars, guest speakers, online continuing education classes, nursery school, and youth ministry—all in tune with modern times.

A more flexible approach to spirituality is a step in the right direction. When individual worship is invigorated, group worship will develop depth. Genuine worship reveals an attitude of giving to God which is developed through our individual, dynamic, and ongoing efforts at knowing God, communing with God, and doing his will. Feeling exhilarated during a service may be a satisfying experience but a short-lived "weekly spiritual dose" hardly affects social progress. The exquisite experience of unbroken communion with God flowing from a heart full of worship is the ultimate achievement of our sincere and ongoing efforts to know God and do the Father's will.

A congregational worship experience can be enlivened and deepened when members are inspired to cultivate the experience of individual worship. Group worship can be a collective outburst of adoration to God that increasingly energizes the souls of every individual in the congregation, flowing into their communities. The growing harmony of the personality will be reflected in the quality of the social interactions as members increasingly express love, happiness, and compassion in their everyday lives.

My Favorite Prayers

Oh God, help me to perceive Thee. Help me to perceive myself. For in understanding Thee, I will know about myself. And once I understand myself, I will know about Thee. Thus, I beseech thee my God, to discover me to myself.　　　 ~ *St. Augustine*, Confessions

Grant me, O Lord my God, a mind to know you, a heart to seek you, wisdom to find you, conduct pleasing to you, faithful perseverance in waiting for you, and a hope of finally embracing you.　　　 ~ *Thomas Aquinas*

I am a daughter (son) of God in tune with my Indwelling Spirit.

I surround myself with a robe of white light comprised of the Love, Power and Wisdom of God. Not only for my protection, but that so all who come into contact with it, may be drawn to God and healed.
　　　 ~ *Gift from Sandy Thomas (author unknown)*

I commit myself to the Will of God. I give my heart and soul to God. I deserve the best in life. I serve the best cause in life. I am a divine manifestation of God.　　　 ~ *Barbara-Ann Brennan*

My Judge and my Knower! Give me Thy Light and the Light of Thy Knower. Let me always be conscious of Thee, that I may do my duties, consciously one with Thee.　　　 ~ *Author unknown*

Thy will be done this day! Today is a day of completion. I give thanks for this perfect day. Miracle shall follow miracles and wonders shall never cease.
　　　 ~ *Florence Scovel Shinn*, Law of Nonresistance

My soul praises you, Oh Lord, and in all things I give thanks. ~ *J. K. Primm*

32.

Attuning to Spirit Guidance

When my children once become self-conscious of the assurance
of the divine presence, such a faith will expand the mind, ennoble the soul,
reinforce the personality, augment the happiness, deepen the spirit perception,
and enhance the power to love and be loved.

The Urantia Book

From a spiritual and cosmic perspective, attuning to spirit guidance is to first become keenly aware of all the circuitry and beings of universe ministry to mortals—from the lowest adjutant to the very presence of God within. This expanded grasp of living spirit realities increases receptivity to the divine guidance, which invariably enhances the worship experience. Our moral choices and spiritual motivation provide leverage for the Indwelling Spirit to function, orchestrating spirit harmony and registering in our minds his personal development plan for us with growing clarity and conviction. We increase attunement to the spirit within us by:

" 1. Choosing to respond to divine leading; sincerely basing the human life on the highest consciousness of truth, beauty, and goodness, and then coordinating these qualities of divinity through wisdom, worship, faith, and love.

2. Loving God and desiring to be like him—genuine recognition of the divine fatherhood and loving worship of the heavenly Parent.

3. Loving man and sincerely desiring to serve him—wholehearted recognition of the brotherhood of man coupled with an intelligent and wise affection for each of your fellow mortals.

4. Joyful acceptance of cosmic citizenship—honest recognition of your progressive obligations to the Supreme Being, awareness of the

interdependence of evolutionary man and evolving Deity. This is the birth of cosmic morality and the dawning realization of universal duty."[1]

We can develop attunement to our Indwelling Spirit through the regular practice of meditation. My personal understanding of meditation underwent a major restructuring through the process of writing *Heaven Is Not the Last Stop*. This chapter was a huge challenge because lingering beliefs clouded my objectivity. I had been a practitioner and teacher of Transcendental Meditation for over twenty-five years, and certainly believed I knew the mechanics, purpose, and benefits of meditation! However, one of my commitments in creating this book was that I would honestly question all my existing beliefs on the subject of meditation. After a long period of research and reconciliation with epochal revelation, new insights did emerge, which evolved into lessons about solitude, meditation, and relaxation.

Solitude

Philosophically, solitude means coping positively with time spent alone; it is in solitude that we can spend quiet time alone with God.

Many people are uncomfortable being alone, and they find silence hard to take. They use noise, excitement, and busy jobs to distract them from the higher calling of worshipful reflection. This busy-ness is an escape from the boredom (resulting from our own choices), which many of us remedy with diversions. We thwart raising the level of cooperation, peace, and harmony that would be of benefit to us in our daily lives by refusing to take a few moments to really feel silence and experience solitude.

Although the terms "solitude" and "loneliness" are often used interchangeably, there is a significant difference between them. In solitude, we are content in our own company and deal constructively with our time; but "[l]oneliness is a negative state, marked by a sense of isolation. One feels that something is missing. It is possible to be with people and still feel lonely— perhaps the bitterest form of loneliness."[2]

Our aversion to loneliness is surely one reason why silence is so rarely a parenting priority, yet silence can help our children develop the capacity to feel comfortable with being alone. It is a valuable component of child development that fosters creativity and expression, increases awareness, and helps children achieve their full potential.

It is in solitude that children and adults alike find the space to think and to reflect on life, to become fully aware of their deepest needs, feelings, and impulses. In silence, we learn to feel comfortable just *being* rather than *doing*. In quietness, as we come to recognize the leadings of our inner guidance, we discover that we are never alone. Jesus of Nazareth often spent time in solitude, reflecting on his mission and planning his strategy for revealing the divine nature of the Father to humankind.

Solitude is learned behavior. It is an acquired attitude that is beneficial to cultivate. The experience of being healthily alone is not only a step toward physical renewal, but is also a stairway to productive reflection. The following suggestions can help create a quiet environment and cultivate a comfortable silence:

- Start the day by taking at least five minutes in the morning to sit and enjoy a quiet wakefulness.

- Look for moments throughout the day when you can sit quietly for a few minutes. At a convenient time, occasionally close your eyes, take a few deep breaths, and let them out very, very slowly.

- Do an exercise routine without external input (e.g., exercise tape, class, or exercise partner).

- Read in silence.

- Take leisure walks in natural environments near you.

- Do household chores in silence.

- Enjoy an occasional quiet meal alone.

- When driving, occasionally drive in silence.

- Turn off controllable external input (e.g., the cell phone, TV, and radio) for short intervals during the day.

Meditation

Meditation is defined as ". . . a practice of concentrated focus upon a sound, object, visualization, the breath, movement, or attention itself in order to increase awareness of the present moment, reduce stress, promote relaxation, and enhance personal and spiritual growth."[3]

Modern definitions of meditation generally reflect an Eastern influence. Even the Christian tradition of contemplation is now sometimes referred to as meditation. There are many styles of meditation, each having its unique intellectual foundation and methods of practice. In this chapter, meditation is explored and defined in the light of epochal revelation, giving it a fresh and fuller perspective. The phrases "spiritual communion," "divine attunement," and "worshipful meditation" are all interchangeable and the word "meditation" will refer to all meditative practices.

Jesus spent much of his time communing with his own soul, for it is through our inner thought that we contact God. To this remarkable man, out of the silence of his own soul, came a direct revelation of his Sonship, his Oneness with God.

The Urantia Book

The basic benefits of meditation are acclaimed throughout the spiritual and medical communities. These benefits include stress reduction, deep relaxation, improved cardiovascular health, emotional cleansing and balancing, increased creativity, focused intelligence, increased self-control, and clearer intuition and alertness. Meditation is often accompanied by sentiments such as love, serenity, and joy, which enrich social interactions. In addition, regular meditation as a spiritual discipline enlivens a sense of integral connection between our planet and its inhabitants; individuals feel environmentally concerned, attuned to economic and social justice, and more concerned with attaining peace in the world. The psychophysical benefits of a meditation practice are proven valuable for a healthier, happier, and more balanced life.

Meditation supports the development of the emotional maturity that is essential to the self-control and moral growth that fosters spiritual progress and unselfish urges. Honesty, devotion, and self-control produce the ideal soil for the growth of spiritual aspirations and enhancement of spiritual insight.

According to Dr. Michael J. Baime, in his article "Meditation and Mindfulness," "Meditation cultivates an emotional stability that allows the meditator to experience intense emotions fully while simultaneously maintaining perspective on them."[4] Such an experience of emotional stability not only increases confidence and control of life, but it also leads to useful insights into our thoughts, feelings, and actions.

Studies with an electroencephalograph (EEG) of the brain during meditation have shown that the practice induces alpha and theta brainwaves. Alpha waves are generated when a person is relaxed, focused, and aware, and is most evident during light meditation. Alpha meditations are effective in reducing stress, which in turn promotes a positive functioning individual. Theta brainwaves are associated with deeper meditation and prayer and support a free flow of ideas that occur without censorship or guilt. The mind is clear, highly receptive to information and inspiration, and rapidly makes associations based on personal beliefs and understandings. Regular practice of theta meditation can increase creativity, enhance learning ability, reduce stress, and awaken intuition.

The goals of meditation are best appreciated when we recognize the transcendence of a personal God and the indwelling presence of a fragment of that same God. It's also helpful to acknowledge our spirit nature—the soul—and understand its relationship to the mind, personality, and the God-fragment within. Meditation, when used as a spiritual practice, is rooted in direct awareness of the divine presence, rather than in the striving to achieve and continually reproduce a certain state of consciousness. To discover new and higher spiritual meanings in our concept of meditation, we'll explore the experience of divine presence in the light of epochal revelation and relate it to the development of God-consciousness.

Divine Presence

As we saw in chapter 4, God in his transcendent aspect maintains parental contact with all personal creatures through his personality circuit and also acts *directly* in the human mind via the prepersonal fragment of Deity that comes to reside in each one of us at the moment of our first moral decision. The concept that God is present in each human being is shared by many religious traditions, though they may understand God's indwelling in different ways, and each has its own terminology to express this.

The fact that human beings are endowed with personality means they are able to recognize the presence of another consciousness, even a divine consciousness. This indwelling divine presence can be felt by anyone regardless of age, faith, or gender. "You can argue over opinions about God, but experience with him and in him exists above and beyond all human controversy and mere intellectual logic."[5]

Epochal revelation affirms that as civilization advances, interpretation of religious experiences must be examined critically for reasonability. "The experience of God-consciousness remains the same from generation to generation, but with each advancing epoch in human knowledge the philosophic concept and the theologic definitions of God *must* change. God-knowingness, religious consciousness, is a universe reality, but no matter how valid (real) religious experience is, it must be willing to subject itself to intelligent criticism and reasonable philosophic interpretation; it must not seek to be a thing apart in the totality of human experience."[6]

Awareness of divine presence is usually associated with one or more of the following:

- A sense of union
- Perception of infinity and eternity, often sensed along with a cessation of time
- A sense of spiritual growth
- Light
- Lingering feelings of love and joy
- An impulse to express virtues through action

These experiences remain constant from generation to generation because of the factual indwelling presence of the spirit of the Father. Likewise, the similarities of mystical experience that religious seekers of all beliefs and background share is due to the identical nature of the Indwelling Spirit within us all.

The significant difference between theistic (God-centered) and nontheistic religionists arises because the latter discern reality from the level of direct experience of this internal and impersonal divinity but do not recognize its origin—the transcendent personal God. This is understandable. The experience of *immanence* does not by itself facilitate the realization of *transcendence*: "The prepersonal divine spirit which indwells the mortal mind carries, in its very presence, the valid proof of its actual existence, but the concept of the divine personality can be grasped only by the spiritual insight of genuine personal religious experience. Any person, human or divine, may be known and comprehended quite apart from the external reactions or the material presence of that person."[7]

The Indwelling Spirit may be impersonal, but being a fragment of the personal God, it emanates a sense of divinity that is personal in the highest sense. This is why this divine entity acting upon and within human personality is experienced as the wellspring of love, the impulse that propels us toward unselfish interest in the welfare of others, and signals awareness that we are possessed of a well-nigh infinite spiritual potential. But since no two mortals are alike, there is no singular interpretation of the leadings and urges of the spirit of divinity that lives within their minds. "The divine presence which any child of the universe enjoys at any given moment is limited only by the capacity of such a creature to receive and to discern the spirit actualities of the supermaterial world."[8]

The Indwelling Spirit has such a luminous nature that when experienced by the human mind it tends to diminish the importance of matter, even to the point where some religious systems declare matter to be an illusion or a projection. Epochal revelation explains that matter, mind, and spirit are equally real, with mind being the mediator between physical and spiritual realities. "The eye of the material mind perceives a world of factual knowledge; the eye of the spiritualized intellect discerns a world of true values. These two views, synchronized and harmonized, reveal the world of reality, wherein wisdom interprets the phenomena of the universe in terms of progressive personal experience."[9] Mind can never reconcile the various levels of the cosmos, nor can the spiritually advancing human fully appreciate her certain destiny, unless the mind chooses to harmonize its relationship to spirit *and* matter.

When we recognize the reality of the transcendent Universal Father as well as experience the indwelling presence of the spirit of the Father, meditation as a spiritual practice becomes not only a technique to increase awareness of divine presence but also a means to facilitate fellowship with God. While the Universal Father, through the personality circuit, is aware of all the thoughts and acts of every individual in the universes of time and space, the love and adoration for God that we cultivate must first be acknowledged as bona fide by the Indwelling Spirit before it is forwarded to the Universal Father through the personality circuit. Growth in the recognition and appreciation of the transcendence and immanence of God progressively aligns human will with divine will and increases the quality of worship.

Epochal revelation greatly expands our understanding of divine presence while it clarifies the role of meditation. It does all this within the framework of the Divine Plan of Progress to inform and inspire the discovery of new and higher spiritual meanings and values.

Realizing God

The Divine Plan of Progress is twofold in nature: God reaching down to embrace his children, and planetary creatures reaching up in faith for their divine parent. Seekers intuitively know this and set out to attain divinity—not to *be* God but to realize God. God-realization reflects personal growth in cosmic understanding, spiritual vision, and experience with ascending levels of Deity; the ultimate achievement is standing in the presence of the Universal Father in Paradise as a perfected spirit. Progress in God-realization is directly linked to progress in the development of God-consciousness, a process that begins with the first inkling of faith and continues throughout eternity. "Were it possible for the lower orders of intelligence to be transported instantly into the presence of the Father himself, they would not know they were there. They would there be just as oblivious of the presence of the Universal Father as where they now are.

There is a long, long road ahead of mortal man before he can consistently and within the realms of possibility ask for safe conduct into the Paradise presence of the Universal Father. Spiritually, man must be translated many times before he can attain a plane that will yield the spiritual vision which will enable him to see even any one of the Seven Master Spirits."[10]

Growth in spiritual vision, in God-realization, embraces those adjustments of the human will and those transformations in the human mind that enable the God-conscious intellect to gradually become spirit-taught and eventually spirit-led:

- Recognition of God begins with the choice to believe in Deity, personal or impersonal. *Faith is not optional.*

- Belief in God evokes the impulse of prayer, vocal or mental—genuine acts of petition, adoration, contrition, or thanksgiving. *Sincerity is required.*

- Belief in Deity is personally validated when a person experiences divine presence as profound feelings of gratitude, joy, or divine union during heartfelt prayer, meditation, or immersion in sacred scripture. It is sometimes expressed in spontaneous episodes of deep wonder for the miracle of life. Sensitivity to divine presence is the precursor to the personal realization of the factual indwelling presence of divinity. *Progressive spirit attunement.*

  - However, when the experience of divine presence is not supported by depth of Deity comprehension—personal and impersonal—the transformative power of the Indwelling Spirit is neglected and the cosmic scheme of self-identification with the Universal Father is disrupted. Meditation may drift into passive receptivity where the intensity of the experience and the manifestation of divine gifts become the indicators or even the motive of spiritual growth.

- Expanding knowledge of the cosmic family leads to a deeper appreciation for the spirit of God—the Indwelling Spirit, the Spirit of Truth, the Holy Spirit, the adjutant mind-spirits and the evolving nature of the Supreme. All these divine impulses of God's love inspire dynamic, personal, and subtly interactive spiritual communion. *Sharing the inner life with God.*[11]

- Balanced growth in God-consciousness and increased receptivity and obedience to the guidance of the Indwelling Spirit develop the soul, the human personality's companion to the afterlife. Determined motive ensures immortality, the eventual fusion of human will with divine will—unity of the evolving nature of the creature with the perfect nature of the Creator. "Only as a creature becomes God-identified, does he become truly real in the universes."[12] *The quest for true spirit status.*

- In the afterlife, progress in acquiring spiritual vision continues with the sequential recognition of successive levels of Deity as spirit persons. First we find the Creator Son of the local universe; then recognition expands to the Ancients of Days and Master Spirit of the superuniverse. In Havona, ascending mortals achieve personality comprehension of God the Supreme.[13] In Paradise, as perfected spirits, we ultimately behold, first the Infinite Spirit, then the Eternal Son, and finally the spirit person of the Universal Father. *Entering the Corps of the Finality.*

Without cognitive recognition of the Universal Father and the cosmic relationships between God and humanity, meditation can become merely a self-serving contemplation of Deity. It can also mistakenly lead to seeing the soul/self as divine—higher human consciousness perceived as divine consciousness—ironically fostering an attitude of self-aggrandizement, even spiritual narcissism. "True, many apparently religious traits can grow out of nonreligious roots. Man can, intellectually, deny God and yet be morally good, loyal, filial, honest, and even idealistic. Man may graft many purely humanistic branches onto his basic spiritual nature and thus apparently prove his contentions in behalf of a Godless religion, but such an experience is devoid of survival values, God-knowingness and God-ascension. In such a mortal experience only social fruits are forthcoming, not spiritual. The graft determines the nature of the fruit, notwithstanding that the living sustenance is drawn from the roots of original divine endowment of both mind and spirit."[14]

To God-loving individuals who have not had an experience of God's presence, intellectual acknowledgement of the Indwelling Spirit and efforts to gain greater understanding of cosmic relationships will expand their capacity to discern the indwelling presence of God and their ability to receive its guidance. Those who have felt the expansive presence of God through contemplative prayer or group worship, for example, will gratefully graduate to the next stage of *reciprocal* communion with God. Harmony between cosmic understanding and spiritual perception will be evidenced in the growing selflessness expressed when serving others. "Religion is not a technique for attaining a static and blissful peace of mind; it is an impulse for organizing the soul for dynamic service. It is the enlistment of the totality of selfhood in the loyal service of loving God and serving man."[15] Growth in identification with the Universal Father and recognition of the Indwelling Spirit foster attunement with the divine consciousness that engenders a harvest of the fruits of the spirit: divine worship, brotherly love, and selfless service—essential not only to evolving spiritual selfhood but also to collective peace.

All human beings are equally privileged to seek intimate personal communion with the Indwelling Spirit of divine origin, and all can choose to accept the uniform spiritual leadings. But we are encouraged to be practical and grounded in this pursuit, by constantly progressing in a firm intellectual grasp of true universe realities. Otherwise, we may be unable to distinguish authentic spiritual experiences from their look-alike counterfeits. Or we may become addicted to feeling the thrill of exalted states but unable to transfer the essence of real experiences of the divine into meaningful activities that serve the Father's plan. "The characteristics of the mystical state are diffusion of consciousness with vivid islands of focal attention operating on a comparatively passive intellect. All of this gravitates consciousness toward the subconscious rather than in the direction of the zone of spiritual contact, the superconscious. Many mystics have carried their mental dissociation to the level of abnormal mental manifestations."[16] Locutions, visions, psychic gifts, or extraordinary religious practices are not necessarily evidence of attunement with the spirit of the Father.

Spiritual humility and the wholehearted desire to do God's will ensure growth in identification with the Universal Father. These superior attitudes allow the human mind to gravitate toward the superconscious—the domain of the Indwelling Spirit, whose guidance forever leads us toward intelligent worship, progressive intellectual and factual expansion, and selfless social service.

Worshipful Meditation

The acts of meditation and genuine prayer add to spiritual growth; they can transform attitudes and generate a fulfillment that results from connecting with divinity. When we recognize the indwelling presence of the spirit of the Father and understand its significance in our lives, prayer and meditation take on a new meaning. We develop a longing, not only to connect with this indwelling divine presence, but to grow in the experience of worship.

"The divine presence cannot, however, be discovered anywhere in nature or even in the lives of God-knowing mortals so fully and so certainly as in your attempted communion with the indwelling Mystery Monitor, the Paradise Thought Adjuster."[17]

The essence of worshipful meditation is to intentionally open our minds and hearts—our whole being—to the presence and guidance of God within. The mystery of this inner presence exists beyond thoughts, words, or emotions. When we consent to the divine presence, it becomes a wellspring of inner peace, leading to a more intimate relationship with God and all persons in our life. This intention to personally interact with the Indwelling Spirit supercharges worshipful meditation and unleashes dynamic spiritual energy that invigorates personal and social transformation. Although we may reach the state of pure awareness, the goal of many practices, we are tethered *in relationship* with God; we identify ourselves *with* spirit rather than *as* spirit. This faith movement reflects the existence of God in human experience, justifies intelligent worship, and validates the hope of personality survival.[18]

Spiritual communion through prayer is the soul's urge to identify itself with the spiritual nature of heavenly ideals. Spiritual communion through the practice of worshipful meditation, however, is the personal realization of our divine fellowship with God that summons his *real presence*. Worshipful meditation is an elevated form of prayer that acknowledges and reciprocates the faith-insight that "Man does not have to go farther than his own inner experience of the soul's contemplation of this spiritual-reality presence to find God and attempt communion with him."[19]

Worshipful meditation positions the mind away from self and directs it toward the superconscious circuit, where the Indwelling Spirit awaits our sincere call. Worshipful meditation is effortless attention on God the Father and faithful receptivity to the guidance of the Indwelling Spirit. This mode of building "friendship with God"[20] becomes the means to gather strength and wisdom for the ordinary conflicts in our lives, and appropriates the energy to solve the higher problems of a moral and spiritual nature.

During his teen years, Jesus was known to spend time in "profound meditation and serious contemplation"[21] and frequently journeyed to the hilltop to pray. This was his way of getting to know his heavenly Father. He was faced with many difficulties as he grew up, and the time taken in communion with his Father summoned the insight he needed to make wise decisions. Astonishingly, we have the same opportunity in our lives. A part of God lives within us, and we can draw close to his presence. When we do this, we open a great treasure chest of wisdom and compassion to help with the decisions and difficulties in our lives. Ever-increasing happiness is always the experience of every person who nurtures a relationship with the Divine Indwelling. "This worshipful practice of your Master brings that relaxation which renews the mind; that illumination which inspires the soul; that courage which enables one bravely to face one's problems; that self-understanding which obliterates debilitating fear; and that consciousness of union with divinity which equips man with the assurance that enables him to dare to be Godlike. The relaxation of worship, or spiritual communion as practiced by the Master, relieves tension, removes conflicts, and mightily augments the total resources of the personality."[22]

Worshipful meditation is ". . . a transforming experience whereby the finite gradually approaches and ultimately attains the presence of the Infinite."[23] But our interpretation of the inner experience of divine presence is limited without an expansion in our concept of Deity. We can indeed eventually experience the unity of the human and divine natures (fusion); but not ". . . as a drop of water might find unity with the ocean. Man attains divine union by progressive reciprocal spiritual communion, by personality intercourse with the personal God, by increasingly attaining the divine nature through wholehearted and intelligent conformity to the divine will. Such a sublime relationship can exist only between personalities."[24]

Sincere hearts crave to worship, to grow in attunement with the Indwelling Spirit, and follow its guidance. Patience, restraint, and balanced zeal induce the Spirit to help the human host; all this is facilitated through worshipful meditation.

The Practice

Worshipful meditation brings us into relationship and harmony with God: it quiets the senses so as to better connect with the indwelling divine presence. An attitude of genuine humility and gratitude enhances the experience. Below is a simple five-step worshipful meditation with components common to ancient traditions as well as more modern practices such as Transcendental Meditation and Centering Prayer.

The use of a mantra—a sacred word, sound, or phrase—is generally considered an acceptable way to quiet the senses. However, it is by no means the only way. You might, for example, be more familiar with using the breath as a way to focus. Whatever technique keeps you open and attentive to the presence of the Divine can be substituted here.

1. **Choose a sacred word as the symbol of your intention to invite the presence and guidance of the Divine within.** The sacred word should be chosen carefully so that it most fully expresses your intention. Examples might be: "Father," "Mother," "Abba," "Eema," "Allah," "Jesus," "peace," "shalom," and "love."

2. **Find a place and time that is comfortable for you, and be seated in a relaxed position.** Try to meditate in a quiet, undisturbed area. Turn off the phone, ask others to respect your meditation time, and make sure that pets or other potential distractions are taken care of. Taking a sitting position will facilitate the practice, rather than inclining us to sleep.

3. **Close your eyes, settle briefly, and then allow yourself mentally and emotionally to receive God.** Silently introduce your sacred word. Remaining in a state of relaxed attention, your eyes should be closed throughout the meditation.

4. **When you become aware of thoughts, return ever so gently to the sacred word.** "Thoughts" is an umbrella term for every perception that flows through consciousness, including sense perceptions, feelings, images, memories, reflections, insights, and commentaries. You may experience attractions or aversions, insights or breakthroughs, self-reflection or thoughts that are a product of stress release. When any of these arise, use your sacred word as often as needed to bring you back to your intention to be with God. If you are interrupted, take care of what is necessary but then return to your meditation.

5. **At the end of the meditation period, stop thinking your sacred word and remain in silence with eyes closed for two to three minutes.** "The spirit of the Father speaks best to man when the human mind is in an attitude of true worship."[25] Then allow your awareness to slowly return as you gently open your eyes. Remain in that relaxed state, enjoying the peace it has brought. This is an important time for readjusting to the outer world, and to allow the physiology of the body to shift back gracefully to normal waking consciousness.

Below are answers to generally asked questions about meditation:

How often and for how long should I meditate?

Two twenty-minute periods of meditation daily are recommended—one in the morning before you begin your day's regular activities, and one in the afternoon or early evening. Try to meditate before a meal. If this is not practical, be sure to allow enough time for digestion before meditating. Light exercise before meditating is okay, but save heavy exercise until later. Because meditation can make the mind more alert, it is best not to meditate just before bedtime. Remember that regularity of meditation is very important. Even if you don't have time for a full session, meditate for whatever time you have available.

What if thoughts keep mingling with my sacred word?

Gently favor the sacred word and remain detached in relation to anything else. You might think of the distractions as a flock of birds moving across a still, calm lake. Just let them pass without attachment.

What if I fall asleep?

This means that your mind and body probably needed the rest. However, if sleep often interrupts your session, consider examining your lifestyle for ways to alleviate constant fatigue.

What if I have constant thoughts or am always restless?

If your thoughts, restlessness, anxiety or boredom are constant companions during your meditation, it means you are releasing stress. This is good, because it is a process of purification. Continue meditating while assuming a neutral attitude toward such interruptions; when you realize you are no longer centered in your intention toward God, gently return to your sacred word.

What if I lose awareness of time passing while I'm in meditation?

There may be moments during your meditation when you slip into a state of timeless awareness, beyond thoughts. Upon returning from this state you will recognize that it was not sleep but that some time has passed. As in all meditation experiences, avoid putting too much emphasis on them. The only way to judge the effects of your meditation practice is through the results you see in your life.

Relaxation

If meditation opens the communication channel with our Indwelling Spirit, relaxation increases our capacity to recognize its guidance. In a delightful paradox, relaxation—humor and play—enhances the effect of worshipful meditation, invigorates the soul, deepens our connection with God, and opens us up to spirit guidance.

Relaxation helps release emotional pressure, checking nervous tension and overserious self-contemplation. Life becomes lucid when we mix our pursuit of spiritual advancement with savoring our successes and engaging in activities with people who bring joy in our lives. Likewise, taking time away from work or a problem, as Jesus taught, is essential to clearer thinking: "'My brethren, you must all learn the value of rest and the efficacy of relaxation. You must realize that the best method of solving some entangled problems is to forsake them for a time. Then when you go back fresh from your rest or worship, you are able to attack your troubles with a clearer head and a steadier hand, not to mention a more resolute heart. Again, many times your problem is found to have shrunk in size and proportions while you have been resting your mind and body.'"[26]

When I started Transcendental Meditation, I enjoyed attending meetings with discussion and interpretation of subjective experiences. I also participated in New Age spiritual activities such as empowerment seminars, guru encounters, channeling, alternative healing sessions, psychic readings, and studying self-help and inspirational books—shared with others of similar interests but all centered on me. It was not until I began to question the intellectual basis of my spiritual practice and pursue the reconciliation of my beliefs with epochal revelation that relaxation took on new meaning.

When the intention to worship became the focus of my meditation practice, the way I perceived personal relationships began to change—every person gave me an opportunity to serve. The insights that guided me didn't come during meditation or as visions, but while relaxing—watching a movie, walking and laughing with friends, or simply listening to music. To my surprise, my volunteer work took on a greater passion and began to address larger community needs. The growing reverence for God that I felt during my meditation began to spill into my everyday life. Epochal revelation explains: "Meditation makes the contact of mind with spirit; relaxation determines the capacity for spiritual receptivity. And this interchange of strength for weakness, courage for fear, the will of God for the mind of self, constitutes worship."[27]

One of my greatest achievements has been taking time to laugh and to enjoy humor. We can get so absorbed in our development and so passionate about serving God that we forget that humor is essential to spiritual growth. Great humor does not mean laughing at the misfortunes of the weak or the erring, nor does it blaspheme the goodness and glory of divinity. Uplifting humor refreshes the soul and is found in three levels of appreciation:

1. Jokes that grow from memories of our past experiences of combat, struggle, and sometimes episodes of fear.

2. Joy from realizing the insignificance of so much personal anxiety.

3. Recognition that all things work together for good. This phase of humor grows out of our faith in the loving guidance of our Indwelling Spirit and care of the many spirit beings involved in our development.

Section Four Summary

Our efforts to develop and harmonize spiritual perception with cosmic understanding have a cascading effect in our relationship with God and one another. Personal salvation can be taken for granted when the certitude of our spiritual experiences is complemented with an attitude of faith in a multilevel universe, extending from the spiritual to the most physical. A deeper appreciation for the personality of God as Universal Father and increased attunement to the guidance of the Indwelling Spirit expand our capacity to love others, enhancing the quality of our personal service to humanity. "A human being can find truth in his inner experience, but he needs a clear knowledge of facts to apply his personal discovery of truth to the ruthlessly practical demands of everyday life."[1]

When our spiritual development efforts are centered in a universal framework that cultivates a cosmic and balanced God-knowing personality, the spirit of love and service will increasingly dominate the collective consciousness in our beloved world.

In Closing

If you know you are on the right track, if you have this inner knowledge,
then nobody can turn you off. Regardless of what they say.
Barbara McClintock (1902–1992), genetic botanist and Nobel Prize winner

Heaven Is Not the Last Stop would not have been written if I had held on to the comfort of my beliefs and the familiar spiritual framework that influenced my outlook and behavior. For certain, the journey would not have begun if my curious spirit had been defeated by fears and skepticism. In this adventure of writing (and growth), I came to realize that what humanity knows of spiritual realities is but a small fragment of the Big Picture of Existence—the tip of a cosmic iceberg that we are only now beginning to fathom.

This book is a decisive step in the long process of rediscovering the true meaning of religion and reconciling it with the development of human consciousness. By expanding the concept of God and the universe, elaborating upon the uniqueness of personality, and presenting crucial distinctions between soul and spirit, *Heaven Is Not the Last Stop*

Our lives begin to end the day we become silent about things that matter.
Martin Luther King, Jr.

brings new depth to the study of spiritual evolution. It will revolutionize the dialogue among spiritual leaders while it affirms the work of the great nineteenth- and twentieth-century mystic-philosophers who sought to bridge the gap between God and humanity and reveal the complementary realities of the transcendent and the immanent.

The indwelling presence of divinity leavens the human yearning for a relationship with God and coordinates those urges to reconcile the facts of the material universe with the inner world of spiritual experience. When we harmonize facts, meanings, and values in the light of epochal revelation, we expand our understanding of origins, gain deeper appreciation for our history, and find unity in our shared destiny. A balanced philosophy of living nurtures devotion to divine ideals, increasing the quality of our decisions and expressions of compassion. Radical new meanings have always been the catalyst of human efforts to improve our world and heighten our appreciation of divinity. The insights offered in *Heaven Is Not the Last Stop* will contribute to the spiritual culture of our world, dispelling confusion and fueling the spiritual power of transformation.

The years I spent developing this project taught me the role that spiritual humility plays in our individual and social evolution. By admitting our spiritual poverty, we break the barricade of self-righteousness and cultivate the wonder that opens our minds to deeper perspectives and higher potentials. In the embrace of sincere spiritual humility we discover the heart of devotion and dare to venture from stagnant systems to enlightened solutions in socio-religious reengineering.

Ancient beliefs and halfhearted practices do not have the dynamic force to thrust this civilization into a moral and spiritual renaissance; true progress will come from *living* the practical and spiritual insights discovered in the pursuit of more meaningful meanings and valuable values. To end the worn-out recourse to war, we have to walk the path of inner change that gradually moves the outer world forward; we must liberate ourselves from intellectual and spiritual comfort zones.

The presumptive adage that we are spirit beings having a human experience will eventually evolve to the realization that we are amazingly gifted physical creatures growing in divine attainment. We are constantly surrounded and guided by *actual* spirit beings and even indwelt by the spirit that both represents and is the Father himself. This reverent attitude acknowledges our *potential to become* full-fledged spirit beings. Recognition that immortality is a choice and must be earned engenders a renewed commitment to spiritual growth, supported by a humble attitude that expands spiritual vision and exposes cosmic truth. It is with this renewed vision of our purpose and destiny that collective efforts at development will truly yield higher levels of compassion, wisdom, and love toward others—reflected in a world growing in peace.

Without the guidance of spiritual wisdom, science has the potential for great destruction. Without doctrinal overhaul, religious institutions will continue to breed dissension, intolerance, and disunity. Without the progressive recognition of eternal cosmic realities, spirituality will continue to focus on self-centered enlightenment.

While we proudly quibble over which religion has the superior belief, our world suffers deeply. It is painfully obvious that progressive evolution mandates that we transcend religious differences—that we live the ideals of the spiritual brotherhood of man.

Do we have the courage to take the steps that will actualize such a worthy vision, beginning with the commitment to critically examine our current understanding of spiritual evolution in the light of epochal revelation? A brave vow of faith from every child of God regardless of religious affiliation and beliefs can overcome the inhibiting apathy that confronts us.

If every individual refines the ability to think, act, and live honestly, loyally, fearlessly, and truthfully, we can wisely adapt to the rigorous realities of the human experience. We can devote effort to the adventure of expanding our knowledge of God and emulating his nature. Neither science nor religion alone can deliver a full understanding of universal truths and relationships—they need the alliance of a new human philosophy and the illumination of divine revelation.

While we honor the past chapters in our approach to God and the universe, we must now give epochal revelation the opportunity to broaden and deepen that legacy, so that we can truly proclaim the brotherhood of man.

Let us not just clamor for peace; let each of us, in faith, cultivate the universal intelligence that will herald world peace. We owe it to ourselves and to future generations.

"The ideals of one generation carve out the channels of destiny for immediate posterity. The quality of the social torchbearers will determine whether civilization goes forward or backward. The homes, churches, and schools of one generation predetermine the character trend of the succeeding generation. The moral and spiritual momentum of a race or a nation largely determines the cultural velocity of that civilization."[1]

Notes

For your convenience, citations for material quoted or paraphrased from *The Urantia Book* are listed in two ways: (first) by the Paper number and the section number(s) within that Paper, and (second) by the corresponding page and paragraph number(s). For example, "Paper 103:6, p. 1136:2" refers to the second paragraph on page 1136, which is found in section six of Paper 103.

The citations reflect the pagination of the original Urantia Foundation printing, copyright 1955, which is duplicated in all of the Foundation's subsequent printings. Please note that the page numbering may not be the same in versions of *The Urantia Book* by other publishers. However, Paper/section citations will be the same across all editions.

Please also note that all Papers begin with a nonnumbered introduction; hence the designation 0 (zero) for references to material located in the introduction of a cited Paper.

Unless otherwise indicated, all Internet links were rechecked for viability in September 2009. If you have difficulty accessing a specific website, try entering into your browser the topic and source names given in the notes, for example, "Book of the Dead Encyclopedia Britannica" to locate the material you are seeking.

Chapter 1

1. The Urantia Foundation, *The Urantia Book* (Chicago: The Urantia Foundation, 1955). Hereafter cited as *The Urantia Book*. Paper 103:6, p. 1136:2 and Paper 103:9, p. 1141:4.
2. Hebrews 11:1.
3. Carl Jung, *Alchemy*, Modern Psychology, vol. 5, 6, 1940–41. (Zurich: Karl Schippert, 1941), p. 63 (out of print).
4. Richard Tarnas, *The Passion of the Western Mind: Understanding the Ideas That Have Shaped Our World View* (New York: Harmony Books, 1991), p. 119.
5. Ibid. p. 166.
6. Ibid. p. 418.
7. Ibid. pp. 285–286.
8. *The Urantia Book*, Paper 102:6, p. 1125:1.
9. Leigh Eric Schmidt, *Restless Souls: The Making of American Spirituality* (New York: Harper Collins, 2005), p. 9.
10. William Sloane Coffin, *Credo* (Louisville, KY: Westminster John Knox Press, 2004), p. 8.
11. Steve McIntosh, *Integral Consciousness and the Future of Evolution: How the Integral Worldview is Transforming Politics, Culture, and Spirituality* (St. Paul, MN: Paragon House, 2007), pp. 207–208.
12. Richard Tarnas, *The Passion of the Western Mind: Understanding the Ideas That Have Shaped Our World View* (New York: Harmony Books, 1991), p. 422.

Chapter 2

1. Kenneth C. Davis, *America's Hidden History: Untold Tales of the First Pilgrims, Fighting Women, and Forgotten Founders Who Shaped a Nation*, repr. (New York: Harper Paperbacks, 2009), introduction, p. xiii.
2. Joshua Cooper Ramo, *The Age of the Unthinkable* (New York: Little, Brown, 2009), p. 8.

3. *The Urantia Book,* Paper 101:0, p. 1104:1.
4. Ibid. Paper 93:3, p. 1089:1–6.
5. Ibid. Paper 101:5, p. 1110:4.
6. Ibid. Paper 92:3, p. 1006:2.
7. Ibid. Paper 101:4, pp. 1109:6–1110:3.
8. *The Gift of Scripture* (London: The Catholic Truth Society, 2005), p. 18. A teaching document of the Bishops' Conference of England and Wales, and of Scotland.
9. *The Urantia Book,* Paper 101:4, p. 1109:3.
10. Ibid. Paper 99:2, p. 1087:5.
11. Ibid. Paper 99:1, p. 1087:3.
12. Ibid. Paper 94:4, p. 1032:2.

Chapter 3

1. *The Urantia Book,* Paper 132:1, p. 1457:2.
2. Ibid. Paper 140:5, p.1575:3.
3. Richard Rosecrance, *The Rise of the Trading State: Commerce and Conquest in the Modern World* (New York: Basic Books, 1986), pp. 13–14 and 24–25.
4. Sri Aurobindo, *The Human Cycle: Ideal of Human Unity; War and Self-Determination,* 2nd ed. (Twin Lakes, WI: Lotus Press, 1970), p. 587.
5. *The Urantia Book,* Paper 196:3, p. 2097:2.
6. Ibid. Paper 100:6, p. 1101:3.
7. Ibid. Paper 99:4, p. 1090:4.

Chapter 4

1. *The Urantia Book,* Foreword, p. 1:2.
2. Stephen Hawking and Roger Penrose, *The Nature of Space and Time,* The Isaac Newton Institute Series of Lectures (Princeton, NJ: Princeton University Press, 1996), p. 20.
3. Paul Davies, "The Birth of the Cosmos," in *God, Cosmos, Nature and Creativity,* ed. Jill Gready (Edinburgh: Scottish Academic Press, 1995), pp. 8–9.
4. Arthur Eddington, *The Expanding Universe* (New York: Macmillan, 1933), p. 124.
5. *The Urantia Book,* Paper 102:6, p. 1125:1.
6. Ibid. Paper 3:6, p. 53:5.
7. Exploration of the eternal past involves the study of complex concepts that are outside the scope of this book. The appearance of the central universe is one concept never before considered. To better understand the Deity union of Father, Son, and Spirit and the accompanying events, I found it very useful to study the book *A Study of the Master Universe: A Development of Concepts of the Urantia Book* by William S. Sadler, Jr., especially the section titled "Prologue in Eternity" (Chicago: Second Society Foundation, 1968). An animated and extremely helpful version of this section is available at the Satania 606 website, http://www.satania606.com /index.html. Sadler's book may be purchased from the Urantia Foundation (telephone: 1-888-URANTIA) or read online at The Urantia Book Fellowship website, http://urantiabook.org/studies/smu.
8. *The Urantia Book.* Paper 8:4, p. 94:7.
9. Ibid. Paper 56:10, p. 646:4.
10. Ibid. Paper 117:1, p. 1278:5.
11. Ibid. Paper 94:3, p. 1030:4.
12. *Columbia Encyclopedia,* 6th ed., s.v. "Friedrich Wilhelm Joseph von Schelling," 2008, Encyclopedia.com, http://www.encyclopedia.com/doc/ 1E1-Schelling.html.
13. *The Urantia Book,* Paper 1:7, p. 31:6.
14. Ibid. Paper 1:5, p. 29:2.
15. Ibid. Paper 6:6, p. 78:5.
16. Ibid. Paper 103:8, p. 1140:6.
17. Ibid. Paper 1:7, p. 31:1.
18. Ibid. Paper 169:4, p. 1856:5.
19. Ibid. Paper 104:1, p. 1143:6.
20. Ibid. Paper 96:1, p. 1053:6.
21. Ibid. Paper 104:1, 1144:5.
22. Ibid. Paper 96:4, p. 1057:5.
23. Ibid. Paper 104:1, p.1144:7.
24. Ibid. Paper 104:1, p. 1144:8.
25. Ibid. Paper 94:6, p. 1033:6.
26. Lao Tse, *Tao Te Ching,* unabridged, trans. James Legge, (New York: Dover Publications, 1997), p. 39.
27. Richard L. Strauss, *Three Persons: One God, Truth for Today: Biblical Essays* by Pastor Paul Mizzi, http://www. tecmalta. org/tft127.htm.
28. *The Urantia Book,* Paper 10:1, p. 108:5.
29. Ibid. Paper 4:1, p. 54:4.
30. Ibid. Paper 1:7, p. 31:6.
31. Ibid. Foreword: II, p. 4:10. "God the Sevenfold—Deity personality anywhere actually functioning in time and space," including the Paradise Creator Sons, the Ancients of Days, and the Seven Master Spirits.
32. Ibid. Paper 8:5, p. 96:2.
33. Ibid. Foreword: VIII, p. 12:2.
34. Ibid. Paper 101:1, p. 1105:2.
35. Ibid. Paper 5:5, p. 69:1.
36. Ibid. Paper 40:5, p. 445:4.

37. Ibid. Paper 107:5, p. 1181:4.
38. Ibid. Paper 107:5, p. 1181:5.
39. Ibid. Paper 109:1, p. 1196:2.
40. Ibid. Paper 109:1, p. 1196:1.
41. Ibid. Paper 1:0, p. 21:3; Paper 1:0, p. 22:3; Paper 7:4, p. 86:1; Paper 26:9, p. 295:1; Paper 40:7, p. 449:2; Paper 56:0, p. 637:1 (cf. Matthew 5:48).
42. Ibid. Paper 1:1, p. 22:1.
43. Ibid. Paper 111:5, p. 1221:5.
44. Ibid. Paper 3:2, p. 47:3.
45. Ibid. Paper 117:4, p. 1285:3.
46. Ibid. Paper 180:2, p. 1946:3.
47. Ibid. Paper 7:4, p. 85:2.
48. Ibid. Paper 2:2, p. 36:3.

Chapter 5

1. *The Urantia Book*, Paper 103:6, p. 1135:5.
2. Ibid. Paper 103:6, p. 1135:7.
3. Ibid. Paper 103:7, p. 1138:3.
4. *Stanford Encyclopedia of Philosophy Online*, s.v. "Georg Willhelm Friedrich Hegel," sec. 2.1: "The traditional 'metaphysical' view of Hegel's philosophy," 1997, rev. Jun 26, 2006, http://plato.stanford.edu/entries/hegel/.
5. Sri Aurobindo, *The Life Divine* (Twin Lakes, WI: Lotus Press, 1985), p. 752.
6. Pierre Teilhard de Chardin, *The Phenomenon of Man*, trans. Bernard Wall, introduction by Sir Julian Huxley, 23rd printing (New York: Harper Perennial, 1975), p. 13.
7. Bernhard Haisch, "Brilliant Disguise: Light, Matter and the Zero-Point Field," *Science & Spirit* 10, no. 3 (September/ October 1999): pp. 30-31. Author is an astrophysicist, the scientific editor of the *Astrophysical Journal*, and editor-in-chief of the *Journal of Scientific Exploration*.
8. *The Urantia Book*, Paper 12:8, pp. 140:11–141:0.
9. Ibid. Paper 12:8, p. 140:6–8.
10. J. Edward Wright, *The Early History of Heaven* (New York: Oxford University Press, 2000), pp. 29, 34.
11. John F. Hawley and Katherine A. Holcomb, "Cosmology Becomes a Science," chap. 2 in *Foundations of Modern Cosmology*. Quote taken from website chapter summaries of the book, http:// www.astro.virginia.edu/~jh8h/Foundations/Foundations_1/chapter2.html.
12. Jose Wudka, "The Middle Ages," article dated 9/24/1998, http://phyun5. ucr.edu/~wudka/Physics7/Notes_www/node40.html.
13. E. Hummel, *The Galileo Connection* (Downers Grove, IL: InterVarsity Press, 1986), pp. 43–45.
14. The Board of Trustees of the University of Illinois, *Einstein's Legacy* (Chicago: University of Illinois, 1995). http://archive.ncsa.illinois.edu/Cyberia/NumRel/EinsteinLegacy.html.
15. David Parrish, *Nothing I See Means Anything: Quantum Questions, Quantum Answers* (Boulder, CO: Sentient Publications, 2005), p. 63.
16. Raymond L. Orbach and Michael Turner, *Quantum Universe: The Revolution in 21st Century Particle Physics* (report). From executive summary titled "Are There Extra Dimensions of Space?" p. 1, Interactions.org, http://www.interactions.org/cms/?pid=1012346. Dr. Orbach is director of the Office of Science of the U.S. Department of Energy and Dr. Michael Turner is assistant director for mathematics and physical science of the National Science Foundation.
17. *The Urantia Book*, Paper 103:7, p. 1139:1.
18. Ibid. Paper 81:6, p. 907:7 and Paper 101:5, p. 1110:4.
19. Ibid. Paper 12:1, p. 129:10.
20. Ibid. Paper 14:0, p. 152:1.
21. David Lindley, "A Fleeting Attraction? Does the Great Attractor Exist?" Discover: Science, Technology, and the Future, September 1992, http://discovermagazine.com/1992/sep/afleetingattract126
22. *The Urantia Book*, Foreword: IV, p. 7:10.
23. Joel Achenbach, "The God Particle," *National Geographic*, March 2008.
24. *The Urantia Book*, Paper 42:4, p. 473:4.
25. Ibid. Paper 42:3, p. 472:1.
26. Ibid. Paper 41:9, p. 465:2 and Paper 42:4, p. 473:1.
27. Ibid. Paper 12:8, p. 140:6.1.
28. Ibid. Paper 42:4, p. 474:1.
29. Ibid. Foreword: IV, p. 7:9.
30. Ibid. Paper 195:6, p. 2077:1.
31. Ibid. Paper 29, p. 319:1.
32. Ibid. Paper 15:4, p. 169:4.
33. Ibid. Paper 15:4, p. 169:2.
34. Ibid. Paper, 15:8, p. 176:5.
35. Ibid. Paper 104:4, p. 1149:11.
36. Ibid. Paper 12:8, p. 139:4.
37. Ibid. Paper 42:9, p. 479:7.
38. Ibid. Paper 42:9, p. 480:1.
39. Ibid. Paper 42:6, p. 476:4.

40. Ibid. Paper, 42:1, p. 467:3.
41. Ibid. Paper 103:6, p. 1136:2.
42. Ibid. Paper 48:6, p. 553.4.

Chapter 6

1. *The Urantia Book*, Paper 2:2, p. 36:3.
2. Ibid. Paper 30:1, p. 334:8.
3. Ibid. Paper 95:6, p. 1049:5.
4. Ibid. Paper 13:4, p. 150:1.
5. Ibid. Paper 18:0, p. 207:10.
6. Ibid. Paper 92:5, pp. 1008:8–1009:0.
7. Ibid. Paper 6:1, p. 73:5.
8. Ibid. Paper 6:2, p. 74:6.
9. Ibid. Paper 6:2, p. 74:8.
10. Ibid. Paper 6:2, p. 75:1.
11. Ibid. Paper 6:3, p. 75:6.
12. Ibid. Paper 6:3, p. 75:7.
13. Ibid. Paper 6:1, p. 74:2.
14. Ibid. Paper 6:5, p. 77:4.
15. Ibid. Paper 6:5, p. 77:7.
16. Ibid. Paper 7:4, p. 85:6.
17. Ibid. Paper 21:2, p. 236:2–4.
18. Ibid. Paper 5:3, p. 66:2.
19. Ibid. Paper 8:5, p. 95:6.
20. Ibid. Paper 119:0, p. 1308:4.
21. Ibid. Paper 119:0, p. 1308:5.
22. Ibid. Paper 21:4, p. 239:10.
23. Ibid. Paper 35:9, p. 393:1.
24. S. C. Malan, *First Book of Adam and Eve* (Whitefish, MT: Kessinger Publishing, 2004), p. 37. Kessinger Publishing utilizes advanced technology to publish and preserve rare, scarce, and out-of-print books.
25. *Encyclopædia Britannica Online*, s.v. "Judaism," May 2007, http://www.britannica.com/eb/article-35260.
26. Dionysius the Areopagite, *The Celestial Hierarchy*, (Whitefish, MT: Kessinger Publishing, 2004), p. 13.
27. Ibid. chap. 9, p. 20.
28. *The Urantia Book*, Paper 38:2, p. 419:1, and Paper 113:2, p. 1243:2.
29. *Strong's Concordance: Blue Letter Bible Lexicon*, s.v. "host," http://blue letterbible.org/lang/lexicon/lexicon.cfm?strongs=06635&t=KJV.
30. *The Urantia Book*, Paper 113:4, p. 1245:1.
31. Ibid. Paper 39:5, p. 436.
32. Ibid. Paper 39:5, p. 437.3.
33. Ibid. Paper 39:5, p. 437:5.
34. Ibid. Paper 39:5, p. 438:2.
35. Ibid. Paper 39:2, p. 430:4.
36. *Catholic Encyclopedia*, s.v. "Guardian Angel" by Hugh T. Pope, New Advent, http://www.newadvent.org/cathen/07049c.htm.
37. *The Urantia Book*, Paper 113:1, p. 1241:3 (cf. Matthew 18:10).

38. Ibid. Paper 113:1, p. 1241:5.
39. Ibid. Paper 113:1, p. 1241:6 and 1242: 2 and 3.
40. Ibid. Paper 113:1, p. 1241:7.
41. Ibid. Paper 113:2, p. 1242:4.
42. Ibid. Paper 113:3, p. 1244:6.
43. Ibid. Paper 113:5, p. 1246:3.
44. Ibid. Paper 37:3, p. 409:3.
45. *Dictionary of the Bible, Compton's Interactive Bible* NIV, s.v. "Gabriel" (SoftKey Multimedia, 1994, 1995, 1996), CD-ROM.
46. *The Urantia Book*, Paper 37:1, p. 407:11.
47. Ibid. Paper 33:4, p. 370:3.
48. Ibid. Paper 37:3, p. 408:4.
49. Ibid. Paper 37:3, p. 409:4.
50. Ibid. Paper 37:3, p. 409:1.
51. Ibid. Paper 34:5, p. 379:2.

Section 1 Summary

1. *The Urantia Book,* Paper 4:1, p. 54:2.
2. Ibid. Paper 56:10, p. 648:3.

Section 2 Introduction

1. *The Urantia Book*, Paper 92:4, p. 1007:1.
2. Ibid. Paper 4:1, p. 54:5.

Chapter 7

1. Frank Newport, "Almost Half of Americans Believe Humans Did Not Evolve," June 5, 2006, Gallup, http://www.gallup.com/poll/23200/almost-half-americans-believe-humans-did-evolve.aspx.
2. David Quammen, "Was Darwin Wrong?" *National Geographic*, November 2004, National Geographic.com, http://ngm.nationalgeographic.com/ngm/0411/feature1/fulltext.html.
3. "How Did Life Begin? RNA That Replicates Itself Indefinitely Developed for First Time," Science News, *Science Daily*, January 10, 2009, http://www.sciencedaily.com/releases/2009/01/090109173205.ht.
4. *The Urantia Book*, Paper 102:6, p. 1125:5.
5. Ibid. Paper 42:1, p. 468:2.
6. Ibid. Paper 36:3, p. 399:3.
7. Ibid. Paper 58:0, p. 664:1.
8. Ibid. Paper 65:4, p. 735:1.
9. Ibid. Paper 36:3, p. 400:2.
10. Ibid. Paper 58:1, p. 664:4.
11. Ibid. Paper 58:4, p. 667:6.
12. Ibid. Paper 49:1, p. 560:4.
13. Ibid. Paper 58:6, p. 669:3–5.

14. Howard Hughes Medical Institute, "Human Brain Is Still Evolving," *HHMI Research News*, September 9, 2005, http://www.hhmi.org /news/lahn4.html. Also, UBtheNEWS at www.ubthenews. com offers detailed academic reports of scientific advances and new discoveries that corroborate information in *The Urantia Book*.
15. *The Urantia Book*, Paper 62:3, p. 706:2.
16. Ibid. Paper 62:3, p. 706:3–4.
17. "Before Lucy Came Ardi, New Earliest Hominid Found," *New York Times*, October 1, 2009, http://www. nytimes.com/aponline/2009/10/01/ science/AP-US-SCI-Before-Lucy.html.
18. *The Urantia Book*, Paper 62:4, p. 707:5 and Paper 79:0, p. 878:1.
19. Ibid. Paper 63:0, p. 711:3.
20. Ibid. Paper 62:5, p. 708:2.
21. Ibid. Paper 62:6, p. 709:6 and Paper 63:1, p. 711:7.

Chapter 8

1. Bryan T. Huie, "Genesis 6: Who Were 'The Sons of God?'" revised April 8, 2009, Here a Little, There a Little, http://www.herealittletherealittle.ne t/index.cfm?page_name=Genesis-6-Sons-of-God.
2. *The Urantia Book*, Paper 66:2, p. 742:8.
3. Ibid. Paper 35:9, p. 393:5.
4. John J. Collins, ed., *The Encyclopedia of Apocalypticism*, vol. 1, *The Origins of Apocalypticism in Judaism and Christianity*, (London: Continuum, 2004), pp. 15–19.
5. *The Urantia Book*, Paper 53:4, p. 604:3.
6. Ibid. Paper 53:2, p. 603:1.
7. Ibid. Paper 54:2, p. 615:1.
8. Ibid. Paper 67:3, p. 756:2.
9. Ibid. Paper 53:7, p. 609:3.
10. Ibid. Paper 67:4, pp. 757:5–758:0.
11. Ibid. Paper 53:8, p. 609:6.
12. Ibid. Paper 68:3, p. 766:5.
13. Ibid. Paper 67:0, p. 754:1.
14. Ibid. Paper 67:5, p. 758:6.
15. Ibid. Paper 67:4, p. 758:1.
16. Ibid. Paper 77:2, p. 857:1.
17. Ibid. Paper 67:4, p. 758:1.
18. Ibid. Paper 67:4, p. 758:2.
19. Ibid. Paper 50:7, p. 578:6.
20. Ibid. Paper 87:4, p. 961:6.
21. Ibid. Paper 87:4, p. 961:7.
22. Ibid. Paper 87:6, p. 964:12.
23. Ibid. Paper 87:4, p. 962:1.
24. Ibid. Paper 77:7, p. 864:0.
25. Ibid. Paper 66:8, p. 753:2.
26. Ibid. Paper 134:8, p. 1492:0 (cf. Matthew 4:1–11).
27. Ibid. Paper 53:8, p. 610:5.
28. Ibid. Paper 54:3, p. 615:3.
29. Ibid. Paper 54:4, p. 616:6.
30. Ibid. Paper 54:5, pp. 617:11–618:0.
31. Ibid. Paper 54:2, p. 615:2.
32. Ibid. Paper 53:7, p. 609.3.
33. Ibid. Paper 54:1, p. 614:1.

Chapter 9

1. *The Urantia Book*, Paper 92:5, p. 1009:0.
2. Ibid. Paper 74:8, p. 838:2.
3. *Dictionary of the Bible*, *Compton's Interactive Bible* NIV, s.v. "Adam," (SoftKey Multimedia, 1994, 1995, 1996), CD-ROM.
4. s.v. "Eve," Ibid.
5. *The Urantia Book*, Paper 51:0, p. 580:1.
6. Ibid. Paper 73:3, p. 823:1.
7. Ibid. Paper 73:3, p. 823:4.
8. Ibid. Paper 73:7, p. 826:6.
9. *Discovery of Atlantis* book description, Discovery of Atlantis website, http: //www.discoveryofatlantis.com/.
10. The similarities between Plato's Atlantis and *The Urantia Book's* Garden of Eden are listed on http://www.squarecircles.com/articl es/edenproject/atlantiseden.htm.
11. *The Urantia Book*, Paper 73:3, p. 823:4.
12. Project Update, May 24, 2007. Discovery of Atlantis. http://www. discoveryof atlantis.com/.
13. *The Urantia Book*, Paper 74:8, p. 837:3.
14. John J. Collins, ed., *The Encyclopedia of Apocalypticism*, vol. 1, *The Origins of Apocalypticism in Judaism and Christianity*, (London: Continuum, 2004), pp. 11–12.
15. *The Urantia Book*, Paper 74:8, p. 837:1.
16. Ibid. Paper 74:4, p. 832:6.
17. Ibid. Paper 51:3, p. 583:4.
18. Ibid. Paper 74:8, p. 837:7.
19. Ibid. Paper 81:5, p. 905:6.
20. Howard Hughes Medical Institute, "Human Brain Is Still Evolving," *HHMI Research News*, September 9, 2005, http://www.hhmi.org/news /lahn4.html. Also, UBtheNEWS at www.ubthenews.com offers detailed academic reports of scientific advances and new discoveries that corroborate information in *The Urantia Book*.
21. *The Urantia Book*, Paper 89:2, p. 975:5.
22. Ibid. Paper 89:2, p. 975:7.
23. Ibid. Paper 121:6, p. 1339:1.
24. Ibid. Paper 67:7, p. 761:6.

25. Ibid. Paper 54:0, p. 613:1.
26. Ibid. Paper 89:10, p. 984:5.
27. Ibid. Paper 67:7, p. 761:3.
28. Ibid. Paper 78:1, p. 868:4.

Chapter 10

1. *The Urantia Book*, Paper 93:3, p. 1017:2.
2. Ibid. Paper 93:1, p. 1014:5.
3. Ibid. Paper 93:5, p. 1018:8.
4. Ibid. Paper 93:2, p. 1015:1.
5. Ibid. Paper 93:4, p. 1018:3.
6. Ibid. Paper 93:3, p. 1017:1.
7. Ibid. Paper 93:5, p. 1018:6.
8. Ibid. Paper 93:6, p. 1020:7.
9. Ibid. Paper 93:6, p. 1021:3.
10. Ibid. Paper 93:7, p. 1022:1.
11. Ibid. Paper 93:8, p. 1022:3.
12. Ibid. Paper 93:9, p. 1023:4–5.
13. Ibid. Paper 93:9, p. 1023:5.
14. Ibid. Paper 95:4, p. 1046:6.
15. Ibid. Paper 95:5, p. 1047:1.
16. Ibid. Paper 95:5, p. 1047:6.
17. Ibid. Paper 95:5, p. 1049:3.
18. Ibid. Paper 96:2, p. 1055:1.
19. Ibid. Paper 96:3, p. 1055:4.
20. Ibid. Paper 96:5, p. 1058:1.
21. Ibid. Paper 96:3, p. 1056:2.
22. Ibid. Paper 96:4, p. 1057:3.
23. Ibid. Paper 96:4, p. 1057:1.
24. Ibid. Paper 96:6, p. 1059:3.
25. Ibid. Paper 97:1, p. 1062:3.
26. Ibid. Paper 97:1, p. 1062:4.
27. Ibid. Paper 97:3, p. 1065:2.
28. Ibid. Paper 97:4, p. 1066:2.
29. Ibid. Paper 97:5, p. 1066:6.
30. Ibid. Paper 97:5, p. 1067:1.
31. Ibid. Paper 97:5, p. 1067:3.
32. Ibid. Paper 94:6, p. 1033:4.
33. Ibid. Paper 97:6, p. 1067:5.
34. Ibid. Paper 97:7, p. 1070:3.
35. Ibid. Paper 94:8, p. 1037:1.
36. Ibid. Paper 94:9, p. 1037:4.
37. Ibid. Paper 94:6, p. 1033:8.
38. Ibid. Paper 94:6, p. 1034:4.
39. Ibid. Paper 95:6, p. 1049:5.
40. Ibid. Paper 98:2, p. 1078:6.
41. Ibid. Paper 97:7, p. 1068:3.
42. Ibid. Paper 93:9, p. 1024:1.

Chapter 11

1. *Manuscripts from Qumran Cave* 4, M. A. Hoselton's Dead Sea Scrolls Resources, http://home. flash.net/~hoselton/deadsea/deadse a.htm. Click on "Inventory of Caves"; scroll down to "The Qumran Manuscript Inventory"; click on "Cave Four."

2. *The Urantia Book*, Paper 169:4, p. 1856:3.
3. Ibid. Paper 169:4, p. 1856:7.
4. Ibid. Paper 169:4, p. 1857:1.
5. Ibid. Paper 104:1, p. 1144:8.
6. Ibid. Paper 149:2, p. 1670:5.
7. Ibid. Paper 104:1, p. 1145:1.
8. Ibid. Paper 120:4, p. 1331:3.
9. Ibid. Paper 32:0, p. 357:3.
10. Ibid. Paper 188:4, p. 2016:8.
11. Ibid. Paper 128:7, p. 1417:5.
12. Ibid. Paper 122:0, p. 1344:2.
13. Ruth Glendhill, "Clergy Who Don't Believe in God," *Times* Online, July 4, 2005, http://www.timesonline.co.uk/.
14. "More Americans Believe in the Devil, Hell and Angels Than in Darwin's Theory of Evolution," news release, December 14, 2008, Information Liberation: The News You're Not Supposed to Know, http://www.informationliberation.com/?id=26260.
15. *The Urantia Book*, Paper 80:7, p. 895:7.
16. Cesar Vidal, *The Myth of Mary* (Chino, CA: Chick Publications, 1995), pp. 74–75.
17. *The Urantia Book*, Paper 119:7, p. 1317:1.
18. Ibid. Paper 122:2, p. 1345:4.
19. Ibid. Paper 122:2, p. 1346:1.
20. Ibid. Paper 122:3, p. 1347:2.
21. Ibid. Paper 122:3, p. 1346:4.
22. Ibid. Paper 122:4, p. 1347:3.
23. Ibid. Paper 126:2, p. 1388:1 and Paper 126:3, p. 1389:5.
24. Ibid. Paper 187:4, p. 2010:0.
25. Ibid. Paper 196:0, p. 2088:2.
26. *Catholic Encyclopedia*, vol. 3 (1967 edition), p. 656.
27. John P. Pratt, "Yet Another Eclipse for Herod," sec. 1, "Evidence for 4 B.C.," reprinted from *The Planetarium* 19, no. 4 (December 1990): pp. 8–14. "Josephus states that Herod captured Jerusalem and began to reign in what we would call 37 B.C., and lived for 34 years thereafter, implying his death was in 4-3 B.C. Other evidence both from Josephus and coins indicates that his successors began to reign in 4-3 B.C. Moreover, Josephus also mentions a lunar eclipse shortly before Herod's death . . . For centuries the evidence from astronomy has appeared decisive: a lunar eclipse occurred on March 13, 4 B.C., whereas there was no such eclipse visible in Palestine in 3 B.C.

Thus, the eclipse has played a crucial role in the traditional conclusion that Herod died in the spring of 4 B.C." Online version at johnpratt.com, http://www.johnpratt.com/items/docs/herod/herod.html.#fn3

28. Maurice Sartre, Catherine Porter, and Elizabeth Rawlings, *The Middle East under Rome* (Cambridge, MA: Belknap Press, 2005), pp. 94–95; cf. Matthew 2:22.

29. Jack Kilmon, "History and the New Testament," article at The Scriptorium, http://www.historian.net/NTHX.html.

30. *The Urantia Book*, Paper 122:7, p. 1350:3.

31. Ibid. Paper 122:8, p., 1352:3.

32. Ibid.

33. Ibid. Paper 122:8, p. 1352:1–2.

34. Ibid. Paper 122:10, p. 1354:3, and Paper 121:2, p. 1334:5.

35. Ibid. Paper 126:3, p. 1390:3.

36. Ibid. Paper 122:4, p. 1347:6.

37. Ibid. Paper 136:1, p. 1510:3.

38. Thomas O. Lambdin, trans., *The Gospel of Thomas*, saying #16, from The Nag Hammadi Library, a section within The Gnostic Society Library online, http://www.gnosis.org/naghamm/gthlamb.html.

39. *The Urantia Book*. Paper 135:5, p. 1500:2.

40. Ibid. Paper 170:2, p. 1861:1.

41. Ibid. Paper 196:0, p. 2089:3.

42. Ibid. Paper 170:5, p. 1865:1.

43. Ibid. Paper 170:2, p. 1861:6.

44. Ibid. Paper 170:2, p. 1861:9.

45. Ibid. Paper 170:5, p. 1865:7.

46. Ibid. Paper 170:5, p. 1865:4.

47. Ibid. Paper 170:4, p. 1863:13.

48. Ibid. Paper 170:4, p. 1863:14.

49. Ibid. Paper 176:2, p. 1915:2.

50. Ibid. Paper 176:0, p. 1912:1.

51. Ibid. Paper 176:1, p. 1913:1.

52. Ibid. Paper 176:4, p. 1918:5.

53. Ibid. Paper 176:2, p. 1915:5.

54. Ibid. Paper 134:8, p. 1493:5.

55. Ibid. Paper 136:2, p. 1512:3.

56. Ibid. Paper 136:2, p. 1512:2.

57. Ibid. Paper 136:2, p. 1511:2–3.

58. Ibid. Paper 136:4, p. 1515:1–2.

59. Ibid. Paper 136:6, p. 1517:3.

60. Ibid. Paper 136: 6, p. 1518:1.

61. Ibid. Paper 136:6, p. 1519:3.

62. Ibid. Paper 136:9, p. 1522:1.

63. Ibid. Paper 149:2, p. 1671:3.

64. Ibid. Paper 150:1, p. 1679:2.

65. Ibid.

66. Ibid. Paper 150:2, p. 1680:1.

67. Ibid. Paper 121:8, p. 1342:5.

68. Ibid. Paper 120:3, p. 1330:3.

69. Ibid. Paper 127:5, p. 1403:2.

70. Ibid. Paper 127:5, p. 1403:3.

71. Ibid. Paper 127:6, p. 1403:5.

72. NationMaster.com Encyclopedia, s.v. "Miracles of Jesus," http://www.statemaster.com/encyclopedia/Miracles-of-Jesus

73. Mary Vallis, "Jesus may have walked on ice, study says; Cold snap in Galilee," *National Post*, April 5, 2006.

74. *The Urantia Book*, Paper 102, p. 1128:3.

75. Ibid. Paper 152:2, p. 1702:1.

76. Ibid. Paper 152:4, p. 1703:4.

77. Ibid. Paper 137:4, p. 1530:4.

78. Ibid. Paper 145:1, p. 1629:1.

79. Ibid. Paper 151:5, p. 1695:1.

80. Ibid. Paper 168:1, p. 1845:2.

81. Ibid. Paper 146:6, p. 1646:1.

82. Ibid. Paper 152:1, p. 1699:1.

83. Ibid. Paper 153:4, p. 1714:0.

84. Ibid. Paper 151:6, p. 1696:4.

85. Ibid. Paper 145:2, pp. 1630:8–1631:0.

86. Ibid. Paper 145:2, p. 1631:1.

87. Ibid. Paper 156:1, pp. 1734–35.

88. Ibid. Paper 146:4, p. 1644:1.

89. Ibid. Paper 146:4, pp. 1643:4–5.

90. Ibid. Paper 146:5, p. 1645:0.

91. Ibid. Paper 148:7, p. 1665:3.

92. Ibid. Paper 148:9, p. 1667:1.

93. Ibid. Paper 152:0, p. 1698:3.

94. Ibid. Paper 164:3, p. 1811:2.

95. Ibid. Paper 145:2, p. 1631:3.

96. Ibid. Paper 152:1, p. 1699:4.

97. Ibid. Paper 121:5, p. 1337:7.

98. Ibid. Paper 121:7, p. 1340:7–9.

99. Ibid. Paper 149:2, p. 1670:4.

100. Ibid. Paper 2:6, p. 41:3.

101. Ibid. Paper 187:3, p. 2008:7.

102. Ibid. Paper 188:5, p. 2018:5.

103. Ibid. Paper 188:4, p. 2017:2.

104. Ibid. Paper 188:4, p. 2017:7.

105. Ibid. Paper 188:5, p. 2019:6.

106. *Catholic Encyclopedia*, s.v. "General Resurrection," New Advent, http://www.newadvent.org/cathen/12792a.htm.

107. *The Urantia Book*, Paper 189:2, p. 2023:5.

108. Ibid. Paper 189:2, p. 2023:2.

109. Ibid. Paper 189:1, p. 2021:3.

110. Ibid. Paper 189:1, p. 2021:0.

111. Ibid. Paper 189:1, p. 2021:6.

112. Ibid. Paper 189: p. 2021:7.

113. Ibid. Paper 189:2, p. 2023:6 and p. 2024:1.

114. Ibid. Paper 189:2, p. 2023:3.

115. Ibid. Paper 189:2, p. 2023:4.

116. Ibid. Paper 189:2, p. 2024:2.

117. *Dictionary of the Bible, Compton's Interactive Bible* NIV, s.v. "Ascension

of Christ," (SoftKey Multimedia, 1994, 1995, 1996).

118. *The Urantia Book*, Paper 193:5, p. 2057:5.
119. Ibid. Paper 193:5, p. 2057:7.
120. Ibid. Paper 194:1, p. 2060:5.
121. Ibid. Paper 194:0, p. 2059:1.
122. Ibid. Paper 194:0, p. 2059:3.
123. Ibid. Paper 194:0, p. 2059:4.
124. Ibid. Paper 194:3, p. 2063:3.
125. Ibid. Paper 194:2, p. 2061:2.
126. Ibid. Paper 194:3, p. 2065:5.
127. Ibid. Paper 194:3, p. 2064:3.
128. Ibid. Paper 194:3, p. 2064:4.
129. Ibid. Paper 194:3, p. 2065:6.
130. Ibid. Paper 194:3, p. 2065:1.
131. Ibid. Paper 140:10, p. 1585:1.
132. Ibid. Paper 192:2, p. 2048:0.
133. Ibid. Paper 196:1, p. 2090:4.

Chapter 12

1. "Mount Toba Eruption: Ancient Humans Unscathed, Study Claims," July 6, 2007, Anthropology.net, http://anthropology.net/2007/07/06/mount-toba-eruption-ancient-humans-unscathed-study-claims/#comments.
2. "Neanderthal Facts: 150 Years of Discovery; Key Neanderthal Finds," Channel 4.com, http://www.channel4.com/history/microsites/N/neanderthal/facts/discovery.html. The first significant discovery was made in August 1856. A partial skeleton was found at the Feldhofer Cave in the Neander Valley, near Dusseldorf in Germany. This was the find that gave the species its name.
3. Excerpted from the section titled "Genetic Anthropology, Ancestry, and Ancient Human Migration" on the U.S. government website genomics.energy.gov, Human Genome Project Information, http://www.ornl.gov/sci/techresources/Human_Genome/elsi/humanmigration.shtml.#2.
4. Ibid.
5. *The Urantia Book*, Paper 67:4, p. 758:1 and Paper 148:4, p. 1660:6.
6. Ibid. Paper 64:2, p. 719:5.
7. Ibid. Paper 64:2, p. 720:1.
8. Ibid. Paper 64:2, p. 719:6.
9. Ibid. Paper 64:3, p. 720:6.
10. Ibid. Paper 64:5, p. 722:4.
11. Ibid. Paper 64:6, p. 722:6.
12. Ibid. Paper 79:5, p. 883:6.
13. Ibid. Paper 64:7, pp. 728:8–729:0.
14. Ibid. Paper 64:7, p. 727:2.
15. Ibid. Paper 78:4, p. 871:7.
16. Ibid. Paper 64:7, p. 728:5.
17. Ibid. Paper 67:4, p. 758:1, and Paper 148:4, p. 1660:6.
18. The Nag Hammadi Library is a collection of thirteen ancient papyrus codices (hidden approximately 390 AD) containing more than fifty texts, that was discovered in upper Egypt in 1945; their translation was completed in the 1970s. The text includes a large number of primary Gnostic Scriptures once thought to have been entirely destroyed during the early Christian struggle to define "orthodoxy"—scriptures such as the Gospel of Thomas, the Gospel of Philip, and the Gospel of Truth. Accessed from The Gnostic Society Library, http://www.gnosis.org/naghamm/nhl.html.
19. Samuel Noah Kramer, *History Begins at Sumer: Twenty-seven "Firsts" in Man's Recorded History* (New York, Doubleday Anchor Books, 1959), p. 144.
20. "Noah, Not Adam, Ate the Apple: Sumerian Bible, 1,000 Years Older Than the Old Testament, Startles Theologians," *New York Times*, August 15, 1915, http://query.nytimes.com/gst/abstract.html.?res=9F04E5DD133FE233A25756C1A96E9C946496D6CF.
21. *The Urantia Book*, Paper 77:4, p. 860:3.
22. "The Epic of Atrahasis: Atrahasis' Dream Explained," Livius.org. http://www.livius.org/as-at/atrahasis/atrahasis.html.#Atrahasis_Dream_Explained.
23. *The Urantia Book*, Paper 67:5, p. 759:2.
24. Ibid. Paper 78:7, p. 874:7.
25. Ibid. Paper 78:7, p. 875:1.
26. "Tablet Tells World Reconstruction After Flood: Fragment of the Ancient Epics, Written 4,000 Years Ago on the Nippur Tablets, Deciphered by Dr. Stephen Herbert Langdon," *New York Times*, September 24, 1916, http://query.nytimes.com/gst/abstract.html.?res=9501E0D91439E233A25757C2A96F9C946796D6CF.
27. *The Urantia Book*, Paper 78:7, p. 875:2.
28. Ibid. Paper 78:7, p. 874:8.
29. Ibid. Paper 77:3, p. 858:3.
30. Ibid. Paper 77:3, p. 858:4.
31. Ibid. Paper 77:3, p. 859:3.
32. Ibid. Paper 67:3, p. 757:1.
33. Ibid. Paper 73:6, p. 826:2.
34. Çatal Höyük, *"The Forked Mound,"* Ancient-Wisdom.co.uk, http://

www.ancient-wisdom.co.uk/turkey
catalhuyuk.htm.
35. *The Urantia Book*, Paper 77:4, p. 860:2.
36. Ibid. Paper 51:1, p. 580:6.
37. Ibid. Paper 81:1, p. 900:3.
38. Ibid. Paper 78:8, p. 876:2–3.
39. Ibid. Paper 78:8, p. 876:4.
40. Ibid. Paper 78:8, p. 876:5.
41. Amelie Kuhrt, *The Ancient Near East* (New York: Routledge, 1997), p. 56.
42. *The Urantia Book*, Paper 80:1, p. 889:5.
43. Leonard Cottrell, *The Quest for Sumer* (New York: Putnam, 1965), p. 203.
44. *The Urantia Book*, Paper 80:6, p. 894:2.
45. *Encyclopædia Britannica*, s.v. "Book of the Dead," http://www.britan nica.com/EBchecked/topic/73503/ Book-of-the Dead.
46. *The Urantia Book*, Paper 95:2, p. 1044:0.
47. Ibid. Paper 95:3, p. 1045:4.
48. Ibid. Paper 80:7, p. 895:2.
49. Ibid. Paper 80:7, p. 895:4.
50. Ibid. Paper 80:7, p. 895:5.
51. Ibid. Paper 79:2, p. 880:2.
52. Ibid.
53. Ibid. Paper 79:4, p. 882:6.
54. Ibid. Paper 94:2, p. 1028:4.
55. Ibid. Paper 94:1, p. 1028:3.
56. Ibid. Paper 79:3, p. 881:3.
57. Ibid. Paper 80:4, p. 893:1.
58. Ibid. Paper 64:6, p. 725:5.
59. Ibid. Paper 68:1, p. 764:2.
60. Ibid. Paper 38:9, p. 424:3.
61. Ibid. Paper 38:9, p. 424:4.
62. Ibid. Paper 77:1, p. 856:3.
63. Ibid. Paper 77:9, p. 866:8.
64. Ibid. Paper 77:8, p. 865:5.
65. Ibid. Paper 77:9, p. 866:0.
66. Ibid. Paper 77:7, p. 863:7 (cf. Matthew 4:24).
67. Ibid. Paper 77:7, p. 863:5.

Chapter 13

1. *The Urantia Book*, Paper 42:12, p. 483:11.
2. James L. Oschman, "Science Measures the Human Energy Field," The International Center for Reiki Training, http://www.reiki.org/ reikinews/ScienceMeasures.htm.
3. *The American Heritage Dictionary of the English Language*, 4th ed., s.v. "brain," http://dictionary.reference.com/sear ch?q=brain.
4. *The Urantia Book*, Paper 12:8, p. 140:7.2.
5. Ibid. Foreword: V, p. 8.8.
6. Ibid. Paper 111.1, p. 1216:4.
7. Ibid. Foreword: VI, p. 9:10.
8. Ibid. Paper 9:5, p. 103:1.
9. Ibid. Paper 12:9, p. 142:1.
10. Ibid. Paper 103:6, p. 1136:1.
11. Ibid. Paper 16:6, p. 192:5.
12. Ibid. Paper 16:6, p. 192:7.
13. Ibid. Paper 108:2, p. 1187:1.
14. Ibid. Paper 66:8, p. 753:2.
15. Ibid. Paper 159:3, p. 1766:8.
16. Ibid. Paper 100:5, p. 1099:4.
17. Source unknown.
18. *The Urantia Book*, Paper 133:6, p. 1478:6.
19. Ibid. Paper 111:0, p. 1215:3.
20. John A. Sanford, *Soul Journey: A Jungian Analyst Looks at Reincarnation* (New York: Crossroad, 1991), p. 85.
21. Ibid. p. 75.
22. *The Urantia Book*, Paper 133:6, p. 1478:4.
23. Ibid. Paper 130:2, p. 1431:3.
24. Ibid. Paper 36:6, p. 404:3.
25. Ibid. Paper 3:6, p. 53:5.
26. Ibid. Paper 2:7, p. 43:5.
27. Ibid. Paper 12:9, p. 142:1.
28. Ibid. Paper 16:9, p. 196:5.
29. Ibid. Paper 16:8, p. 194:6.
30. Ibid. Paper 16:9, p. 196:5–9.
31. Ibid. Paper 130:2, p. 1431:5.
32. Ibid. Paper 132:7, p. 1467:5.
33. Ibid. Paper 112:5, p. 1233:1.
34. Ibid. Paper 16:8, p. 194:7.
35. Ibid. Paper 5:6, p. 71:3.
36. Ibid. Paper 112:2, p. 1229:7.

Chapter 14

1. *The Urantia Book*, Paper 16:7, p. 192:8
2. Ibid. Paper 16:6, p. 192:7.
3. Ibid. Paper 65:6, p. 738:3.
4. Ibid. Paper 196:3, p. 2095:1.
5. Ibid. Paper 133:6, p. 1478:4.
6. Ibid. Paper 195:10, p. 2084:4.
7. Ibid. Paper 100:1, p. 1095:2.
8. Ibid. Paper 101:6, p. 1111:7.
9. Ibid. Paper 196:3, p. 2095:4.
10. Ibid. Paper 87:5, p. 963:4.
11. Ibid. Paper 87:5, p. 963:5–8.
12. Ibid. Paper 103:3, p. 1132:5.
13. Ibid. Paper 196:3, p. 2096:3.
14. Ibid. Paper 195:5, p. 2075:12.
15. Ibid. Paper 170:3, p. 1862:6.
16. Ibid. Paper 66:7, p. 751:4–11.
17. Ibid. Paper 93:4, pp. 1017:8–1018:2.
18. Ibid. Paper 93:4, p. 1017:7.
19. Ibid. Paper 142:3, p. 1599:2–12.
20. Ibid. Paper 89:1, p. 975:1.
21. Ibid. Paper 96:4, p. 1056:4.
22. Ibid. Paper 88:2, p. 969:3.
23. Ibid. Paper 142:3, p. 1599:13.
24. Ibid. Paper 88:2, p. 969:4.
25. Ibid. Paper 142:3, p. 1600:0.
26. Ibid. Paper 140:5, p. 1573:3.
27. Ibid. Paper 180:5, p. 1949:7.

28. Ibid. Paper 180:5, p. 1950:3.
29. Ibid. Paper 19:1, p. 215:8.
30. Ibid. Paper 102:5, p. 1124:2.
31. Ibid. Paper 83:7, p. 928:7.
32. The Barna Group, *Marriage and Divorce Statistics* (March 31, 2008), Blisstree.com, www.blisstree.com/articles/marriage-divorce-statistics-the-barna-group-232/.
33. America's Children: Key National Indicators of Well-Being, 2009; Family Structure and Children's Living Arrangements, ChildStats.gov, http://www.childstats.gov/americaschildren/famsoc1.asp. Source: U.S. Bureau of the Census, Current Population Survey, http://www.childstats.gov/americaschildren/surveys2.asp?popup=true#cps.
34. "French Out-of-Wedlock Birthrate Shows Impact of Marriage Substitutes," Christian News Wire, January 23, 2008, http://www.christiannewswire.com/news/673115457.html.
35. "Teen Birth Rates Up Slightly in 2007 for Second Consecutive Year," Press Release, CDC National Center for Health Statistics, March 18, 2009, http://www.cdc.gov/media/pressrel/2009/r090318.htm.
36. Caitlin Flanagan, "Why Marriage Matters," *Time*, July 13, 2009.
37. Ibid.
38. *The Urantia Book*, Paper 82:0, p. 913:2.
39. Ibid. Paper 133:2, p. 1471:1.
40. Ibid. Paper 68:2, p. 765:5.
41. Ibid. Paper 84:7, p. 939:7.
42. Ibid. Paper 47:1, p. 531:4.
43. Ibid. Paper 84:7, p. 940:1.
44. Ibid. Paper 84:8, p. 943:1.
45. Ibid. Paper 84:7, p. 940:3.
46. Ibid. Paper 84:7, p. 942:1.
47. Ibid. Paper 8:1, p, 92:1.
48. Ibid. Paper 84:7, p. 941:9.

Section 2 Summary

1. *The Urantia Book*. Paper 1:6, p. 30:7.
2. Ibid. Paper 60:1, p. 686:5.
3. Saskia Praamsma Raevouri, "The Human Race, Part Two: The Six Sangik Races—from 500,000 BC," SquareCircles.com, http://www.squarecircles.com/studyaids/race/sixsangiks/SIXSANGIKS.htm.

Section 3 Introduction

1. *The Urantia Book*, Paper 2: 7, p. 43:3.
2. Ibid. Paper 1:5, p. 28:5.

Chapter 15

1. *Major Religions of the World Ranked by Number of Adherents*, http://www.Adherents.com. Click on "List of the Major World Religions ordered by size." Adherents.com has a growing collection of more than 43,870 adherent statistics and religious geography citations: references to published membership/adherent statistics and congregation statistics for over 4,200 religions, churches, denominations, religious bodies, faith groups, tribes, cultures, movements, ultimate concerns, etc.
2. *The Urantia Book*, Paper 86:4, p. 953:5.
3. Ibid. Paper 95:5, p. 1049:1.
4. James H. Breasted, *Development of Religion and Thought in Ancient Egypt* (London: Hodder and Stoughton, 1912), p. 277.
5. *The Urantia Book*, Paper 79:3, p. 881:4.
6. Ibid. Paper 94:1, p. 1028:0.
7. S. Radhakrishnan, *The Principal Upanishads* (London: George Allen and Unwin, 1968), p. 433.
8. *The Urantia Book*, Paper 94:3, p. 1030:2.
9. Ibid. Paper 1:7, p. 31:2.
10. Ibid. Paper 94:8, p. 1037:3.
11. *Grolier Multimedia Encyclopedia* (created with Grolier Online), s.v. "Hinduism" by Karl. H. Potter, http://teacher.scholastic.com/scholasticnews/indepth/upfront/grolier/hinduism.htm.
12. *The Urantia Book*, Paper 94:4, p. 1032:1.
13. Ibid. Paper 98:2, p. 1079:6.
14. Samos is an ancient region of southwestern coastal Anatolia (now in Turkey), on the Aegean Sea.
15. John A. Sandford, *Soul Journey: A Jungian Analyst Looks at Reincarnation* (New York: Crossroad, 1991), p. 75.
16. Ibid. pp. 75–76.
17. *The Urantia Book*, Paper 121:6, p. 1338:6.
18. Ibid. Paper 164:3, p. 1811:5.
19. Ibid. Paper 135:4, p. 1499:4.
20. Ibid. Paper 135:4, p. 1499:5.
21. Quintus Septimius Florens Tertullianus, *A Treatise on the Soul*, chap. 35, "The Opinions of Carpocrates: Another Offset from the Pythagorean Dogmas, Stated and Confuted," IntraText Edition CT, (copyright Éulogos 2007), Intratext Digital Library, http://www.intratext.com/IXT/ENG0254/_PZ.HTM. Biblical quotes from Matthew 17:12 11:14.

22. *The Urantia Book*, Paper 158:2, p. 1754:2.
23. Ibid. Paper 136:1, p. 1509:5.
24. Ibid. Paper 94:2, p. 1029:1.
25. Aaron, Rita, et al., "Suicides in Young People in Rural Southern India," *The Lancet* 363, issue 9415 (April 2004): pp. 1117–1118. Statistics taken from the summary at http://www.the lancet.com/journals/lancet/article/PIIS0140-6736(04)15896-0/abstract.
26. Phil Zuckerman, *The Cambridge Companion to Atheism*, ed. by Michael Martin (Cambridge, UK: Cambridge University Press, 2005), p. 56.
27. Russell Ash, *The Top 10 of Everything* (New York: DK Publishing, 1997), pp. 160–161.
28. *The Urantia Book*, Paper 79:6, p. 885:7–8.
29. Ibid. Paper 79:8, p. 887:4.
30. Ibid. Paper 79:8, p. 887:7.
31. Richard Hooker, *China Glossary*, Washington State University, 1996, updated July 14, 1999, http://www.wsu.edu:8080/~dee/GLOSSARY/CHIGLOSS.HTM.
32 *The Urantia Book*, Paper 94:6, p. 1034:3.
33. Ibid. Paper 94:6, p. 1034:4.
34. Ibid. Paper 94:6, p. 1034:6.
35. Ibid. Paper 94:6, 1035:0.
36. Ibid. Paper 94:11, pp. 1038:8–1039:0.
37. Ibid. Paper 94:9, p. 1038:4.
38. Ibid. Paper 160:5, p. 1781:1.
39: Ming Wan, *Human Rights in Chinese Foreign Relations: Defining and Defending National Interests* (Philadelphia: University of Pennsylvania Press, 2001), p. 29. "This was a national poll conducted entirely by Gallup staff based on over 3700 hour-long, in-home interviews in every province, municipality, and autonomous region of the country" (note 31 on p. 152). Also "1997 Survey: The People's Republic of China Consumer Attitudes and Lifestyle Trends" (Princeton, NJ: Gallup, October 27, 1997).
40. William J. McEwen, "The Chinese: A New Wave of Entrepreneurs?" December 26, 2007, Gallup.com, http://www.gallup.com/poll/103444/chinese-new-wave-entrepreneurs.aspx.
41. Simon Elegant, "China's Me Generation," *Time* magazine November 5, 2007.
42. *China Human Rights Fact Sheet*, Robert F. Kennedy Memorial Center for Human Rights, March 1995. Based on information provided by Amnesty International—USA, the Committee to Protect Journalists, the Francois-Xavier Bagnoud Center for Health and Human Rights, Human Rights in China, the International Campaign for Tibet, the Puebla Institute, and the RFK Memorial Center for Human Rights. Support Democracy in China, http://www.christusrex.org/www1/sdc/hr_facts.html.
43. *Amnesty International Report 2005: The State of the World's Human Rights*, Amnesty International, http://www.amnesty.org/en/library/info/POL10/001/2005.
44. Fareed Zakaria, "Does the Future Belong to China?" Newsweek, Inc., May 9, 2005, http://www.newsweek.com/id/51964/.
45. *The Urantia Book*, Paper 195:10, p. 2084:7.
46. Evan Osnos, "Jesus in China: Life on the Edge," *Chicago Tribune* Web Edition, June 26, 2008.
47. *The Urantia Book*. Paper 195:5, p. 2075:4.
48. Daniel V. A. Olson, *The Secularization Debate* (paperback), (Lanham, MD: Rowman and Littlefield, 2000), p. 45.
49. "Facts and Figures of Reincarnation Belief in Europe," spiritual-wholeness.org, http://www.spiritual-wholeness.org/faqs/reinceur/reineuro.htm. An analysis of the European Values Systems Study, which was conducted on a Europe-wide scale in 1981 and 1990.
50. E. Haraldsson, "Popular psychology, belief in life after death and reincarnation in the Nordic countries, Western and Eastern Europe," *Nordic Psychology* 58, no. 2 (2006): pp. 171–180, http://www3.hi.is/~erlendur/english/Nordic_Psychology_erlhar06.pdf.
51 Alec Gallup and Frank Newport, "Three in Four Believe in Paranormal," *The Gallup Poll: Public Opinion 2005* (Lanham, MD: Rowman & Littlefield, 2007), p. 221.
52. "Facts and Figures of Reincarnation Belief in Europe" (see note 49), http://www.spiritual-wholeness.org/faqs/reinceur/reineuro.htm.
53. "Generation Y embraces choice, redefines religion," *Washington Times*, April 12, 2005, http://www.washingtontimes.com/news/2005/apr/12/2

0050412-121457-4149r/. Statistics in this article are taken from 2004 Reboot's study, "OMG! How Generation Y is Redefining Faith in the iPod Era," by Anna Greenberg, Greenberg Quinlan Rosner Research, http://www.greenbergresearch.com/index.php?ID=1218.

54. *The Urantia Book*, Paper 195:8, p. 2082:2.

55. Ibid. Paper 102:8, p. 1127:8.

56. William J. Bennet, "Quantifying America's Decline," *Wall Street Journal*, March 15, 1993, The Augustine Club at Columbia University, http://www.columbia.edu/cu/augustine/arch/usadecline.html.

57. Ibid.

58. The United States crime index rates per 100,000 inhabitants went from 1,887.2 in 1960 to 5,897.8 in 1991, as reported in *United States Crime Rates 1960–2008*, Disaster Center, http://www.disastercenter.com/crime/uscrime.htm. Scroll down to "United States Crime Index Rates Per 100,000 inhabitants."

59. Lea L. Bryant, *Self-Esteem and Aggressive Behavior: Who's More Aggressive?* National Undergraduate Research Clearinghouse, 2006. Results of a survey of 68 participants from Missouri Western State University conducted by the Department of Psychology. http://clearinghouse.missouriwestern.edu/manuscripts/826.php.

60. Tom Huston, "The Dumbest Generation?" *EnlightenNext: The Magazine for Evolutionaries*, December 2008–February 2009.

61. "Crime is Down, According to Our Preliminary Stats," highlights from the *2008 Preliminary Annual Uniform Crime Report*, Federal Bureau of Investigation, June 1, 2009, http://www.fbi.gov/page2/june09/ucr_statistics060109.html.

62. *FBI Preliminary Annual Uniform Crime Report*, 2005, Federal Bureau of Investigation, http://www.fbi.gov/ucr/2005preliminary/index.htm.

63. *The Urantia Book*, Paper 4:1, p. 54:5.

64. Geoffrey A. Barborka, *The Divine Plan*, 6th repr. (Wheaton, IL: Theosophical Publishing House, 1998), pp. 20–22.

65. *The Urantia Book*, Foreword, Section V, p. 9.

66. Ibid. Paper 16:6, p.191:6.

67. Ibid. Paper 118:8, p.1302:5.

68. Ibid. Paper 26:3, p. 288:2 and Paper 28:3, p. 310:9.

Chapter 16

1. *The Urantia Book*, Paper 98:4, p. 1081:4.

2. "Barna Survey Examines Changes in Worldview Among Christians over the Past 13 Years," March 6, 2009, Barna Group, http://www.barna.org/barna-update/article/21transformation/252-barna-survey-examines-changes-in-worldview-among-christians-over-the-past-13-years.

3. *The Urantia Book*, Paper 103:9, p. 1141:3.

4. Ibid. Paper 132:3, p. 1459:6.

5. Ibid. Paper 169:1, p. 1853:2.

6. Ibid. Paper 101:6, p. 1112:4.

7. Ibid. Paper 101:6, pp. 1112:4–1113:4.

8. Ibid. Paper 101:6, p. 1113:5.

9. Ibid. Paper 133:6, p. 1478:4.

10. Ibid. Paper 101:2, p. 1106:2.

11. Ibid. Paper 196:3, p. 2096:8.

12. Ibid. Paper 133:6, p. 1478:5.

13. Ibid. Paper 188:4, p. 2017:8.

14. National Conference of Commissioners on Uniform State Laws, *Uniform Determination of Death Act*, 1980, Penn Law, the University of Pennsylvania website, http://www.law.upenn.edu/bll/archives/ulc/fnact99/1980s/udda80.htm.

15. *The Urantia Book*, Paper 24:2, p. 267:5.

16. Ibid. Paper 55:2, p. 623:11.

17. Ibid. Paper 112:5, p. 1232–1235.

Chapter 17

1. Michelle Vu, "Poll: Most Americans Reject Resurrection of the Body," *Christian Post*, April 13, 2006, http://www.christianpost.com/article/20060413/poll-most-americans-reject-resurrection-of-the-body/index.html.

2. *The Urantia Book*, Paper 1:3, p. 26:1.

3. Ibid. Paper 40:5, p. 447:4.

4. Ibid. Paper 110:4, p. 1206:3.

5. Ibid. Paper 30:4, p. 341:1.

6. Ibid. Paper 112:5, p. 1234:3.

7. Michelle Vu, "Poll: Most Americans Reject Resurrection of the Body," *Christian Post*, April 13, 2006, http://www.christianpost.com/article/20060413/poll-most-americans-reject-resurrection-of-the-body/index.html.

8. *The Urantia Book*, Paper 98:4, p. 1081:9.
9. Ibid. Paper 174:3, p. 1900:4.
10. Ibid. Paper 42:12, p. 483:11.
11. Ibid. Paper 48:1, p. 542:2.
12. Ibid. Paper 30:4, p. 341:1.
13. Ibid. Paper 49:6, p. 568:5.
14. Ibid. Paper 90:1, p. 986:5.
15. Ibid. Paper 90:1, p. 987:1.
16. Ibid. Paper 112:3, p. 1230:5.
17. Susan Blackmore, "All in the Mind," *New Internationalist* 237, November 1992, http://www.newint.org/issue237/all.htm.
18. Greg Barrett, "Can the Living Talk to the Dead?" *USA Today*, sec. D, June 20, 2001.
19. *The Urantia Book*, Paper 111:3, p. 1218:9.
20. Ibid. Paper 45:4, p. 514:3. (cf. Genesis 5:24 and Hebrews 11:5).
21. Ibid. Paper 40:8, p. 449:4.
22. Ibid. Paper 40:8, p. 450:0.

Chapter 18

1. Arnobius, *Against the Heathen*, book 2, passage 14, New Advent, http://www.newadvent.org/fathers/06312.htm. Source quoted on page: "Translated by Hamilton Bryce and Hugh Campbell. From Ante-Nicene Fathers, Vol. 6. Edited by Alexander Roberts, James Donaldson, and A. Cleveland Coxe. (Buffalo, NY: Christian Literature Publishing Co., 1886.) Revised and edited for New Advent by Kevin Knight."
2. Alec M. Gallup, *The Gallup Poll: Public Opinion 2007* (Lanham, MD: Rowman and Littlefield, June 28, 2008), p. 258.
3. *The Urantia Book*, Paper 86:4, p. 953:6.
4. Pope John Paul II, "Heaven, Hell, and Purgatory," papal document reproduced on Eternal Word Television Network website, http://www.ewtn.com/library/PAPALDOC/JP2HEAVN.HTM. Based on material appearing in the newspaper of the Holy See, *L'Osservatore Romano*: "Heaven" (28 July 1999), "Hell" (4 August 1999), and "Purgatory" (11/18 August 1999). The weekly English edition of *L'Osservatore Romano* is published for the U.S. by the Cathedral Foundation in Baltimore, MD.
5. Matthew 5:22, 29, 30; 10:28; 18:9; 23:15, 33; Mark 9:43, 45, 47; Luke 12:5; James 3:6.
6. *Encyclopædia Britannica Online*, s.v "gehenna," http://dictionary.reference.com/browse/gehenna.
7. *The Urantia Book*, Paper 67:7, p. 760:6.
8. Ibid. Paper 2:3, p. 37:0.
9. Ibid. Paper 2:4, p. 38:1.
10. Ibid. Paper 54:4, p. 616:5.
11. Ibid. Paper 2:3, p. 37:2.
12. Ibid. Paper 1:1, p. 22:5.
13. Ibid. Paper 100:4, p. 1098:3.

Chapter 19

1. *Catholic Encyclopedia*, s.v. "particular judgment," New Advent, http://www.newadvent.org/cathen/08550a.htm.
2. *The Urantia Book*, Paper 5:5, p. 69:8.
3. Ibid. Paper 110:3, p. 1205:6.
4. Ibid. Paper 2:4, p. 38:5.
5. Ibid. Paper 112:5, p. 1233:6.
6. Ibid. Paper 33:7, p. 372:8.
7. Ibid. Paper 28:6, p. 314:3.
8. Ibid. Paper 28:6, p. 314:4.
9. Ibid.
10. Ibid. Paper 28:6, p. 314:5.
11. Ibid. Paper 28:6, p. 314:6.
12. Ibid. Paper 21:5, p. 241:1.
13. Ibid. Paper 28:6, p. 315:2–3.
14. Ibid. Paper 28:6, p. 315:6.
15. Ibid. Paper 28:6, p. 316:1.
16. Ibid. Paper 28:6, p. 316:6.
17. Ibid. Paper 28:6, p. 317:1.
18. Ibid. Paper 28:6, p. 317:2.
19. Ibid. Paper 28:5, p. 313:1.
20. Ibid. Paper 22:2, p. 245:1.
21. Ibid. Paper 2:3, p. 38:4.

Chapter 20

1. *Encyclopædia Britannica Online*, s.v. "culture," http://www.britannica.com/EBchecked/topic/146289/culture.
2. Andrew Cohen and Ken Wilber in dialogue, "The Leading Edge of the Leading Edge," *What Is Enlightenment?* Issue 38, October–December 2007. Also, *Kosmic Consciousness*, CD 4, track 4, 6:38.
3. *The Urantia Book*, Paper 19:1, p. 215:8.
4. Ibid. Paper 50:6, p. 578:4.
5. Ibid. Paper 111:6, p. 1222:6.
6. Ibid. Paper 50:6, p. 578:4.
7. Ibid. Paper 102:3, p. 1122:1.
8. Ibid. Paper 49:4, p. 564:9.
9. Ibid. Paper 50:5, p. 576:6.
10. Ibid. Paper 50:5, p. 567:7.
11. Ibid. Paper 81:5, p. 905:6.
12. Howard Hughes Medical Institute, "Human Brain Is Still Evolving,"

HHMI Research News, September 9, 2005, http://www.hhmi.org/news/lahn4.html. Also, UBtheNEWS at www.ubthenews.com offers detailed academic reports of scientific advances and new discoveries that corroborate information in *The Urantia Book*.

13. *The Urantia Book*, Paper 135:5, p. 1500:2.
14. David Mathews, "Hal Lindsey's Prophecies: A Study of *The Late Great Planet Earth*," from David Mathews's website, http://www.geocities.com/athens/agora/3958/hal1.htm.
15. *The Urantia Book*. Paper 139:4, p. 1555:7.
16. Ibid. Paper 12:7, p. 138:6.
17. Ibid. Paper 195:8, p. 2082:5.
18. Ibid. Paper 41:9, p. 465:5.
19. Ibid. Paper 51:2, p. 582:3.
20. David Deutsch, "Problems or Prophecies?" review of *What Remains to Be Discovered* by John Maddox, Physicsworld.com, December 4, 1998, http://physicsworld.com/cws/article/indepth/2494.
21. *The Urantia Book*, Paper 195:10, p. 2085:6.

Chapter 21

1. *The Urantia Book*, Paper 71:4, pp. 804:17–1805:0.
2. Ibid. Paper 71:6, p. 805:7.
3. Ibid. Paper 55:4, p. 627:6.

Chapter 22

1. The Supreme Being is not likely to be attained until ascending personalities ". . . have achieved seventh-stage-spirit status, and until the Supreme has become actually functional in the activities of the future outer universes." *The Urantia Book*, Paper 56:6, p. 641:5. Also see "Corps of Mortal Finaliters" section in this chapter.
2. Ibid. Paper 101:6, p. 1111:7.
3. Ibid. Paper 12:8, p. 139:4.
4. Ibid. Paper 101:5, p. 1111:3.
5. Ibid. Paper 44:0, pp. 497:1–499:2.
6. Ibid. Paper 47:3, p. 533:4.
7. Ibid. Paper 47:1, p. 531:4.
8. Ibid. Paper 47:3, p. 534:2.
9. Ibid. Paper 47:5, p. 536:1.
10. Ibid. Paper 47:6, p. 536:4.
11. Ibid. Paper 47:7, p. 537:5.
12. Ibid. Paper 108:3, p. 1188:5.
13. Ibid. Paper 43:8, p. 494:2.
14. Ibid. Paper 35:3, p. 388:1.

15. Ibid. Paper 18:4, p. 211:4.
16. Ibid. Paper 14:1, p. 152:11.
17. Ibid. Paper 31, p. 345.
18. Ibid. Paper 31:0, p. 345:8.
19. Ibid. Paper 31:3, p. 348:3.

Section 4 Introduction

1. *The Urantia Book*. Paper 25:4, p. 279:13.
2. Ibid. Paper 155:5, p. 1729:6.
3. Ibid. Paper 155:6, p. 1731:2.

Chapter 23

1. *The Urantia Book*. Paper 101:7, p. 1114:0.
2. Ibid. Paper 156:5, p. 1738:1.
3. Jiddu Krisnamurti, *The Book of Life: Daily Meditations with Krishnamurti*, R. E. Mark Lee, ed., May 4 entry titled "Intellect vs. Intelligence, p. 131; September 3 entry titled "Unity of Mind and Heart," p. 258 (New York, HarperOne, 1995).
4. *The Urantia Book*, Paper 92:2, p. 1005:2.
5. W. John Murray, *Mental Medicine* (New York: Divine Science Publishing, 1923), p. 80.
6. *The Urantia Book*, Paper 2:2, p. 36:3.
7. Sarah Belle Dougherty, "Spiritual Growth or Spiritual Behaviorism?" *Sunrise* magazine, Theosophical University Press, June–July 1988.
8. *The Urantia Book*. Paper 101:8, p. 1114:5.
9. Ibid. Paper 101:3, p. 1107:8.
10. Ibid. Paper 132:3, p. 1459:5.
11. Ibid. Paper 132:2, p. 1457:5.
12. Ibid. Paper 130:3, p. 1433:2.
13. Ibid. Paper 5:2, p. 65:0.
14. Ibid. Paper 100:2, p. 1095:6.
15. Ibid. Paper 126:2, p. 1388:5.
16. Ibid. Paper 110:3, p. 1206:2.
17. Ibid. Paper 139:8, p. 1562:1.
18. Ibid. Paper 117:4, p. 1285:3.
19. Ibid. Paper 102:2, p. 1120:4.
20. Ibid. Paper 152:6, p. 1705:1.

Chapter 24

1. *The Urantia Book*, Paper 101:1, p. 1104:6.
2. Ibid. Paper 91:7, p. 1001:4.
3. Ibid. Paper 101:5, p. 1110:12.
4. Ibid. Paper 1:3, p. 26:1.
5. Ibid. Paper 2, p. 1095:6.
6. Ibid. Paper 49:6, p. 569:3.
7. Ibid. Paper 110:6, pp. 1209–1212.
8. Ibid. Paper 123:2, p. 1357:5.
9. Ibid. Paper 140:4, p. 1572:8.

10. Ibid. Paper 123:3, p. 1360:4.
11. Ibid. Paper 123:5, p. 1363:1.
12. Ibid. Paper 124:4, pp. 1372:6–1373:0.
13. Carolyn Myss, *Anatomy of the Spirit: The Seven Stages of Power and Healing* (New York: Three Rivers Press, 1997), p. 187.
14. *The Urantia Book*. Paper 126:2, p. 1388:5.
15. Ibid. Paper 127:6, p. 1405:7.
16. Ibid. Paper 127:6, p. 1405:4.
17. Ibid. Paper 134:1, p. 1484:4.
18. Ibid. Paper 134:8, p. 1493:4.
19. Ibid. Paper 134:8, p. 1493:3.
20. Ibid. Paper 100:6, p. 1100:6.
21. Ibid. Paper 133:5, p. 1477:3.
22. Ibid. Paper 43:9, p. 494:10.
23. Ibid. Paper 141:5, p. 1592:1.
24. Ibid. Paper 100:2, p. 1095:6.

Chapter 25

1. Daniel Day Williams, "Love and the Intelligent," chap. 13 in *The Spirit and the Forms of Love* (New York: Harper and Row, 1968).
2. *The Urantia Book*, Paper 16:9, p. 196:3.
3. Ibid. Paper 149:6, p. 1676:4.
4. Ibid. Paper 111:5, p. 1221:7 and Paper 118:8, p. 1303:1.
5. Ibid. Paper 84:7, p. 941:7.
6. Ibid. Paper 174:1, p. 1898:5.
7. William Barclay, *New Testament Words: The Greatest of the Virtues* (Westminster: John Knox Press, 2000), p. 21.
8. *The Urantia Book*, Paper 180:5, p. 1950:5.
9. Ibid. Paper 82:1, p. 913:4.
10. Ibid. Foreword: V, p. 8:8.
11. J. Andrew Armour, *Neurocardiology: Anatomical and Functional Principles*, http://www.heartmathstore.com/cgi–bin/category.cgi?item=enro.
12. "Waking Up to the Holographic Heart: Starting Over with Education," a conversation between Joseph Chilton Pearce and Casey Walker, editor and publisher of the *Wild Duck Review*, on May 20, 1998, with the production assitance of KVMR, a community-supported radio station in Nevada City, CA, http://www.ratical.org/many_worlds/JCP98.html.
13. The Urantia Book. Paper 155:6, p. 1733:1.
14. Ibid. Paper 100:4, p. 1097:5.
15. Ibid. Paper 111:5, p. 1221:7 and Paper 118:8, p. 1303:1.
16. Ibid. Paper 193:2, p. 2054:3.

Chapter 26

1. *The Urantia Book*. Paper 122:8, p. 1352:3.
2. A CD-ROM of *The Urantia Book* with searchable text is available from the Urantia Foundation. Telephone: 1-888-URANTIA, or from outside the U.S. and Canada, 1-773-525-3319. Study aids and secondary source books are available for exploration. Study groups—informal, familial associations of readers of *The Urantia Book*—can be found worldwide.
3. *The Urantia Book*, Paper 2:7, p. 42:7.
4. "Majority of Adult Americans Believe That Religious Differences are the Biggest Challenge for World Peace," Reaching Common Ground, Pressroom section, http//www.reachingcommonground.com (website now discontinued).
5. *The Urantia Book*, Paper 133:5, p. 1477:2.
6. Ibid. Paper 87:7, p. 966:2.

Chapter 27

1. Michael Scriven and Richard Paul, *Defining Critical Thinking*, a statement for the National Council for Excellence in Critical Thinking Instruction, The Critical Thinking Community, Foundation for Critical Thinking, http://www.criticalthinking.org/aboutCT/definingCT.cfm.
2. *The Urantia Book*, Paper 148:1, p. 1657:6.
3. Ruth A. Rosenbaum, "Factoids, Facts, Information, Knowledge, Wisdom: Systemic Analysis in the Information Age," *Starting Points* newsletter, vol. 4, no 2 (2004), Center for Reflection, Education and Action, http://www.crea-inc.org. To locate the article, enter into your browser the first four words of the article name.
4. Richard Paul and L. Elder, "The Critical Mind Is a Questioning Mind," Foundation For Critical Thinking, May 1996, http://www.critical thinking.org/resources/articles/critical-mind.shtml.
5. Michael Scriven and Richard Paul, *Defining Critical Thinking*, a statement for the National Council for Excellence in Critical Thinking Instruction, The Critical Thinking Community, Foundation for Critical

Thinking, http://www.criticalthink
ing.org/aboutCT/definingCT.cfm.
6. *The Urantia Book*, Paper 92:7,
p. 1012:6.

Chapter 28

1. I.K. Taimni, *Gayatri* (Adyar, India:
The Theosophical Publishing House),
pp. 29–30.
2. Dwight G. Dean, "Emotional
Maturity and Marital Adjustment,"
Journal of Marriage and the Family 28,
no. 4, (November 1966): p. 454–457.
Adapted for this book.
3. *The Urantia Book*, Paper 149:4,
p. 1674:1.
4. Ibid. Paper 149:3, p. 1672:5.
5. Ibid. Paper 160:1, p. 1773:4.
6. Ibid. Paper 132:3, p. 1460:3.
7. Robert Reasoner, "The True Meaning
of Self-Esteem," National Association
for Self-Esteem, http://www.self-
esteem-nase.org/what.php.
8. *The Urantia Book*, Paper 156:5,
p. 1740:1.
9. Jill Elish, "Sociologists find low self-
esteem at age 11 predicts drug
dependency at 20," April 3, 2006,
FSU News, Florida State University.
From the article: "FSU sociology
professors John Taylor and Donald
Lloyd, along with University of
Miami professor emeritus George
Wahrheit, found that low self-esteem
and peer approval of drug use at age
11 predicted drug dependency at age
20. The researchers came to that
conclusion after analyzing data from
a multiethnic sample of 872 boys
collected over a period of nine years.
The study was published in the
Journal of Child and Adolescent
Substance Abuse." The Florida State
University, http://www.fsu.edu/
news/2006/04/03/self.esteem.
10. *The Urantia Book*, Paper 159:3,
p. 1765:5.
11. Jill Elish, "FSU Study Finds Self-
Esteem Programs Don't Work,"
March 1, 2004, Florida State
University, FSU.com,
http://www.fsu.com/News-
Archive/2004/20040301self_esteem.
12. Ibid. Findings of study were
presented at the annual meeting of
the American Association for the
Advancement of Sciences (AAAS).
13. *The Urantia Book*, Paper 100:6,
p. 1100:5.
14. James J. Messina, "Developing Self-
Control," April 26, 2006,

Addictioninfo.org, http://www.
addictioninfo.org/articles/754/1/
Developing-Self-Control/Page1.html.
15. *The Urantia Book*, Paper 89:3, p. 976:5.
16. Clayton E. Tucker-Ladd, *Psychological
Self-Help*, ch. 4, p. 54, online book
at http://www.psychologicalself
help .org/.
17. Ibid. p. 53.
18. Ibid. p. 54.
19. Mark Gorkin, "The Four Faces of
Anger," *SelfhelpMagazine*, April 26,
1998, revised 8/4/09 by Marlene M.
Maheu, http://www.selfhelp
magazine.com/article/anger-
management.
20. *The Urantia Book*, Paper 48:7, p. 557:4.
21. Ibid. Paper 149:4, p. 1673:2.
22. Alex Pattakos, *Prisoners of Our
Thoughts: Viktor Frankl's Principles for
Discovering Meaning in Life and Work*
(San Francisco: Berrett-Koehler,
2008), foreword, p. viii.
23. Aristotle, *The Nicomachean Ethics*,
trans. David Ross (New York: Oxford
World's Classics, 1998), p. 45.
24. Thomas Hine, *The Rise and Fall of the
American Teenager* (New York: Avon
Books, 1999), p. 277.
25. *The Urantia Book*, Paper 82:1, p. 914:6.
26. Ibid. Paper 54:1, p. 613:7.
27. Ibid. Paper 131:2, p. 1458:1.
28. Rabbi Michael Lerner, "The Ten
Commitments," Tikkun website,
http://www.tikkun.org/rabbi_lerner
/tencommitments.
29. *The Urantia Book*, Paper 82:1, p. 914:6.
30. Ibid. Paper 140:5, p. 1575:1.

Chapter 29

1. *Encyclopedia of the Self*, s.v. "taste,"
website of Mark Zimmerman,
http://www.selfknowledge.com/
96869.htm.
2. Mark Akenside, *Poetical Works of
Akenside*, part 2 of 7, http://www.
fullbooks.com/Poetical-Works-of-
Akenside2.html.
3. Ronald H. Silverman, "Art Criticism:
judgment versus taste," from the
website *Learning About Art: A
Multicultural Approach*, http://
instructional1.calstatela.edu/laa/
aesthetics_2.html.
4. Kevin F. McCarthy, Elizabeth H.
Ondaatje, Laura Zakaras, and Arthur
Brooks, *Gift of the Muse: Reframing the
Debate About the Benefits of the Arts*
(2004 RAND Corporation Report),
p. xv.
5. Ibid. p. 52.

6. Ronald H. Silverman, "What do you study when you study art?, from the website *Learning About Art: A Multicultural Approach*, http://instructional1.calstatela.edu/laa/study_1.html.
7. Kevin F. McCarthy, Elizabeth H. Ondaatje, Laura Zakaras, and Arthur Brooks, *Gift of the Muse: Reframing the Debate About the Benefits of the Arts* (2004 RAND Corporation Report), p. 52.
8. *The Urantia Book*, Paper 34:6, p. 381:1.
9. Ibid. Paper 2:7, p. 43:4.
10. Ibid. Paper 110:1, p. 1204:3.
11. Durant Drake, *Problems of Conduct*, (Charleston, SC: Bibliobazaar, 2006), p. 166. Author is associate professor of ethics and philosophy of religion at Wesleyan University.
12. Anthony Blunt. *Artistic Theory in Italy* (London: Oxford University Press, 1940), p. 69.
13. Kenneth Clark, *The Nude: A Study in Ideal Form* (New York: Doubleday, 1956), paperback ed., p. 474.
14. *The Urantia Book*, Paper 56:10, p. 646:4.

Chapter 30

1. Randy Ruffin, *What Does it Mean to Be Moral?* June 3, 2005, Initiatives of Change International, http://www.iofc.org/node/22689.
2. *The Urantia Book*, Paper 16:7, p. 193:8.
3. Ibid. Paper 101:9, p. 1115:6.
4. Ibid. Paper 162:7, p. 1796:4; Paper 141:7, p. 1594:0, cf. John 8:32.
5. Joel Osteen, *Your Best Life Now: 7 Steps to Living at Your Full Potential* (Brentwood, TN: FaithWords, 2004), p. 287.
6. *The Urantia Book*, Paper 67:1, p. 754:4.
7. Ibid. Paper 102:6, p. 1125:4.
8. Ibid. Paper 171:8, p. 1876:8.
9. Ibid. Paper 194:3, p. 2064:4.
10. Ibid. Paper 141:3, p. 1590:3.
11. Robert Enright, *Proposed Activities within the International Forgiveness Institute*, undated. International Forgiveness Institute (based at the University of Wisconsin, USA), http://homepage.uab.edu/pedersen/a20.htm.
12. Ibid.
13. Ibid.
14. Frederic Luskin, *Forgive for Good*, (New York: HarperOne 2003), Introduction, p. xii.
15. Ibid. pp. 71–73.
16. *The Urantia Book*, Paper 174:1, p. 1898:5.
17. Ibid. Paper 142:7, p. 1604:6.
18. Ibid. Paper 174:1, p. 1898:4.
19. John F. MacArthur, *The Freedom and Power of Forgiveness* (Crossway Books, 1998), p. 112.
20. *The Urantia Book*, Paper 100:4, p. 1098:2.
21. Ibid. Paper 2:6, p. 41:4.
22. Ibid. Paper 174:1, p. 1898:3.
23. Ibid. Paper 170:3, p. 1862:1.
24. Stephen Post and Jill Neimark, *Why Good Things Happen to Good People* (New York: Broadway Books, 2007), pp. 8–9.
25. *The Urantia Book*, Paper 100:6, p. 1101:3.
26. Ibid. Paper 170:3, p. 1862:6.
27. Bill Clinton. *Giving: How Each of Us Can Change the World* (New York: Knopf, 2007), p. 70.
28. *The Urantia Book*, Paper 12:5, p. 135:9.
29. Ibid. Paper 142:3, p. 1600:0.
30. Ibid. Paper 142:4, p. 1602:3.

Chapter 31

1. *The Urantia Book*, Paper 1:1, p. 22:5.
2. Ibid. Paper 160:1, p. 1774:5.
3. Ibid. Paper 100:4, p. 1098:3.
4. *Encyclopædia Britannica Online*, s.v. "prayer," http://www.britannica.com/eb/article-9375817 (accessed February 18, 2008).
5. *The Urantia Book*, Paper 91:1, p. 995:1.
6. Ibid. Paper 91:6, p. 999:5.
7. Ibid. Paper 146:2, p. 1640:3.
8. Ibid. Paper 111:7, p. 1223:4.
9. Ibid. Paper 91:6, p. 1000:1.
10. Ibid. Paper 146:2, p. 1641:1.
11. Kieran Kavanaugh and Otilio Rodriguez, trans., *Teresa of Avila: The Book of Her Life* (Indianapolis, IN: Hackett Publishing, 2008), p. 44.
12. *The Urantia Book*, Paper 7:3, p. 84:5–6. (cf. 1 Corinthians 13:1).
13. Ibid. Paper 91:5, p. 998:5.
14. Ibid. Paper 27:7, p. 303:5.
15. Ibid. Paper 5:3, p. 66:4.
16. Ibid. Paper 143:7, p. 1616:8–10.
17. Ibid. Paper 1: 1, p. 22:5.
18. Ibid. Paper 146:2, p. 1641:1.
19. Ibid. Paper 99:6, p. 1092:2.
20. Jimmy Cutter, "Worship: Definition and Purpose of Worship," Advocate Old Paths website, February 1, 1986, http://www.newtestamentchurch.org/OPA/Articles/1986/02/worship_definition_and.htm.

Chapter 32

1. *The Urantia Book*, Paper 110:3, p. 1206:5–8.
2. Hara Estroff Marano "What Is Solitude?" *Psychology Today*, July 1, 2003, http://psychologytoday.com/articles/index.php?term=pto-2965.html.&fromMod=popular.
3. Answers.com., s.v. "meditation," http://www.answers.com/topic/meditation?cat=health.
4. Michael J. Baime, "Meditation and Mindfulness" in *Essentials of Complementary and Alternative Medicine*, Wayne B. Jonas and Jeffrey S. Levin, eds. (New York: Lippincott Williams and Wilkins, 1999).
5. *The Urantia Book*. Paper 1:6, p. 30:5.
6. Ibid. Paper 5:5, p. 69:7.
7. Ibid. Paper 1:6, p. 30:3.
8. Ibid. Paper 1:4, p. 27:1.
9. Ibid. Paper 130:4, p. 1435:2.
10. Ibid. Paper 5:1, p. 62:3.
11. Ibid. Paper 111:5, p. 1221:2.
12. Ibid. Paper 118:7, p. 1301:2.
13. See note 1, chapter 22.
14. *The Urantia Book*, Paper 102:7, p. 1126:4.
15. Ibid. Paper 100:3, p. 1096:6.
16. Ibid. Paper 100:5, pp. 1099:7–1100:0.
17. Ibid. Paper 5:2, p. 64:6.
18. Ibid. Paper 5:5, p. 69:1.
19. Ibid. Paper 5.0, p. 62.1.
20. Ibid. Paper 159:3, p. 1766:5.
21. Ibid. Paper 124.3, p. 1371.3.
22. Ibid. Paper 160:1, p. 1774:4.
23. Ibid. Paper 146:2, p. 1641:1.
24. Ibid. Paper 1:7, p. 31:2.
25. Ibid. Paper 146.2, p. 1641:1–16.
26. Ibid. Paper 143:3, p. 1611:1.
27. Ibid. Paper 160:3, p. 1777:2.

Section 4 Summary

1. *The Urantia Book*. Paper 111:6, p. 1222:6.

In Closing

1. *The Urantia Book*, Paper 81:6, p. 909:7.

Select Bibliography

This is a selection of the sources that I found especially helpful in providing a context for my work by presenting contrasting, supporting, or complementary viewpoints and data. It also includes some sources I used for my research that are additional to those in the chapter endnotes.

Achenbach, Joel. "The God Particle." *National Geographic*, March 2008.

Aurobindo, Sri. *The Human Cycle: Ideal of Human Unity; War and Self-Determination*. Twin Lakes, WI: Lotus Press, 1970.

———— *The Life Divine*. Twin Lakes, WI: Lotus Press, 1985.

Barborka, Geoffrey A. *The Divine Plan*. Wheaton, IL: Theosophical Publishing House, 1998.

Barclay, William. *New Testament Words: English New Testament Words Indexed with References to the Daily Study Bible*. Westminster: John Knox Press, 2000.

Breasted, James H. *Development of Religion and Thought in Ancient Egypt*. London: Hodder and Stoughton, 1912.

Clark, Kenneth. *The Nude: A Study in Ideal Form*. New York: Doubleday, 1956.

Clinton, Bill. *Giving: How Each of Us Can Change the World*. New York: Knopf, 2007.

Coffin, William Sloane. *Credo*. Louisville, KY: Westminster John Knox Press, 2004.

Collins, John J. *The Encyclopedia of Apocalypticism*, vol. 1, *The Origins of Apocalypticism in Judaism and Christianity*. London: Continuum, 2004.

Cottrell, Leonard. *The Quest for Sumer*. New York: Putnam, 1965.

Davis, Kenneth C. *America's Hidden History: Untold Tales of the First Pilgrims, Fighting Women, and Forgotten Founders Who Shaped a Nation*. New York: Harper Paperbacks, 2009.

Dionysius the Areopagite. *The Celestial Hierarchy*. Whitefish, MT: Kessinger Publishing, 2004.

Drake, Durant. *Problems of Conduct*. Charleston, SC: Bibliobazaar, 2006.

Eddington, Arthur. *The Expanding Universe*. New York: Macmillan, 1933.

Frankl, Viktor E. *Man's Search for Meaning*, Boston, MA: Beacon Press, 2006.

Freeman, Charles. *The Closing of the Western Mind: The Rise of Faith and the Fall of Reason*. New York: Vintage Books, 2005.

Haisch, Bernhard. "Brilliant Disguise: Light, Matter and the Zero-Point Field," *Science & Spirit* 10, no. 3 (September/October 1999).

Hine, Thomas. *The Rise and Fall of the American Teenager*. New York: Avon Books, 1999.

Kramer, Samuel Noah. *History Begins at Sumer: Twenty-seven "Firsts" in Man's Recorded History*. New York, Doubleday Anchor Books, 1959

Krishnamurti, Jiddu. *The Book of Life: Daily Meditations with Krishnamurti*, R. E. Mark Lee, ed. New York, HarperOne, 1995.

Luskin, Frederic. *Forgive for Good*. New York: HarperOne, 2003.

MacArthur, John F. *The Freedom and Power of Forgiveness*. Crossway Books, 1998.

McCarthy, Kevin F., Elizabeth H. Ondaatje, Laura Zakaras, and Arthur Brooks. *Gift of the Muse: Reframing the Debate About the Benefits of the Arts*. Rand Corporation Report, 2004.

McIntosh, Steve. *Integral Consciousness and the Future of Evolution: How the Integral Worldview is Transforming Politics, Culture, and Spirituality*. St. Paul, MN: Paragon House, 2007.

Murray, W. John. *Mental Medicine*. New York: Divine Science Publishing, 1923.

Olson, Daniel V. A. *The Secularization Debate*. Lanham, MD: Rowman and Littlefield, 2000.

Osteen, Joel. *Your Best Life Now: 7 Steps to Living at Your Full Potential*. Brentwood, TN: FaithWords, 2004.

Peck, M. Scott. *A World Waiting To Be Born: Civility Rediscovered*. New York: Bantam Books, 1993.

Post, Stephen, and Jill Neimark. *Why Good Things Happen to Good People*. New York: Broadway Books, 2007.

Ramo, Joshua Cooper. *The Age of the Unthinkable*. New York: Little, Brown, 2009.

Paul, Richard. *The Miniature Guide to Critical Thinking: Concepts and Tools*. Dillon Beach, CA: Foundation for Critical Thinking, 2001.

Sadler, William S., Jr. *A Study of the Master Universe: A Development of Concepts of the Urantia Book*. Chicago, IL: Second Society Foundation, 1968. Also, the Urantia Book Fellowship website, http://urantiabook.org/studies/smu.

Sanford, John A. *Soul Journey: A Jungian Analyst Looks at Reincarnation*. New York: Crossroad, 1991.

Schmidt, Leigh Eric. *Restless Souls: The Making of American Spirituality*. New York: Harper Collins, 2005

Spinoza, Benedictus de. *Short Treatise on God, Man, and His Well-Being*. Charleston, SC: BiblioBazaar, 2009.

Sprunger, Meredith J. *Spiritual Psychology: A Primer*. Jemenon Inc., 1992.

Tarnas, Richard. *The Passion of the Western Mind: Understanding the Ideas That Have Shaped Our World View*. New York: Harmony Books, 1991.

Teilhard de Chardin, Pierre. *The Phenomenon of Man*. trans. Bernard Wall. New York: Harper Perennial, 1975.

Tertullianus, Quintus Septimius Florens. *"A Treatise on the Soul."* IntraText Edition CT, (copyright Éulogos 2007), Intratext Digital Library, http://www.intratext.com /IXT/ENG0254/_PZ.HTM.

Tucker-Ladd, Clayton E. *Psychological Self-Help*. E-book at http://www.psychological selfhelp.org.

Urantia Foundation. *The Urantia Book*, Chicago: The Urantia Foundation, 1955.

Wilber, Ken. *Integral Spirituality: A Startling New Role for Religion in the Modern and Postmodern World*. Boston, MA, Integral Books, 2006.

Williams, Daniel Day. *The Spirit and the Forms of Love*. New York: Harper and Row, 1968.

Wuthnow, Robert. *After Heaven: Spirituality in America Since the 1950s*. Los Angeles: University of California Press, 1998.

Zuckerman, Phil. *The Cambridge Companion to Atheism*, ed. Michael Martin. New York: Cambridge University Press, 2007.

Index

Illustrations are indicated by *fig* following the page number.

Deified universe reality, 33
Deists, 7
Deity, 33–45
    See also God
    functional levels in religions, 21
    The I AM as, 33–36
    impersonal, 34
    Indwelling Spirit as prepersonal, 43–45,
        203–204
    Paradise Trinity as existential, 38–40
    personal, 36–38
    trinitization and personality of, 41–43
Demeter, 146
Demons, 115–116, 166, 198
Descartes, René, 7
Descending Sons of God, 71, 72*fig*
Destiny of humanity, 293–311
    challenge to, 309–311
    consciousness development and, 295–296
    cultural factors and, 294–296
    dispensations of divine Sons and, 296–297
    end of the world and, 306–309
    epochs and dispensations and, 296–299,
        302–305*fig*
    golden age and, 313–315
    history and, 295
    judgment of the realm and, 299, 306
Devil, 77, 112, 115–116, 198
Devotion, 417–419
Dhammakaya, 33
Diderot, Denis, 7
Dies natalis solis invicti (birthday of the
    invincible sun), 148
Digges, Thomas, 51
Dilmun, 128, 183, 187
Din-gir, 107
Dionysius Exiguus, 148
Dionysius the Areopagite, 65, 78, 80*fig*
Discerners of Spirits, 291
Discovery of Atlantis (Sarmast), 122
Dispensations, 296–299
    Christianity and, 298
    of divine Sons, 296–297
    Earth and schedule of, 297, 300–301*fig*
    seven developmental epochs and, 298–299,
        300*fig*
    termination of, 299
A Divine Comedy (Dante), 51, 77
Divine Consciousness-Force, 32
The Divine Plan (Barborka), 261–262
Divine Plan of Creation, 117
Divine Plan of Progress, 46–47
    death and eternal life in, 208
    evolution, survival and ascension aspects
        of, 288
    free will and, 46, 288
    Garden of Eden and, 121
    God-realization and, 434–437
    phases of, 47
    three components of, 46–47
    of Universe Organization, 55, 55*fig*
Divine Science, 257
Divine Sons, 34, 41, 60, 75, 296–297
Djibril, 85
Dobbelaere, Karel, 258
Draught of fish miracle, 165
Dravidians, 193, 194, 245, 246
Dreams, 264

Dual-origin beings of grand universe, 42
Dual spiritism, 115
"The Dumbest Generation" (Huston), 260
Dvaita (dualist school), 252
Dysfunctional behavior recognition, 379–381

E

Earth
    Andon and Fonta on, 104
    arrival of Adam and Eve, 122–126, 218
    Atlantis location on, 122, 191
    Caligastia as Planetary Prince of, 108–109,
        114, 217
    Cosmic location of, 54*fig*
    Darwin theory of evolution and, 99, 100
    dispensations schedule and, 297,
        300–301*fig*
    as experimental decimal planet, 101
    Jesus reappearances after death on, 171,
        172
    Machiventa Melchizedek bestowed on, 76,
        131, 132, 134, 218
    midwayers on, 196–198
    as mortal bestowal planet of Creator Son,
        75, 145
    Nebadon as local universe of, 53, 54*fig*, 105
    as part of Satania System, 108
    planetary rebellion and, 110–114
    Satan and Caligastia on, 116
    Satan and Lucifer and, 76–77
    theories of creation of life on, 99–101
Eastern gurus, 9
Ecclesiasticus, 52
Economic interdependence, 27
Ecumenical Council (first) in 325 AD, 7
Eddington, Sir Arthur, 31
Edentia, 62, 321, 322
Edict of Milan, 7
Education and cultural progress, 28–29, 372
Edward, John, 279
Ego, 249, 261–262, 261*fig*
Egypt
    migration of human races and, 190–191
    Moses and, 136–137
    Pyramid texts of, 190, 273
    Salem teachings in, 135, 190
    Sethite missionaries and Trinity concept in,
        38
    Seven Mystery Gods of, 65
    Sumerian influence on, 190, 244
Egyptian
    Akh (ba and ka), 207
    belief of "winged beings," 83
    Hunmanit as guardian angel, 84
    mother goddess Isis, 146
    papyri depictions of Gods, celestial beings,
        65
    quest for eternal life, 244–245, 273, 287
    religious worldview, 6
    seer Amenemope, 135
    spiritual resurrection beliefs, 273
Einstein, Albert, 50, 52, 56, 57
Elam (Persia), 146
El Elyon (Constellation Father), 132, 135, 136
Elijah, 138, 250–251, 280
Elisha, 138
Eloah, 39
Elohim, 39, 132, 143, 144